CONFLICT IN THE CLASSROOM

The Education of Emotionally Disturbed Children

Fourth Edition

CONFLICT IN THE CLASSROOM

The Education of Emotionally Disturbed Children

Fourth Edition

Nicholas J. Long
American University

William C. Morse
University of Michigan

Ruth G. Newman
Washington School of Psychiatry

Wadsworth Publishing Company
Belmont, California
A Division of Wadsworth, Inc.

Education Editor: Roger Peterson
Production Editor: Kathie Head
Designer: Janet Wood
Copy Editor: Zipporah Collins
Technical Illustrator: Carlton Brown
Cover Photograph: © Philip Jon Bailey/Jeroboam, Inc.

Printed in the United States of America

4 5 6 7 8 9 10—84

ISBN 0-534-00791-0

Library of Congress Cataloging in Publication Data
Long, Nicholas James, 1929–   ed.
    Conflict in the classroom.

    Includes bibliographies.
    1. Emotional problems of children.
2. Mentally handicapped children—Education—
United States. I. Morse, William Charles.
II. Newman, Ruth G.   III. Title.
LC4631.L6 1980   371.9'4   79-20955
ISBN 0-534-00791-0

Contents

Preface

The field of special education has come a long way since the first edition of *Conflict in the Classroom*. There was, originally, no other book of readings and we had to hunt, peck, and burrow to glean good pieces that would reflect the dilemmas posed by the many emotionally disturbed children in the classroom, to say nothing of the many more who were kept out of school. There was also very little material useful to people attempting to teach and/or help these children. Now there are many schools and classrooms, some good, some mediocre, and some sadly inadequate.

Now, although there are many books, we believe ours remains unique, because of the material chosen and because of our psychoeducational point of view. This book reflects our belief that behavior is caused, and that teachers must understand and deal with the causes of behavior to help children grow, develop, and learn beyond the rote performance of tasks to earn rewards or avoid punishments. While we do not disapprove of any techniques and strategies that work well, we believe that these strategies need to be grounded in understanding of the dynamics of a given child. We also believe in the power of the child's inner life, in the power of relationships with adults and peers, in the power of changing educational practices, and in the power of societal pressures, both on the child and on the school system.

While various theories of emotional disturbance are included in the selections, our psychoeducational biases are clear. We think the psychoeducational approach will be useful to those who seek to teach or to help emotionally disturbed children whether mainstreamed in a regular class, in a special class, in a residential treatment setting, or in a mental hospital.

We have opted for wide variety in material and in proven methods. We have tried to cover as many aspects of the experience of emotional disturbance as we can and to offer the reader both the insights of theory and the wisdom of successful ideas and methods.

In this edition, there is much new and pointed material. To include it, we sometimes had to eliminate articles we would have liked to keep, but we had limited space. There is a new chapter on mainstreaming. There is dramatic material on the increasing use of alcohol by children and on the damaging effects of child abuse. There are new original articles on autistic children, adolescent programs, working with parents, group dynamics, teaching frustration tolerance, physical education, the stress and coping cycles, behavior modification cautions, and predictions about the future of this fascinating field as a whole. Our commitment is to help implement new clinical and educational services for the many emotionally disturbed children in our society. To do this, we need aware and interested teachers, administrators, counselors, psychologists, psychiatrists, social workers, pediatricians, and parents. We believe that the future of this field will be more exciting, challenging, and productive than the present and that this fourth edition can help in the task of bringing that future to fruition.

We would like to thank the following people for their helpful suggestions: Edward Gickling, University of Nevada; Ronald F. Kingsley, Kent State University; and James R. Tompkins, Appalachian State University.

Nicholas J. Long
William C. Morse
Ruth G. Newman

Dedicated to Fritz Redl

...who has devoted his life to caring and thinking about the needs of children, especially children in trouble, regardless of the reasons and of how the trouble is exhibited. He has served these children's needs by transmitting his tremendous understanding, not only to them but also to the adults who work with them—parents, teachers, mental health professionals, administrators, lawmakers, and child advocates. He has accomplished this by the force of his own background, training, and understanding and by means of his tireless teaching and consultation, his powerful speeches, his seminars, books, and articles.

His professional life began during the period when the psychological structure of the human personality was being reconceptualized. He worked in Vienna, in the first part of the twentieth century, close to the thinking and feeling revolution that Sigmund Freud had set in motion. He worked closely with Anna Freud when she was developing her theories of child psychoanalysis and with August Aichorn, the pioneer of work with "acting out delinquent youth."

First in Europe, and then in this country from the 1930s on, Redl was himself one of the greats and worked with many of the great psychologists who have affected our thinking and practices. At no time did he sacrifice his standards for tough thinking on the altar of expedience. He has fought and is still fighting against the cheap ploy, the easy answer, the instant formula, the panacea.

In a society like ours, which tends to leap on immediate solutions, he continues to fight for the less dramatic and often submerged deep understanding and treatment, rather than the popular approach or the quick cure.

He has taught many people around the world. His impact on some of us has been lasting. We three authors have had the privilege of having him as a teacher and as a colleague. Each of us, like so many others, is incalculably in his debt.

1

How Does It Feel to Be Emotionally Disturbed?

Editors' Commentary

How It Feels Inside Looking Out

Emotional disturbance in childhood is not a new problem, but only recently has it been recognized as a condition that can be alleviated through early diagnosis and careful treatment. Although scientists battle over the causes of emotional disturbance and the relative importance of genetic, constitutional, and environmental factors, everyone agrees that its form is in some degree dependent on the cultural and social values of the times.

Each of us contains the whole range of emotional health and disease within ourselves. Our nightmares, if they serve no other purpose, enable us to share the ways in which many psychotics experience life. If our legs "go to sleep" and refuse to behave as they should, we can briefly experience the helpless and often outraged feelings of the organic spastic. The sudden loss of temper nearly all of us have experienced gives a momentary empathy with the feelings of uncontrollable rage, helplessness, confusion, guilt, and self-hate felt by the child with no impulse control. Most of us have shared a variety of neurotic symptoms: the terrifying fear of something that we know rationally should not in itself cause fear; the magical, protective cloak of knocking on wood, crossing fingers, counting to ten, holding our breath; the compulsive need to get one thing done, no matter how inane or how inconvenient, before we can do something else; the piece of work that can never be finished because it is never good enough; the headaches, stomach pains, or shortness of breath (unexplainable in the doctor's office) that often occurs at a family reunion, at exam time, or at the appearance of a certain person; the need to eat greedily though we are not hungry, or the reverse—being unable to swallow a mouthful; the uncontrollable blush or stutter; the immobilizing lapse of memory; or the urge to take something, to break something, to say the very thing that will get us into trouble, or to be silent when speaking up might simplify our lives and reduce the hostility of others.

Such illogical behavior does not mean that most of us are neurotic—only that some emotional disorder is as much a part of everyone's life as the common cold. It is not surprising, therefore, that emotional disturbance should play so great a role in childhood—a period of dependence and change, in which the world and its demands are new and often confusing, conflicting, and frustrating. When the case histories of severely disturbed children are examined, we often are amazed that *more* disturbance has not occurred or, indeed, that these children have survived at all.

Many literary artists have chronicled the actions of disturbed children or of adults with disturbances rooted in their childhood. Writers were describing these people long before Freud; and since good writers are skilled in conveying pictures and feelings, their descriptions often have greater impact on us than the clinical descriptions in textbooks. For this reason, we present in this chapter excerpts from a variety of fictional and autobiographical works to illustrate the kinds of mental illnesses and disturbances that beset children. Mostly, the stories are about children of various ages, but there are also some descriptions of adult behavior that show clearly the final development of a childhood disturbance. There are examples of behavior problems and of delinquency in various forms and degrees. There are accounts of trauma, anxiety, and panic. There are descriptions of the workings of several kinds of neuroses, from mild to severe, as well as some psychotic behavior. We have included here the withdrawn child and the acting-out child; the culturally or emotionally disadvantaged and the physically or mentally handicapped; the social rebel and the autistic child, who lives in a world of his or her own making; and even the child murderer and the child suicide. We present portrayals of the feelings and experiences of both young and old people living in today's society and reacting to it, its paraphernalia, its values, and its real or philosophical restrictions in ways that are often destructive to the person reacting and to others. Although destructive reactions to the circumstances of life occur in all social and ethnic groups, certain forms of destructive behavior are often found more prominently among members of a particular economic class. For example, ghetto or poverty society—white, black, brown, yellow, or red—breeds certain kinds of hate, virulence, and acting out against others or oneself. The affluent middle class, with its high priority on material things and achievement, often breeds another kind of reaction, frequently the behavior of the middle-class drug user and addict. In both environments—poverty and the middle class—the reaction, against despair and misery on the one hand and against phony values on the other, may be a healthy one: it may result in the need to do something about the unsatisfactory environmental conditions. But a reaction that signals passive helplessness and ends in greater inadequacy and despair encourages emotional disturbance. Emotional upset in most people results in behavior that is ultimately both intelligent and useful. When a person's initial feeling of rage or apathy becomes destructive of that person or others, however, the behavior can legitimately be called disturbed.

This chapter is divided into three parts: the first pictures basic intrapsychic difficulties that can be found anywhere, anytime; the second presents certain aspects of society—its deprivations, restrictions, and human devaluations—that breed disturbed behavior, or, in conflict with inner needs, cause some people to react destructively. Some react by withdrawing into themselves; some separate feeling from thought; some resort to body language, get headaches or ulcers, or become psychologically deaf or paralyzed; some eat compulsively to build a wall of fat between themselves and others; some drink to numb their pain. The third part discusses drug use. Many young people take drugs, some to such excess that they delude themselves into a state of "nonfeeling" or believe they have grasped the import of their lives or expanded their awareness of the world; others take drugs to do what they might otherwise never be able to countenance.

The selections in this chapter portray some of these basic emotional states, caused by either internal dynamics or external forces or a combination of both. Of course, we cannot cover every circumstance—these selections were chosen as particularly insightful or descriptive samples.

At the beginning of each reading, if the author does not already do so, we give a description of the kind of child so that a teacher might recognize this child in the actual classroom. Also, to familiarize the teacher with the language of psychiatric or psychological reports, we give the clinical terms that would be used in diagnosing the children in these readings. These terms are shortcut descriptions that imply a general pattern of personality or behavior. They have limited meaning and, with careless use, lose even that. In most cases diagnostic terms are as meaningless to laypeople as Latin terms for medicines. The words are given here simply to remove their aura of mystery, so that we may look deeper, as William James says, "like a child staring a fact in the face."

The fundamental purpose of this chapter, however, is to offer the reader an intense experience of *how it feels* to be emotionally disturbed, a victim of psychological forces that control and sometimes choke off one's sense of acceptance, adequacy, and love.

The Use of Force

William Carlos Williams

They were new patients to me, all I had was the name, Olson. Please come down as soon as you can, my daughter's very sick.

When I arrived I was met by the mother, a big startled looking woman, very clean and apologetic who merely said, Is this the doctor? and let me in. In the back, she added, You must excuse us, doctor, we have her in the kitchen where it is warm. It is very damp here sometimes.

The child was fully dressed and sitting on her father's lap near the kitchen table. He tried to get up, but I motioned for him not to bother, took off my overcoat and started to look things over. I could see that they were all very nervous, eyeing me up and down distrustfully. As often, in such cases, they weren't telling me more than they had to, it was up to me to tell them; that's why they were spending three dollars on me.

The child was fairly eating me up with her cold, steady eyes, and no expression to her face whatever. She did not move and seemed, inwardly, quiet; an unusually attractive little thing, and as strong as a heifer in appearance. But her face was flushed, she was breathing rapidly, and I realized that she had a high fever. She had magnificent blonde hair, in profusion. One of those picture children often reproduced in advertising leaflets and the photogravure sections of the Sunday papers.

She's had a fever for three days, began the father, and we don't know what it comes from. My wife has given her things, you know, like people do, but it don't do no good. And there's been a lot of sickness around. So we tho't you'd better look her over and tell us what is the matter.

As doctors often do I took a trial shot at it as a point of departure. Has she had a sore throat?

Both parents answered me together, No . . . No, she says her throat don't hurt her.

Does your throat hurt you? added the mother to the child. But the little girl's expression didn't change nor did she move her eyes from my face.

Have you looked?

I tried to, said the mother, but I couldn't see.

As it happens we had been having a number of cases of diphtheria in the school to which this child went during that month and we were all, quite apparently, thinking of that, though no one had as yet spoken of the thing.

Well, I said, suppose we take a look at the throat first. I smiled in my best professional manner and asking for the child's first name I said, come on, Mathilda, open your mouth and let's take a look at your throat.

Nothing doing.

Aw, come on, I coaxed, just open your mouth wide and let me take a look. Look, I said opening both hands wide, I haven't anything in my hands. Just open up and let me see.

Such a nice man, put in the mother. Look how kind he is to you. Come on, do what he tells you to. He won't hurt you.

At that I ground my teeth in disgust. If only they wouldn't use the word "hurt" I might be able to get somewhere. But I did not allow myself to be hurried or disturbed but speaking quietly and slowly I approached the child again.

As I moved my chair a little nearer suddenly with one cat-like movement both her hands clawed instinctively for my eyes and she almost reached them too. In fact she knocked my glasses flying and they fell, though unbroken, several feet away from me on the kitchen floor.

Both the mother and father almost turned

themselves inside out in embarrassment and apology. You bad girl, said the mother, taking her and shaking her by one arm. Look what you've done. The nice man . . .

For heaven's sake, I broke in. Don't call me a nice man to her. I'm here to look at her throat on the chance that she might have diphtheria and possibly die of it. But that's nothing to her. Look here, I said to the child, we're going to look at your throat. You're old enough to understand what I'm saying. Will you open it now by yourself or shall we have to open it for you?

Not a move. Even her expression hadn't changed. Her breaths however were coming faster and faster. Then the battle began. I had to do it. I had to have a throat culture for her own protection. But first I told the parents that it was entirely up to them. I explained the danger but said that I would not insist on a throat examination so long as they would take the responsibility.

If you don't do what the doctor says you'll have to go to the hospital, the mother admonished her severely.

Oh yeah? I had to smile to myself. After all, I had already fallen in love with the savage brat, the parents were contemptible to me. In the ensuing struggle they grew more and more abject, crushed, exhausted while she surely rose to magnificent heights of insane fury of effort bred of her terror of me.

The father tried his best, and he was a big man but the fact that she was his daughter, his shame at her behavior and his dread of hurting her made him release her just at the critical moment several times when I had almost achieved success, till I wanted to kill him. But his dread also that she might have diphtheria made him tell me to go on, go on though he himself was almost fainting, while the mother moved back and forth behind us raising and lowering her hands in an agony of apprehension.

Put her in front of you on your lap, I ordered, and hold both her wrists.

But as soon as he did the child let out a scream. Don't you're hurting me. Let go of my hands. Let them go I tell you. She shrieked terrifyingly, hysterically. Stop it! Stop it! You're killing me!

Do you think she can stand it, doctor? said the mother.

You get out, said the husband to his wife. Do you want her to die of diphtheria?

Come on now, hold her, I said.

Then I grasped the child's head with my left hand and tried to get the wooden tongue depressor between her teeth. She fought, with clenched teeth, desperately! But now I also had grown furi-

ous—at a child. I tried to hold myself down but I couldn't. I know how to expose a throat for inspection. And I did my best. When finally I got the wooden spatula behind the last teeth and just the point of it into the mouth cavity, she opened up for an instant but before I could see anything she came down again and gripping the wooden blade between her molars she reduced it to splinters before I could get it out again.

Aren't you ashamed, the mother yelled at her. Aren't you ashamed to act like that in front of the doctor?

Get me a smooth-handled spoon of some sort, I told the mother. We're going through with this. The child's mouth was already bleeding. Her tongue was cut and she was screaming in wild hysterical shrieks. Perhaps I should have desisted and come back in an hour or more. No doubt it would have been better. But I have seen at least two children lying dead in bed of neglect in such cases, and feeling that I must get a diagnosis now or never I went at it again. But the worst of it was that I too had got beyond reason. I could have torn the child apart in my own fury and enjoyed it. It was a pleasure to attack her. My face was burning with it.

The damned little brat must be protected against her own idiocy, one says to one's self at such times. Others must be protected against her. It is social necessity. And all these things are true. But a blind fury, a feeling of adult shame, bred of a longing for muscular release are the operatives. One goes on to the end.

In a final unreasoning assault I overpowered the child's neck and jaws. I forced the heavy silver spoon back of her teeth and down her throat till she gagged. And there it was—both tonsils covered with membrane. She had fought valiantly to keep me from knowing her secret. She had been hiding that sore throat for three days at least and lying to her parents in order to escape just such an outcome as this.

Now truly she *was* furious. She had been on the defensive before but now she attacked. Tried to get off her father's lap and fly at me while tears of defeat blinded her eyes.

Editors' Commentary

Diagnosis: Behavior problem—resistance to adult authority, hostility, aggressiveness; might be the beginning signs of a "character" neurosis.

The story shows a power struggle—a sick, frightened, but powerful child who is accustomed to defeating adults and who will try to do so even when one adult is there to save her life. Confronted with incompetent grown-ups, she renders them more incompetent, testing their power with her own. In so doing, she alienates herself from others, refusing to accept the help she so badly needs. The ingredient of trust (which Erikson's[1] developmental scale postulates as basic to growth) has been distorted, and her growth inevitably will be distorted also, unless she and her parents can change. She needs adults who care and who can show they care by setting limits and providing consistent protection.

1. **Erik Erikson,** *Childhood and Society* (New York: W. W. Norton, 1960).

An Incident

Anton Chekhov

Morning. Brilliant sunshine is piercing through the frozen lacework on the window-panes into the nursery. Vanya, a boy of six, with a cropped head and a nose like a button, and his sister Nina, a short, chubby, curly-headed girl of four, wake up and look crossly at each other through the bars of their cots.

"Oo-oo-oo! naughty children!" grumbles their nurse. "Good people have had their breakfast already, while you can't get your eyes open."

The sunbeams frolic over the rugs, the walls, and nurse's skirts, and seem inviting the children to join in their play, but they take no notice. They have woken up in a bad humor. Nina pouts, makes a grimace, and begins to whine:

"Brea-eakfast, nurse, breakfast!"

Vanya knits his brows and ponders what to pitch upon to howl over. He has already begun screwing up his eyes and opening his mouth, but at that instant the voice of mamma reaches them from the drawing-room, saying: "Don't forget to give the cat her milk, she has a family now!"

The children's puckered countenances grow smooth again as they look at each other in astonishment. Then both at once begin shouting, jump out of their cots, and filling the air with piercing shrieks, run barefoot, in their nightgowns, to the kitchen.

"The cat has puppies!" they cry. "The cat has got puppies!"

Under the bench in the kitchen there stands a small box, the one in which Stepan brings coal when he lights the fire. The cat is peeping out of the box. There is an expression of extreme exhaustion on her grey face; her green eyes, with their narrow black pupils, have a languid, sentimental look. . . . From her face it is clear that the only thing lacking to complete her happiness is the presence in the box of "him," the father of her children, to whom she had abandoned herself so recklessly! She wants to mew, and opens her mouth wide, but nothing but a hiss comes from her throat; the squealing of the kittens is audible.

The children squat on their heels before the box, and, motionless, holding their breath, gaze at the cat. . . . They are surprised, impressed, and do not hear nurse grumbling as she pursues them. The most genuine delight shines in the eyes of both.

Domestic animals play a scarcely noticed but undoubtedly beneficial part in the education and life of children. Which of us does not remember powerful but magnanimous dogs, lazy lapdogs, birds dying in captivity, dull-witted but haughty turkeys, mild old tabby cats, who forgave us when we trod on their tails for fun and caused them agonizing pain? I even fancy, sometimes, that the patience, the fidelity, the readiness to forgive, and the sincerity which are characteristic of our domestic animals have a far stronger and more definite effect on the mind of a child than the long exhortations of some dry, pale Karl Karlovitch, or the misty expositions of a governess, trying to prove to children that water is made up of hydrogen and oxygen.

"What little things!" says Nina, opening her eyes wide and going off into a joyous laugh. "They are like mice!"

"One, two, three," Vanya counts. "Three kittens. So there is one for you, one for me, and one for somebody else, too."

"Murrm . . . murrm . . ." purrs the mother, flattered by their attention. "Murrm."

After gazing at the kittens, the children take them from under the cat, and begin squeezing them in their hands, then, not satisfied with this, they put them in the skirts of their nightgowns, and run into the other rooms.

"Mamma, the cat has got pups!" they shout.

Mamma is sitting in the drawing-room with some unknown gentleman. Seeing the children unwashed, undressed, with their nightgowns held up high, she is embarrassed, and looks at them severely.

"Let your nightgowns down, disgraceful children," she says. "Go out of the room, or I will punish you."

But the children do not notice either mamma's threats or the presence of a stranger. They put the kittens down on the carpet, and go off into deafening squeals. The mother walks round them, mewing imploringly. When, a little afterwards, the children are dragged off to the nursery, dressed, made to say their prayers, and given their breakfast, they are full of a passionate desire to get away from these prosaic duties as quickly as possible, and to run to the kitchen again.

Their habitual pursuits and games are thrown completely into the background.

The kittens throw everything into the shade by making their appearance in the world, and supply the great sensation of the day. If Nina or Vanya had been offered forty pounds of sweets or ten thousand kopecks for each kitten, they would have rejected such a barter without the slightest hesitation. In spite of the heated protests of the nurse and the cook, the children persist in sitting by the cat's box in the kitchen, busy with the kittens till dinner-time. Their faces are earnest and concentrated and express anxiety. They are worried not so much by the present as by the future of the kittens. They decide that one kitten shall remain at home with the old cat to be a comfort to her mother, while the second shall go to their summer villa,

and the third shall live in the cellar, where there are ever so many rats.

"But why don't they look at us?" Nina wondered. "Their eyes are blind like the beggars'."

Vanya, too, is perturbed by this question. He tries to open one kitten's eyes, and spends a long time puffing and breathing hard over it, but his operation is unsuccessful. They are a good deal troubled, too, by the circumstance that the kittens obstinately refuse the milk and the meat that is offered to them. Everything that is put before their little noses is eaten by their gray mamma.

"Let's build the kittens little houses," Vanya suggests. "They shall live in different houses, and the cat shall come and pay them visits. . . ."

Cardboard hat-boxes are put in the different corners of the kitchen and the kittens are installed in them. But this division turns out to be premature; the cat, still wearing an imploring and sentimental expression on her face, goes the round of all the hat-boxes, and carries off her children to their original position.

"The cat's their mother," observed Vanya, "but who is their father?"

"Yes, who is their father?" repeats Nina.

"They must have a father."

Vanya and Nina are a long time deciding who is to be the kittens' father, and, in the end, their choice falls on a big dark-red horse without a tail, which is lying in the store-cupboard under the stairs, together with other relics of toys that have outlived their day. They drag him up out of the store-cupboard and stand him by the box.

"Mind now!" they admonish him, "stand here and see they behave themselves properly."

All this is said and done in the gravest way, with an expression of anxiety on their faces. Vanya and Nina refuse to recognize the existence of any world but the box of kittens. Their joy knows no bounds. But they have to pass through bitter, agonizing moments, too.

Just before dinner, Vanya is sitting in his father's study, gazing dreamily at the table. A kitten is moving about by the lamp, on stamped note paper. Vanya is watching its movements, and thrusting first a pencil, then a match into its little mouth. . . . All at once, as though he has sprung out of the floor, his father is beside the table.

"What's this?" Vanya hears, in an angry voice.

"It's . . . it's the kitty, papa. . . ."

"I'll give it you; look what you have done, you naughty boy! You've dirtied all my paper!"

To Vanya's great surprise his papa does not share his partiality for the kittens, and, instead of being moved to enthusiasm and delight, he pulls Vanya's ear and shouts:

"Stepan, take away this horrid thing."

At dinner, too, there is a scene. . . . During the second course there is suddenly the sound of a shrill mew. They begin to investigate its origin, and discover a kitten under Nina's pinafore.

"Nina, leave the table!" cries her father angrily. "Throw the kittens in the cesspool! I won't have the nasty things in the house! . . ."

Vanya and Nina are horrified. Death in the cesspool, apart from its cruelty, threatens to rob the cat and the wooden horse of their children, to lay waste the cat's box, to destroy their plans for the future, that fair future in which one cat will be a comfort to its old mother, another will live in the country, while the third will catch rats in the cellar. The children begin to cry and entreat that the kittens may be spared. Their father consents, but on the condition that the children do not go into the kitchen and touch the kittens.

After dinner Vanya and Nina slouch about the rooms, feeling depressed. The prohibition of visits to the kitchen has reduced them to dejection. They refuse sweets, are naughty, and are rude to their mother. When their uncle Petrusha comes in the evening, they draw him aside, and complain to him of their father, who wanted to throw the kittens into the cesspool.

"Uncle Petrusha, tell mamma to have the kittens taken to the nursery," the children beg their uncle, "do-o tell her."

"There, there . . . very well," says their uncle, waving them off. "All right."

Uncle Petrusha does not usually come alone. He is accompanied by Nero, a big black dog of Danish breed, with drooping ears, and a tail as hard as a stick. The dog is silent, morose, and full of a sense of his own dignity. He takes not the slightest notice of the children, and when he passes them hits them with his tail as though they were chairs. The children hate him from the bottom of their hearts, but on this occasion, practical considerations override sentiment.

"I say, Nina," says Vanya, opening his eyes wide. "Let Nero be their father, instead of the horse! The horse is dead and he is alive, you see."

They are waiting the whole evening for the moment when papa will sit down to his cards and it will be possible to take Nero to the kitchen without being observed. . . . At last, papa sits down to cards, mamma is busy with the samovar and not noticing the children. . . .

The happy moment arrives.

"Come along!" Vanya whispers to his sister.

But, at that moment, Stepan comes in and, with a snigger, announces:

"Nero has eaten the kittens, madam."

Nina and Vanya turn pale and look at Stepan with horror.

"He really has . . ." laughs the footman, "he went to the box and gobbled them up."

The children expect that all the people in the house will be aghast and fall upon the miscreant Nero. But they all sit calmly in their seats, and only express surprise at the appetite of the huge dog. Papa and mamma laugh. Nero walks about by the table, wags his tail, and licks his lips complacently . . . the cat is the only one who is uneasy. With her tail in the air she walks about the rooms, looking suspiciously at people and mewing plaintively.

"Children, it's past nine," cries mamma, "it's bedtime."

Vanya and Nina go to bed, shed tears, and spend a long time thinking about the injured cat, and the cruel, insolent, and unpunished Nero.

Editors' Commentary

Diagnosis: Childhood trauma caused by parental insensitivity to children's feelings, identifications, and projections.

Sometimes this story is entitled "A Trivial Incident." On the continuum of disturbance, these two children are quite normal: fighting with each other, irritable when thwarted, quickly diverted, and deeply involved when the matter at hand (the kittens) interests them. From such a trivial incident, however, the children can grasp, sometimes with only half-awareness, the real attitudes of the signficant adults in their world. The parents' callousness and lack of concern for important issues of life, death, and designs for the future shake the very foundations of the children's belief in adults. These two children have had the door opened on adult cruelty, evil, and unconcern; on the lack of imagination or ability to project feelings, characteristic of self-centered people. The children's natural sympathies have been shocked by recognition that others feel, see, and act in quite a different way. From such an event defenses are built. Whether these take the form of hiding vulnerability, of cloaking feelings with cruelty, or of rebellion against the world, will depend on the children's own genetic constitutions and the amount of love they have already received, as well as on the strength and humanness they are able to feed each other.

Children can be shocked into disillusion by crudity and lack of concern from teachers as well as from parents. Since the child's initial major sojourn into the world at large occurs at school, teachers represent the world the child is to cope with, for good or ill. If both parents and teachers affirm the evil, hypocrisy, and carelessness in the world, the child's adjustment to injustice or rebellion against injustice can become a major problem and provide the soil in which pathology can grow. Likewise the school can mitigate the difficulty by providing experiences with kind adults who are sensitive to children's feelings.

The Runaway

Anton Chekhov

The doctor began seeing the patients. He sat in his little room, and called up the patients in turn. Sounds were continually coming from the little room, piercing wails, a child's crying, or the doctor's angry words:

"Come, why are you bawling? Am I murdering you, or what? Sit quiet!"

Pashka's turn came.

"Pavel Galaktionov!" shouted the doctor.

His mother was aghast, as though she had not expected this summons, and taking Pashka by the hand, she led him into the room.

The doctor was sitting at the table, mechanically tapping on a thick book with a little hammer.

"What's wrong?" he asked, without looking at them.

"The little lad has an ulcer on his elbow, sir," answered his mother, and her face assumed an expression as though she really were terribly grieved at Pashka's ulcer.

"Undress him!"

Pashka, panting, unwound the kerchief from his neck, then wiped his nose on his sleeve, and began deliberately pulling off his sheepskin.

"Woman, you have not come here on a visit!" said the doctor angrily. "Why are you dawdling? You are not the only one here."

Pashka hurriedly flung the sheepskin on the floor, and with his mother's help took off his shirt. . . . The doctor looked at him lazily, and patted him on his bare stomach.

"You have grown quite a respectable corporation, brother Pashka," he said, and heaved a sigh. "Come, show me your elbow."

Pashka looked sideways at the basin full of bloodstained slops, looked at the doctor's apron, and began to cry.

"May-ay!" the doctor mimicked him. "Nearly old enough to be married, spoilt boy, and here he is blubbering! For shame!"

Pashka, trying not to cry, looked at his mother, and in that look could be read the entreaty: "Don't tell them at home that I cried at the hospital."

The doctor examined his elbow, pressed it, heaved a sigh, clicked with his lips, then pressed it again.

"You ought to be beaten, woman, but there is no one to do it," he said. "Why didn't you bring him before? Why, the whole arm is done for. Look, foolish woman. You see, the joint is diseased!"

"You know best, kind sir . . ." sighed the woman.

"Kind sir. . . . She's let the boy's arm rot, and now it is 'kind sir.' What kind of workman will he be without an arm? You'll be nursing him and looking after him for ages. I bet if you had had a pimple on your nose, you'd have run to the hospital quick enough, but you have left your boy to rot for six months. You are all like that."

The doctor lighted a cigarette. While the cigarette smoked, he scolded the woman, and shook his head in time to the song he was humming inwardly, while he thought of something else. Pashka stood naked before him, listening and looking at the smoke. When the cigarette went out, the doctor started, and said in a lower tone:

"Well, listen, woman. You can do nothing with ointments and drops in this case. You must leave him in the hospital."

"If necessary, sir, why not?"

"We must operate on him. You stop with me, Pashka," said the doctor, slapping Pashka on the shoulder. "Let mother go home, and you and I will stop here, old man. It's nice with me, old boy, it's first-rate here. I'll tell you what we'll do, Pashka, we will go catching finches together. I will show you a fox! We will go visiting together! Shall we? And mother will come for you tomorrow! Eh?"

Pashka looked inquiringly at his mother.

"You stay, child!" she said.

"He'll stay, he'll stay!" cried the doctor gleefully. "And there is no need to discuss it. I'll show him a live fox! We will go to the fair together to buy candy! Marya Denisovna, take him upstairs!"

The doctor, apparently a light-hearted and friendly fellow, seemed glad to have company; Pashka wanted to oblige him, especially as he had never in his life been to a fair, and would have been glad to have a look at a live fox, but how could he do without his mother? . . .

A long time passed, but the doctor still did not appear. The nurse brought in tea, and scolded Pashka for not having saved any bread for his tea; the assistant came once more and set to work to wake Mihailo. It turned blue outside the windows, the wards were lighted up, but the doctor did not appear. It was too late now to go to the fair and catch finches; Pashka stretched himself on his bed and began thinking. He remembered the candy promised him by the doctor, the face and voice of his mother, the darkness in his hut at home, the stove, peevish granny Yegorovna . . . and he suddenly felt sad and dreary. He remembered that his mother was coming for him next day, smiled, and shut his eyes.

He was awakened by a rustling. In the next ward someone was stepping about and speaking in a whisper. Three figures were moving about Mihailo's bed in the dim light of the night-light and the ikon lamp.

"Shall we take him, bed and all, or without?" asked one of them.

"Without. You won't get through the door with the bed."

"He's died at the wrong time, the Kingdom of Heaven be his!"

One took Mihailo by his shoulders, another by his legs and lifted him up: Mihailo's arms and the skirt of his dressing-gown hung limply to the ground. A third—it was the peasant who looked like a woman—crossed himself, and all three tramping clumsily with their feet and stepping on Mihailo's skirts, went out of the ward.

There came the whistle and humming on different notes from the chest of the old man who was asleep. Pashka listened, peeped at the dark windows, and jumped out of bed in terror.

"Ma-a-mka!" he moaned in a deep bass.

And without waiting for an answer, he rushed into the next ward. There the darkness was dimly lighted up by a night-light and the ikon lamp; the patients, upset by the death of Mihailo, were sitting on their bedsteads: their disheveled figures, mixed up with the shadows, looked broader, taller, and seemed to be growing bigger and bigger; on the furthest bedstead in the corner, where it was darkest, there sat the peasant moving his head and his hand.

Pashka, without noticing the doors, rushed into the smallpox ward, from there into the corridor, from the corridor he flew into a big room where monsters, with long hair and the faces of old women, were lying and sitting on the beds. Running through the women's wing he found himself again in the corridor, saw the banisters of the staircase he knew already, and ran downstairs. There he recognized the waiting-room in which he had sat that morning, and began looking for the door into the open air.

The latch creaked, there was a whiff of cold wind, and Pashka, stumbling, ran out into the yard. He had only one thought—to run, to run! He did not know the way, but felt convinced that if he ran he would be sure to find himself at home with his mother. The sky was overcast, but there was a moon behind the clouds. Pashka ran from the steps straight forward, went round the barn and stumbled into some thick bushes; after stopping for a minute and thinking, he dashed back again to the hospital, ran round it, and stopped again undecided; behind the hospital there were white crosses.

"Ma-a-mka!" he cried, and dashed back.

Running by the dark sinister buildings, he saw one lighted window.

The bright red patch looked dreadful in the darkness, but Pashka, frantic with terror, not knowing where to run, turned towards it. Beside the window was a porch with steps, and a front door with a white board on it; Pashka ran up the steps, looked in at the window, and was at once possessed by intense overwhelming joy. Through the window he saw the merry affable doctor sitting at the table reading a book. Laughing with happiness, Pashka stretched out his hands to the person he knew and tried to call out, but some unseen force choked him and struck at his legs; he staggered and fell down on the steps unconscious.

When he came to himself it was daylight, and a voice he knew very well, that had promised him a fair, finches, and a fox, was saying beside him:

"Well, you are an idiot, Pashka! Aren't you an idiot? You ought to be beaten, but there's no one to do it."

Editors' Commentary

Diagnosis: Panic—anxiety caused by adults' lies to avoid child's tears or anger.

This is the story of a child's terror, induced by adult mishandling. The child, ignorant and afraid, is brought by his ignorant mother to a clinic-hospital, where she, his protector, is cowed, scolded, and dominated by the doctor, who treats his cases in an utterly routine, impersonal manner. The child is left with the doctor and the hospital. He has never been left before, and the circumstances are not explained to him. Moreover, the doctor lies to him, promises him candy and a jaunt to a fair. He is put in a room with adults who are sick and in pain. His bewilderment is increased by the terrifying atmosphere, and he seeks out his "friend," the lying doctor, only to find himself once again helpless in the hands of adults, betrayed by the doctor, deserted by his helpless mother, and living in a nightmare of pain and uncertainty.

Thus are sown the seeds of distrust, suspicion, and terror of helplessness. Chekhov, who himself was a doctor, understood how the bewilderment and helplessness of children could lead to cruelty in adults or to ineffective, cowed adults. Here is a traumatic incident that could well affect a child's entire life, for his trust in his mother and in other adults who were supposed to take care of him was shattered.

Such adult lack of understanding happens daily, and not only in hospitals, clinics, and doctors' offices—though a child's physical helplessness in the hands of doctors and nurses makes the youngster particularly vulnerable in such places. It can also happen the first day of school in a classroom, or whenever a ridiculing or sarcastic teacher holds a child up for shame or makes a false promise to the child simply to get over a potentially unpleasant situation.

The Day of the Last Rock Fight

Joseph Whitehill

Fallbrook Academy

May 16, 195–

Dear Dad,

I expect this will be a very long letter, so I am sending it to your office marked *Personal*. I know you don't like to do family business at the office, but I wanted you to have a chance to read this all by yourself, and I didn't want Mother or Sue reading it before you did.

Thank you for sending my allowance, and also for the subscription to the home paper. Thank you also for the nice new wallet for my birthday. I really needed it, as my old one was afflicted with rot and falling apart.

I apologize for not having written sooner. As you said in your last letter, "*Something* must have happened in the last two months worth writing down." I have been very busy with things here at school, but mainly I haven't written because I didn't know how to say what I wanted to say. I hope this letter will make up for the long delay.

You keep asking me what I think of Fallbrook Academy and if I'm happy here, and so on. Well, I don't like it here, and I want to come home. That's what this letter is for—to tell you that now it's all right for me to come back home. I guess I know why you sent me here, and I admit that I wanted very much to come when I did. It's not that the people here aren't nice or anything. They are. They're so nice it's phony. In all the catalogues of the school they call it a *Special School*, but the boys here call it *Goodbar*. (Mr. Goodbar is a chocolate bar full of nuts.) They all kid about it, and pretend they don't care about being put in a school for misfits and boys with emotional problems. I guess most of them like it here. Most of them say they hate their parents, one or both, and are really glad to get away from them. All the faculty are so sweet and kind and sympathetic that a lot of the boys get away with murder. (That last word was sort of a poor choice, I suppose, but I'll leave it there anyway.) But I don't feel like I belong here any more.

It is going to be very complicated to explain everything in just one letter, because there are lots of different ways of looking at that mess that happened there at home, and I suppose I am the only one who knows the whole story. I guess you sent me here because you thought I was terribly upset by Gene Hanlon getting killed out there at Manning Day School at home, and seeing his body lying in the creek, and so on. Well, that was part of it, but only a little part. The rest of it I couldn't tell anybody until Detective Sergeant Gorman put the story in the paper last week. I got that paper in the mail yesterday and I have been reading the story over and over, and feeling relieved and awful at the same time.

I'm sure you read the same story, so you already know that Gene Hanlon was murdered, instead of getting killed accidentally as they said at first. But neither you nor anybody else knows that I saw the murder done, and knew all the time who did it. I guess if I acted upset afterwards it was from knowing all this and not being able to tell anyone about it. I'm going to work on this letter all night, if it takes that long, because I have to get all this out of my system. (When you stay up after curfew around here they don't actually *make* you go to bed, but the doctor who is on duty looks in on you every half hour or so to see what you're doing, and to try to make you *want* to go to bed.)

I suppose the beginning is the best place to start, so I will tell you first about Gene Hanlon, the boy who got killed. He came to Manning Day School last fall as a senior. They said he was fired from his last school, but I don't know about that. I didn't like him just from looking at him. I know you hate judgments that way on first impressions, but I couldn't help it. I wouldn't ever bring him over to our house, but if I had, you might have seen what I was talking about. He was big and beefy, and he played on the first string last fall. He was also blond, and the girls thought he was cute and from what I heard they fought over him for dates. But he was a bully, and he cheated in the classroom and he borrowed your stuff without asking you and then left it some place where you had to go hunt it up for yourself.

In a school like Manning Day there are always a number of tight little groups—cliques, I guess you call them—that move around independently and generally stay out of the way of the others. I mean there is a football group, and a group of boys who drink beer, and a group who studies hard, and a group who loafs and tries to avoid everything that looks like work, and a group that meets in the locker room to talk about sex and tell dirty jokes. It was probably the same way when you yourself went to school, but you may have forgotten. When you go to a school like that, you pretty soon find the group that suits you best, and you stay there and don't try to mix with any of the others, because if you do you won't be let in.

What I am getting at in this long explanation is that Gene Hanlon was the Big Man in all the groups I wouldn't be seen dead in. He was tops among the football players and their fans. He could tell filthier stories and, he said, hold more liquor than anybody else. And he told stories about the things he had done to girls that you wouldn't believe if anybody else had told them, but with him telling them, you knew they were all possible. I guess he was feared more than he was liked, but one thing sure, he never went anywhere alone. There was always a loud bunch along with him horse-laughing and beating him on the shoulders.

I stayed out of his way. There is something about me that brings out the worst in bullies. That's what Peter Irish used to say. I guess it's because I'm slightly built, and because of those glasses I have to wear. Once, I was going upstairs to lab, and Gene Hanlon was coming down and we met halfway, and for no reason I could see, he belted me as hard as he could on my shoulder. My glasses flew off and bounced halfway down the stairs along with a whole armload of books and papers. I had to grab the banister to keep from following them down myself. Two other guys with him saw him do it and didn't say anything at first, but then they looked at Gene and knew they'd better laugh, so they did. So I sat there on the stairs all confused inside, holding my shoulder to make it stop hurting. Gene Hanlon and the others went on down the stairs laughing to beat all at how I looked there with everything scattered around me. On the way down, Gene kicked my physics book ahead of him, bouncing it all the way to the bottom. When I could stand up all right I went down and got it. When I picked it up it fell apart in my hands with its binding broken and I guess I started to cry. I hate to see books treated that way.

When I had about got everything picked up, Peter Irish came up to where I was and wanted to know what had happened. Peter being my best friend, I told him all about it. Probably there were still tears in my eyes about the physics book because Peter said, "Do you want me to get him for you?"

I thought for a minute how swell that would be, but then I said no. It was almost yes because Peter was the only one in school who could have whipped Gene under any rules, and it was a very satisfying thing to think about. But then I thought about afterwards, when Gene would have gotten over his beating and would begin to wonder why Peter had done it, and he would remember that Peter was my best friend. Then he would put one and one together and start out after me seriously. So I said no.

Peter Irish was a good friend to have. I suppose he was the strongest kid in school, but he didn't ever use his strength to bully people, but just for things that were fun, like squashing a beer can in one hand. You knew him pretty well because of all the times he came over to the house to study with me. I remember the time he beat you at Indian hand wrestling on the dining-room table, and you were a real good sport about it because Mother was watching and laughing at your expression. But anyway, you know how strong Peter was, and you can feature what he would have done to Gene if I'd told him to. Peter always stayed out of fights unless they were for fun, and if they ever got serious he'd quit because he didn't want to hurt anybody. But he would have torn Gene Hanlon apart if I had asked him to.

That was something I don't think you understood—Peter and me, I mean, and why we hung around together. The simplest way to say it is that we swapped talents. I used to write a lot of his themes for him, and help him in labs so he'd finish when the rest of us did, and he'd show me judo holds and how to skin a squirrel, and such things. You would call it a good working agreement.

Now, there are just two more things you have to know about to see the whole picture. The first one is Peter Irish and Angela Pine. Peter and Angela went together all last year and the year before, and neither of them wanted anybody else. Both their folks made them date other kids because they didn't like to see them going steady, but everybody knew that Angela belonged to Peter, and Peter belonged to Angela, and that's all there was to it. He used to talk to me a lot about her, and how they were going to get married and run a riding stable together. And he told me that he would never touch her that way until they were married. They used to kiss good night and that was all, because Peter said that when the great thing happened, he wanted it to happen just right, and it could never be really right while they were both kids in high school. A lot of the fellows thought that more went on between them than I know did, but that's because they didn't understand Peter really. He had a simple set of rules he operated under, and they suited him very well. He was good to Angela and good to animals, and all he asked was to be let alone to do things his own way.

The other thing you have to know about is the noontime rock fights. From the papers and the inquest and all, you know something about them, but not everything. I guess most of the parents were pretty shocked to learn that their little Johnny was in a mob rock fight every day at school, but that's the way it was. The fights started over a year ago, as near as I can recollect, and went on all that time without the faculty ever finding out. The papers made a big scandal out of them and conducted what they called an "exposé of vicious practices at select Manning Day School." It was comical, actually, the way everybody got all steamed up over the things we knew went on all the time, not only at Manning but in all the other schools in town. Of course, we all knew the rock fights were wrong, but they were more fun than they seemed wrong, so we kept them up. (That time I came home with the mouse under my eye, I didn't get it by falling in the locker room. I just forgot to duck.)

We had a strict set of rules in the fights so that nobody would really get hurt or anything, and so the little guys could get into them too without fear of being killed. All sixty of us, the whole school, were divided into two teams, the Union Army and the Confederates, and after lunch in the cafeteria we'd all get our blue or gray caps and head out into the woods behind the school. The faculty thought we played Kick the Can and never followed us out to check up on us.

Each team had a fort we'd built out of sapling logs—really just pens about waist high. The forts were about two hundred yards apart, invisible to each other through the trees and scrub. You weren't allowed to use rocks any bigger than a hazelnut, and before you pegged one at a guy in the opposite army, you had to go *chk, chk* with your mouth so the guy would have a chance to find where it was coming from and duck in time. We had scouting parties and assault teams and patrols, and all the rest of the military things we could think up. The object was to storm the enemy's fort and take it before recess was up and we had to quit.

These rock fights weren't like the papers said at all. I remember the *Morning Star* called them "pitched battles of unrelenting fury, where injuries were frequent." That was silly. If the injuries had been frequent, it wouldn't have been fun any more, and nobody would have wanted to keep doing it. You *could* get hurt, of course, but you could get hurt a lot worse in a football game with the grandstand full of newspaper reporters and faculty and parents all cheering you on.

Now I guess you know everything that was important before the day Gene Hanlon got killed, and I can tell you how it happened so that you'll know why.

After our last morning class, Peter Irish and I went down to the washroom in the basement to clean up for lunch. All morning Peter had acted funny—silent and sort of tied up inside—and it was worrying me some. At first I thought I had done something he didn't like, but if I had, he'd have told me. He'd hardly said two words all morning, and he had missed two recitations in English that I had coached him on myself. But you couldn't pry trouble out of Peter, so I just kept quiet and waited for him to let me in on it.

While he was washing his hands I had to go into one of the stalls. I went in and shut the door and was hanging up my jacket when I heard somebody else come into the washroom. I don't know why, but I sat down—being real careful not to make any noise.

Somebody said, "Hi, Pete, boy." It was Gene Hanlon, and he was alone for once.

"Hi, Gene." That was Peter. (I am trying to put this down as near as I can just the way they said it.)

"Oh, man!" Gene said. "Today I am exhaust pipe!"

"Tired?"

"You said the word, man. Real beat under."

"Why so?"

"Big date last night. Friend of yours, Angela Pine." Just as if that stall door hadn't been there, I could see Gene grinning at Peter and waiting for a rise out of him. Peter didn't say anything, so Gene tried again. "You're pretty sly, Pete."

"What do you mean?"

"I mean about Angela. You've done a real fine job of keeping her in drydock all this time."

"She dates other guys," Peter said, sounding like he ought to clear his throat.

"Aaaah. She goes out with those meatballs and then comes home and shakes hands at the door. What kind of a date is that?"

"Well, that's *her* business."

Gene said, giggling, "I don't know what her business is, but I got a few suggestions for her if she ever asks me."

"What are you getting at?"

"Real coy, boy. She's crazy for it. Just crazy. Real crazy hungry chick, yeah."

"Are you through?"

"What? . . . Oh, sure. *Hey!* You sore or something?"

Peter said, "It's time for you to go eat lunch."

"All right already. Jesus! You don't have to get *that* way about it. A guy gives you a compliment and you go and get sore. You *are* an odd ball. You and your screwy horses too. See you around." And Gene went out scuffing his feet along the floor.

When I came out of the stall Peter was hunched stiff-armed over the wash-basin. He didn't even know I was around. I wished right then that I could have gone back and unlived the last five minutes. I wished they had never happened, and that everything was back just the way it was before. I was hurt and mad, and my mind was whirling around full of all the stuff Gene Hanlon had said. Just to be doing something, I got busy combing my hair, wetting and shaking the comb and all, trying to find a way to say what I was feeling. Peter was very busy turning both faucets on and off again in a kind of splashy rhythm.

Finally, I said, "If you believe all that crap, you're pretty silly. That guy's a bragging liar and you know it."

Peter looked up at me as though he had just noticed I was there. "I've got to believe it," he said.

I jumped on him for that. "Oh, come on," I said. "Give Angela a little credit. She wouldn't give that pile of you-know-what the right time."

Peter was looking down the basin drain. "I called her this morning to say hello. She wouldn't talk to me, Ronnie. She wouldn't even come to the phone."

Now I knew what had been eating him all morning. There wasn't any more a friend could say to Peter, so I made him let go of the faucets and come with me to eat lunch in the cafeteria. All through lunch he just pushed dishes around on his tray and didn't say anything. As we scraped our plates I asked him if he was going out to the fight in the woods, and he surprised me by saying yes, so we got our caps and hiked out to the Confederate fort.

Almost everybody, Gene Hanlon too, was

there before us, and they'd already chosen today's generals. Smitty Rice was General of the Armies of the Confederacy, and Gene Hanlon was the Union Commander. Gene took all his boys off to the Union fort to wait for the starting whistle, and Smitty outlined his strategy to us.

There was to be a feint at the south side of the Union fort, and then a noisy second feint from the north to pull the defenders out of position. Then Smitty and Peter Irish were to lead the real massed assault from the south, under the lip of the hill where the first feint had come from. When five minutes had gone by on my watch, we all got up and Smitty blew the starting whistle and we piled out of the fort, leaving only five inside as a garrison, and a couple of alarm guards a little way out on each side of the fort.

I got the job I usually got—advance observation post. I was to note enemy movements and remember concentrations and directions and elapsed times between sightings. Even though you couldn't see more than a hundred feet through the woods, you could always get a fair idea of the enemy strategy by the way they moved their troops around. So all I had to do was stay in one place and watch and listen and remember, and every so often Smitty would send a runner over from field headquarters to check up on what had happened lately. I had three or four good posts picked out where I could hide and not be seen, and I never used the same one twice running.

Today's was my favorite—Baker Post, we called it. It was a dense thicket of young blackjack oak on a low hill on the inside of a bend in the creek, and because nothing grew on the gravel bars of the creek, you could see a long way to each side. The creek ran generally south, cutting the fighting area between the forts right in two, and it made a good defense line because there were only a few places you could cross it in one jump and not get your shoes wet. The east bank of the creek, directly across from Baker Post, is a vertical bluff about ten feet high so that the ground up there is right on eye level with Baker, and the creek and the gravel bars are spread out between you and the bluff bank. I always knew that Baker Post was good, because every time I took it up I had to flush out a covey of quail or a cottontail.

It was always quiet in the woods during the first few minutes of those fights. Even the birds shut up, it seemed like, waiting for the first troop contacts. Out of the corner of my eye I saw somebody jump the creek at the North Ford, and I rolled over to watch. Because of the brush up there I couldn't see who it was, but I knew he was there because once in a while a bush would stir, or his

foot would slide a little on the gravel. Pretty soon he came out to the edge of the underbrush and crouched there looking around and listening. It was Gene Hanlon. His eyes crossed right over me, without finding me, and after a minute he came out and ran low along the creek. When he got even with Baker Post, he went down to his knees and began filling his cap with rocks. I had to laugh to myself at how stupid that was. He should have collected his ammunition earlier, when he and his army were on their way over to their fort. He was wasting maneuvering time and exposing himself for no good reason. It makes you feel good when a guy you hate does something dumb like that.

I got ready to go *chk, chk* with my mouth just to scare him and see him run. But then I looked up at the bluff above him and my heart flopped over inside me. Peter Irish was there, down on one knee, looking over at Gene Hanlon. Gene never looked up. Peter moves like that—floating in and out of the brush as quietly as if he didn't weigh anything. Peter was a good woods fighter.

So instead of going *chk, chk* I hunkered down lower in my thicket and thought to myself that now it wasn't a game any more. Peter looked a long time over at where I was hiding, then he looked up and down the creek bed, and then he moved back a little from the edge of the bluff. He put all his weight pulling on a half-buried boulder beside him until it turned over in its socket and he could get a good grip on it. Even from where I was I could see the cords come out in his neck when he raised it up in his arms and stood up. I hadn't heard a sound except the creek gurgling a little, and Gene Hanlon scratching around in the gravel. And also the blood roaring in my own ears. Watching this was like being in a movie and seeing the story happen on the screen. Nothing you can do or say will change what is going to happen because it's all there in the unwinding reel.

Peter held the heavy stone like a medicine ball and walked to the edge of the bluff and looked down at Gene Hanlon. Gene had moved a few feet south along the creek, so Peter above him moved south too, until he was even with Gene. Peter made a little grunt when he pushed the rock out and away and it fell. Gene heard the grunt and lifted his head to look up, and the rock hit him full in the face and bent his head away back and made his arms fly out. He sat right down in the water with his red and dirty face turned up to the sky and his hands holding him up behind. Then he got himself up with his head still twisted back like that, so he was looking straight up, and he wandered a little way downstream with the water up to his knees, and then he fell out on a gravel bar on his stomach.

His legs and arms spread out like he was asleep, but his head was up rigid and his mouth was open. I couldn't look any more.

Peter hadn't made a sound leaving, but when I looked up, the bluff above was empty. As soon as I could move without getting sick I faded out of there and went up north a ways to Able Post and lay down in the foxhole there and held myself around the knees and just shook. I couldn't have felt more upset if I had dropped that rock myself. Just like a movie reel had the ends tied together, the whole scene kept rolling over and over in front of my eyes, and I couldn't stop the film or even turn off the light in the projector.

I lay there with my head down waiting for someone to find the body and start hollering. It was little Marvin Herold, Smitty's courier, who started screaming in his high voice, "Safety! . . . Oh, God! . . . Safety safety safety! . . . Help! . . . Help!" "Safety" was the call we used to stop the fights if anyone saw a master coming or somebody got hurt. I lay there for several minutes listening to guys running past me through the brush heading for Baker Post, then I got up and followed them. I couldn't move very fast because my knees kept trying to bend the wrong way.

When I came out of the brush onto the gravel bank, I was surprised that everything looked so different. When I had left just five minutes before, the whole clearing and the creek were empty and lying bright in the sun, and Gene Hanlon was there all alone on the gravel bar. Now, with all the guys standing around and talking at once with their backs to the body, the whole place was different, and it wasn't so bad being there. I saw little Marvin Herold go over and try to take the pulse of Gene Hanlon's body. Marvin is a Boy Scout with lots of merit badges, and I expected him to try artificial respiration or a tourniquet, but he didn't find any pulse so he stood up and shook his head and wobbled over to where we were. He looked terribly blank, as though the *Scout Manual* had let him down.

The assumption going around was that Gene had run off the bluff and landed on his head and broken his neck. I couldn't see Peter anywhere, so I finally had to ask Smitty where he was. Smitty said he had sent Peter in to the school to tell somebody what had happened, and to get the ambulance. Smitty was still being the General, I guess, because there was nothing less for him to do. I tried to think to myself what Peter must be feeling like now, sent off to do an errand like that, but I couldn't get anywhere. My head was too full of what *I* was feeling like, standing with the fellows on the gravel bar looking at Gene Hanlon spread out half in the water like a dropped doll, knowing just how he had gotten there, and not being able to say anything.

Then Smitty got an idea, and he said, "Ronnie, weren't you here at Baker Post all the time?"

I made myself look at him, and then I said, "No, damn it, I got to thinking their army might try a crossing up by Able Post, so I went up there instead."

He said, "Oh," and forgot it.

Not long after, we heard a siren. We all knew what it was, and everybody stopped talking to listen to it as it got nearer. It was the first time I ever heard a siren and knew while hearing it why it had been called, and where it was going. It was sort of creepy, like it was saying to us over the trees, "Wait right there, boys. Don't anybody leave. I'll be there in a minute, and then we'll see just what's going on." I wanted to run and keep on running, until I got away from all the things swarming around inside me. You always wish afterward you had never joggled the wasp ball.

Pretty soon we heard somebody moving in the woods on the bluff and then two big men in white pants, carrying a folded-up stretcher, and another man in a suit, carrying a black bag, came out to the lip of the bluff. They stood there looking at us a minute without saying anything until one of the stretcher-bearers saw Gene Hanlon lying there all alone on the gravel bar. The man said something to the other two, and they all three looked where he pointed. Then the doctor looked at us all bunched up where we were and said, "Well, how do we get down?" He sounded sore. None of us moved or said anything, and in a minute the doctor got tired of waiting and blasted us. "Wake up over there! How do we go to get down?" Smitty came unstuck and gave them directions, and they went back into the brush heading north.

From then on things got pretty crowded in the woods. Two uniformed policemen and a photographer and a plain-clothes man showed up, and then Peter Irish came back leading almost the whole school faculty, and later a reporter and another photographer arrived. Nobody paid any attention to us for a while, so we just sat there in a clump, not moving or saying much. I managed to get right in the middle, and I kept down, hiding behind the guys around me and looking between them to see what was going on. After the police photographer was through taking pictures of Gene Hanlon from all sides, the two ambulance men raised him onto the stretcher and covered him with a piece of canvas or something and carried him away. The photographer took pictures all around by the creek and then went up onto the bluff and took pictures of the ground up there too. The plain-clothes man poking around on the gravel bar found Gene Hanlon's blue cap half full of rocks and gave it, with the rocks still in it, to one of the policemen to save.

I finally got up nerve enough to look for Peter Irish. He was standing with Smitty and Mr. Kelly, the math teacher, and they were talking. Peter didn't look any different. I didn't see how he could do it. I mean, stand right out there in plain sight of everyone, looking natural, with all that in his head. He looked around slowly as though he felt me watching him, and he found me there in the middle of the bunch. I couldn't have looked away if I had tried. He gave me a little smile, and I nodded my head to show him I'd seen it, then he went back to his talking with the other two.

Then the plain-clothes man went over to the three of them, and I got all wild inside and wanted to jump up and say that Peter couldn't possibly have done it, so please go away and let him alone. I could see the plain-clothes man doing most of the talking, and Peter and Smitty saying something once in a while, as though they were answering questions. After a little the plain-clothes man stopped talking and nodded, and the other three nodded back, and then he led them over to where the rest of us were. Smitty and Peter sat down with us and Mr. Kelly collected all the other faculty men and brought them over.

The plain-clothes man tipped his hat back and put his hands in his pockets and said, "My name is Gorman. Sergeant Gorman. We know all about the rock fight now, so don't get nervous that you'll let on something that'll get you into trouble. You're already *in* trouble, but that's not my business. You can settle that with your instructors and your parents. Uh ... you might think some about this, though. It's my feeling that every one of you here has a share in the responsibility for this boy's death. You all know rock fighting is dangerous, but you went ahead and did it anyway. But that's not what I'm after right now. I want to know if any of you boys actually saw this (what's his name?), this Hanlon boy run over the bluff." I was looking straight at Sergeant Gorman, but in the side of my eye I saw Peter Irish turn his head around and look at me. I didn't peep.

Then Sergeant Gorman said, "Which one of you is Ronnie Quiller?"

I almost fainted.

Somebody poked me and I said, "Me." It didn't sound like my voice at all.

Sergeant Gorman said, "Which?"

I said, "Me," again.

This time he found me and said, "Weren't you supposed to be lying there in this thicket all the time?"

"Yes," I said. All the kids were looking at me. "But there wasn't anything doing here so I moved up there a ways."

"I see," he said. "Do you always disobey orders?"

"No," I said, "but after all, it was only a game."

"Some game," said Sergeant Gorman. "Good clean fun."

Then he let me alone. There was only one person there who knew I would never have deserted the post assigned to me. That was Peter Irish. I guess, Dad, that's when I began to get really scared. The worst of it was not knowing how much Peter knew, and not daring to ask. He might have been waiting out of sight in the brush after he dropped that rock, and seen me take out for Able Post. I had always been his friend, but what was I now to him? I wanted to tell him everything was okay and I wouldn't for the world squeal on him, but that would have told him I knew he did it. Maybe he knew without my telling me. I didn't know what to do.

Sergeant Gorman finished up, "Let's all go back to the school now. I want to talk to each of you alone." We all got up and started back through the woods in a bunch. I figured Peter would think it was funny if I avoided him, so I walked with him.

I said, "Lousy damn day."

He said, "Real lousy."

I said, "It seems like a hundred years since lunch."

We didn't say any more all the way back.

It took all afternoon to get the individual interviews over. They took us from Assembly Hall in alphabetical order, and we had to go in and sit across from Sergeant Gorman while he asked the questions. He must have asked us all the same questions because by the time he got to me he was saying the words like they were tired. A girl stenographer sat by him and took down the answers.

"Name?"

"Ronnie Quiller." I had to spell it.

"Were you at the rock fight this afternoon?"

"Yes, I was."

"What side were you on?"

"The Confederates."

"What were you supposed to do?"

"Watch the guys on the other side."

"After this whistle, did you see anyone?"

"No."

"You sure?"

"No, I didn't. That's why I moved from Baker Post up to Able Post. There wasn't anything doing where I was hiding."

"In rock fights before, have you ever changed position without telling somebody?"

"Sure, I guess. You can't run clear back to the field headquarters to tell anyone anything. It's up to them to find *you*."

Sergeant Gorman squinted at me with his eyebrows pulled down. "You know that if you had stayed where you were supposed to be you would have seen him fall over that bluff there?"

"Yes," I said.

"I wish you had."

Afterwards I ran into Smitty out in the hall and I asked him why all this fuss with the police and all. I asked him who called them.

"It was Peter, I think. He told Mr. Kelly to, and Mr. Kelly did."

"What do you suppose they're after?" I asked Smitty.

"Oh, I guess they're trying to get a straight story to tell Gene's parents and the newspapers. From what I get from Mr. Kelly, the school is all for it. They want everybody to know they weren't responsible."

"Do *you* think Gene fell over that bluff?" I couldn't help asking that one.

"I don't know. I suppose so." He cocked his head to one side and grinned a little at me. "Like they say in the papers, 'fell or was pushed,' huh?"

I said, "I guess nobody'd have nerve enough to do that to Gene—push him, I mean." All of a sudden I was thinking about something I had seen. Going back in my mind I remembered seeing Sergeant Gorman pick up Gene's cap half full of rocks. Gravel rocks taken from the low bank of the creek. Now, I figured that Sergeant Gorman wouldn't have been a sergeant if he was stupid, and unless he was stupid he wouldn't go on for long thinking that Gene had fallen from above—*when the cap half full of rocks said he'd been down below all the time!*

I got my bike and rode home the long way to give me time to think about Peter and what he had done, and what I should do. You were real swell that night, and I guess I should have told you the whole story right then, but I just couldn't. I put myself in Peter's place, and I knew he would never have told on me. That's the way he was. He hated squealers. I couldn't think about his ever learning I had squealed on him. That would put me right alongside Angela Pine in his book. To him, I would have been the second person he trusted who let him down.

I felt like a rat in a cage with no place to go and no way out. When you kept me home nights after that, I didn't mind, because I wouldn't have gone out after dark if I'd been paid to. I don't blame you and Mother for thinking I had gone loony over the whole thing. Every noon recess for two whole weeks they pulled us into Assembly Hall and one of the masters would give a speech about group responsibility or public conscience or something awful like that, and then, worst of all, they made us bow our heads for five minutes in memory of Gene Hanlon. And there I'd be, sitting next to Peter Irish on the Assembly Hall bench, thinking back to the day of the last rock fight, and how Peter had looked up there on the bluff with the cords of his neck pulled tight, holding that big rock like it was a medicine ball. I had the crawliest feeling that if anybody in the hall had raised up his head and looked over at us together there on the bench, he would have seen two great fiery arrows pointing down at us. I was always afraid even to look up myself for fear I would have seen my own arrow and passed out on the spot.

It was my nightmares that got you worried, I guess. They always started out with Peter and me on a hike on a dusty country road. It was so hot you could hardly breathe. We would walk along without saying anything, with me lagging a little behind Peter so I could always keep an eye on him. And then the road would come out on the football field there at school, and he would go over to the woodpile and pick up a thin log and hold it in one hand, beckoning to me with the other and smiling. "Let's go over to the drugstore," he'd say, and then I'd start running.

I would follow the quarter-mile track around the football field and I'd know that everything would be all right if I could only get around it four times for a full mile. Every time I turned around to look, there he'd be right behind me, carrying that log and running easily, just like he used to pace me when I was out for the 880. I would make the first quarter mile all right, but then my wind would give out and my throat would dry up and my legs would get heavy, and I'd know that Peter was about to catch me, and I'd never make that full mile.

Then I would jar awake and be sweating and hanging on tight to the mattress, and in a minute you'd come in to see why I'd screamed. Your face was always kind of sad over me, and there in my bed in the dark, with you standing beside, I would *almost* let go and tell you why things were so bad with me. But then as I'd come awake, and the hammering in my heart would slow up, and the sweat would begin to dry, all the things I owed Peter

Irish would stand out again and look at me, and I would know that I could never tell you about it until my telling could no longer get Peter Irish into trouble.

I'm tired now, Dad—tired in so many ways and in so many places that I don't know where to begin resting. This letter took all night, as I thought it would. It's beginning to get light outside and the birds are starting up. I just reread the story in the paper where it says that Sergeant Gorman knew all along that Gene Hanlon had been murdered. I told you he wasn't stupid. He knew what that cap half full of rocks meant, and he knew what it meant to find a big damp socket in the earth on top of the bluff, and the rock which had been *in* the socket down below in the creek. And after he had talked to each of us alphabetically there in the school office, he knew the name of the only boy in school strong enough to lift up a seventy-pound rock and throw it like a medicine ball. He knew all of these things before the sun went down on the day of the last rock fight, but he was two months putting the rest of the story together so he could use it in his business.

As I read it in the paper, Sergeant Gorman went over to Peter's house last Monday and talked to him about the things he had learned, and Peter listened respectfully, and then, when Sergeant Gorman was through and was ready to take Peter along with him, Peter excused himself to go upstairs and get his toilet articles. He got his four-ten shotgun instead and shot himself. I suppose it was the same four-ten he and I hunted squirrels with.

There's only one good thing about this whole stinking lousy mess, Dad. Because Sergeant Gorman talked to Peter and Peter listened, there in the living room; when Peter Irish climbed up those stairs he did it knowing that I, Ronnie Quiller, had not squealed on him. That may have made it easier. I don't know.

Now please, Dad—please may I come home again?

RONNIE

From *Able Baker and Others* by Joseph Whitehill (Boston: Little, Brown and Co., 1957). Reprinted by permission of Candida Donadio & Associates, Inc. Copyright © 1954, 1955, 1956, 1957 by Joseph Whitehill.

Editors' Commentary

Diagnosis: Traumatic or situational neurosis—severe anxiety reaction.

This story deals with a neurosis brought about by conflict between guilt and loyalty. Ronnie was fully aware of the guilt he shared with Peter by concealment. His conscience or superego immobilized him. He was torn between society's demand to report homicide to the authorities and his own love for and loyalty to his friend. Peter had many times protected Ronnie from the cruelty or bullying of other boys, particularly the star bully, Gene Hanlon. Ronnie's guilt was not only that of concealment but also that of shared hostility. He too hated Gene Hanlon and at times may have fantasized the aggression that Peter acted out.

In the adolescent struggle for identity, Peter and Ronnie made up one whole person, each compensating for the other's weaknesses and using the other's strength. "We swapped talents," Ronnie says—Ronnie being the intellectual performer. He considered himself a natural scapegoat and thus regarded Peter, the physical performer, with gratitude and respect. Ronnie sensed he must not under any circumstance betray his friend. His emotions were complicated by partial hostility and jealousy toward Angela (he also had trouble trusting his own mother, as indicated in the first paragraph of his letter); but, as the physically more passive of the two boys, he was taking the feminine role, which made him feel superior to Angela.

As a sensitive boy, Ronnie was aware that Peter must be protected not only from the police or another betrayer, but even from knowing that he, Ronnie, knew of the crime. Thus, Ronnie felt trapped—"like a rat in a cage"—by the necessity for silence and the projection of guilt. His overt symptoms were deep depression, nightmares, sweating, and inability to be with his friends.

His letter, written to a trusted parent as soon as the crime was exposed, without his having participated in its exposure, released him from his anxiety reaction. He was able to see his own part in the drama and also to evaluate realistically and without blame the part of the adults. His trust in his father's ability to listen to him sympathetically indicates he had a basically sound relationship and therefore the capacity to grow out of this incident.

If father listens, good! Ronnie should come home, resume normal life, and receive individual psychotherapy for catharsis of trauma, for his identity problems (including sexual identity), and for his scapegoat feelings. Obviously the boy has great capacity for awareness, introspection, and meaningful relationships.

Between the lines of this story runs an undercurrent of a homosexual relationship between Ronnie and Peter. Such a relationship, as Sullivan[2] states in his theory of interpersonal development, is a normal aspect of growth and a primer for teaching about nonfamilial love. When the culture surrounds such development with opprobrium, dismay, and punitive or horrified responses, this normal tide may be turned to self-doubt, guilt, and immobilization. These factors may have contributed, along with the murder, to Ronnie's severe distress.

2. **Harry Stack Sullivan,** *Theory of Interpersonal Relations* (New York: W. W. Norton, 1953).

Paul's Case

Willa Cather

It was Paul's afternoon to appear before the faculty of the Pittsburgh High School to account for his various misdemeanors. He had been suspended a week ago, and his father had called at the Principal's office and confessed his perplexity about his son. Paul entered the faculty room suave and smiling. His clothes were a trifle outgrown, and the tan velvet on the collar of his open overcoat was frayed and worn; but for all that there was something of the dandy about him, and he wore an opal pin in his neatly knotted black four-in-hand, and a red carnation in his buttonhole. This latter adornment the faculty somehow felt was not properly significant of the contrite spirit befitting a boy under the ban of suspension.

Paul was tall for his age and very thin, with high, cramped shoulders and a narrow chest. His eyes were remarkable for a certain hysterical brilliancy, and he continually used them in a conscious, theatrical sort of way, peculiarly offensive in a boy. The pupils were abnormally large, as though he were addicted to belladonna, but there was a glassy glitter about them which that drug does not produce.

When questioned by the Principal as to why he was there, Paul stated, politely enough, that he wanted to come back to school. This was a lie, but Paul was quite accustomed to lying; found it, indeed, indispensable for overcoming friction. His teachers were asked to state their respective charges against him, which they did with such a rancor and aggrievedness as evinced that this was not a usual case. Disorder and impertinence were among the offenses named, yet each of his instructors felt that it was scarcely possible to put into words the real cause of the trouble, which lay in a sort of hysterically defiant manner of the boy's; in the contempt which they all knew he felt for them, and which he seemingly made not the least effort to conceal. Once, when he had been making a synopsis of a paragraph at the blackboard, his English teacher had stepped to his side and attempted to guide his hand. Paul had started back with a shudder and thrust his hands violently behind him. The astonished woman could scarcely have been more hurt and embarrassed had he struck at her. The insult was so involuntary and definitely personal as to be unforgettable. In one way and another, he had made all his teachers, men and women alike, conscious of the same feeling of physical aversion. In one class he habitually sat with his hand shading his eyes; in another he always looked out of the window during the recitation; in another he made a running commentary on the lecture, with humorous intent.

His teachers felt this afternoon that his whole attitude was symbolized by his shrug and his flippantly red carnation flower, and they fell upon him without mercy, his English teacher leading the pack. He stood through it smiling, his pale lips parted over his white teeth. (His lips were continually twitching, and he had a habit of raising his eyebrows that was contemptuous and irritating to the last degree.) Older boys than Paul had broken down and shed tears under that ordeal, but his set smile did not once desert him, and his only sign of discomfort was the nervous trembling of the fingers that toyed with the buttons of his overcoat, and an occasional jerking of the other hand which held his hat. Paul was always smiling, always glancing about him, seeming to feel that people might be watching him and trying to detect something. This conscious expression, since it was as far as possible from boyish mirthfulness, was usually attributed to insolence or "smartness."

As the inquisition proceeded, one of his instructors repeated an impertinent remark of the boy's, and the Principal asked him whether he thought that a courteous speech to make to a woman. Paul shrugged his shoulders slightly and his eyebrows twitched.

"I don't know," he replied. "I didn't mean to be polite or impolite, either. I guess it's a sort of way I have, of saying things regardless."

The Principal asked him whether he didn't think that a way it would be well to get rid of. Paul grinned and said he guessed so. When he was told that he could go, he bowed gracefully and went out. His bow was like a repetition of the scandalous red carnation.

His teachers were in despair, and his drawing master voiced the feeling of them all when he declared there was something about the boy which none of them understood. He added: "I don't really believe that smile of his comes altogether from insolence; there's something sort of haunted about it. The boy is not strong, for one thing. . . . There is something wrong about the fellow."

The drawing master had come to realize that, in looking at Paul, one saw only his white teeth and the forced animation of his eyes. One warm afternoon the boy had gone to sleep at his drawing board, and his master had noted with amazement what a white, blue-veined face it was; drawn and wrinkled like an old man's about the eyes, the lips twitching even in his sleep. . . .

His teachers left the building dissatisfied and unhappy; humiliated to have felt so vindictive toward a mere boy, to have uttered this feeling in cutting terms, and to have set each other on, as it were, in the gruesome game of intemperate reproach. One of them remembered having seen a miserable street cat set at bay by a ring of tormentors.

As for Paul, he ran down the hill whistling the Soldiers' Chorus from *Faust*, looking wildly behind him now and then to see whether some of his teachers were not there to witness his lightheartedness. As it was now late in the afternoon and Paul was on duty that evening as usher at Carnegie Hall, he decided that he would not go home to supper. . . .

After a concert was over, Paul was often irritable and wretched until he got to sleep—and tonight he was even more than usually restless. He had the feeling of not being able to let down; of its being impossible to give up this delicious excitement which was the only thing that could be called living at all. During the last number he withdrew and, after hastily changing his clothes in the dressing-room, slipped out to the side door where the singer's carriage stood. Here he began pacing rapidly up and down the walk, waiting to see her come out.

Over yonder the Schenley, in its vacant stretch, loomed big and square through the fine rain, the windows of its twelve stories glowing like those of a lighted cardboard house under a Christmas tree. All the actors and singers of any importance stayed there when they were in the city, and a number of the big manufacturers of the place lived there in the winter. Paul had often hung about the hotel, watching the people go in and out, longing to enter and leave schoolmasters and dull care behind him forever.

At last the singer came out, accompanied by the conductor, who helped her into her carriage and closed the door with a cordial *auf wiedersehen*— which set Paul to wondering whether she were not an old sweetheart of his. Paul followed the carriage over to the hotel, walking so rapidly as not to be far from the entrance when the singer alighted and disappeared behind the swinging glass doors which were opened by a Negro in a tall hat and a long coat. In the moment that the door was ajar, it seemed to Paul that he, too, entered. He seemed to feel himself go after her up the steps, into the warm, lighted building, into an exotic, tropical world of shiny, glistening surfaces and basking ease. He reflected upon the mysterious dishes that were brought into the dining-room, the green bottles in buckets of ice, as he had seen them in the supper party pictures of the Sunday supplement. A quick gust of wind brought the rain down with sudden vehemence, and Paul was startled to find that he was still outside in the slush of the gravel driveway; that his boots were letting in the water and his scanty overcoat was clinging wet about him; that the lights in front of the concert hall were out; and that the rain was driving in sheets between him and the orange glow of the windows above him. There it was, what he wanted—tangibly before him, like the fairy world of a Christmas pantomime; as the rain beat in his face, Paul wondered whether he was destined always to shiver in the black night outside, looking up at it.

He turned and walked reluctantly toward the car tracks. The end had to come some time; his father in his night-clothes at the top of the stairs, explanations that did not explain, hastily improvised fictions that were forever tripping him up, his upstairs room and its horrible yellow wallpaper, the creaking bureau with the greasy plush collar-box, and over his painted wooden bed the pictures of George Washington and John Calvin, and the framed motto, "Feed my Lambs," which had been worked in red worsted by his mother [*whom Paul could not remember*]. . . .

The leading juvenile of the permanent stock company which played at one of the downtown theaters was an acquaintance of Paul's, and the boy had been invited to drop in at the Sunday night rehearsals whenever he could. For more than a year Paul had spent every available moment loitering about Charley Edwards's dressing-room. He had won a place among Edwards's following not only because the young actor, who could not afford to employ a dresser, often found him useful, but because he recognized in Paul something akin to what churchmen term "vocation."

It was at the theater and at Carnegie Hall that Paul really lived; the rest was but a sleep and a forgetting. This was Paul's fairy tale, and it had for him all the allurement of a secret love. The moment he inhaled the gassy, painty, dusty odor behind the scenes, he breathed like a prisoner set free, and felt within him the possibility of doing or saying splendid, brilliant things. The moment the cracked orchestra beat out the overture from *Martha*, or jerked at the serenade from *Rigoletto*, all stupid and ugly things slid from him, and his senses were deliciously, yet delicately fired.

Perhaps it was because, in Paul's world, the natural nearly always wore the guise of ugliness, that a certain element of artificiality seemed to him necessary in beauty. Perhaps it was because his experience of life elsewhere was so full of Sabbath-school picnics, petty economies, wholesome advice as to how to succeed in life, and the unescapable odors of cooking, that he found this existence so

alluring, these smartly clad men and women so attractive, that he was so moved by these starry apple orchards that bloomed perennially under the limelight.

It would be difficult to put it strongly enough how convincingly the stage entrance of that theater was for Paul the actual portal of Romance. Certainly none of the company ever suspected it, least of all Charley Edwards. It was very like the old stories that used to float about London of fabulously rich Jews, who had subterranean halls, with palms, and fountains, and soft lamps and richly appareled women who never saw the disenchanting light of London day. So, in the midst of that smoke-palled city, enamored of figures and grimy toil, Paul had his secret temple, his wishing-carpet, his bit of blue-and-white Mediterranean shore bathed in perpetual sunshine.

Several of Paul's teachers had a theory that his imagination had been perverted by garish fiction; but the truth was, he scarcely ever read at all. The books at home were not such as would either tempt or corrupt a youthful mind, and as for reading the novels that some of his friends urged upon him—well, he got what he wanted much more quickly from music; any sort of music, from an orchestra to a barrel organ. He needed only the spark, the indescribable thrill that made his imagination master of his senses, and he could make plots and pictures enough of his own. It was equally true that he was not stage-struck—not, at any rate, in the usual acceptation of that expression. He had no desire to become an actor, any more than he had to become a musician. He felt no necessity to do any of these things; what he wanted was to see, to be in the atmosphere, float on the wave of it, to be carried out, blue league after blue league, away from everything.

After a night behind the scenes, Paul found the school-room more than ever repulsive; the bare floors and naked walls; the prosy men who never wore frock coats, or violets in their buttonholes; the women with their dull gowns, shrill voices, and pitiful seriousness about prepositions that govern the dative. He could not bear to have the other pupils think, for a moment, that he took these people seriously; he must convey to them that he considered it all trivial, and was there only by way of a joke, anyway. He had autographed pictures of all the members of the stock company which he showed his classmates, telling them the most incredible stories of his familiarity with these people, of his acquaintance with the soloists who came to Carnegie Hall, his suppers with them and the flowers he sent them. When these stories lost their effect, and his audience grew listless, he would bid

all the boys good-by, announcing that he was going to travel for a while; going to Naples, to California, to Egypt. Then, next Monday, he would slip
back, conscious and nervously smiling; his sister
was ill, and he would have to defer his voyage until spring.

Matters went steadily worse with Paul at
school. In the itch to let his instructors know how
heartily he despised them, and how thoroughly he
was appreciated elsewhere, he mentioned once or
twice that he had no time to fool with theorems;
adding—with a twitch of the eyebrows and a touch
of that nervous bravado which so perplexed
them—that he was helping the people down at the
stock company; they were old friends of his.

The upshot of the matter was, that the Principal went to Paul's father, and Paul was taken out of
school and put to work. The manager at Carnegie
Hall was told to get another usher in his stead; the
doorkeeper at the theater was warned not to admit
him to the house; and Charley Edwards remorse-
fully promised the boy's father not to see him
again.

The members of the stock company were
vastly amused when some of Paul's stories reached
them—especially the women. They were hard-
working women, most of them supporting indo-
lent husbands or brothers, and they laughed rather
bitterly at having stirred the boy to such fervid and
florid inventions. They agreed with the faculty and
with his father, that Paul's was a bad case. . . .

[Paul steals money from the office where he works
and takes a train to New York, where he buys himself
some expensive clothes and, claiming that he is waiting
for his parents to arrive from Europe, installs himself in
an elegant hotel.]

On the part of the hotel management, Paul excited no suspicion. There was this to be said for
him, that he wore his spoils with dignity and in no
way made himself conspicuous. His chief greedi-
ness lay in his ears and eyes, and his excesses were
not offensive ones. His dearest pleasures were the
gray winter twilights in his sitting room; his quiet
enjoyment of his flowers, his clothes, his wide di-
van, his cigarette and his sense of power. He could
not remember a time when he had felt so at peace
with himself. The mere release from the necessity
of petty lying, lying every day and every day, restored his self-respect. He had never lied for pleasure, even at school, but to make himself noticed
and admired, to assert his difference from other
Cordelia Street boys; and he felt a good deal more
manly, more honest, even, now that he had no
need for boastful pretensions, now that he could,

as his actor friends used to say, "dress the part." It
was characteristic that remorse did not occur to
him. His golden days went by without a shadow,
and he made each as perfect as he could. . . .

[Paul has been in New York for eight days. His
money is running out, and he had too much wine the
night before.]

He rose and moved about with a painful effort,
succumbing now and again to attacks of nausea. It
was the old depression exaggerated; all the world
had become Cordelia Street. Yet somehow he was
not afraid of anything, was absolutely calm; perhaps because he had looked into the dark corner at
last, and knew. It was bad enough, what he saw
there; but somehow not so bad as his long fear of it
had been. He saw everything clearly now. He had
a feeling that he had made the best of it, that he
had lived the sort of life he was meant to live, and
for half an hour he sat staring at the revolver. But
he told himself that was not the way, so he went
downstairs and took a cab to the ferry.

When Paul arrived at Newark, he got off the
train and took another cab, directing the driver to
follow the Pennsylvania tracks out of the town.
The snow lay heavy on the roadways and had
drifted deep in the open fields. Only here and
there the dead grass or dried weed stalks projected,
singularly black, above it. Once well into the country, Paul dismissed the carriage and walked, floun-
dering along the tracks, his mind a medley of irrelevant things. He seemed to hold in his brain an
actual picture of everything he had seen that morning. He remembered every feature of both his drivers, the toothless old woman from whom he had
bought the red flowers in his coat, the agent from
whom he had got his ticket, and all of his fellow-
passengers on the ferry. His mind, unable to cope
with vital matters near at hand, worked feverishly
and deftly at sorting and grouping these images.
They made for him a part of the ugliness of the
world, of the ache in his head, and the bitter burning on his tongue. He stooped and put a handful of
snow into his mouth as he walked, but that, too,
seemed hot. When he reached a little hillside,
where the tracks ran through a cut some twenty
feet below him, he stopped and sat down.

The carnations in his coat were drooping with
the cold, he noticed; all their red glory over. It occurred to him that all the flowers he had seen in
the show windows that first night must have gone
the same way, long before this. It was only one
splendid breath they had, in spite of their brave
mockery at the winter outside the glass. It was a
losing game in the end, it seemed, this revolt

against the homilies by which the world is run. Paul took one of the blossoms carefully from his coat and scooped a little hole in the snow, where he covered it up. Then he dozed a while, from his weak condition, seeming insensible to cold.

The sound of an approaching train woke him, and he started to his feet, remembering only his resolution, and afraid lest he should be too late. He stood watching the approaching locomotive, his teeth chattering, his lips drawn away from them in a frightened smile; once or twice he glanced nervously sidewise, as though he were being watched. When the right moment came, he jumped. As he fell, the folly of his haste occurred to him with merciless clearness, the vastness of what he had left undone. There flashed through his brain, clearer than ever before, the blue of Adriatic water, the yellow of Algerian sands.

He felt something strike his chest—his body was being thrown swiftly through the air, on and on, immeasurably far and fast, while his limbs gently relaxed. Then, because the picture-making mechanism was crushed, the disturbing visions flashed into black, and Paul dropped back into the immense design of things.

Reprinted from *Youth and the Bright Medusa.*

Editors' Commentary

Diagnosis: Severe neurosis bordering on psychosis—hysteria, narcissism—leading to suicide out of desperation.

The number of youthful suicides has increased precipitously. This story, though written many years ago, illustrates beautifully one of the syndromes leading to such an end.

The faculty meeting, which is held to rule on Paul's dismissal from school, demonstrates the amount of anxiety, hostility, and aggression such a child may evoke. Paul's arrogance—his contempt for the mundane world and its mundane teachers, values, and subjects—so enrages those who must try to teach him that they react punitively and hostilely (see "The Use of Force," p. 0). They become ashamed of themselves for allowing a child to get under their skin, and thus they build up guilt. When they meet with no success in further encounters with the child, the guilt spirals to further anger, more guilt, and so on.

The child, meanwhile, has developed a poor opinion of the people about him and conceals his lack of trust behind a strong wall of contempt. His suspicious or contemptuous ways bring out the worst reactions of people, thus alienating them still further.

Paul, in his hatred for his real life, home, neighborhood, school, and teachers, takes refuge in a made-up world of theater, glamour, and make-believe. Only this world of showmanship has any meaning to him. He seeks beauty from outside, beauty that is smooth and unruffled by reality, to make up for the lack of beauty and warmth inside him. Love and understanding have been so far lost in his young life that these values seem to exist only in the wealthy, the glamorous, the dramatic life. His hysterical nature arises from his feeling that, if one poses enough, the pose may become reality. He steals money to buy himself a substitute for love. When the money runs out, the meaning of life runs out for him. His slim grasp on reality depends on the arrogant, grand attitude and picture of life. Without it, he feels he might as well be dead. To the hysteric "might as well" changes from a metaphor to a deed—suicide seems the only and inevitable solution.

To handle and reach such a child requires a great deal of security and self-esteem on the teacher's part—so that the teacher is not hurt by the child's false wall of arrogance and contempt, or repelled by the child's narcissistic manner. The teacher would have to share some of this child's love of the unreal world, encouraging the taste for drama in a useful way, offering aesthetic outlets and rewards for honest work. The ultimate despair

leading to suicide might be averted in such a case if the child were given psychodynamic group or individual treatment and a sympathetic school atmosphere, especially
if he or she were allowed to work out the feelings of emptiness and despair by identifying with someone of the same sex. The child who cannot care deeply (not necessarily
sexually) for someone of the same sex is unlikely to move on to loving someone of the
opposite sex. This explains the necessary preadolescent stage of development in which
girls are interested only in girls, and boys in boys—in the clique, the gang, or the pal.

Another book that discusses the problem of adolescent suicide in depth and with great
sensitivity is a novel, *Ordinary People* by Judith Guest (New York: Viking, 1976). It tells
of a boy who attempts suicide and after hospitalization goes into therapy with a wise,
skillful, unconventional therapist. The book also gives an extremely accurate picture of
skillful, unconventional therapist. The book also gives an extremely accurate picture of
a girlfriend the boy meets in the hospital who needs to deny her psychotic experience
and keep it secret when she gets out. In contrast, the boy, who at first seems to be
having a harder time, does work on his despair and shame and learns by means of his
family's involvement in therapy that even very difficult problems can not only be
talked about, but can be shared to the potential benefit of everyone intimately involved.
The boy comes to a better adjustment; the mother and father are finally able through the
son's expression of his difficulties to deal with the death of their other son as well as the
flaws in their own relationship. The contrast between this happening and the suicide of
the girl who was unable and unwilling to get help through skilled therapeutic intervention is gripping. A similar family involvement and joint responsibility is illustrated
in the next story excerpt.

Lie Down in Darkness

William Styron

[*The family members: Helen, the mother; Milton or
Loftis, the father, whom the daughter, Peyton, calls
Bunny. Edward is Helen's brother and Loftis's brother-
in-law. Carey is an old family friend. Dolly is a woman
friend of Loftis. Harry is the man Peyton is to marry.*]

. . . He heard Edward's laughter somewhere,
Edward who was already tight, with whom he had,
for Helen's sake, enacted the most strained and
touchy friendship, and for some reason the desire
for a drink became hot and powerful. There were
other footsteps in the hall, and he started, but they
faded away; how silly to have this nervous, quar-
relsome conscience, that resentment—yes, he had
had it, just for a moment, at Edward's laughter
which, in turn, had made him think of Helen and
of the ridiculousness of her demands on him, demands he had paradoxically brought on himself—
all in all, how silly to have to pussyfoot about like
this on Peyton's wedding day, dredging up such
ugly conflicts. Or was it silly? Well, my God, just
one. He found two glasses, got the bottle out of the
dresser and went back to Peyton's room, closing
the door behind him.

"Oh, Bunny, you're so clever," she said, "all in
such a cunning little bottle."

Loftis looked at her sharply. "Baby," he murmured, sitting down beside her, "do you really
want a drink? Why don't we wait until afterwards?
There's champagne——"

"Don't be a spoilsport. Make me a drink. This
is just for my nerves." Obediently he poured an
ounce or so into a glass.

"Aren't you going to have one?" she asked.

Why had he suddenly become so depressed? It
was unfair of Peyton to seduce him like this, and
he found himself saying, "You know, baby, I've
found that when everything is going along all
right you don't need anything to drink. When
you're happy——"

But she broke in with a laugh, her face rosy
with some sudden excitement, "Don't be so solemn, Bunny, this is for my nerves, buck up,
sweetie. . . ."

He poured himself a drink and with the first
swallow, his dark mood fading, he gazed at her,
then past her—avoiding those eyes—to say, while
the whisky taste began to seem unfamiliarly sweet

and strong, "So anyway, honey, you're here and you're going to get married to a swell guy and that's all that counts. Isn't it wonderful?"

"Yes. I'm here. Thanks to you."

"It's not my doing," he said, "thank your mother."

"I've thanked her," she said wryly, looking away.

"Now don't——" he began, for it was wrong, unbearably wrong for her to bring up, on this day of all, the faintest suggestion of regrettable memories; those memories had indeed made this day poignantly perfect, childish in its brazen delight, like the day long ago of the circus or the fair, sweet from its apocalyptic dawning to the last, exhausted, bedtime end; all the near-ruined moments in the family had made this particular day even sweeter, but it was absolutely unfair of Peyton to suggest now that anything had ever been wrong one bit. The illusion of serenity would be swept away like so many dew-drenched spider webs leaving only the unsightly façade, the dusty plaster and all the bricks with their weathered holes. So *quit, quit* it, he was trying to say, softly but forcibly. . . .

"Don't you see, Bunny, I've got my own reasons for coming home. I've wanted to be normal. I've wanted to be like everybody else. These old folks wouldn't believe that there are children who'd just throw back their heads and howl, who'd just *die* to be able to say, 'Well now my rebellion's over, home is where I want to be, home is where Daddy and Mother want me.' Not with a sort of take-me-back-I've-been-so-wrong attitude—because, Bunny, you can believe me, most kids these days are not wrong or wrongdoers, they're just aimless and lost, more aimless than you all ever thought of being—not with that attitude, but just with the kind of momentary, brief love recognizing those who fed your little baby mouth and changed your didy and paid your fare all the way. Does that sound silly, Bunny? That's all they want to do, that's what I've wanted to do and I've tried, but somehow today it all seems phony. I don't know why. I lied. I'm really not excited at all. Maybe I've got too many sour memories." She paused and looked at him, her eyes enormously sad, and he approached her, with the day in its crumbling promise going before his vision, tried to put his arms around her. "Baby——"

"Don't," she said, "don't, Bunny. I'm sorry." She held him off without even a look, for she was gazing down at the lawn, at the guests moving toward the house, all together, silent, but with a sort of giddy haste, like picnickers before the storm—holding him off as much by her silence as if she had finished erecting between them a curtain of

stone, then said gently: "I'm sorry, Bunny." She looked up at him. "I can't figure where the trouble starts. Mother. She's such a faker. Look at this circus. Flaunting the blissful family. Oh, I feel so sorry for us all. If just she'd had a soul and you'd had some guts . . . Come on now," she said, grabbing his sleeve, "let's go downstairs, sweetie. I'll put up a real good front for you."

He stood rooted to the rug, wishing to faint there forever. He had been bludgeoned half to death, not so much by these truths, he told himself while he drained the sedative glass, as by necessity.

"O.K., baby," he said. . . .

And this day had really been a triumph for her. No one would ever know. No one would ever know what electric fulfillment she felt, beneath the soft, tender dignity of her manner, behind the wrinkled, rather sad, but gracefully aging serenity of her brow. No one would ever know the struggle, either. The struggle to accomplish just this casual, collected air of the proud mother: the woman who has sacrificed, whose suffering is known to the community, but who, on the day of her daughter's marriage, presents only the face of humility and courage and gentle good will. It had been cruelly difficult to put on this act, and how she had connived, how she had falsified her true feelings! But she knew that any means justified *this* end, *this* day, and after she had murmured into Milton's ear, "Oh, darling, I do want Peyton to come home," she had rejoiced at the sincere and grateful look in his eyes; she could tell he didn't doubt her honesty.

Her honesty. Oh, what was honesty, anyway? After so much suffering, did a woman really have to be honest to fulfill herself? She felt that her marriage had been such a nightmare, she had endured so many insults—the weight of so many outrages had pressed so heavily upon her spirit—that she could discard honest intentions in order to make this one day come true. *Anything, anything,* she had said to herself these past months, *anything at all.* Anything that Peyton should come home. Anything that people should know Helen Loftis was a good mother, a successful mother. Anything that people should know: it was Helen Loftis, that suffering woman, who had brought together the broken family.

Now, in sheer, rash courtliness, Carey bent down and kissed her hand. She knew how Carey saw her: poised, gentle, smiling brightly. Who could tell, she asked herself—and certainly it wasn't Carey who could tell, in his dense, well-meaning charity—that this genteel sprightliness masked the most villainous intentions? Well they *were* villainous. Here a shadow passed over her mind, just briefly, but long enough for Carey to murmur, "What's wrong, Helen?"

"Why, nothing, Carey!"

They were cruel intentions, cruel feelings, and perhaps unnatural, but what could she do? She had suffered too much and too long not to feel them. Or it. This profound and unalterable *loathing* of Peyton. Poor Peyton. Dishonorable, sinful. Her own flesh and blood. . . .

Loftis was aware of the noise but for a solitary instant he felt—looking at Peyton and Helen and Harry—islanded in silence. And during this moment he again tried vainly to recall what he had said or done to bring on such a tense and obvious, such a mutual sense of uneasiness. *Ah, those smiles, those smiles.* Was it the kiss he gave Peyton?

Then all at once he had a flicker of insight and during this moment—so brief that it lasted, literally, one blink of Peyton's eyes—he knew what the smiles were about and he had a crushing, chilling premonition of disaster. Harry smiled politely, but he faded before his sight, for Loftis was watching Peyton. She held her glass in the air, touched it to her lips. But along with her smile there was something else he was conscious of, too: she had already drunk too much. Her face rubbed pink as if by a scrubbing brush, she glowed with a fever, and in the way her eyes sparkled, her lips moist and parted, he knew somehow, with a plummeting heart, that she was beyond recovery. It was a moment of understanding that came sharp and terrible. He felt that he had waited all his life for this moment, this flash of insight to come about. He had just said crazy, unthinking, harmless words, but he had said words like "fickle" and "love" and "death," and they, in their various ways, had sent a secret corrosion through these two women's hearts. God help him, hadn't he known all along that they hated and despised each other? Had he had to spend twenty years deceiving himself, piling false hope upon false hope—only to discover on this day, of all days, the shattering, unadorned, bitter truth? Those smiles . . . of course . . . how Peyton and Helen had always smiled at each other like that! There had been words, too, attitudes, small female gestures which it had been beyond him to divine, or even faintly to understand.

And he had gone on for years deceiving himself—too proud, too self-conscious, maybe just too stupid to realize that it had always been he himself who had been at the focus of these appalling, baffling female emotions. Not anything he had done or had failed to do had made them hate each other. Not even Dolly. None of his actions, whether right

or wrong, had caused this tragedy, so much as the pure fact of himself, his very existence, interposed weaponless and defenseless in a no-man's-land between two desperate, warring female machines. Now he had kissed Peyton, said the wrong words, and he had somehow hurt her. And the smile she wore concealed her hurt—to everyone else, at least—just as Helen's smile, echoing Peyton's, concealed only the wild, envenomed jealousy which stirred at her breast. What had she done? Why had Helen deceived him like this? Those smiles. He was chilled with a sudden horror. Those smiles. They had fluttered across the web of his life like deceptive, lovely butterflies, always leading him on, always making him believe that, in spite of everything, these two women really did love each other. That, deep down, there was motherly, daughterly affection. But no. Now he saw the smiles in a split moment for what they were: women smiles—Great God, so treacherous, so false, displayed here—himself between them—like the hateful wings of bats. . . .

"You just go straight to hell, Edward," Loftis muttered, shoving him away. He plodded on upstairs. In the hallway it was dark and silent. The sounds from below came up muted and indistinct. For a moment he stood at the head of the stairs with his nose in the air, sniffing, reconnoitering. He couldn't see a thing but in the darkness shapes and shadows reeled indiscriminately, and he had to steady himself against the wall. He felt his heart pounding, and a cold dread. He pulled himself together some and moved down the hall on precarious tiptoe, trying to avoid knocking things over. Finally from Helen's room he heard voices. A voice, rather: Helen's. He stole near the door. It was closed but not locked, and a thin wedge of light fell onto the hallway floor. He heard Peyton say, "Words, words, words—why don't you get to the point?" Later he was unable to recollect, because of the fog in his mind, just what came next, but it went something like this:

Helen's voice, unemotional, polite, but direct: "That's what I'm trying to tell *you*, my dear. No, I didn't expect you not to drink some. Do you think I'm a member of the W.C.T.U.? Certainly not. But my dear girl, it's this other thing that matters to me. Really, Peyton, after all we've done to plan this affair for you, do you think——"

Peyton's voice cut in angrily: "Do I think what? What? Will you please explain?"

"This business with your father. Do you really think you have any right to treat him like you have? After all he's done for you? I saw what happened just now. Really, Peyton, you needn't pretend that it didn't happen or no one saw it. Because I saw it. I *saw* it, I tell you."

"*What?*"

"Just this." Her tone grew short and harsh. "Just this. Lashing out at him like that. In front of everybody. I wasn't the only one who saw it. Chess Hegerty saw it, and the Braunsteins. Everybody. After all I've planned. After everything I've tried— not tried but *had* to forget about you, in order to make this whole affair come off right. I said to myself, 'Well, I'll forget everything that she's done.' For the sake of morality, for the sake of Christian principles. For the sake of everything decent I'll overlook the things you've done——"

"What things?"

"Never mind. I said I'd overlook them for the sake of everything decent. So you could be married properly, in your own home. The home you forsook easily, too. That was the irony. Anyway, for all these decent things, for their sake, I said I'd make this wedding a success. If it killed me. For your father's sake, too. Now see what you've done. Everyone knows you hate me. That doesn't matter. But for them to know you hate him, too! After all these years of your faking and your flattery and your seductions——"

There was a sudden thump, a creak of springs, as if someone had fallen abruptly back upon a bed. There was laughter, too, Peyton's, tense and somewhat hysterical but also muffled, the laughter of someone lying horizontal: "Oh, God, really. If that isn't the limit. Poor Helen, you've really suffered, haven't you? Poor Helen. You're a sad case, you know, and I really shouldn't be talking like this. I really should be silent and forbearing, charitable, really, but I just can't. You're such a wretched case I can't even feel pity——"

"You shut up. You respect your elders. Your parents who——"

"You can't even suffer properly," Peyton broke in, her voice solemn now; "You're like all the rest of the sad neurotics everywhere who huddle over their misery and take their vile, mean little hatreds out on anybody they envy. You know, I suspect you've always hated me for one thing or another, but lately I've become a symbol to you couldn't stand. Do you think I'm stupid or something, that I haven't got you figured out? You hate men, you've hated Daddy for years, and the sad thing is that he hasn't known it. And the terrible thing is that you hate yourself so much that you just don't hate men or Daddy but you hate everything, animal, vegetable and mineral. Especially you hate me. Because I've become that symbol. I *know* I'm not perfect but

I'm free and young and if I'm not happy I at least know that someday I *can* be happy if I work at it long enough. I'm free. If I'd hung around in Port Warwick and married some simpleminded little boy who worked in the shipyard and lived in a little bungalow somewhere and came to see you and Daddy every Sunday, you'd be perfectly content. You'd have your claws in me then. I'd be obeying your precious code of Christian morality, which is phony anyway. But it's not that way. I'm free and you can't stand it——"

"You hate——"

Peyton's feet hit the floor; Loftis could hear them, the snapping, outraged heels. "I know what you're going to say! You're going to say I hate Port Warwick, Daddy, everything. Well, it's not true! I don't hate anything that you haven't forced me to hate and, damn you, you've forced me to hate you——"

Helen's voice rose on a high, hysterical wail. "You *tell* me these things and you don't know . . . you don't *know*," she cried wildly, "and you come here and make a mockery—with your—airs . . . and after all your sleeping around . . . you don't know . . . and your filthy little Jew . . ."

Loftis moved toward the door, but it was too late. The moment of silence which lasted between Helen's final word and what came next seemed to possess at once brevity and infinite length; this silence, so brief and so timeless, had, in its sense of awfulness, all the quality of a loud noise. Then Loftis heard it, a scuffling sound and a single, agonized moan, but he was still too late; he threw open the door. Peyton rushed sobbing past him into the hallway, down the stairs. He reached out for her, but she had gone like air, and he stood wobbling in the doorway, watching Helen. With her hands at her face she was moaning, but through her fingers ran trickles of blood and he looked at these, with a sort of remote and objective fascination, and paid no attention to her moans. He never remembered how long he stood there—perhaps half a minute, perhaps more—but when, sensing his presence, she removed her hands and looked at him, her lips moving soundlessly and her cheeks so dead and white beneath the raw, deep slits gouged out by Peyton's fingernails, he only said—making a bad job of it because of his perverse, whisky-thick tongue: "God help you, you monster."

Then he went downstairs.

From *Lie Down in Darkness*, copyright © 1951 by William Styron; reprinted by permission of the publishers, The Bobbs-Merrill Company, Inc.

Editors' Commentary

Diagnosis: Family neurosis—alcoholic father, with poorly repressed incestuous feelings toward daughter, embittered mother who has been completely involved with a severely handicapped older daughter—guilt on both sides and increasingly destructive family relationships.

William Styron's book *Lie Down in Darkness* describes a family neurosis in which the unhappiness of the parents, their frailties, their unmet needs, and their immaturity are played out on their healthy daughter so that she comes to reflect and incorporate in herself the misery of the entire family and cannot separate herself from it except by suicide. This excerpt can give only a glimpse of these complex intertwinings. To fully appreciate this situation, it is strongly recommended that the reader read the entire book.

The first chapter of this long novel reveals that the focal character, Peyton, committed suicide at the age of twenty-two. Her father is a weak, kind, charming alcoholic, deeply involved and overidentified with his daughter. Her mother, Helen, a borderline psychotic, is deeply resentful and jealous of the relationship of these two. She had given all her attention and affection to the older daughter, Maudie, a feebleminded cripple who died before Peyton's suicide. Time and again in the novel the author demonstrates how the beautiful, bright, and miserable Peyton is caught in the crossfire of the parents and is used as a weapon to fight their fight. Finally she learns how to use their hatred and hostile dependence as a way of turning them further against each other.

Family neurosis is a phenomenon too often seen today. Indeed, most neurosis can be said to be a "family" illness. This story illustrates the common tragedy of an interwoven misery, where the illness of one member causes the illnesses of the other family members and, in turn, is fed by their sickness. No one can seem to disengage. Each one chooses an escape that is no escape: the father, alcohol; the mother, withdrawn, delusionary brooding; the daughter, suicide; even the feebleminded sister found comfort in her helplessness and, finally, in death.

This is not so unusual a history as we would like to think. We can see Peytons in our classrooms. They are bright, pretty, social successes, sporadically brilliant and careless. They demand special privileges and special hours and turn in overdue reports and superficial papers. They frequently flunk out but more often get by through charm, manipulation, and cleverness.

We see Bunnys in the classroom as charming youngsters—easily led, kindly, weak, unable to stick the hard subjects out, good at those they can bluff through, glib, seductive with teachers and often successful in the seduction, infantile, passive, too eager to please, and lacking a secure sense of themselves.

We also see Helens in the classroom, strong-willed, stubborn, aggressive, dominating the other children and belittling the weak members of the class, attempting to possess and control the lives of those around them.

For the Peytons and the Bunnys, teachers must set firm limits. They must show full and hearty acceptance of these children's warmth and responsiveness but refuse to be manipulated or fooled by them. The teacher must show them that they are acceptable and worthy, that bluff and pretense are unnecessary and unrewarding.

The Helens need more love and lower standards of perfection. Their standards for themselves are inhumanly rigid and high. They need to learn to accept their own fallibility and, thus, make room for the human foibles of others. Above all, they should not be allowed to cultivate their own sufferings or use them as weapons against classmates or teachers.

In Peyton's family, all the members needed some form of well-designed treatment. Perhaps everybody would not have been cured, or even reached, but some members of the family might have been. At the least, Peyton's suicide might have been averted. The most desirable form of therapy in this case would be family therapy, in which the family is treated as a group. Though individual members might be treated separately, their growth and even survival as individuals are so intimately dependent on their relationships to one another that unless their problems are faced as group problems they may be insoluble and their fates inescapable.

Notes from the Underground

Fyodor Dostoyevsky

But, in the beginning, what agonies I went through in this inner struggle! I didn't believe that there were others who went through all that, so I've kept it a secret all my life. I was ashamed (perhaps even now, I am still ashamed). I reached a point where I felt a secret, unhealthy, base little pleasure in creeping back into my hole after some disgusting night in Petersburg and forcing myself to think that I had again done something filthy, that what was done couldn't be undone. And I inwardly gnawed at myself for it, tore at myself and ate myself away, until the bitterness turned into some shameful, accursed sweetishness and, finally, into a great, unquestionable pleasure. Yes, yes, definitely a pleasure! I mean it! . . .

I, for instance, am horribly sensitive. I'm suspicious and easily offended, like a dwarf or a hunchback. But I believe there have been moments when I'd have liked to have my face slapped. I say that in all seriousness—I'd have derived pleasure from this too. Naturally it would be the pleasure of despair. But then, it is in despair that we find the most acute pleasure, especially when we are aware of the hopelessness of the situation. And when one's face is slapped—why, one is bound to be crushed by one's awareness of the pulp into which one has been ground. But the main point is that, whichever way you look at it, I was always guilty in the first place, and what is most vexing is that I was guilty without guilt, by virtue of the laws of nature. Thus, to start with, I'm guilty of being more intelligent than all those around me. (I've always felt that and, believe me, it's weighed on my conscience sometimes. All my life, I have never been able to look people straight in the eye—I always feel a need to avert my face.) And then, I'm also guilty because, even if there had been any forgiveness in me, it would only have increased my torment, because I would have been conscious of its

uselessness. I surely would have been unable to do anything with my forgiveness: I wouldn't have been able to forgive because the offender would simply have been obeying the laws of nature in slapping me, and it makes no sense to forgive the laws of nature—but neither could I have forgotten it, because it is humiliating, after all. Finally, even if I hadn't wanted to be forgiving at all, but on the contrary, had wished to avenge myself on the offender, I couldn't have done it, for the chances are I'd never have dared to do anything about it even if there had been something I could do. . . .

And there, in its repulsive, evil-smelling nest, the downtrodden, ridiculed mouse plunges immediately into a cold, poisonous, and—most important—never-ending hatred. For forty years, it will remember the humiliation in all its ignominious details, each time adding some new point, more abject still, endlessly taunting and tormenting itself. Although ashamed of its own thoughts, the mouse will remember everything, go over it again and again, then think up possible additional humiliations. It may even try to avenge itself, but then it will do so in spurts, pettily, from behind the stove, anonymously, doubting that its vengeance is right, that it will succeed, and feeling that, as a result, it will hurt itself a hundred times more than it will hurt the one against whom its revenge is directed, who probably won't even feel enough of an itch to scratch himself. . . .

How can one, after all, have the slightest respect for a man who tries to find pleasure in the feeling of humiliation itself? I'm not saying that out of any mawkish sense of repentance. In general, I couldn't stand saying "Sorry, Papa, I'll never do it again."

And it wasn't at all because I was incapable of

saying it. On the contrary, perhaps it was just because I was only too prone to say it. And you should've seen under what circumstances too! *I'd get myself blamed, almost purposely, for something with which I'd had nothing to do even in thought or dream.* [Italics added.] That's what was most disgusting. But, even so, I was always deeply moved, repented my wickedness, and cried; in this, of course, I was deceiving myself, although I never did so deliberately. It was my heart that let me down here. In this case, I can't even blame the laws of nature, although those laws have oppressed me all my life. It makes me sick to remember all this, but then I was sick at the time too. It took me only a minute or so to recognize that it was all a pack of lies; all that repentance, those emotional outbursts and promises of reform—nothing but pretentious, nauseating lies. I was furious. And if you ask me now why I tortured and tormented myself like that, I'll tell you: I was bored just sitting with my arms folded, so I went in for all those tricks. Believe me, it's true. Just watch yourself carefully and you'll understand that that's the way it works. I made up whole stories about myself and put myself through all sorts of adventures to satisfy, at any price, my need to live. How many times did I convince myself that I was offended, just like that, for no reason at all. And although I knew that I had nothing to be offended about, that I was putting it all on, I'd put myself into such a state that in the end I'd really feel terribly offended. I was so strongly tempted to play tricks of this sort that, in the end, I lost all restraint. . . .

But I can't see any justice or virtue in vengeance, so if I indulge in it, it is only out of spite and anger. Anger, of course, overcomes all hesitations and can thus replace the primary reason precisely because it is no reason at all. But what can I do if I don't even have anger (that's where I started from, remember)? In me, anger disintegrates chemically like everything else, because of those damned laws of nature. As I think, the anger vanishes, the reasons for it evaporate, the responsible person is never found, the insult becomes an insult no longer but a stroke of fate, just like a toothache, for which no one can be held responsible. And so I

find that all I can do is take another whack at the stone wall, then shrug the whole thing off because of my failure to find the primary cause of the evil. . . .

[Behind the veil of masochism and anger are dreams of glory and grandiose fantasies.]

But how much love—ah, how much—I experienced in my dreams, when I escaped to "the sublime and the beautiful." Perhaps it was an imaginary love and maybe it was never directed toward another human being, but it was such an overflowing love that there was no need to direct it—that would've been an unnecessary luxury. Everything always ended safely in a leisurely, rapturous sliding into the domain of art, that is, into the beautiful lives of heroes stolen from the authors of novels and poems and adapted to the demands of the moment, whatever they might be. I, for instance, triumph over everyone, and they, of course, are strewn in the dust, acknowledging my superiority; I'm all-forgiving; I'm a great poet and court chamberlain; I fall in love; I inherit millions and donate them to human causes and take advantage of this opportunity to publicly confess my backslidings and disgrace which, of course, is no ordinary disgrace but contains much that is "sublime and beautiful" in it, something in the Manfred style. Everyone is weeping and kissing me (they could hardly be so thickskinned as not to); then I leave, hungry and barefoot, to preach new ideas and rout the reactionaries at Austerlitz. Then, a triumphal march is played, an amnesty is declared, the Pope agrees to leave Rome for Brazil, there's a ball for all of Italy at the Villa Borghese on the shores of Lake Como, which lake, for this occasion, is moved to the vicinity of Rome. Then there's a scene in the bushes, and so on and so forth; see what I mean? . . .

From Fyodor Dostoyevsky's *Notes from the Underground and Selected Stories* translated by Andrew R. MacAndrew. Copyright © 1961 by Andrew R. MacAndrew. Reprinted by arrangement with The New American Library, Inc., New York.

Editors' Commentary

Diagnosis: Masochist solution—repressed or concealed rage, impotent anger covering fantasies of grandeur, glory, and supremacy, which are never risked by being acted upon.

These "notes from the underground" reflect the very core of the masochistic solution, demonstrating great self-imposed suffering. They indicate the unending hostility and rage behind the abject *mea culpa* attitude, anger that can never be expressed directly, because, if it is, the masochistic structure falls. Should the structure fall, the lurking, secret contempt and grandiose fantasies would have to be tested in the light of the real world, where they are bound to fail. Failure, though devastating, is less upsetting to the masochist than success. Strange? Think of the children who continually get hurt, always appear put upon, are always the scapegoats. At first we tend to side with them. Later, we observe that it is always the same little Johnny or Jane who gets in the way of the flung ball or book or rock; who sometimes by his or her very posture provokes Bill to bullying. It is the same Johnny or Jane whose paper gets torn just as it is to be passed in, or who always has obstacles in the way of completing the assignment that would assure the expected A or B. This child always—whether academically, physically, or socially— falls short and looks sad and beaten. Sadness and indirectness can cover up the child's fantasy that it is outward circumstances that are keeping him or her from success, though the person who feels this way is often unwilling to give circumstances a chance, because it would mean risking failure.

Why? There are many possible causes. The answer may lie in a mother who "suffers" all the time, so that joy is not in the child's perception of life and seems somehow wrong. A too-successful and proud parent or sibling may leave no room for Johnny or Jane to be anything special except a special failure. The parents may transmit to this child, consciously or unconsciously, a feeling that he or she is alive only for the purpose of erasing their troubles or complementing their lives. Because these are impossible tasks, there is nothing left for Johnny or Jane to do but live out an apology: to say, "I can't, I can't, I can't, I'm sorry, I'm sorry, I'm sorry." And "I hate you for asking this of me, for then I feel I must, but it is too much for me." This last is never said aloud and is often not consciously felt, but it is at the root of many a miserable life dedicated to masochistic suffering and failure.

Of Human Bondage

W. Somerset Maugham

. . . But meanwhile he had grown horribly sensitive. He never ran if he could help it, because he knew it made his limp more conspicuous, and he adopted a peculiar walk. He stood still as much as he could, with his club-foot behind the other, so that it should not attract notice, and he was constantly on the lookout for any reference to it. Because he could not join in the games which other boys played, their life remained strange to him; he only interested himself from the outside in their doings; and it seemed to him that there was a barrier between them and him. Sometimes they seemed to think that it was his fault if he could not play football, and he was unable to make them understand. He was left a good deal to himself. He had been inclined to talkativeness, but gradually he became silent. He began to think of the difference between himself and others.

Two years passed, and Philip was nearly twelve. He was in the first form, within two or three places of the top, and after Christmas when several boys would be leaving for the senior school

he would be head boy. He had already quite a collection of prizes, worthless books on bad paper, but in gorgeous bindings decorated with the arms of the school: his position had freed him from bullying, and he was not unhappy. His fellows forgave him his success because of his deformity.

"After all, it's jolly easy for him to get prizes," they said, "there's nothing he *can* do but swat."

He had lost his early terror of Mr. Watson. He had grown used to the loud voice, and when the headmaster's heavy hand was laid on his shoulder Philip discerned vaguely the intention of a caress. He had the good memory which is more useful for scholastic achievements than mental power, and he knew Mr. Watson expected him to leave the preparatory school with a scholarship.

But he had grown very self-conscious. The new-born child does not realize that his body is more a part of himself than surrounding objects, and will play with his toes without any feeling that they belong to him more than the rattle by his side; and it is only by degrees, through pain, that he understands the fact of the body. And experiences of the same kind are necessary for the individual to become conscious of himself; but here there is the difference that, although everyone becomes equally conscious of his body as a separate and complete organism, everyone does not become equally conscious of himself as a complete and separate personality. The feeling of apartness from others comes to most with puberty, but it is not always developed to such a degree as to make the difference between the individual and his fellows noticeable to the individual. It is such as he, as little conscious of himself as the bee in a hive, who are the lucky in life, for they have the best chance of happiness: their activities are shared by all, and their pleasures are only pleasures because they are enjoyed in common; you will see them on Whitmonday dancing on Hampstead Heath, shouting at a football match, or from club windows in Pall Mall cheering a royal procession. It is because of them that man has been called a social animal.

Philip passed from the innocence of childhood to bitter consciousness of himself by the ridicule which his club-foot had excited. The circumstances of his case were so peculiar that he could not apply to them the ready-made rules which acted well enough in ordinary affairs, and he was forced to think for himself. The many books he had read filled his mind with ideas which, because he only half understood them, gave more scope to his imagination. Beneath his painful shyness something was growing up within him, and obscurely he realized his personality. But at times it gave him odd surprises; he did things, he knew not why, and afterwards when he thought of them found himself all at sea. . . .

The King's School at Tercanbury, to which Philip went when he was thirteen, prided itself on its antiquity. The masters had no patience with modern ideas of education, which they read of sometimes in *The Times* or *The Guardian,* and hoped fervently that King's School would remain true to its old traditions. The dead languages were taught with such thoroughness that an old boy seldom thought of Homer or Virgil in after life without a qualm of boredom; and though in the common room at dinner one or two bolder spirits suggested that mathematics were of increasing importance, the general feeling was that they were a less noble study than the classics. Neither German nor chemistry was taught, and French only by the form-masters; they could keep order better than a foreigner, and, since they knew the grammar as well

as any Frenchman, it seemed unimportant that none of them could have got a cup of coffee in the restaurant at Boulogne unless the waiter had known a little English. Geography was taught chiefly by making boys draw maps, and this was a favorite occupation, especially when the country dealt with was mountainous: it was possible to waste a great deal of time in drawing the Andes or the Apennines. . . .

[A new headmaster, Mr. Perkins, disturbs the older masters by occasionally taking their classes.]

The results were curious. Mr. Turner, who was the first victim, broke the news to his form that the headmaster would take them for Latin that day, and on the pretense that they might like to ask him a question or two so that they should not make perfect fools of themselves, spent the last quarter of an hour of the history lesson in construing for them the passage of Livy which had been set for the day; but when he rejoined his class and looked at the paper on which Mr. Perkins had written the marks, a surprise awaited him; for the two boys at the top of the form seemed to have done very ill, while others who had never distinguished themselves before were given full marks. When he asked Eldridge, his cleverest boy, what was the meaning of this the answer came sullenly:

"Mr. Perkins never gave us any construing to do. He asked me what I knew about General Gordon."

Mr. Turner looked at him in astonishment. The boys evidently felt they had been hardly used, and he could not help agreeing with their silent dissatisfaction. He could not see either what General Gordon had to do with Livy. He hazarded an enquiry afterwards.

"Eldridge was dreadfully put out because you asked him what he knew about General Gordon," he said to the headmaster, with an attempt at a chuckle.

Mr. Perkins laughed.

"I saw they'd got to the agrarian laws of Caius Gracchus, and I wondered if they knew anything about the agrarian troubles in Ireland. But all they knew about Ireland was that Dublin was on the Liffey. So I wondered if they'd ever heard of General Gordon."

Then the horrid fact was disclosed that the new head had a mania for general information. He had doubts about the utility of examinations on subjects which had been crammed for the occasion. He wanted common sense.

Sighs grew more worried every month; and he hated the attitude the head adopted towards classical literature. And Squirts, the master of the middle-third, grew more ill-tempered every day.

It was in his form that Philip was put on entering the school. The Rev. B. B. Gordon was a man by nature ill-suited to be a schoolmaster: he was impatient and choleric. No master could have been more unfitted to teach things to so shy a boy as Philip. He had come to the school with fewer terrors then he had when first he went to Mr. Watson's. He knew a good many boys who had been with him at the preparatory school. He felt more grown-up, and instinctively realized that among the larger numbers his deformity would be less noticeable. But from the first day Mr. Gordon struck terror in his heart; and the master, quick to discern the boys who were frightened of him, seemed on that account to take a peculiar dislike to him. Philip had enjoyed his work, but now he began to look upon the hours passed in school with horror. Rather than risk an answer which might be wrong and excite a storm of abuse from the master, he would sit stupidly silent, and when it came towards his turn to stand up and construe he grew sick and white with apprehension. His happy moments were those when Mr. Perkins took the form. He was able to gratify the passion for general knowledge which beset the headmaster; he had read all sorts of strange books beyond his years, and often Mr. Perkins, when a question was going round the room, would stop at Philip with a smile that filled the boy with rapture, and say:

"Now, Carey, you tell them."

The good marks he got on these occasions increased Mr. Gordon's indignation. One day it came to Philip's turn to translate, and the master sat there glaring at him and furiously biting his thumb. He was in a ferocious mood. Philip began to speak in a low voice.

"Don't mumble," shouted the master.

Something seemed to stick in Philip's throat.

"Go on. Go on. Go on."

Each time the words were screamed more loudly. The effect was to drive all he knew out of Philip's head, and he looked at the printed page vacantly. Mr. Gordon began to breathe heavily.

"If you don't know why don't you say so? Do you know it or not? Did you hear all this construed last time or not? Why don't you speak? Speak, you blockhead, speak!"

The master seized the arms of his chair and grasped them as though to prevent himself from falling upon Philip. They knew that in past days he often used to seize boys by the throat till they almost choked. The veins in his forehead stood out and his face grew dark and threatening. He was a man insane.

Philip had known the passage perfectly the day before, but now he could remember nothing.

"I don't know it," he gasped.

"Why don't you know it? Let's take the words one by one. We'll soon see if you don't know it."

Philip stood silent, very white, trembling a little, with his head bent down on the book. The master's breathing grew almost stertorous.

"The headmaster says you're clever. I don't know how he sees it. General information." He laughed savagely. "I don't know what they put you in his form for. Blockhead."

He was pleased with the word, and he repeated it at the top of his voice.

"Blockhead! Blockhead! Club-footed blockhead!"

That relieved him a little. He saw Philip redden suddenly. He told him to fetch the Black Book. Philip put down his Caesar and went silently out. The Black Book was a sombre volume in which the names of boys were written with their misdeeds, and when a name was down three times it meant a caning. Philip went to the headmaster's house and knocked at his study-door. Mr. Perkins was seated at his table.

"May I have the Black Book, please, sir?"

"There it is," answered Mr. Perkins, indicating its place by a nod of his head. "What have you been doing that you shouldn't?"

"I don't know, sir."

Mr. Perkins gave him a quick look, but without answering went on with his work. Philip took the book and went out. When the hour was up, a few minutes later, he brought it back.

"Let me have a look at it," said the headmaster. "I see Mr. Gordon has black-booked you for 'gross impertinence.' What was it?"

"I don't know, sir. Mr. Gordon said I was a club-footed blockhead."

Mr. Perkins looked at him again. He wondered whether there was sarcasm behind the boy's reply, but he was still much too shaken. His face was white and his eyes had a look of terrified distress. Mr. Perkins got up and put the book down. As he did so he took up some photographs.

"A friend of mine sent me some pictures of Athens this morning," he said casually. "Look here, there's the Acropolis."

He began explaining to Philip what he saw. The ruin grew vivid with his words. He showed him the theatre of Dionysus and explained in what order the people sat, and how beyond they could see the blue Aegean. And then suddenly he said:

"I remember Mr. Gordon used to call me a gipsy counter-jumper when I was in his form."

And before Philip, his mind fixed on the photographs, had time to gather the meaning of the remark, Mr. Perkins was showing him a picture of Salamis, and with his finger, a finger of which the nail had a little black edge to it, was pointing out how the Greek ships were placed and how the Persian. . . .

From *Of Human Bondage* by W. Somerset Maugham. Copyright 1915 by Doubleday & Company, Inc. Reprinted by permission of Doubleday & Company, Inc., A. P. Watt & Son (Literary Executor of the late W. Somerset Maugham), and William Heinemann Limited.

Editors' Commentary

Diagnosis: Withdrawal because of physical handicap—use of handicap to foster neurosis, masochism.

The question of emotional disturbance of children with physical handicaps is the problem of "Which came first, the chicken or the egg?" There is no doubt that some children with severe, even multiple, physical handicaps have no more than an ordinary dose of emotional problems. These children generally have excellent physical health along with their disability, and they have warm, accepting, unpitying relationships at home, where reasonable expectations are blended with acceptance of limitations.

It is equally certain that many children who have physical handicaps also suffer from emotional disorders. Being different is hard for children; restriction by edict of fate breeds resentment and is hard on the ego. When parents cannot accept the disability, or when they use it as a means of tying their children to them, damage ensues. When, further, schoolmates and teachers ridicule or set the child apart by too little or too much sympathy, difficulties mount.

Philip's case is a good example. A lonely child, bereft of warmth and understanding, he feels different from and unaccepted by his peers. He turns inward to reading and fantasy and removes himself from friendship. Here good teachers could come to the rescue. He looks toward religion—or, in his adolescent view, magic or miracle—to solve his problem. When this fails, he turns further inward and escapes to compulsive reading. Bad teachers underline his troubles. His school work falls off, and a pattern of failure follows through early manhood, until he finds a way out via projection, or identity with the sufferings of others.

We all have seen this child—whether a Philip with a club foot, a stutterer like Maugham himself, or a child with a disability that makes it impossible for him or her to read. These children need careful watching, sympathy but not pity, understanding without overindulgence, acceptance but not resignation. At a further extreme, the brain-damaged child, the epileptic, the blind youngster, and the deaf child (who feels the most isolated) bear similar marks. Special skills and teaching techniques are needed for various severely handicapped children; the severer the handicap and the greater the difference these children feel between themselves and others, the greater the chance for emotional disturbance.

Silent Snow, Secret Snow

Conrad Aiken

Just why it should have happened, or why it should have happened just when it did, he could not, of course, possibly have said; nor perhaps could it even have occurred to him to ask. The thing was above all a secret, something to be preciously concealed from Mother and Father; and to that very fact it owed an enormous part of its deliciousness. It was like a peculiarly beautiful trinket to be carried unmentioned in one's trouser-pocket—a rare stamp, an old coin, a few tiny gold links found trodden out of shape on the path in the park, a pebble of carnelian, a sea shell distinguishable from all others by an unusual spot or stripe—and, as if it were any one of these, he carried around with him everywhere a warm and persistent and increasingly beautiful sense of possession. Nor was it only a sense of possession—it was also a sense of protection. It was as if, in some delightful way, his secret gave him a fortress, a wall behind which he could retreat into heavenly seclusion. This was almost the first thing he had noticed about it—apart from the oddness of the thing itself—and it was this that now again, for the fiftieth time, occurred to him, as he sat in the little schoolroom. It was the half hour for geography. Miss Buell was revolving with one finger, slowly, a huge terrestrial globe which had been placed on her desk. The green and yellow continents passed and repassed, questions were asked and answered, and now the little girl in front of him, Deirdre, who had a funny little constellation of freckles on the back of her neck, exactly like the Big Dipper, was standing up and telling Miss Buell that the equator was the line that ran round the middle.

Miss Buell's face, which was old and grayish and kindly, with gray stiff curls beside the cheeks, and eyes that swam very brightly, like little minnows, behind thick glasses, wrinkled itself into a complication of amusements.

"Ah! I see. The earth is wearing a belt, or a sash. Or someone drew a line round it!"

"Oh, no—not that—I mean—"

In the general laughter, he did not share, or only a very little. He was thinking about the Arctic and Antarctic regions, which of course, on the globe, were white. Miss Buell was now telling them about the tropics, the jungles, the steamy heat of equatorial swamps, where the birds and butterflies, and even the snakes, were like living jewels. As he listened to these things, he was already, with a pleasant sense of half-effort, putting his secret between himself and the words. Was it really an effort at all? For effort implies something voluntary, and perhaps even something one did not especially want; whereas this was distinctly pleasant, and came almost of its own accord. All he needed to do was to think of that morning, the first one, and then of all the others—

But it was all so absurdly simple! It had amounted to so little. It was nothing, just an idea—and just why it should have become so wonderful, so permanent, was a mystery—a very pleasant one, to be sure, but also, in an amusing way, foolish. However, without ceasing to listen to Miss Buell, who had now moved up to the north temperate zones, he deliberately invited his memory of the first morning. It was only a moment or two after he had waked up—or perhaps the moment itself. But was there, to be exact, an exact moment? Was one awake all at once? or was it gradual? Anyway, it was after he had stretched a lazy hand up towards the headrail, and yawned, and then relaxed again among his warm covers, all the more grateful on a December morning, that the thing had happened. Suddenly, for no reason, he had thought of the postman, he remembered the postman. Perhaps there was nothing so odd in that. After all, he heard the postman almost every morning in his life—his heavy boots could be heard clumping round the corner at the top of the little cobbled hill-street, and then, progressively nearer, progressively louder, the double knock at each door, the crossings and recrossings of the street, till finally the clumsy steps came stumbling across to the very door, and the tremendous knock came which shook the house itself.

(Miss Buell was saying "Vast wheat-growing areas in North America and Siberia."

Dierdre had for the moment placed her left hand across the back of her neck.)

But on this particular morning, the first morning, as he lay there with his eyes closed, he had for some reason *waited* for the postman. He wanted to hear him come round the corner. And that was precisely the joke—he never did. He never came. He never had come—*round the corner*—again. For when at last the steps *were* heard, they had already, he was quite sure, come a little down the hill, to the first house; and even so, the steps were curiously different—they were softer, they had a new secrecy about them, they were muffled and indistinct; and while the rhythm of them was the same, it now said a new thing—it said peace, it said remoteness, it said cold, it said sleep. And he had understood the situation at once—nothing could have seemed simpler—there had been snow in the night, such as all winter he had been longing for; and it was this which had rendered the postman's first footsteps inaudible, and the later ones faint. Of course! How lovely! And even now it must be snowing—it was going to be a snowy day—the long white ragged lines were drifting and sifting across the street, across the faces of the old houses, whispering and hushing, making little triangles of white in the corners between cobblestones, seething a little when the wind blew them over the ground to a drifted corner; and so it would be all day, getting deeper and deeper and silenter and silenter.

(Miss Buell was saying "Land of perpetual snow.")

All this time, of course (while he lay in bed),

he had kept his eyes closed, listening to the nearer progress of the postman, the muffled footsteps thumping and slipping on the snow-sheathed cobbles; and all the other sounds—the double knocks, a frosty far-off voice or two, a bell ringing thinly and softly as if under a sheet of ice—had the same slightly abstracted quality, as if removed by one degree from actuality—as if everything in the world had been insulated by snow. But when at last, pleased, he opened his eyes, and turned them towards the window, to see for himself this long-desired and now so clearly imagined miracle— what he saw instead was brilliant sunlight on a roof; and when, astonished, he jumped out of bed and stared down into the street, expecting to see the cobbles obliterated by the snow, he saw nothing but the bare bright cobbles themselves.

Queer, the effect this extraordinary surprise had had upon him—all the following morning he had kept with him a sense of snow falling about him, a secret screen of new snow between himself and the world. If he had not dreamed such a thing—and how could he have dreamed it while awake?—how else could one explain it? In any case, the delusion had been so vivid as to affect his entire behavior. He could not now remember whether it was on the first or the second morning—or was it even the third?—that his mother had drawn attention to some oddness in his manner.

"But my darling—" she had said at the breakfast table— "what has come over you? You don't seem to be listening. . . ."

And how often that very thing had happened since!

(Miss Buell was now asking if anyone knew the difference between the North Pole and the Magnetic Pole. Deirdre was holding up her flickering brown hand, and he could see the four white dimples that marked the knuckles.) . . .

"Now Paul—I would like very much to ask you a question or two. You will answer them, won't you—you know I'm an old, old friend of yours, eh? That's right! . . ."

His back was thumped twice by the doctor's fat fist—then the doctor was grinning at him with false amiability, while with one finger-nail he was scratching the top button of his waistcoat. Beyond the doctor's shoulder was the fire, the fingers of flame making light prestidigitation against the sooty fireback, the soft sound of their random flutter the only sound.

"I would like to know—is there anything that worries you?"

The doctor was again smiling, his eyelids low against the little black pupils, in each of which was a tiny white bead of light. Why answer him? why answer him at all? "At whatever pain to others"— but it was all a nuisance, this necessity for resistance, this necessity for attention: it was as if one had been stood up on a brilliantly lighted stage, under a great round blaze of spotlight; as if one were merely a trained seal, or a performing dog, or a fish, dipped out of an aquarium and held up by the tail. It would serve them right if he were merely to bark or growl. And meanwhile, to miss these last few precious hours, these hours of which every minute was more beautiful than the last, more menacing—? He still looked, as if from a great distance, at the beads of light in the doctor's eyes, at the fixed false smile, and then, beyond, once more at his mother's slippers, his father's slippers, the soft flutter of the fire. Even here, even amongst these hostile presences, and in this arranged light, he could see the snow, he could hear it—it was in the corners of the room, where the shadow was deepest, under the sofa, behind the half-opened door which led to the dining room. It was gentler here, softer, its seethe the quietest of whispers, as if, in deference to a drawing room, it had quite deliberately put on its "manners"; it kept itself out of sight, obliterated itself, but distinctly with an air of saying, "Ah, but just wait! Wait till we are alone together! Then I will begin to tell you something new! Something white! something cold! something sleepy! something of cease, and peace, and the long bright curve of space! Tell them to go away. Banish them. Refuse to speak. Leave them, go upstairs to your room, turn out the light and get into bed—I will go with you, I will be waiting for you, I will tell you a better story than Little Kay of the Skates, or The Snow Ghost—I will surround your bed, I will close the windows, pile a deep drift against the door, so that none will ever again be able to enter. Speak to them! . . ." It seemed as if the little hissing voice came from a slow white spiral of falling flakes in the corner by the front window— but he could not be sure. He felt himself smiling, then, and said to the doctor, but without looking at him, looking beyond him still—

"Oh, no, I think not—"

"But are you sure, my boy?"

His father's voice came softly and coldly then—the familiar voice of silken warning.

"You needn't answer at once, Paul—remember we're trying to help you—think it over and be quite sure, won't you?"

He felt himself smiling again, at the notion of being quite sure. What a joke! As if he weren't so sure that reassurance was no longer necessary, and all this cross-examination a ridiculous farce, a grotesque parody! What could they know about it? These gross intelligences, these humdrum minds so bound to the usual, the ordinary? Impossible to tell them about it! Why, even now, even now, with the proof so abundant, so formidable, so imminent, so appallingly present here in this very room, could they believe it?—could even his mother believe it? No—it was only too plain that if anything were said about it, the merest hint given, they would be incredulous—they would laugh—they would say "Absurd!"—think things about him which weren't true. . . .

"Why no, I'm not worried—why should I be?"

He looked then straight at the doctor's low-lidded eyes, looked from one of them to the other, from one bead of light to the other, and gave a little laugh.

The doctor seemed to be disconcerted by this. He drew back in his chair, resting a fat white hand on either knee. The smile faded slowly from his face.

"Well, Paul!" he said, and paused gravely, "I'm afraid you don't take this quite seriously enough. I think you perhaps don't quite realize—don't quite realize—" He took a deep quick breath, and turned, as if helplessly, at a loss for words, to the others. But Mother and Father were both silent—no help was forthcoming.

"You must surely know, be aware, that you have not been quite yourself, of late? don't you know that? . . ."

It was amusing to watch the doctor's renewed attempt at a smile, a queer disorganized look, as of confidential embarrassment.

"I feel all right, sir," he said, and again gave the little laugh.

"And we're trying to help you." The doctor's tone sharpened.

"Yes, sir, I know. But why? I'm all right. I'm just *thinking*, that's all."

His mother made a quick movement forward, resting a hand on the back of the doctor's chair.

"Thinking?" she said. "But my dear, about what?"

This was a direct challenge—and would have to be directly met. But before he met it, he looked again into the corner by the door, as if for reassurance. He smiled again at what he saw, at what he heard. The little spiral was still there, still softly whirling, like the ghost of a white kitten chasing the ghost of a white tail, and making as it did so the faintest of whispers. It was all right! If only he could remain firm, everything was going to be all right.

"Oh, about anything, about nothing—*you* know the way you do!"

"You mean—day-dreaming?"

"Oh, no—thinking!"

"But thinking about *what?*"

"Anything."

He laughed a third time—but this time, happening to glance upward towards his mother's face, he was appalled at the effect his laughter seemed to have upon her. Her mouth had opened in an expression of horror. . . . This was too bad! Unfortunate! He had known it would cause pain, of course—but he hadn't expected it to be quite so bad as this. Perhaps—perhaps if he just gave them a tiny gleaming hint—?

"About the snow," he said.

"What on earth!" This was his father's voice. The brown slippers came a step nearer on the hearth-rug.

"But my dear, what do you mean?" This was his mother's voice.

The doctor merely stared.

"Just *snow*, that's all. I like to think about it."

"Tell us about it, my boy."

"But that's all it is. There's nothing to tell. *You* know what snow is?"

This he said almost angrily, for he felt that they were trying to corner him. He turned sideways so as no longer to face the doctor, and the better to see the inch of blackness between the window-sill and the lowered curtain—the cold inch of beckoning and delicious night. At once he felt better, more assured.

"Mother—can I go to bed, now, please? I've got a headache."

"But I thought you said—"

"It's just come. It's all these questions—! Can I, mother?"

"You can go as soon as the doctor has finished."

"Don't you think this thing ought to be gone into thoroughly, and *now?*" This was Father's voice. The brown slippers again came a step nearer, the voice was the well-known "punishment" voice, resonant and cruel.

"Oh, what's the use, Norman—"

Quite suddenly, everyone was silent. And without precisely facing them, nevertheless he was aware that all three of them were watching him with an extraordinary intensity—staring hard at him—as if he had done something monstrous, or was himself some kind of monster. He could hear the soft irregular flutter of the flames; the cluck-click-cluck-click of the clock; far and faint, two sudden spurts of laughter from the kitchen, as quickly cut off as begun; a murmur of water in the pipes; and then, the silence seemed to deepen, to spread out, to become world-long and worldwide, to become timeless and shapeless, and to center inevitably and rightly, with a slow and sleepy but enormous concentration of all power, on the beginning of a new sound. What this new sound was going to be, he knew perfectly well. It might begin with a hiss, but it would end with a roar—there was no time to lose—he must escape. It mustn't happen here—

Without another word, he turned and ran up the stairs.

Not a moment too soon. The darkness was coming in long white waves. A prolonged sibilance filled the night—a great seamless seethe of wild influence went abruptly across it—a cold low humming shook the windows. He shut the door and flung off his clothes in the dark. The bare black floor was like a little raft tossed in waves of snow, almost overwhelmed, washed under whitely, up again, smothered in curled billows of feather. The snow was laughing: it spoke from all sides at once: it pressed closer to him as he ran and jumped exulting into his bed.

"Listen to us!" it said. "Listen! We have come to tell you the story we told you about. You remember? Lie down. Shut your eyes, now—you will no longer see much—in this white darkness who could see, or want to see? We will take the place of everything. . . . Listen—"

A beautiful varying dance of snow began at the front of the room, came forward and then retreated, flattened out toward the floor, then rose fountainlike to the ceiling, swayed, recruited itself from a new stream of flakes which poured laughing in through the humming window, advanced again, lifted long white arms. It said peace, it said remoteness, it said cold—it said—

But then a gash of horrible light fell brutally across the room from the opening door—the snow drew back hissing—something alien had come into the room—something hostile. This thing rushed at him, clutched at him, shook him—and he was not merely horrified, he was filled with such a loathing as he had never known. What was this? this cruel disturbance? this act of anger and hate? It was as if he had to reach up a hand toward another world for any understanding of it—an effort of which he was only barely capable. But of that other world he still remembered just enough to know the exorcising words. They tore themselves from his other life suddenly—

"Mother! Mother! Go away! I hate you!"

And with that effort, everything was solved, everything became all right: the seamless hiss advanced once more, the long white wavering lines rose and fell like enormous whispering sea-waves, the whisper becoming louder, the laughter more numerous.

"Listen!" it said. "We'll tell you the last, the most beautiful and secret story—shut your eyes—it is a very small story—a story that gets smaller and smaller—it comes inward instead of opening like a flower—it is a flower becoming a seed—a little cold seed—do you hear? we are leaning closer to you—"

The hiss was now becoming a roar—the whole world was a vast moving screen of snow—but even now it said peace, it said remoteness, it said cold, it said sleep.

Editors' Commentary

Diagnosis: Schizophrenic breakdown—delusions and hallucinations, both visual and auditory; gradual withdrawal from world of reality into autistic or fantasy world.

This secret world of snow is unbearably tempting or beckoning to Paul, like the Sirens to Ulysses, until this twelve-year-old boy is magnetized away from the world of home and school. Exactly what, in his middle-class home and daily life, was so painful for him that he needed to retreat? It could have been the clinging to mother or the overidentification and unconscious hostility of one of the parents, so frequently found in schizophrenic breakdowns. We are told only how his delusionary cocoon spread from home to school. Mother, father, and teacher become aware of the increasing withdrawal of this boy, of his "not-thereness." The ways the doctor mishandles the child and the father's understandable irritation under the strain of anxiety are typical reactions to the frightening phenomenon of watching the child disappear into another world before their eyes. They find they are unable to stop him and probably even unconsciously encouraging that very withdrawal.

The story indicates well the kind of child this is. In a classroom, he or she is shy, quiet, withdrawn—no behavior problem except that more and more often the youngster is miles away when a question is asked. Sometimes his or her answers are puzzlingly inappropriate, rooted in the question but winding off into outer space. This is the kind of child Miss Buell would describe in a conference as being very well prepared sometimes, but just not there most of the time. The seemingly sudden onset of the illness is misleading. A keen and sensitive teacher can recognize signs of increasing withdrawal if prepared to see them. An adequately prepared teacher would consult the psychology department of the school before actual breakdown occurred.

Editors' Commentary

The Abused Child

The following is the true story of a boy who was born into a protected home but had experienced, by the time he was ten, all the horrors, cruelties, and bestialities humans are capable of inflicting. He was a Polish-Jewish child whose parents gave him to a peasant in order to spare him the horrors and probable death of a Nazi prison camp. His peasant helper died several months after he arrived, however, and he was left at age seven to roam for three years, homeless, helpless, ill-fed, and ill-treated. Because of his dark skin, he was thought to be either Gypsy or Jewish and therefore subjected to a variety of cruelties by the ignorant, highly superstitious peasants of the villages he wandered through. His journey from farm to village to town to city, through the Nazi and then the Russian occupations of Poland, was a living nightmare. He was exploited, beaten, mauled, sexually abused, and treated like an animal. In one episode, when he was beaten, whipped, tied, and buried deep in a human manure heap, he lost his speech. Each time he reached out for minimal sustenance and care, he met with physical violence.

Although his story reflects the intense ugliness, horror and cruelty that people may inflict on a child, it lacks one aspect of hideousness that happens daily to children throughout our nation—it was not this boy's own parents who perpetrated the horrors on him. He thought his parents were dead, but they had survived, and after the war they fought through years of red tape to find him again. He was then living in a Russian-run orphanage—the most secure home he had found since his wanderings began. Even after his return to his parents, he did not regain his speech until caught one time in a blizzard, when his survival was once more at stake.

This author knows at first hand the abuse of children: their suffering, fantasies, susceptibility to superstition, defenses against utter invasion, vulnerability to cruelty, hope for nurture, and immobilizing despair under the yoke of mistreatment.

Child abuse is as old as history itself. It occurs when adults who are wrapped in feelings of helplessness about their own lives take out their rage and distress, their twisted and thwarted sexual and affectional desires, on helpless children. It occurs most often in the family setting. Often, it goes too long without comment by neighbors and community, because people believe that no one should interfere in the parents' handling of their own child, that the child is the "property" of the parents. It is time we discarded the notion that others have no right to save a child from mistreatment even when death or crippling can result.

The Painted Bird

Jerzy Kosinski

Garbos was waiting for me at home. As soon as I entered he dragged me to an empty room in the corner of the house. There at the highest point of the ceiling two large hooks had been driven into the beams, less than two feet apart. Leather straps were attached to each as handles.

Garbos climbed on a stool, lifted me high, and told me to grab a handle with each hand. Then he left me suspended and brought Judas into the room. On his way out he locked the door.

Judas saw me hanging from the ceiling and immediately jumped up in an effort to reach my feet. I brought my legs up and he missed them by a few inches. He started another run and tried again, still missing. After a few more tries he lay down and waited.

I had to watch him. When freely hanging, my feet were no more than six feet above the ground and Judas could easily reach them. I did not know how long I would have to hang like this. I guessed that Garbos expected me to fall down and be attacked by Judas. This would frustrate the efforts I had been making all these months, counting Garbos's teeth, including the yellow, ingrown ones at the back of his mouth. Innumerable times when Garbos was drunk with vodka and snored open-mouthed I had counted his loathsome teeth painstakingly. This was my weapon against him. Whenever he beat me too long I reminded him of the number of his teeth; if he did not believe me he could check the count himself. I knew every one of them, no matter how wobbly, how putrefied, or how nearly hidden under the gums. If he killed me he would have very few years left to live. However, if I fell down into the waiting fangs of Judas, Garbos would have a clear conscience. He would have nothing to fear, and his patron, St. Anthony, might even give him absolution for my accidental death.

My shoulders were becoming numb. I shifted my weight, opened and closed my hands, and slowly relaxed my legs, lowering them dangerously near to the floor. Judas was in the corner pretending to be asleep. But I knew his tricks as well as he knew mine. He knew that I still had some strength left and that I could lift my legs faster than he could leap after them. So he waited for fatigue to overcome me.

The pain in my body raced in two directions. One went from the hands to the shoulders and neck, the other from the legs to the waist. They were two different kinds of pain, boring toward my middle like two moles tunneling toward each other underground. The pain from my hands was easier to endure. I could cope with it by switching my weight from one hand to the other, relaxing the muscles and then taking the load up again, hanging on one hand while blood returned to the other. The pain from between my legs and abdomen was more persistent, and once it settled in my belly it refused to leave. It was like a woodworm that finds a cozy spot behind a knot in the timber and stays there forever.

It was a strange, dull, penetrating pain. It must have been like the pain felt by a man Garbos mentioned in warning. Apparently this man had treacherously killed the son of an influential farmer and the father had decided to punish the murderer in the old-fashioned manner. Together with his two cousins the man brought the culprit to the forest. There they prepared a twelve-foot stake, sharpened at one end to a fine point like a gigantic pencil. They laid it on the ground, wedging the blunt end against a tree trunk. Then a strong horse was hitched to each of the victim's feet, while his crotch was leveled with the waiting point. The horses, gently nudged, pulled the man against the spiked beam, which gradually sank into the tensed flesh. When the point was deep into the entrails of the victim, the men lifted the stake, together with the impaled man upon it and planted it in a previously dug hole. They left him there to die slowly.

Now hanging under the ceiling I could almost see the man and hear him howling into the night, trying to lift to the indifferent sky his arms which hung by the bloated trunk of his body. He must have looked like a bird knocked out of a tree by a slingshot and fallen flabbily onto a dried-out, pointed stalk.

Still feigning indifference, Judas woke up below. He yawned, scratched behind his ears, and hunted the fleas in his tail. Sometimes he glanced slyly at me, but turned away in disgust when he saw my hunched legs.

He only fooled me once. I thought he had really gone to sleep and straightened out my legs. Judas instantly bounced off the floor, leaping like a grasshopper. One of my feet did not jerk up fast enough and he tore off some skin at the heel. The fear and pain almost caused me to fall. Judas licked his chops triumphantly and reclined by the wall. He watched me through the slits of his eyes and waited.

I thought I could not hold on any longer. I decided to jump down and planned my defense against Judas, though I knew that I wouldn't even have time to lift a hand before he would be at my throat. There was no time to lose. Then suddenly I remembered the prayers.

I started shifting weight from one hand to the other, moving my head, jerking my legs up and down. Judas looked at me, discouraged by this display of strength. Finally he turned toward the wall and remained motionless.

Time went by and my prayers multiplied. Thousands of days of indulgence streaked through the thatched roof toward heaven.

Late in the afternoon Garbos came into the room. He looked at my wet body and the pool of sweat on the floor. He took me off the hooks roughly and kicked the dog out. All that evening I could neither walk nor move my arms. I lay down on the mattress and prayed. Days of indulgence came in hundreds, in thousands. Surely by now there were more of them in heaven for me than grains of wheat in the field. Any day, any minute, notice of this would have to be taken in heaven. Perhaps even now the saints were considering some radical improvement of my life.

Garbos hung me up every day. Sometimes he did it in the morning and sometimes in the evening. And had he not been afraid of foxes and thieves and needed Judas in the yard, he would have done it at night too.

It was always the same. While I still had some strength the dog stretched out on the floor calmly, pretending to sleep or casually catching fleas. When the pain in my arms and legs became more intense, he grew alert as though sensing what was going on inside my body. Sweat poured from me, running in rivulets over my straining muscles, hitting the floor with regular plip-plops. As soon as I straightened my legs Judas invariably leapt at them.

Months went by. Garbos needed me more around the farm because he was often drunk and didn't want to work. He hung me up only when he felt he had no particular use for me. When he sobered up and heard the hungry pigs and the lowing cow he took me off the hooks and put me to work. The muscles of my arms became conditioned by the hanging and I could endure it for hours without much effort. Although the pain that came

to my belly began later now, I got cramps which frightened me. And Judas never missed a chance to leap at me, though by now he must have doubted he would ever catch me off guard.

While I hung on the straps I concentrated on my prayers to the exclusion of all else. When my strength ebbed I told myself that I should be able to last another ten or twenty prayers before I dropped down. After these were recited I made another promise to myself of ten or fifteen prayers. I believed that something could happen at any moment, that every extra thousand days of indulgence could save my life, perhaps at this very instant.

Sometimes, to divert my attention from the pain and from my numb arm muscles, I teased Judas. First I swung on my arms as though I were about to fall down. The dog barked, jumped, and raged. When he went to sleep again I would wake him with cries and the smacking of lips and grinding of teeth. He could not understand what was happening. Thinking that this was the end of my endurance, he leapt about madly, knocking into the walls in the darkness, overturning the stool standing by the door. He grunted with pain, heaved heavily, and finally rested. I took the opportunity to straighten my legs. When the room resounded to the snoring of the fatigued beast, I saved strength by setting prizes for myself for endurance: straightening one leg for every thousand days of indulgence, resting one arm for every ten prayers, and one major shift of position for every fifteen prayers.

At some unexpected moment I would hear the clatter of the latch and Garbos would enter. When he saw me alive he would curse Judas, kick and beat him until the dog cried and whimpered like a puppy.

His fury was so tremendous that I wondered if God Himself had not sent him at this moment. But when I looked at his face, I could find no trace of the divine presence. . . .

Rough hands tore me up from the floor and pulled me toward the doorway. The crowd parted in stupefaction. From the balcony a male voice shouted "Gypsy vampire!" and several voices took up the chant. Hands clamped my body with excruciating hardness, tearing at my flesh. Outside I wanted to cry and beg for mercy, but no sound came from my throat. I tried once more. There was no voice in me.

The fresh air hit my heated body. The peasants dragged me straight toward a large manure pit. It had been dug two or three years ago, and the small outhouse standing next to it with small windows cut in the shape of the cross was the subject of special pride to the priest. It was the only one in the area. The peasants were accustomed to attending to the wants of nature directly in the field and only used it when coming to church. A new pit was being dug on the other side of the presbytery, however, because the old pit was completely full and the wind often carried foul odors to the church.

When I realized what was going to happen to me, I again tried to shout. But no voice came from me. Every time I struggled a heavy peasant hand would drop on me, gagging my mouth and nose. The stench from the pit increased. We were very close to it now. Once more I tried to struggle free, but the men held me fast, never ceasing their talk about the event in the church. They had no doubt that I was a vampire and that the interruption of the High Mass could only bode evil for the village.

We halted at the edge of the pit. Its brown, wrinkled surface steamed with fetor like horrible skin on the surface of a cup of hot buckwheat soup. Over this surface swarmed a myriad of small white caterpillars, about as long as a fingernail. Above the surface circled clouds of flies, buzzing monotonously, with beautiful blue and violet bodies glittering in the sun, colliding, falling toward the pit for a moment, and soaring into the air again.

I retched. The peasants swung me by the hands and feet. The pale clouds in the blue sky swam before my eyes. I was hurled into the very center of the brown filth, which parted under my body to engulf me.

Daylight disappeared above me and I began to suffocate. I tossed instinctively in the dense element, lashing out with my arms and legs. I touched the bottom and rebounded from it as fast as I could. A spongy upswell raised me toward the surface. I opened my mouth and caught a dash of air. I was sucked back below the surface and again pushed myself up from the bottom. The pit was only twelve feet square. Once more I sprang up from the bottom, this time toward the edge. At the last moment, when the downswell was about to pull me under, I caught hold of a creeper of the long thick weeds growing over the edge of the pit. I fought against the suction of the reluctant maw and pulled myself to the edge of the pit, barely able to see through my slime-obscured eyes.

I crawled out of the mire and was immediately gripped with cramps of vomiting. They shook me so long that my strength vanished and I slid down completely exhausted into the stinging, burning bushes of thistle, fern, and ivy.

I heard the distant sound of the organ and human singing and I reasoned that after the Mass the people might come out of the church and drown me again in the pit if they saw me alive in the bushes. I had to escape and so I darted into the forest. The sun baked the brown crust on me and clouds of large flies and insects besieged me.

As soon as I found myself in the shade of the trees I started rolling over in the cool, moist moss, rubbing myself with cold leaves, and vomiting. With pieces of bark I scraped off the remaining muck. I rubbed sand in my hair and then rolled in the grass and vomited again.

Suddenly I realized that something had happened to my voice. I tried to cry out, but my tongue flapped helplessly in my open mouth. I had no voice. I was terrified and, covered with cold sweat, I refused to believe that this was possible and tried to convince myself that my voice would come back. I waited a few moments and tried again. Nothing happened. The silence of the forest was broken only by the buzzing of the flies around me.

I sat down. The last cry that I had uttered under the falling missal still echoed in my ears. Was it the last cry I would ever utter? Was my voice escaping with it like a solitary duck call straying over a huge pond? Where was it now? I could envision my voice flying alone under the high-arched, vaulting ribs of the church roof.

Editors' Commentary

Diagnosis: Varies from extent and meaning of abuse. Frequently leads to violent, uncontrolled behavior or deep, paralyzing depression and little sense of self-worth. Ego development arrested unless reliable relations and help are found.

The Dynamics of Child Abuse

Adults perpetrating child abuse often were abused themselves as children or grew up with violence as the major means of expression. These parents are reluctant to bring their children to medical facilities for treatment and loath to confess. Although the emergency room of every children's hospital or clinic sees cases of deaths caused by beatings, burnings, and maulings, it is only recently that medical personnel have attempted to get proper records, make inquiries, and follow up on incidents. Even now, adequate protection of abused children, particularly infants, is tragically lacking. Sometimes child abuse is an outlet for rage, sometimes it is a means of punishing another person in the family. The results are scarred and bruised bodies. In some cases, hair can no longer grow, because hot grease poured has burned the source of growth. Whip scars and bruises to face and body are everyday occurrences. Damaged penises and ripped vaginas and anuses are common in every hospital. Blindness and deafness are frequent results, as are crippling and maiming.

The psychological results, if the child survives, are every bit as scarring. The most familiar are lack of trust, stultification of mind and speech, inability to relate, and, most common of all, total self-hate that results in the development either of a permanent victim or of an abuser, one who is as physically violent and uncontrolled as the parent. Sometimes, to protect themselves the personalities of abused children split and then severe alienation from self and others appears. Sometimes paranoid delusions spread to other adults. In cases where the abused child cracks, psychoses rather than neuroses are more likely to develop. An abused child who survives always feels intrinsically worthless, as if he interprets his abusing parents' acts as a value judgment on his worth. A child reasons that a rationale must explain the violent acts done to him; he must deserve ill treatment.

One of the most paradoxical elements found in child abuse is the frequent loyalty of children for the abusing parent. Children will sometimes even defend parents within minutes after a beating. They will deny their very obvious wounds. Children can thus see the parent as good and loving despite all evidence and all pain.

The best treatment, where treatment is possible, is family treatment with much support given to the offending adult(s). Despite the repulsiveness of the acts, the parent's behavior must be looked at as an uncontrollable illness that must be stopped. Usually, one child in a family is selected as victim. However, if the selected child is placed elsewhere, it is likely that another child will be selected. Often the chosen child is the most vulnerable of the children: the quiet, the very sensitive, or the handicapped child. The offending parent perhaps sees his or her own vulnerability in the selected child.

Though only one of two parents may be engaged in actual physical abuse, the other participates or acquiesces in the act—even when he or she does not overtly know what is going on. The nonabusing parent tries to remain unaware of the facts or belittles the seriousness of them. Part of the treatment involves confronting the inactive partner with his or her own role in the family act.

Thus the abused child is the human sacrifice to the untapped unconscious of the couple. The child becomes the target for the parent's anger and despair. This anger is expressed by whip, or fist, or boiling oil, or hanging rope. Sometimes it is the unconscious or repressed sexual needs of one partner, the homosexual panic, the need to be the raped infant, or child, the unsatisfied lust that expresses itself in violent assault. So close is sexual activity to aggression in primitive levels of human development that this is a common attribute of child abuse. Therefore, treatment involves close scrutiny of sexual patterns as well as of patterns of anger and their causes.

The number of child abuse cases that are reported is staggering, running into the thousands annually. The number of unreported cases is even more staggering. The conditions of poverty breed despair, and lack of education limits means of expressing frustrations—the choice of verbal substitutes for physical impulses. Hence, poverty is the most fertile ground for acting out and for child abuse. Among ethnic minorities who themselves have been ill-treated, often with external violence, and where hatred cannot be turned outward for lack of power and means, it is turned inward towards self or family, so that one of the concomitants of racism can be child abuse.

However, child abuse by no means belongs exclusively to the economically deprived or to racial minorities. The middle and upper class are better able to keep the physical scars and signs of child abuse concealed from others. Severe beatings and sadistic acts go unreported and private doctors try to believe the lies they are told to explain peculiar and unlikely injuries; often, they have no proof to bring the cases out in the open, so they pretend to believe and go along with the families. Especially in the more privileged groups, where violence is not the normal mode of expression and verbal skills are the major currency of communication unlike the more deprived groups, it is hard to tell what goes on, hard to believe, and as long as the lie is maintained it is next to impossible to work with the family.

There is debate about whether Christina Crawford's book *Mommie Dearest*, a story of her own abuse by her mother Joan Crawford, is or is not true. Because of the kind of details on provoking incidents, I have little doubt as to its accuracy. It is a typical middle-class case even to the ease with which it is disbelieved. One such case that I supervised was E, a middle-class, bright and attractive young woman with severe symptoms, physical and mental. E was punished by her mother in her father's frequent absence by having her head pushed down unflushed toilets, or she was beaten, or she was stuck in half-filled garbage cans with the lids closed. At three years of age, she was set on fire, and saved by her five-year-old brother. She remembers being strapped to a table with legs and arms apart and sometimes her mother would stick forks or fingers up her vagina, sometimes she would get the dog to lick her vagina. So often was her vagina pulled and mauled that at college in a physical examination and at gynecological examinations she was accused of excessive masturbation to a point of misshape. Feces were pulled out of her and her mother forced her to eat them. Until very recently the mother has burst in on her while she was toileting and has attempted homosexual rape. Typical of such cases, her father, in all these years, was never available to help even when home, nor did he seem to know anything about what was going on in his house. Never once did E tell on her mother to her father. This was because she feared that she must, in some way, have colluded with her mother, or that she herself must have done something that would justify such acts. Though she sometimes hated, and always feared her mother's rantings, she rarely blamed her mother and always thought the abuse was founded in something debased or wrong about herself. When the time came for all this hidden material to pour forth in therapy, she refused to believe her mother was at fault and it horrified her to recognize her mother was at such times mad. At length she got confirming evidence of her memories by her brother who had witnessed much of the abuse. She became aware of body scars and mutilations she had long chosen to overlook. One day while she was in therapy, her mother in a rage threw a breadknife at her. When she was visiting her home on another day, her mother burst into the bathroom and physically attempted to rape her. Then she believed the evidence of her memories.

For years she had cowered helplessly before her mother's attacks. But finally, she could no longer deny the facts of her mother's acts—sexual, petty, cruel—and her own fears concerning them. Slowly she recognized and was enraged at her father's removal from the arena and her own collusion in the whole pattern. She began, with great fear, to defend herself, to keep herself as much as possible out of any situation where she would be alone with her mother. Finally, when her own physical symptoms, a kind of body language, disappeared, they left in their wake vivid memories. She then became aware of her conflict between loving her mother and hating her. She became able to experience her rage, although she remains terrified of all incidents of violence. She was able to be effectively angry with both her mother and her father. She confronted him with the fact that he had never been there to support or help her. Since then she is less prone to find herself in the victim position not only at home but with friends and at work. She has not yet been able to blot out her self-loathing and self-doubts. Though very beautiful, she thinks of herself as ugly and misshapen. Though very bright, she doubts her ability to grasp concepts, take exams, and express herself in groups. By believing herself unworthy she curtails her considerable gifts. She doubts her ability to attract men and feels repulsive. But she is beginning to accept herself and see some future for herself, having had great personal determination and intensive individual and group therapy.

This actual case serves as a supplement to the excerpt from Jerzy Kosinski's "The Painted Bird." Both are examples of cruelty wreaked upon children by adults, an all too common occurrence. The child mortality records in our hospitals tell us how common, though they understate the facts.

Dr. Vincent Fontana, Medical Director of New York Foundling Hospital Center and Professor of Pediatrics at New York University College of Medicine, as well as Chairman of the Mayor's Task Force on Child Abuse and Neglect for the city of New York, says the following:[3]

> Child abuse is a symptom of the violence running rampant in our society today. This disease, if it is allowed to continue at its present pace, will threaten the future of our society and the entire fabric of our civilization. Child abuse is one form of violence which results in social disorganization and disintegration. Persons who engage in violence tend to have been victims of violence. This generation's battered children if they survive will be the next generation's battering parents. It has been shown that many infants and young children that have been abused and neglected at the hands of their own parents, if they survive, tend to carry out their injuries into adolescence. These children, as they approach adolescence begin to show evidence of psychological and emotional disturbances leading to juvenile delinquency. Dr. Karl Menninger has stated that "every criminal was an unloved and maltreated child." He feels that the criminal is the child who survives his maltreatment physically but who suffers at the hands of unrestrained, aggressive and psychotic adults. . . . When a child is exposed to repeated episodes of violence—physical abuse, verbal abuse, neglect or rejection—the child grows with anger and patterns his behavior on that of the model or the parent by imitation. The child learns particularly during the first 3 to 4 years, the imprinting years, a manner of behavior patterned on the parental behavior—namely one of acting out in a violent manner. Psychologists tell us that this type of child can develop a perception of the world as a hostile and dangerous place to be dealt with in an aggressive antisocial destructive fashion. It is of course highly unlikely that there is a one to one relationship between child abuse and later crimes of violence.
>
> Strong consideration should be given to the thesis that treating the syndrome of the battered child not only may be a means of preventing possible permanent physical or mental injury or death of a child but may also be a means of breaking the violence generational cycle, assuming the sad fact that violent children and violent adults are mainly taught to be that way by their parents.
>
> In the course of many years as a pediatrician and as an activist in the field of child maltreatment, I have been able to observe and come to know countless parents who have battered, neglected, and abused their children. These observations during the past decade have led me to believe that adult attitudes and the love for their children vary. There are ambivalent latent feelings concerning children in all adults, admixtures of love and hate. It is false for anyone to assume that every parent loves his or her children and that abuse, neglect and battering are unthinkable and rare entities. Unfortunately, an appreciable number of parents cannot or do not adequately care for their children. . . . Child abuse is our responsibility; it hurts everybody—the child, the parents and the community. There are positive steps that can be taken to help the little children who become tragic statistics—hospital child abuse teams; Parents Anonymous groups; parental stress hotlines; homemakers; parent aides; community child abuse prevention and treatment centers; child advocate community groups; family health clinics; and expansion, funding, and the realistic staffing with trained social workers of the Child Protective Units responsible for the investigation of the child abuse and neglect reports.
>
> It is my belief, a belief in which virtually all my colleagues concur, that a large proportion of abusive and neglectful parents do not willfully harm their children. Willfully is the operative word. They know they are neglecting. They know a cry of pain when they hear one. Many would like to stop themselves if only they knew how, but they don't. They are inadequate, frightened people, incapable of parenting, and they don't like what they are.

3. "Child Abuse and Neglect," *American Journal of Orthopsychiatry*, 48 (1978): pp. 580–605.

Editors' Commentary

Some Reasons Why It Feels the Way It Does (Poverty; Slums; and Racial, Ethnic, Class, and Economic Differences)

E. R. Braithwaite, author of the first excerpt in this section, is an Oxford-trained black engineer. Unable to find a job that made use of his professional training and experience, he took a teaching job at an experimental day school in the poorest white slums of London. The school, run by an inspired educator, takes on the obstreperous rejects from other schools. The entire book Braithwaite wrote about his experiences there would be valuable reading for anyone working with disturbed or deprived children. Braithwaite's understanding of group dynamics as a sine qua non of teaching is impressive. The excerpt here invites comparison with the selections from Malcolm X and Piri Thomas that follow.

To Sir, with Love

E. R. Braithwaite

Just about this time a new supply teacher, Mr. Bell, was sent to our school as supernumerary to the Staff for a few weeks. He was about forty years old, a tall, wiry man, who had had some previous experience with the Army Education Service. It was arranged that he should act as relief teacher for some lessons, including two periods of P.T. with the senior boys. One of Mr. Bell's hobbies was fencing: he was something of a perfectionist and impatient of anyone whose co-ordination was not as smooth and controlled as his own. He would repeat a P.T. movement or exercise over and over again until it was executed with clockwork precision, and though the boys grumbled against his discipline they seemed eager to prove to him that they were quite capable of doing any exercise he could devise, and with a skill that very nearly matched his own.

This was especially true in the cases of Ingham, Fernman and Seales, who would always place themselves at the head of the line as an example and encouragement to the others. The least athletic of these was Richard Buckley, a short, fat boy, amiable and rather dim, who could read and write after a fashion, and could never be provoked to any semblance of anger or heat. He was pleasant and jolly and a favorite with the others, who, though they themselves chivvied him unmercifully, were ever ready in his defense against outsiders.

Buckley was no good at P.T. or games; he just was not built for such pursuits. Yet, such is the perversity of human nature, he strenuously resisted any efforts to leave him out or overlook him when games were being arranged. His attempts at accomplishing such simple gymnastic performances as the "forward roll" and "star jump" reduced the rest of the P.T. class to helpless hilarity, but he persisted with a singleness of purpose which, though unproductive, was nothing short of heroic.

Buckley was Bell's special whipping boy. Fully aware of the lad's physical limitations, he would encourage him to try other and more difficult exercises, with apparently the sole purpose of obtaining some amusement from the pitiably ridiculous results. Sometimes the rest of the class would protest; and then Bell would turn on them the full flood of his invective. The boys mentioned this in their "Weekly Review," and Mr. Florian decided to discuss it at a Staff Meeting.

"The boys seem to be a bit bothered by remarks you make to them during P.T., Mr. Bell."

"To which remarks do you refer, Mr. Florian?" Bell never used the term "Sir," seeming to think it "infra dig." Even when he granted him the "Mr. Florian," he gave to this form of address the suggestion of a sneer.

"From their review it would seem that you are unnecessarily critical of their persons."

"Do you mean their smell?"

"Well, yes, that and the state of their clothing."

"I've advised them to wash."

"These are the words which appear in one review." The Headmaster produced a notebook, Fernman's, and read:

"'Some of you stink like old garbage.'"

His tone was cool, detached, judicial.

"I was referring to their feet. Many of them never seem to wash their feet, and when they take their shoes off the stink is dreadful."

"Many of them live in homes where there are very few facilities for washing, Mr. Bell."

"Surely enough water is available for washing their feet if they really wanted to."

"Then they'd put on the same smelly socks and shoes to which you also object."

"I've got to be in contact with them and it isn't very pleasant."

"Have you ever lived in this area, Mr. Bell?"

"No fear."

"Then you know nothing about the conditions prevailing. The water you so casually speak of is more often to be found in the walls and on the floors than in the convenient wash basin or bath to which you are accustomed. I've visited homes of some of these children where water for a family in an upstairs flat had to be fetched by bucket or pail from the single back-yard tap which served five or six families. You may see, therefore, that so elementary a function as washing the feet might present many difficulties."

Bell was silent at this.

"I've no wish to interfere, or tell you how to do your work; you're an experienced teacher and know more about P.T. than I ever will,"—the Old Man was again patient, encouraging—"but try to be a little more understanding about their difficulties." He then turned to other matters, but it was clear that Bell was considerably put out by the rebuke.

Matters came to a head that Monday afternoon. I was not present in the gym, but was able to reconstruct the sequence of events with reasonable accuracy from the boys' reports and Bell's subsequent admissions.

During the P.T. session he had been putting them through their paces in the "astride vault" over the buck, all except Buckley, who was somewhat under the weather and wisely stood down from attempting the rather difficult jump, but without reference to or permission from Bell, who was not long in discovering the absence of his favorite diversion.

"Buckley," he roared.

"Yes, Sir."

"Come on, boy, I'm waiting." He was standing in his usual position beside the buck in readiness to arrest the fall of any lad who might be thrown off balance by an awkward approach or incorrect execution of the movement. But the boy did not move, and the master stared at him amazed and angry at this unexpected show of defiance by the one generally considered to be the most timid and tractable in the whole class.

"Fatty can't do it, Sir, it's too high for him," Denham interposed.

"Shut up, Denham," Bell roared. "If I want your opinion I will ask for it." He left his station by the buck and walked to where Buckley was standing. The boy watched his threatening approach, fear apparent in his eyes.

"Well, Buckley," Bell towered over the unhappy youth, "are you going to do as you're told?"

"Yes, Sir," Buckley's capitulation was as sudden as his refusal.

The others stopped to watch as he stood looking at the buck, licking his lips nervously while waiting for the instructor to resume his position. It may have been fear or determination or a combination of both, but Buckley launched himself at the buck in furious assault, and in spite of Bell's restraining arms, boy and buck crashed on the floor with a sickening sound as one leg of the buck snapped off with the sound of a pistol shot. The class stood in shocked silence watching Buckley, who remained as he fell, inert and pale; then they rushed to his assistance. All except Potter; big, good-natured Potter seemed to have lost his reason. He snatched up the broken metal-bound leg and advanced on Bell, screaming:

"You bloody bastard, you fucking bloody bastard."

"Put that thing down, Potter, don't be a fool," Bell spluttered, backing away from the hysterical boy.

"You made him do it; he didn't want to and you made him," Potter yelled.

"Don't be a fool, Potter, put it down," Bell appealed.

"I'll do you in, you bloody murderer." Bell was big, but in his anger Potter seemed bigger, his improvised club a fearsome extension of his thick forearm.

That was where I rushed in. Tich Jackson, frightened by the sight of Buckley, limp and white on the floor, and the enraged Potter, slobbering at the instructor in murderous fury, had dashed upstairs to my classroom shouting: "Sir, quick, they're fighting in the gym." I followed his disappearing figure in time to see Bell backed against a wall, with Potter advancing on him.

"Hold it, Potter," I called. He turned at the sound of my voice and I quickly placed myself between them. "Let's have that, Potter." I held out my hand towards the boy, but he stared past me at Bell, whimpering in his emotion. Anger had completely taken hold of him, and he looked very dangerous.

"Come on, Potter," I repeated, "hand it over and go lend a hand with Buckley."

He turned to look towards his prostrate friend and I quickly moved up to him and seized the improvised club; he released it to me without any resistance and went back to join the group around Buckley. Bell then walked away and out of the room, and I went up to the boys. Denham rose and faced me, his face white with rage.

"Potts should have done the bastard like he did Fatty, just 'cos he wouldn't do the bloody jump."

I let that pass; they were angry and at such times quickly reverted to the old things, the words, the discourtesies. I stooped down beside Buckley, who was now sitting weakly on the floor, supported by Sapiano and Seales, and smiling up at them as if ashamed of himself for having been the cause of so much fuss.

"How do you feel, old man?" I inquired.

"Cor, Sir," he cried, smiling, "me tum does hurt."

"He fell on the buck. You should have seen 'im, Sir."

"Gosh, you should've heard the noise when the leg smashed."

"Mr. Bell couldn't catch Fatty, Sir, you should've seen him."

Most of them were trying to talk all at once, eager to give me all the details.

"Bleeding bully, always picking on Fats." This from Sapiano, whose volatile Maltese temperament was inclined to flare up very easily.

"If I'd had the wood I'd have done the fucker in and no bleeding body would have stopped me." Denham was aching for trouble and didn't care who knew it. Bell had slipped away unharmed after hurting his friend, and Denham wanted a substitute. But I would not look at him, or even hear the things he said. Besides, I liked Denham; in spite of his rough manner and speech he was an honest, dependable person with a strong sense of independence.

"Can you stand up, Buckley?"

With some assistance from Seales and Sapiano the boy got to his feet; he looked very pale and unsteady. I turned to Denham: "Will you help the others take Buckley up to Mrs. Dale-Evans and ask her to give him some sweet tea; leave him there and I'll meet you all in the classroom in a few minutes."

Without waiting for his reply I hurried off to the staffroom in search of Bell.

I was in something of a quandary. I knew that it was quite possible Buckley was all right, but there was no knowing whether he had sustained any internal injury not yet apparent. The Council's rules required that all accidents be reported and logged; the Headmaster should be informed forthwith, and in the light of what he had said to Bell so very recently, there would most certainly be a row.

I went up to the staffroom and found Bell washing his face at the sink.

"I've sent Buckley upstairs for a cup of tea," I said. "I suppose he'll be all right, anyway he was walking under his own steam."

"What happens now?" His voice was querulous.

"You should know as well as I do," I replied. "Shouldn't you see the Old Man and make some kind of report?"

"Yes, I suppose I'd better get over to his office right away. I should have attended to the Buckley boy, but the other one rushed me. Thanks for helping out."

"Oh, that's all right," I replied. "But why did you insist on the boy doing the vault?"

"I had to, don't you see; he just stood there refusing to obey and the others were watching me; I just had to do something." His whole attitude now was defensive.

"I'm not criticizing you, Mr. Bell, just asking. Buckley's a bit of a mascot with the others, you know, and I suppose that is why Potter got out of hand."

"I guess it was the way he jumped or something, but I couldn't grab him. He hit the buck too low and sent it flying."

"He's a bit awkward, isn't he; anyway I'm sure the Old Man will understand how it happened."

"He might be a bit difficult, especially after what he said the other day."

"Not necessarily. After all, it was an accident and thank Heaven it's not very serious."

He dried his hands and moved towards the door. "I suppose they'll really go to town on this in their weekly reviews," he remarked.

"I'll ask the boys to say nothing about it. I don't suppose Potter is now feeling any too pleased with himself at his conduct."

As he left Clinty came into the staffroom.

"What's happening, Rick?" she asked. "I just saw some of your boys taking Fatty Buckley upstairs. What's happened to him?"

I told her about the incident and added: "Bell has just gone to the Old Man's office to report the matter."

"Well, what do you know?" she chuckled.

"Fancy Potter going for Bell like that. I always thought that boy a bit of a softie, but you never know with those quiet ones, do you?"

"He was not the only one. Sapiano and Denham were just as wild, I think, but they were too busy fussing over Buckley to bother with Bell."

"He is a bit of a tyro, isn't he. This might make him take it a bit easier."

"I don't think the boys mind his being strict during P.T. It's just that Buckley's a bit of a fool and they resented his being hurt. If it had been Denham or someone like that, I'm sure they would have done nothing."

"Yes, I guess you're right. Bell is a good teacher. I wonder how long the Divisional Office will let him stay here. I hope he hasn't had too much of a fright."

"Oh, he'll get over that. Now I must go and have a word with my boys."

I left her. For some inexplicable reason I felt nervous about being alone with Clinty; I felt that there was something she wanted to say to me, and for my part I did not want to hear it.

In the classroom the boys were sitting closely grouped together, looking rather sheepish. I knew they were feeling aggrieved and, according to their lights, justifiably so; but nevertheless the matter of Potter's behavior had to be dealt with.

"How's Buckley?" I asked.

"We left him upstairs with Mrs. Dale-Evans, Sir. He didn't want to stay, he kept saying he was all right. But she told him if he wasn't quiet she'd give him some castor oil, Sir. Ugh!" They all managed a smile at Seales' remark.

"Good," I replied, "I expect he'll be quite all right. But there is something I want to say to you about this unfortunate incident." I sat down on the edge of Fernman's desk.

"Potter, there is nothing I can think of which can excuse your shocking conduct in the gym."

Potter's mouth fell open; he looked at me in surprise, gulped a few times and stammered:

"But it was him, Sir, Mr. Bell, making Fatty fall and that." His voice was shrill with outrage at my remark.

"Mr. Bell was the master there, Potter, and anything that happened in the gym was his responsibility. Buckley's mishap was no excuse for you to make such an attack on your teacher."

"But Fatty told him he couldn't do it, Sir, and he made him, he made him, Sir."

Potter was very near tears. His distress was greater because of what he believed was the further injustice of my censure. The others, too, were looking at me with the same expression.

"That may be, Potter. I am not now concerned with Mr. Bell's conduct, but with yours. You came very near to getting yourself into very serious trouble because you were unable to control your temper. Not only was your language foul and disgusting, but you armed yourself with a weapon big enough and heavy enough to cause very serious harm. What do you think would have happened if everyone had behaved like you and had all turned on Mr. Bell like a pack of mad wolves?" I waited for this to sink in a bit, but Potter interjected:

"I thought he had done Fatty in, Sir, he looked all huddled up like, Sir."

"I see. So you didn't wait to find out but rushed in with your club like a hoodlum to smash and kill, is that it? Your friend was hurt and you wanted to hurt back; suppose instead of a piece of wood it had been a knife, or a gun, what then?" Potter was pale, and he was not the only one.

"Potts didn't think. He was narked, we was all narked, seeing Fatty on the deck. I wasn't half bleeding wild myself."

"You're missing the point, Denham. I think you're all missing the point. We sit in this classroom day after day and talk of things, and you all know what's expected of you; but at the first sign of bother you forget it all. In two weeks you'll all be at work and lots of things will happen which will annoy you, make you wild. Are you going to resort to clubs and knives every time you're upset or angered?" I stood up. "You'll meet foremen or supervisors or workmates who'll do things to upset you, sometimes deliberately. What then, Denham? What about that, Potter? Your Headmaster is under fire from many quarters because he believes in you—because he really believes that by the time you leave here you will have learned to exercise a little self-control at the times when it is most needed. His success or failure will be reflected in the way you conduct yourselves after you leave him. If today's effort is an example of your future behavior I hold out very little hope for you."

At this moment Buckley walked in, smiling broadly and seemingly none the worse for wear. I waited until he was seated then went on:

"I've no wish to belabor this matter, but it cannot be left like this. Potter, you were very discourteous to your P.T. instructor, and it is my opinion that you owe him an apology." Potter stared at me, his mouth open in amazement at my remark; but before he could speak Denham leapt to his feet.

"Apologize?" His voice was loud in anger. "Why should Potts apologize? He didn't do him any harm. Why should he apologize to him just because he's a bleeding teacher?" He stood there, legs slightly apart, heavy-shouldered and truculent, glaring at me. The others were watching us, but agreeing with him; I could feel their resentment hardening.

"Please sit down Denham, and remember that in this class we are always able to discuss things, no matter how difficult or unpleasant, without shouting at each other."

I waited, fearful of this unexpected threat to our pleasant relationship; he looked around at his colleagues indecisively, then abruptly sat down. I continued, in a very friendly tone:

"That was a fair question, Denham, although you will agree it was put a little, shall we say, indelicately?"

I smiled as I said this, and, in spite of his anger, Denham smiled briefly too. I went on:

"Potter, are you quite pleased and satisfied with the way you behaved to your P.T. teacher?"

Potter looked at me for a moment, then murmured, "No, Sir."

"But he couldn't help it," Denham interjected.

"That may be so, Denham, but Potter agrees that his own actions were unsatisfactory; upon reflection he himself is not pleased with what he did."

"How's about Mr. Bell then: How's about him apologizing to Buckley?" Denham was not to be dissuaded from his attitude.

"Yes, how about him?" echoed Sapiano.

"My business is with you, not with Mr. Bell," I replied.

This was not going to be easy, I thought. Denham was getting a bit nasty; the usual "Sir" had disappeared from his remarks, and Sapiano was following suit.

"It's easy for you to talk, Sir, nobody tries to push you around." Seales' voice was clear and calm, and the others turned to look at him, to support him. His question touched something deep inside of me, something which had been dormant for months, but now awoke to quick, painful remembering. Without realizing what I was doing I got up and walked to where he sat and stood beside his desk.

"I've been pushed around, Seales," I said quietly, "in a way I cannot explain to you. I've been pushed around until I began to hate people so much that I wanted to hurt them, really hurt them. I know how it feels, believe me, and one thing I learned, Seales, is to try always to be a bit bigger than the people who hurt me. It is easy to reach for a knife or a gun; but then you become merely a tool and the knife or gun takes over, thereby creating new and bigger problems without solving a thing. So what happens when there is no weapon handy?"

I felt suddenly annoyed with myself for giving way to my emotion, and abruptly walked back to my desk. The class seemed to feel that something had touched me deeply and were immediately sympathetic in their manner.

"The point I want to make, Potter," I continued, "is whether you are really growing up and learning to stand squarely on your own feet. When you begin work at Covent Garden you might some day have cause to be very angry; what will you do then? The whole idea of this school is to teach you to discipline yourself. In this instance you lost your temper and behaved badly to your teacher. Do you think you are big enough to make an apology to him?"

Potter fidgeted in his seat and looked uncertainly at me, then replied: "Yes, Sir."

"It's always difficult to apologize, Potter, especially to someone you feel justified in disliking. But remember that you are not doing it for Mr. Bell's sake, but your own."

I sat down. They were silent, but I realized that they understood what I meant. Potter stood up:

"Is he in the staffroom, Sir?"

"I think he should be there now, Potter."

Denham and Seales stood and joined Potter and together they went to find Bell. I called Buckley.

"How are you feeling, Buckley?"

"Okay, Sir," he replied, as jovial as ever.

"What will your parents say about all this, Buckley?" I was being devious but, I thought, necessarily so.

"I shan't tell 'em, Sir. Must I, Sir?"

"It's up to you, Buckley. If you feel fine there's no need to bother; but if in the next few days or weeks you feel any pain, it would be best to mention it so that they'd know what to do."

In a few minutes the boys were back, Potter looking red and embarrassed; behind them came Mr. Bell.

"May I speak to your boys for a moment, Mr. Braithwaite?" He came in and stood beside my desk and I nodded to him.

"I want to say to all of you," he began, "that I'm sorry about what happened in the gym a little while ago. I think that one way or another we were all a bit silly, but the sooner we forget the whole thing, the better.

"How're you feeling now, boy?" He addressed himself to Buckley.

"Okay, Sir," the boy replied.

"Fine. Well, I suppose we'll see each other as usual next week." And with that he was gone, having made as friendly a gesture as his evident nervousness would allow.

The boys seemed not unwilling to let the matter drop, so we turned our attention to the discussion of other things.

Editors' Commentary

Diagnosis: Impulse breakthrough—acting-out children—the syndrome of the socially and economically deprived child.

In this case the behavior of Potter was clearly provoked. However, the reason for losing control, as Potter did, is frequently neither so visible nor so apparently justified to the outsider. In very disturbed cases the provocation may come from inner fantasies, such as distorted images of the people around the child, which evoke tortured memories or half-memories. It may come from a tone of voice, a seemingly harmless phrase, a frustration that makes the child feel foolish, helpless, inept. Here, Potter's anger was aroused by injustice; and children, even disturbed ones, are happily committed to justice—even though their definitions may not coincide with society's. The crucial factor in Potter's case was not his anger but the way he handled it. Rage is an overwhelming experience. Inability to handle it in an acceptable fashion leads to tragedy.

Braithwaite is careful to make this point to the boys themselves as he details the precarious life ahead for one who is at the mercy of rage instead of its master. His handling of the problem in the group of children, where all could hear and express themselves, displays the kind of skill that comes from human understanding.

This selection also highlights the contagion of rage among children. It indicates, too, that the teacher's revelation of his own deep personal feeling communicated real, emotional understanding far more powerfully than intellectual reasoning. This, more than the proper words, got across to the boys. Children, even badly disturbed ones, respond to genuineness. In many cases the more troubled the child, the more therapeutic can a teacher's genuine feelings be, provided they are not overexploited or used to gain sympathy for the teacher.

Doctor Jack-o'-Lantern

Richard Yates

All Miss Price had been told about the new boy was that he'd spent most of his life in some kind of orphanage, and that the gray-haired "aunt and uncle" with whom he now lived were really foster parents, paid by the Welfare Department of the City of New York. A less dedicated or less imaginative teacher might have pressed for more details, but Miss Price was content with the rough outline. It was enough, in fact, to fill her with a sense of mission that shone from her eyes, as plain as love, from the first morning he joined the fourth grade.

He arrived early and sat in the back row—his spine very straight, his ankles crossed precisely under the desk and his hands folded on the very center of its top, as if symmetry might make him less conspicuous—and while the other children were filing in and settling down, he received a long, expressionless stare from each of them.

"We have a new classmate this morning," Miss Price said, laboring the obvious in a way that made everybody want to giggle. "His name is Vincent Sabella and he comes from New York City. I know we'll all do our best to make him feel at home."

This time they all swung around to stare at once, which caused him to duck his head slightly and shift his weight from one buttock to the other. Ordinarily, the fact of someone's coming from New York might have held a certain prestige, for to most of the children the city was an awesome, adult place that swallowed up their fathers every day, and which they themselves were permitted to visit only rarely, in their best clothes, as a treat. But anyone could see at a glance that Vincent Sabella had nothing whatever to do with skyscrapers. Even if you could ignore his tangled black hair and gray skin, his clothes would have given him away: absurdly new corduroys, absurdly old sneakers and a yellow sweatshirt, much too small, with the shredded remains of a Mickey Mouse design stamped on its chest. Clearly, he was from the part of New York that you had to pass through on the train to Grand Central—the part where people hung bedding over their windowsill and leaned out on it all day in a trance of boredom, and where you got vistas of straight, deep streets, one after another, all alike in the clutter of their sidewalks and all swarming with gray boys at play in some desperate kind of ball game.

The girls decided that he wasn't very nice and turned away, but the boys lingered in their scrutiny, looking him up and down with faint smiles. This was the kind of kid they were accustomed to thinking of as "tough," the kind whose stares had made all of them uncomfortable at one time or another in unfamiliar neighborhoods; here was a unique chance for retaliation.

"What would you like us to call you, Vincent?" Miss Price inquired. "I mean, do you prefer Vincent, or Vince, or—or what?" (It was purely an academic question; even Miss Price knew that the boys would call him "Sabella" and that the girls wouldn't call him anything at all.)

"Vinny's okay," he said in a strange, croaking voice that had evidently yelled itself hoarse down the ugly streets of his home.

"I'm afraid I didn't hear you," she said, craning her pretty head forward and to one side so that a heavy lock of hair swung free of one shoulder. "Did you say 'Vince'?"

"Vinny, I said," he said again, squirming.

"Vincent, is it? All right then, Vincent." A few of the class giggled, but nobody bothered to correct her; it would be more fun to let the mistake continue.

"I won't take time to introduce you to everyone by name, Vincent," Miss Price went on, "because I think it would be simpler just to let you learn the names as we go along, don't you? Now, we won't expect you to take any real part in the work for the first day or so; just take your time, and if there's anything you don't understand, why, don't be afraid to ask."

He made an unintelligible croak and smiled fleetingly, just enough to show that the roots of his teeth were green.

"Now then," Miss Price said, getting down to business. "This is Monday morning, and so the first thing on the program is reports. Who'd like to start off?"

Vincent Sabella was momentarily forgotten as six or seven hands went up, and Miss Price drew back in mock confusion. "Goodness, we do have a lot of reports this morning," she said. The idea of the reports—a fifteen-minute period every Monday in which the children were encouraged to relate their experiences over the weekend—was Miss Price's own, and she took a pardonable pride in it. The principal had commended her on it at a recent staff meeting, pointing out that it made a splendid bridge between the worlds of school and home, and that it was a fine way for children to learn poise and assurance. It called for intelligent supervision—the shy children had to be drawn out and the show-offs curbed—but in general, as Miss Price had assured the principal, it was fun for everyone. She particularly hoped it would be fun today, to help put Vincent Sabella at ease, and that was why she chose Nancy Parker to start off; there was nobody like Nancy for holding an audience.

The others fell silent as Nancy moved gracefully to the head of the room; even the two or three girls who secretly despised her had to feign enthrallment when she spoke (she was that popular), and every boy in the class, who at recess liked nothing better than to push her shrieking into the mud, was unable to watch her without an idiotically tremulous smile.

"Well—" she began, and then she clapped a hand over her mouth while everyone laughed.

"Oh, *Nancy*," Miss Price said. "You *know* the rule about starting a report with 'well.'"

Nancy knew the rule; she had only broken it to get the laugh. Now she let her fit of giggles subside, ran her fragile forefingers down the side seams of her skirt, and began again in the proper way. "On Friday my whole family went for a ride in my brother's new car. My brother bought this new Pontiac last week, and he wanted to take us all for a ride—you know, to try it out and everything? So we went into White Plains and had dinner in a restaurant there, and then we all wanted to go see this movie, 'Doctor Jekyll and Mr. Hyde,' but my brother said it was too horrible and everything, and I wasn't old enough to enjoy it—oh, he made me so mad! And then, let's see. On Saturday I stayed home all day and helped my mother make my sister's wedding dress. My sister's engaged to be married you see, and my mother's making this wedding dress for her? So we did that, and then on Sunday this friend of my brother's came over for dinner, and then they both had to get back to college that night, and I was allowed to stay up late and say goodbye to them and everything, and I guess that's all." She always had a sure instinct for keeping her performance brief—or rather, for making it seem briefer than it really was.

"Very good, Nancy," Miss Price said. "Now, who's next?"

Warren Berg was next, elaborately hitching up his pants as he made his way down the aisle. "On Saturday I went over to Bill Stringer's house for lunch," he began in his direct, man-to-man style, and Bill Stringer wriggled bashfully in the front row. Warren Berg and Bill Stringer were great friends, and their reports often overlapped. "And then after lunch we went into White Plains, on our bikes. Only we *saw* 'Doctor Jeckyll and Mr. Hyde.'" Here he nodded his head in Nancy's direction, and Nancy got another laugh by making a little whimper of envy. "It was real good, too," he went on, with mounting excitement. "It's all about this guy who—"

"About *a man who*," Miss Price corrected.

"About a man who mixes up this chemical, like, that he drinks? And whenever he drinks this chemical, he changes into this real monster, like? You see him drink this chemical, and then you see his hands start to get all scales all over them, like a reptile and everything, and then you see his face start to change into this real horrible-looking face—with fangs and all? Sticking out of his mouth?"

All the girls shuddered in pleasure. "Well," Miss Price said, "I think Nancy's brother was probably wise in not wanting her to see it. What did you do *after* the movie, Warren?"

There was a general "*Aw-w-w!*" of disappointment—everyone wanted to hear more about the scales and fangs—but Miss Price never liked to let the reports degenerate into accounts of movies. Warren continued without much enthusiasm: all they had done after the movie was fool around Bill Stringer's yard until suppertime. "And then on Sunday," he said, brightening again, "Bill Stringer came over to *my* house, and my dad helped us rig up this old tire on this long rope? From a tree? There's this steep hill down behind my house, you see—this ravine, like?—and we hung this tire so that what you do is, you take the tire and run a little ways and then lift your feet, and you go swinging way, way out over the ravine and back again."

"That sounds like fun," Miss Price said, glancing at her watch.

"Oh, it's *fun* all right," Warren conceded. But then he hitched up his pants again and added, with a puckering of his forehead, "'Course, it's pretty dangerous. You let go of that tire or anything, you'd get a bad fall. Hit a rock or anything, you'd probably break your leg, or your spine. But my dad said he trusted us both to look out for our own safety."

"Well, I'm afraid that's all we'll have time for, Warren," Miss Price said. "Now, there's just time for one more report. Who's ready? Arthur Cross?"

There was a soft groan, because Arthur Cross was the biggest dope in class and his reports were always a bore. This time it turned out to be something tedious about going to visit his uncle on Long Island. At one point he made a slip—he said "botormoat" instead of "motorboat"—and everyone laughed with the particular edge of scorn they reserved for Arthur Cross. But the laughter died abruptly when it was joined by a harsh, dry croaking from the back of the room. Vincent Sabella was laughing too, green teeth and all, and they all had to glare at him until he stopped.

When the reports were over, everyone settled down for school. It was recess time before any of the children thought much about Vincent Sabella again, and then they thought of him only to make sure he was left out of everything. He wasn't in the group of boys that clustered around the horizontal bar to take turns at skinning-the-cat, or the group that whispered in a far corner of the playground, hatching a plot to push Nancy Parker in the mud. Nor was he in the larger group, of which even Arthur Cross was a member, that chased itself in circles in a frantic variation of the game of tag. He couldn't join the girls, of course, or the boys from other classes, and so he joined nobody. He stayed on the apron of the playground, close to school, and for the first part of the recess he pretended to be very busy with the laces of his sneakers. He would squat to undo and retie them, straighten up and take a few experimental steps in a springy, athletic way, and then get down and go to work on them again. After five minutes of this he gave it up, picked up a handful of pebbles and began shying them at an invisible target several yards away. That was good for another five minutes, but then there was still five minutes left, and he could think of nothing to do but stand there, first with his hands in his pockets, then with his hands on his hips, and then with his arms folded in a manly way across his chest.

Miss Price stood watching all this from the doorway, and she spent the full recess wondering if she ought to go out and do something about it. She guessed it would be better not to.

She managed to control the same impulse at recess the next day, and every other day that week, though every day it grew more difficult. But one thing she could not control was a tendency to let her anxiety show in class. All Vincent Sabella's errors in schoolwork were publicly excused, even those having nothing to do with his newness, and all his accomplishments were singled out for special mention. Her campaign to build him up was painfully obvious, and never more so than when she tried to make it subtle; once, for instance, in explaining an arithmetic problem, she said, "Now, suppose Warren Berg and Vincent Sabella went to the store with fifteen cents each, and candy bars cost ten cents. How many candy bars would each boy have?" By the end of the week he was well on the way to becoming the worst possible kind of teacher's pet, a victim of the teacher's pity.

On Friday she decided the best thing to do would be to speak to him privately, and try to draw him out. She could say something about the pictures he had painted in art class—that would do for an opening—and she decided to do it at lunchtime.

The only trouble was that lunchtime, next to recess, was the most trying part of Vincent Sabella's day. Instead of going home for an hour as the other children did, he brought his lunch to school in a wrinkled paper bag and ate it in the classroom, which always made for a certain amount of awkwardness. The last children to leave would see him still seated apologetically at his desk, holding his paper bag, and anyone who happened to straggle back later for a forgotten hat or sweater would surprise him in the middle of his meal— perhaps shielding a hard-boiled egg from view or wiping mayonnaise from his mouth with a furtive hand. It was a situation that Miss Price did not improve by walking up to him while the room was still half full of children and sitting prettily on the edge of the desk beside his, making it clear that she was cutting her own lunch hour short in order to be with him.

"Vincent," she began, "I've been meaning to tell you how much I enjoyed those pictures of yours. They're really very good."

He mumbled something and shifted his eyes to the cluster of departing children at the door. She went right on talking and smiling, elaborating on her praise of the pictures; and finally, after the door had closed behind the last child, he was able to give her his attention. He did so tentatively at first; but the more she talked, the more he seemed to relax, until she realized she was putting him at ease. It was as simple and as gratifying as stroking a cat. She had finished with the pictures now and moved on, triumphantly, to broader fields of praise. "It's never easy," she was saying, "to come to a new school and adjust yourself to the—well, the new work, and new working methods, and I think you've done a splendid job so far. I really do. But tell me, do you think you're going to like it here?"

He looked at the floor just long enough to make his reply—"It's awright"—and then his eyes stared into hers again.

"I'm so glad. Please don't let me interfere with your lunch, Vincent. Do go ahead and eat, that is, if you don't mind my sitting here with you." But it was now abundantly clear that he didn't mind at all, and he began to unwrap a bologna sandwich with what she felt sure was the best appetite he'd had all week. It wouldn't even have mattered very much now if someone from the class had come in and watched, though it was probably just as well that no one did.

Miss Price sat back more comfortably on the desk top, crossed her legs and allowed one slim stockinged foot to slip part of the way out of its moccasin. "Of course," she went on, "it always does take a little time to sort of get your bearings in a new school. For one thing, well, it's never too easy for the new member of the class to make friends with the other members. What I mean is, you mustn't mind if the others seem a little rude to you at first. Actually, they're just as anxious to make friends as you are, but they're shy. All it takes is a little time, and a little effort on your part as well as theirs. Not too much, of course, but a little. Now for instance, these reports we have Monday mornings—they're a fine way for people to get to know one another. A person never feels he has to make a report; it's just a thing he can do if he wants to. And that's only one way of helping others to know the kind of person you are; there are lots and lots of ways. The main thing to remember is that making friends is the most natural thing in the world, and it's only a question of time until you have all the friends you want. And in the meantime, Vincent, I hope you'll consider *me* your friend, and feel free to call on me for whatever advice or anything you might need. Will you do that?"

He nodded, swallowing.

"Good." She stood up and smoothed her skirt over her long thighs. "Now I must go or I'll be late for *my* lunch. But I'm glad we had this little talk, Vincent, and I hope we'll have others."

It was probably a lucky thing that she stood up when she did, for if she'd stayed on that desk a minute longer Vincent Sabella would have thrown his arms around her and buried his face in the warm gray flannel of her lap, and that might have been enough to confuse the most dedicated and imaginative of teachers.

At report time on Monday morning, nobody was more surprised than Miss Price when Vincent Sabella's smudged hand was among the first and most eager to rise. Apprehensively she considered letting someone else start off, but then, for fear of hurting his feelings, she said, "All right, Vincent," in as matter-of-fact a way as she could manage.

There was a suggestion of muffled titters from the class as he walked confidently to the head of the room and turned to face his audience. He looked, if anything, too confident: there were signs, in the way he held his shoulders and the way his eyes shone, of the terrible poise of panic.

"Saturday I seen that pitcha," he announced.

"Saw, Vincent," Miss Price corrected gently.

"That's what I mean," he said; "I sore that pitcha. 'Doctor Jack-o'-Lantern and Mr. Hide.'"

There was a burst of wild, delighted laughter and a chorus of correction: "Doctor *Jekyll!*"

He was unable to speak over the noise. Miss Price was on her feet, furious. "It's a *perfectly natural mistake!*" she was saying. "There's no reason for any of you to be so rude. Go on, Vincent, and please excuse this very silly interruption." The laughter subsided, but the class continued to shake their heads derisively from side to side. It hadn't, of course, been a perfectly natural mistake at all; for one thing it proved that he was a hopeless dope, and for another it proved that he was lying.

"That's what I mean," he continued. "'Doctor Jackal and Mr. Hide.' I got it a little mixed up. Anyways, I seen all about where his teet' start comin' outa his mout' and all like that, and I thought it was very good. And then on Sunday my mudda and fodda come out to see me in this car they got. This Buick. My fodda siz, 'Vinny, wanna go for a little ride?' I siz, 'Sure, where yiz goin'?' He siz, 'Anyplace ya like.' So I siz, 'Let's go out in the country a ways, get on one of them big roads and make some time.' So we go out—oh, I guess fifty, sixty miles—and we're cruisin' along this highway, when this cop starts tailin' us? My fodda siz, 'Don't worry, we'll shake him,' and he steps on it, see? My mudda's gettin' pretty scared, but my fodda siz, 'Don't worry, dear.' He's tryin' to make this turn,

see, so he can get off the highway and shake the cop? But just when he's makin' the turn, the cop opens up and starts shootin', see?"

By this time the few members of the class who could bear to look at him at all were doing so with heads on one side and mouths partly open, the way you look at a broken arm or a circus freak.

"We just barely made it," Vincent went on, his eyes gleaming, "and this one bullet got my fodda in the shoulder. Didn't hurt him bad—just grazed him, like—so my mudda bandaged it up for him and all, but he couldn't do no more drivin' after that, and we had to get him to a doctor, see? So my fodda siz, 'Vinny, think you can drive a ways?' I siz, 'Sure, if you show me how.' So he showed me how to work the gas and the brake, and all like that, and I drove to the doctor. My mudda siz, 'I'm prouda you, Vinny, drivin' all by yourself.' So anyways, we got to the doctor, got my fodda fixed up and all, and then he drove us back home." He was breathless. After an uncertain pause he said, "And that's all." Then he walked quickly back to his desk, his stiff new corduroy pants whistling faintly with each step.

"Well, that was very—entertaining, Vincent," Miss Price said, trying to act as if nothing had happened. "Now, who's next?" But nobody raised a hand.

Recess was worse than usual for him that day; at least it was until he found a place to hide—a narrow concrete alley, blind except for several closed fire-exit doors, that cut between two sections of the school building. It was reassuringly dismal and cool in there—he could stand with his back to the wall and his eyes guarding the entrance, and the noises of recess were as remote as the sunshine. But when the bell rang he had to go back to class, and in another hour it was lunchtime.

Miss Price left him alone until her own meal was finished. Then, after standing with one hand on the doorknob for a full minute to gather courage, she went in and sat beside him for another little talk, just as he was trying to swallow the last of a pimento-cheese sandwich.

"Vincent," she began, "we all enjoyed your report this morning, but I think we would have enjoyed it more—a great deal more—if you'd told us something about your real life instead. I mean," she hurried on, "For instance, I noticed you were wearing a nice new windbreaker this morning. It *is* new, isn't it? And did your aunt buy it for you over the weekend?"

He did not deny it.

"Well then, why couldn't you have told us about going to the store with your aunt, and buying the windbreaker, and whatever you did afterwards. That would have made a perfectly good report." She paused, and for the first time looked steadily into his eyes. "You do understand what I'm trying to say, don't you, Vincent?"

He wiped crumbs of bread from his lips, looked at the floor, and nodded.

"And you'll remember next time, won't you?"

He nodded again. "Please may I be excused, Miss Price?"

"Of course you may."

He went to the boys' lavatory and vomited. Afterwards he washed his face and drank a little water, and then he returned to the classroom. Miss Price was busy at her desk now, and didn't look up. To avoid getting involved with her again, he wandered out to the cloakroom and sat on one of the long benches, where he picked up someone's discarded overshoe and turned it over and over in his hands. In a little while he heard the chatter of returning children, and to avoid being discovered there, he got up and went to the fire-exit door. Pushing it open, he found that it gave onto the alley he had hidden in that morning, and he slipped outside. For a minute or two he just stood there, looking at the blankness of the concrete wall: then he found a piece of chalk in his pocket and wrote out all the dirty words he could think of, in block letters a foot high. He had put down four words and was trying to remember a fifth when he heard a shuffling at the door behind him. Arthur Cross was there, holding the door open and reading the words with wide eyes. "Boy," he said in an awed half-whisper. "Boy, you're gonna get it. You're really gonna *get* it."

Startled, and then suddenly calm, Vincent Sabella palmed his chalk, hooked his thumbs in his belt and turned on Arthur Cross with a menacing look. "Yeah?" he inquired. "Who's gonna squeal on me?"

"Well, nobody's gonna *squeal* on you," Arthur Cross said uneasily, "but you shouldn't go around writing—"

"Arright," Vincent said, advancing a step. His shoulders were slumped, his head thrust forward and his eyes narrowed, like Edward G. Robinson. "Arright. That's all I wanna know. I don't like squealers, unnastand?"

While he was saying this, Warren Berg and Bill Stringer appeared in the doorway—just in time to hear it and to see the words on the wall before Vincent turned on them. "And that goes fa you too, unnastand?" he said. "Both a yiz."

And the remarkable thing was that both their faces fell into the same foolish, defensive smile that Arthur Cross was wearing. It wasn't until they had glanced at each other that they were able to meet his eyes with the proper degree of contempt, and by then it was too late. "Think you're pretty smart, don'tcha, Sabella?" Bill Stringer said.

"Never mind what I think," Vincent told him. "You heard what I said. Now let's get back inside."

And they could do nothing but move aside to make way for him, and follow him dumfounded into the cloakroom.

It was Nancy Parker who squealed—although, of course, with someone like Nancy Parker you didn't think of it as squealing. She had heard everything from the cloakroom; as soon as the boys came in she peeked into the alley, saw the words and, setting her face in a prim frown, went straight to Miss Price. Miss Price was just about to call the class to order for the afternoon when Nancy came up and whispered in her ear. They both disappeared into the cloakroom—from which, after a moment, came the sound of the fire-exit door being abruptly slammed—and when they returned to class Nancy was flushed with righteousness, Miss Price very pale. No announcement was made. Classes proceeded in the ordinary way all afternoon, though it was clear that Miss Price was upset, and it wasn't until she was dismissing the children at three o'clock that she brought the thing into the open. "Will Vincent Sabella please remain seated?" She nodded at the rest of the class. "That's all."

While the room was clearing out she sat at her desk, closed her eyes and massaged the frail bridge of her nose with thumb and forefinger, sorting out half-remembered fragments of a book she had once read on the subject of seriously disturbed children. Perhaps, after all, she should never have undertaken the responsibility of Vincent Sabella's loneliness. Perhaps the whole thing called for the attention of a specialist. She took a deep breath.

"Come over here and sit beside me, Vincent," she said, and when he had settled himself, she looked at him. "I want you to tell me the truth. Did you write those words on the wall outside?"

He stared at the floor.

"Look at me," she said, and he looked at her. She had never looked prettier: her cheeks slightly flushed, her eyes shining and her sweet mouth pressed into a self-conscious frown. "First of all," she said, handing him a small enameled basin streaked with poster paint, "I want you to take this to the boys' room and fill it with hot water and soap."

He did as he was told, and when he came back, carrying the basin carefully to keep the suds from spilling, she was sorting out some old rags in the bottom drawer of her desk. "Here," she said, selecting one and shutting the drawer in a businesslike way. "This will do. Soak this up." She led him back to the fire exit and stood in the alley watching him, silently, while he washed off all the words.

When the job had been done, and the rag and basin put away, they sat down at Miss Price's desk again. "I suppose you think I'm angry with you, Vincent," she said. "Well, I'm not. I almost wish I could be angry—that would make it much easier—but instead I'm hurt. I've tried to be a good friend to you, and I thought you wanted to be my friend too. But this kind of thing—well, it's very hard to be friendly with a person who'd do a thing like that."

She saw, gratefully, that there were tears in his eyes. "Vincent, perhaps I understand some things better than you think. Perhaps I understand that sometimes, when a person does a thing like that, it isn't really because he wants to hurt anyone, but only because he's unhappy. He knows it isn't a good thing to do, and he even knows it isn't going to make him any happier afterwards, but he goes ahead and does it anyway. Then when he finds he's lost a friend, he's terribly sorry, but it's too late. The thing is done."

She allowed this somber note to reverberate in the silence of the room for a little while before she spoke again. "I won't be able to forget this, Vincent. But perhaps, just this once, we can still be friends—as long as I understand that you didn't mean to hurt me. But you must promise me that you won't forget it either. Never forget that when you do a thing like that, you're going to hurt people who want very much to like you, and in that way you're going to hurt yourself. Will you promise me to remember that, dear?"

The "dear" was as involuntary as the slender hand that reached out and held the shoulder of his sweatshirt; both made his head hang lower than before.

"All right," she said. "You may go now."

He got his windbreaker out of the cloakroom and left, avoiding the tired uncertainty of her eyes. The corridors were deserted, and dead silent except for the hollow, rhythmic knocking of a janitor's push-broom against some distant wall. His own rubber-soled tread only added to the silence; so did the lonely little noise made by the zipping-up of his windbreaker, and so did the faint mechanical sigh of the heavy front door. The silence made it all the more startling when he found, several yards down the concrete walk outside, that two boys were walking beside him: Warren Berg and Bill Stringer. They were both smiling at him in an eager, almost friendly way.

"What'd she do to ya, anyway?" Bill Stringer asked.

Caught off guard, Vincent barely managed to put on his Edward G. Robinson face in time. "Nunnya business," he said, and walked faster.

"No, listen—wait up, hey," Warren Berg said, as they trotted to keep up with him. "What'd she do, anyway? She bawl ya out, or what? Wait up, hey, Vinny."

The name made him tremble all over. He had to jam his hands in his windbreaker pockets and force himself to keep on walking; he had to force his voice to be steady when he said "Nunnya business, I told ya. Lea' me alone."

But they were right in step with him now. "Boy, she must of given you the works," Warren Berg persisted. "What'd she say, anyway? C'mon, tell us, Vinny."

This time the name was too much for him. It overwhelmed his resistance and made his softening knees slow down to a slack, conversational stroll. "She din say nothin'" he said at last; and then after a dramatic pause he added, "She let the ruler do her talkin' for her."

"The ruler? Ya mean she used a ruler on ya?" Their faces were stunned, either with disbelief or admiration, and it began to look more and more like admiration as they listened.

"On the knuckles," Vincent said through tightening lips. "Five times on each hand. She siz, 'Make a fist. Lay it out here on the desk.' Then she takes the ruler and Whop! Whop! Whop! Five times. Ya think that don't hurt, you're crazy."

Miss Price, buttoning her polo coat as the front door whispered shut behind her, could scarcely believe her eyes. This couldn't be Vincent Sabella—this perfectly normal, perfectly happy boy on the sidewalk ahead of her, flanked by attentive friends. But it was, and the scene made her want to laugh aloud with pleasure and relief. He was going to be all right, after all. For all her well-intentioned groping in the shadows she could never have predicted a scene like this, and certainly could never have caused it to happen. But it was happening, and it just proved, once again, that she would never understand the ways of children.

She quickened her graceful stride and overtook them, turning to smile down at them as she passed. "Goodnight, boys," she called, intending it as a kind of cheerful benediction; and then, embarrassed by their three startled faces, she smiled even wider and said, "Goodness, it is getting colder, isn't it? That windbreaker of yours looks nice and warm, Vincent. I envy you." Finally they nodded bashfully at her; she called goodnight again, turned, and continued on her way to the bus stop.

She left a profound silence in her wake. Staring after her, Warren Berg and Bill Stringer waited until she had disappeared around the corner before they turned on Vincent Sabella.

"Ruler, my eye!" Bill Stringer said. "Ruler, my eye!" He gave Vincent a disgusted shove that sent him stumbling against Warren Berg, who shoved him back.

"Jeez, you lie about *everything*, don'tcha, Sabella? You lie about *everything!*"

Jostled off balance, keeping his hands tight in the windbreaker pockets, Vincent tried in vain to retain his dignity. "Think *I* care if yiz believe me?" he said, and then because he couldn't think of anything else to say, he said it again. "Think *I* care if yiz believe me?"

But he was walking alone. Warren Berg and Bill Stringer were drifting away across the street, walking backwards in order to look back on him with furious contempt. "Just like the lies you told about the policeman shooting your father," Bill Stringer called.

"Even *movies* he lies about," Warren Berg put in; and suddenly doubling up with artificial laughter he cupped both hands to his mouth and yelled, "Hey, Doctor Jack-o'-lantern!"

It wasn't a very good nickname, but it had an authentic ring to it—the kind of a name that might spread around, catch on quickly, and stick. Nudging each other, they both took up the cry:

"What's the matter, Doctor Jack-o'-Lantern?"

"Why don'tcha run on home with Miss Price, Doctor Jack-o'-Lantern?"

"So long, Doctor Jack-o'-Lantern!"

Vincent Sabella went on walking, ignoring them, waiting until they were out of sight. Then he turned and retraced his steps all the way back to school, around through the playground and back to the alley, where the wall was still dark in spots from the circular scrubbing of his wet rag.

Choosing a dry place, he got out his chalk and began to draw a head with great care, in profile, making the hair long and rich and taking his time over the face, erasing it with moist fingers and reworking it until it was the most beautiful face he had ever drawn: a delicate nose, slightly parted lips, an eye with lashes that curved as gracefully as a bird's wing. He paused to admire it with a lover's solemnity; then from the lips he drew a line that connected with a big speech balloon, and in the balloon he wrote, so angrily that the chalk kept breaking in his fingers, every one of the words he had written that noon. Returning to the head, he gave it a slender neck and gently sloping shoulders, and then, with bold strokes, he gave it the body of a naked woman: great breasts with hard little nipples, a trim waist, a dot for a navel, wide hips and thighs that flared around a triangle of fiercely scribbled pubic hair. Beneath the picture he printed its title: "Miss Price."

He stood there looking at it for a little while, breathing hard, and then he went home.

From *Eleven Kinds of Loneliness* by Richard Yates. Reprinted by permission of Monica McCall—International Famous Agency. Copyright © 1961 by Richard Yates.

Editors' Commentary

Diagnosis: Culturally and affectionally deprived child in a middle-class environment.

The story is a realistic description of how a new child in a strange environment tries to find his way. His clothers, manner, and speech make him a stranger. His difference is felt keenly by classmates, the teacher, and himself. His attempt to be like the others by lying or make-believe is understandable enough. Equally understandable is his well-intentioned teacher's overinvolvement with him. Her behavior, although well-meaning and sympathetic, singles him out and further alienates him from the class. Teacher's pet is at best a hard role, particularly when a child is starving for attention and expression.

Vincent's reaction to the teacher's moralistic, middle-class approach to him is confused. In despair, anger, loneliness, and a sense of isolation, he uses the very tools that shock middle-class society most—bad language and lewd pictures.

Overinvolvement often results in a teacher's withdrawal and disappointment. The danger of the teacher's pet role is clear. A gradual welcome that would give the boy a chance to be different and an understanding that a weekend report from him is bound to be a fiasco, one way or another, are what were needed. Sadly, even teachers who come from the same ethnic groups as their students tend not to be trained in an awareness of their middle-class myopia. Though this condition is improving, it is still much too familiar.

The Autobiography of Malcolm X

... My restlessness with Mason—and for the first time in my life a restlessness with being around white people—began as soon as I got back home and entered eighth grade.

I continued to think constantly about all that I had seen in Boston, and about the way I had felt there. I know now that it was the sense of being a real part of a mass of my own kind, for the first time.

The white people—classmates, the Swerlins, the people at the restaurant where I worked—noticed the change. They said, "You're acting so strange. You don't seem like yourself, Malcolm. What's the matter?"

I kept close to the top of the class, though. The topmost scholastic standing, I remember, kept shifting between me, a girl named Audrey Slaugh, and a boy named Jimmy Cotton.

It went on that way, as I became increasingly restless and disturbed through the first semester. And then one day, just about when those of us who had passed were about to move up to 8-A, from which we would enter high school the next year, something happened which was to become the first major turning point of my life.

Somehow, I happened to be alone in the classroom with Mr. Ostrowski, my English teacher. He was a tall, rather reddish white man and he had a thick mustache. I had gotten some of my best marks under him, and he had always made me feel that he liked me. He was, as I have mentioned, a natural-born "advisor," about what you ought to read, to do, or think—about any and everything. We used to make unkind jokes about him: why was he teaching in Mason instead of somewhere else, getting for himself some of the "success in life" that he kept telling us how to get?

I know that he probably meant well in what he happened to advise me that day. I doubt that he meant any harm. It was just in his nature as an American white man. I was one of his top students, one of the school's top students—but all he could see for me was the kind of future "in your place" that almost all white people see for black people.

He told me, "Malcolm, you ought to be thinking about a career. Have you been giving it thought?"

The truth is, I hadn't. I never have figured out why I told him, "Well, yes, sir, I've been thinking I'd like to be a lawyer." Lansing certainly had no Negro lawyers—or doctors either—in those days, to hold up an image I might have aspired to. All I really knew for certain was that a lawyer didn't wash dishes, as I was doing.

Mr. Ostrowski looked surprised, I remember, and leaned back in his chair and clasped his hands behind his head. He kind of half-smiled and said, "Malcolm, one of life's first needs is for us to be realistic. Don't misunderstand me, now. We all here like you, you know that. But you've got to be realistic about being a nigger. A lawyer—that's no realistic goal for a nigger. You need to think about something you *can* be. You're good with your hands—making things. Everybody admires your carpentry shop work. Why don't you plan on carpentry? People like you as a person—you'd get all kinds of work."

The more I thought afterwards about what he said, the more uneasy it made me. It just kept treading around in my mind.

What made it really begin to disturb me was Mr. Ostrowski's advice to others in my class—all of them white. Most of them had told him they were planning to become farmers. But those who wanted to strike out on their own, to try something new, he had encouraged. Some, mostly girls, wanted to be teachers. A few wanted other professions, such as one boy who wanted to become a county agent; another, a veterinarian; and one girl wanted to be a nurse. They all reported that Mr. Ostrowski had encouraged what they had wanted. Yet nearly none of them had earned marks equal to mine.

It was a surprising thing that I had never thought of it that way before, but I realized that whatever I wasn't, I *was* smarter than nearly all of those white kids. But apparently I was still not intelligent enough, in their eyes, to become whatever *I* wanted to be.

It was then that I began to change—inside.

I drew away from white people. I came to class, and I answered when called upon. It became a physical strain simply to sit in Mr. Ostrowski's class.

Where "nigger" had slipped off my back before, wherever I heard it now, I stopped and looked at whoever said it. And they looked surprised that I did.

I quit hearing so much "nigger" and "What's wrong?"—which was the way I wanted it. Nobody, including the teachers, could decide what had come over me. I knew I was being discussed. . . .

In this year, 1965, I am certain that more—and worse—riots are going to erupt, in yet more cities, in spite of the conscience-salving Civil Rights Bill. The reason is that the *cause* of these riots, the racist malignancy in America, has been too long unattended.

I believe that it would be almost impossible to find anywhere in America a black man who has lived further down in the mud of human society than I have; or a black man who has been any more ignorant than I have been; or a black man who has suffered more anguish during his life than I have. But it is only after the deepest darkness that the greatest joy can come; it is only after slavery and prison that the sweetest appreciation of freedom can come.

For the freedom of my 22 million black brothers and sisters here in America, I do believe that I have fought the best that I know how, and the best that I could, with the shortcomings that I have had. I know that my shortcomings are many.

My greatest lack has been, I believe, that I don't have the kind of academic education I wish I had been able to get—to have been a lawyer, perhaps. I do believe that I might have made a good lawyer. I have always loved verbal battle, and challenge. You can believe me that if I had the time, right now, I would not be one bit ashamed to go back into any New York City public school and start where I left off at the ninth grade, and go on through a degree. Because I don't begin to be academically equipped for so many of the interests that I have. For instance, I love languages. I wish I were an accomplished linguist. I don't know anything more frustrating than to be around people talking something you can't understand. Especially when they are people who look just like you. In Africa, I heard original mother tongues, such as Hausa, and Swahili, being spoken, and there I was standing like some little boy, waiting for someone to tell me what had been said; I never will forget how ignorant I felt.

Aside from the basic African dialects, I would try to learn Chinese, because it looks as if Chinese will be the most powerful political language of the future. And already I have begun studying Arabic, which I think is going to be the most powerful spiritual language of the future.

I would just like to *study*, I mean ranging study, because I have a wide-open mind. I'm interested in almost any subject you can mention. I know this is the reason I have come to really like, as individuals, some of the hosts of radio or television panel programs I have been on, and to respect their minds—because even if they have been almost steadily in disagreement with me on the race issue, they still have kept their minds open and objective about the truths of things happening in the world. Irv Kupcinet in Chicago, and Barry Farber, Barry Gray and Mike Wallace in New York—people like them. They also let me see that they respected my mind—in a way I know they never realized. The way I knew was that often they would invite my opinion on subjects off the race issue. Sometimes, after the programs, we would sit around and talk about all kinds of things, current events and other things, for an hour or more. You see, most whites, even when they credit a Negro with some intelligence, will still feel that all he can talk about is the race issue; most whites never feel that Negroes can contribute anything to other areas of thought, and ideas. You just notice how rarely you will ever hear whites asking any Negroes what they think about the problem of world health, or the space race to land men on the moon. . . .

Editors' Commentary

Diagnosis: Intelligence and motivation thwarted by an environment of cultural bigotry and ignorance.

The *Autobiography of Malcolm X* is the story of a man who grew to responsible leadership from a background that offered almost no encouragement. Malcolm X fulfilled much of his exceptional ability in an environment of poverty and racial discrimination and with an education that ended at the ninth grade. The despair and bitterness he felt as a young man led him from virulent self-hatred to hatred of others, delinquency, and crime, which resulted in his imprisonment. In prison he found a protective therapeutic agent in the form of the prison library and a channel toward growth in the form of the Black Muslim organization, a group he later left as he came to adopt a less sectarian view of the need for social change. Prison and poverty are miserable schools to have to learn in, but neither did the public school system provide positive learning experiences. The less motivated and less gifted residents of racial ghettos are frequently trapped in the despair from which Malcolm X emerged.

The excerpts here describe one painful incident with an unconsciously prejudiced teacher whose thoughtless words were a partial source of lifelong despair and regret for Malcolm. The schools should be a source of hope and fulfillment for students, but for many—especially for members of racial minorities—they are the agents of despair, convincing students that their personal goals are unreachable.

Most of the residents of New York's East Harlem, Spanish Harlem, are immigrants from Puerto Rico, a racially mixed population. Piri Thomas is the son of a black father and a white mother from Puerto Rico. The combination of alien language, alien culture, poverty, and racial mixture in his own family made his adolescence unusually difficult. He describes some of his experiences in these selections.

Down These Mean Streets

Piri Thomas

. . . We were moving—our new pad was back in Spanish Harlem—to 104th Street between Lex and Park Avenue.

Moving into a new block is a big jump for a Harlem kid. You're torn up from your hard-won turf and brought into an "I don't know you" block where every kid is some kind of enemy. Even when the block belongs to your own people, you are still an outsider who has to prove himself a down stud with heart.

As the moving van rolled to a stop in front of our new building, number 109, we were all standing there, waiting for it—Momma, Poppa, Sis, Paulie, James, José, and myself. I made out like I didn't notice the cats looking us over, especially me—I was gang age. I read their faces and found no trust, plenty of suspicion, and a glint of rising hate. I said to myself, *These cats don't mean nothin'. They're just nosy.* But I remembered what had happened to me in my old block, and that it had ended with me in the hospital.

This was a tough-looking block. That was good, that was cool; but my old turf had been tough, too. *I'm tough,* a voice within said. *I hope I'm tough enough. I am tough enough. I've got* mucho corazón, *I'm king wherever I go. I'm a killer to my heart. I not only can live, I will live, no punk out, no die out, walk bad; be down, cool breeze, smooth.* My mind raced, and thoughts crashed against each other, trying to reassemble themselves into a patter of rep. I turned slowly and with eyelids half-closed I looked at the rulers of this new world and with a cool shrug of my shoulders I followed the movers into the hallway of number 109 and dismissed the coming war from my mind.

The next morning I went to my new school, called Patrick Henry, and strange, mean eyes followed me.

"Say, pops," said a voice belonging to a guy I later came to know as Waneko, "where's your territory?"

In the same tone of voice Waneko had used, I answered, "I'm on it, dad, what's shaking?"

"Bad, huh?" He half-smiled.

"No, not all the way. Good when I'm cool breeze and bad when I'm down."

"What's your name, kid?"

"That depends. 'Piri' when I'm smooth and 'Johnny Gringo' when stomping time's around."

"What's your name now?" he pushed.

"You name me, man," I answered, playing my role like a champ.

He looked around, and with no kind of words, his boys cruised in. Guys I would come to know, to fight, to hate, to love, to take care of. Little Red, Waneko, Little Louie, Indio, Carlito, Alfredo, Crip, and plenty more. I stiffened and said to myself, *Stomping time, Piri boy, go with heart.*

I fingered the garbage-can handle in my pocket—my homemade brass knuckles. They were great for breaking down large odds into small, chopped-up ones.

Waneko, secure in his grandstand, said, "We'll name you later, *panín*."

I didn't answer. Scared, yeah, but wooden-faced to the end, I thought, *Chevere, panín*.

It wasn't long in coming. Three days later, at about 6 P.M., Waneko and his boys were sitting around the stoop at number 115. I was cut off from my number 109. For an instant I thought, *Make a break for it down the basement steps and through the back yards—get away in one piece!* Then I thought, *Caramba! Live punk, dead hero. I'm no punk kid. I'm not copping any pleas.* I kept walking, hell's-a-burning, hell's-a-churning, rolling with cheer. *Walk on, baby man, roll on without fear. What's he going to call?*

"Whatta ya say, Mr. Johnny Gringo?" drawled Waneko.

Think, man, I told myself, *think your way out of a stomping. Make it good.* "I hear you 104th Street coolies are supposed to have heart," I said. "I don't know this for sure. You know there's a lot of streets where a whole 'click' is made out of punks who can't fight one guy unless they all jump him for the stomp." I hoped this would push Waneko into giving me a fair one. His expression didn't change.

"Maybe we don't look at it that way."

Crazy, man. I cheer inwardly, the cabrón is falling into my setup. We'll see who gets messed up first, baby! "I wasn't talking to you," I said. "Where I come from, the pres is president 'cause he got heart when it comes to dealing."

Waneko was starting to look uneasy. He had bit on my worm and felt like a sucker fish. His boys were now light on me. They were no longer so much interested in stomping me as in seeing the outcome between Waneko and me. "Yeah," was his reply.

I smiled at him. "You trying to dig where I'm at and now you got me interested in you. I'd like to see where you're at."

Waneko hesitated a tiny little second before replying, "Yeah."

I knew I'd won. Sure, I'd have to fight; but one guy, not ten or fifteen. If I lost I might still get stomped, and if I won I might get stomped. I took care of this with my next sentence. "I don't know you or your boys," I said, "but they look cool to me. They don't feature as punks."

I had left him out purposely when I said "they." Now his boys were in a separate class. I had cut him off. He would have to fight me on his own, to prove his heart to himself, to his boys, and most important, to his turf. He got away from the stoop and asked, "Fair one, Gringo?"

"Uh-uh," I said, "roll all the way—anything goes." I thought, *I've got to beat him bad and yet not bad enough to take his prestige all away.* He had *corazón*. He came on me. *Let him draw first blood,* I thought, *it's his block.* Smish, my nose began to bleed. His boys cheered, his heart cheered, his turf cheered. "Waste this chump," somebody shouted.

Okay, baby, now it's my turn. He swung. I grabbed innocently, and my forehead smashed into his nose. His eyes crossed. His fingernais went for my eye and landed in my mouth—crunch, I bit hard. I punched him in the mouth as he pulled away from me, and he slammed his foot into my chest.

We broke, my nose running red, my chest throbbing, his finger—well, that was his worry. I tied up with body punching and slugging. We rolled onto the street. I wrestled for acceptance, he for rejection or, worse yet, acceptance on his terms. It was time to start peace talks. I smiled at him. "You got heart, baby," I said.

He answered with a punch to my head. I grunted and hit back, harder now. I had to back up my overtures of peace with strength. I hit him in the ribs, I rubbed my knuckles in his ear as we clinched. I tried again. "You deal good," I said.

"You too," he muttered, pressuring out. And just like that, the fight was over. No more words. We just separated, hands half up, half down. My heart pumped out, *You've established your rep. Move over, 104th Street. Lift your wings, I'm one of your baby chicks now.*

Five seconds later my spurs were given to me in the form of introductions to streetdom's elite. There were no looks of blankness now; I was accepted by heart.

"What's your other name, Johnny Gringo?"

"Piri."

"Okay, Pete, you wanna join my fellows?"

"Sure, why not?"

But I knew I had first joined their gang when I cool-looked them on moving day. *I was cool, man,* I thought. *I could've wasted Waneko any time. I'm good, I'm damned good, pure corazón. Viva me!* Shit, I had been scared, but that was over. I was in; it was *my* block now.

Not that I could relax. In Harlem you always lived on the edge of losing rep. All it takes is a one-time loss of heart. . . .

When you're a kid, everything has some kind of special meaning. I always could find something to do, even if it was doing nothing. But going to school was something else. School stunk. I hated school and all its teachers. I hated the crispy look of the teachers and the draggy-long hours they took out of my life from nine to three-thirty. I dug being outside no matter what kind of weather. Only chumps worked and studied.

Every day began with a fight to get me out of bed for school. Momma played the same record over an' over every day: "Piri, get up, it's time to go to school." And I played mine: "Aw, Moms, I don't feel so good. I think I got a fever or something."

Always it ended up the same old way: I got up and went to school. But I didn't always stay there. Sometimes, I reported for class, let my teacher see me and then began the game of sneaking out of the room. It was like escaping from some kind of prison. I waited for the teacher to turn her back, then I slipped out of my seat and, hugging the floor, crawled on my belly toward the door. The other kids knew what I was doing; they were trying not to burst out laughing. Sometimes a wise guy near me made a noise to bring the teacher's attention my way. When this happened, I lay still between the row of desks until the teacher returned to whatever he or she had been doing.

I sneaked my way to the door, eased it open and—swoom!—I was on my way. It was a great-o game, slipping past the other classes and ducking the other teachers or monitors.

One class I didn't dig at all was the so-called "Open Air Class" for skinny, "underweight" kids. We had to sleep a couple of half hours every day, and we got extra milk and jelly and peanut butter on brown bread. The teacher, Miss Shepard, was like a dried-up grape. One day I raised my hand to go to the toilet, but she paid me no mind. After a while, the pain was getting bad, so I called out, "Miss Shepard, may I leave the room?"

She looked up and just shook her head, no.

"But I gotta go, Miss Shepard."

"You just went a little while ago," she said.

"I know, Miss Shepard, but I gotta go again."

"I think it's sheer nonsense," said the old bitch. "You just want an excuse to play around in the hallways."

"No, ma'am, I just wanna take a piss."

"Well, you can't go."

I had to go so badly that I felt the tears forming in the corners of my eyes to match the drops that were already making a wet scene down my leg. "I'm goin' anyway," I said and started toward the door.

Miss Shepard got up and screamed at me to get back to my seat. I ignored her.

"Get back to your seat, young man," she screamed. "Do you hear me? Get right back—"

"Fuck you," I mumbled. I reached the door and felt her hands grab out at me and her fingers hook on to the back of my shirt collar. My clean, washed-a-million-times shirt came apart in her hand.

I couldn't see her face clearly when I turned around. All I could think about was my torn shirt and how this left me with only two others. All I could see was her being the cause of the dampness of my pants and hot pee running down my leg. All I could hear was the kids making laughing sounds and the anger of my being ashamed. I didn't think of her as a woman, but as something that had to be hit. I hit it.

"Ohhhhhh, you *struck* me," she cried, in surprise as much as pain.

I thought, *I did not, you fuckin' liar. I just hit you.*

"You struck me! You *struck* me! Oh, help, help!" she cried.

I cut out. Man, I ran like hell into the hallway, and she came right after me, yelling, "Help, help!" I was scared now and all I could think about was getting back to my Moms, my home, my block, where no one could hurt me. I ran toward the stairway and found it blocked off by a man, the principal. I cut back toward the back stairs.

"Stop him! Stop him!" dear Miss Shepard yelled, pointing her finger at me. "He struck me, he struck me."

I looked over my shoulder and saw the principal talk to her for a hot second and then take off after me, yelling: "Stop! Stop!" I hit the stairs and went swooming down like it was all one big step. The principal was fast and I could hear him swearing right behind me. I slammed through the main-floor door that led to the lunchroom and jumped over benches and tables, trying like hell to make the principal trip and break a leg. Then I heard a muted cry of pain as a bench caught him in the shin. I looked over my shoulder and I dug his face. The look said that he was gonna hit me; that he wasn't gonna listen to my side of the story; that I had no side. I figured I better not get caught.

I busted my legs running toward the door that led to the outside and freedom, and with both hands out in front of me I hit the brass bar that opens the door. Behind me I heard a thump as the principal smacked into it. I ran down the block, sneaking a look behind me. The principal was right behind me, his face redder and meaner. People were looking at the uneven contest.

I tore into my hallway, screaming as loud as I could for help. The apartment doors opened up, one right after another. Heads of all colors popped out. "*Qué pasa?*" asked a Puerto Rican woman. "Wha's happenin'?" said a colored lady.

"They wanna beat me up in school and that's one of them," I puffed, pointing at the principal, who was just coming into view.

"Hoo, ain't nobody gonna hurt you, sonny," said the colored lady, whose name was Miss Washington. She gently pushed me behind her with one hand and with the other held it out toward the principal roaring down at us.

The principal, blocked by Miss Washington's 280 pounds and a look of "Don't you touch that boy," stopped short and puffed out, "That—that—kid—he—punched a teacher and—he's got to be chastised for it. After all, school disci—"

"Now hol' on, white man," Miss Washington interrupted. "There ain't nobody gonna chaz—whatever it is—this boy. I knows him an' he's a good boy—at least good for what comes outta this heah trashy neighborhood—an' you ain't gonna do nuttin' to him, unless you-all wan's to walk over me."

Miss Washington was talking real bad-like. I peeked out from behind that great behind.

"Madam, I assure you," the principal said, "I didn't mean harming him in a bodily manner. And if you knew the whole issue, you would agree with me that he deserves being chastised. As principal of his school, I have his best interest at heart. Ha, ha, ha," he added, "you know the old saying, madam, 'A stitch in time saves nine.' Ha, ha, ha—ahurmph."

I could see him putting that stitch in my head.

"I assure you, madam," he continued, smiling pretty, "we have no intention of doing him bodily harm."

Once again I peeked out from behind Miss Washington's behind. "Yeah, that's what you say," I said. "How about alla time you take kids down to your office for some crap and ya start poking 'em with that big finger of yours until they can't take it any more?"

There were a lot of people in the hall by this time. They were all listening, and I knew it. "Yeah, ask any of the kids," I added. "They'll tell ya." I looked sorry-like at the crowd of people, who were now murmuring mean-like and looking at the principal like he didn't have long on this earth.

Smelling a Harlem lynch party in the making, I said, "An'—you—ain't—gonna—do—it—to—me. I'll get me a forty-five an'—"

"Hush your mouth, boy," Miss Washington said; "don't be talkin' like that. We grownups will get this all straightened out. An' nobody's gonna poke no finger in your chest"—she looked dead at the principal—"is they?"

The principal smiled the weakest smile in this smiling world. "I—I—I—er, assure you, madam, this young man is gifted with the most wonderful talent for prevarication I've ever seen."

"What's that mean?" Miss Washington asked suspiciously.

"Er, it means a good imagination, madam. A-ha-ha—yes, a-hurmph."

"That's a lie, Miss Washington," I said. "He's always telling the kids that. We asked Mrs. Wagner, the history teacher, and she said it means to lie. Like he means I'm a liar."

The look in the principal's eye said, "Oh, you smarty pants bastard," but he just smiled and said nothing.

Miss Washington said, "Iffen thar's any pokin' ta be done, we all heah is gonna do it," and she looked hard at the principal. The crowd looked hard at the principal. Hard sounds were taking forms, like, "So this is the way they treat our kids in school?" and "What you-all expect? These heah white people doan give a damn," and "If they evah treats mah boy like that, I'd . . ."

The principal, smiling softly, began backing up.

I heard Momma's voice: "Piri, Piri, qué pasa?"

"Everything all right, Mis' Thomas," Miss Washington assured her. "This heah man was tryin' to hit your son, but ain't, 'cause I'll break his damn head wide open." Miss Washington shifted her weight forward. "Damn, Ah got a good mind to do it right now," she added. . . .

I'd turn and head back to my block, noticing the overflow wash strung out on front fire escapes and thinking about the people who complain that clothes on front-side fire escapes make the block look cheap, that people who do that have no sense of values and destroy the worth of the neighborhood. But I liked it; I thought it gave class to the front fire escapes to be dressed up with underwear, panties, and scrubbed work clothes.

I'd meet my boys, and all the other hearing and seeing suddenly became unimportant. Only my boys were the important kick, and for good reasons—if I had boys, I had respect and no other clique would make me open game. Besides, they gave me a feeling of belonging, of prestige, of accomplishment; I felt grande and bad. Sometimes the thoughts would start flapping around inside me about the three worlds I lived in—the world of home, the world of school (no more of that, though), and the world of street. The street was the best damn one. It was like all the guys shouting out, "Hey, man, this is our kick."

The worlds of home and school were made up of rules laid down by adults who had forgotten the feeling of what it means to be a kid but expected a kid to remember to be an adult—something he hadn't gotten to yet. The world of street belonged to the kid alone. There he could earn his own rights, prestige, his good-o stick of living. It was like being a knight of old, like being ten feet tall. . . .

Editors' Commentary

These selections from Thomas's book illustrate a number of significant points. One impressive element is the high degree of sophistication of the bright boys of the street in terms of group behavior: leadership is established, challenged without being overthrown, enhanced, and maintained; a new member enters the group, participates in the appropriate verbal and nonverbal rituals, and finds a place in the pecking order. If teachers studied group behavior with such sophistication, their lives would be easier. The boys know when to be tough, when to ignore, and when to barge in, and with whom.[4] The teacher's lack of sensitivity is by no means an uncommon characteristic. She refuses to recognize the boy's needs because she is intent on humiliating him and asserting her power by imposing a formal rule. The neighborhood loyalty to its own against the alien establishment as represented by the principal is significant. The fact is that physical mistreatment of children often does occur in the privacy of a principal's office, and when it does the neighborhood knows it. As a defender, Miss Washington is careful both to protect the boy and to quash his fantasy of shooting the principal. She speaks as an adult—"We grownups will get this all straightened out"—and she does so both to Piri and to the principal.

Drugs: What Some People Do about Their Feelings and What That Does to Them

Anxiety is hard to bear. Yet none of us can live without learning to tolerate a certain amount of it. Anxiety arises from the self-preserving instinct of fear, to which all animals react with either fleeing or fighting mechanisms; anxiety's basic purpose is to send us alarms and warnings, to alert us to whatever threatens, so that we can do something about it. There is a good bit of evidence to support the theories of the biophysiologist John Cannon and the psychiatrist Harry Stack Sullivan[5] that without some degree of anxiety we would not learn to learn, and as a result our very survival would be endangered.

Yet as society grows increasingly complex, human-generated anxieties haunt us. Competition, anger, feelings of inadequacy and unworthiness, guilt, loneliness, confusion, problems of sexual identity, and dependence—to name a few—are the lot of people who live together and are by nature dependent on each other. When anxiety rises too high, it is sometimes more than we can handle. Immobilized, we may revert to the crudest, most primitive forms of combating danger and acute discomfort. In the moment of anxiety, everything we know can be forgotten, and everything we have repressed, often at great cost, may come pouring in: we may give way to overwhelming bursts of anger and violence, or we may take flight. Anxiety is often the reason teenagers run away or students who have ability show apathetic lack of effort. Over the years, we all learn certain defenses, and sometimes they serve us worse than the anxiety they are combating. The particular defense we choose is determined by our temperament and by our environment, past and present. Some of us develop pusillanimous abjectness, some combativeness and irritability. For some, psychosomatic ills such as headaches, stomach upsets, and hives are the outward signs of the terror underneath. Many of us choose escape. Some find it in books, some in TV. (Many people, especially preadolescents, use TV as a kind of drug.) Some escape in alcohol, which can be as effective as any of the hard drugs at damaging human relationships, job effectiveness, and physical or mental health.

---

4.   An exciting and informative description of the power focus games in this subculture can be found in **Herbert L. Foster**, *Ribbin', Jivin', and Playin' the Dozens* (Cambridge, Mass.: Ballinger Publishing, 1974).

5.   **Harry Stack Sullivan**, *Collected Works* (New York: W. W. Norton, 1965), 112.

To escape anxiety and society's deficiencies and onslaughts many young people today have turned to drugs, just as those in earlier generations turned to alcohol. Some drugs, such as marijuana, are not in themselves harmful physiologically to most people, though any drug, aspirin included, can be harmful to some. The overuse of some drugs, such as the amphetamines (which are stimulants) or barbiturates (downers), and glue-sniffing can cause long-term physical damage. Inconclusive evidence suggests that the popular hallucinogen LSD may do permanent physical harm. Other drugs are so addictive that they become the controlling force in a person's life. For the addictive drugs the craving is both physical and psychological. Those addicted to alcohol, the barbiturates, or the opiates (such as heroin, opium, and morphine) suffer not only an overwhelming desire for the drug but also extreme physical discomfort upon withdrawal—shaking, stomach cramps, and wracking pain. They also incur a great risk of death from taking unknown mixtures or an overdose. Addiction brings helplessness, abject dependence, misery to oneself and others, and self-loathing.

More and more young people are using addictive drugs, and increasing numbers of them are very young indeed. In New York City there were three reported heroin-caused deaths of children under ten years old in 1970. Some children get on drugs because bucking the crowd or being called square is too much for their essentially conforming, infantile, and dependent social natures. Some young people take a hard drug once or twice and then leave it alone. But others become addicted with few exposures. Some young people may turn to drugs out of frustration at their inability to tell their parents about their unhappiness. It may be the normal unhappiness of any adolescent growing up, but it sometimes seems especially acute in a world where so much is demanded, a world whose values often appear phony and hypocritical, a world whose problems seem nearly insoluble. Given a sufficient sense of powerlessness, a young person in today's culture is often tempted to give up. Sometimes the adolescent then chooses an alternative life without knowing much about its terrors and consequences.

Some of the drug takers have been disturbed for a long time, but, because their parents were insensitive or unprepared or simply didn't want to see, or because their teachers were afraid of alarming someone or of "overstepping boundaries," drug use was left to go on until it was too late. These youngsters found no way to tell someone they were in trouble inside, except through actions that seriously limit, if they do not end, their futures. The disturbances were always there; drugs made them manifest. Of course, drugs often make matters worse—at times irremediably worse. A familiar type of drug abuser is the gifted adolescent with middle- and upper-middle-class parents. Sensitive to the ills of the environment, unable to communicate with his or her family, the gifted adolescent sometimes shares with that family a tendency to avoid looking facts in the face. The drug abuser of the poor ghetto, like this wealthier counterpart, is dependent, frightened, and unwilling to grow up. Both may be disturbed in a psychiatric sense as well as for social causes. Both have little sense of self, and both share an inability to be direct or to communicate feelings; they have little ability to tolerate anxiety or to foresee that the future will largely derive from their present choices—for good or bad. The younger the child (and some are only nine to twelve years old), the more the will is affected, and training for coping with life is sacrificed.

Many adults are not nearly as learned as their children are about the varieties of pills, serums, powders, and plants that will take a person up, out, or down. But there is a terrifying ignorance about the actual effects of drugs among many young users themselves as well as among adults who ought to know better, including supposed experts. So little is known that there is still a great deal of work to be done by people in medicine, physiology, psychiatry, psychology, social work, sociology, and anthropology, as well as by educators. The realistic handling of young drug abusers requires the active engagement of physicians, psychologists, researchers, lawyers, educators, and law enforcement officers in evaluating, preventing, and treating drug abuse—not simply in punishing it. Whatever other needs drug use may fill, its illegality has given it the added attraction among young people of being another channel for the common adolescent rebellion against authority. It is altogether a very complicated issue, and we cannot begin to understand it without making a differentiation among the drugs, their effects, and the individuals and groups who use them.

Teachers and school officials seeking a sensible approach to student drug use will probably adopt at least one principle from their handling of other, less emotionally loaded, subjects: certain things are appropriate to do in school or during work hours, and others are not; some things are appropriate to bring to school, and others are not. A person does not drink in school or at work or come drunk to school or work without consequences. Likewise, a person does not get high on drugs in school. But when a student fails to abide by this principle, as many do, it should be a major concern of the school to assist the drug abuser in coping with the sources of the problem in anxiety, frustration, and the painful process of growing up.

Though heavy drug takers often fantasize great creations, they seldom act on them; the act of creation itself seems to require too much effort, to make too great a demand on the infantile orientation of the drug user. The addictive drugs reduce the appetite, so that undernourishment and consequent lack of energy make productivity the exception rather than the rule among addicted users. Baudelaire's selection below describes this seductive and enervating state where, if the drugs take hold, particularly in children and youth, they can burn out a zest for learning and living.

Although the literature on drug use among the young is increasing, remarkably little has been written that accurately conveys the experience and helps adults to recognize and deal with the problem. However, teachers are now aware of certain signals of student drug use: large pupils and heavy eyelids, leaden or slack bodies, atypical or inappropriate speech, excessive giggling or tears, or reports of fantasies. (Of course, these may be caused by other things besides drugs.)

Marijuana, hashish, and peyote are in a different category from synthetic drugs, hallucinogens, and hard drugs, because they are, according to most reports, *not in themselves* any more addictive than tobacco, except for certain people who have psychologically addictable personalities or are allergic to specific chemicals. The hallucinogens are well-described in a passage below by Alan Watts and in *The Electric Kool-Aid Acid Test* by Tom Wolfe.[6] His account of Ken Kesey's crew is strongly recommended for anyone interested in reading about a total drug life-style.

The hard drugs are represented in the excerpt from Piri Thomas's *Down These Mean Streets* (dealing with heroin).

Marijuana, Hashish, and Peyote These three natural hallucinogens are extracted from plants; LSD, the amphetamines, and the barbiturates are made synthetically. Most evidence indicates that moderate use of natural hallucinogens is not dangerous for most people. Yet some people are allergic or sensitive to them, as others may be to aspirin or any drug, and for such people they can have destructive physiological and psychological effects. The desired effects can range from relaxation to intense excitement, from social pleasure to a spiritual experience of an occult or mystical nature. Their use is worldwide and has a long history. With overuse or use by young people, hallucinogens appear to affect the will and the abilities to concentrate and to persevere. The drugs may be used to escape from hard or unpleasant tasks that are necessary for the achievement of ultimate goals. Their illegality has caused some of the serious psychological and perhaps moral damage to our young people. The fact that very young children, from eight or nine years up, use them is frightening; the younger the user, the more these drugs appear to affect the will or energy level and thus interfere with concentration on a work task, motivation, and the acquisition of necessary skills.

Natural hallucinogens have always been used to induce altered dimensions of time, space, sound, and visual experience. For some, their use represents a life-style. For

6. **Tom Wolfe,** *The Electric Kool-Aid Acid Test* (New York: Farrar, Straus & Giroux, 1968).

others, they provide a way to feel apart from and above the crowd, able to be or do anything. In the excerpt that follows, Baudelaire recognizes that he found this experience damaging and isolating as well as pleasurable.

The Poem of Hashish

Charles Baudelaire

"What does one experience? What does one see? Wonderful things, eh? Amazing sights? Is it very beautiful? Very terrible? Very dangerous?" . . .

The intoxication of hashish . . . will not bring us beyond the bounds of the natural dream. It is true that throughout its whole period the intoxication will be in the nature of a vast dream—by reason of the intensity of its colors and its rapid flow of mental images; but it will always retain the private tonality of the individual. The man wanted the dream, now the dream will govern the man; but this dream will certainly be the son of its father. . . .

It is right then, that sophisticated persons, and also ignorant persons who are eager to make acquaintance with unusual delights, should be clearly told that they will find in hashish nothing miraculous, absolutely nothing but an exaggeration of the natural. The brain and organism on which hashish operates will produce only the normal phenomena peculiar to that individual—increased, admittedly, in number and force, but always faithful to their origin. A man will never escape from his destined physical and moral temperament: hashish will be a mirror of his impressions and private thoughts—a magnifying mirror, it is true, but only a mirror.

Let me now revert to the normal development of the intoxication. After the first phase of childish mirth comes a sort of momentary lull. But soon new adventures are heralded by a sensation of chilliness in the extremities (for some people this becomes an intense cold), and a great weakness in all the members. In your head, and throughout your being, you feel an embarrassing stupor and stupefaction. Your eyes bulge, as if under the pull, both physical and spiritual, of an implacable ecstasy. Your face is flooded with pallor. Your lips shrink and are sucked back into your mouth by that panting movement that characterizes the ambition of a man who is a prey to great projects, overwhelmed by vast thoughts, or gaining breath for some violent effort. The sides of the gullet cleave together, so to speak. The palate is parched with a thirst that it would be infinitely pleasant to satisfy, if only the delights of idleness were not still more agreeable, and did they not forbid the slightest disarrangement of the body's posture. Hoarse, deep sighs burst forth from your chest, as if your *old* body could not endure the desires and activity of your *new* soul. Now and then a jolt passes through you, making you twitch involuntarily. It is like one of those sharp sensations of falling that you experience at the end of a day's work, or on a stormy night just before finally falling asleep. . . .

Notes of music turn into numbers; and, if you are endowed with some aptitude for mathematics, the melody or harmony you hear, whilst retaining its pleasurable and sensuous character, transforms itself into a huge arithmetical process, in which numbers beget numbers, whilst you follow the successive stages of reproduction with inexplicable ease and an agility equal to that of the performer. . . .

Let us suppose that you are sitting and smoking. Your gaze rests a moment too long on the bluish clouds emerging from your pipe. The notion of a slow, steady, eternal evaporation will take hold of your mind, and soon you will apply this notion to your own thoughts and your own thinking substance. By a singular transposition of ideas, or mental play upon words, you will feel that you yourself are evaporating, and that your pipe (in which you are huddled and pressed down like the tobacco) has the strange *power to smoke you.*

Luckily this apparently interminable fancy has lasted only for a single minute—for a lucid interval, gained with a great effort, has enabled you to glance at the clock. But a new stream of ideas carries you away: it will hurl you along in its living vortex for a further minute; and this minute, too, will be an eternity, for the normal relation between time and the individual has been completely upset by the multitude and intensity of sensations and ideas. You seem to live several men's lives in the space of an hour. You resemble, do you not? a fantastic novel that is being lived instead of being written. There is no longer any fixed connection between your organs and their powers; and this fact, above all, is what makes this dangerous exercise, in which you lose your freedom, so very blameworthy. . . .

So by this time my hypothetical man, this soul of my choosing, has reached the pitch of joy and serenity at which he is *compelled* to admire himself. Every contradiction effaces itself, all the problems of philosophy become crystal-clear, or at least appear to be so. Everything is a matter for rejoicing. The fullness of his life at this moment inspires him with a disproportionate pride. A voice speaks within him (alas! it is his own), saying to him: "You are now entitled to consider yourself superior to all men; nobody knows, or could understand, all that you think and feel; men would be incapable even of appreciating the benevolence with which they inspire you. You are a king unrecognized by the passers-by, a king who lives in the solitude of his own certainty. But what do you care? Do you not possess that sovereign pride which so ennobles the soul?" . . .

Editors' Commentary

Stronger Hallucinogens   The synthetic hallucinogens, such as LSD, are well described by Alan Watts (excerpted below) and by Tom Wolfe in his remarkable book *The Electric Kool-Aid Acid Test.*

In the mid-sixties the so-called psychedelic drugs, particularly the synthetic LSD, were very popular, especially among middle-class high school and college students. Despite a great deal of publicity on the ill effects of LSD, the scientific evidence on its effects is still uncertain. Yet its use has diminished partly because of reports of its severely bad effects on people, because the impurities in its manufacture cause physical and emotional damage, and because of its gross misuse by some people on unsuspecting others. It has been claimed that LSD sometimes causes permanent psychological damage (actually producing psychosis and sometimes leading to suicide) and physical damage (leading to birth defects and chromosome breakdown), but there is much less reliable scientific information about the effects of LSD than about those of most other drugs. It is possible that lingering psychological reactions to LSD are occasioned not by the drug itself but by the attempts of a user who is more or less unstable to cope with the profound changes experienced during the relatively long period (eight to ten hours) of the drug's action. Likewise, there is no proof that LSD has any permanent physical effect on people. Under controlled therapeutic conditions, LSD has for some time been useful in treating various psychological disorders. It has, of course, played a disastrous part in the experiences of a number of emotionally disturbed adolescents. Though LSD is not addictive, the practice of taking the drug has become a way of life for some and a way of avoiding life for others; and though it has long-range, often terrifying, effects on some users, there is so far no way of knowing whether any individual will be susceptible to "bad trips" or recurring effects. The following selections focus on various aspects of the psychedelic experience.

A Psychedelic Experience: Fact or Fantasy?

Alan Watts

To come . . . to an effective evaluation of these [psychedelic] chemicals and the changed states of consciousness and perception which they induce, we must begin with a highly detailed and accurate description of what they do, both from the standpoint of the subject and of the neutral observer, despite the fact that in experiments of this kind it becomes startlingly obvious that the observer cannot be neutral, and that the posture of "objectivity" is itself one of the determinants of the outcome. As the physicist well knows, to observe a process is to change it. But the importance of careful description is that it may help us to understand the kind or level of reality upon which these changes in consciousness are taking place.

For undoubtedly they are happening. The dancing, kaleidoscopic arabesques which appear before closed eyes are surely an observation of *some* reality, though not, perhaps, in the physical world outside the skin. But are they rearranged memories? Structures in the nervous system? Archetypes of the collective unconscious? Electronic patterns such as often dance on the TV screen? What, too, are the fernlike structures which are so often seen—the infinitude of branches upon branches upon branches, or analogous shapes? Are these a glimpse of some kind of analytical process in the brain, similar to the wiring patterns in a computer? We really have no idea, but the more carefully observers can record verbal descriptions and visual pictures of these phenomena, the more likely that neurologists or physicists or even mathematicians will turn up the physical processes to which they correspond. The point is that these visions are not *mere* imagination, as if there had ever been anything mere about imagination! The human mind does not just perversely invent utterly useless images out of nowhere at all. Every image tells us something about the mind or the brain or the organism in which it is found.

The effects of the psychedelics vary so much from person to person and from situation to situation that it is well nigh impossible to say with any exactitude that they create certain particular and invariable changes of consciousness. I would not go so far as to say that the chemical effects are simply featureless, providing no more than a vivid mirror to reflect the fantasies and unconscious dispositions of the individuals involved. For there are certain types of change which are usual enough to be considered characteristic of psychedelics: the sense of slowed or arrested time, and the alteration of "ego boundary"—that is, of the sensation of one's own identity.

The feeling that time has relaxed its pace may, to some extent, be the result of having set aside the better part of a day just to observe one's own consciousness, and to watch for interesting changes in one's perception of such ordinary things as reflected sunlight on the floor, the grain in wood, the texture of linen, or the sound of voices across the street. My own experience has never been of a distortion of these perceptions, as in looking at oneself in a concave mirror. It is rather that every perception becomes—to use a metaphor—more resonant. The chemical seems to provide consciousness with a sounding box, or its equivalent, for all the senses, so that sight, touch, taste, smell, and imagination are intensified like the voice of someone singing in the bathtub.

The change of ego boundary sometimes begins from this very resonance of the senses. The intensification and deepening of color, sound, and texture lends them a peculiar transparency. One seems to be aware of them more than ever as vibration, electronic and luminous. As this feeling develops it appears that these vibrations are continuous with one's own consciousness and that the external world is in some odd way inside the mind-brain. It appears, too, with overwhelming obviousness, that the inside and the outside do not exclude one another and are not actually separate. They go together; they imply one another, like front and back, in such a way that they become polarized. As, therefore, the poles of a magnet are the extremities of a single body, it appears that the inside and the outside, the subject and the object, the self and the world, the voluntary and the involuntary, are the poles of a single process which is my real and hitherto unknown self. This new self has no location. It is not something like a traditional soul, using the body as a temporary house. To ask *where* it is, is like asking where the universe is. Things in space have a where, but the thing that space is in doesn't need to be anywhere. It is simply what there is, just plain basic isness!

How easily, then, an unsophisticated person might exclaim, "I have just discovered that I am God!" Yet if, during such an experience, one retains any critical faculties at all, it will be clear that anyone else in the same state of consciousness will also be God. It will be clear, too, that the "God" in question is not the God of popular theology, the Master Technician who controls, creates, and understands everything in the universe. Were it so, a person in this state should be able to give correct answers to all questions of fact. He would know the exact height of Mount Whitney in millimeters. On the other hand, this awareness of a deeper and universal self would correspond exactly with that other type of God which mystics have called the "divine ground" of the universe, a sort of intelligent and superconscious space containing the whole cosmos as a mirror contains images . . . though the analogy fails in so far as it suggests something immense: we cannot picture sizelessness.

Anyone moving into completely unfamiliar territory may at first misunderstand and misinterpret what he sees, as is so evident from the first impressions of visitors to foreign lands where patterns of culture differ radically from their own. When Europeans depicted their first impressions of China, they made the roofs of houses exaggeratedly curly and people's eyes slanted at least 45 degrees from the horizontal. Contrariwise, the Japanese saw all Europeans as red-haired, sunked-eyed goblins with immensely long noses. But the unfamiliarities of foreign cultures are nothing to those of one's own inner workings. What is there in the experience of clear blue sky to suggest the structure of the optical nerves? Comparably, what is there in the sound of a human voice on the radio to suggest the formations of tubes and transistors? I raise this question because it is obvious that any chemically induced alteration of the nervous system must draw the attention of that system to itself. I am not normally aware that the sensation of blue sky is a state of the eyes and brain, but if I see wandering spots that are neither birds nor flying saucers, I know that these are an abnormality within the optical system itself. In other words, I am enabled, by virtue of this abnormality, to become conscious of one of the instruments of consciousness. But this is most unfamiliar territory.

Down These Mean Streets

Piri Thomas

I sat down on the edge of the roof ledge. My mind refused to get off its kick of reminiscing. Man, like how many times some cat's come up to me with his old man's watch or sister's coat and swap for a three-cent bag. Heh, a three-cent bag—like a grain of rice crushed to powder, that's how much it is for a cost of three dollars, and you couldn't beat down that hell-like look as the begging took place in exchange for that supertranquilizing ca-ca powder. I sniffed back a tear that came out of my nose. And how about the time I plowed through that falling snow with no pride at all in my Buster Brown shoes—like brown on top and bustered on the bottoms—knowing without a doubt in the world that the only thing that would get me warm again so I could care about being cold was the connecting—the blending of my vein's blood and dogie drug.

Shit, man, how far can pride go down? I knew that all the help in the world could get that stuff out of my system, but only some kind of god would be able to get it out of my swinging soul and mind. What a sick mudder scene! If you didn't get gypped outta your stuff, you'd get beat on some weak, cutdown shit. If you didn't get dead on an overdose, you'd get deader on a long strung-out kick. Everything in the world depended on heroin. You'd go to bed thinking about stuff and wake up in the morning thinking about it. Love and life took second place to it and nothing mattered except where, and how soon. It was like my whole puking system had copped a mind bigger than the one in my head.

I walked toward the roof landing. I was thinking. I was gonna kick for good. "I can do it. I swear ta God and the Virgin. Gonna get me li'l shit and cut down good. *I ain't no fuckin' junkie.*"

I went looking for Waneko. I found him in *El Viejo's* candy store. I put my want to him in fast words.

"Help me kick, man?" It was a question. Waneko knew how it was. Even though he was pushing now, he wasn't using, but he'd been through that kicking road *mucho* times. Waneko nodded, "Sure, *panín*—sure I will." We walked into Waneko's place. He explained to his moms what was shaking. She smiled nice-like and said everything was gonna be all right. Waneko followed that assurance up with, "Moms helps most of the cats that want to kick and even some of the chicks. She should be some kind of church worker or something." He laughed. I tried a weak smile.

They put me in a room that just had a bed and chair and a window that had a metal gate across it to keep the crooks out and kicking junkies in. I laid down, and after a while Waneko brought in a small radio so I could dig some music, to take my mind off what was coming. Both he and I knew that the li'l taste of stuff I had shot up on the roof a while ago was gonna wear off and then World War III was gonna break out inside of me. Billie was wailing some sad song. I wailed along with her in a soft hum. Then some kinda time started to go by and my system was better than a clock. And then Judgment Day set in . . .

Man, talk about wantin' to die—everything started off as it should. First like always, the uncomfortable feeling as you knew your system wanted its baby bottle. And nose running ever so gently at first and the slow kind of pain building up not so gently. I tried hard to listen to some wailin' on the radio, but all I could hear was my own. I got up and went to the door. It was locked from the outside. "Hey, Waneko, open the door," I yelled.

"*Quê es?*"

"I feel real bad, like in bad, man."

"Man, lay down, you ain't been in there long enough to work up any kind of sweat. I'll tell you when, and only then I'll give you a li'l taste to ease you off. So cool it, *panín.*"

I don't know how many hours ran crawling by. I just knew I couldn't make it. *But I hadda. I just hadda.* "Lemme out, Waneko—lemme out, you mother-fucker." I swam to the door and hit at it.

"Waneko is not home right now." It was Waneko's moms.

"Let me out, *señora.* I kicked already."

"He said not to let you come out until he comes back, *hijo.*"

"Did he leave something for me?" My voice sounded like tears. I went back to bed and just rolled and moaned all alone.

I don't know how many hours ran crawling by. It was a lot of them. At one time I heard the lock being taken off the door and heard it fall from someone's hand. I felt Waneko's mom's voice—I felt her cool hand on my face and felt her wipe my cold sweating face. I heard sounds of comfort coming from her.

"*No te apures, hijo,* you weel soon be fine."

I tried to get up and make it, but she was faster. I felt the iron gates on the window. I shook them. I turned and flopped back on the bed. I was shaking. I was in bad pain. I was cold and I couldn't stop my snots from flowing. I was all in cramps and my guts wouldn't obey me. My eyes were overflowing real fast.

"Lemme out, Waneko—lemme out, you mother-fucker." Shit, I was like screaming out of veins.

Nobody answered and I just lay there and moaned and groaned all alone and turned that mattress into one big soaking mopful of my sweat.

I don't know how many hours went crawling by. Millions maybe. And then a real scared thought hit me. Waneko wasn't coming back. He was gonna let me make it—cold-turkey—*a la canona.* I kept trembling and my whole swinging soul full of pain would make my body lurch up and tie itself up into one big knot and then ease itself almost straight and then retie itself. I felt like a puke coming afar. I thought, didn't I puke before? I felt it come out of my mouth like a green river of yellow-blue bile. I couldn't control nothing, and all the strength I had was enough just to turn my head away. I think I made some soft ca-ca on myself. I think I made some hard ones too.

Sometimes I think I heard Waneko telling me, "It's almost over, baby, it's almost over—we got it beat." But I couldn't answer. I'd just hold myself together with my arms holding me tight and rockaby baby myself to some kind of vague comfort. In a dream I'd eat mountains and mountains of sweet, sweet candy. I opened my eyes and Waneko had me sitting in a chair and I saw Moms cleaning the toilet I had made out of the room—and then I was back in the bed. I still had all the pain, all the cramps. I still had the whole bad bit, but I knew I was gonna make it. I rocked myself to and fro.

I don't know how many hours ran crawling by. Jillions maybe. At last the pain cut itself down. I felt all dried out. Waneko came into the room and rubbed my body down, like trying to work all the knots to straighten out. Waneko and his moms kept me with them for a week or so putting me into shape with hot pigeon soup, liquids, and later heavier stuff like I mean, rice and beans. They were great, Waneko and Moms. My body was kicked free from H—gone was dogie. They said it takes seventy or so hours to kick a habit. I think it seemed like seventy years. Now all I had to do was kick it outta my mind.

I left Waneko's house after really thanking them from way down. I hit the street thinking, "Wow, dying is easier than this has been. Never—never—*nunca mâs.*"

Editors' Commentary
The Alcoholic Child

The use of alcohol by children and adolescents in the United States has increased alarmingly. It is becoming a more pervasive problem in schools than the use of other drugs and narcotics. Alcohol is easily available to children, although it is illegal for minors to buy or drink it (the age of minority varies according to state law). Youngsters can get liquor from people older than themselves, from illegal sales and use of false identification cards, and at their own or at friends' homes. Though liquor prices run high, the cost is small compared to that of the illegal drugs. What's more, liquor can be obtained by theft from businesses or homes. Teenagers hold up and loot liquor stores more frequently than any other type of store.

Many children grow up seeing their parents drink, whether socially or heavily. The use of alcohol permeates American culture. The "happy hour" is frequently advertised by restaurants and bars, while liquor stores abound in every village, town, and city. The corner tavern is as much a part of the scenery to children as the gas station or drugstore. It is highly unlikely that a child could grow up today without seeing TV programs or movies depicting drinkers and drunks.

Any child whose family drinks can taste wine with dinner, beer with snacks, or hard liquor at parties. Some ethnic groups give children alcohol as a matter of course. In many cases, these children do not abuse alcohol, but some family practices may instigate its overuse. Although stereotypes are always dangerous, there are clinical observations that, given low income and low employment opportunities, some ethnic groups are more susceptible to alcoholism than others. For example, the Irish and the American Indians tend to find alcohol a particularly difficult chemical to handle. However, all ethnic groups are prone to misuse alcohol when their conditions in life appear to be or are overwhelming. Children from these families grow up considering alcohol a way to veil misery.

Children who drink too much may start for any reason: so they can be one of the gang, or because they saw their parents reach for drinks when under stress, or because they found a bottle on the playground and found that drinking erased their problems temporarily. They may become severe drinkers if their home life is miserable, if they feel imprisoned in untenable situations by dependence on their parents or caretakers because they cannot yet fend for themselves. Sometimes the child is neglected or mistreated by one or more drunken parents. In an effort to erase the feelings of being uncared for, he or she proceeds to do what the elders do—opt for escape. In some ways alcoholism is a contagious disease: it is so difficult to relate to an alcoholic family member that spouses and children may give up and join what they cannot fight. Sometimes the precipitating cause is fear of sexual impulses, particularly homosexual ones, or fear of inability to perform sexually without the prop of alcohol (although excessive drinking leads to impotence and disinterest in sex). Sexual fears tend to be rampant at adolescence anyway, and they simply contribute to the teenage drinker's primitive neediness and sense of general inadequacy.

Like many drugs, alcohol numbs—it depresses the rigid controls most people live by. For a short while it permits a child who feels lonely, unhappy, and unsure to feel okay—likable and affectionate, entertained and amusing, strong and able. At the very moment liquor makes the child feel in control, he or she is usually most out of control, however; illusion is the essence of excessive alcohol intake. Often drink gives these children an initial glow of ability to cope, while the numbness that follows momentarily loosens the pressures they feel and makes the world seem rosier, if unreal.

As different as alcoholics are from each other, there are some basic similarities. Whether adults or children, they are fundamentally very dependent, needy, and infantile, while presenting a facade that is often poised and charming, seductive and winning, indirect and manipulative. They have great expectations of themselves, often because of explicit or implicit parental demands or because they want to prove to neglectful parents that they are worth loving. Their aspirations tend to be grandiose, and they are given to extremes of elation and despair. They are either the most wonderful or the most terrible, or they want to be one or the other, never in-between, never ordinary. They must be special or nothing.

Their need for reassurance and support is as bottomless as their thirst. Although they make demands for closeness, when push comes to shove they keep a wall or protective distance between themselves and others, because they feel so empty, so needy, so thirsty inside. They fear that others will discover their emptiness, what they see as their fakery or deficiencies, and will despise them. They are therefore filled with self-hate and guilt. This self-hate is exacerbated by drinking, but to drown it they drink more.

For alcoholics of every age the symbol of a bottle is apt. Inside the alcoholic personality, no matter how sophisticated, is an infant needing the complete nurture one gets only at the breast. Underneath the grandiose goals or the "out-of-it" manner there hides a fearful, self-critical, and pervasively guilty person with unendingly voracious needs that are not met by what the world is offering.

Alcohol becomes a poison for a child even more, and sooner, than for an adult. It destroys not only liver and kidneys but also self-esteem, will, and motivation. It ultimately can affect the nervous system and the brain. It feeds on fantasy rather than fact. To drinking children, alcohol represents a return to the nipple or the bottle, a wish for the warm oblivion of infancy before expectations and demands became overwhelming. Often alcoholism is an unspoken message that a child is not ready to grow up. This is particularly true where a child is under heavy pressure to act grown up or to undertake responsibility that he or she is not ready to bear. The escape from burdens that can't be shouldered is frequently through the bottle, which offers comfort and oblivion for a little while. Such children often behave and perform very well for periods, but mysteriously fall apart from time to time. They have become secret drinkers (and secrecy and shame are part of the essence of alcoholism).

If a child comes to school drunk, it would be helpful for a teacher to know whether the home life is so unsatisfying, or whether parents are modeling drinking behavior. Teachers can observe to see if the alcoholic child fears other children in or outside the classroom, or fears being exposed as unprepared or ridiculous or stupid in school. Both home and school have to be examined. Are the pressures and the rigidity of standards and expectations too great? When a pupil is drunk in school more than once, it is essential to take a good look at the youngster and the family, through interviews and, if possible, home visits. When teachers report that a child is drinking, parents may deny it and refuse to believe the facts until the habit is too far advanced to be easily curtailed. Often a child is devastated by realizing he or she is addicted and cannot stop drinking. Parents usually need help to acknowledge that, directly or indirectly, their habits, attitudes, pressures, or unrealistic dreams for their children have brought on addictive behavior.

Help can come through appropriate attention and recognition. Training can help the student to be comfortable with honesty and to develop more openness. Realistic expectations can be opened up along with opportunities for the pupil to relax and be childish when he or she needs to be. The family may need guidance in helping the child to order his or her social horizons. Finally, offering group therapy as a mode of treatment can ameliorate the student's drinking problem and the problems underlying it. Alcoholics Anonymous continues to be one of the very best organized groups dealing with both alcoholics and their families (through its auxiliary group Alanon). The patient joins an A.A. group while his or her family joins an Alanon group to help the families of alcoholics understand the problems of the alcoholic while drinking and while withdrawing from drink. It helps them with their problems as well. Individual, group, or family therapy may also be used.

School personnel need to understand the part they can play in referral and in setting clear limits without overmoralizing or making unrealistic expectations. The parents or family of a drunk child must understand that the teacher attempting to deal with the child will try to furnish basic satisfaction of the youngster's needs while setting firm and clear limits on behavior. The child will not be permitted to disrupt the class by becoming the center of attention. If too drunk to work, he or she may be allowed to sleep at the nurse's office and then be seen by someone expert in the field of alcohol abuse. The therapist or other helping person needs to find out what factors in the child's life set off the desire to take to drink, and then to guide the child and the family to recognition and appropriate treatment of the problem.

Interview with a Patient—the Alcoholic Teenager

I began to drink when I was twelve and my parents went out, which they did often. I would raid the liquor cabinet. At first it burnt and made me sick, but I kept trying—and I don't know why. It made me feel smart when I felt dumb. It made me laugh and made me forget things like bad report cards and the beatings I'd get for them. I made people laugh with me, or maybe at me, but anyway— Only then I couldn't do anything without a drink. It was like punctuation marks: I needed a drink to be with people, or a drink to be alone; a drink before homework so I could tackle it, and another after, for reward. I carried vodka with me to school in my milk thermos, I chewed chlorophyll mints to keep away any smell. I'd steal liquor from my parents and put water in the bottles. They fired the maid because they thought she did it.

They found out when I was drunk and stole a guy's car and ran into a pole and I landed in the hospital. The social worker here saw my parents and the A.A. people came to see me. They said I could get well, and they'll help me, and my parents will go to Alanon, though I don't believe they'll go to their meeting. But I still want a drink right now so bad. You see when I'm drunk I know I'm good at things. I'm the best car designer. I'm the best basketball player like my father was. The girls are crazy for me instead of turning me down. Anything, everything looks ok, and I don't even have to try—it just is there, one drink away . . . maybe.

Printed with patient's permission.

Patient's Reminiscence of the Alcoholic Parent

I never told anyone, you see, that my mother was mostly drunk when I came home from school. Sometimes, she was very drunk and had fallen down in the house or even outside and, though I was little, I had to pull her into the bedroom so no one would find out—not my friends, or the neighbors or the teachers who passed by. So, of course, I couldn't have friends over. I didn't have many friends. I tried to buy them things so they'd like

me and make me feel like other people, but I couldn't invite them in. They would have seen my mother like that.

It was worse when she yelled or ranted. She wanted me with her all the time. The first time I stayed out overnight was in high school at a friend's. My mother got drunk and came and got me, yelling curses at my friend's family. My father left us when I was two, and there was never a man around I could count on. Oh, she'd bring drunk dates home from time to time, but no one lasted and in between she'd rave and rant about men and my father and how awful he was—so I grew up hating men. I still don't trust them. I always felt her drunkenness was his fault for leaving. But now I wonder if he left her because she was a drunk.

The worst was graduation day from the parochial eighth grade school I went to. For weeks, the nuns asked us to get dresses or have them made. My mother promised and promised—weeks went by and nothing happened. I had no money but I took little jobs and saved up and bought the material and my mother promised to sew it. When she was sober she could sew. Dress rehearsal came and went; the Sister was furious at me because I had no dress. I promised I would have it on graduation day and pleaded with my mother to get it done. She began working on it the night before graduation, but then she got very drunk and as usual yelled and screamed at me because I wanted something. In her rage and drunkenness, she tore the dress in ribbons, and threw them at me.

All the long day of graduation the phone rang. My mother passed out and I knew it was one of the Sisters from school. I couldn't answer. I just cried and cried, and I never got to graduation. The one Sister in charge of my class was furious with me because I had spoiled her processional line, and called me to come in. She said I couldn't graduate because I'd been so unreliable. I went myself to see the head Sister—the Mother Superior—and burst into tears and, for the first time ever, told the truth about my mother. She was nice and put her arm around me, and I wept with shame and hurt. My mother couldn't come to explain. She got upset about what she had done, so she went out to a bar and got drunk.

I never could think at school since I was busy worrying about what was happening to her—and my worst thoughts always happened.

Printed with patient's permission.

Alienation of Today's Youth

Ruth G. Newman

Closely related to the use of drugs—sometimes the cause and sometimes the effect—is the basic problem of alienation among young people. Alienation is particularly prevalent among the economically privileged, but it is also found among the very poor. Here, the sensitive child indirectly experiences his parents' struggle against the steel-like bonds of the system; to the parents (and thus the child), there seems no hope of escaping from squalor and poverty. The child often gives up in early adolescence and sinks into apathy, numbness, or antisocial behavior. Each of these states is a kind of personal protest against society, but quite a different protest from the organized, politically oriented youth rebellions. Rather, it is a withdrawal of feeling and energy from anything society represents.

For less obvious reasons, the economically privileged exhibit alienation more frequently. Usually it emerges in adolescence. Young people look at their parents' lives and judge them to be empty of meaning or destructive to others. They answer their parents' pleas for achievement, industry, ambition, and competition with "Why? To be like you?" The alienated young see their parents' hard-earned material prizes as false gods. They view the impersonal, automated society as sick. They respond to social problems by despair, by resigning from the fray. Refusing to engage in the external world, they are forced to enter the arena within themselves, subjectively exploring their own inner worlds. The search for life's meaning attracts many to Eastern religions, whose practices of meditation, retreat, and diet enrich their lives by yielding a more universal answer than any they have found in their inherited religions. Thus, they become Buddhists of various types or "Jesus Freaks," who simplify Christian principles and rituals to suit more basic human values.

Some youngsters "drop out" while accepting money from their families, whose money-making goals they deplore. Such action probably indicates that underneath the talk of love, spiritual values, care for the land and nature, crafts, etc., there lie deep, unconfessed (perhaps unconscious) dependence and hostility. Although these young people cannot relate to their parents, neither can they leave the nest.

Because adolescents have traditionally viewed their elders critically, today's revolution is not a unique phenomenon, but the means, style, and results are different from those of other generations. Alienation probably reflects our complex society at the moment—its coldness, lack of personal individual communication, opportunistic values, and corruption in high places. The result is that millions of young people have banded together (as adolescents have in the past), although now their common bond is unrelated to work or achievement. Instead, they congregate on the street, or in communes, coffeehouses, and church basements, searching for leadership in charismatic leaders or gurus.

Understanding and relating to these young people is difficult for adults, particularly privileged parents who often try to force their children into what they consider "the good life"—education and training for professions. For a time, the young reject and scorn these benefits, and few tasks undertaken through coercion or cajolement are completed. Instead of attending college, some drop out of high school, take jobs as dishwashers, construction workers, waiters or waitresses, or service-station helpers. They quit when they tire of the routine or don't like their bosses. Parents look in horror at the children's lack of perseverance and loss of valuable time. They also object to the appearance and behavior of the young, their experiments in sexually open living, their lack of interests outside their own minds and desires. The parents become stymied by the weapon of aggressive passivity by which their children fight by not fighting. What does it all mean and why?

Although alienation stems from the adolescent search for identity, it is also a commentary on the older generation's lack of personal joy, on the computerized, mechanized takeover of a society where loneliness abounds and self-realization has been lost in the service of externals. The gains in self-knowledge that come from communal living and the attempt to establish a sound personal base are considerable for the young. There are many admirable values in such a life-style, especially those concerned with the importance of being more human. Society needs such a commentary. But it also needs skilled people who can work within society as well as within themselves.

Given time, however, the less disturbed young people come back to socially accepted roles. They find that they are ready to adapt to life in society, go back to school, learn a skill or profession, or bring up a family. Some return having profited from their time out: they hold stronger values and with more certainty than their elders.

Some, however, cannot or do not wish to return. They may have been burned out by drugs and become unable to attempt the tasks they would once have found easy. This minority of young people are sometimes lost, often sickly, and lacking motivation. Even when they come back to high school or college classrooms they are unable to get "with it" again. Some are stuck in hospitals and clinics, trying to separate reality from delusion, struggling to live. Adults worry whether these young people are forever lost to society, and they worry about what will be the future of that society, which, with its myriad complexities, needs special skills to accomplish its work and ameliorate its ills and a social responsibility lacking in those who don't come back. In the meantime, alienated youth have taught us a great deal about the society from which they have turned away: temporarily or forever.

1. They have taught us about the rigidity and sterility of our sexual norms, based on outmoded patterns, when many children, not few, were needed, when homosexuality was societally wasteful, when the penalty of sexual contact between the sexes was often unwanted babies and disgrace. True, the philosophy of the young has often been seriously flawed, but society is nonetheless forced to come to grips with its present need to establish more meaningful family relationships. It is too early to tell whether or not the more sexually liberated will be happier in their families than their elders have been. Indeed, the biggest risk is the welfare and bringing up of children in less permanent family constellations.

2. They have pointed out the real failures in our society: inhumanity, phony values, lack of ability to listen, loneliness, and waste of spiritual values.

3. They have shown us the worth of simple skills, arts and crafts, and the necessity of conserving our land and resources.

4. They have revealed that in our great efforts to gain the "good life" we have lost much of the good in life. The goals of achievement and success have become so important that we have forgotten just what it is that we are trying to achieve.

The amount of damage to the alienated generation—and to society because of it—is still to be measured. Literature in this field abounds. Keniston[1] and Friedenberg[2] have made important contributions in the social sciences, and in fiction the problem has been illuminated by Samuel Beckett among others.

The seventies have changed tone and produced a different form of alienation. It has not been a period of political activism nor one of extreme withdrawal or changed life-styles. Rather it goes along with the values and goals of the middle-class definition of The Good Life, whether this be material goodies or intellectual ones or fame and power benefits. Adolescents and adults are not alienated from the culture's values—they are alienated from each other. There is an upsurge of self-centeredness, of goals of self-aggrandizement, of indifference to the needs of others if those needs interfere with personal ambitions or dreams. There is heavy competition, and often great competence, but this is more frequently centered in a virtuoso, prima donna, solo skill than attuned to collaborative efforts or to serving social goals.

There is great interest, however, in health, and in conservation of the world's natural resources, reflecting a more global purpose than the self-centered view of the world that is sometimes implicit in conservationism.

One prevalent trend is the continuing interest in the mystical religions, many of which offer a nonmaterialist but very individually centered value system. Often these sects, Eastern and Western alike, are antiscientific and antirational—a rebellious reaction to the mechanization and computerization so dominant in the nonspiritual world. Many cults have developed which have great power over their youthful converts. The joiners give up to their guru responsibility for their own behavior—always a risky business. Some find it impossible to break away and many prefer to follow without question rather than face growing up and making adult decisions. The most flagrant of such sects were the "family" of Charles Manson, whose leadership led to murder; the People's Temple of Jim Jones, whose leadership in Guyana led to mass suicide of gigantic proportions; and Reverend Moon, whose methods and organization have been sharply attacked. These and many other sects are troubling because they reflect a desire to give up personal autonomy and authority, without which democracy cannot survive.

Notes

1. **Kenneth Keniston,** *The Uncommitted—Alienated Youth in American Society* (New York: Harcourt, Brace and World, 1965).

2. **Edgar Z. Friedenberg,** *The Vanishing Adolescent* (New York: Dell, 1962).

2

Identification and Assessment of Disturbance

Editors' Commentary

Identification and assessment of the disturbed child have never been simple matters. The reasons are many and overlap to some degree. First, different theoretical views provide selective foci. We shall start with a brief examination of the behavioral, psychodynamic, and several other orientations. The choice of a theoretical perspective affects what we examine for data. Is it the person or the setting that is the "cause"? Second, there is the matter of who contributes the data that lead to an assessment of disturbance—teachers, clinicians, parents, peers, or the person being assessed? Third, are decisions to be based on tests, interviews, observations, or judgments? Finally, there is the matter of sequence: *screening* those who should be considered for complete *assessment*, and then gathering the information base for designing relevant *interventions*. In special education, the intervention format now required is the IEP—the individual educational plan.

The Joint Commission on the Mental Health of Children and Youth has stated that an emotionally disturbed child is one who has (a) impairment of age-relevant capacity to perceive the external environment realistically, (b) inadequate impulse control, (c) a lack of rewarding interpersonal relationships, and (d) a failure to achieve appropriate learning levels. Studies of American children in the commission reports estimate that fewer than 0.2 percent of all children are psychotic, 2 to 3 percent are severely disturbed, and an additional 8 to 10 percent have emotional problems needing specialized services. Thus, approximately 10 million people under twenty-five years old need professional help. Yet, less than 7 percent of them receive that help. Some 85 percent of the total who need care can be treated by school personnel, clergy, general practitioners, social workers, and paraprofessionals who have been oriented in mental health work. The vast responsibility of the public schools is obvious. The commission indicates that the percentage of institutionalized children is increasing at twice the rate of the child population.

Teachers' perceptions differ from these statistics, as Kelly and his colleagues found.[1] Some 20 percent of the pupils were considered by teachers to have behavioral disorders,

1. **T. J. Kelly, L. M. Bullock, and M. K. Dykes,** "Behavioral Disorders: Teachers' Perceptions," *Exceptional Children* 43 (1977): 316–321.

over 12 percent mild, over 5 percent moderate, and over 2 percent severe. The percentage increased from kindergarten to the end of elementary school and then decreased (except for grade 9) in secondary school. Twice as many males as females were considered disturbed.

Rhodes[2] points out that a valid definition of "disturbance" should explicate a system in distress, a "disrupted pattern of human–environment exchanges." Too often, only one part of this pattern is examined. Has the child, as a consequence of biological limitation and/or prior learning, developed a repertoire of deviant behaviors that assert themselves even in a "normal" nonprovoking environment? Or is the youngster's behavior a "normal" or reasonable response to a deviant, overstressful life milieu?

Some approaches place the entire problem within the patient; some go to the other extreme, attributing individual disturbances to contemporary social conditions. In past educational settings, the pupil always was at fault when dissonance occurred; supposedly objective teachers and clinicians screened and diagnosed the *child's* problem. Now some would say that it is always the problem of the teacher or the school—the child is innocent. In an *interactive* view of behavior,[3] however, such diverting polemics do not cloud the real issue, which is to find valid and reliable assessment devices attending to both aspects.

Behavior is a consequence of a unique combination of *both* the self and the environment. Thus, identification must eventually include systematic coverage of both the individual and the environment in the distressed system.[4] To illustrate this concept in the school environment, Kelleher[5] has diagramed the "teacher–pupil interactive chain"; there are also pupil–peer and pupil–task interactions and reactions to the physical environment. The psychological potential of environmental stimuli, however, still depends on how the stimuli are perceived by the pupil: the same teacher's behavior may agitate one pupil and soothe another. We should remember that, psychologically, *all* of the child's behavior is "reasonable" and "normal" given the internal and external conditions operating at that given moment; only when these responses are judged against some standard of desired or acceptable behavior are given responses considered "impaired."

This concept introduces another complication in assessing children's behavior. The role of an infant, a child, or even an adolescent is a subservient and difficult one. The child's dependence, combined with adult arbitrary judgments about behavior, may produce highly subjective standards of deviance. The standard may be merely adult irritation or expectation of undue perfection. Disturbing behavior to one teacher may be evidence of highly valued independence or creativity to another. Because teachers are group workers, they are particularly sensitive to behavior that upsets the group process. Differences in tolerance, setting, and concept all enter into individual judgments of the behavior labeled "impaired." Various identification processes have been developed to reduce variance in individual judgments, to provide common baselines, and to safeguard the pupil against idiosyncratic decisions. An explanation of these processes is the concern of this section.[6]

2.   **William C. Rhodes and Michael L. Tracy,** *A Study of Child Variance,* ISMRRD (Ann Arbor: University of Michigan Press, 1972).

3.   **Carol Cheney and William C. Morse,** "Psychodynamic Interventions in Emotional Disturbance," in *A Study of Child Variance,* vol. 2: *Interventions,* ISMRRD, eds. William C. Rhodes and Michael L. Tracy (Ann Arbor: University of Michigan Press, 1972).

4.   The leader in this aspect is **Rudolf Moos.** See *Evaluating Treatment Environments: A Social Ecological Approach* (New York: John Wiley & Sons, 1974).

5.   **Daniel Kelleher,** "A Model for Integrating Special Educational and Community Mental Health Services," *Journal of Special Education* 2–3 (1968): 263–272.

6.   A complete discussion of this and related matters can be found in **W. C. Morse,** "Concepts Related to Diagnosis of Emotional Impairment" in *State of the Arts: Diagnosis and Treatment,* ed. K. F. Kramer and R. Rosonke (Washington, D.C.: Bureau of Education of Handicapped, 1974), contract no. OEC-0-9-252901-4539(608).

Before examining the details of these processes, however, three other problems must be noted that confound interpretation of conditions surrounding deviance. The first is philosophical: How much latitude should be allowed for freedom and how much conformity should be required? Deviance is always from some norm of behavior. Schools, with their classic emphasis on conformity, are often overrigid and demanding. And yet the democratic ethos requires adherence to certain minimum standards of behavior.

The second problem is whether the implied blame falling on a child for deviance is justified. Historically, the implication has been that deviant behavior was "bad," "willful," and "volitional." Thus, a disturbed child became ipso facto a bad child by choice. Yet the child has "learned" the current behavior through life experiences. The converse—that no child is accountable for his or her behavior—is equally perplexing. Like the nondeviant child, the deviant youngster has acquired behavior patterns through learning experiences and individual potential. Given the behavior patterns that deviant children internalize and the external conditions with which they are confronted, their responses are normal for them. If we wish to change the responses, we must teach them something new or change their external conditions.

The third problem is that child screening and diagnosis are often a prelude to a label (e.g., "delinquent," "childhood schizophrenic"), which in turn is a prelude to a self-fulfilling prophecy that encapsulates these children and sometimes even condemns them. True, diagnosis is the basis of planning a specific program of assistance, but categorizing children discourages attention to individual differences, and these differences are the key to prescriptive planning. Two "disturbed" children are not alike, nor are two delinquents or two autistic children. Each child must be understood in his or her uniqueness and must be seen as part of a unique milieu. Although autistic children tend to bring a repertoire with them wherever they go, variation in setting can mitigate chronic patterns over time. The very anxious, depressed youngster may be slow to respond, even in the most healthful setting. A milieu with very few limits might stimulate action from the quiescent pupil. A punitive setting (e.g., where the staff shames, shocks, or applies physical punishments) accentuates counterhostility. (More subtle punitive settings may have sterile routines, perfunctory adult–child relationships, and a lack of concern for the child's rights as a human being.) A child who is relatively mute and withdrawn among peers may warm up in a one-to-one relationship with a kind and gentle reading teacher, for example.

As we shall see, it is possible to organize a set of descriptions to clarify the child's state. The youngster's standing on *particular* dimensions is far more important than any general label. Adequate descriptors of the environmental press in which the child must react (especially as perceived by the youngster personally) are more difficult to define at present but are just as critical. Moreover, the intervention model must be sensitive to both inner state and external press. Identification and treatment require recognition of distortions in the inner life space (incorporated attitudes and feelings about the self and others, ego capacities, recognized attitudes and values, and social skills) and outer life space, which contains the milieu elements Redl[7] has described so well (the power system, the overt and covert individual and peer codes, staff interactions, grouping patterns, gratifications and punishments, and many others).

These difficulties in screening and assessment are very real. They demand a sophisticated professional awareness that is always primarily concerned with the welfare of the youngster. Until the culture achieves a more positive and effective socializing climate, teachers will encounter problem situations with deviant pupils.

One method of considering the identification of the disturbed child rests upon a theoretical orientation. Dr. William Rhodes has completed a monumental study funded by the Bureau of Education of the Handicapped (BEH), called the Conceptual Project in

---

7. **Fritz Redl,** *When We Deal with Children* (New York: Free Press, 1966).

Emotional Disturbance.[8] As a sequel to the study, Morse and Smith developed a series of five Video Tape Training Packages in Child Variance. The tapes portray sixteen vignettes of classroom behavior problems, while nationally known experts discuss their contrasting theoretical views of the situations. Brief summaries of several of these contemporary views are reprinted here. (The tapes and complete workshop units are available for individual or group instruction from Dr. Herman Saetler of the U.S. Office of Education, Division of Pupil Personnel, 400 Maryland S.W., Washington, D.C. 20202, the distributor of this material.)

Theoretical Position Statements

The following statements, prepared for the Bureau of Education of the Handicapped by William C. Morse and Judy Smith, are oversimplifications but do indicate major distinctions between theoretical viewpoints.

Behavioral Position   The behavioral view regards the behavior and its settings as of primary concern. The behaviorist wants to know how often a behavior occurs, what event precedes it, and what event follows it. He is less concerned about internal motivation. A behavior is seen as either appropriate or inappropriate for a given setting. That judgment is a social or cultural one. The behaviorist intervenes to build appropriate behaviors by rewarding them. Inappropriate behaviors are discouraged in one of three ways: (1) by punishing them, (2) by ignoring them, or (3) by reinforcing a competing behavior, i.e., rewarding the person for doing something else instead.

Psychodynamic Position   The psychodynamic view regards the individual and his internal motivation as of primary concern. The psychodynamic practitioner wants to know as much as possible about how the individual sees his life and behavior. Explanations are sought in prior interpersonal relationships, especially in the family and school history. He is also concerned with developmental growth stages. Behaviors which are appropriate at one stage in life may be seen as inappropriate at another stage. He will intervene by helping the individual to understand his needs and to express them in socially acceptable ways. To do this he will use individual and group counseling, and bring out the therapeutic potential of various activities (games, dances, art, etc.), which may be done in conjunction with parents, teachers, and others.

Biophysical Position   The biophysical view regards the physiological state of the human organism as of primary concern in accounting for deviant behaviors. The biophysical practitioner attributes many behaviors to physiological causes, and therefore wants to know the current state of the individual's health, as well as his past history, including factors of heredity and accidental damage to his body. Concern is directed toward physiological abnormalities that are medically detectable, and also abnormalities that are inferred through the observation of behavioral symptoms. Interventions often consist of the inducement of physiological changes through drugs, alterations of diet, correction of biochemical imbalances, or surgical operations. Biophysical interventions may also include measures which compensate for defects through restructuring the environment or through retraining the individual.

Sociological Position   The sociological view regards society and the groups within society as of primary concern. The sociologist is interested in describing the existing social patterns because he views deviant behavior as resulting from forces in society rather than arising from individual pathology. He examines the behavioral norms and values of society. He identifies roles of individuals and groups, and the process by which these roles are assigned. He wants to know the process by which change occurs, and what strain and conflict it causes. Thus, when a sociologist intervenes, he is likely to suggest changes in the larger system, rather than dealing with the particular individual. Educational innovations such as compensatory education, bilingual education, and racial integration and delabeling have been based on the sociological view. At the level of the

8.   **William Rhodes and Michael L. Tracy**, *A Study of Child Variance*, 5 vols. (Ann Arbor: University of Michigan Press, 1972).

individual classroom, interventions which seek to adapt the class to meet the needs of deviant individuals and sub-groups are preferable to those which attempt to change the deviants by imposing alien societal norms, or which do not recognize the positive value of deviant behavior for society itself.

Traditional and Alternative Positions   Traditional views of behavior and education are based on some common assumptions.

1.   There are standards of behavior to which children should conform.

2.   Children who do not conform are a problem to themselves and to others.

3.   Teachers must intervene to solve behavior problems indirectly (by modifying the environment) or directly (by modifying the child).

4.   The purpose of education is to prepare children to deal with the reality of the outside world, and to carry out their responsibilities as citizens.

Some alternative writers, however, dispute these assumptions. They suggest that no one standard of behavior is innately more desirable than any other, and that children should be free to choose their own mode of behavior (providing they understand the social consequences of their behavior). They hold that the variety of human experience should be celebrated rather than eliminated, and that education should serve to expand awareness of the full range of individual human potential. They point out that "reality" is socially constructed rather than objectively existing apart from human experience. Nontraditional theorists have suggested that the present educational system must be drastically changed, perhaps eliminated. Many have started alternative schools, employing radically different educational modes, particularly those stressing a close personal teacher–student relationship.

Ecological Position   The ecological view regards the individual and the environment with equal concern in analyzing behavior. Behavior is seen as resulting from the interaction of characteristics of the individual and factors in the setting. Thus, similar settings may prompt different behaviors in different individuals. A deviant behavior is one which is not appropriate to a particular setting. That judgment is a socio-cultural one, and the same behavior may be considered positive or negative by different cultures.

When an ecologist intervenes, he may attempt to change: (1) the behavior, (2) the setting, and/or (3) the perceptions of those who view the behavior as deviant. He may intervene in any aspect of the setting or directly on the individual in order to bring about these changes. Ecologists often use techniques consistent with other models. For example, a behavior might be changed through behavior modification (behavioral view), or through medication (biophysical view). Aspects of the environment might be changed using sociological approaches. Group perceptions might be altered using group dynamics techniques (psychodynamic view). Thus, the ecological approach is not a unitary model with specific techniques of intervention. Rather, it locates the source of disturbance by looking at the individual's total environment, and utilizes any intervention technique which will bring about change.

The Basis of Assessment

Looking at the excerpts in Chapter 1, it is obvious that the children's behavior was a product of both inner and external forces. The balance of the two generators changes from case to case and situation to situation. This fits Rhodes's definition of disturbance as a *system* in distress. The importance of this obvious but often neglected fact is increasingly evident when teachers are required to make IEPs and to document accountability. What is the goal for each child, and what are the reasonable interventions to achieve it—both interventions directly focused on the child and interventions in the setting? The following article by Prieto and Rutherford makes a strong case for the ecological position and provides specific processes as well.

An Ecological Assessment Technique for Behaviorally Disordered and Learning Disabled Children

Alfonso G. Prieto
Robert B. Rutherford, Jr.

There appear to be few screening procedures for behaviorally disordered and learning disabled children that can be carried out by classroom teachers with relative ease and without consuming a great deal of time. Bower (1961) has provided an instrument for teachers to screen children with emotional handicaps. His technique utilizes self, peer, and teacher perceptions in the identification of children's behavioral and emotional problems. Hobbs (1966), Rhodes (1967), and Lewis (1974), in the development of Project Re-Ed, have provided a broader philosophical position by which to examine problems associated with children who are labeled behaviorally disordered. This ecological philosophy assumes that dysfunctions do not occur in isolation; they are not exclusive to the child or the environment. Instead these dysfunctions often occur within the interface, that is, where the child and the environment meet or interact. Bower's position, based on the concept of "the earlier the identification the easier the cure" (1971, p. 100) denotes a traditional deviant child model. Hobbs (1966), Rhodes (1967), and Lewis (1974), on the other hand, move away from the assumption that behavior disorders are child centered by examining deviance from an interaction perspective.

Assessment of children's learning/behavioral problems from an interactional or ecological viewpoint makes more relevant data available to the teacher, thus increasing the teacher's options for intervention. An ecological assessment technique combines an ecological philosophy with Bower's teacher centered method of data collection for assessing the child and his environment.

Ecological Assessment Technique

Central to ecological theory is the concept of the ecosystem, which is simply the interaction of an organism with its environment. Viewing the classroom as an ecosystem, classroom teachers can systematically assess the child's ecological niche in each encounter or interaction, as well as the magnitude of his niche breadth. The ecological niche is the role the child plays in each ecosystem. The niche breadth is the range of roles that he plays within the ecosystem. Ecological assessment involves teachers trained to assess each of the child's niches as either positive or negative and then to examine the range of positive or negative roles he plays. The evaluation should not follow a norm referenced model but should be based on a criterion referenced approach, that is, the assessment should reflect whether the child is approximating previously established goals for both academic and social performance. It is recognized that this judgment may well be subjective, but the subjectivity will be controlled for at a later point in the assessment process. At this time, the idea is to not restrict the teacher from indicating a problem area because she does not have objective data. Rather the teacher is encouraged to indicate a problem area which will either be confirmed or denied when the objective data are gathered.

Assessment information is gathered by going through several steps. (1) The teacher develops a hypothesis as to whether the child's niche is a positive or negative one. (2) She or he then examines the child's niche breadth by the use of the Niche Breadth Assessment Card, which indicates how many positive and negative roles the child is playing in the ecosystem in relation to the various interactions that take place. (3) If the original hypothesis is confirmed, namely that the child has one or more negative niches, the teacher can then use the Ecological Baseline Assessment Card to objectively state the problem and to begin to collect data related to the stated problem.

This assessment procedure is based upon a modification of Hobbs's Ecological Model (see Figure 1) which provided the conceptual framework for Project Re-Ed (1966), and which was also used by Harth in developing Project CASA (1975).

This model lends itself well to the concept of mapping which involves graphically portraying the areas of dysfunctions within the ecosystem (Cantrell and Cantrell, 1970). Mapping focuses on the interactions that take place between the child and the activities and people in the school. The school–child component of Hobbs's model must be isolated to adequately map these interactions (see Figure 2).

While the purpose of the proposed classroom assessment technique is not to exclude all interactions outside the classroom from assessment, the classroom is considered the primary target area for most classroom teachers to begin assessment. The various functions and activities that take place in the classroom, in relation to the child, are mapped. A sample of the mapping process is graphically represented in Figure 3. Areas of dysfunction can be noted and the specific problems indicated.

Problems may be depicted by an X at the interface as shown in Figure 3. Concurrent difficulties may be represented by the dotted line. It is possible to structure maps to represent most of the activities associated with the child and classroom in question. It may then be possible to examine the niche breadth of the child by ascribing a positive or negative valence to each ecological niche represented in the diagram.

Although there is a need to collect preliminary data on the child as he interacts within each of the ecosystems, it must be remembered that these data are often subjective. As has already been indicated, this subjectivity allows the teacher to express a concern and that concern will be verified by the use of the Ecological Baseline Card. The only assumption to be made at this level is that the teacher is able to assess whether the behavior is excessive or defi-

cient, based on previously established criteria, to such an extent that the possibility of intervention needs to be examined further. Again, it is assumed that assessment is based upon criterion referenced rather than norm referenced data. As can be noted on the Niche Breadth Assessment Card (see Figure 4), the teacher must indicate whether the niche is positive or negative. This places the teacher in the position of making a forced choice; he or she cannot take a neutral position. The rationale for this structure is to have the teacher indicate problem areas that need to be assessed. The specific interface in which there is some suspicion of dysfunction, and where possible intervention must be directed, is indicated on the Niche Breadth Assessment Card. By using the mapping model in Figure 3, the teacher can formulate the interface section of the Niche Breadth Assessment Card. This section obviously is subject to change depending on the various ecosystems available to the child.

The next step is for the teacher to utilize the Ecological Baseline Card to behaviorally state the problems indicated by the Niche Breadth Assessment Card, and begin to objectively record data. It will be noted that the idea is to move away from the deviant child concept and address the significant antecedents and consequences in the ecosystems that may affect the child's behavior.

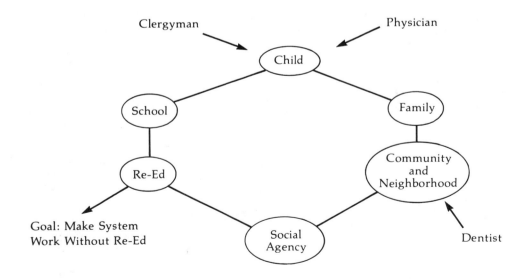

Figure 1. Hobbs's Conceptual Model: The Ecological System

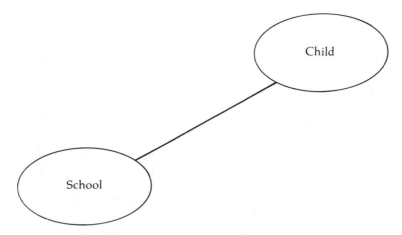

Figure 2. School–Child Component of Hobbs's Conceptual Model

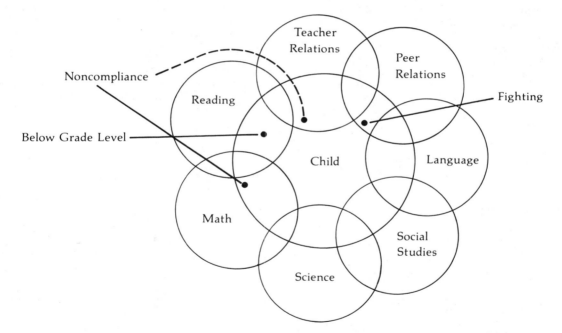

Figure 3. School–Child Mapping Diagram

Collecting an Ecological Baseline

Information about specific problems which the child has with the systems in which he lives or, conversely, which the systems have with the child, must be identified and data collected about them. When there is discordance between the child and his settings, we can either attempt to change the child's competencies in relation to those settings or we can change the expectations of the settings toward the child.

The Ecological Baseline involves an effort by the teacher to pinpoint the specific problem areas of the child, to critically observe the problem areas of the child, to critically observe the problem in its

CHILD'S NAME Jock Mahoney   DATE September 10, 1976

	POSITIVE	NEGATIVE
INTERFACE		
Teacher Relations		X
Peer Relations		X
Other Adults Relations		X
Math	X	
Science	X	
Social Studies	X	
Reading		X
Language		X

Figure 4. Sample Niche Breadth Assessment Card

natural setting(s), and to record the quality and quantity of the problem. The Ecological Baseline provides a means for specifying the problem area and identifying the environmental antecedents and consequences of the problem. By analyzing the situation from an ecological point of view, the teacher can isolate events that may maintain that problem.

The term Ecological Baseline is drawn from two distinct but complementary approaches to resolving child–environment conflict, ecological theory and applied behavior analysis. Again, ecological theory (Hobbs, 1966; Rhodes, 1970; and Lewis, 1974) holds that when a problem arises for a child in his environment, simultaneous interventions must be made on both the conditions of the child and the surroundings of the child. The premise of ecological theory is that the point of discordance is at the interaction or interface between the child and his environment. Since the child's behavior is only part of the problem, interventions into the surroundings of the child should occur concurrently with any interventions into the conditions of the child. While Rhodes, Hobbs, and Lewis developed a theory for moderate behavioral disorders of children, ecological theory applies to many areas of child–environment discord, from mild to severe. When the teacher initiates an ecological baseline, he or she is assuming that the discordance is, in part, the result of an agitated exchange between the individual child and his various ecosystems. More specifically, the teacher is interested in assessing the effects of these environmental settings on the child's academic and social behavior in the classroom. Interventions which are developed by the teacher are aimed not only at remediating the individual child's problem, but at strengthening the environmental components which will maintain positive changes. These environmental components consist of where and with whom the child spends his time—the child's natural behavior settings (Lewis, 1974). When an Ecological Baseline is established, the teacher observes the totality of the situation from an ecological or environmental perspective rather than from solely a deviant child perspective.

Applied behavior analysis (Baer, Wolf & Risley, 1968) provides the concept of the baseline or recording of the level of the behavior or problem before interventions are initiated to change or eliminate the problem. The purpose of the baseline is: 1) to have sufficient information about the problem to ascertain whether it warrants intervention, 2) to determine where the problem lies—with the child, with his ecosystems, or with the interaction between the child and his ecosystems, and 3) to have a basis of evaluation for changes in the level of the problem before and after an intervention has been initiated. The purpose of the ecological baseline, then, is to measure problems of children in their natural settings before interventions are initiated with either the child, or the environment, or the interaction between the two.

Teachers must have three skills in order to be able to initiate an Ecological Baseline. The first skill involves the ability to precisely and concisely specify the problem. The skill here is to be able to identify what the problem appears to be without making subjective judgments as to the causation and reasons for maintenance of the problem. The second skill that teachers must have is to be able to critically observe in order to establish the ecology of the problem. This skill involves the ability to see the problem not in isolation but in relation to the environment where the problem occurs. These observation skills take time to develop but are crucial to establishing the baseline for possible future interventions. The final skill centers on the ability of teachers to accurately record the quality and quantity of the problem. Recording the intensity and duration, as well as the frequency, of the problem is essential to eventual success in changing the problem.

Ecological Baseline Card

The Ecological Baseline Card (see Figure 5) provides a means for collecting the information necessary for analyzing and changing the problem in various ecological settings. The *statement of the problem* calls for a clear, precise phrase identifying *what* the problem is and *who* has the problem. Problem statements are phrased: "Jim cries when I ask him questions," "Johnny hits and kicks the other students on the playground," "The children in the class will not play with Susan," "Sally complains of headaches," "Steve comes to school high on drugs or alcohol," "Debbie drools." The problem statement involves those problems of the child that the teacher continues to observe over time and which appear to occur with such intensity, duration, or frequency as to warrant special teacher attention.

The statement of the problem is essentially meaningless unless the teacher identifies the probable antecedents and consequences of the problem. *Antecedents* include *where* the problem occurs, e.g.,

on the school bus, in language training time, on the playground, in study hall, in the restrooms; *when* the problem occurs, e.g., just before lunch, during the first hour of school, around 2:30 every day, every Monday morning, all day; and *who* is present when the problem occurs, e.g., the teacher or aide who gives directions, with two or more other girls, with his older brother on the playground, with three younger boys after school. Antecedents, then, involve those places, times, and/or people which appear to set off the problem. The Ecological Baseline Card provides space for listing several potential antecedents to the problem in question. Additional space is provided on the card for elaborating on the time and place where the problem occurs most often. By observing the events which occur immediately preceding the problem, teachers can begin to pinpoint those environmental cues which may set the problem off. The skill involved here does not call for the ability to specify exact relationships between antecedents and problems, but to observe the problem in its natural environment and attempt to isolate as many different possible antecedents which are present just before the problem occurs.

The skills involved in isolating environmental antecedents of a problem are similar to the skills necessary to isolate the environmental consequences of the problem. Critical and objective observation skills are important for the precise noting and recording of what happens immediately after a problem behavior occurs. The teacher who develops this skill will quickly begin to identify patterns of consequences which may maintain the problem. The *consequences* section of the Ecological Baseline Card provides space for identifying what patterns of events appear to occur repeatedly over time following the problem in question. Teacher's and aide's reactions and responses to the problem behavior, as well as the reactions of the child's parents, other children's reactions, the child's own reactions to his behavior, and direct or indirect changes in the physical environment due to the problem, must be pinpointed in order to determine the consequences that may maintain the problem. There are three classes of consequences to any behavior: 1) consequences can be pleasant and thus reinforce the behavior, increasing the likelihood that the behavior will be increased, or at least maintained, 2) consequences can be aversive and thus punish behavior, resulting in the suppression of the problem behavior, and 3) consequences can be neutral and thus have no direct effect on the behavior. The only way that the teacher can determine whether the consequences of a given behavior or problem are positive, aversive, or neutral is

Child's Name: Date:

ECOLOGICAL BASELINE CARD

Antecedents to Problem:	Statement of Problem:	Consequences of Problem:
_____	_____	_____
_____	_____	_____
_____	_____	_____
_____	_____	_____
_____	_____	_____

Time (When does problem occur?):

_____

_____

Place (Activities/location problem occurs):

_____

_____

Frequency (How often or long does problem occur?):

Day 1		Day 6	
Day 2		Day 7	
Day 3		Day 8	
Day 4		Day 9	
Day 5		Day 10	

Figure 5. Ecological Baseline Card

to observe and record their effects on the behavior itself. If the problem increases, the consequences are positive; if the problem is suppressed, the consequences are aversive, or at least not reinforcing; and if the problem remains unchanged, the consequences are neutral.

When the teacher fills out an Ecological Baseline Card, he or she is attempting to identify patterns of antecedents and consequences that surround the problem behavior and may actively maintain the behavior. In conjunction with analyzing the antecedents and consequences of a given problem behavior, the teacher should count the frequency or duration of the behavior over a limited time span. A baseline, by definition, is a statement of the level of occurrence of the problem before a change strategy is initiated. Obviously, if a child comes in off the playground with his clothes torn and his nose bloodied, the teacher is not going to count how many times this occurs over a two week period before initiating an intervention. However, most problems have been identified as such because they have recurred repeatedly over time with such intensity as to warrant some type of teacher intervention. The Ecological Baseline Card provides space to record the baseline frequency of the problem over a ten day period.

Thus, in order for teachers to solve problems and serve the child effectively, they first establish an ecological baseline on the problem. This screening procedure provides a method for initial assessment. By utilizing this technique, attention is focused on antecedent and consequent variables which affect and maintain the child's behavior in the classroom. With this information, the problem can be analyzed and probable solution strategies devised.

References

Baer, D. M., Wolf, M. M. & Risley, T. R. Some current dimensions of applied behavior analysis. *Journal of Applied Behavior Analysis*, 1968, 1, 91–97.

Bower, E. M. A process for identifying disturbed children. In Harth, R. (Ed.) *Issues in Behavior Disorders*. Springfield, Illinois: Charles C Thomas, 1971.

Cantrell, R. & Cantrell, M. L. Systematic decision-making and children's problems: A heuristic attempt. Prevention-Intervention Project Working Paper, 1970.

Harth, R. Ecological Design of Special Education Programs. Paper presented at the Annual Meeting of the Teacher Educators for Children with Behavior Disorders, Atlanta, Georgia, 1975.

Hobbs, N. Helping disturbed children: Psychological and ecological strategies. *American Psychologist*, 1966, 21, 1105–1115.

Lewis, W. W. From Project Re-Ed to ecological planning. *Phi Delta Kappan*, 1974, 55, 538–540.

Rhodes, W. C. The disturbing child: A problem of ecological management. *Exceptional Children*, 1967, 33, 449–455.

Rhodes, W. C. A community participation analysis of emotional disturbance. *Exceptional Children*, 1970, 36, 309–314.

Editors' Commentary

For those particularly interested in the assessment of young high-risk children, a 1978 article by Bradley and Caldwell[9] discusses the national effort called EPSDT (Early and Periodic Screening, Diagnosis, and Treatment Program), designed to identify at an early age and prevent further development of problems in children. The authors point out that screening must start while the child is in the home. They delve into the theory, specific instruments, and a critical evaluation of the state of the field.

Teachers and Screening Processes

The school itself has been seen by some as one huge screening operation to determine who will be successful in the culture. Of course this is not accurate: many who have problems in school do not have significant mental health problems, and some who would be evaluated as having serious adjustment problems overall are not "screened out" by the school. We read about the "perfect pupil" who suddenly murders a classmate, teacher, or parent. Since the school is the major community agency that sees almost every child, and since school personnel are now mandated to find all children who need help—search them out—it is incumbent on the educational establishment to perform this screening function with much more objectivity and thoroughness than it has in the past.

9. **R. H. Bradley and B. M. Caldwell,** "Screening the Environment," *American Journal of Orthopsychiatry* 1 (1978): 114–130.

Screening consists of securing a roster of pupils who, at least on the basis of first-level scrutiny, deserve further study. Further study should result in clarification: the youngster has no problem; the problem is transitory; the problem is a response to a situational complex of social or academic stresses in school, which could and should be altered; or the problem is evident in school, home, and neighborhood and will necessitate careful analysis and specialized assistance.

Teachers have a unique role in screening and its counterpart, evaluation of change. Teachers are the only trained professionals who see all children in many settings, and this tends to give them a broad perspective. In school, a youngster has tasks (work), authority (bosses), and peer relationships (colleagues). In this microcosm the many out-pourings of the child's inner feelings will be evident whether or not special attention is given to them. Teachers' broad experience in the range of normal, age-related behavior can serve as a base for evaluation. In many cases, the teacher's contact with the child's home or community life gives added awareness.

Yet all teachers have biases, set expectations, sensitivities, and the capacity to distort. A study by Fremont et al.[10] shows that teachers and school counselors view emotional disturbances as conduct and behavior manifestations. In contrast, other mental health disciplines emphasize personality factors. This difference seems a natural one, since the disruptive pupil is a highly pragmatic problem to anyone who has to manage groups of children. However, the contrast among disciplines emphasizes the need for multidisciplinary approaches. This need is corroborated by Bloom, who found that behavior problems and emotional disturbances are separate identifications.[11] Of the many approaches to screening, some provide more objectivity than others. In the following articles, we examine certain devices that teachers can use in screening. The search for devices is endless, and there are several source books devoted to procedures.[12]

It should also be recognized that, in traditional terms, diagnosis and treatment are not entirely separate processes. The adult continually discovers new aspects of the child's world in a diagnosis, and the adult's sharing of and reaction to the child's problems are an integral part of the treatment. Diagnosis is progressive, often specific in focus, and existential in appearance, and prescriptive planning must be flexible, open, and always progressing.

Quay and his colleagues, the authors of the next excerpt, have conducted a persistent search for individual behavior symptoms that can be observed by teachers and at the same time provide information about recognized patterns of behavior. In a series of studies, their factor analyses have resulted in delineating three scales of deviance: personality, conduct, and immaturity. The following study reports on application of the scales to a population of disturbed children.

10.   **T. S. Fremont, M. J. Klingsporn, and J. H. Wilson,** "Identifying Emotional Disturbances in Children—the Professionals Differ," *Journal of School Psychology* 14 (1976): 275–282.

11.   **Robert B. Bloom,** "Teacher–Pupil Compatibility and Teachers' Ratings of Children's Behavior," *Psychology in the Schools* 13 (1976): 142–145.

12.   **Oscar K. Buros, ed.,** *The Sixth Mental Measurements Yearbook* (Highland Park, N.J.: Gryphon Press, 1965); J. P. Robinson and P. R. Shaver, *Measures of Social Psychological Attitudes* (Ann Arbor: Institute for Social Research, 1972); A. L. Comrey, T. E. Backer, and E. W. Glaser, *A Source Book for Mental Health Measures* (Los Angeles: Human Interaction Research Institute, 1973); M. J. Kaufman, M. Semmel, and J. A. Agard, *Supplementary Materials to Year 1,* Interim Report, Part II (Bloomington: University of Indiana, no date); **Orval G. Johnson,** *Tests and Measurements in Child Development: Handbook II,* vols. 1 and 2 (San Francisco: Jossey-Bass, 1976); **Bert A. Goldman and John L. Saunders,** *Directory of Unpublished Experimental Mental Measures,* vol. 1 (New York: Behavioral Publications, 1974). An excellent analytical study of behavior checklists can be found in **John D. Cone and Robert Hawkins,** eds., *Behavioral Assessment,* chap. 4 (New York: Brunner/Mazel, 1977).

Personality Patterns of Pupils in Special Classes for the Emotionally Disturbed

Herbert C. Quay
William C. Morse
Richard L. Cutler

Although there has been considerable interest in the kinds of children who might be considered for special class placement and in the ways these children might best be grouped, there has been no systematic investigation of the behavioral characteristics of children in the schools already defined, by whatever process, as emotionally disturbed. This paper reports the analysis of teacher ratings of problem behavior in a large group of children in special classes for the emotionally disturbed in a variety of school systems. The purpose of the research was to investigate the basic dimensions which might underlie the observed interrelationships of a representative number of deviant behavior traits.

Procedure

In the context of a much larger research effort (Morse, Cutler, and Fink, 1964), ratings of problem behavior traits of 441 children were made by 60 different teachers. The sample of classes varied widely in geographic locus and represented many different philosophies of placement and program operation. The sample was composed of approximately 80 percent boys and 20 percent girls; the mean ages were 9.4 and 9.8 years, respectively. More complete information about the classes is provided in the earlier publication.

The problem behavior rating scale employed was first developed by Peterson (1961) and represents the most common problem behaviors of children referred to a child guidance clinic. Since its publication, the items of the scale have been subjected to a series of factor analyses on a variety of populations (Quay, 1964a; Quay and Quay, 1965; Quay, 1966). These studies have almost uniformly shown that three factorially independent dimensions account for about two-thirds of the variance of the interrelationships among the problem behaviors.

The first dimension is composed of aggressive, hostile, and contentious behavior which has been labeled, at various times, conduct disorder, unsocialized aggression, or psychopathy. The second dimension represents anxious, withdrawn, intro-

vertive behavior and has been labeled personality problem or neuroticism. The third dimension involves preoccupation, lack of interest, sluggishness, laziness, daydreaming, and passivity. This factor generally has accounted for much less of a variance than the first two dimensions, and its meaning is less easily decided upon. The labels of inadequacy-immaturity and autism have been suggested.

While the design of this study did not permit the assessment of two rater reliability, the results of prior research have suggested that the scale can be used reliably by parents and teachers alike.

For statistical analysis, those traits rated present in at least 10 percent of the cases were intercorrelated and subjected to a principal axis factor analysis using the squared multiple correlation as the communality estimate. Factors having at least one variable with a loading of .40 or greater were then rotated to Kaiser's (1958) Varimax criterion.

Results

Rotated factor loadings are presented in Table 1. The three factors rotated accounted for 76 percent of the variance.

The first factor is clearly that of the conduct problem or unsocialized aggressive dimension, with the largest loadings appearing on such behaviors as defiant, impertinent, uncooperative, irritable, boisterous, etc. As noted above, the rating scale has been used in other studies; it is thus possible to compare the factors found in this research with those previously identified. Table 2 presents the variables common to both the present research and a number of the earlier studies, along with their respective factor loadings. Inspection of the pattern of loadings suggests a high degree of comparability across all of the analyses for the conduct problem factor. This apparent comparability was assessed by the calculation of Tucker's coefficients of factor similarity (Quay and Quay, 1965) which are presented in Table 3. As can be seen, the values are uniformly high among those factors labeled as "conduct problem."

Table 1. Rotated Factor Loadings

		Factors		
Variable	Conduct Problem	Inadequacy Immaturity	Personality Problem	b^2
Defiant, disobedient	69	10	−14	50
Impertinent	68	09	−05	47
Uncooperative in group	65	20	07	47
Irritable	64	07	14	43
Boisterous	63	06	04	41
Show off, attention-seeking	64	00	03	41
Bullies	60	−01	03	36
Temper tantrums	59	−04	15	37
Hyperactive	59	−12	12	39
Restless	58	−12	11	36
Negative	53	24	−08	35
Irresponsible	53	38	−05	44
Swears, profane language	52	04	06	28
Destructive	53	06	07	29
Jealous	52	04	21	31
Inattentive	42	46	00	38
Tense	37	−08	39	31
Hypersensitive	32	03	57	42
Short attention span	32	32	12	22
Dislikes school	32	46	02	32
Shy	−40	27	42	40
Withdrawn	−32	40	36	39
Sluggish	−09	59	15	39
Lack of interest	14	57	06	34
Lazy	19	52	−02	31
Preoccupied	−03	51	18	29
Daydreams	−03	46	20	25
Drowsy	00	45	08	21
Reticent	03	44	31	29
Passive, suggestible	−18	30	22	17
Inferiority	11	02	64	42
Self-conscious	−09	07	60	38
Lacks self-confidence	02	02	57	33
Easily flustered	25	20	52	37
Fearful, anxious	23	09	48	29
Depressed	11	21	34	17
Clumsy	−01	18	27	11
Inability to have fun	−15	22	23	12
Aloof	−13	25	25	14
Plays with younger children	08	10	24	07
Masturbates	12	16	14	06
Headaches	10	15	12	05
Stomach aches	14	24	15	10

Decimal points omitted.

Factor two, loading such variables as sluggishness, laziness, lack of interest, preoccupation, dislike for school, and inattentiveness, seems a representation of the factor identified in earlier studies as inadequacy-immaturity. It has also been suggested (Himmelweit, 1953; Peterson, Becker, Shoemaker, Luria, and Hellmer, 1961) that this factor is perhaps associated with autism or a prepsychotic condition. Unfortunately, none of the samples studied to date has contained adequate numbers of clearly autistic or frankly psychotic children to test this hypothesis. At present it seems best to con-

Table 2. Rotated Factor Loadings of Common Variables from Present Research and Prior Studies

Variable	8th Grade Students (Quay and Quay 1965)			Adolescent Delinquents (Quay, 1964)			Preadolescent Delinquents (Quay, 1966)			Present Study		
	P	C	I	P	C	I	P	C	I	P	C	I
Restless	−04	70	15	14	46	37	03	44	04	11	58	−12
Attention seeking	−08	61	19	−07	70	20	01	49	−09	03	64	00
Inability to have fun	31	−15	03	60	23	22	39	−12	10	23	−15	22
Self-conscious	54	00	−11	48	−05	39	59	−08	00	60	−09	07
Disruptive	−12	70	21	−05	77	11	00	67	15			
Feelings of inferiority	57	−07	17	47	05	29	65	06	05	64	11	02
Boisterousness	−03	60	15	−14	71	18	00	69	08	04	63	06
Preoccupation	21	−04	62	60	14	28	18	−21	48	18	−03	51
Shyness	38	−42	00	54	−28	13	59	−27	08	42	−40	27
Withdrawal	15	−18	12	67	−06	04	41	−34	27	36	−32	40
Short attention span	11	44	56	11	59	28	19	37	55	12	32	32
Lack of confidence	63	−17	22	66	12	30	57	03	22	57	02	02
Inattentive	−08	46	58	24	64	18	22	50	52	00	42	46
Easily flustered	34	14	02	55	19	46	60	21	25	52	25	20
Lack of interest	−02	−02	48	49	49	−02	29	−03	47	06	14	57
Reticence	18	−23	08				14	−04	25	31	03	44
Laziness in school	−15	22	59	20	55	00	09	24	66	−02	19	52
Irresponsibility	00	29	51	34	75	00				−05	53	38
Daydreaming	20	13	57	70	08	26	−07	41	50	20	03	46
Disobedience	00	62	22	11	74	00	−03	64	06	−14	69	10
Uncooperativeness	−07	36	25	15	74	01	−04	59	13	07	65	20
Aloofness	22	−32	20	29	−01	02	20	−30	27	25	−13	25
Passive, suggestible	14	13	38	21	47	30	28	12	27	22	−18	30
Hyperactivity	08	54	−01	03	37	53	−05	60	09	12	59	−12
Distractibility	−11	59	36	30	34	62	03	46	53			
Impertinence	07	33	11	21	62	29	−16	57	02	−05	68	09
Lethargy	02	−17	27	62	22	−05	29	−16	58	08	00	45
Nervous, jittery	35	28	−14	42	22	43	40	39	17	39	37	−08

Decimal points omitted.

Table 3. Coefficients of Factor Similarity for Studies of Ratings of Problem Behavior

		Present Study			Eighth Grade Students			Adolescent Delinquents		
		P	C	I	P	C	I	P	C	I
Eighth	Personality	.94	−.42	−.28						
Grade	Conduct	−.58	.93	−.39						
	Immaturity	−.51	.04	.70						
Adolescent	Personality	.59	−.72	.41	.75	.02	.60			
Delinquent	Conduct	−.83	.85	−.04	.00	.84	.72			
	Immaturity	.48	.09	−.59	.58	.55	.44			
Pre-	Personality	.85	−.66	.00	.72	−.09	.27	.86	.23	.63
Adolescent	Conduct	−.54	.92	−.44	−.06	.93	.45	.27	.87	.48
Delinquent	Immaturity	−.22	−.29	.81	.26	.29	.89	.62	.62	.49

sider this dimension as representing behavioral immaturity. Whether the basis is developmental or regressive remains a question for further research. The pattern of coefficients in Table 3 indicates that, despite difficulties of interpretation, this factor is comparable to those identified earlier in terms of salient variables.

Factor three, composed primarily of such behaviors as inferiority feelings, self-consciousness, lack of self-confidence, fearfulness, and depression, is clearly the dimension of personality problem or neuroticism identified in the earlier research. In this study, however, this dimension accounts for less of the variance than does inadequacy-immaturity—a reversal of the usual state of affairs. Comparability with previous studies is again indicated by Table 3.

Discussion

The results of this study indicate clearly that the behavior problems of children in a wide sampling of special public school classes for the emotionally disturbed can be understood within the three dimensional framework identified in earlier studies of ratings of problem behavior in other kinds of children. Prior research has also demonstrated that these three dimensions can be found in the analysis of both life history data (Quay, 1964b; Quay, 1966) and responses to personality questionnaires (Peterson, Quay, and Tiffany, 1961). Certainly these behavior dimensions, objectively observable and reliably rated, provide a potentially more useful way of looking at problem behavior children than does the application of psychiatric nosological labels which are of doubtful reliability even when applied to adults (Schmidt and Fonda, 1956).

The fact that, in the present group of children, the inadequacy-immaturity dimension accounted for a relatively greater proportion of the variance than has usually been the case suggests that children displaying these behavioral characteristics are perhaps more likely to find their way into special classes than are children whose behavior is more anxious and withdrawn. Whether this is due to the Wickman effect (Wickman, 1928) or whether children with immaturity characteristics are perceived as "more disturbed" or even frankly autistic by school personnel is not clear. What does seem clear is that despite a lack of overt aggression, such children are less able to function in the regular classroom than are the more neurotic children. In a later publication it is planned to report on the relationship of the scores of the children on the three

factors to many of the other variables reported in the earlier monograph (Morse et al., 1964).

In other research, in addition to the dimensions reported here, there has frequently appeared a constellation of behavior traits which has been labeled subcultural or socialized delinquency. The failure of this syndrome to emerge in this study is likely due both to the fact that few items in the rating scale tap this factor, and to the fact that children representative of this syndrome are not quite so likely to be found in classes for the emotionally disturbed. As one of us has indicated elsewhere (Quay, 1963), these children are not truly emotionally disturbed and represent a quite different educational problem.

Even at this juncture it seems clear that differential programs are likely to be required to remediate both the behavioral and academic difficulties of "emotionally disturbed" children. While we can expect to find few children who are so clearly representative of a given syndrome as to be clearly one "type" or another, we nevertheless can experiment with classifying children with the three dimensional framework for the study of the effects of differential treatment methods. One of us has commented at greater length elsewhere (Quay, 1965) to the effect that present theory, however rudimentary, does suggest different ways to approach different children.

References

Himmelweit, Hilde T. A factorial study of "children's behavior problems." Cited in H. J. Eysenck. *The structure of human personality.* London: Methuen, 1953. P. 88.

Kaiser, H. F. The Varimax criterion for analytic rotation of factor analysis. *Psychometrika,* 1958, **23,** 187–200.

Morse, W. C., Cutler, R. L., and Fink, A. H. *Public school classes for the emotionally handicapped: a research analysis.* Washington: The Council for Exceptional Children, 1964.

Peterson, D. R. Behavior problems of middle childhood. *Journal of Consulting Psychology,* 1961, **25,** 205–209.

Peterson, D. R., Becker, W. C., Shoemaker, D. J., Luria, Zella, and Hellmer, L. A. Child behavior problems and parental attitudes. *Child Development,* 1961, **32,** 151–162.

Peterson, D. R., Quay, H. C., and Tiffany, T. L. Personality factors related to juvenile delinquency. *Child Development,* 1961, **32,** 355–372.

Quay, H. C. Some basic considerations in the education of emotionally disturbed children. *Exceptional Children*, 1963, **30,** 27–31.

Quay, H. C. Personality dimensions in delinquent males as inferred from the factor analysis of behavior ratings. *Journal of Research in Crime and Delinquency,* 1964, **1,** 33–37. (a)

Quay, H. C. Dimensions of personality in delinquent boys as inferred from the factor analysis of case history data. *Child Development,* 1964, **35,** 479–484. (b)

Quay, H. C. Dimensions of problem behavior in children and their interactions with approaches to behavior modification. Paper read at a symposium, University of Kansas, Kansas City, March, 1965.

Quay, H. C. Personality patterns in preadolescent delinquent boys. *Educational and Psychological Measurement,* 1966, **26,** 99–110.

Quay, H. C. and Quay, Lorene C. Behavior problems in early adolescence. *Child Development,* 1965, **36,** 215–220.

Schmidt, H. O. and Fonda, C. P. The reliability of psychiatric diagnosis: a new look. *Journal of Abnormal and Social Psychology,* 1956, **52,** 262–267.

Wickman, E. K. *Children's behavior and teachers' attitudes.* New York: Commonwealth Fund, 1928.

Editors' Commentary

H. K. Walker's Behavior Problem Checklist is a useful screening device that also measures the degree or intensity of the behavior.

Behavior Problem Checklist

Col. No.	Please complete each question carefully.
(1–8)	1. Name (or number) of child_____
(9–10)	2. Age (in years)_____
(11)	3. Sex_____(M 1, F 2)
(12)	4. Father's occupation_____
(13)	5. Name of person completing this checklist
	_____
(14)	6. What is your relationship to this child? (circle one)
	a. Mother b. Father c. Teacher d. Other_____
	(Specify)

Please indicate which of the following constitute problems, as far as this child is concerned. If an item does *not* constitute a problem, encircle the zero; if an item constitutes a *mild* problem, encircle the one; if an item constitutes a *severe* problem, encircle the two. Please complete every item.

0	1	2	1. Oddness, bizarre behavior
0	1	2	2. Restlessness, inability to sit still
0	1	2	3. Attention-seeking, "show-off" behavior
0	1	2	4. Stays out late at night
0	1	2	5. Doesn't know how to have fun; behaves like a little adult
0	1	2	6. Self-consciousness; easily embarrassed

0	1	2	7. Fixed expression, lack of emotional reactivity
0	1	2	8. Disruptiveness; tendency to annoy & bother others
0	1	2	9. Feelings of inferiority
0	1	2	10. Steals in company with others
0	1	2	11. Boisterousness, rowdiness
0	1	2	12. Crying over minor annoyances and hurts
0	1	2	13. Preoccupation; "in a world of his own"
0	1	2	14. Shyness, bashfulness
0	1	2	15. Social withdrawal, preference for solitary activities
0	1	2	16. Dislike for school
0	1	2	17. Jealousy over attention paid other children
0	1	2	18. Belongs to a gang
0	1	2	19. Repetitive speech
0	1	2	20. Short attention span
0	1	2	21. Lack of self-confidence
0	1	2	22. Inattentiveness to what others say
0	1	2	23. Easily flustered and confused
0	1	2	24. Incoherent speech
0	1	2	25. Fighting
0	1	2	26. Loyal to delinquent friends
0	1	2	27. Temper tantrums
0	1	2	28. Reticence, secretiveness
0	1	2	29. Truancy from school
0	1	2	30. Hypersensitivity; feelings easily hurt
0	1	2	31. Laziness in school and in performance of other tasks
0	1	2	32. Anxiety, chronic general fearfulness
0	1	2	33. Irresponsibility, undependability
0	1	2	34. Excessive daydreaming
0	1	2	35. Masturbation
0	1	2	36. Has bad companions
0	1	2	37. Tension, inability to relax
0	1	2	38. Disobedience, difficulty in disciplinary control
0	1	2	39. Depression, chronic sadness
0	1	2	40. Uncooperativeness in group situations
0	1	2	41. Aloofness, social reserve
0	1	2	42. Passivity, suggestibility; easily led by others
0	1	2	43. Clumsiness, awkwardness, poor muscular coordination
0	1	2	44. Hyperactivity; "always on the go"
0	1	2	45. Distractibility
0	1	2	46. Destructiveness in regard to his own &/or other's property
0	1	2	47. Negativism, tendency to do the opposite of what is requested
0	1	2	48. Impertinence, sauciness
0	1	2	49. Sluggishness, lethargy
0	1	2	50. Drowsiness
0	1	2	51. Profane language, swearing, cursing
0	1	2	52. Nervousness, jitteriness, jumpiness; easily startled
0	1	2	53. Irritability; hot-tempered, easily aroused to anger
0	1	2	54. Enuresis, bed-wetting
0	1	2	55. Often has physical complaints, e.g. headaches, stomach ache

Quay has worked out specific educational designs for each of the three dimensions.[13]

Another screening procedure relies on observations of specific behavior in the classroom. Such processes are in keeping with behavioristic approaches because they are

13. **H. C. Quay,** "Facets of Educational Exceptionality: A Conceptual Framework for Assessment, Grouping, and Instruction," *Exceptional Children* 35 (1968): 25–32.

neither clinical nor inferential. Werry and Quay[14] have contributed in this area. Walker[15] presents both a conceptual rationale and a device for obtaining information on three levels: (1) a fifty-five-item behavior checklist; (2) a seventy-five-item rating scale, which includes frequency, teacher reaction, and pupil response, and (3) a ten-minute observation form for task orientation. Walker suggests uses for the information that make it a teaching as well as a screening device. The "teacher-reaction, pupil-response" is also the start of an ecological analysis. Because many behavior observation schemes deal with "on-task" or "in-seat" behavior, the meaning of the deviance still must be inferred. Withdrawn pupils might score well and yet still have problems in such instances.

Long, Fagen, and Stevens[16] have developed a schema that is educationally oriented, useful to the teacher, requires only twenty minutes per pupil, and has an interesting four-part format. The "Pupil Assessment of Self in School" assesses the pupil's perception of (a) his or her functions in school, (b) performance of the work, and (c) relationships to peers and the teacher. The eight-item "Self Control Behavior Inventory" is rated by the teacher on a four-point scale. Sample items include "remembers directions," "anticipates consequences of behavior," and "can delay actions even when excited," each with behavioral examples. The third part concerns "Patterns of Achievement." Seven styles are suggested, such as "slow start but sudden increase," "slow constant increase," and "erratic achievement." The fourth part, "Significant Life Events Inventory," presumes that ecological aspects such as injury, illness, economic stress, and separation from parents are significant. Although these external conditions can be assessed only in terms of how the pupil responds to them, this aspect of screening is certainly an important contribution.

Interest in preschool and early screening has encouraged the development of rating devices for this age group. Bell, Waldrop, and Weller[17] have provided an explicit eleven-point rating scale for each of nine dimensions ranging from "frenetic play" and "emotional aggression" to "vacant staring" and "chronic fearfulness." To use the teacher's knowledge, Kohn and Rosman[18] have done considerable analysis of their dual social competence scale and symptom checklist. Walker[19] has discussed in detail 143 socioemotional measures and discussed theoretical problems involved in assessing young children.

The *Pupil Behavior Inventory*[20] has both an elementary and a junior high school form. Teachers have responded well to it for several reasons: it is fast, the thirty-four items and the rating scale are comfortable to use, and the final dimensions (classroom conduct, academic motivation, socioemotional state, teacher dependence, and personal behavior) represent areas of high interest to the educational community.

14. **J. S. Werry and H. C. Quay,** "Observing the Classroom Behavior of Elementary School Children," *Exceptional Children* 35 (1969): 461–470.

15. **H. K. Walker,** "Empirical Assessment of Deviant Behavior in Children," *Psychology in the Schools* 6 (1969): 93–97.

16. **N. J. Long, S. A. Fagen, and D. J. Stevens,** *Psychoeducational Screening System for Identifying Resourceful, Marginal, and Vulnerable Pupils in Primary Grades* (3565 Brandywine St., N.W., Washington, D.C.: Psychoeducational Resources, Inc., 1971).

17. **R. Q. Bell, M. F. Waldrop, and G. M. Weller,** "A Rating System for the Assessment of Hyperactive and Withdrawn Children in Preschool Samples," *American Journal of Orthopsychiatry* 42 (1972): 23–34.

18. **M. Kohn and B. L. Rosman,** "A Social Competence Scale and Symptom Checklist for the Preschool Child," *Developmental Psychology* 6 (1972): 430–444.

19. **D. K. Walker,** *Socioemotional Measures for Preschool and Kindergarten Children* (San Francisco: Jossey-Bass, 1973).

20. **R. D. Vinter et al.,** *Pupil Behavior Inventory* (Ann Arbor: Campus Publishers, 1966).

Hammer[21] has provided a rating scale of fifty-seven items for the following disturbances: classroom behavior; attitudes toward self; behavior with the teacher; relationship with peers; inappropriate infantile behavior; physical functioning or appearance; speech; sexuality; and difficulties in learning. The individual items provide significant screening and appraisal cues for teachers.

One screening device used in considerable research is the DESB (Devereux Elementary School Behavior Rating Scale), which uses a teacher rating on a five- to seven-point scale, based on comparison to the average pupil.[22] The dimensions are of considerable teacher interest: disturbance, defiance, external blame, anxiety, inattention, etc. Spivack, who developed the scale, and Swift have also done a critical review of teacher rating devices.[23] They found that the major dimensions on such scales are control problems, recessive behavior, school adjustment, and cognitive functioning.

Doughton and Fix[24] have tied their checklist to behavior clusters that identify hyperkinetic activity, learning disabilities, depression, psychosis, and sociopathy. These syndromes are then tied to teaching approaches, and in that sense can be considered for IEP preparation.

Bower and Lambert, our next authors, have designed a multiple approach that covers the pupil in a broader context, though it does not deal with the environmental conditions. Follow-up studies[25] have verified the utility of their process, which consists of a combination of teachers' ratings on eight dimensions, peer perceptions recorded through age-appropriate role analyses, and finally self-perceptions recorded on a scale. The evidence is collated to provide one total assessment.

21. **M. Hammer,** "A Teacher's Guide to the Detection of Emotional Disturbance in the Elementary School Child," *Journal of Learning Disabilities* 3, no. 10 (1970): 35–37.

22. **G. Spivack and M. Swift,** *Devereux Elementary School Behavior (DESB) Scale Manual* (Devon, Penn.: Devereux Foundation, 1967).

23. **G. Spivack and M. Swift,** "The Classroom Behavior of Children: A Critical Review of Teacher-Administered Rating Scales," *Journal of Special Education* 7 (1973): 55–89.

24. **D. Doughton and J. A. Fix,** "The Educational Implications of Five Behavioral Clusters," *Journal of Special Education* 12 (1978): 37–44.

25. **N. M. Lambert,** "Intellectual and Nonintellectual Predictors of High School Status," *Journal of Special Education* 6 (1972): 247–259.

In-School Screening of Children with Emotional Handicaps

Eli M. Bower
Nadine M. Lambert

What Is Meant by "Emotionally Handicapped"?

An understanding of what is meant by "emotionally handicapped" is a prerequisite for effective use of the screening process. Mental or emotional health is inferred from the degree of freedom an individual has in choosing from among alternative kinds of behavior. Conversely, mental or emotional disturbance can be inferred from individual behavior which is limited, inflexible, and restricted. Such limitations or restrictions serve to reduce the individual's relative freedom of choice in social and educational endeavors. The reduction of personal maneuverability and flexibility in a changing environment increases the individual's difficulties in adapting to the pressures and changes of life. As a result, the emotionally handicapped person shows increasing susceptibility to behavioral difficulties and interpersonal friction. . . .

Specifically, the emotionally handicapped child is defined as having moderate to marked reduction in behavioral freedom, which in turn reduces his ability to function effectively in learning or working with others. In the classroom, this loss of freedom affects the child's educative and social experiences and results in a noticeable susceptibility to one or more of these five patterns of behavior:

1. *An inability to learn which cannot be adequately explained by intellectual, sensory, neurophysiological, or general health factors.* An inability to learn is, perhaps, the single most significant characteristic of emotionally handicapped children in school. Nonlearning of this kind may be manifested as an inability to profit from *any* school learning experiences as well as an inability to master skill subjects. The non-learner may fall behind almost imperceptibly in the first few grades but finds himself in deep water by the time he reaches 4th grade. There are some students, too, who seem to be keeping pace until they reach junior high school, when they begin to flounder badly.

By whatever symptoms the inability manifests itself, we will, as educators, seek the cause or causes. And once we have ruled out intellectual, sensory, neurophysiological, and general health factors, there remain emotional conflicts and resistances to be investigated as major causes of learning disabilities.

2. *An inability to build or maintain satisfactory interpersonal relationships with peers and teachers.* It is not just "getting along" with others that is significant here. The term "satisfactory interpersonal relations" refers to the ability to demonstrate sympathy and warmth toward others, the ability to stand alone when necessary, the ability to have close friends, the ability to be aggressively constructive, and the ability to enjoy working and playing with others as well as to enjoy working and playing by oneself. In most instances, children who are unable to build or maintain satisfactory interpersonal relationships are noticed by their peers, or are most clearly *visible* to their peers. Teachers, however, are also able to identify many such children after a period of observation.

3. *Inappropriate or immature types of behavior or feelings under normal conditions.* Inappropriateness of behavior or feeling can often be sensed by the teacher and peer groups. "He acts like a baby almost all the time," or "He acts funny lots of times,"

are judgments often heard that describe such behavior. The teacher may find some children reacting to a simple command, like "Please take your seat," in wildly disparate or incongruous ways. What is appropriate or inappropriate, mature or immature, is best judged by the teacher using his professional training, his daily and long-term observation of the child, and his experience working and interacting with the behavior of large numbers of children.

4. *A general pervasive mood of unhappiness or depression.* Children who are unhappy most of the time may demonstrate such feelings in expressive play, art work, written composition, or in discussion periods. They seldom smile and usually lack a "joy of living" in their school work or social relationships. In the middle or upper grades a self-inventory is usually helpful in confirming suspicions about such feelings.

5. *A tendency to develop physical symptoms, such as speech problems, pains, or fears, associated with personal or school problems.* Often, this tendency is first noted by the child himself. Illness may be linked regularly to school pressures or develop when a child's confidence in himself is under stress. Speech difficulties resulting from emotional distress are usually painfully audible to the teacher and parent.

To sum up, then: the significant patterns of behavior in children indicating a need for closer scrutiny by a teacher are: inability to learn, unsatisfactory interpersonal relationships, inappropriate behavior, unhappiness, repetitive symptoms of illness after stress. . . .

What Is Meant by "Screening"?

A major caution in the use of the instruments and process described in this *Technical Report* is to be aware of the fact that this is a *screening* process, and is *not* intended for diagnosis or classification.

A second caution: the screening process has little to say about the causes of emotional difficulties. It has been designed to answer the question: Which children are not functioning well in a particular behavioral dimension? It cannot answer these questions: What caused the difficulty? Is the difficulty serious or minor and transitory? What can be done about it?

The purpose of screening in the area of emotional handicaps is similar to the purposes of other screening activities carried on by the school, for example, the screening programs for vision and hearing problems. To illustrate: the vision screening program in California public schools has four objectives which would be equally applicable in screening for emotional handicaps:

1. To insure early in their school careers a more adequate identification of pupils with defects;

2. To help pupils with defects to receive more intensive individual study and, if necessary, remedial services;

3. To help teachers become aware of such disabilities and to help teachers to cope with disabilities educationally;

4. To provide necessary educational adjustments for groups of pupils in the school who can profit from such programs.

Effective screening for emotional handicaps is dependent on procedures or instruments which can be administered, scored, and interpreted with the same ease and effectiveness as those for screening visual handicaps. The efficacy and economy of screening for emotional handicaps are based on the assumption that some defects or handicaps can be detected early and remedied with greater ease and less effort than handicaps allowed to develop fully. The same thoughtful professional care and discretion need to be exercised in this type of screening as in any other. Parents need to be informed about the objectives of the process and to be assured that the school will follow up the screening by advising and consulting with those parents whose children may need additional help. The administrator and the teaching staff need to understand the purposes of the program and to carry out the procedures of the process in an informed and motivated manner. The entire procedure, including the administration and scoring of each instrument, has been developed to ease the burden of work for the teacher. Effective screening, however, does not occur through effortless magic. Teachers and administrators will need to put the same effort and attention into the details of this screening process as they would into testing vision, hearing, or achievement. . . .

Certain broad criteria emerged as likely to be important in any process for the screening of children subject to or susceptible to emotional disturbance, especially in a process to be used on a large scale in many schools:

1. It should be possible to complete the screening procedure with only such information as the teacher could obtain without outside technical or professional assistance;

2. The procedure should be sufficiently simple and straightforward for the average teacher to undertake without long training or daily supervision;

3. The results of the procedure should be *tentative identification* of children with emotional problems—leading the teacher to *refer* to competent specialists those children who could benefit most from thorough diagnosis;

4. As a corollary to 3 above, the procedure should *not* encourage the teacher to diagnose emotional problems, nor to draw conclusions about their causes, nor to label or categorize children; in fact, the procedure should actively discourage the teacher from undertaking any of these highly technical interpretations;

5. The procedure should be one which neither invades the privacy of individuals nor violates good taste;

6. The procedure should be one which does not offer a threat to any child;

7. The procedure should be inexpensive to use.

With these criteria, and others that emerged as the work progressed, development was begun of screening procedures for identification of emotionally disturbed children at several different levels of schooling.

Behavior Rating of Pupils (All Grades)

One of the most important and useful kinds of information obtained by the school is the teacher's professional judgment of children's behavior. Teachers see children over a period of time in a variety of circumstances: in stress situations, at work and at play. Their judgment and observation have been sharpened by professional training and by day-to-day experience with the normal behavior of children. Often the teacher's rating can be the single most effective index of a pupil's growth and development.

Few professional persons, no matter how well-trained, can make ratings of others with absolute certainty and complete comfort. Don't spend too much time worrying about whether your rating for a particular child is "right" or "wrong." Make your best judgment of each student, then go on to the next. Remember that it is not your judgment alone that will be used to determine whether or not a pupil is developing emotional difficulties. Your perception of a child's behavior will be combined with the perceptions of the child himself and those of his peers—to make the final judgment about screening a child.

The Class Pictures (Peer Rating—Kindergarten to Grade 3)

After you have completed the *Behavior Rating of Pupils*, your next step in screening is to plan for administration of the peer ratings. The peer rating instrument for kindergarten and primary grades, *The Class Pictures*, must be given to each child in your class individually. This may take fifteen to twenty minutes of time for each child. Administration of *The Class Pictures* to the entire class, however, may be spread over a period of time—up to, but not exceeding, one month.

Administer the instrument to children one at a time when the rest of the class is engaged in seat work of some kind or occupied in other activities which do not require constant supervision. Such a schedule will require a minimum of interruption in your regular teaching program.

The Class Pictures are composed of twelve picture cards with a total of twenty scoring items (one or two items on a card). Five of the items are pictures of boys in situations related to emotionally maladjusted behavior; five are pictures of girls in situations related to emotionally maladjusted behavior; five are pictures of boys in situations related to positive or neutral types of behavior; and five are pictures of girls in situations related to positive or neutral types of behavior.

The Class Pictures have been developed as a means of analyzing, in a systematic and measurable way, how children are perceived or "seen" by their peers. The responses of most pupils to the pictures will not surprise you. Some responses, however, may seem unrealistic and inappropriate. *Accept each child's responses without comment unless the child obviously misunderstands directions.* Your role during the administration of *The Class Pictures* is one of test proctor and recorder of responses.

The Class Pictures are used with children who have not yet learned to read or write well. Therefore, the responses of each child will need to be recorded individually by you. You will, of course, have to make special provision for the rest of the class while you are administering *Class Pictures* to individual children. If an additional school person is available, he may work with the class while you administer *Class Pictures*. The actual administration should always be done by you. If you are able to organize the class into working groups, *Class Pictures* may be administered to a few individuals daily during such work periods—but you will decide for yourself how best to accomplish this task.

On the test each child is asked to consider which of his classmates is most like the child in every one of the twenty situations. Some children will pick twenty different names. Others may name one or two peers for several or many different items. Still others may make no response for one or more items. *Do not expect any fixed pattern of responses.*

When the responses for every child in the class are collected, the teacher can tally the number of times a particular child is chosen for each of the twenty pictures. The total number of times a child is chosen for *all* of the pictures indicates how clearly or how vividly he is "seen," or perceived, by his peers.

The number of times a pupil is picked for the ten *negative* pictures indicates the degree to which he or she is *negatively* perceived by his peers. By dividing the number of times a child is picked for the ten negative pictures by the total number of times he is picked for all twenty of the pictures, a per cent, indicating the ratio of negative perception by peers, is obtained and used in screening.

The mean or average number of negative selections of emotionally handicapped boys and girls has been found to be significantly different from the mean number of negative selections in the general school population of that grade and sex. Consequently, the per cent of negative perception has been found to be a reliable indicator of those children whose behavior, as observed by peers, indicates some degree of emotional difficulty. The higher the per cent, the greater the possibility that the child has emotional problems. The per cent of negative selections on *The Class Pictures*, when combined with teacher ratings and self-ratings, has been found effective in primary grades for screening children with emotional handicaps.

A Class Play (Peer Rating—Grades 3–7)

A Class Play is a peer rating instrument with greatest applicability in grades 4, 5, and 6, though it has been used with success in grades 3 and 7. It should be administered reasonably soon after you have completed the *Behavior Rating of Pupils*. It should take no more than 35 to 45 minutes.

Section I of the instrument contains descriptions of twenty hypothetical roles in a play, with instructions directing each pupil to choose a classmate who would be most suitable and natural in each of the roles. A second section of the *Play* (Section II) elicits from each pupil an indication of the roles he would prefer, or which he thinks other people would select for him. This section has thirty different quartets of the twenty roles, with a question aimed at finding out how the child sees himself in relation to each role.

The scoring of *A Class Play* is very much like

the scoring of *The Class Pictures*. Each pupil names a classmate for each of the roles in the play. By counting the number of times a pupil is picked for each of the roles in the play, and then counting the number of times each pupil is picked for the *even numbered* (negative) roles, a percentage is obtained indicative of the positive or negative perception of each pupil by his classmates. This score is used in the screening. . . .

Student Survey (Peer Rating— Grades 7–12)

The *Student Survey* is the peer rating instrument for use in the junior and senior high schools. In order for this test to have validity, it is necessary to administer it to a class in which the students have had an opportunity for some social and intellectual interaction, as well as for observation of one another in a variety of classroom situations. Previous work with this test has shown that social studies or English classes are usually best for this purpose.

Some students in the junior and senior high school may be sensitive to the kinds of questions asked on the *Student Survey*. It is important, therefore, that you anticipate the possibility of such sensitivity and take steps to allay any suspicion or resentment. For example, some teachers have found it helpful to have ready an envelope into which all the tests can be placed when the students are finished. This helps to reassure the class that the test results are confidential and reinforces statements made in the instructions that the results will not be discussed with others.

Section I of the *Student Survey* consists of twenty items. Ten are illustrative of maladjusted or emotionally disturbed behavior and ten are illustrative of neutral or positive behavior. For each statement of behavior, the students are asked to list the name of a classmate who is most like the student described in the item.

Section II of the *Student Survey* contains the same twenty behavior statements randomly arranged in thirty groups of four statements each. The student is asked to select one of the four statements in each group as the one which he thinks others in the class might apply to himself. The responses to Section II can be used to compare the peer ratings of a student with his self-rating. The value of providing two sections in the *Student Survey*, a peer rating and a self-rating on the same items, is that, after scoring both sections, the teacher is able to measure and analyze how a student sees himself in relation to how he is seen by others. . . .

A Picture Game (Self Rating— Kindergarten to Grade 3)

A Picture Game is designed to give a measure of young children's perception of *self*. It is used along with the *Behavior Rating of Pupils* (teacher rating) and *The Class Pictures* (peer rating) to identify pupils who are vulnerable to, or handicapped by, emotional problems.

A Picture Game consists of 66 pictures, including two sample pictures. Each picture is illustrative of normal home and school relationships and events. With the exception of the two sample cards and the first ten pictures, each picture is emotionally neutral in the portrayal of the relationship or event. The child is asked to sort each picture into one of two categories: "This is a happy picture" or "This is a sad picture." The sorting is done by placing each picture in the "happy" or "sad" side of a two-compartment box which has a happy face shown on one compartment and a sad face on the other. The child categorizes each picture in accordance with his perception of it.

The first ten pictures the child sorts are stereotypes: obviously happy or obviously sad situations. The purpose of including them in the test items is to check on each pupil's understanding of the task. If a child sorts the first ten pictures correctly, you can be fairly sure that he has understood the process well enough for you to use his score in screening. If, on the other hand, he does not sort the first ten pictures correctly, you will need to meet with him individually and ask him to sort the pictures again for you, making certain that he understands the process. Some children *choose* to place pictures differently from others. If you find that such children understand the process but continue, on readministration, to sort the pictures in an independent fashion, make a note of it on the "Class Record Sheet," and use the child's score in screening. . . .

Thinking about Yourself (Self Rating—Grades 3–7)

The purpose of *Thinking about Yourself* is to elicit from the pupil himself an *intra-self* measure of the relationship between a pupil's perception of his environment and his conception of what it ought to be. What is looked for is the degree of discrepancy between a pupil's self perception and an ideal self, between his perception of himself as he *is* and as he would like to be.

Many pupils with serious emotional problems cannot bring themselves to disclose their difficulties in writing, or are uncomfortable about disclosing them. Their responses will therefore very much resemble those of other children in the class. These youngsters are most likely to be screened by teachers and peers.

There are other pupils, however, who do not manifest their difficulties to teachers or peers, but who rise to the opportunity to express inner discomfort and *can* communicate their disturbance on a self rating instrument. Since the average discrepancy between self and *ideal* self has been found to discriminate between pupils with emotional problems and those with normal behavior adjustment, *Thinking about Yourself* provides a meaningful and useful screening dimension not available from teacher or peer ratings. . . .

A Self Test (Self Rating— Grades 7–12)

A Self Test is intended to obtain a measure of the difference between the way a pupil sees himself and the way he would like to be—in other words, a measure of the difference between self and ideal self. To the extent that a student is able to disclose the differences or similarities between these two aspects of self, the instrument is useful in screening. However, some pupils with moderate or serious emotional problems cannot bring themselves to disclose the discomfort or dissatisfaction which this instrument invites them to disclose. Their responses, therefore, will very much resemble those of other students in the class. These youngsters are more likely to be identified by teachers and peers in the screening process.

There are other pupils, however, who do not manifest their difficulties to teachers or peers, but who rise to the opportunity to express inner discomfort and *can* communicate their disturbance on a self rating. For these students, the *Self Test* provides the opportunity. Since the average discrepancy between self and *ideal* self has been found to discriminate between pupils with emotional problems and those with normal behavior adjustment, *A Self Test* provides a meaningful screening dimension not available from teacher or peer ratings.

A Self Test contains forty statements describing people behaving in a number of different ways. In Section I, the student is asked to indicate how strongly he *would like* to be or *would not like* to be the person described. In Section II, the items are repeated and the student is asked to indicate how strongly he feels he *is* like or *is not* like the person described. The two responses by the student (i.e., whether or not he *wants* to be like and whether or not he *is* like) are then compared in the scoring process, after which the amount of discrepancy between the two "selves" is compared. . . .

Editors' Commentary

These procedures cover three domains—teacher, pupil, and peers. Other domains—parents, specialists, and institutional stress—complete the inner and outer ecological model. What is needed is a total institutional mental health index of the stress-support provided a particular pupil by a given school environment. Sarason's School Anxiety Scale[26] and other devices that sense the pupil's perception of his or her relationship to teachers and subject matter contain the makings of such an index. Many existing rating scales, each with a specific purpose, help the teacher objectify judgments about pupils. For example, Kvaraceus has developed the *KD Proneness Scale and Check List* for early identification of delinquents.[27] His insightful work contains observations for all types of screening.

More complex screening batteries have been proposed by many authors. One is Bruce Saunders, excerpted below, who has proposed a screening-identification-diagnosis-prescriptive sequence, which depends initially on the teacher and turns subsequently to more specialized personnel for intensive diagnostic efforts.

26. **Seymour B. Sarason,** *Anxiety in Elementary School Children* (New York: John Wiley & Sons, 1960).

27. **William C. Kvaraceus,** "Early Identification and Prediction," in *Anxious Youth: Dynamics of Delinquency* (Columbus, Ohio: Charles E. Merrill, 1966).

A Procedure for the Screening, Identification, and Diagnosis of Emotionally Disturbed Children in the Rural Elementary School

Bruce T. Saunders

Several problems have been delineated that seriously interfere with the development of educational programs for the emotionally disturbed child in rural areas (Saunders, 1971). Noted among these problems are specific demographic-geographic considerations, low per-capita income, lack of trained personnel, and the lack of any real impetus and direction from any authoritative sources within the rural states. For example, at the time of the preparation of this manuscript there are two classes for the emotionally disturbed in the state of Maine on the public school level, one in Waterville and one in Bangor. In addition to these two classes, the Division of Special Education, Area of the Emotionally Disturbed, University of Maine at Orono will operate three or four Special Resource Classes for emotionally disturbed children as internship experiences for graduate students. Essentially, there will be six classes for emotionally disturbed children in the public schools of Maine. The current level of services for the education of disturbed children is quite minimal in Maine, and it is very unlikely we can expect any serious commitments to programs within the near future.

If one considers the current school enrollment in the state of Maine as of June 1970 (241,198 Total, 175,525 K-8, 65,673 High School[1] in relation to the generally accepted estimate of incidence of serious emotional disturbance in children, which ranges from 4 percent to 12 percent (Lambert & Bower, 1961), we are concerned with a minimum of 7,000 children. Further, Glidewell and Swallow (1968) have reported that if one considers mild as well as moderate and severe emotional handicapping conditions the estimate of incidence is as high as 30 percent, and we then are concerned with 52,658 children in K-8 alone. Glidewell and Swallow (1968) have indicated clearly that estimates of incidence vary considerably with individual screenings of emotionally disturbed children and, obviously, once an initial screening has been completed there exists some responsibility on the part of the schools to provide programs for those children for whom such programming is indicated.

The SID Program

The author, in conjunction with several graduate students, has developed a relatively efficient and inexpensive procedure for the screening, identification, and diagnosis of emotionally disturbed children in the rural elementary school. The procedure is referred to as SID (Screening, Identification, and Diagnosis) and has been developed to be directed by an SID Coordinator and administered by the classroom teacher. The goal of this program was twofold: (a) to provide a badly needed service to children in rural school communities; and (b) to continue to develop the level of sophistication and competence of the graduate student to deal with emotionally disturbed children (Saunders, 1971).

Screening

Screening refers to a gross estimate of the total number of children in a school system who are in need of specific identification in order to determine the actual incidence of emotional disturbance. Screening is based upon the use of a modified form of the Lambert and Bower Behavior Rating of Pupils. Screening indicates which children, by name, should be considered for the identification phase of the SID program.

The screening phase of the SID program is organized by an SID Coordinator and is administered by the teacher. SID Coordinators are trained at the University of Maine, and the SID program is considered a tool in the special educators' areas of specialization. The procedure requires approximately one minute per child of the teacher's time. It requires 30 minutes for a teacher to complete a BRS [Behavior Rating Scale] for each of 30 children in her class, which then are returned to the SID Coordinator for analysis.

The SID Coordinator scores each BRS by adding the ratings for each of the eight categories, but omits the rating 3. The total score is referred to as the BRS raw score. After the BRS raw scores from high to low are calculated, the child with the highest raw score on the BRS in the class is given rank number 1. Tied ranks are handled in the traditional manner; namely, the mean rank for the tied-rank position is utilized for the tied scores.

After the SID Coordinator has rank ordered the BRS, the highest 40 percent of the rank-ordered BRS then are considered in the identification phase of the SID procedure. Our initial research in the

SID procedure indicated that the top 30 percent of the rank ordered BRS will have areas of significant emotional disturbance or behavior disorder in the identification phase of the program. With many classes, the correlation was still significant when we included the top 35 percent of the BRS. Therefore, the top 40 percent of the BRS must be utilized in the identification phase. If a teacher has a class of 30 pupils, at least the top 12 rank-ordered BRS scores should be considered in the identification phase of the SID program. In each of 11 classes studied in developing the SID program, correlations significant at the .05 level consistently were observed between the BRS X Burke Behavior Rating Scales for the top 35 percent of the ranked BRSs (Ayer, 1971).

The screening phase of the SID program is utilized because it provides a considerable saving in time and money. The screening of a class of 30 pupils takes approximately one hour, including the work of the Coordinator. The identification phase requires approximately 20 minutes per child of teacher's time. The screening phase saves a great deal of time, since only 40 percent of the original class needs to be considered in the identification phase. If the identification phase were utilized without the initial screening, the teacher would be required to spend 11 hours of her time for a class of 30 pupils and the Coordinator would spend an additional 7½ hours. Further, the screening costs the school $.25 per child and the identification costs $1.00 per child. A considerable financial savings is realized through initial screening prior to the identification phase.

Identification

Identification refers to a considerably more sophisticated procedure that generally indicates which children will require specific diagnostic evaluation and indicates the nature of the diagnostic evaluation, i.e., personality assessment, intelligence testing, testing for specific learning disability, neurological assessment, etc.

The identification phase of the SID program employs the Burke Behavior Rating Scales, which also are organized by the SID Coordinator and administered by the classroom teacher. The Burke Scales are best employed subsequent to a brief training session with the teachers conducted by the SID Coordinator. Approximately half an hour should be allotted for this purpose. The SID Coordinator should instruct the teacher to complete the Burke Scales on the top 40 percent of the rank-ordered BRS and supply the teacher with the names of the children whose BRS scores placed

them in the referred group. The SID Coordinator should not indicate specifically why these children have been selected for further evaluation. After the teacher completes the Burke Scales, they are returned to the Coordinator for analysis.

After he has scored the Burke Behavior Rating Scales as indicated in the manual, the Coordinator interprets the profile to determine whether the pupil will require further diagnostic evaluation (Burke, 1969).

The Burke Scales contain 116 items that cluster into the following 20 factors:

1. Excessive self-blame
2. Excessive anxiety
3. Excessive withdrawal
4. Excessive dependency
5. Poor ego strength
6. Poor physical strength
7. Poor coordination
8. Poor intellectuality
9. Poor academics
10. Poor attention
11. Poor impulse control
12. Poor reality contact
13. Poor sense of identity
14. Excessive suffering
15. Poor anger control
16. Excessive sense of persecution
17. Excessive sexuality
18. Excessive aggressiveness
19. Excessive resistance
20. Poor social conformity

When he analyzes the profiles, the SID Coordinator will observe that each of the 20 factors will have three columns into which the raw scores obtained on the factor (sum of the items included in the factor) will fall. The raw score will fall into one of the three columns: Not Significant, Significant, or Very Significant. Any child who attains a score in the Significant or Very Significant range should be considered for further diagnostic evaluation. The determination for specific referral for diagnostic evaluation follows careful consideration of the meaning of the factor and the extent of the deviation. Further, pattern analysis as well as spike analysis should be considered in referral for diagnostic evaluation (Burke, 1968).

The Burke Behavior Rating Scales provide diagnostic information by identifying:

1. Patterns of disturbed behavior that distinguish among several groups of children.

2. Changes in behavior patterns over a period of time.

3. Areas in a child's personality where further evaluation might take place advantageously.

4. Information useful to school personnel to be utilized in parent conferences.

5. Which children will do well in special classes.

Diagnosis

When further diagnosis is not indicated, the Burke Manual suggests specific programming for mild and moderate levels of difficulty. When diagnosis is indicated, the SID Coordinator will determine whether the referral should be a request for a complete evaluation or whether specific diagnostic information is indicated. The SID Coordinator may determine whether neurological, educational, psychological, psychiatric, or pediatric consultation is indicated. In some cases, social welfare agencies should be consulted.

Diagnosis refers to the integrated evaluation of specific areas of psychological-educational functioning and includes intellectual, achievement, projective, educational, developmental, and sociometric assessment. In addition, specific medical and neurological evaluation may be indicated. The diagnosis phase of the SID program may follow from a recommendation based upon the results of the screening and identification phase or, in the case of clinically observable false negative, from direct behavioral observation and teacher referral.

Generally, the SID Coordinator is not prepared to complete a full diagnostic evaluation. When a child requires specific diagnostic evaluation beyond the training of the Coordinator, three resources for evaluation are available in the state of Maine: Community Mental Health Centers, licensed psychological examiners, and licensed psychologists. Some of the SID Coordinators are prepared and qualified to perform specific diagnostic evaluations.

The diagnostic evaluation should be reported in a manner that is meaningful to school personnel. It is the responsibility of the SID Coordinator to provide appropriate feedback of the diagnostic evaluation and to prescribe specific educational programming for each child based upon the results of the evaluation.

Some of the more frequently employed diagnostic instrumentation includes:

1. Detailed developmental history

2. Detailed educational history

3. Wechsler Intelligence Scale for Children (WISC)

4. Stanford-Binet (Form L-M)

5. Illinois Test of Psycholinguistic Ability (ITPA)

6. Peabody Picture Vocabulary Test (PPVT)

7. Children's Apperception Test (CAT)

8. Thematic Apperception Test (TAT)

9. Bender-Gestalt

10. Wide Range Achievement Test (WRAT)

11. Vineland Social Maturity Scale

12. Rorschach Psychodiagnostic Techniques

13. Rating Scales (Devereux Elementary School Behavior Rating Scale, Burke Behavior Rating Scale, etc.)

14. Standardized achievement testing

15. Detroit Tests of Learning Aptitude

The SID Coordinator should be responsible for items 1, 2, 13, and 14, which should accompany a referral for diagnostic evaluation.

It is crucial that the reader understand and be committed to the principle stated by Caplan (1964):

It is insufficient merely to identify the vulnerable child. One serious limitation even of highly sensitive early identification is the lack of available resources for remediation and follow-through.

The SID Coordinator is thoroughly trained in appropriate prescriptive techniques and further is able to utilize community resources to the child's best advantage. School personnel should be committed to programming for individual children before they request the SID program in their districts. In addition, the Division of Special Education is preparing an authoritative manuscript that will detail a number of models for the delivery of Special Education Programming in rural areas. This manuscript will be available to interested educators and will be subject to constant revision as new models are developed.

The author is involved in a continuing research and demonstration project, the objective of which is to refine the SID program. Further research will be reported in the literature as projects are completed.

Note

1. Telephone conversation between Commissioner of Education, State of Maine, and David Johnson, graduate student at the University of Maine.

References

Ayer, J. The paired use of the Teacher Rating Scale of the Lambert and Bower Behavior Rating Scale and the Burke's Behavior Rating Scale to screen public school population for deviant behavior. Unpublished manuscript, University of Maine.

Burke, H. H. *Manual for the Burke's Behavior Rating Scale.* El Monte, Calif.: Arden Press, 1969.

Caplan, G. *Principles of preventive psychiatry.* New York: Basic Books, 1964.

Glidewell, J. C., & Swallow, C. S. The prevalence of maladjustment in elementary schools. *Joint Commission on Mental Health of Children.* Chicago: University of Chicago Press, 1968.

Lambert, N. M., & Bower, E. M. A process for in-school screening of children with emotional handicaps. *Technical Report,* California State Department of Education, Sacramento, California. Princeton, N.J.: Educational Testing Service, 1961.

Saunders, B. T. Emotional disturbance and social position within the non-graded classroom. *Psychology in the Schools,* 1970, 7, 269–271.

Saunders, B. T. Meeting special educational needs in rural Maine. Paper presented at Council for Exceptional Children, Topical Conference, Memphis, Tennessee, December 1971.

From *Psychology in the Schools,* vol. 9, no. 2 (1972), pp. 159–164. Reprinted with permission.

Strategies for Diagnosis and Identification of Children with Behavior and Learning Problems

Elizabeth Munsterberg Koppitz

The selection of strategies for the diagnosis and identification of behavior and learning problems in children will depend in part on the youngsters' age and on the purpose of such diagnoses. Older pupils are usually evaluated in order to provide effective remedial or therapeutic help for existing problems; while school beginners are frequently assessed so as to prevent or minimize potential problems. Most children, age 8 and older, with serious emotional or learning disorders have already had difficulties in kindergarten and the primary grades, but not all pupils with problems in the early grades have serious difficulties later on (Keogh, 1970; Koppitz, 1973b; Kraus, 1973).

The strategies a diagnostician employs will also be influenced by his or her theoretical frame of reference and the basic assumptions held concerning behavior and learning problems. On the basis of my own research and experience I hypothesize that behavior and learning problems are not two distinct and separate types of disorders, but that both are highly interrelated and are usually different aspects of children's overall functioning (Koppitz, 1971, 1973a). Children with serious diffi-

culties in school tend to demonstrate more than just one type of symptom or problem. For instance, a pupil referred for psychological evaluation because of severe reading problems may also show difficulties in language skills and memory, as well as hyperactivity, distractibility, emotional maladjustment, poor peer relationships, and he may have a very unstable home situation to contend with.

There is no one-to-one relationship between any single symptom or characteristic of a child and his social adjustment or progress in school (Koppitz, 1973b). A pupil's behavior and achievement result from an interaction of many factors both within the child and in the environment.

I have also learned that the most obvious symptom or problem of a youngster is not necessarily the most serious one. Take the case of Willie, age eight, who did not talk until he was three, and was unintelligible long after that. From age four on his concerned parents, teachers and a language therapist treated Willie like a child whose only problem was the language impairment. They focussed all their remedial efforts on his language development. They neglected to discover that

Willie also had severe problems in visual-motor perception, oral-visual integration, and memory, that he was highly distractible, restless, and concretistic, that his self-concept was poor, and that he could not relate to his peers. In fact some of these other problems exceeded in severity his language impairment.

The diagnostic label a child receives depends often on whether he was seen by a psychiatrist, a reading specialist, an optometrist, a language therapist, or a psychologist. Each expert tends to concentrate on his area of expertise, yet a meaningful evaluation has to involve the whole child and, if possible, a team of diagnosticians. A youngster's diagnostic label determines too often the treatment and educational program the pupil will receive. Diagnostic labels have their place, but they rarely provide useful information for educators or therapists working with a child. A detailed description and explanation of the child's areas of strengths and weaknesses are usually much more instructive.

It is important to realize that pupils' symptoms and characteristics change as they get older. The majority of children seen for evaluation in the primary grades are referred for "learning problems." They tend to exhibit many so called "soft" neurological signs such as impulsivity, hyperactivity, disorganization, poor coordination and intersensory-integration, perceptual and memory problems. When middle or high school students are referred for evaluation their teachers regard them as being primarily "emotionally disturbed," or "behavior problems." In fact, they do tend to have emotional and social problems, but these are only part of their difficulties. The school records usually show that these pupils also had "soft" neurological signs and learning problems in the early grades. As youngsters mature many of the earlier symptoms disappear or become less obvious, while secondary emotional and behavior problems become more apparent. It is therefore important to take the entire school history of older pupils into account while making a diagnosis. When developing an educational program for a child, a description of his past and present functioning is more meaningful than a diagnostic label.

With these considerations in mind, I propose that we need to explore at least six different areas in order to understand a child with behavior and learning problems. Each of these six areas exists as a continuum and may reveal various degrees of strengths or weaknesses. Furthermore the six dimensions all interact, yet they are also quite distinct from each other in that a pupil can have problems in any one of them and not in the other five. The six areas are:

1. *Inner control* involves a child's concentration, attention span, frustration tolerance, ability to cope with sudden changes or failure, restlessness, hyper- or hypoactivity, rigidity, perseveration, moodiness, etc.

2. *Intersensory integration* is concerned with the youngster's perceptual-motor integration, sequencing and recall in the various sense modalities, integration within and across sense modalities, short- and long-term memory, and oral and written expression.

3. *Reasoning* encompasses pupils' common sense, abstracting reasoning, and their ability to benefit from experience.

4. *Emotional adjustment* reflects the child's self-concept, his fears, motivation, anxieties, ways of coping with problems, and satisfactions.

5. *Social adjustment* relates to youngsters' attitudes toward parents, siblings, peers, and teachers; it involves their functioning in group situations, their acceptance by others, and the degree of their being influenced by leading others.

6. *Developmental and social background* deals with the developmental and medical history of children, their socio-cultural affiliations, value system, and significant events in their families, such as the birth of a sibling, serious illness or death of a family member, intense parental conflict or separation, frequent moves or changes of school.

It is hypothesized that the areas of *Inner Control, Intersensory Integration*, and *Reasoning* depend on the maturity and intactness of children's Central Nervous System, that is, that they have an organic basis. Obviously very young children whose Central Nervous System has not yet fully developed will have less adequate inner control, intersensory integration, and reasoning ability than older more mature youngsters. Minimal brain dysfunction, regardless of its etiology, will also affect these three areas. Minimal brain dysfunction may result from many different causes, including prenatal or birth trauma, serious accidents or illnesses, developmental lags, genetic factors, severe early deprivation, chemical poisoning, or other as yet unknown causes. Children's *Emotional* and *Social Adjustment* are mainly based on their experiences with the significant people in their home and in the community. Thus neurological, developmental, medical, and social factors all have to be taken into consideration when diagnosing children's problems and when planning for them.

Pupils may have difficulties in any one of the six areas outlined above and may still be average or even above average students *provided* the other five areas are intact and strong. For example, it is no great handicap for children to be hyperactive, if they are bright, well integrated, have self-confidence, can get along with others, and have a stable, supportive home. In fact such youngsters often become successful athletes, teachers, or salesmen (Steward and Olds, 1973).

Similarly children with poor visual-motor perception may be good students, if they are intelligent, well controlled, if their motivation and language skills are good, and if they have good social relationships and interested, helpful parents (Koppitz, 1973b). It is also apparent that limited reasoning ability (but not retardation) need not grossly interfere with a youngster's school progress, if he has outstanding athletic ability and no other marked difficulties. Teachers will also put up with children who have emotional or social problems, as long as the pupils are not too disruptive, have sufficient control, are of average mental ability, and are able to learn. Most remarkable are the "invulnerable" children (Pines, 1975) who come from deprived or unstable homes and who are nevertheless well adjusted and good students; the same is often true of youngsters with histories of birth trauma or neurological impairment. A single symptom or factor will not determine children's behavior or achievement.

It seems that a youngster can compensate for problems in any one of the areas, if the difficulties are not too extreme and if there are no serious problems in the other five areas. Children who are referred for evaluation because of behavior or learning problems tend to have difficulties in at least two, more often in three or four of the six areas. It is not uncommon to find that pupils with learning disabilities exhibit poor inner control, immaturity in intersensory integration and recall, emotional and social maladjustment, and a history of high fever attacks with convulsions in infancy.

The question to be asked is not whether a child is emotionally disturbed *or* neurologically impaired, or whether he is educationally handicapped *or* socially maladjusted, but rather whether he suffers *more* from one problem and *less* from another one. A hierarchy of difficulties has to be determined for each youngster. All six areas should be evaluated for each child, and the findings should then be ranked according to their severity; the educational and treatment program devised for a given pupil should be based on this hierarchical system rather than on a diagnostic label. For some children immediate psychiatric intervention or family counseling is essential before they can even begin to cope with an academic school program.

For others a realistic adjustment of the teacher's expectations and of the demands made at home and in school will automatically lead to a reduction in anxiety and to a lessening of behavior problems.

What is the best strategy for obtaining information about the six areas for an individual child? There are at least five different sources that can provide such information:

(a) *Observation of the child* in class, in the halls, in the cafeteria, on the playground. A great deal can be learned about a pupil's inner control, intelligence, emotional and social adjustment just from observing the youngster in different situations.

(b) *Teachers' reports* are indispensable; teachers work with the children daily and know more about them than any diagnostician can find out in one brief diagnostic session.

(c) *The Cumulative School Record* of a pupil can provide valuable information about the youngster's learning pattern over the years. Especially for older pupils it is essential to find out how they functioned in the primary grades, and whether there was any sudden change in their behavior and achievement. Children's school histories can show their rate of progress and the type of help they have received in the past and how much they were able to benefit from it.

(d) *A conference with the parents* and a look at the school health records can provide much information about the pupil's developmental and medical histories and about their socio-cultural background. Such information is important in order to understand the attitudes of the family toward the youngster's problems. For instance, a serious learning difficulty in the only son of an ambitious family will be viewed very differently by the parents than learning problems in one of several daughters of a family that does not consider education for girls very important. If possible, information about children should also be obtained from any clinic, social agency, therapist, or tutor who is working with the youngsters.

(e) *Testing and an interview with the child* can give first hand information about the youngster's own perception of his problems, and can gather objective data about his integration and recall, his reasoning and his achievement level. The child's functioning can then be compared with that of other pupils of his age and grade level, and with his own previous record. Personality tests can shed light on the youngster's conflicts, concerns, and attitudes.

A meaningful evaluation and diagnosis should make use of all of these sources of information. If at all possible the youngsters should be seen by a diagnostic team consisting of a psychologist, language and reading specialists, and pediatric neurologist or psychiatrist. But even if this is not feasible, a considerable amount of information can be gathered from available sources. The amount of information needed will depend to some extent on the age of the youngsters, on the severity of the problems presented, and on the purpose of the evaluation. A complete evaluation of an individual child will require, of course, more information than would the screening of groups of pupils for the identification of learning and behavior problems.

A word about screening school beginners is in order. It is difficult to diagnose serious learning problems in kindergarten or first grade pupils who have not yet been taught how to read and write and who are, for the most part, still too immature to be able to do so. At the time of school entry one can only identify "high risk" (Keogh, 1970) or vulnerable children who may or may not develop serious difficulties in school later on. Despite this uncertainty it seems both more beneficial and economical to use a preventive approach and to give special consideration and support to all vulnerable youngsters, even if some of them might be able to function in school without extra assistance, than waiting and offering special help only after serious problems have fully developed. Elsewhere (Koppitz, 1971, 1975) I have outlined screening procedures for identifying high risk children at the beginning and end of kindergarten or at the beginning of the first grade. With very young children particular attention has to be given to developmental and medical factors, to behavior observations by an experienced teacher, to some brief screening tests, and to the youngsters' birthdates. A child who is very immature for his age *and* who is also young for his class has a double handicap.

When older children are seen for evaluation it is just as important to determine what they are good at as [it is to determine] what their problems are. Even though every effort should be made to remediate specific learning difficulties most children learn best and are taught most successfully by building on their areas of strength. Since most learning problems have at least in part an organic basis they do not just disappear. They tend to improve in time with good teaching and with maturation, but even at best educationally handicapped pupils have to learn to compensate for remaining difficulties and have to learn to function in spite of their weaknesses. It is suggested that middle and high school students with behavior and learning problems participate in conferences with their parents and teachers and share in the diagnostic findings and in the planning of educational programs.

Summary

Children with behavior and learning problems tend to show a combination of different symptoms and difficulties rather than any single difficulty. The youngsters' symptoms change as they get older. Furthermore the most obvious symptom is not necessarily the most serious problem a pupil has. Most children with behavior problems also have some learning difficulties and vice versa. The diagnostic label a child receives often depends on the person who evaluates the youngster. Diagnostic labels are often of limited usefulness when designing a meaningful educational or therapeutic program for children. A description of the pupil's functioning in different areas is of greater value.

In order to understand and diagnose problems in a pupil it is important to evaluate the entire child, and to consider at least six different areas. Three of these, Inner Control, Intersensory Integration and Memory, and Reasoning, are based on the Central Nervous System; two other areas, Emotional and Social Adjustment, are mainly based on the youngster's experiences; the sixth area involves the children's developmental, medical, and social backgrounds. Information concerning these six areas can be derived from observation of the child, teachers' reports, cumulative school records, parent interviews, and from interviewing and testing the pupils.

The screening of school beginners is essential to identify "high risk" or vulnerable children. Even though not all vulnerable children necessarily develop serious problems later on, all children with severe behavior and learning problems in later years had difficulty in kindergarten and are vulnerable. Many later learning difficulties can be avoided or minimized if the high risk children are identified early and are permitted to progress at their own slow rate without undue pressure in small, supportive classes, and are given special help.

References

Keogh, B. K. *Proceedings of a Conference: Early Identification of Children with Potential Learning Problems.* University of California at Los Angeles, 1970.

Koppitz, E. M. *Children with Learning Disabilities: A five year follow-up study.* New York: Grune & Stratton, 1971.

Koppitz, E. M. Visual Aural Digit Span Test performance of boys with emotional and learning problems. *Journal of Clinical Psychology*, 1973, 29, 463–466. (a)

Koppitz, E. M. Bender Gestalt Test performance and school achievement: A nine year study. *Psychology in the Schools*, 1973, 10, 280–284. (b)

Koppitz, E. M. *The Bender Gestalt Test for Young Children. Volume 2: Research and Application 1963–1973.* New York: Grune & Stratton, 1975.

Kraus, P. E. *Yesterday's Children.* New York: John Wiley & Sons, 1973.

Pines, M. In praise of "Invulnerables." *APA Monitor*, 1975, 6(12), 7.

Steward, M. A. and Olds, S. W. *Raising a Hyperactive Child.* New York: Harper & Row, 1973.

Reprinted from *Journal of Behavioral Disorders* 2 (May 1977), pp. 136–140, by permission of The Council for Exceptional Children. Copyright 1977 by The Council for Exceptional Children.

Editors' Commentary

The selection reprinted next, by Rabinovitch and Ingram, is notable for the insight of its observations of a series of cases seen in a psychiatric setting. The article is part of a series of studies leading to the development of a new scale through the examination of test data and the "sensing" of interview and case-history material. Three major diagnostic groupings are formulated. We do not know in what percentages these types are found, but we do see clearly what they are. Then the syndrome of "primary retardation" is developed in detail with concrete examples. The generalizations drawn from the cases and the etiology are woven into the practical implications for treatment.

Neuropsychiatric Considerations in Reading Retardation

Ralph D. Rabinovitch
Winifred Ingram

A close, interdependent relationship between our schools and our psychiatric clinics and hospitals is generally recognized as essential for effective work with school age children. Two relatively new developments have further highlighted the need for this integration of effort. On the one hand there is the rapid growth of special education classes for the emotionally disturbed in the public schools, and on the other hand expansion of specialized classroom programs in psychiatric day-care and in-patient centers (6).

In our work in both public school and psychiatric settings we have been impressed with the high incidence of reading and language problems among the total referrals. We have been particularly interested to note that in those schools that have developed special psychiatric or social adjustment rooms, the regular classroom teachers have tended to recommend children with both personality and gross reading problems. Even severe distur-

bance tends to be found tolerable in the classroom if the child is making adequate academic progress. This was not anticipated when some of these programs were established and we now find teachers trained to work with the emotionally disturbed faced with virtually illiterate children whose special remedial needs they do not feel competent to meet. Similarly, through bitter experience, we have learned that for a significant percentage of the *boys* admitted to Hawthorn Center's day-care or in-patient units, psychotherapy and milieu therapy alone are insufficient for rehabilitation; intensive specific remedial reading therapy must be added. Of necessity, then, our multidiscipline group has been forced to give major research and clinical attention to reading problems.

A severe burden imposed on child, family and clinic worker alike is the tendency of many school people and pediatricians to refer the child with the assumption that the psychiatric clinic will find the learning problem to be due to an "emotional block" and that through the magic of psychotherapy, perhaps limited to a few interviews, the child will be "released" to learn adequately. Unfortunately some of us in child psychiatry and clinical psychology have fostered this attitude in the past, overgeneralizing dynamic formulations. The problem is much more complex and there is a need for careful differential diagnosis in each case studied.

Two broad factors in the child's reading functioning must be assessed: (1) The mastery of specific techniques and skills necessary for reading; (2) The application of skills in the learning situation.

In recent years there has been a valid emphasis by educators on content in learning, on the social meaningfulness of what is taught, and this has led to many positive changes in curriculum. Repetitive drill work has been reduced in both language and arithmetic, much to the benefit of the victims of schooling. In the large majority of children, reading skills tend to evolve spontaneously, stimulated and directed by good teachers. With these children content becomes the major concern. But, unfortunately, there are some for whom written material remains meaningless and for whom there can be no content because the *technique* of reading itself is lacking. Despite the highest level of motivation and effort, they have difficulty learning to translate letter symbols into concepts. The *process of symbolization* is impaired and learning through "normal" teaching methods cannot be expected.

In some of these cases history indicates brain injury (encephalopathy) as the probable cause of disability. In other cases no history is found and the disability is felt to be due to a developmental neurological deficit.

Using the broad term "reading retardation" to describe all cases in which there is a significant discrepancy between mental age on performance tests and level of reading achievement, we can, then, define three major diagnostic groupings (7, 8):

1. Capacity to learn to read is impaired without definite brain damage suggested in history or on neurological examination. The defect is in the ability to deal with letters and words as symbols, with resultant diminished ability to integrate the meaningfulness of written material. The problem appears to reflect a basic disturbed pattern of neurologic organization. Because the cause is biologic or endogenous, these cases are diagnosed as *primary reading retardation*.

2. Capacity to learn to read is impaired by frank brain damage manifested by clear-cut neurologic deficits. The picture is similar to the early-described adult dyslexic syndromes. Other definite aphasic difficulties are generally present. History usually reveals the cause of the brain injury, common agents being prenatal toxicity, birth trauma or anoxia, encephalitis, and head injury. These cases are diagnosed as *brain injury with resultant reading retardation*.

3. Capacity to learn to read is intact but is utilized insufficiently for the child to achieve a reading level appropriate to his mental age. The causative factor is exogenous, the child having a normal reading potential that has been impaired by negativism, anxiety, depression, emotional blocking, psychosis, limited schooling opportunity or other external influence. We diagnose these as *secondary reading retardation*.

Unfortunately the criteria for definite differential diagnosis are still uncertain and the problem is complicated by much overlap in etiology in individual cases. It is difficult to be certain in the cases of suspected secondary reading retardation, the problem being to rule out a basic developmental deficiency mild in degree. Through the years our research group has come to view the incidence of secondary retardation as lower than we had at first anticipated. While the meaningfulness to the child of what he reads will be strongly conditioned by his life experience and personality, and while the rapidity of his progress in learning will be much influenced by his social opportunities, his basic mastery of symbolization is probably much more neurologically determined than we had once thought. Detailed studies of the reading skills of severely disturbed inpatients, presenting a wide range of psychopathology and attending school in residence, should provide helpful in assessing the effects of specific relationship and life experience distortions on the reading process and its application. Such studies are now in progress at Hawthorn Center.

Of all the children with reading problems those with primary retardation present the greatest challenge. In our research we have devoted major attention to this group. Beginning with the surface symptom we can define the syndrome in terms of the following levels of process disturbance:

1. *Reading retardation:* The level of disability is usually severe and apart from a small sight vocabulary, learned by rote, and sporadic simple phonic skills there may be almost no functional reading ability. Arithmetic competence is usually also low although it may be somewhat higher than the reading level. Greatest impairment may be in spell-

ing, reflected in the child's attempts at writing to dictation.

2. *Reading process disturbance:* Analysis of the child's reading performance indicates difficulties in both visual and auditory areas and directionality also tends to be impaired. Visual recognition and discrimination on a perceptual level are intact but letter forms and combinations cannot be translated into meaningful concepts. In a similar way, in the auditory sphere, differences in vowel sounds are appreciated when presented orally, but the sounds cannot be translated into their letter symbols. For example, when a series of short vowel sounds "i, i, e, i" are presented orally, the "e" is readily recognized as different from the "i's" but the crucial step required for reading and spelling, the translation of the sound into its appropriate letter symbol, is impaired. The difficulty then is in symbolization in both visual and auditory fields. Complicating the problem may be left-right directional confusion with or without mixed laterality. Some typical illustrative examples of writing to dictation by children with a severe primary syndrome follow (5):

Paul is aged twelve, referred for psychiatric study because of severe depression. He is in the fifth grade, having repeated both the third and fourth grades. On the Wechsler Test performance I.Q. is 114, verbal I.Q. 82. Tested reading level is preprimer despite a performance mental age of fourteen years. Diagnosis is severe primary retardation. Paul produces the following when asked to write to dictation "The boy came home":

Paul's production reveals total confabulation with no capacity to deal with letters as symbols. Both visual and auditory skills are grossly deficient.

Bill, aged nine, was referred because of school truancy and acting-out behavior in the classroom. Originally considered mentally retarded because of inability to learn at school, psychometric testing indicates that Bill is of normal intellectual potential, performance I.Q. being 94; verbal I.Q. is 72. Reading level is low first grade. Bill writes "The boy came home" as follows:

This child depends totally on his visual memory and has virtually no phonic skills. He recalls "nor" as a word and just hopes that by chance it will turn

out to be "came." He struggles with "boy," but cannot differentiate from "dog" and the contamination "doy" emerges.

Tom is diagnosed as having primary reading retardation at age seven, midway through the first grade, which he had repeated. At that time he wrote "The boy came home" as follows:

An intensive remedial program was instituted and at age nine he has progressed to this point:

Tom still reverses "b's" and "d's" but he is well on the road to reading competence.

3. *Broader language deficits:* While in everyday conversation the child may appear to manage relatively well, careful attention to the language pattern reveals frequent difficulties in specific name finding, imprecise articulation and primitive syntax. Typical examples drawn from the responses by severe primary cases to test questioning follow:

Why is it better to build a house of brick than of wood? "Well just in case a hurricane the house can break down, but you put the brick on, it can just hit it but not break nothing down." (Age nine years)

What must you do to make water boil? "You should put it under a fire." (Age ten years)

How did he get hurt? "He sprang a thing, a arm when he felled out of that tree." (Age eleven years)

Is it night-time or day-time now? "Day-time. It's, well, clouds are out and stuff. It's white the clouds, it's lightsen up, the clouds and stuff." (Age nine years)

Is it morning or afternoon? "It's in the noon-time. Noon. In the noon." (Age nine years)

These tend to represent extreme examples, but we look for similar disturbances in expressive language in all cases of the primary syndrome.

4. *Specific concept-symbolization deficiency in orientation:* The symbolization defect is not limited to the reading processes alone, but is found to be more basic. There is difficulty in translating orientational concepts into symbols. Thus while the child has no trouble appreciating which of two people is taller, he cannot define their height in feet. Similarly, while he knows clearly that he wakes up in the morning, he may be unable to express this

knowledge in terms of a specific hour. To explore further this orientational factor we have devised the Hawthorn Center Concept-Symbolization Test with questions relating to personal information, time, quantity and dimension, number, directionality and laterality. Drs. Ingram, Katz, Kauffman, Langman and Lynn of our group are now completing standardization of the test which we hope may prove helpful as a diagnostic and prognostic instrument, especially with young children, and as a partial key to therapy need (4).

5. *Body image problems:* Even more basic, there may be disturbances in personal-orientation or body image but these have been much less clearly demonstrated. Now we are using Benton's Laterality and Finger Localization Test and other approaches to study further this aspect of the pathology (1).

All of us working with children with severe reading problems recognize the need for more precise differential diagnostic criteria. We are approaching this problem in two ways. First, a longitudinal study of reading progress of classes of children in public schools is under way. A large battery of tests has been given, starting with first grade, and two groups have been isolated for detailed comparative investigation, those at the highest and at the lowest end of the scale of reading competence; from this study, now in its fourth year, we hope to isolate prognostic indices. Second, our psychologists are attempting to refine differential diagnostic criteria through detailed analysis of psychologic test data, obtained from children presenting a wide range of psychopathology, including language and reading disabilities. Tests used are the Wechsler, the Stanford-Binet LM, Bender-Gestalt, Draw-A-Family, Hawthorn Center Concept-Symbolization Scale and Benton Laterality and Finger Localization Battery. Thus far all data point at least in one direction: the problem is not one in perception per se, but rather in the translation of perceptions and concepts into meaningful symbols that can be used in reading and related language functions.

The total symptom complex of the primary reading retardation syndrome gives, we feel, a clue to the etiology: a neurological deficit, often familial in origin, and expressing parietal cerebral dysfunction (2, 3).

No discussion of neuropsychiatric considerations in reading problems can avoid mention of the inordinate suffering experienced by otherwise normal children, cut off from communication channels, increasingly vital for survival today. With limited resources to meet their specific needs we are obliged all too often to limit our involve-

ment with them to documenting their successive psychological reactions from initial anger to guilt feelings, depression and ultimate resignation and compromise with their aspirations. Work in clinics throughout the country has encouraged us to hope that early intervention by well trained language therapists may permit many children with primary reading retardation to develop at least functional reading competence. Major needs are for early diagnosis and the provision of intensive remedial programs in the public schools. In addition, an adjusted curriculum throughout the school years, relying minimally on literacy, must be devised for some students. It is interesting, if disconcerting, to note how much further advanced our speech correction programs are, in comparison with those for reading therapy. It may be that the speech correction workers have been more aggressive in presenting their reasonable demands and have in the past had more clearcut programs to offer. But now, as reading diagnostic issues are becoming clarified and as specific remedial techniques are evolving, the time is ripe for implementation of large-scale special education reading services in our public schools. Such programs, financed by special reimbursements available in many States, must take their place alongside those already established for children with speech, visual, hearing, orthopedic and other handicaps. In view of the fact that no responsibility of the public school is greater than to teach all children to read, the inclusion of remedial reading as a recognized branch of special education would seem as logical as it is essential.

References

1. **Benton, A. L.** *Right-Left Discrimination and Finger Localization: Development and Pathology.* New York: Hoeber, 1959.

2. **Critchley, M.** *The Parietal Lobes.* Baltimore: Williams and Wilkins, 1953.

3. **Drew, A. L.** "A Neurological Appraisal of Familial Congenital Word-Blindness." *Brain,* 79:440, 1956.

4. **Langman, M. P.** "The Reading Process: a Descriptive Interdisciplinary Approach." *Genetic Psychol. Monographs,* 62:3, 1960.

5. **Missildine, H., and L. Eisenberg.** "Physician's Role in Management of Retarded Reader." *Feelings,* 3, No. 9, October 1961.

6. **Morse, W. C.** "Education of the Socially Maladjusted and Emotionally Disturbed Children," in W. M. Cruickshank and G. O. Johnson, eds., *Education*

and Exceptional Children and Youth. New York: Prentice-Hall, 1958.

7. **Rabinovitch, R. D.** "Learning and Reading Disabilities," in S. Arieti, ed., *Handbook of Psychiatry.* New York: Basic Books, 1959.

8. **Rabinovitch, R. D., A. L. Drew, R. N. DeJong, W. Ingram, and L. Withey.** "A Research Approach to Reading Retardation," in R. McIntosh, ed., *Neu-*

rology and Psychiatry in Childhood. Baltimore: Williams and Wilkins, 1956.

From Ralph D. Rabinovitch and Winifred Ingram, "Neuropsychiatric Considerations in Reading Retardation," *Reading Teacher,* XV (May 1962), 433–439. Reprinted with permission of Ralph D. Rabinovitch and Winifred Ingram and the International Reading Association.

Editors' Commentary

A rare follow-up study of serious learning disability cases gives a pessimistic view of the future.[28, 29]

Procedures combining elements of screening with diagnosis have also been developed. The purpose is to identify a problem and to seek out general patterns or syndromes of behavior—to diagnose the specific nature of the problem. As we review the procedures for assembling this information we find many facets and styles. Zax and Cowen and their associates have done some of the most extensive work on identification and prevention over the years.[30] They have found it possible to identify pupils in the first grade who will be problems by the third grade. Their detection procedures include a group intelligence test, the Goodenough Draw-a-Person test, and behavioral observation by the psychologist. Teachers rate ability and adjustment, and social workers interview the parents concerning the child's developmental history, adjustment, and other family conditions. This investigation produces a general evaluative criterion rather than specific familial situations that predict particular pathologies.

One of the most frequently used methods for analysis of deviant behavior is the case study. Its basic purpose is to integrate the total life experience. When done well, it serves as a compendium of information and understanding by combining identifying information, psychological test data, gleanings from observation and interviews, and in-depth interpretation. A conceptual system is necessary for organizing a case study. Without it, the study may lack appreciation of the sociological press under which the child lives in the home, school, and community.

Rothney[31] has a well-rounded discussion of the content needed in a case study. He differentiates between census and personal data.

28. **Cruickshank, William M.,** *Education of Exceptional Children* (Englewood Cliffs, N.J.: Prentice-Hall, 1967).

29. **John G. Frauenheim,** "A Follow-up Study of Adult Males Who Were Clinically Diagnosed as Dyslexic in Childhood" (Ph.D. diss. Wayne State University, 1975); **William Cruickshank and Daniel P. Hollahan,** *Perceptual and Learning Disabilities in Children,* vol. 1, *Psychoeducational Practices* (Syracuse, N.Y.: Syracuse University Press, 1975).

30. **Melvin Zax and Emory L. Cowen,** "Early Identification and Prevention of Emotional Disturbance in a Public School," in *Emergent Approaches to Mental Health Problems,* ed. Emory Cowen, Elmer Gardner, and Melvin Zax (New York: Appleton-Century-Crofts, 1967), pp. 331–351; and David R. Beach, Emory L. Cowen, Melvin Zax, James D. Laird, Mary Ann Trost, and Louis D. Izzo, "Objectification of Screening for Early Detection of Emotional Disorder," *Child Development* 39 (1968): 1177–1188.

31. **John W. M. Rothney,** *Methods of Studying the Individual Child* (Waltham, Mass.: Blaisdell, 1968). See especially chap. 2.

By census data we mean items such as name, age, height, weight, place of residence, and place of birth which may be essential in the identification of the person and his setting. Personal data are derived from the observation of any subject, regardless of his census classifications. The difference between these kinds of data is that the census materials are verifiable items which can be obtained from records but which do not permit interpretations that apply solely to an individual. The personal data permit interpretations by an investigator from his observations of how a particular individual performs and behaves. (P. 6.)

Rothney does not believe that any outline should be followed arbitrarily, but he gives the following general guides for data gathering. First, any information that will help in understanding the child should be considered, which means that screening personnel examine a wider scope of behavior than has traditionally been studied. Second, because of the variations in reliability of information, all data must be evaluated. Third, the child's cultural situation is considered part of the matrix. The reader is encouraged to consult Rothney's book for details.

Many times, additional specific studies are needed to deepen the case study. However, some investigators spend more time collecting detailed information than in developing plans. Additional assessment is needed when we cannot devise a plan because of a lack of understanding, but in many cases careful thinking with the available knowledge is sufficient to create plans within available resources. In short, diagnostic studies should not be substituted for interventions. It is easier to study a problem than to develop plans for change, and to some it is more fascinating to examine than to confront.

But often examination in more depth is necessary to comprehend a problem. We may need sociological information: What forces in the community—such as gangs in a slum or the "achievement neurosis" in a suburb—operate on the pupil? We may need to know how the family interrelates—the roles and configurations of mother, father, and siblings. (This information is particularly important if the disturbed child is the family scapegoat.)

The psychologist contributes by study of the intellectual and affective nature of the child. Individual intelligence tests reveal both the overall IQ and where functioning may be relatively high or low. For example, is the memory, reasoning, or perception below expected limits? Particularly for children who may have learning capacity deficiencies, the quality of performance is as important as the quantity. (However, to go from test results to a concrete classroom prescription is difficult, and the teacher can make significant additions to the psychological findings.) Projective tests, used to gauge anxiety, fear, and hate, often indicate the particular life area that is the source of difficulty. Drawing, creative writing, stories told about semiambiguous pictures, and responses to inkblots are examples of the psychologists' exploration devices. The most difficult result to obtain is a quantified appraisal of moral or values development. Basically, the psychologist tries to reveal underlying emotional states.

Engel[32] has written a classic article on the parameters of the psychologist's testing role with children. The first parameter is control. Because the child is "forced" to the situation, he or she reacts with uncanny skill to control the situation by using a range of "actions" from silence to hyperactivity. Under pressure the child may regress. The conditions Engel discusses are present in any interview with a child, but giving a test under absolutely set conditions adds more stress.

Social workers and psychiatrists contribute to the case study through insights gained in diagnostic interviews with families and children. Although this mode has been seriously criticized for its subjectivity, it is also true that the trained human mind is a highly sensitive receptor which can pick up and respond to hidden messages and nonverbal

---

32. **Mary Engel,** "Some Parameters of the Psychological Evaluation of Children," *Archives of General Psychiatry* 2 (1960): 593–605.

behavior. Essentially the interview is an interaction between two human beings. When the interviewer is responding to his or her own cues, giving hints, or forcing issues, the results will be suspect. However, training and self-regulation minimize these factors and make interviews an important source of insight.

The Problem of Incidence and Differential Diagnosis

Differential diagnosis is critical in designing intervention programs. For example, to set the proper rewards for operant conditioning, one must know what the individual considers a reward. No problem arises when a hungry rat is offered food or a deprived boy is offered new toys, but it is more difficult to predict when a pupil may find a teacher's strong reprimand more rewarding than being ignored. The response depends on that child's motivational system. When a child seeks punishment, is gratified by making an adult angry, or listens but doesn't feel because he or she lacks empathic concern, differential diagnosis becomes focal for therapeutic planning. Suppose a boy says "I can't do it" when confronted with a math problem. If he makes this statement because he is afraid of failure, the teacher's strategy should be different from that used if the child sees no value in learning anything about numbers. We need to know the reason behind the behavior so that we can design proper approaches.

Labeling a child neurotic or psychotic is not the level of differential diagnosis that the teacher needs. Although labels should have the same connotation for all who use them, they often do not, because the categories are too general. Chapter 1 of this book illustrated the individuality of youngsters, even those with the same general diagnoses. The purpose of differential diagnosis is to plan differential treatment. Although no two children are alike, particular types show recognizable contrasts. To a degree, symptoms are arrayed in patterns that indicate certain handling methods. A psychopath does not benefit from the same adult response as does an anxious neurotic.

Although many psychiatric interviews with disturbed young children and adolescents are brief "verifying" snapshots, a skilled child psychiatrist has the potential of offering first-hand diagnostic information on how the child sees life and where the basic problems lie. With young children, the psychiatrist may use play therapy; with older children, semiprojective interactions in completing stories or making up a TV play.[33] Drawings may be encouraged. Talking with adolescents, especially defensive ones, requires great skill, for the interview is also a relationship experience for the youngster. The importance of the interview is to help the youngster express personal ideas and fantasies. Werkman[34] considers the most important interview question to be: "Why are you here?" Asking about three wishes the child would make, or about family, school, and peer life, gives direction to further probes in important areas. Before the interview is over, however, there should be closure to help the child regain defenses and know that help will be given. Goodman has an excellent series of suggestions on the interview.[35]

The purpose of screening is to locate potential problems. The purposes of further study are (1) to be certain the behavior is not a normal response to a situation that must be changed; and, if it is not, (2) to reach a diagnosis of the problem. The conclusions from these studies lead to planning. Thus, it is necessary to collect material from various sources to understand what interventions are appropriate. Morse and Rabinovitch[36] call

33. **R. A. Gardner,** *Therapeutic Communication with Children: The Mutual Storytelling Technique* (New York: Science House, 1971).

34. **S. L. Werkman,** "The Psychiatric Diagnostic Interview with Children," *American Journal of Orthopsychiatry* 35 (1965): 764–771.

35. **Jerome D. Goodman,** "The Psychiatric Interview," in *Manual of Child Psychopathology,* ed. Benjamin B. Wolman (New York: McGraw-Hill, 1972), pp. 743–766.

36. **W. C. Morse and Ralph Rabinovitch,** *The Nature and Education of Disturbed Children and Adolescents* (New York: McGraw-Hill, forthcoming).

Table 1. Functional Diagnostic Dimensions

Level of intellectual performance: abstraction, problem solving, etc.
    Verbal IQ
    Performance IQ
    Rote learning
    Social concepts

Neurological integration
    Large-muscle coordination
    Small-muscle coordination
    Visual-motor coordination

Language skills
    Oral comprehension
    Oral expression
    Reading: oral
              sight vocabulary
              phonetic skills
              comprehension
    Spelling
    Arithmetic

Clarity of ego boundaries

Level of depth relationships: empathy

Self-concept, self-esteem

Relationships and identifications

Freedom from disabling anxiety

Acculturalization: opportunities and exposure to learning experiences

---

this procedure "clinical ledger and functional diagnosis." From the presented symptoms, the investigator goes to the dynamic situation. Although some dimensions are easier to scale than others, the goal is to gather the information into the profile summary shown in table 1.

Where one goes from here is described in following chapters and in a summary outline by Cheney and Morse.[37]

As we bring this chapter to a close, we turn to an examination of the overall incidence and nature of childhood mental illness, which is presented in some detail. Various recent studies by the Joint Commission on the Mental Health of Children have found that estimates of the amount of school maladjustment range from a low of 3 and 4 percent to highs of 12 and 22 percent of the pupils. But no consistency in definition or process of identification exists, and we can expect considerable variation from one community to another.

---

37. **C. Cheney and W. C. Morse,** "Psychodynamic Interventions in Emotional Disturbance," in *A Study of Child Variance: Interventions*, vol. 2, ed. W. C. Rhodes and M. L. Tracy, Institute for the Study of Mental Retardation and Related Disabilities (Ann Arbor: University of Michigan Publications Distribution Services, 1972).

Perhaps the most recent comprehensive compendium of information on elementary school disturbance is found in a study done by Glidewell and Swallow[38] for the joint commission. The authors summarized both studies and theory concerning maladjustment in the elementary school. Their figures suggest that 30 percent of the children studied had some difficulties: 5 to 25 percent had intrapersonal tensions; and 10 to 30 percent had interpersonal difficulties, ranging from withdrawal to aggression. Obviously a child may have more than one kind of difficulty.

A comprehensive examination of the problem is presented in the *Report of the Joint Commission on Mental Health of Children.*[39] A few summary statements may stimulate the reader to study the entire volume.

The Commission considered in its study nearly one-half of the American population—that is, the approximately 95,000,000 persons under 25 years of age. Of this number, it is estimated:

Two percent are severely disturbed and need immediate psychiatric care.

Another eight to 10 percent are in need of some type of help from mental health workers.

Of the approximately 10 million under 25 who need treatment and/or care the Commission estimates:

Eighty percent suffer from emotional disorders due to faulty training, faulty life experiences, and externalized situational conflicts, such as difficulties with school, sex, siblings, parent–child relations, and social problems. These groups can usually be treated by general practitioners or pediatricians trained in mental health; school counselors; child development specialists; social workers; paraprofessionals who have been sufficiently oriented; and other persons working in settings not primarily established for treatment of mental illness.

Ten percent show deeper conflicts, which have become internalized within the self and create emotional conflicts (the so-called neuroses). The services needed by this group range from outpatient services to Re-Ed and/or residential care; however, all these services need to be interrelated in harmonious working referral and treatment arrangements, so the child can easily move from one to another of these services as each is required for his needs.

Five percent show physical handicaps and require specialized facilities and intensive care. Of the estimated 7.6 million physically handicapped children who need services, 5.6 million receive some services. The present services, however, require many improvements. Mental health services and educational services particularly need to be increased and improved.

The remaining five percent suffer severe mental disorders (for example, schizophrenia, severe mental retardation, etc.) and require more intensive care and often institutionalization.

According to our best estimates, only about 500,000 children are currently being served by psychiatric facilities (clinics, hospitals, private therapists). (P. 38.)

The commission indicates the need for early identification and goes on to state:

The admission of teenagers to state hospitals has risen something like 150 percent in the last decade . . . Instead of being helped, the vast majority are the worse for the experience. The usual picture is one of untrained people working with outmoded facilities within the framework of long abandoned theory (where there is any consistent theory), attempting to deal with a wide variety of

---

38. **John C. Glidewell and Carolyn S. Swallow,** "The Prevalence of Maladjustment in Elementary Schools," a report for the Joint Commission on the Mental Health of Children, mimeographed (Chicago: University of Chicago, 1968).

39. *Crisis in Child Mental Health: Challenge for the 1970s* (New York: Harper and Row, 1970).

complex and seriously sick youngsters and producing results that are more easily measured by a recidivism rate that is often 30 to 50 percent, and occasionally higher. (P. 6.)

It is clear that special education has a major role to play for all disturbed children, but the commission has a sorry status report.

We have many reasons to point with pride to our educational system. Yet, few would deny that there are glaring deficiencies. There are old goals which have yet to be realized. There is the unfulfilled dream of an equal education for all—one fitted to the unique nature, needs, and aspirations of each child, one which develops the competence and skill necessary for an individual sense of mastery and accomplishment. For many children, we have made little or no advance toward these goals. For example:

Only 13 percent of the 800,000 emotionally disturbed children identified as needing special education currently receive such assistance.

Of the estimated 5,500,000 handicapped children who need special education because of their disabilities, only one-third receive any educational assistance.

An estimated 50,000 migrant children must travel each year when they should be in school; many of these children are excluded from attending local schools on the basis of their transient status.

Millions of poor children and those oppressed ethnic minorities are still herded into old, inferior and segregated schools where they lag further behind their more affluent counterparts as they advance into higher grades. (Pp. 72–73.)

Two important questions remain to be answered. First, for what reasons are children referred to clinical help? Second, what syndromes are found when the children are studied?

Table 2 shows the types of problems found in children *referred* to community and school clinics. Roughly 3 percent of the child population is referred when resources are available. Most of them can be classified as problems for teachers. However the problems of children placed in special classes for the emotionally disturbed are perceived by the teachers as somewhat different. Aggression and management problems occur most often, academic problems are second, and hyperactivity, withdrawn behavior, and perceptual problems are much less frequent.[40]

Table 3 adds recent figures to some of the material presented. It is quoted from *The 1966 Survey of the American Association of Psychiatric Clinics for Children,* part of a longer report to the Joint Commission on Mental Health for Children.

Comparing these percentages with the diagnoses in the Morse, Cutler, and Fink study referred to in footnote 40, we find that 60 percent of the children in the special classes, including those who internalized or acted out, are neurotic, corresponding to "psychoneurotic disorder" in table 3. In the classes 18 percent have disorders similar to the "personality disorder" in the table. Brain syndromes account for 7 percent of the children in Morse's classes, and academic failure (an added category) accounts for 7 percent.

Although the final article in this chapter, by Bower, is built around the concept of prevention, it speaks lucidly to the issue of identification and screening, with particular focus on the educator's role. If Bower's conclusions are correct, mental health experts may well be taking their cues from teachers. Bower, an outstanding researcher and theoretician in the school mental health field, has shown many ramifications of current mental health mystiques.

40. **William C. Morse, Richard L. Cutler, and Albert H. Fink,** *Public School Classes for the Emotionally Handicapped: A Research Analysis* (Washington, D.C.: Council for Exceptional Children, 1964).

Table 2. Referral Problems of 2,500 Outpatient Children*

Referral Problem	Under 6 M	Under 6 F	6–10 M	6–10 F	10–14 M	10–14 F	14–18 M	14–18 F	All Ages M	All Ages F	All Ages Total	Total as % of N	In 2 Community Clinics	In 2 School Clinics
Academic difficulties	3	0	358	126	322	117	146	54	829	297	1126	45	27	56
Mental retardation	16	9	166	94	180	123	50	35	412	261	673	27	6	40
Aggressive, antisocial behavior	45	12	242	65	192	39	115	45	594	161	755	30	45	20
Passive, withdrawn, asocial behavior	38	15	174	74	110	50	60	25	382	164	546	22	32	14
Emotional irritability and anxiety symptoms	45	16	205	86	108	46	49	25	407	173	580	23	34	16
Hyperactivity and motor symptoms	24	12	139	59	69	24	20	5	252	100	352	14	22	8
Sexual behavior problems	6	1	12	10	13	6	6	6	37	23	60	2.5	4	1
Toilet training	27	7	50	25	36	14	0	2	113	48	161	6.5	12	1
Speech defects	25	9	62	19	26	9	10	1	123	38	161	6.5	6	7
Miscellaneous	14	17	90	38	71	51	34	29	209	135	344	14	20	9
Total	243	98	1498	596	1127	479	490	227	3358	1400	4758	190.5	208	172

Number of Referrals by Age and Sex; Percentage of All Cases

From G. M. Gilbert, "A Survey of 'Referral Problems' in Metropolitan Child Guidance Centers," Journal of Clinical Psychology 13 (1957): 37–42.

*Average number of complaints per child: 1.9

Slicing the Mystique of Prevention with Occam's Razor

Eli M. Bower

Prevention is a word with many shades and ranges of meaning. I have read somewhere that in colonial days Philadelphia health officials sought to prevent an epidemic of yellow fever by repeatedly firing a cannon from the steps of City Hall. This was certainly a unique preventive approach; however, it lacked any evaluation, since no one really knows how many mosquitoes were killed by this procedure.

Occam's Razor turns out to be a more formidable preventive weapon than Philadelphia cannon.

Occam's Razor was tempered by a few cutting remarks about human functioning which, loosely translated and brought up to date, could be stated thus: "Don't complicate simple things." For those who prefer a more literal translation, Occam's words were: "Assumptions introduced to explain something should not be multiplied beyond necessity."

The focus in this paper is not so much on the hard-nosed data about early identification of children with potential problems, but the mythologies

Table 3. Comparison of Distribution of Diagnostic Categories for National Institute of Mental Health and American Association of Psychiatric Clinics for Children Facilities

Diagnostic Category	79 AAPCC Facilities		1,301 NIMH Facilities	
	Diagnosis	Treatment	Not Treated*	Treated
Brain syndrome	7%	5%	10%	6%
Mental deficiency	6	3	14	3
Psychotic disorder	8	12	5	6
Psychophysiological disorder		4	3	1
Psychoneurotic disorder	21	26	8	14
Personality disorder	27	25	23	22
Transient situational personality disorder	26	25	39	48
Total	100	100	100	100

*Omits "undiagnosed" and "without mental disorder."

Note: AAPCC clinics tend to see more psychotic and psychoneurotic children, and clinics reporting to NIMH see more transient situational disorders. This difference is probably based more on differences in diagnostic terminology than on differences in symptoms.

and encrustations about mental health and education which have kept this kind of an attempt feeble and ineffective. We will need to change blades in Occam's Razor more than once, before we get any program of real significance and impact operating in this area. Now what is the mystique which needs slicing and why?

The state of a child's mental health or ill health is best known and judged by a mental health professional (psychiatrist, clinical psychologist or psychiatric social worker) rather than by less "sophisticated" professional persons who live with the child on a day-to-day basis.

About ten years ago, the State of California decided to invest a sizable amount of money and some of my time to find out whether emotionally disturbed children could be identified early in their school life and, if so, could something be done to immobilize, interrupt, or intercept this kind of development. We found we could identify children with beginning learning and behavior problems, if we effectively and economically used perceptual ratings of students by teachers, peers, and the students themselves. Not surprisingly, we found our measures of the state of emotional development of students to be highly reliable and, on the basis of what good sense and little research we had, to be valid. At this point, however, some of

our mental health colleagues began to shake their heads. Remember, they said, the old Wickman study in which considerable doubt was raised about the ability of teachers and schools to recognize the symptoms of serious emotional problems. How do we know that the children you have identified are *really and truly* the mental health problems of our society? Are children identified by teachers (and peers and themselves) really emotionally disturbed? And what is more important, how do you know that these are the children who will eventually become mentally ill? The last question was always posed with the all-knowing scowl of the pipe-smoking scholar searching for the first star in the night sky.

Let me resurrect Wickman's study for those too young to have been exposed or too old to remember. Wickman asked a group of 511 teachers and a group of 30 mental hygienists to rate the seriousness of 50 behavior traits of children. What set the fulminating cap sizzling was the finding that ratings made by the mental hygienists and those made by the teachers had zero correlation. Wickman himself was not at all dismayed by this result, and was most emphatic in pointing out that the directions to each group had been significantly different. The teachers had been asked to rate the behavior as problems in the present reality of the classroom, while the mental hygienists were directed to rate the behavior on the basis of its effect on the future life of the child. Teachers were also told to define the seriousness of a problem by the amount of difficulty it produced in the classroom. The mental health group was asked to rate problem behavior in relation to its importance to a child's mental health. When the smoke cleared and the ratings of the two groups were compared, it became obvious that teachers were concerned with behavior that related to classroom disruption; mental health people, on the other hand, focused attention on behavior that was disturbing the child's inner psyche. Each group was looking at the problem in terms of their own professional biases and from their job-related firing lines.

Although Wickman was careful to point out the limitations of his study, this did not prevent many alexic professionals from jumping to unwarranted conclusions. Two educators examined 12 texts in psychology and educational psychology which mentioned Wickman's study, and found only two which gave a clear and concise statement of the study and its findings. Most discussed the study as indicating that, as judges of the mental health status of children, teachers were way off base. The basic assumption, of course, was that the mental health experts were right and that teachers were wrong.

The myth still exists that someone, somewhere, somehow, knows how to assess behavior and/or mental health as positive or negative, good or bad, healthy or nonhealthy, and independent of the social context wherein the individual is living and functioning. It is possible that the teacher who focuses on the child's observable behavior in school is closer to an operational reality of mental health than can be determined in an office examination. What a teacher is judging is how a specific behavior affects him as a key professional person in a primary social system and how well a child can play the role of student in a school. Similarly, when a child in a play group can not play the play role (adhere to the rules of the game), the nursery school supervisor will find his behavior a problem in that setting. In both instances, the lack of these role skills isolates the child from his peers. A child with an absence of emotional responsiveness to a parent will be a problem in a family setting where such responsiveness is one of the expected behaviors of children and of satisfaction to parents. But each behavior can only be judged as positive or negative in relation to the social system in which feelings or behavior are expected and prescribed.

Each of the social contexts in which children function has specific goals, rules, and competencies that act as guides for assessing prescribed and expected behavior. A school is a system which demands learning competence; a play group requires rule-abiding behavior; a family should provide an opportunity for some interchange of healthy hostility and affection. Life is lived by children within primary humanizing institutions, each of which requires specific functioning skills and behavior appropriate to its goals. I have no idea what mental health is in the abstract, but I would like to define it as comprising the kinds of competence and reality-testing which allow a child to function effectively in the humanizing institutions where he is asked to live. Specifically, these are the home, the peer or play group, and the school.

The fact is that teachers gather enough information about children in their routine operations to make highly accurate professional predictions about the course of a child's school life. However, there is little or no magic in such predictive data unless, in the process of gathering such data, the key professional person in the system is moved to act. For example, there is very good evidence that it is possible to detect potential delinquents at an early age if the Social Prediction Scale, developed by the Gluecks, is used. Why is it not used as a preventive tool? By and large, I would guess because the process of prediction requires operations not consistent with the goals and processes of the institution. In addition, the prediction itself has little curriculum implication or program consequences for the key professional worker in the school—the teacher. Prediction processes must lead to positive action by someone in the system, and this is especially critical in the case of problems which have not as yet become major crises to the teacher. How often one hears a kindergarten or first-grade teacher in a teachers' room react to a fifth- or sixth-grade teacher's description of the gory adventures of a problem child. "Oh, him—he was somewhat of a problem in the first grade," is the likely comment. "I thought he might get over it." The upper-grade teacher sadly shakes her head, indicating a less optimistic state of affairs.

But can teachers and schools be effective screeners of children with beginning mental health problems? In a 1963 study, teachers were asked to rate children on five steps, ranging from the first which was: the child has no problems and is obviously extremely well adjusted; there is absolutely no need for referral, to the last: the child has problems of sufficient severity to require referral. Following this, a sample of children were seen by psychiatrists in privately conducted interviews of, predictably enough, about 50 minutes each. There was a marked lack of agreement between professional groups in classifying children who had severe adjustment problems and needed referral. The investigator thereupon concluded that teachers cannot adequately serve as case finders in mental health screening.

In discussing this research with the investigator, two questions were posed: (1) to what extent do you feel that a 50-minute appraisal by psychiatrists is a more valid assessment of a child's functioning capabilities and liabilities in a school setting than a teacher's day-in-day-out experience; (2) how, exactly, do teachers react to the concept and meaning of the terms "adjustment" and "referral"? One teacher explained her meaning of adjustment: "I guess it means how well a student gets along in school and with others. Now I have this one student who gets along pretty well and I guess is well adjusted, but can't seem to learn anything." While the concept of adjustment is understood by teachers, its operational implementation is somewhat out of the frame of reference and functioning of teachers. Most feel that in rating "adjustment," they are attempting to fill the role of a psychiatrist; somehow, they rate the degrees of intrapsychic conflict and chaos in the minds of their students. Whatever rating adjustment means, teachers should stick to school-related behaviors and roles which can be operationally defined and observed. Does the child get into fights? Can he pay attention when necessary? Does he learn to read? Is he always in a blue funk? Does he get sick? Does he get hurt? Can he express an idea?

To put the shoe on the other foot, another study compared the predictive skill of a teacher, psychologist, and child psychiatrist in judging which kindergarten children would learn up to their IQ potential in first grade. A total of 56 kindergarten children were included in the study. Each professional person related to the children as he would normally. The teacher taught and observed, the psychologist tested, and the child psychiatrist used a standard play situation. All three did a good job of predicting the achievement, but the teacher's was best. The psychiatrist had a tendency to predict underachievement more frequently than it occurred. He suggested that the reason may be that some of the clinical anxiety which the psychiatrist picked up in the children—and which he expected to lead to underachievement—actually produced overachievement. This is, of course, the nub of the problem. Only when the teacher observes how a child may use different aspects of his personality and self can he assess the nuances of how the child mediates what he has, be it anxiety, IQ, shyness, or aggressivity. The investigation confirms Robins' study (discussed later) that

(1) raters in general are better at spotting potential positive achievers than the negative ones; (2) teacher judgments provide the most economical and efficient guides to predictions of school success.

The Nonmagic of Teacher Referrals

Another wicked slice with Occam's Razor needs to be taken at the notion and concept of "the referral." In the past, teachers have been so convinced of their lack of mental health expertise and so impressed with the competence of their mental health colleagues that the only significant help for problems which they could verbalize was: "If we only had adequate referral resources." We have invested this process, at least for teachers, with a penicillin-like magic which, unfortunately, is dissipated in the realities of limited knowledge and manpower. The referral concept for the majority of teachers is one where the child is taken elsewhere, where something magical is done to straighten him out, and then returned to school a healthy, well-motivated student. This rarely turns out to be the case. Occasionally, referrals are consummated to the satisfaction of the teacher. When this happens, it is evident that some mental health expert has learned to translate what he knows clinically and psychodynamically into the frame of reference of the teacher and into educational processes and objectives. Unfortunately, there are only a few referral agencies that have the competence to do this or know how to begin to do this. Most teachers have high regard for mental health persons and their professional competence. When the secrets of a problem are revealed to a teacher, she often stands aghast at the marvels of modern psychiatry, psychology, or casework. Indeed, she is thrilled to be a partner to such mighty revelations. She may re-enter the class with a better understanding of the "why" and "what" of the student's difficulty, but with her major problem still unanswered: "How do I teach this child?"

There is another assumption about teachers and referrals which needs slicing. If, in a hypothetical community, there were available immediate, convenient, and useful referral services (each of these will affect the process significantly) and teachers were encouraged to refer children who needed help, one would not get the most serious or the most difficult problems. A referral is the result of a dyadic relationship between a teacher and a child in the context of a class and a school. One psychologist who attempted to help teachers in an inner city school wanted to know why he got so few referrals. The teachers laughed at the question, and pointed out that if he were serious they would be happy to send him three-fourths of their class. There is also the phenomenon that when a teacher refers a child, she does so because *she* is puzzled or anxious about his behavior. Many teachers will not refer students with serious problems if they feel they understand some of the background and causes of the problems, but will refer less serious problems when the behavior or learning difficulty is puzzling or anxiety-provoking to them.

It is no longer possible in this day and age to think of referral services as desirable or necessary, if one is concerned with the basic preventive question: how do you increase the ecological competence of a humanizing institution to serve more children more effectively? One way would be to develop mental health professionals (clinical behavioral workers) who would not be walled off from the primary institutions by having to deal with its casualties, but could become an active partner with the teacher, principal, and parents in monitoring and enhancing the behavior of all children in the school.

The Object of Early Identification Is to Identify Cases Early

It took me quite a while to realize that the notion of early identification meant different things to different professional groups. One of my psychiatric colleagues used to puzzle me by his lack of enthusiasm for research in this field. Once, when I confronted him with this, he replied: "I don't see why you get worked up about this early identification of emotionally disturbed children. We've got more cases than we can handle right now without finding some more."

His notion of early discovery had to do with what is known in the profession as "cases." My notion of early discovery has to do with the discovery of a child in a primary institution, such as a school, who is having beginning trouble in coping with the demands and processes of that institution. The essential assumption is that, left alone, a beginning problem either finds a wise and highly competent teacher or it continues to grow. In our California studies, children identified as emotionally handicapped fell further and further behind in reading and arithmetic achievement, and were increasingly deemed by their peers to be negative or inadequate students. After five years, they were seen in child guidance clinics and appeared in the Juvenile Index for vehicle code and penal code violations in stark contrast to a randomly selected group of their classmates. This was replicated and amplified by the Minnesota Study which confirmed the fact that children identified by the California materials as emotionally handicapped fall further and further behind their classmates in achievement, and get stuck on a track which leads to severe educational embarrassment and incompetence.

The humanizing institutions to which children are mandated are unfortunately social systems that tend to reward those who succeed in them and punish those who fail. Programs of early identification in schools must therefore not only find failing and problem children early; but, in the process of finding them, must provide for the institutional changes which will make the discovery worth while. This means that processes of early identification must be carried out by key persons in specific humanizing institutions in the context of the goals and processes of that institution, and in such a way that alternative possibilities for action are natural outcomes of the process. Programs of early identification which require teachers to do non-teacher-like jobs will not last and cannot be effective. Moreover, such programs cannot enlist mental health workers to visit homes to make clinical appraisals of how a child is disciplined at home, the degree of affection shown to him by his parents, and so on, critical as this kind of information may be. Early identification processes which solely aim at identifying children with "mental health" problems are no more than exercises. They must lead to and be conceptualized in a program framework, and must be translatable into valid interventions within the humanizing institution where the child is living and is attempting to function.

Nobody believes it is possible for all children to experience our humanly constructed humanizing institutions in a positive and ego-enhancing way.

If one can remove one's home-grown complexities and professional blinkers about this sordid world and its people, it is possible to conceptualize humanizing institutions which can carry out their goals and processes for greater ranges of children and eventually for all children. Either we do this or pay the cost in lives and money for remedial or rehabilitative institutions such as prisons, mental hospitals, welfare programs, alcoholic and drug wards. It is also well to remember that when children cannot function in institutions devised for their benefit, they hurt and they bleed. One does not have to ask whether they have broken a leg or cut an artery before administering first aid. It is questionable whether the children identified as emotionally disturbed in school are really and truly disturbed or if they represent the group who will later become mentally ill. I suspect more of them later become antisocial, inadequate, dependent, alcoholic, drug-addicted, and physically ill than a random group of adults. This conclusion is supported by an interesting study of 524 adults who were seen as children in a child guidance clinic and 100 controls of the same age, sex, neighborhood, race and IQ. The purpose of the study was to describe, through a longitudinal natural history, the kinds of childhood behavior problems that present serious danger signals and those that do not. Robins' study is interesting in that there was an unexpected dividend in the data on the control group.

Let us first look at what happened to the 524 adults who had been seen as children in the child guidance clinic. Robins divided them into two categories, antisocial and nonantisocial, on the basis of behavior which led to referral. She found that antisocial children by and large became antisocial adults. Not only were these adults more often arrested and imprisoned than expected, but they were more mobile, had more marital difficulties, poorer occupational and armed service histories, used alcohol and drugs excessively, and had poorer physical health. "But," Robins adds, "from one point of view . . . what we have found is not so much a pathological patient group as an extraordinarily well-adjusted control group."

Such a control group was selected from the files of the St. Louis public schools by setting quotas for year of birth, sex, census tract, no clinic visit, IQ above 80, no grade repeats, and no record of expulsion or transfer. Microfilm reels were spun and selection made in the Las Vegas tradition. This, however, turned out to be a winner. Using these four not high standard criteria (IQ over 80, not seen at the municipal psychiatric clinic, no grade repeated, and no expulsion from school), Robins had selected a group of 100 adults of whom only two ever appeared in juvenile court and who, as adults, had good psychiatric adjustment and social competence. She concludes that while having repeated grades in elementary school certainly does not efficiently predict serious adult problems, having not had serious school difficulties may be a rather efficient predictor of the absence of gross maladjustment as adults. Perhaps we have been so concerned with the prediction of deviant behavior that we were not aware how well we could do in predicting effective behavior.

In light of our earlier comment about predicting eventual mental illness, Robins found no clear connection between type of deviance in childhood and type of problem in adulthood. For example, those adults with antisocial behavior in childhood not only showed antisocial adult behavior, but also showed a greater degree of social alienation and more psychiatric and physical disabilities. As a result, Robins found that children referred for antisocial behavior have a less promising prediction than children referred for other reasons. This is a group that vitally needs mental health services, as teachers have repeatedly pointed out to their principals and mental health consultants.

Conclusion

Don't complicate simple things. Prevention is getting children through our health, family, and school institutions "smelling like a rose." A little soap, a little affection, and a little learning are the holy trinity of prevention. If we can send rockets to the moon, we certainly can do these three little things for the human condition on earth.

Reprinted from *American Journal of Public Health*, Vol. 59, No. 3, March, 1969. Copyright by the American Public Health Association, Inc., New York. Reprinted by permission.

Editors' Commentary

Summary

The combination of culture and individual biological limitations produces a significant amount of deviation. The interaction between biological limitations (i.e., neurological, perceptual, and genetic) and environment is responsible for the seriousness and magnitude of atypical, neurotic, and psychotic patterns. These patterns may occur in various combinations; seldom is there a pure example of any one. Theories on the causes of deviation have recently undergone thorough scrutiny, and a concept of interaction is gradually replacing the theories that behavior malfunctions are either person-caused or society-caused.

Acting-out children and adolescents, an increasing proportion of the total maladjusted child population, are receiving inadequate help. Besides the typical psychoses and neuroses, we must deal with new patterns of alienation, delinquency, violence, drugs, sex, and fear. To an increasing extent, the schools will have a key role in this effort. Confronted with mandatory legislation and legal action, the schools can no longer ignore these children.[41] Nor can school programs be primarily custodial, for the "right to treatment" will be the quality control for future school provisions.

Teachers are often the first to encounter children who need help; they can screen out cases that require careful diagnosis and plan healthful measures within the educational system.

The teacher has a verified and central role to play in the screening process. Child-rearing institutions must become more humanized; the school must incorporate the necessary identifying, supporting, and correcting resources within its structure. Teachers and education are keystones in mental health screening and interventions. As educational accountability increases and the line between special and regular education is lost, a threefold program will develop following identification: (1) primary prevention through affective educational programs; (2) secondary prevention, with provisions such as the crisis teacher (described in chapter 4); and (3) tertiary prevention, the specialized programs presented in detail in chapter 6, p. 467. The proper outcome of screening and assessment is properly planned interventions and not labeling or categorizing. The proper outcome is development of an IEP that reflects goals based on the assessment data and includes environmental changes as well as intrapersonal changes. In chapter 8 on evaluation, this will again become our concern.

41. **J. Regal et al.,** *The Exclusion of Children from School: The Unknown, Unidentified, and Untreated* (Reston, Va.: Council for Children with Behavioral Disorder; Council for Exceptional Children, 1972).

3

What Kinds of Therapeutic Help Are Available to Schools?

Editors' Commentary

The children described in the previous chapters can be helped. If circumstances go well, they may simply grow up and out of some problems, especially if they have encouragement from teachers, a good school system, and supportive peers. Their chances are improved if they have families who can face difficulties with honesty and accept them without becoming immobilized by self-blame. This asks a lot—often too much—from people who are intimately involved with the hurdles and holocausts of children in distress. If experiences are not sufficiently regenerative, however, or if a disturbance is too firmly established to be outgrown naturally, troubles are likely to increase and to cripple the child's life and the lives of others.

Fortunately, many kinds of help are available. The most pervasive kind is given by carefully planned school programs staffed by talented, trained teachers. Besides school programs there are many other sources of treatment or therapy for children with emotional problems. Types of therapy vary almost as widely as types of disturbances. One method may be more appropriate to a particular child at a given stage of development than others. Sometimes more than one kind of treatment may be necessary, either simultaneously or sequentially. Treatment can take place in the school setting, therapist's office, clinic, or mental health center.

This section summarizes some of the major forms of psychotherapy now used to treat children. We approach the subject more or less historically, beginning with individual psychotherapy and going on to group psychotherapy, including one of the newer and more important developments of the past twenty years—family therapy. The discussion on groups also covers therapeutic use of media (art, dance, music, psychodrama, bibliotherapy [literature], and writing); group therapy for adolescents; excerpts from a therapeutic classroom session; family therapy; a discussion on a group of black children; and the necessity of staff training for group leadership.

Many therapies now used differ vastly from one-to-one Freudian psychoanalysis. As a matter of fact, the first analysis of a child did not even directly include the child; it was conducted by Freud and the father of a severely phobic child. However, Freud's first method implied that success in treating the child was contingent on the parent's active cooperation.

Anna Freud and Melanie Klein both developed theories of personality and child treatment based on Freud's, although they are quite divergent. Anna Freud worked closely with parents and teachers of the children treated and developed a theory of defense mechanisms that is still important in practice. Melanie Klein developed a theory about primitive forms of thinking and acting. These divergent paths have enriched the variety of therapy now available.

There are also exciting, new, dynamic approaches that help agencies and schools deal with families without making the family or child assume the role of patient. These are based on the premise that most adults and children are motivated to do better and can do better if the specifics needed for change are made evident. These briefer, ego level programs are described by Leventhal and Weinberger[1] and by Love et al.[2]

Individual Psychotherapy and Psychoanalysis

Freud predicted that he would be remembered for formulating a theory that really wasn't new—about the forces underlying human behavior. Particularly, he said, philosophers, writers, and artists knew and described the inner human drives. He felt his contribution was to take their observations and insights and to systematize them. His theory came from experience with hundreds of sick people who could not be helped by other medical disciplines. His prescription for treatment came from philosophy rather than pharmacology: "Know the truth and it shall set you free." The method rested on leading or helping the patient to become aware of the truths about himself or herself.

Freud's theory might be called an education theory. The therapist is a teacher. The subject matter is the individual patient; the curriculum is the patient's past experience, present world, and unconscious feelings. The methods used to help the patient gain awareness, insight, and consequent change were set down by Freud in specific terms for treating adult neurotics. They have been modified according to the knowledge and convictions gained from treating more seriously disturbed adults—psychotics and criminals—as well as children suffering from emotional illnesses.

Freud's basic premises resulted in an intense study of children and their development. His theory of the libido, which might be defined as affectional energy, starts at the breast. This energy can develop naturally in a child who is able to put up with the pressures of society; or it can be blocked, deterred, or turned in ill-fated directions. Freud's emphasis on early childhood experiences focuses psychoanalytic, psychiatric, and educational thought on parent–child and teacher–child relationships. His theory of the unconscious makes sense out of seemingly senseless behavior. Failure to achieve where potential exists, somatic complaints without perceptible causes, crime or misdeed without apparent reason become understandable in the light of unsuspected human needs and conflicts that, if blocked too long, find alternative means of making their presence felt.

Since the psychoanalytic treatment of adults focused largely on childhood, it was natural that children themselves be scrutinized. If illness began in the early years, could it be prevented or caught before it developed further? Could society or education help from the outside? Could the therapist help from the inside? Could parents and teachers alter the course of a child's development to free energy for constructive living instead of pathological living?

The first case of child therapy was undertaken by Freud himself. Little Hans was treated indirectly by Freud for a phobia of horses. That is to say, Freud supervised the treatment through Hans's father. The father would come to Freud frequently, reporting in detail

1. **Theodore Leventhal and Gerald Weinberger,** "Evaluation of a Large-Scale Brief Therapy Program for Children," *American Journal of Orthopsychiatry* 45 (1975): 119–133.

2. **Lenore Love et al.,** *Troubled Children: Their Families, Schools and Treatment* (New York: John Wiley and Sons, 1974).

his son's actions, angers, pouts, tears, and joys. When he could, he would report little Hans's dreams as they had been told to him; the interrelations of mother, father, governess, and Hans were also reported. Freud would interpret what he heard, explaining to Hans's father what the information implied for the management of little Hans in the context of the social mores and goals that were expected of that child in Austria at that time. By this means, little Hans's phobia of horses, which like most phobias spread to other things and consequently decreased his ability to play and learn, was ultimately cured. This was the first child analysis.

In the early years of psychoanalysis, Anna Freud, Sigmund Freud's daughter, and Melanie Klein both worked with children. Although both based their work on Freud's formulations, they disagreed with each other on many basic questions of treatment, such as the relationship between therapist and child, the use of dreams and symbols, the length and conditions of treatment, and the handling of parents. Melanie Klein took the major part of Freud's adult theory and applied it to children. Anna Freud, however, modified her father's theory in a way that was consistent with a child's basic dependence on parents. She was more concerned with the child's total environment—friends, neighborhood, teacher. Space limitations unfortunately prevent us from including any selections from the work of Anna Freud or Melanie Klein. They were, with G. Stanley Hall in the United States, the founders of child psychiatry, and the reader is urged to examine some of their work. An important book by each is listed in our bibliography.

During World War II, Anna Freud lived in England, where she cared for and treated hundreds of children who had been bombed out of their London homes or whose parents had sent them to her to escape the bombing. Her studies of these children's reactions to trauma, disaster, death, and separation are fascinating. Melanie Klein also lived in England, where she developed loyal followers. Her work has had less appeal to American therapists, but her dramatic theories have proved particularly successful with borderline psychotic children and in application of the principles of groups and group structure and behavior to adults as well as children. They have found expression in the Tavistock theory of group relations and in the work of Wilfred Bion, both of which are described below in the section on groups.

The mental health movement in the United States has a rather different history from that of the corresponding movement in Europe, where interest first centered on the adult incapacitated by emotional illness. In America, on the other hand (true to our reputation for being all wrapped up in our children), the mental health movement began through child guidance clinics, which were started by the psychologist G. Stanley Hall in the 1890s. It is interesting that psychology rather than psychiatry instigated our major efforts.

The following article is an excerpt from the work of an American child psychoanalyst, Dorothy Baruch, who works along the lines described by Anna Freud. The case excerpted here should be of particular interest to school people, since it is the story of a boy (Kenneth) who acted out his unconscious conflict through severe physical symptoms and through school failure. This child was operating at a 101 IQ at the beginning of treatment, at 140 at the close of treatment.

In this selection the parents' involvement in the child's pathology is emphasized. Dr. Baruch saw the mother (Cathy) individually on a regular basis and the father (Vic) from time to time. Both parents also participated in group therapy for parents with children in treatment. These two techniques are used increasingly when treatment of children is undertaken. It is rare today, except in hospital or residential treatment settings, that therapists will work with children under the age of fifteen without insisting that the parents also participate in some form of regular therapy. Sometimes parents are seen by the child's therapist, as they were in Dr. Baruch's case; sometimes separate therapists are used. Multitherapeutic measures are used with parents, as in the example given here. Frequently, teachers, too, are interviewed by the therapist for the purpose of getting, and sometimes giving, information relevant to the child's growth.

The following selection was chosen for four major reasons:

1. It is the case of a child who was treated for a learning problem, in reading and spelling.

2. It is an example of the most typical kind of therapy done in this country: work with a child and a parent in a child guidance clinic. The child's therapist was a psychoanalyst; the mother's therapist was a psychiatric social worker.

3. It is the record of one complete case.

4. It indicates the use of one type of group therapy with parents—the psychoanalytically oriented group.

One Little Boy

Dorothy Baruch

At home Kenneth wheezed steadily for the four days and nights between that session and the next. He was quiet. He was good. But he coughed and struggled for air during the night and breathed with painful tightness during the day. The doctor did what he could.

But Kenneth kept on wheezing.

The doctor questioned me: Were we moving too fast? I said I'd watch it; perhaps we were. Kenneth had been such a good boy for so long that it was frightening him to open up to his own view this other part of himself—a part that lies deep in every one of us—hidden but ready to splash out in the bitter word, in the twisted temper, or in the flood-burst of mass riot, lynchings and war. In small or large measure we manage, each in our own way, to keep it underground, according to the smallness or largeness of the hurts we have suffered, according to the onus we have leveled at ourselves for unwelcome feelings and according to the quantity and depth of the bitter gall we have stored.

Kenneth had been hurt. I knew only part of it all at the moment. Anger had, as a result, accumulated inside him, and had given rise to fantasies mixed with tremendous fear and guilt. He could not show this anger or he might do too much. He might lose the last remnants of his mother's love. Therefore, unconsciously he did let the anger turn back on its course till he himself was both donor and recipient in the pain of illness, in the tragedy of failure, and in the fantasied hurts more dreaded than that of the wounded soldier and more dreadful to bear.

He would have to bring anger to the surface where he could look at it and with my help gradually understand and integrate it into the portrait that he painted of himself in his mind.

Release had to come as a primary step if he was to survive in wholeness. I knew this. But I knew also that if it came too fast, it would threaten to inundate him so that he might close up the floodgates anew with reinforced blockades.

In his next session, Kenneth again chose the soldiers. At the start, he dared not follow his impulse to strike down the enemy. Hesitance encased him like lead-gray fog. But at last his desire broke through—throwing a spotlight on terrain that had been veiled from view. And with it, his face was illuminated.

His bombs struck not only mountains but men. His bullets, born in swift flight by his hand from enemy to enemy, crackled mercilessly. Faster and faster. The open voice replaced the closed whisper. Free breath in and out of lungs replaced the stoppered sibilance of his wheeze.

"The bomb got em!" jubilantly. "One man. Two. Three...." He went down on one knee, crouching in triumph over the strewn men, his yellow head bent to inspect the havoc he had finally managed to deal after such struggle. His words spilled out. And with them, in the risen excitement, a small trickle of saliva dribbled from his mouth to the floor.

He looked at the dark spot of spittle on the linoleum in stunned silence.

"I—I'll clean it up," he whispered.

Stiffly he rose from his bombs and his soldiers. He walked to the closet hook where a cloth hung and to the sink where he wet it. He wrung out the cloth like a well-taught robot, and brought it back to the spot on the floor.

"I—I didn't mean to get the floor messy."

"I know it, Ken. But really, in here it doesn't

matter. You can do lots of things in here that you think aren't proper outside."

But he could not hear me or dared not show that he'd heard.

Slowly and with painstaking thoroughness he mopped the wet space, went back to the sink, washed the cloth out, wrung it, mechanically hung it back on the hook. And with not another word but with the rasp of his wheezes breaking the silence, he came straight into my lap.

I thought: To him messing means being bad. So also do injuring and killing, even in play, mean being bad. They're different sides of the same coin, different facets of resentment, or anger, or hostility—call it what one will. Inside of Ken, the reservoir was full to spilling over. In his play, when it was draining out through the drama of killing, it did not need for the moment to drain out in asthma. In such play, though, it showed more of its true form. Ken could not escape its meaning as completely as he could when it came out in sickness or failure. Sickness and failure were great camouflagers. With them he could say in the space beyond words where unrecognized thoughts exist more as feelings: I'm being good, not naughty. I can't help it, after all, if I fail or am sick.

Since messing was less bad than injuring or killing and since injury and killing had frightened him so much, it was obviously not the messy spittle in itself that had sent Ken back in fear to being a baby seeking arms' shelter. The spittle was merely the proverbial last straw.

I would try to help Kenneth get firmly acquainted with the milder forms in which his "badness" showed itself before tackling what to him seemed more dangerous. I would arrange materials and set up the playroom so that it would automatically limit what Kenneth brought out. Instead of waiting for him to get the soldiers from the cupboard, I would have clay or paints out on the floor in readiness, as an invitation to mess rather than injure or kill.

Then bit by bit as he tackled what was less frightening to him and saw that he could live through it without being overpowered by his feelings or deserted by me, he might perhaps gain courage to explore more deeply. I would try as we went along to help him feel less guilty and less afraid and to understand his feelings better, not through mere words of explanation but through the experiences which we would share. Perhaps then—very gradually—the more dreaded feelings might lessen until he could say, in effect, I can handle what's left of them. I'm not really so bad! I don't need to be afraid any longer that my feelings will push me into such terrible actions that I'll ei-

ther be deserted or destroyed. I needn't turn them back on myself and punish myself with illness and failure. I needn't keep them walled off and hidden as if I were telling myself, "These feelings, they're *not* part of *me*." Instead, I'll be able to let them slip into place as part of what I am. If he could reach this point, he would no longer need to stand over himself, cruelly denying himself and trying to relish denial in place of pleasure. He would no longer have to drain energy from his school work, for instance, in order to keep reinforcing the walls. The energy that had been used for hiding would be freed for work and play, for enjoyment and laughter, for friendship and love.

All this I hoped might eventually happen. I would try to help Kenneth achieve it. But essentially it was Kenneth himself who had to do it. Would he be able to? Was there sufficient courage and vigorous urge left in him, not only for living, but for aliveness? How far would Kenneth be able to go?

I had finger paints waiting ready for him next time, right in the middle of the floor.

"What are they? . . . Where are the brushes? . . . Where are pictures to color? . . . I don't do well in free art in school. I like paint-books better. I almost never go outside of the line."

Poor, tight little Kenneth, afraid of what his brush's unsteadiness might mean, feeling that he must not go beyond the line—seeking the shelter of its neat constraint.

I told him you did this kind of painting with your hands, that was why it was called "finger painting."

He wanted gray. And when we got a blob of it onto the paper, he touched it very gingerly with one finger. "Look how dirty my finger got."

He stared unhappily at it.

"Will my finger get clean again? Will the mess come off?"

"Let's try with the soap and water at the sink." We did. And he saw.

He took a big breath. "It does come off."

He started afresh. With the tips of all the fingers on one hand. With whole fingers down. With palm in, slithering, until the sticky paint was covering the inside of his hand. "See how dirty?"

Again doubt. "Will *this much* come off?"

Back to the sink. "I'd better see."

He scrubbed until I wondered if he'd left any skin.

To the paints with both hands sliding in. Back to the sink. Again to the paints. Again to the sink. Paint and scrub. Prove that he wouldn't have to keep tell-tale signs of dirt on him, then he could get dirty. But the proof was hard to believe. And so it had to be sought again and again until he could finally say with more certainty, "I *can* get them clean."

Both hands went in, then, and the paint slid up past the wrists. "I'll make them real, real dirty." He was smearing the paint now, over the backs of his hands and between his fingers. "I'll get them all dirty. Ahrrr, ahhrrrr, I'm messy! Ahhrrrr!" He growled and stuck up his hands toward my face in a menacing gesture as if he were going to smear me. A pouncing gesture, his fingers spread like claws. His head was back, his eyes guardedly on me, and a sound came from his lips. It was laughter but it was not the full-throated sound that rises from the gay heart. Rather the ghost-sound of an echoed, hollow denial of fear.

I wondered if he saw me swallow.

Even though it was thin and shallow, coming from no farther back it seemed than his palate, still this was the first time in the short long month he'd been with me that I'd heard Kenneth laugh. . . .

Blaine did not call Cathy. But he called Vic into his private office, and from behind Mr. Taylor's great mahogany desk, he told Vic that he was reorganizing the business and for the time being would not need Vic's services.

Vic said, "That's all right." Nothing more. Next day, however, he went back and doggedly questioned, "What's wrong, Blaine? Why are you letting me out? It's important for me to know."

Blaine had said there was nothing against Vic. Only right now he needed men of a different type, more aggressive. "You're the research type, Vic; the inventor, the investigator. Right now that's not what this place needs. We need people who can promote. Push. Why don't you open a consulting service? When we come up with a tough problem we'll use you. It's a deal. But at present we don't need your kind of a man here full time."

That night there was a group psychotherapy session. Cathy came in, the air of a crusader about her, her dark head high. Vic followed, dragging his feet.

Glancing around the already gathered circle, Cathy chose the straight-backed chair from the two that were still empty and Vic, looking helpless, sank into the low armchair and huddled over himself.

The hum of greetings between the group members stopped as the doctor glanced at his watch. "Well," he said, swiftly surveying each face in the circle, "it's time for us to get to work."

There was silence and a few moments of waiting for some group member to spontaneously start to talk about whatever lay on his mind. For into this warm, big room with the quiet of shadows on the wall and the circle of waiting faces, these people once a week brought their troubles and feelings and fantasies just as Kenneth brought his into the room where he played. Here, the doctor and I, as joint psychotherapists, had come to stand as a new father and mother. Under our guidance, these men and women with their diverse problems had grown to speak as freely as they would alone.

Tonight it was Cathy, not Vic, who began.

"It isn't fair," she protested. "It shouldn't have happened to Vic!"

She went on to recount what Vic had told her. She was angry, she said, at Mr. Taylor for not having protected Vic. "After all the years that Vic's been there. Why, he's been Mr. Taylor's right hand man. I think it's a darn rotten deal. Especially being told he's not the aggressive type!"

Cathy's voice was patiently sweet with martyred indignation. "That's like a slap in the face! What if Vic isn't the aggressive type? Vic's got a lot of other qualities . . ."

With quick perspicacity, several group members picked up Cathy's feelings. They now came out with thoughts that people ordinarily keep unsaid.

This is part of group psychotherapy. For when a person sees in the group how others react to him with the covers of pretense shorn off, he can at one and the same time see how he affects people outside the group. How he reacts in turn with hurt or anger, with impotence or with gestures of appeasement, stands out in clean silhouette. He can see more clearly what he is and how he is and what there is in him that upsets others and brings trouble onto himself. In the circle of the group he experiences safely and without harm in microcosm the under-cover reactions which in the macrocosmic circle of his life outside the group bring him trouble.

With perceptiveness reaching with honesty toward honesty, one group member now hit on the falseness in Cathy's exaggerated sympathy.

"Come on off your pedestal, Cathy."

And another, "You're damned mad at Vic for not being more aggressive and you know it."

"I'm not." Cathy sat straighter and stared around the circle of faces, her hands trembling. "I'm not mad at Vic. Why should I be? I feel sorry for him. I'm mad at that damned Taylor."

"How do you feel, Vic?" another group member asked.

"I *don't* feel, I guess. That's still the trouble. I don't think it matters too much, if you know what I mean. I think Blaine's suggestion about my opening a consulting office is a good one and that's what I'm planning to do, and some of the clients

I've worked with will come to me, I'm sure, as soon as they know I'm on my own. I think Blaine himself will use me, and I'll do all right. I'm not really worried."

This time the group reacted to his feelings. Some were friendly, some were challenging, some were frankly angry at him for the absence of vigor in his response. He persisted passively, "It doesn't bother me!" He showed no anger at their anger. No backfiring to their challenges. No appreciation, either, for the friendly concern.

Finally the doctor pointed out, "You have the same problem here, don't you, Vic, that you had on the job? You take all the criticism here without protest. You don't work up any aggressiveness. Let's see, now, how does it really make you feel when the rest of the group jumps all over you?"

Vic looked at the floor and swallowed. He uncrossed his long legs and recrossed them. "It doesn't matter, if you know what I mean."

"What do you mean, Vic?"

He swallowed again and turned toward Cathy, his great hands hanging limply over the arms of his chair. "It doesn't matter," he said and added without change in pace or pitch, "It doesn't matter as long as Cathy thinks I'm all right."

The response rose quickly from various people.

"You sound like a little boy feeling fine as long as his mama says he's O.K. Just like me."

"As long as mother thinks you're wonderful, you don't have to struggle. The world can go by."

Vic's eyes were narrowed like blue slits of water almost lost in their hollows a great distance off. "My mother did think I was wonderful. My mother and Cathy."

His voice did not as usual plod on in monotone to indecisive end without ending. It paused in distinct waiting as if for something to rise from inside him rather than to come from the group.

"My father was away a lot, traveling for a firm he worked for. When he was at home, he was cold and aloof and disapproving of everything I did. I never felt close to him. I'd try to do things to please him when he was around, like getting his slippers for him or kissing him goodnight because he expected it of me, but I'd kiss him gingerly and notice how sharp his whiskers were, like barbed wires telling me to stay on my own side of the fence and not to get in his way or his territory or something, if you know what I mean. I tried to do things to please him, but it never did any good. He'd pack up and leave. I never really had a father. We never were close. I took Mr. Taylor as a father, I guess. I looked up to him and admired him and felt close to him and showed him I was there to do

whatever he said. I guess that's got something to do with it, my always doing what he said. If I'd shown more initiative I might be managing the firm now. But I always looked to Mr. Taylor as the one who held the reins. He was so much older . . ."

"The man with the whiskers!"

"Well, I took him that way. As a father."

"And now the only father you ever had walks out and leaves you. But it doesn't really matter, you say, because you have Cathy. I used to say my father could walk out and go to hell and I wouldn't care. But I've seen recently that it mattered a hell of a lot. I was just covering up that I cared, so that the caring wouldn't hurt quite so much."

The doctor came in again. "You thought it didn't matter then, Vic, because you had Mother. You tell yourself it doesn't matter now because you have Cathy."

Vic nodded slowly. "Mother and I were close. But somehow I guess it did matter. I had to be man of the house, if you know what I mean . . ."

"What, Vic?" I asked.

"Well, I did things for Mother. Took care of the furnace and chopped wood and shoveled snow and other things, too, that were more just for her. Just between the two of us, if you know what I mean." He looked for all the world like a frightened overgrown boy who wanted to slink out and hide in some dark street with his guilty but cherished secret.

"What, Vic? What sort of things?" I hoped he could share with me now the secret things he'd shared with his mother earlier, only now show them openly in front of these other people, discovering as he did so that in reality he had nothing to fear.

"Well," he swallowed and cleared his throat, "things like brushing her hair. She had blond hair, long and like silk. When she had it unbraided it came to below her waist. She'd let me unbraid it. And I'd run my fingers through its length, straightening it all the way . . ." Vic's eyes were now very blue, focused as if off into distance. "She had a white ivory hair brush with a woman's figure carved on the back. Only a hole had been burned into the girl someway by a branding iron. That's silly, by a cigar or cigarette, I don't remember. And I forget where the hole was in her, what part of her was missing, just that there was a hole somewhere. I'd like to brush her hair; it felt soft and good and there were other things, too, like that, if you know what I mean."

"That felt good?"

He nodded.

"Well," he looked down at the floor. "Well, she'd like me to sleep in bed with her when *he* was away, and I'd wash her back for her when she bathed. She liked me to do it, take care of her, sort of . . ."

"She thought you were wonderful, Vic," the doctor said gently. "How did you feel, Vic? Protected and safe?"

Vic's eyes almost closed till the blue scarcely showed. He looked down at the floor away from everybody, as if he were afraid to meet anyone squarely. Then, in a voice that was duller and flatter and yet tighter and less flaccid, he answered, "No. Not safe really. No. I didn't really feel safe with my mother. I don't understand it. There was something about it. Well, it seems to me somehow . . . It came to me just at this moment . . . I never thought so before, but . . . Well, as if she had in some way expected too much."

"Like Cathy now?"

He scuffed his great feet on the floor in a helpless gesture, and very slowly shook his head. . . .

"I can't club her!" Kenneth had said. "But I can do other things."

"If I were Hamburger," he elaborated one day, "I'd show her I was angry. I'd jump on her bed and get paw marks all over it. I'd get real mad and growl and bark. I'd chew up her purse and get mud on it. I'd be a real mad and happy Hamburger. Really happy to be mad."

He looked at me soberly. "I'd like to be like that. I'd like to do things, too, to show her how I feel. I'd like to be a real-happy-to-be-mad-Kenneth. But if I got too outspoken it would just get me into a mess of trouble. I can't do it with her. I know that. But I can get the mad out in here with you."

He became freer and easier in reporting what had gone on at home and in the neighborhood. "My boy friend Gene took me to a movie. He treated me. I feel more like a friend!". . . "And me and a couple of other boys got some flower seeds and planted them in the empty lot.". . . "And we're working on a model airplane."

He was freer, too, in expressing his feelings. He was angry at his mother when she was late to meet him at the dentist's one afternoon. He was angry when she forgot to pick him up at school as she'd promised to do. He was angry at her and at his father when they proposed taking back his room for their study and moving him in again with Brad.

"It makes me furious," he announced, glowering. "It'll put me right down again at Brad's level, three years younger than I am. I'll have to turn the lights off earlier and turn the radio off earlier. Just the idea of the whole business makes me mad . . . They don't care how much Brad disturbs me. I don't know what I'll do if I have to move in with that brat . . ."

He stopped and a crafty look came into his face. "Oh, yes, I do know. I'll cough and I'll sneeze and I'll wheeze. I'll get the asthma again. I'll annoy them with it every night. Every night about every half-hour I'll call them in and I'll be such a nuisance keeping Brad awake that he'll be all peevish and shrieky and they won't be able to stand either of us together, and then they'll *have* to give me back my own room. . . ."

Even though he thought he could not manage to talk about it to his parents, he had.

At dinner that evening when Brad was especially silly, Ken saw an opening. He threw a glance in Brad's direction, and then turning to his mother, he announced with utter disdain, "That there's my brother. I love him. I could murder him. And if you put me into that room with him, I will."

He reported to me a few days later, "I was surprised. She took it O.K."

He grew more expansive. "It's really remarkable. She really can take it from me better than she used to. I guess because she's learning to bring her own crossness out in little fire-cracker explosions. She doesn't hold it all in the way she did. You should see her at home sometimes. She looks like a witch.

"But it's still hard for me to say things to her. It's still easier to say them to you."

He looked pensive. And then very slowly, as if he were pushing to see his direction through fog, he struggled to bring into words what had long been one of his greatest fears. "Sometimes I want to let go. Over some little nothing, almost. Some little thing happens; only it isn't little when it gets to me. It seems big. I guess because it sets off something *big* inside me. The biggest wish to SOCK that you ever knew. It's so big that if I socked anybody with that much steam I—I—think I'd explode."

In great simplicity, Kenneth had elucidated what many people never come to understand. He had been so afraid that he might act on his inner anger and carry out to the full what it dictated that he had kept himself tightly in check. Immobilized almost. So afraid had he been of the push and the force of hostility in him that he had closed up and denied that any was there. In his unconscious mind, however, it had continued to propel him until again and again he had turned it back onto himself, punishing himself for the bad wishes and thoughts, getting sick, feeling guilty, cringing and failing.

If a child's emotional hungers are satisfied by his mother in the helpless beginnings of life when he cannot fend for himself, then he can take in better stride the necessary denials which must be imposed on him as he grows. If he were to put the matter into words, he might say, "I get angry, yes, at big people for their forbidding me things I want. But still I know they are fundamentally with me and for me. They care about me. They proved that to me when I was small."

On the other hand, when forbiddings follow early deprivations and a child has not come to the place where he feels he can trust his parents to love and understand him, he is apt to feel they deny him because they don't care about him. Then hurt and anger and rage and fury mount far more stormily. They must be barricaded all the more tightly. It's as if he said to himself, "I must not even look to see that these feelings exist. If I acknowledge them, they may burst and destroy me and my world."

Kenneth, however, had looked. With me to support him, he had come through pain and fear to a place of seeing. The pain and fear had grown small enough to endure, and Kenneth had built inner courage enough to tolerate the remnants that still were there and always would be. The trust in me that he had come to feel so profoundly had helped him to make up for his earlier lack of trust in his mother and father. It had helped him move forward toward trust in himself.

Now, since he trusted himself more securely, he could trust himself to manage feelings that he had not felt capable of managing earlier.

Before coming into therapy, he had built up a way of managing himself that was in truth self-demolishment. His way of checking himself had not lain in control but in paralysis. He had virtually immobilized effective functioning in his fear lest unwanted feelings come through. As a result he had not been able to bring out normal aggressiveness. The drive and the push had been so checked that he could not even tackle school subjects with the verve that comes when feelings flow freely into any act. It was as if he had posted a demon of punishment at the streets' intersection, always keeping the "Go" sign off and the "Stop" sign on.

But now he felt it less necessary to call on the demon. Kenneth felt himself more able to judge and choose and guide what he should do. He could use his eyes and look over the terrain and take into account what the traffic could bear. He could say to himself, "I'll not go up that street; it's better not to. I'll move along this other street instead. The first street's not safe; the second one is." He could say to himself, "It's not possible to let my feelings run along this action pathway. But along this other one, it's all right.

"I can't let my feelings run out in the act of clubbing my mother. That way is no good.

"But I can talk to my mother sometimes about my feelings. Though only very occasionally.

"I can talk my feelings out to you and to myself . . .

"I've been mad at my mother lots. I was mad at her the other day because she promised me I could go to the store with her and then she went off and completely forgot that I was waiting. I'd like to have called her an idiot. But I knew if I did, she'd get too sore. So I drew little idiot pictures and knew in my mind who they were."

Or again, "I'd like to sock her really. But she's a woman and so I can't. I went and socked my ball, though, all around the block."

He could manage these feelings now more consciously without shoving them all into his unconscious mind. He had acquired the basis for true *self-control*—for managing the outflow of feelings, neither denying nor letting them run wild. He saw what he could do and what he could not do in more realistic terms.

Reprinted from *One Little Boy* by Dorothy Baruch (New York: The Julian Press, 1952; Delta Paperback, 1964) by permission of the publisher.

Editors' Commentary
Emerging Group Forms of Therapy

We have indicated some of the major pathways in which psychotherapy has been traveling in its effort to help individuals lead more fulfilled and productive lives. Because of the increasing pressures and complexities of modern, particularly urban, society, there are greater needs for treating the severely emotionally disabled, the somewhat incapacitated, and the victims of society-bred illness. Treatment for emotional disturbance is needed for couples, families, and larger groups as well as individuals; the needs for treatment are apparent in such places as private offices, clinics, hospitals, schools, and churches, as well as on street corners and playgrounds. There are many forms of treatment. One of the most commonly used is group therapy. Both the mental health worker and the educator need to understand the forces at work in groups and how they can be effectively used to teach or treat.[3]

The structure, leadership, and methods of groups vary according to their purposes. In examining those described below, readers should keep in mind their own varied experiences of groups. There are bound to be a number of enlightening parallels.

3. *Psychoanalytic Study of the Child*, Vol. III (New York: International Press, 1948).

Groups: How They Grew and What They Do

Ruth G. Newman

These days the Group is the Thing. There are haphazard groups; groups emphasizing verbal communication; nonverbal groups; long-term therapy groups; short-term groups; groups to study group behavior; groups to train for leadership in groups; discussion groups; meditative groups; marathon groups; role-playing groups; psychodrama groups; sensitivity groups; and encounter groups. There are groups for delinquents, for debutantes, for miners, for ministers, for alcoholics, for drug addicts, for adolescents, for kindergarteners, for couples, for the divorced, for the old people, for teachers, for students, for principals, and for politicians. Groups abound to study interracial relations and international relations. There are even groups broken up into subgroups which study the interaction of their constituent groups. Consequently, it is no wonder that many people, responding to a phenomenon that has much of the appearance of a fad, look askance at groups or are frightened or repelled by them. At the other extreme, there are those who are so imbued with the experience that they become group-addicted, getting their "kicks" from group experience and, like any other addict, are unable to do without that experience, sometimes even permitting the group experience to replace any efforts at sustaining relations in ordinary unscheduled life situations. It is understandable that, with such varieties of response, there is a wide variety in the methods of groups and in the quality and kind of group leadership.

With all this groupiness, what is seldom understood by loyal advocates of one or another particular kind of group is that the underlying aims and primary tasks of groups vary as much as does the quality or method of leadership, and that the only fair way to judge the effectiveness of a group is to ask whether or not it accomplishes or approaches its aims or primary tasks. Its task may be to learn how to solve a specific problem, or to alter behavior, or to arrive at some insight, or to treat the emotional disturbances of group members, or to discuss something of mutual interest. It may achieve other things as well, but the important question is whether or not it does what it sets out to do. If a group is fundamentally for teaching or learning, the group cannot be held responsible for the fact that someone who joined it for therapeutic experiences failed to get what he wished or had, as sometimes happens, an overwhelming emotional experience. He was not in the right group.

It is the responsibility of the group leadership and of the person joining a group to be clear about just what the group's primary goal is. An ideal group leader understands what is happening in a group on many levels at every moment. Without a general awareness among its members of which direction the group is to go, the group will at best probably fail in its purpose and may at worst be destructive. This is true for a teaching group, a staff meeting, a therapy group, a seminar, or a political policy-making group. A group needs a knowledgeable leader who is clear about the group's task and aware of potential pitfalls.

All groups need far better tools for screening group members in order to avoid some of the worst hurdles and hazards. But the screening methods presently in use are either overly pedantic or too loose to be effective. There are few experiences more immobilizing, for instance, than that of the child who is placed in a group which repeatedly excludes him. Eventually he develops a pattern of self-exclusion, so that he holds himself apart whenever he meets new groups of people. There is a need for some good research into the requirements of grouping as well as into the training of leaders appropriate to the tremendous variety of groups required by modern society. Some understanding of groups as such is essential to an understanding of families; of schools; of the types of teaching appropriate to different children; of local, national, and international politics; and of the interrelations among various groups within single institutions (such as the schools, which encompass to one or another extent boards of education, administrations, teaching and non-teaching staffs, parents, students, in some respects the entire community). The present high interest in groups is a graphic indicator of their importance in modern society.

Far from being a new concept, groups are of course one of the oldest means of human survival. Like other animal species, early man grouped himself into herds, and the herds subdivided themselves into leaders and followers according to the task at hand. From the herds there evolved the more differentiated tribes, and from the tribes the clans—the groups at each level more specialized and finely differentiated than those above. Warring, working, and negotiating with each other, the smaller groups defined for themselves territorial boundaries, and nations developed. Various forms of cultural ethics emerged as different groups developed differently. Some of the sources of differentiation were psychodynamic, some were economic, and some were ecological and climatic. The various hostile forces of nature solidified the group-proneness of humans all over the earth. Within larger groups there developed subgroups for the purpose of achieving one or another of the particular goals of the society. Tribal custom, personal abilities, and hereditary roles helped determine grouping (much as they do in contemporary schools and classes). Religious groups, food-acquiring groups (hunting groups, herding groups, planting groups), women's groups, children's groups, and even out-groups (the excommunicated or the especially venerated) all found a place, their power varying according to the particular needs of the large group at the moment. Human society would not have survived if there were not in the human species an instinct for grouping. (The word

instinct is to be taken literally, on the basis of anthropological and historical data.) There is in men a need for simultaneous difference and sameness in relation to one another.

Perhaps because of its instinctual sources, man's group-proneness has never, as such, received much attention. Perhaps the most self-conscious use of groups has been among statesmen and churchmen. From Ikhnaton to Lenin, from Moses to Martin Luther King, the democratic Jefferson, the manipulative Machiavelli, the power-driven Napoleon or Hitler, the socially conscious Roosevelt—none would have achieved what they did without knowing how to relate to and manipulate the groups they dealt with directly and those they dealt with indirectly through representatives. They knew how to use man's instincts for group life to serve the purposes in which they believed, for good or for ill.

Even in the little arena of the classroom, no teacher would survive a school day without knowing how to deal with a group. All of the teacher's actions have some effect—productive, destructive, or something in between—on the members of the group, the class. "Johnnie, move your chair to the back of the room," "Susie, come sit by me," "Laurie, you help Ken," "Nancy, it's your turn to choose your spelling team." How did the students accept these instructions? Why? What was the price? What was the value? Did the teacher have any unconscious motivations? Did the students perceive them? What task did the teacher want to achieve? Was that the best way to do it or just the way everybody had done it—or the way the syllabus or the supervisors had said to do it?

The teacher faces similar questions in his association with other groups, such as the other teachers he works with and the parents of his students. What *did* happen at the teachers' meeting yesterday? Why didn't he speak up? Why didn't he say what he wanted to say and had planned to say? Why did what he said come out too weak, too strong, too wheedling, too belligerent? What about the parents' meeting he had to lead? What went wrong? What went right and why? Did he or did he not accomplish the task? Did he spend too much time with the N's to the rejection of the B's? Why did he shut himself off when the racial issue came up? Was he scared by it or was it right to do so at that time and place?

A person in a group finds himself in a variety of roles—roles which are continually changing. He is violent. He is withdrawn. He is convincing. He is misunderstood. He reaches one or more people. He is isolated. He is the leader one minute and the dependent follower the next. He considers himself guided by rational methods, yet he finds himself acting on utterly irrational, overwhelming motives. He is hated for leading although he has been made to lead. He is scorned for following although no one would follow *him*. He is singled out by one member and ignored by the others. He is the doctor, and therefore isolated or the patient, and therefore the center of everyone's attention. He incorporates in himself everyone in the group, and yet he remains, if he is at all healthy, his own unique self.

The knowledge that a person acquires about himself in groups helps him to understand his colleagues and his pupils. Experience with the emotionally disturbed is especially good at teaching a person his own defenses and vulnerabilities. More intensely perhaps than any other groups, the emotionally disturbed represent all the phases of oneself and of everyone else; that is one reason these groups often make a person so anxious: they strike chords of intense anger, of hopelessness, of withdrawal, of isolation, of loneliness, of the struggle to succeed, of competition, of winning, of losing, of hatred, of need, of love, of hunger, of the whole gamut of human conditions. But though some of these conditions may be uncomfortable and unattractive, a teacher needs to know what it's like to experience all of them in order to deal with them intelligently in his students.

When working with groups of children, a teacher must beware of thinking he can improve the group by ridding it of the child who is causing a disturbance. If he removes such a child, he can be certain that another child will assume the role of disturber, and he can be fairly sure that both are being egged on by that seemingly quiet fellow in the third row. To try to eliminate the uncomfortable parts of that whole which is a group is to restrict experience and to imply that life is something it is not. To accept the inconvenient elements of group experience and to channel them constructively is to enrich that experience for both teacher and students.

Classroom groups are best organized around the task at hand. What does the teacher want the children to achieve? An academic skill? Personal insight? An exchange of ideas or feelings? A cooperative project such as a mural or a play? A different kind of group is appropriate for each of these purposes, and a teacher should choose each group with leaders who will be able to inspire confidence in the group's ability to achieve the particular task at hand, leaders who can lead without demanding that other group members abdicate all responsibility. From his experience with groups as participant

and observer, a teacher finds in time reasonably workable rules for grouping according to the task at hand, be it short- or long-range.

Groups That Study Groups

With the recent upsurge of interest in groups and group theory, a number of organizations have arisen with the purpose of studying groups and group behavior. The National Training Laboratory is one of the sources of such study. It is in this center that the concepts of the "sensitivity group" and "sensitivity training" evolved, the idea being to develop a program through which a participant might become more sensitive to himself in relation to the other members of a group under a variety of experiences. The task is *not*, as many people interpret it, to make one a more sensitive person (it may or may not do that); the task is to make each individual member more effective in terms of the total group. The major center of the National Training Laboratory is in Washington, D.C. It also has a summer center in Bethel, Maine, and other centers in California and elsewhere. Although many kinds of group experience are offered, it is best known for its small groups consisting of about eight to twelve people and a group trainer. They are called T-groups, for training groups. As with any group, the T-group's quality and the direction it takes depend largely on the leader, though these are of course modified by all of the group's members. Such groups emphasize informality (first names, any kind of dress, familiarity with the leader), openness, intimacy, and emotionality, since one premise of these groups is the belief that the inhibition of these qualities creates barriers among people that affect them in all of their dealings. The emphasis given to these qualities varies tremendously from group to group.

The National Training Laboratory has attracted many industries, departments of government, social agencies, and schools, for the training of groups among their staff members. Some varieties of these groups, such as encounter groups and those of the Esalen Institute, have been criticized for being anti-intellectual and undisciplined as well as for arousing more feelings, letting loose more hostility, and breaking down more defenses than some group members are able to handle; it has been said that organizations need to be run by rational rather than emotional means. But in spite of the criticism, many people continue to find group experiences of these kinds useful. Many varieties have developed: bio-energetics; massage groups; all kinds of encounter groups, which are an intensely emotional undertaking; the contact group, which is often nonverbal; the transactional or game-theory group, which uses group games as models of pressure situations (deriving from the theory presented by Dr. Eric Berne in a bestselling book, *Games People Play*); and the gestalt group developed by Dr. Fritz Perls, in which a group member dramatizes some partially conscious tendency in himself with the help of the other group members. *Please Touch* by Jane Howard is a readable book that describes NTL groups and their off-shoots.

The center for a different approach to the study of group behavior is the Institute of Group Relations at the Tavistock Institute in England. In America, similar studies are being done at the A. K. Rice Institute for Human Relations. These groups have their theoretical sources in the ideas of Dr. Wilfred Bion, whose work began with the rehabilitation of Royal Air Force fliers during World War II. These groups were subsequently developed among various people in England and later in the United States: doctors and hospital staffs, trade unionists, churchmen, government workers, educators, and people generally who are interested in social change. Many, including this author, feel that the Tavistock model contributes more to an understanding of the subtleties and covert processes within groups in relation to leadership— particularly important to the complexities of to-day's society—than any other theory.

The emphasis in the Tavistock groups is on learning through experiencing groups and simultaneously being able to reflect about the experience. One of the goals of Tavistock groups is to determine which factors encourage and which discourage a work group in achieving its task. These groups examine the relationship between a group and its leadership; they are interested in the sources of authority within a group and in the question of the responsibility of individual group members for the direction a group takes and the decisions it makes. They come to recognize the power of the group in determining the roles, active or passive, of individual members, and they learn what it is to accept or reject those roles. The meaning of leadership and the significance of the various barriers that exist between people, such as the leader and the led, are important considerations of these groups.

In addition to the small group, similar in size to the T-group of the National Training Laboratories, the A. K. Rice–Tavistock model makes use of larger groups, a format which has many applications to modern, particularly urban, society, where

such groups as the school assembly and the student protest meeting are increasingly familiar. The large group experience on the Tavistock model is often disconcerting and confusing, though it is also enlightening in that it demonstrates the difficulty of communicating in a group too large for face-to-face confrontation.

The A. K. Rice groups hold periodic conferences, lasting from a few days to two weeks, at which their exercises in the study of small group, large group, and intergroup behavior take place. The intergroup exercise offers dramatically instructive experience in the difficulties of relationship, communication, and negotiation among various groups. It has obvious analogies in the United Nations, in national politics, in labor–management relations, in school board–administration relations, in staff–administration relations of schools and hospitals, and in relations among different racial and ethnic groups. The formation of conservative, liberal, and radical attitudes often takes place in groups, and various individual roles emerge, such as the stranger, the belonger, the excommunicated, the defector, the informer, the rebel, and the go-between. One of the most revealing aspects of these exercises is the difficulty groups have simply in agreeing on a method for the study of group behavior, the difficulty of agreeing on the means for carrying out the group's task once the task itself is agreed on, the difficulty of negotiations among groups, and the chaos and sense of futility that often ensue from these efforts. A most dramatic presentation of the complicated concepts demonstrated by the Tavistock groups can be found in Kenneth Rice's book, *The Conference in Group Relations*. A particularly moving account of the interpersonal dynamics among a small group of men faced with actual life and death decisions regarding the future of a whole nation and perhaps even the world is provided in Robert Kennedy's *Thirteen Days*, a first-hand account of the Cuban missile crisis as it was handled by the top advisors to President John Kennedy.

The National Training Laboratory directs its attention to the individual within a group: how he comes across, how his behavior affects others in the group, and how he reacts to others. The A. K. Rice–Tavistock groups concentrate on the *gestalt* of the group: what forces are released by the group; what pressures and what unconscious group attitudes, covert and overt, are aroused. Because leadership, the authority to work, and responsibility are the foci of this model, the staff behave in a much more formal manner, carefully keeping time and space boundaries between themselves and individual members while work is in progress, so as to be able to keep their full attention on the group and its conscious and unconscious behavior as they study problems of roles within the group, forces that emerge, leadership, competence, and the consequences of taking on or abdicating responsibility.

In addition to Wilfred Bion's *Experience in Groups*,[1] see the excellent articles by Margaret J. Rioch, "The Work of Wilfred Bion on Groups"[2] and "We, Like Sheep."[3]

Notes

1. **Wilfred Bion,** *Experience in Groups* (New York: Basic Books, 1962).

2. **Margaret J. Rioch,** "The Work of Wilfred Bion on Groups," *Psychiatry,* 33 (1970): 56–66.

3. **Margaret J. Rioch,** "We, Like Sheep," *Psychiatry,* 38 (1972): 38–46.

Editors' Commentary

The following article is an excerpt from a book about all aspects of groups in schools: the school as a miniature social system; classroom groups, staff groups, parent and community-action groups, administration and teachers' union groups; the nature of group forces and group roles in the school; and the treatment of children in and out of the school setting. The excerpt deals with treatment in groups of children and youths who can stay within the school setting in regular or special classes. The children range on a problem continuum from ordinary to severe disturbances, but all can benefit from group treatment properly administered.

Treatment Groups

Ruth G. Newman

Living sometimes brings to children, as it also sometimes does to adults, problems of such a nature that they may become immobilized. Anxiety or panic besets them to such an extent that they cannot concentrate, and even when they appear to be doing their work, they can neither comprehend nor retain it. Like as not, they are unable to sit still long enough to hear the task assigned, let alone to pursue it. When these problems come only from the outside and are temporary—let's say, when a child's parents have separated, or his father has lost his job; or when his mother is ill or the gang has ostracized him or when a beloved pet has died—tension abounds in the family, and the child may become morose or cross. He may feel ignored, belittled, picked on, rejected or unworthy. Or he may be recovering from a bad flu or suffering from undernourishment, both of which conditions make for low tolerance of anxiety, easy loss of temper and clouds of depression. These things he will get over, but if they go on too long beyond their causes, in order to keep the situation from becoming worse, to keep what began as superficial from turning into a deepset response, the child often needs help, usually of a temporary nature.

Help for problems of this kind may be given as therapy within the school building, or it may be given in a clinic or private office outside the school. In most cases recognition that a child needs help comes first from the school. In these instances, therapy is usually preceded by parent conferences and a diagnostic work-up by a school psychologist, a referral clinic or a private facility. In the latter cases, the school needs to have some way of determining whether the child is actually getting help outside and if so of what kind; it needs to know whether the therapist wants to keep in touch with the school or not. The therapy decided on may be individual and may or may not include the family or it may be in a group of peers. There are sometimes special and good reasons for treatment to be individual, but if these are not apparent, this kind of child will probably be very well able to use a group, for in a group he can discover that, as well as his peers, the adults involved can help him gain insight.

If the problems are in fact largely born of circumstance, this type of child tends to be that boon to group therapists, the child who himself takes to therapy as a thirsty man to water, and who is able also to be helpful to others in the group. When he leaves the group, he has learned something more about himself, about his interpersonal style. He has become more aware of the habitual ways in which he has defended himself in situations that make him anxious, and of how he comes across to others; he gains, as well, many more insights that can be of use to him throughout his life. If he is too young for such self-recognition and ability to do something about it, his parents, through parallel or collaborative group work, will have gained the ability to hear his cues and act upon them, and to seek counseling themselves. At the time of crisis, the problems of this group of children *feel* to them no less bad or intense than those of far more distressed children, and sometimes their actions in class are as disturbing or even more so, but the distress lasts less long, and the situation, if caught and recognized, does far less damage to the child or the class, and can be handled more readily. This type of child is well served both by short-term group psychotherapy where some unconscious material can be dealt with, some basic needs served, and coping mechanisms explored, and by interactive groups such as sensitivity training offers. These groups can meet either in or out of school. There are many kinds of therapy groups. I will describe the basic ones briefly.

Non-Treatment Groups

What do we mean by the term "non-treatment group"? Most commonly, the kind of circumstances that beset a youth above the age of twelve may be alleviated by responsibly led encounter or sensitivity groups in which the group concentrates on its collective behavior and feelings in the here and now, groups in which the individual members get and give feedback on what is happening to them, from and with each other, as well as from and to the adult leader(s).

The leaders of such groups usually behave and dress in a very open and familiar manner. They not only use their own feelings, as every good therapist does, but relay these feelings and the behavior they generate to the individuals in the group in order to indicate how what a person is doing may make others feel. The leaders and the group attempt to explore alternative modes of behavior which might be more successful, or at least more satisfying and so presumably more easing to one's own soul and relationships. Groups serve as a laboratory: they offer a safe place to try on different roles to see which ones fit one's own temperament and needs most usefully. Different leaders use different styles and techniques, but in general the sensitivity or "encounter" type of group attempts to deal with problems in the here and now, largely using past material only where it seems relevant to present behavior or feelings. It emphasizes relationships, closeness, caring, as therapeutic tools to help the individual. Though it often arouses unconscious or reminiscent material and sets up anxiety-provoking happenings, it is not a sine qua non of the sensitivity group dogma that the unconscious be looked at as it is in most psychodynamic therapy or in the Tavistock Model groups. The aim is to enable an individual to see himself and others in a group, and to get help from the group and the leader toward personal growth and development. This is often all that is needed to alleviate the pain and paralysis that derive from these circumstances and to allow them to come close enough to the surface, in time and place, to be looked at and appraised.

Adolescents as well as adults who are shy of "psychotherapy" are often very willing to try this kind of experience. It is particularly apt for adolescents, with their loneliness, their struggle to find themselves, their dependence on group approval, and their need to test out adult authority. The search for the self fits in well with the identity struggle adolescents face. When led by skillful leaders, such a group does well in helping the person without deepset problems who needs to grapple with developmental changes, which by themselves at crisis periods of growth (such as adolescence or aging) can cause great anguish.

Sensitivity or encounter groups are often held in the school, though sometimes they are held outside. It is essential that if the school is the sponsoring agency the leaders have some contact with the counselor and teacher—not to breach confidentiality, but so that school people can be made aware that the child is working on his problems, and that while he is doing so, his behavior in class may, for a while, seem more tense or dreamy, and even, at times, bizarre. It is equally important, or more so, that the parents be fully aware of the groups their children are in. It needs to be made absolutely sure that the parents have given their permission. Again, with younger children especially, the group's value is enhanced appreciably if the parents too are involved in a group, or in individual counseling experience.

Sensitivity and encounter groups are also used widely for staff training.... Although "sensitivity" and "encounter" groups may differ in technique, the goal of *individual* growth through interaction is paramount in both kinds of group. The difference between the two depends on the particular school of thought or techniques used by the leaders.[1]

Leaders of the two types of group differ not only because of differing professional interests but also because of different theoretical biases. Right now, the largest number form a cluster around what is called "Gestalt" and "transactional therapy." "Gestalt" is represented in the practices of the late Fritz Perls and Laura Perls. "Transactional therapy" is exemplified by Eric Berne in his *Games People Play.* A similar kind of eliciting interaction and insight is that of Virginia Satir who emphasizes a role-playing dramatic approach. Her interests have been largely in family therapy, where the family is seen as a group, but her methods have since been extended to other groups as well.

"Marathon" groups—groups based on the principle that when people are tired their usual sets or behavior patterns can be broken down more easily, and that insight and change can thus occur—are used by most sensitivity and encounter leaders. Sessions may run anywhere from eight to forty-eight hours at a stretch. Some more conventional groups who meet regularly once a week for one and a half hours include a few modified marathons in which the participants can go home to sleep for brief periods. For many reasons such exercises are clearly inappropriate for young children.

There can be dangers for adolescents (in fact for everyone) in the extremist types of groups. Some adolescents can't take the kind of closeness forced on them, because they are not yet sufficiently clear about their own identity and unity as persons to have whatever patterns they have developed for themselves battered down without time to assimilate the why and the how and the what it all means. Many, who in their daily lives are overexposed to badgering, cannot take the force of group-badgering which insists that a person feel what the group thinks he should-ought to-must feel. He may not feel what the group wants him to feel and may either fake it—which is not useful—or get group-pressured into feelings, phony or real, he can't deal with. Another danger, when these groups are adapted to children, lies in precisely that quality which appeals to adolescents and to many adults. Since one of the goals is to develop closeness, intimacy, sharing, the procedures involve the breaking down of existing boundaries. But such boundaries are needed, especially by young children, to give some steering power, some individual sense of how the skin separates one person from another, of where the limits of do and don't, can and can't really fall.

Where boundaries are not a problem, such groups are appealing and useful, and when they are led by people who know adolescents, they are particularly useful with that age group. They can be invaluable to facilitate open communication, to help one realize feelings, to make one aware that the supposedly unacceptable parts of oneself are often liberating and energy-producing. A responsible leader of a sensitivity type of group for adolescents in the school or outside would give careful attention to the problem of who should join and who should be eliminated. He would be careful not to mix adults who are emotionally adolescent with chronological adolescents.

A leader may use many Gestalt and transactional techniques, but he must not allow the activity to reach a point where the adolescents are forced into a closeness they cannot tolerate, or led into sexual fantasies or acting-out which would make them too frightened or too guilty. Fooling around with people's defenses while setting loose group forces is at best a precarious business. The safeguards lie in the leadership. Still, keeping this in mind, groups which concern themselves with the three areas of particular moment to adolescents—peer relations, self, and authority—can be valuable aids.

Before we leave the subject of sensitivity groups for school-age children, it should be said that in modified form a sensitivity group may be useful in the earlier years as far down as the second or third grade. It may include all or only some members of a class; and it can be a useful device when included as a means to teach sex education or social values and to stimulate intellectual growth as well.

Psychotherapy Groups

There are certain children whose problems have deeper roots than those we have so far discussed. In their lives too, circumstances may arise which cause traumas, and these may bring to light or exacerbate pre-existent difficulties. It requires careful diagnostic procedures to distinguish the problems with deep roots from the more superficial ones. Children with deep-rooted problems fit well into psychotherapy groups.

To pass over the perennial debate about whether the problems that beset humans are rooted in physical constitution, chemical imbalance, genetic fault, environmental happenstance, or cultural pressures, let us agree that all these factors do exist and do create stresses. It is rare to be able to say with any validity that a particular individual's misery or mis-adaptation is caused by one aspect and not by the others. Whatever the causes, the difficulties in living exist, and all we can do is take the best information we have available and try to find the best way we now know to work with a particular child, given his assets as well as his liabilities. We do know *some things* beyond trial-and-error methods. If the chosen mode of approach does not work, we try another and another, or we combine two or more, or we eliminate the ones that don't work. Since people are the instruments of these methods, we have to consider not only the receiver of treatment, but the giver as well—and most of all, in nearly all therapies, no matter how mechanical or "controlled," we have to look at the relationship that exists between the giver and the receiver of treatment. Moreover, at the same time that we become more sophisticated in what we know, we have learned that with all humans, but particularly with children, we have to look at the homes they live in, the culture and values they absorb, and the school and the people who teach and treat them. With this assortment of factors in mind, we can proceed to review—we can only skim over them—the various types of therapy where groups become a central aspect of treatment.

Many times it has become clear that certain children do far better in working out their problems—no matter how deep-seated—in a group with children roughly about their own age level than in individual therapy. Their fear of adults is mitigated and their fear of exposure is lessened by the knowledge that others have problems too. Groups confront difficulties in relationships with peers, a prime cause of problems. From these confrontations, understanding, whether vocalized or acted upon, can be gained. For children, a group is a more everyday setting than what Fritz Redl calls the "pressurized cabin" atmosphere of the therapist alone with one child, in a situation outside the context of daily life. Sometimes groups are made up of children with the same kinds of problems. Most often it has been found that a mixture of many kinds of children, exhibiting many different kinds of behavior and exemplifying within themselves a variety of inner dynamics, do better together than children all of one kind or type. Depending on the need, family and group treatment are offered either simultaneously or in sequence. If the therapists of each—the family and the group—collaborate closely, this can be very successful.

Sometimes a child is so emotionally deprived, or so beset by his inner dynamics, that he requires individual one-to-one treatment. He may need only this form of treatment, or he may need it as a prelude to group therapy. The group therapy then becomes a safe testing ground for what he has learned, a kind of graduation exercise from individual treatment, where the child makes transition from the complete attention of one adult to the more difficult and more usual situation where one must share adult attention, and find a way to have one's own needs met while leaving room for the needs of others. Sometimes a child is so fearful of adults, so tight and clammed-up, that he can better manage to get help from a group of peers than from one adult. If this is all he needs, well and good. If he needs more, the group may serve as a prelude or a support to his use of individual therapy, either after the group or simultaneously.

Three Special Forms of Group Psychotherapy

There have been two broad lines of thinking out of which group therapy as it is practiced today has developed. The first has come from the medical model or the psychoanalytic school; in this each patient comes with his individual problems as he would for individual treatment, but is seen within a group. The group happily profits from listening to one of its members work on his problems with the trained leader. The group members may have more or less opportunity to react to the material presented, depending on the convictions of the group leader. With some group leaders—those whose interest is more in group interaction—the group that is listening may be led to relate to the problems with their own experience and insights, and thus play more of a role in being therapeutic agents; with others, the procedure is largely a dialogue, with the leader engaged with one member after another.

This "classical" approach, as it is called, is typically represented by Slavson, the man who is the father of activity groups for youngsters. Its leaders are all professionals, usually trained in individual one-to-one treatment, who have come to group therapy later in their experience.

The second broad line of thinking may be represented by such groups as Alcoholics Anonymous and Synanon. Here people with a common problem get together to keep guard over each other, with the conviction that the force of a group whose common experience binds them together can help each member in times of stress or temptation. The group mitigates loneliness, satisfies dependency, and serves as a cathartic agency. It tries to mobilize itself, often by faith either in an overseeing agent, such as God, or, if not God, the group itself and its leadership. The leaders here are often people from the ranks of the group, though sometimes professional leaders will be brought in to work alone or in unison with the indigenous leaders. The power of the group has been seen to be extraordinarily helpful for motivated individuals, especially for those given to an addiction of some sort: alcohol, drugs, obesity, gambling, smoking, and the like. (About the only type of group that has not so far been constructed on these principles is a group to deal with people who have become addicted to groups as a substitute for direct life experience.) Here the group is paramount, and group process is the therapeutic tool. Dependency is the prime mover and the attempt is to transfer the dependency from a drug or a consuming obsessive pattern to the group. At this stage this therapy may be likened to methadone treatment as a means to get someone off the habit. Later, at least in some cases, the goal may be to free the person from gripping dependency needs, but for some it is clear that, once formed, the group must always be behind one to rescue one and to use one as rescuer in turn. Thus, along with caring for dependency needs, this type of group makes for a lifestyle, a social life, a release from isolation and loneliness; it is a route for helping and being helped that makes an individual feel needed and necessary.

The Bion-type group is quite different from the first two ... yet in some ways combines elements of both: for here the psychoanalytic unconscious material is basic and so is the treatment of the *group* as an entity. Treatment is of the group as a group; it is not focused on individuals. Thus, group process here too is paramount. The leader is trained in group behavior, covert and overt, and the recognition of covert processes is a sine qua non of insight. Dependency may be one phase of the process, but others are considered equally important as life-factors: Fight, Flight, and Pairing must be continually dealt with as well for the group to do its work and become a work-group. In Bion group therapy, in contrast to group education, the task is allowing individuals within a group structure to deal with conscious and unconscious ways of coping with life, and thereby to free them from crippling aspects of their lives by offering alternatives.

These three broad categories of group psychotherapy cover most of the types of groups that are now used in therapy, including behavior modification groups, hypnosis groups, and drug-induced groups, as well as activity groups, art and music and body therapy groups, psychodrama and scream therapy groups. Some theories and some techniques are applicable to classroom teaching; however, since the task is a quite different one, the application needs to be effected with discrimination and care to avoid confusion of goals. Having said so much, I believe it is clear that the sensitivity and encounter groups talked of above fit better into the second and third categories than the first. The Gestalt (despite the fact that the word itself means "the whole") fits better into the first category, since in Gestalt groups people are treated in a coupling between leader and subject with the rest of the members of the group looking on, relatively inactive until their turns arrive. The network group, whether its developers are conscious of that fact or not, is in some ways more Bionesque; in others, more like communes and self-help groups.

In view of the existence of all this potpourri of group structures, it is difficult to know which child in trouble will fit into what group and why. That decision is best left to the diagnostic process once the child is referred. The trouble is that conventional diagnosis seems to be getting rustier all the time. Since the school is nowadays laden with looking after a child's behavior as well as his intellectual development, and since that behavior is linked to the use of his intelligence, and both to his inner dynamics and the stress of developmental changes, it would seem mandatory that the school, or one of its delegates—teacher or counselor—be automatically included in the diagnostic process. Though this is indeed sometimes done, especially if the treatment planned is to come from within the school, it is not done often enough. True, teachers and counselors could use more skill in sharpening their observations and translating them, but if their summaries were included automatically along with records of testing and interviewing, we could cut down considerably on mistaken placement in both classroom and treatment modality, and the damaging consequences of doing the wrong thing or nothing would be much mitigated.

As a rule adolescents who need treatment do better in a group than in individual treatment, but there are many exceptions. Many younger children do better in a group or in family sessions than in individual therapy, since individual therapy often divides their loyalties and their ability to work out ways of relating to peers and parents. Here too there are many exceptions. In both cases the exceptions depend on the amount of pressure internal forces are placing on the child. If those forces tend to be so all-consuming that the child cannot deal with a group, or so idiosyncratic that no group seems appropriate, or if they are such as to lead him to destroy any group he is part of, then individual treatment is mandatory. Most workers still think first of individual therapy and then of group in diagnostic placement. It is useful to have diagnosis include a group experience of two or more sessions; that would make it possible to judge whether a child would do better with individual or group treatment, and if group treatment is indicated, might tell what kind of group the child would do best in.

In making a decision about the kind of treatment group to send a child to, if indeed he is to be sent to any group, the school could add essential information concerning the extent to which the child fears classmates, how he handles himself in those toughest of all periods in the school day—the transition periods—and how he acts in the lunchroom, playground, study hall, or rest rooms. What is his concentration span? Can he get started? And once started, can he stop? Does he talk excessively? How does he show how he feels—or does he? How does he play? How does he win and how does he lose? What is his attendance record like? His health record? Does the nurse have data? The gym teacher? Is he one who waits in the principal's office, and if so for what kinds of offense? What role does he play in the classroom—bully, scapegoat, clown, or sad sack? Do his parents come to meetings? What are their superficial attitudes toward him? How does he make the teacher feel—pitying, furious, indulgent, amused, bewildered? Is he over-intellectual? Is everything always the other guy's fault? If so, would an art therapy group or a psychodrama group help? Is he a loner or a mixer or a leader? If any of these, a low-keyed talk group might be a good choice. What developmental phase has he reached? Does he need work in behavior control, or does he need the chance to explore his body and mind in an activity group or encounter group? Are parental pressures such that he needs a place to help him relax and meet only minimal demands, or does he require higher expectations of himself? Is he ashamed of being tall, small, fat, dumb, bright, different? Is his or her sexual development a terror to him, and the thought of sex a nightmare? Does he try to act older or younger than his years? Does he attach himself to one person? Does he bribe or steal or brag to get friends? All of these are questions to which an alert teacher can contribute answers for the use of the diagnostician, along with the picture his parents give of how he behaves at home. Both accounts, compared with what the psychologist or psychiatrist finds, tell us how the child sees himself, how others see him, what his emotional and mental capacities are.

The composite picture may indicate what group he will fit into and be able to use, and whether individual treatment should be considered simultaneously or uniquely.

All of the above assumes that a teacher or counselor, the school social worker and the psychologist all agree that a child would benefit by help. A conference of school people that decides that Tessa has really been crying too many days in class, or that Louis has been running into the locker room to hide under people's coats too many times, will strengthen the recommendations given at a parent conference, and will give the person responsible for diagnosis and placement a clearer prescription as to how to proceed and what kind of treatment to seek.

Behavior Modification

We have not gone into the various kinds of therapy—those which may be offered in or out of school—which are based on principles of Behavior Modification. This particular form of therapy has become more and more popular among psychologists and in schools in these last years. There are a complex set of reasons why Behavior Modification therapeutic techniques are particularly popular in the schools. Schools have good pragmatic reasons for being concerned with behavior. "Deportment," as it used to be called, has always been the teacher's concern, and the teacher is often rated on how well her children behave. Misbehavior is usually defined as anything that "doesn't go" in Mr. N's or Miss M's classroom or in Mrs. P's or Mr. Q's school. Behavior is rarely seen as the psychologists see it—as any action or reaction, verbal or otherwise, that responds to stimuli from the environment. Behavior is even more rarely seen from the psychodynamic point of view—as not only reactive to outside stimuli, but as symptomatic of what is going on in the inside world of the child to make him perceive outside stimuli as he does and make him react to them as he does. Behavior Modification gives school people a tool they can apply to many situations in the realms of both cognitive learning and "deportment." Since Behavior Modification therapy derives from learning theory, the psychologist's domain, it is a natural alliance between education and psychology. It can deal with the behavior that bothers the teacher at the moment; it need not concern itself with bringing in past happenings in the family or personal history.

Behavior Modification is an outgrowth of Pavlovian conditioning psychology in which animals were taught to produce a number of responses by means of punishment or reward. By the same means they were taught to avoid other behavior, to "unlearn" it. The process of "unlearning" was called "extinction" (of a habit or response). Pavlovian theory was later applied to people—both reward and punishment have been used to teach new modes of behavior or new cognitive material. In the Soviet Union, Pavlovian theory is the basis for most psychological therapy. It is often used both here and abroad to make extinct various patterns considered undesirable, such as stuttering and smoking and drug-taking.

In its more sophisticated form, now in use in some parts of this country, Behavior Modification involves a thorough inquiry into a child's total pattern of behavior, and an even more detailed exploration of the problem that is of particular concern—for example, school-phobia (which lends itself well to this form of treatment) or poor study habits, or not being able to control actions, anger, or body movement. The detailed inquiry tells the therapist all he can learn from everyone involved—child, parent, teacher, friends—about the patterns of behavior and what kind of thing sets the problem in motion. It also tells him what is seen as a *reward* in the case of a particular child. The famous M & M candy may work for some small children, but it may not work at all for others—it certainly does not work for older children. Money may work for some, records for others; chits to be used toward the purchase of a guitar or a motorcycle, or a TV or a sleeping bag or a trip to the seashore, may work for a good many. Once a program is worked out, detailed as any program designed for a computer, and 'once a reward system is evolved, the plan can be put into effect. From then on, any avoidable stimulus that would work to upset the new learning is avoided; any stimulus that would work toward the goal is encouraged. This means, for instance, that if a given piece of behavior is considered undesirable and therefore to be made extinct, it must be ignored; in behavioral terms, not the slightest word is said about it, for ignoring is "punishment." If such an act is performed, a scolding, or even a mention, may act as a reward in the form of attention-getting, and the aim is literally to get the child to forget it. After each success, rewards appropriate to the particular child, or tokens that will mount up to realize the reward, are given because desired behavior requires attention to impress it on the child. After the behavior is "conditioned," harder and harder assignments are made until the desired goal is reached. Though rewards continue to be given, it takes more and more work to get them. The goal is finally to have the wanted behavior so ingrained, and the satisfaction from it so clear, that rewards

are no longer needed to "reinforce" the learning. The success of the process is measured by what happens when rewards and programming stop. Is the new learning really learned or do old patterns re-emerge in an orgy of backsliding? How much reinforcement is needed, and at what intervals? Results vary.

Many behavior modification people began as purists, insisting that all that was needed was the program and the reward. Though punishment in the form of shock, electric or verbal, has been used in some instances—electric shock with, for example, autistic children; psychological shock, visual or oral, in a remedial reading institute for children with learning disabilities—punishment is not really commonly used. This is partly because there are some data that tend to prove people respond more lastingly to reward than to shock; there is too the fact that public opinion reacts more favorably to the use of rewards than to the use of punishment.

Behavior Modification has been found to be most successful when carried out in groups, since the presence of the group and competition among members seem to act as reinforcements in themselves.

More recently Behavior Modification people have found it most helpful when working with children and youth, rather than with rats, cats, and dogs, to "reinforce" the learning by means of adding talks with the group leader—a kind of combined psychodynamic and Behavior Modification practice. Clearly, since the leader or the people who are directing the program dictate what must be done with the children, this kind of group falls within the dependency AA-type model. But of course, the leaders must be professionals, well-trained in Behavior Modification techniques.

There has been considerable success with this method, especially when the relationship between the group leader and the children is seen as being as basic to the treatment as are the program and the reward-systems themselves. But the method does not work for all children. For some it does not work at all; for others, results may be temporary. It does seem to work particularly well for many children with severe learning disabilities, especially those whose psychological problems appear to be more the result than the cause of school failure—children whose inability to conquer a basic skill has led to severe feelings of incompetence and apathy.

For the successful use of Behavior Modification in groups, no matter where they are, within the classroom or as an addition to the class offices outside the school, it is essential that parents be involved. The younger the child, the more important is this axiom. The reason is obvious. The purpose is to get rid of certain behaviors or learnings and to instill new or different ones, and this is to be achieved by completely ignoring the old pattern and continuously reinforcing the new. If then the child goes home and is scolded or punished for the very behavior that is to be assiduously ignored and is ignored in the behavior that is to get immediate notice and reward, the outcome will at best be highly questionable. Parents are usually seen either singly or, more economically and more usually, in groups. They are given explanations of what is going on in the treatment of their children, and told why and how they must help, and what will hinder progress. These parent groups are basically educational in function, but they may and often do turn into discussions of dynamic issues, such as feelings, causes, traps parents fall into, and traps they themselves set, with or without awareness.

The danger lies in the fact that since Behavior Modification *seems* easy to do, it is often looked at as a panacea for all troubles, instead of as simply a tool—one tool among many—to approach some problems, but not all. It also causes many people to be concerned about the obvious possibilities for misuse, for Behavior Modification carries about with it an Orwellian, brainwashing character, generating fear that someone up there or out there will decide what people ought to think, how they ought to act, what they ought to like; the fear that someone's thinking—the psychologist's, the teacher's, the dictator's—will "condition" all of us to be robot-automatons, all uniform assembly-line products. Particularly frightening is the political misuse the technique can be put to—e.g., in the service of the status quo or of a dictatorship or a religious fanaticism.

Nevertheless, with proper monitoring and caution, and in the hands of people who are aware that they are using potential dynamite, Behavior Modification can be a helpful group tool in the classroom and in the clinic. As a group, delinquents or children caught in the immobilizing trap of unusual learning disabilities are often particularly appropriate choices for a program of Behavior Modification when it is combined with an understanding of what is going on and why, so that they may have some awareness about what is happening to them. But this is true of any theory.

Before we leave the subject of Behavior Modification, it should be said that in diluted form, and not in its pure culture, this technique is frequently used in all of the groups we are to be concerned with in the rest of this chapter, especially at the early stages of group formation and definition of the task and the methods. This is true particularly with those groups of children who have a hard time with impulse control and sitting still. For instance, at the outset of a program, even though the methods chosen for the group are psychodynamic, an activity group leader may distribute Cokes to the children to reward a few minutes of sitting silent so that he can suggest to the children what activity is available today and where the materials for it are. The handing out of Cokes is a diluted form of reward, but it serves its purpose. The collaboration of a group psychotherapist with someone who knows Behavior Modification techniques has proved successful with persons who are hyperactive, or those who suffer from apathy and withdrawal.

Once it is decided that a child (or a youth) needs a group, the problem becomes what kind of group to choose and what kind of group leadership will best meet the needs of this child at this particular stage of his physical, mental, and emotional development.

Many children have a hard time talking, especially about their feelings. So of course do many adults, especially men who have been trained not to talk about their feelings. To make it possible for such children (or adults) to benefit by psychotherapy, an education or re-education job must be undertaken to open them to treatment—much as a surgeon will not operate until the patient is in good enough health to tolerate an anesthetic and the strain of the surgery. In psychotherapy, ability to receive therapy is even more important, for the treatment depends entirely upon the give-and-take process between patient and therapist. Unlike other treatments, it cannot be done *to* a patient; it must be done with him. The unhappy myth that the psychiatrist knows all, that the psychologist comes equipped with a crystal ball, is often encouraged by the practitioners themselves with their mystique-laden jargon and props. Given a therapist who is able and willing to give up this voice-from-on-high role, group process can break the myths down. Even in adult or pure talking-groups, it becomes impossible to keep up the myth of unseen voices making wise, oracular comments. Children's therapy has always been a nail in the cross of this mystique, since from its inception child-therapy forms of play have substituted for or have supplemented talk. Messages about feelings and circumstances of life are given through toys, puppets, games, pictures, charades, and other materials as clearly as through words, or even more clearly. The therapist, depending on whether he came from the Anna Freud, Melanie Klein, or Virginia Axline schools of training, may talk a little or a lot, may interpret or only reflect what the messages given out by the child's use of material mean, but it is still the child who expresses the messages by his play or by his use of materials.

Play and materials, as much as or more than talk, are the language of children. This is especially true of slum or ghetto children whose parents are beset with work and weariness, and who themselves have not been trained to use words as either tool or weapon, and therefore find the demand that they say how they feel overwhelming.[2]

Even if language were available as a tool, even if in itself learning abstraction and symbolization were more familiar, the question of using these techniques with people whom you have no reason to trust becomes a gigantic hurdle. Why should any child trust a strange adult with his feelings when clearly his family, whom he is expected to trust, have not understood them or been able to use them—when his teachers, with whom he is at least acquainted, seem not to be able to understand them, and when these very feelings appear to be the reason he is in enough trouble to need special help? Besides, he probably isn't sufficiently at home with his own feelings to know what they are, let alone to name them. Even God took a few days before he named things in the world, so the troubled child, especially the nonverbally educated child, has legitimate precedent! It becomes the therapist's job to ease the pathways of communication and hack out new paths where none existed before.

A group therapist may, for a time, have a hectic and bewildering experience, but his task is made easier by the fact that he is dealing with a group, who by their manner and interests and separate means, suggest materials, games, images, which he can follow up and use as channels for getting feelings expressed and dealt with. Interestingly enough, a by-product of successful therapy is usually the ability of a child to use speech more ably than ever before, not only in the realm of feelings, but as a tool for thinking—that is, for solving cognitive problems as well as emotional ones. The therapy, itself, if successful, is educative, and the therapist (along with the group) has been the teacher. This is amusing, because many therapists vigorously deny their teaching role just as they too often object to the teacher's playing a therapeutic role. Yet many of the children without any intervention other than psychotherapy in their lives, do far better in the conceptual school subjects after therapy. One may say that this is true because their emotional problems have been sufficiently solved to allow them to use their energy in school study; it is hard to disentangle emotional from intellectual effort, but there is much evidence to indicate that the mere ability to translate feelings and thought into words is indeed a successful by-product of the group venture.

Keeping all this in mind, we turn now to those forms of group therapy that use materials as the focal point of group organization, and where words only supplement or come out of the materials being used. The group leader, depending on his point of view and personal style, may interpret much or little. His interpretations will, to be sure, affect the course of the ideas and the problems produced, but the primary point here is that the group itself use the materials to state and to work on the problems of its members.

Activity Groups

Slavson, as I mentioned earlier, was the grandfather of activity group theory. F. Redl, W. Morse and many others could also be mentioned as utilizing a natural child-group structure in the service of treatment. Such a group, often called a club, may meet together at regular intervals, anywhere from once a week for a few hours, to several afternoons or evenings a week after school, or in school or at a designated camp. The group is together because all the members exhibit some kind of behavior which troubles either them or, more often, their schools, homes, or community. They may meet indoors or out; there is usually a room or "clubhouse" set apart for their use. They may, with the leader's help, or at first on the leader's initiative, find projects that they are interested in—building a playing field, fixing over the clubhouse, etc. They may play checkers, monopoly, pool, card games, baseball, basketball, etc. They may box, trampoline-jump, learn acrobatics, or dance. They may work in crafts and make things in wood, plastic, clay, basketry. They may cook or sew or sing. The activities, though directed and sometimes suggested by the group leader(s), derive from the age-level interests and needs of the members. At first, it is unlikely that they will, no matter what their ages, all be able to do the same thing at the same time. That may come in time, if it comes. How they win, how they lose at games, the effect on them of competition, how they cheat and how they get found out, how they steal or lie within the group—all these things are significant and make great group material to work on. How do they handle a fight? Do they look for a fight, start one, run from one—always get licked, always bully, or get bullied? How do they handle the use of tools, a tool that won't work, an object that will not work? How does a member act if the object was broken by himself, by another group member, by the group leader? Observations based on these questions offer a direct route to basic problems. How do the members handle the problems of attendance—their own or other people's? How do they handle lateness or no-shows, trips that are postponed, defections of particular pals, switches in loyalties, their own inclusion or exclusion and that of others, new members, the loss of old members, change of adult leadership? How are crises handled—crises that arise out of the group itself or in their lives? How do they relate to the leader, to the others in times of stress or need, to their own needs or to the needs of others? These are all basic problems to everyone; with skillful handling and appropriate interpretation or restraint of interpretation, depending on the state and readiness of that particular child at that particular time, working them out is the therapy.

Activity groups can be geared for children as young as three and four, and as old as eighteen and nineteen. The materials used, the games played, the projects engaged in, will differ of course according to age, sexual development, and sex interest, but, if well led, groups of this kind are excellent for children and young people of all ages. The age range needs to be fairly homogeneous, though in day-camp settings or residential-camp settings where there is a sufficient number of group workers or leaders so that subgroups can be formed and so that the older members can, as part of their advanced treatment, help younger or newer ones, the age range can profitably be quite wide.

Leading activity groups is a demanding job. It requires certain skill and a certain kind of temperament. In many cases, the kind of ability to handle children exhibited by talented recreation teachers, nursery-school teachers, and camp counselors is more valuable than the more intellectualized talent of the garden-variety psychotherapist. In other words, the prime essential here is a feel for children at a given age level, ease with them and enjoyment of them, and the kind of sense of humor that children understand and can share and respond to. In addition to such a temperament in its various phases, what is most important is empathy with what it feels like to be a child and in trouble—in trouble beyond the power of a child to mend or alter. Actual skill at games, crafts, arts, can be learned. But imagination, the ability to use ideas, the flexibility to let something you have planned drop and to take on something that seems more youth- or child-motivated—these are rarer traits, harder to use and equally necessary to success in this field. Many sophisticated psychiatrists who are good at other forms of therapy are not comfortable in this kind of group and need training to relax into para-verbal modes. Many times it has been found helpful to use group leaders who are themselves relatively untrained in psychiatric know-how or in psychologic know-what-for as the major leaders, under the supervision of a psychiatrist or psychologist or with the professional taking the role of assistant. In such groups co-workers or teams of leaders are especially useful. Collaboration and supervision time is of the essence, since with the best will in the world, and even with the help of tape recorders and videotape, one person cannot help but miss much significant material. Lest I be misunderstood, let me add that I am not saying that trained therapists should never lead activity groups, but simply that they need more training and some re-educating to do so, for their professional training itself has in many cases trained them out of or beyond the flexibility and ease with the nonverbal messages and language of childhood that are required. This kind of retraining is essential to any good group leadership, especially with children and young people.

Art Therapy Groups

Over the past years, art therapy has grown up to be an entity in itself. It has left the area of occupational therapy and now has its own theory and practices, and of course its own group differences in point of view. It could be said that art therapy began through acceptance of Hermann Rorschach's projective tests, tests in which diagnosis is based in significant part on how the client perceived the world. Perceptions, anxieties, distortions, conflicts, and quality of mind were revealed by what one read into the white cards on which there were only ink blots in black and mixed colors. As the projective tests grew and multiplied, material from them yielded much useful data about the functioning and nonfunctioning of adults and children alike. The study was further advanced by the use of many additional kinds of materials: story pictures, self-created pictures of persons, houses, trees, etc. Models were provided with which people, especially children, would create mini worlds according to their own perceptions; mosaic blocks were introduced too, and games and mazes and comments on films, scenes, and anything imaginable.

What a person creates is clearly a projection of himself. Any artist knows this. Conceal himself as he may school himself to do through techniques and skill, somewhere the personality shines through—if one can read the message, even the message the person does not intend to give. That message may come through to anyone, but the skilled psychologist is especially trained to read it. The less skilled a person is in using a medium to express himself, the more clearly he reveals himself. For that reason, especially in pure diagnosis, it is better, when using drawing, painting, or clay productions, to have one of those many people who say "I can't draw anything" or "I never touch a paint brush" than an aspiring Picasso. What one is after is not a product, but a communication from the inside of a person.

This seeming paradox is relevant to the selection of an art therapy group, especially for children and youth. The group leader may want children who like to use art materials. Those that do like to tend to be better at it than those who turn away from these media. Yet one doesn't necessarily want skilled artists; indeed, it is more difficult to read the messages of those who are so naturally skillful that they can glibly cover over and conceal their inner selves. The dilemma is a far more conscious one among art therapists than among therapists who deal with verbal wares. It is true one hears of too great ease or glibness with words, of intellectualizing as a form of resistance, of talking too much in order not to say anything important, but people are not excluded from talk groups because of their verbal skills. Still, it might be wise to get verbally gifted people into art, dance, or pantomime activity therapy. The point I am making here is twofold: (1) simply being willing to use art materials is enough to admit one into an art group; and, (2) the quality of the products, though sometimes surprisingly good, is not the important thing. The important thing in an art therapy group is the same as in other groups: the decision about what to do; the time it takes to get started; the throwaways, the erasures and crossings out, the slips and errors, the mess; the disgust and frustration; the rage with the leader, with others, with oneself; the envy expressed; the comments before, during, and after a picture or other art form is made; as well as the fun, joy, recognition, and even ecstasy over finding new ways to express one's feelings and thoughts. The heaviness of the lines, the overlap of colors, the personal symbolism of the colors selected, and the personal forms, abstract and/or concrete, that emerge to express oneself and one's own image; the mood of the pictures and the changes in that mood; the joint interpretations and comments of the group; the kind of contribution each member makes to a joint production such as a group mural or group clay structure: all of these are the essentials out of which the therapy grows. The group therapists—at least one of whom should be cognizant of and comfortable with the use of art materials, and one, or preferably both, of whom should

be aware of the processes of personality development and its pathology—may, depending on their point of view, interpret much or little. They may use group processes and group awareness; they may be direct or indirect in their approach. They may wish to limber people up with body or at least arm exercises; they may or may not use music; they may meet many times a week or once a week. They may themselves see individuals in the group aside from the art therapy sessions for talk sessions, or they may prefer not to do so, but rather to send individuals elsewhere if, through the art groups, material comes up that the child needs extra work on, as indeed often happens. When this occurs, the leaders, if they are group-wise, will let the group know what is happening, so that the issues arising out of being special, or the worries over having problems, can emerge. Having more come up than can be handled in one session a week, let's say, can be a common group concern.

Many art therapists leave the choice of subject completely free. Others, especially those working with school age and adolescent children, find it useful to assign topics to serve as a basis for drawing, painting, modeling, or sculpting. The following suggestions have been found to be useful to groups, both because they get children unstuck from the "I don't know what to draw" defeat before it defeats them, and because the topics are such excellent starters for group discussions:

Make pictures of all the people you live with, or of your family; label the people. Draw something happy, something sad, something frightening, exciting, or funny. Make an angry picture; make a happy one. Make a picture of the group. Make a picture of someone in the group you think could help you. Let's make a joint picture about fun, about dating, about girls and boys, about parents or teachers. These pictures can be either realistic or abstract. When I was first involved in this sort of work, I thought it would be hard to get children to use art media abstractly. I was dead wrong. Children catch on right away, and the comments that are made about their own and other people's abstract pictures or products are tremendously revealing and helpful in the group. So impressive are the results of well-led art therapy groups for ghetto children, for torn-apart adolescents, for tied-up, constricted children, for children who find talking—especially to adults—next to impossible, that I would like to see all adults who want to become therapists go through an art therapy experience. They would not only find out much about themselves and about the children they think uncommunicative, but would find themselves more in touch with a children's world.

Music and Dance Therapy Groups

The same principles that operate in art therapy operate also in the use of dance or music as therapy. Just as in the case of art, music and dance were first used with hospitalized patients. It was found that many patients who could not and would not communicate in words would do so when they were allowed to use one of these other expressive forms. We have found that catatonic schizophrenics—patients whose body postures are so rigidly held that they seem (but often only seem) not to take in stimuli, and who do in fact emit no reactions or next to none—react especially well to the use of music, rhythm, and body movement. In doing so, they often assume postures and positions or go into patterns of movement that relay to the insightful therapist what they are experiencing in their inner world; they may even give some clues as to how they got that way.

When dance and music therapy was taken out of the hospital and into psychiatric offices and some schools, we established the truth of something that had been guessed before, and even applied by a few experimentally minded, gifted teachers: that brain-damaged children and hyperactive children, especially those with minimal brain damage, respond extraordinarily well to music and dance treatment. Aside from the gains that can be achieved, first toward communication and through that toward relationship with the therapists and other group members, it is a useful cue to teachers that music and body movement can be used well in the classroom for this kind of child. There is something so basic in telling what is going on in oneself by physical stance, kinesthetic sensation and rhythmic movement, that children like the very ill respond to it (once their embarrassment or awkwardness is overcome) with ease. Likewise, there is a part of all of us that helps us reach out of ourselves and respond to the sounds and rhythms, tunes and harmonies, related to nature. A good leader, with the help of music and dance, can set this element in ourselves in motion more easily in a group. Helping patients to do the choreography is as therapeutic as it is revealing.

It is important in using these forms, whether interpretive as in dance or listening, or active as in choreography and instrument playing, that boundaries be set to fit the personality of the group members. That is to say, hyperactive children and brain-damaged children with few controls need more formalized, less free, dance and music forms, while rigid, inhibited, tense youngsters require greater freedom. For this reason, the group leaders (or at least one of them) must be aware, beyond their use of music and dance, of the significance of the disturbance the children are burdened with, so as not to exacerbate the difficulty while they are trying to alleviate it.

Writing and Reading Therapy

It seems paradoxical that many of the people who most love words and what they can do, and who depend on writing words or reading them as their major solace, often have so much trouble communicating orally, face to face with other people. Yet that is true for many. Among this group are many adolescents. Experience has shown that often those who fear any face-to-face encounter, especially in a group, respond well, *even in a group*, when they are allowed to write at home or alone in privacy, and then share what they have written with the group. They may be asked, too, to write comments on what they have read, and to share these as well. Sometimes, at the beginning of such a group, anonymity is used to ensure privacy for the shy person. The progress of the group can in part be measured by the willingness of the members to own their productions and ideas. At the end of such a group, we may hope to find that the members are able to say what they feel to one another and in front of one another, without needing a piece of paper with words on it to protect them or to hide behind. Sometimes in such groups, journals are kept and shared—the teens are diary-keeping years. Sometimes the device is used of having letters written either from one member to another, or by a group member to the group leaders or to the group as a whole. This brings to mind a story about Abe Burrows: In talking to a class of aspiring writers at the University of Pennsylvania, he answered their questions about how to write by advising practice. "Write," he said. "Write all the time. Write letters. Try writing home!" People in writing therapy groups write. Some write poetry, some stories or essays or scenes from plays. They experiment with forms old and new. They write to one another and collaborate with one another. They try group writing and group reading. It is often an exciting experience which develops skills in thinking as well as writing. It gives a community of interest and a pathway out of isolation, loneliness, shyness, and self-consciousness. Stutterers, whose trouble often lies in self-consciousness and hostility, do particularly well in such groups. Writing becomes an avenue for the expression of difficult feelings such as anger, hurt, competitiveness, and affection. The difference between such a group and a good writing seminar is that the task of the group is therapeutic, and therefore the quality of the product, which is sometimes first class and sometimes pretty awful, is secondary to the fact of communication itself. The important thing is getting to be at home with one's own feelings and being able to own them in public, changing one's attitudes so as to be able to live a more satisfying life within oneself and among others.

Psychodrama

Of all the therapies which use nonverbal (as well as verbal) ways of expressing feelings, conflicts, and dilemmas, probably the best-known and most widely used is psychodrama. Since this form requires group participation, whether playing a role in a play or being part of the actively engaged audience, it is essentially a group form. Many people have developed psychodrama in many ways and have adapted the technique, or parts of it, to their own uses. Curiously, the term is not generally associated with the name of its founder, Moreno, though he has written extensively on the theory, practice, and application of psychodrama. Moreno heads an institute where he trains people to use the technique, and he has trained many psychodrama leaders in hospitals and institutions and agencies all over the country, and in fact, in foreign countries as well. There are too many skilled followers of Moreno's ideas to mention here, and too many innovators whose work is based on his. Suffice it to say the field is still being explored, and uses for the method broadened and deepened. Gestalt theory and transactional theory use snatches of psychodrama in their exercises and in their dream work. Transactional therapy also uses the technique to demonstrate the games that take place among people and to indicate less dangerous alternatives than those employed in these games. Virginia Satir and her school use psychodrama in family therapy in the technique known as family sculpturing. Other groups use it too in moments or full sessions of role-playing. (See Viola Spolin's *Theatre Games.*)

Essentially psychodrama is an opportunity for people to "act out" in a useful way their fantasies, dreams, fears, and preoccupations, on the one hand, and the situations which do already, or which later on may, give them trouble, on the other. For example, a member of a group might report a dream and have various members of the group act out parts of his dream. Perhaps they switch roles in the middle, perhaps not. The dreamer may act as director and actor or as either one, or he may serve as audience. Fritz Perls and others exploited the technique of using objects: the chairs and cars and attic windows in the dream are

mimed by the dreamer and personified by him. Another example: a child may report an obsessive fear of dogs. He is asked to choose others to help him, and all with him act out his fear, which may be general or may have arisen out of a frightening experience. Or a youth may be going to an interview that means a great deal to him—a job, college-admission, a first date with a girl he likes. He tells the group his concerns and with him they act out the interview or date.

The uses of psychodrama for children or youth of all ages are many. Children like to play-act and like making their own plays as they go along, so it is a popular activity. Children like to create their own experiences and feel them out in a safe place away from outside criticism and belittling. One adaptation has been used by a theatrical group in which the players are actors and respond to requests from an audience of children: Act out this or that. The actors do so, and the children respond. One can deal with material once it has emerged, and the audience helps get the problem posed and sees solutions being added before their eyes. There is no age above three that cannot use psychodrama as therapy.

It is amazing to note the different feelings one gets by becoming for a moment another person or object in one's own life-drama. Attitudes and patterns of thought alter and are often helpful.

Family Therapy

[Family therapy is discussed in detail in the excerpt by Salvador Minuchin that follows this article. In essence, the nuclear family is a small group, governed by group forces.]

Since the family constitutes the central group in anyone's life, but especially in the life of the young, and since the younger one is, the more closely one tends to replicate relationships known, heard, hated, or yearned for, in the original family, we find family-group sessions useful in diagnosing the major cause of a child's trouble and in getting at the characteristic modes of family interaction. Since family therapy is a relatively new form of treatment, there are many theories about it, some conflicting and some overlapping.

The least group-centered of the lot is the Systems Approach represented by Dr. Murray Bowen. In this approach, the family is understood to be a group, but is not treated as one. Instead, the therapist sees the mother and father and treats them as a couple, first talking and listening to one, then to the other—allowing some dialogue between them, but not using group process. Like all the theories of family therapy, the Systems Approach sees the child who is in trouble . . . as "The Index Member" of the family, the one in whom the family trouble is stored. The child is seen as acting out the unconscious—or at least unspoken—difficulties of the family. To Bowen and his group the clue to the difficulty is to be found in a detailed and thorough study of the genealogy and present network of the family—their physical story, their economic status, their job choices and educational histories, their divorces and deaths and illnesses. The further back one can go and the more widely one can study the offshoots of the family, the better for the purposes of this kind of approach. Therefore, even though the Bowenites say with passion that they eschew the treatment of the central family as a group, they are, curiously enough, ready to engage in the study of unusually large groups, not to offer them therapy, but rather to use them as information sources. The literature of this type of therapy abounds in fascinating studies of family happenings: reunions, births, funerals, weddings, anniversaries, and birthday parties. The patients are asked to study these rites and occasions to determine patterns; some therapists try, when possible, to get themselves invited so that they may explore and see at first-hand what goes on. In this way the large live family is used as a group tool.

Network Theory

There is only one . . . branch of psychological treatment I know of that uses the large group . . . for therapy. That branch is Network Theory, a new outgrowth of family therapy that is used in families where the crises derive from sticky chronic conditions that have not yielded to other forms of treatment, no matter how lengthy or how drastic. Such treatments may have ranged from long years of individual treatment to hospitalizations; they may have moved from group to family therapy and back, with all stages in between. The formulator of Network Theory is Dr. Ross Speck.

In this form of treatment, the organizing therapist and a team of therapists act as consultants to the family in trouble for a definite and short-term series of "network" meetings, anywhere from two to about six in number. For example, a mother and daughter in a family have such severe trouble that neither can leave the other alone. Neither can let the other live separately; yet neither can live with the other without terrible battles. Thus serious destruction ominously hovers about them as well as over the rest of the family and their friends. Suicide and murder attempts are not unusual in such severe situations, whether between husband and wife, or between parent and child. The two

central figures, together with the whole family, are asked to invite to a group meeting everyone they know—relatives, ex-wives, lovers, teachers, friends, doctors, counselors, service people who have become involved, bosses—any and everyone. The bigger the group, the theory goes, the better: it dilutes the problem. The idea is to get all these people involved and so to generate a kind of anxiety that has been severely aroused in the focal pair of miserable people. After group anxiety has been aroused—and that's not hard to get going in a large group—and the feelings expressed, the group breaks up—in the same room—into committees (small groups) each to tackle one aspect of how they can help with the problem. The notion is that in this way the spiraling trials and failures of the focal couple can be broken into, diluted, and monitored by a concerned multitude. The family-trap is thus hopefully broken by sheer weight of concerted pressure from all sides. A further concept here is that the extreme differences between the pair in trouble, by being taken on by a network of people, can be worked out by compromise, and through compromise alternate ways of acting and reacting be found, if the support of a large enough group is insured. After setting up these "networks," the team of therapists vanishes—as any good business consultant does after he has finished doing all he has contracted to do for the firm. If therapy is needed, either the committees of the network take over or they see . . . that it is arranged for. If housing, a job, school placement, or money is needed, ways of taking care of the problem are worked out. In this context, one of the most fascinating and unusual things Network Theory offers is the use of the chaos engendered by a large group as a therapeutic tool. Gossip too is used, as one offshoot of ways to get opinions whether sound and based on fact, or not. Network Theory suggests an intriguing but as yet unworked-out possibility of using this kind of treatment for school children in deep trouble with their peers or the staff, or for crisis (with a capital C!) in the staff itself.

Some other forms of family therapy, although they differ from one another, can be talked of together, since the therapists who offer them conceive the family as a group and use the interaction between members as a treatment tool. Some are more group-process oriented than others, but all use the way a family interacts and the roles each is supposed to play for the other and for themselves as a key to the problems of the child in trouble—the Index Member—and the family as a whole. Some family therapists insist on home visits to see the family in its habitat. Some do most of their work in offices. Some invite in-laws and grand-parents and close family friends, if this seems important; others stick to the core family. Some use speech alone; others use art and psychodrama and role-playing and a technique called family-sculpturing. In family-sculpturing one derives a whole family situation or character from the inter-action of therapist and one family member, creat-ing the script with body movement and words.

Family therapy as a systematized way of deal-ing with people in trouble grew out of work with families in which there was a very damaged schiz-ophrenic son or daughter, often one who was hos-pitalized. Time and again it became clear that on those occasions when the family was seen in com-bination with the sick child, the family guilt about that child seemed not to give way even when the child got better. It came to light that the group guilt had a genuine reason for existing beyond the constant useless jumping back and forth between periods of mea-culpa and woe-saying, and periods of anger and withdrawal of all interest. The proof-of-the-pudding was seen time and time again as lying in the fact that when the sick one (the Index Member) got well, the family as a whole would fall apart, or would appear to be in danger of doing so, until either the sick one got sick again, or the fam-ily dealt with its problem otherwise. Without out-side help it would seem each member felt he could not afford to take on his own problems and allow the elected one a measure of health without re-sponsibility for keeping the whole rickety struc-ture from collapsing. A second proof was seen in the great number of families (any school, like any mental health agency, knows the number is legion) in which as soon as one child who has come as "The Patient" has been treated, and has become well, another family member, usually a sibling, at once gets into trouble just as bad as the first child's, or even worse. The therapists developing this form of therapy began with hospitalized schizophrenic patients whose families illustrated this group phe-nomenon to the extreme; it was taken up soon thereafter by agencies where the repetitive pattern of breakdown in the family, a recatching of the dis-ease after "the cure" of one member, was part of a vast intake picture. Names often associated with exploration in this field are: Ackerman, Wynn, Shapiro, Bloch, Jackson, Whittaker, Minuchin, Rycoff, and Paul; many of these (along with Bowen) are still working in the field, as are many others.

. . . The record indicates that a common and damaging group phenomenon can affect the core group structure, the family, as well as people out-side the family group. One member of a group is made the scapegoat—that is, he is sacrificed to keep the group together, to take away the pain and unacceptable feelings from others in the group, thus dumping the pain on the chosen group mem-ber. We have seen this phenomenon in the class-room of the teacher who is shaky about her own leadership, or the teacher whose personality does not allow expression of hostility, affection, rage, or fear. The cure for such scapegoating in any group, just as in family therapy, is to try to get each mem-ber, along with the leadership, to own his "un-acceptable" feelings by exploring them, and to help each member not to allow himself to play the lethal game of being the scapegoat or sacrificial lamb.

Notes

1. The National Training Labs launched the sensitivity groups. National Training Labs is an or-ganization associated with the National Education Association. Its program is based on the work of Kurt Lewin; its founders are Leland Bradford, Ron-ald Lippitt, and Kenneth Benne. Sensitivity train-ing has gone through many phases since its incep-tion, and now has centers throughout the country. Its staff and trainees are active in many groups, some in business, many in education and training, some in therapy, and some as an expression of so-cial concern.

2. See John Dewey and Alfred North White-head, as well as Joseph Barrett's "Cognitive Thought and Affect in Organizational Experience" in *Science and Psychoanalysis*, Vol. 12 (N.Y., Grune & Stratton, 1965); and James McWhinner, "Forms of Language Usage in Adolescence and Their Rela-tionships to Disturbed Behavior and Its Treatment" in G. Caplan and S. Lebovic (eds.), *Adolescence: Psychosocial Perspective* (N.Y.: Basic Books, Inc., 1969).

Editors' Commentary

The selection below gives a sample of one type of family therapy (taught by Salvador Minuchin and others) and describes the history of this new and important branch of therapy. If the families described below were treated by Whittaker or Ackermann, the methods of treatment would be quite different from those outlined by Minuchin; each would use his personality theory to focus the family on new alignments. Similarly, if Paul were the therapist, he would search for the families' hidden secrets and denied grief. Shapiro and Wynn would search out the interlocking and interdependent psychopathology gluing the family together, Bower would select the two key members of the family group for study, while Haley, whose work most closely resembles that of Minuchin, would use structural family treatment and paradoxical approaches.

Structural Family Therapy: Activating Alternatives Within a Therapeutic System

Salvador Minuchin

It is noteworthy that at a point in which the family as an institution is undergoing great changes, interest in family therapy is rapidly increasing. In this decade, we have seen a significant rise in the number of divorces, with the natural corollary of a fantastic rise in blended families. A small but interesting group of people has been experimenting with alternative family styles, like the different types of communes, and many others are choosing or being forced to try alternative styles, like two single-parent families sharing a household. National concern has been aroused by the growing reports of abused and neglected children, by the sharp increase in the number of teenaged mothers and single-parent families. The framing of "the family" is becoming a matter of increasing complexity, and "the family's" performance of its vital functions is coming under increasing concern, and even attack.

Nevertheless, family therapy, the newest significant approach to therapy, is growing at an exponential rate. This may be due in part to a concern for buttressing one repair mechanism in a fraying social fabric, but the interest in family therapy springs from more than its effectiveness in healing. What we are seeing is an epistemological change in psychiatry, following the changes in other scientific and philosophical disciplines that are bringing us to the realization that our orientation to search for truth by fragmenting data into smaller units is obsolete, and that new paradigms are required to understand the dynamic interrelation between people and their significant context.

The sense of despair with which we look at the changes in the family today is due to the utilization of an incorrect observational framing. Separating the family from its socioecological niche we see changes as evidence of a dangerous trend challenging the viability of the family. But if we look at the family as a subsystem of society, we see that the changes are necessary adaptations so that the family can continue to survive as a viable institution in the complexities of the modern era.

The structural family therapist sees a family as a natural group which has, over time, evolved transactional patterns that are economical and effective for this particular group. Just as there are many forms of family composition, there are many forms of family functioning, and many of them are compatible with healthy development. Some forms may appeal more than others, but families with widely differing value systems, child-rearing practices, and ways of negotiating may all offer reasonable environments for growth and support. The essential tasks—supporting individuation while providing a sense of belonging—can be carried out in many ways. But carrying them out successfully will depend on some sort of viable family structure.

A family structure is expressed in the rules that regulate interactions. These rules form a governing superstructure on which the behavior of each group member depends. This is not unique to the family, of course. All natural groups are similarly regulated by rules, explicit and implicit. This governing structure restricts individual behavior, but it also makes it possible to carry on the business of life without constant consideration and negotiation.

When a family comes into therapy, the structural family therapist postulates that some stress has overloaded this system's adaptive and coping mechanisms, thus handicapping the optimal functioning of all system members. The family's own diagnosis of the problem is usually that one of their members is behaving in ways that are stressing the family. They want the therapist to change the person who is experiencing or causing difficulties. But the therapist focuses on the whole group. One of its members may be expressing the family stress in the most clearly visible ways. But the problem is not restricted to that identified patient. The whole system is responding to some overloading stress.

Therefore, the therapist joins the family, forming a new system—the therapeutic system. He helps the family members explore and activate alternative ways of dealing with each other. The goal of therapy is a family system that can now continue its own enhanced growth—encouraging, supportive, and reparative functions.

Family Structure

Since the family therapist relies on the family members and the family system for the development of a healing context, it is necessary to understand the concept of the family as a context of growth and actualization.[1] To recapitulate, a family structure is a set of rules that govern the behavior of each family member and subsystem. This may sound negative to some of us, with our orientation to individual rights and potentials. And it is quite true that a family structure constrains the individual, inhibiting behavior that differs from the family norm. But the family structure also encourages growth and autonomy, protecting the individual, and giving each family member a sense of stability and belonging that is essential for individual well-being.

I have always found it useful to postulate that a family has its beginning at a point in time. I set the beginning of a family arbitrarily: the agreement to join with the purpose of forming a family.

In the nuclear family model, the family begins with two adults, a man and a woman. Each of these new partners has a set of values and expectations,

both recognized and unconscious, ranging from the value of self-determination to whether people should eat breakfast. These two value sets must be reconciled over time to make possible a life in common. Differences will emerge, and they must be negotiated. Each spouse will have to give up part of his own ideas and preferences. In the process, a new system is formed, and the transactional patterns that are slowly evolved express the structure of this spouse subsystem.

Transactional patterns usually are not recognized as such. They are simply part of the underpinnings of life—there, and necessary, but not really thought about. Many are evolved with little or no effort. If both spouses come from patriarchal families, for instance, they may simply take it for granted that the woman will do the dishes. Other transactional patterns are the result of specific agreement: "It's your turn to cook." But in either case, the established patterns govern the way each spouse experiences self and partner in the spouse context. Behavior that differs from the customary pattern will hurt, and spark a sense of betrayal, even if neither partner has any conscious idea of what the trouble is.

The formation of the spouse subsystem is the first step in the formation of the family, but establishing patterns for its internal workings is not the only task the spouse subsystem faces. It must also establish ways of dealing with the extrafamilial. Later, as children are born, the spouse subsystem must also differentiate to carry out parenting and other tasks.

Families, therefore, are highly complex systems. They are subsystems of larger social systems—the extended family, the neighborhood, the city, and so on. Their interaction with these larger entities will be a significant part of the family's problems, tasks, and supportive network. In addition, families themselves differentiate into subsystems. Individuals are subsystems within a family, as are dyads like husband and wife. Larger subgroupings can be formed by generation (e.g., sibling subsystem), by gender, or by task. People accommodate kaleidoscopically in these different subsystems. A son has to act like a child so his father can act like an adult in the parent-child subsystem. But the child may take on executive powers when he is left in charge of his younger brother.

I want to emphasize that many types of family composition are seen, and therefore, many types of family structure.[2] All may be viable. This presentation focuses on the nuclear family, because that is still the model that largely governs our thinking about the family. But structural family therapy is applicable to families with widely varying composition and circumstances.

Within the nuclear family it is useful to look at three characteristic subsystems.[3] These are particularly significant for family health, especially for child growth and development.

The spouse subsystem, already described, is generally a system of parity. Spouses negotiate the distribution of functions, cooperating in some areas and differentiating to perform other tasks. Eventual differences must be negotiated in such a way that neither partner feels that when he gives, he gives in.

One of the important tasks of this subsystem is the development of boundaries that protect the spouses, giving them an area for the satisfaction of their own psychological needs without the intrusion of in-laws, children, and others. By definition, then, the spouse subsystem is vital for the child's growth. Any major dysfunction in the spouse subsystem will reverberate throughout the family, upsetting all members. In pathogenic situations, a child may be scapegoated, or perhaps co-opted into an alliance by one spouse against the other.

The spouse subsystem is also important to the child as a model for intimate relationships, as expressed in visible daily interaction. The child sees ways of expressing affection, of relating to a partner who is stressed, and of dealing with conflict as equals. What he sees will become part of the child's values and expectations as he comes in contact with the outside world.

A second major family subsystem is the parenting subsystem, a subsystem that may include a grandmother (or other significant adult) or a "parental child" in addition to the familiar parents-child composition. Transactions within this subsystem involve the familiar child-rearing and socializing functions. However, many other aspects of the child's development are also affected by his interaction within the parenting subsystem. Here the child learns what to expect from people who have greater resources and strength. He learns to think of authority as rational or as arbitrary. He learns whether his needs will be supported, and he learns the most effective ways of communicating what he wants within his own family's style. His sense of adequacy is shaped by how his elders respond to him, and by whether this response is appropriate for his age. He learns which behaviors are rewarded and which are discouraged. Finally, within the parental subsystem, the child experiences his family's style of dealing with conflict and negotiation.

As the child grows and his needs change, the parental subsystem must change as well. As the child's capacity increases, he must be given more opportunities for decision making and self-control. Families with adolescent children will negotiate differently from families with younger children. Parents will give more authority to the children while demanding more responsibility from them.

The adults in the parental subsystem have the responsibility to care for, protect, and socialize the children, but they also have rights. The parents have the right to make decisions that are related to the survival of the total system: relocation, selection of schools, and the determination of the rules that protect all family members. They have the right, and indeed the duty, to protect the privacy of the spouse subsystem, and to determine what role the children will play in the family's functioning.

In our child-oriented culture, we tend to stress the obligations of the parents and pay less attention to their rights. But the subsystem that is given tasks must also have the authority to carry them out. And while a child must have the freedom to explore and grow, he will feel safe to explore only if he has the sense that his world is predictable.

The third major significant subsystem is the sibling subsystem. Siblings form a child's first peer group. Within this context, children support each other, enjoy, attack, scapegoat, and generally learn from each other. They develop their own transactional patterns for negotiating, cooperating, and competing. They learn how to make friends and deal with enemies, how to learn from others, and how to achieve recognition. They generally take different positions in the constant give and take, and the process furthers both the sense of belonging to a group and the sense of individual choices and alternatives within a system. These patterns will be significant as they move into extrafamilial peer groups, the classroom system, and later the world of work.

Each family system must have boundaries that protect its functioning. Each subsystem must fulfill its tasks and resolve its problems. These boundaries do not preclude the possibility of summoning other family members to resolve specific subsystem problems, but they do have to delineate the subsystem adequately. A child who always calls his mother because his brother is picking on him, for example, is missing the experience of self-reliance that ought to be provided within the sibling subsystem.

The family, then, is a differentiated social unit structured by transactional patterns. In some areas, the system is flexible, offering a broad range of choices. In other areas, preferred patterns are tightly maintained. Though alternative patterns would be possible, they are unused, and the family counterdeviation mechanisms are quickly activated when behavior changes.

Structural Adaptation

A family must retain the stability to give its members a sense of belonging. But it cannot exist unchanged. The family must constantly adapt to meet the demands of changing circumstances, and the changing developmental needs of its members. In a real sense, therefore, crisis is the norm. The family is always in transition, but it has to accommodate to new circumstances in such a way that family members' sense of stability is not seriously undermined.

The most obvious, inevitable source of family disequilibrium comes from growth. Children and adults move through developmental stages. These changes produce pressures that push the system, challenging the usual positions of family members in relation to each other. The family must summon alternative patterns and try them out, selecting and discarding in terms of how they work and feel. If one child moves toward greater independence, all members of the system must reorganize themselves. The whole family must cope with the distress of strangeness and change.

Family stress may also spring from idiosyncratic problems, like a child's retardation or chronic illness. Or stress may spring from one member's contact with the extrafamilial world, like a parent's having trouble at work. Or it may come from total family contact with the extrafamilial world. The family may be stressed by poverty, discrimination, separation from natural systems of support, and so on. Whatever the source, the family must adapt in a way that continues to protect its members without unduly restricting freedom.

Sometimes, however, families cannot respond to a demand for change. Instead of activating and experimenting with alternative patterns, they increase the rigidity of patterns that have become preferred. The range of choices narrows. Responses to each other and to the extrafamilial world become stereotyped, but even if the accustomed patterns are perceived as dysfunctional, no alternatives seem possible. Family members experience themselves as trapped and impotent:

The Bryant family, for example, came to therapy because Julie, 21, suffers from psychosomatic vomiting. Her symptoms started a year ago, interrupting her college studies. The vomiting became so intense that Julie was hospitalized in a psychiatric ward. After two months without improvement, her parents took her home against medical advice. At that point the GI specialist referred the Bryants for family therapy.

In the first session the Bryants, father and mother in their 50's, Julie, and Don, 18, presented themselves as an upper middle-class conventional—even proper-suburban family. Father, a successful executive, is a good provider and a distant father and husband, "protected" by his wife from the children's demands. Mother, a bright, sensitive, giving woman, is very close to the children, and has always protected them from "father's ugly temper." That temper has been so successfully "controlled" by mother's peacekeeping tactics that the children have never seen it, but it is talked about in the family as a terrible possibility.

Julie's vomiting started when Don began college in a nearby city. Mrs. Bryant, unsuccessful in finding new targets for her energy and talent, became depressed, phoning both children daily and confiding deeply in her daughter. Mr. Bryant began spending more and more time at work. Julie, whose accommodation to college had been tenuous at best, returned home and enrolled in a nearby college as a day student until her worsening symptoms made it impossible for her to continue her studies.

The GI specialist recommended treatment with metachlopramide, which controlled the frequency of vomiting. But it was clear to both specialists that more than the treatment of Julie's symptoms was needed here. The Bryants are in a situation of developmental crisis, and the necessary structural adaptation has not taken place. The Bryants will need the help of the family therapist so that both Julie and Don can separate from the family to form their own lives, and the parents, particularly Mrs. Bryant, can develop other sources, inside the spouse subsystem as well as outside the family group, to meet their needs.

The Therapeutic Approach

Suppose a family has a vulnerable child—a mildly retarded boy, for example. He has developed well, within his potential, at home. But when he enters school and comes into contact with the social system of school and peers, he begins to signal distress. It may be that the school as a system can handle this reaction, and the family can develop an adapted system of guidance and support, enabling the child to deal with his new life circumstances competently. But suppose the school cannot respond appropriately, and/or the family has scarce resources or is stressed by problems in other areas. If this is the case, the family may be unable to adapt or respond to their child's heightened need. Instead, they may relate to him with a tightening of the patterns used in relation to him when he was younger. The family structure is crystallizing and maintaining pathology. The child may become withdrawn, isolated from social contact, and overly dependent on the family.

The diagnosis might be that the child is disturbed. But it would be equally valid to say that the family organization is supporting and maintaining a child's dysfunctional reactions to a life stress.

If the diagnosis focuses on the child alone, so will the main therapeutic input. Secondary efforts may be made with the parents and the school. But both the family members and the school will be considered normal, and the child, sick. The second diagnosis, however, locates pathology in the child *in his context*. Therefore, intervention is directed toward the child, toward his family, toward his school, and the ways they all affect one another. The system is considered dysfunctional, and intervention is conceptualized in these terms.

Note that in a systems framework, the traditional cause-and-effect model disappears. There is no assumption that there is a straight line from etiology to illness to treatment to cure. The unit is not the symptomatic individual. It is the individual in interaction with his human and physical environment. The individual self in this concept is multifaceted. It is a whole which includes *both* significant elements of the context *and* the individual characteristics elicited by those elements.

Growing up in the family, the individual has learned that the participation in different subsystems at different times requires the actualization of different segments of the self, i.e., a child in an overinvolved dyad with his mother operates by eliciting nurturance. In the sibling subsystem, he operates shrewdly and competitively to get what he wants from his older brother. A man who is an authoritarian husband and father in the family system must accept a lower hierarchical position in the world of work. A young adolescent who is dominant in the peer group when in coalition with his older brother learns the rules of courtesy when his brother isn't there. Different contexts call forth different facets. The rules that apply to some subsystems do not apply to others, and the behaviors that are functional in certain subsystems will not serve in other subsystems.

The concept of self developed through participation in different familial and extrafamilial contexts suggests that humans are always functioning with only some of the possibilities. Alternatives are not used because the contextual structure—family or otherwise—discourages their appearance. But alternatives exist. The therapist who searches for strength can find unused areas of coping capacity in the individuals, subsystems, and family system in therapy. Activating these possibilities can restore a healthy flexibility to the system.

The Family in Therapy

To recapitulate, when a family comes into therapy, the structural family therapist assumes that some stress has overloaded the system. Instead of adapting to changed circumstances, the family has been reifying malfunctional patterns. The therapist's goal, therefore, is to search out and activate the submerged alternatives possible in this group. Once the family can continue its own tasks of supporting and encouraging growth, therapy will terminate.

Therapy begins with the therapist's joining the family, forming a therapeutic system. The therapist must be a member of the system that he will attempt to transform. Only as a participant can he experience the invisible pushes and pulls that form the web of the family structure: the pathways that are open, the rules that forbid. And only as a participant can he perceive the cues that will orient him to the possibilities for family transformation.

Experiencing the family's transactions, the therapist draws a "family map"—an experiential diagnosis of family functioning. This map indicates the position of the family members vis à vis each other. It indicates proximity and peripherality. It indicates coalitions, affiliations, explicit and implicit conflicts, and how family members group themselves in conflict resolution. It indicates family members who operate as detourers of conflict and members who function as family "switchboards." The map demarcates the nurturers, the healers, and the scapegoaters. The delineation of boundaries indicates what movement there is, and suggests possible areas of strength and dysfunction.

The therapist, a participant in the therapeutic system, is constrained by the demands of the system. But he is also an outsider, free to shift positions, participate in alternative subsystems, and challenge the family members' own delineation of role. Because he has the freedom to participate or withdraw, he can challenge the proximity of distance of the family members vis à vis each other. And because areas of dysfunction in the family frequently involve over- and/or underaffiliation, therapy in great measure is the process of monitoring proximity and distance, and introducing alternative ways of relating.

The world view of family members depends to a great extent on their positions in family subsystems. If there is overinvolvement, the member's freedom to function is restricted by membership participation. If there is underinvolvement, members may be isolated and undersupported. Increasing or decreasing distance between members of significant subsystems brings forth alternative ways of thinking, feeling, and acting that were inhibited by subsystem participation.

Therapeutic Techniques

We will present three broad categories of techniques that are used in family therapy to transform the family: changing boundaries, changing epistemology, and changing realities. They all require the capacity of the family therapist to join with the family in the formation of the therapeutic system.

Changing Boundaries

The Thomas family, two parents in their 30's and two boys, Mark, 9, and Ronny, 4, came into therapy because Ronny's very serious eczema was exacerbated by uncontrollable scratching. Mrs. Thomas was overinvolved with Ronny and whenever she paid attention to Mark, Ronny began to scratch, irritating his eczema and reinvolving his mother with himself. Father, a competent teacher, had the capacity for involvement with his children, but his wife's overinvolvement with Ronny left him in a peripheral relationship with his younger son. The relationship of the spouses was somewhat distant. Mr. Thomas thought his wife was too involved with Ronny, but both of them were overprotective but concerned parents.

The family therapist watched Ronny's constant engagement with his mother for a few minutes, and then organized a task. He instructed the parents to talk without accepting Ronny's intrusion. Whenever Mrs. Thomas looked at Ronny, Mr. Thomas was to engage her.

This boundary delineation produced the usual activity in Ronny. He began to whimper and cry, jumping up and down in his chair, and scratching furiously. But with the therapist's help his parents ignored him, talking only to each other. Mark, obviously a parental child, tossed a toy to Ronny, engaging him in a playful, slightly aggressive transaction. Soon Ronny threw the toy at Mark and ran to his mother, touching her. But Mr. Thomas attracted his wife's attention again. At first Ronny returned to his mother every minute or so. But as she did not respond, he began to function differently. He began to explore the room and finally took a large poodle toy and tossed it to Mark. His motor activity became less hesitant, and his scratching ceased completely. At the same time, his mother's almost tic-like hovering over her younger son disappeared, and she became more direct in her contact with her husband, responding to some criticism not by engaging with Ronny, but by confronting her husband directly.

It seems that certain behaviors were signaled in the overinvolvement dyad of mother and Ronny. The disappearance of this signaling due to the therapist's boundary delineation allowed the appearance of usually underutilized skills. The therapist's intervention in this situation has changed the context of the family members. An overinvolved pair has been slightly distanced. As a result, Ronny has moved to participation with his older

sibling—a situation that requires more competent functioning from him. Mother has moved from a situation in which she is exclusively nurturer and controller to a situation of involvement with her husband—a conflict negotiation between peers. The change in subsystem participation has produced a change in functioning, and coping capacities have appeared.

The result of such context modification is a change in experience. Family members perceive themselves as functioning in a different way. By challenging the rules that constrain people's experience, the therapist actualizes aspects of the family members' repertoire that are possible, but submerged.

Changing Epistemology

Other techniques that family therapists use have to do with changing the epistemology of family members. People tend to see themselves as acting or reacting. They say, "my husband nags me," or "my wife is overdependent." Consequently, when a family member develops a symptom, this member becomes "the problem." Other family members see themselves as accommodating to his illness.

One agitated, depressed patient I worked with started the first family session saying, "I am the problem."[1] The rest of the family and psychiatrists who treated him when he was hospitalized agreed with this linear formulation: "The world starts with me, and I am the problem." In effect, everyone was saying, "You are depressed and upset, and we are trying to help you."

In family therapy, however, I told him, "Don't be so sure." I was relating to the same data, but in terms of how people act and are activated in a system. My next statement was, "If your problem were caused by somebody outside of you, somebody in the family, whom do you think would cause you to be so depressed?" I was not introducing new data; I was introducing a different way of "punctuating" reality.

This type of intervention has major significance in therapy. The family therapist attempts to change the epistemology of family members, moving them from a definition of self as separate, responding to others, to a definition of self as a part of a whole. An individual therapist tells the individual, "Change yourself." "Work with yourself so you will grow." "Look inside, and change what you find there." The family therapist makes a paradoxical statement. He says, "Help the other change." But in this world view, people cannot change unless the context changes, eliciting alternative behaviors. Therefore, the real message is, "Help the other change by changing yourself as you relate to him."

Who is superior, who is inferior, who caused, and who reacted—these concerns lose their salience in a conceptualization that deals with the way each family member integrates in a larger picture. The assignment of responsibility for an act and the consequent allocation of blame both recede in the more complex frame of the larger design.

Presenting Alternative Realities

Patients come to therapy because reality, as they have constructed it, is unworkable. Therefore, all types of therapy depend on a challenge to that construct. Psychodynamic therapy says that the patient's conscious reality is too narrow. There is an unconscious world, inside the patient, that he must explore. Behavioral therapy suggests that the patient has mislearned aspects of how to deal with his context. Family therapists also deal with the reorganization of reality in a way that offers the possibility of alternatives. Transactional patterns depend on (and contain) the way family members look at reality. Therefore, changing the way family members look at reality helps them develop new ways of interacting.

The therapist takes the data that the family offers and regroups it. In therapy, family members learn a different framework of experiencing themselves and each other. The conflictual and stereotyped reality of the family is given a new framing, one which suggests solutions.

A family composed of a father and mother in their 40's, a daughter, 15, and a son, 10, came to therapy because the daughter had anorexia nervosa.[4] The family presentation of the problem was that they were a typical normal family with a daughter who had been perfect up to the moment in which the illness transformed her. They had been trying to help the daughter for the last year, changing their own relationship to her, depending on advice by friends, minister, pediatrician, and child psychiatrist, but felt, at this point, helpless, frightened, and somewhat hopeless.

I met with the family at lunch and we all ate together. During the meal I asked the parents to help their daughter survive by helping her to eat. The daughter's response to the parents was refusal to eat accompanied by a broad range of the most sophisticated insults. I proceeded to point out the strength of the daughter, who could defeat both parents, and focused on the insulting quality of her response to the parents.

The family reality was reframed: the parents (who were overinvolved with their daughter and triangulated her in their own unresolved conflicts) closed ranks in a subsystem that felt attacked and defeated, and simultaneously increased their distance from their daughter (diminishing their overprotection and overcontrol). The daughter was in the strange position of being labeled stubborn, strong, and competent, and of being demanded to monitor her own body. This type of construction elicited from family members a startled new look at their reality.

In another case, a single mother brought her nine-year-old daughter to therapy because she was growing disobedient, staying up past bedtime, and sometimes faking stomachaches to avoid school. In a session with mother and daughter, the therapist explored the mother's social relationships. He learned that she was a lonely person with no close friends. Recently fired from her job, she was now collecting her unemployment insurance and making only minimal efforts to find another job.

In the mother's framing, the daughter was disobeying. A therapist following this framing might suggest an increase in the mother's executive functioning. But looking at the two together, the problem could not be seen only as behavior initiated by the daughter. This was a complementary relationship of two people who needed each other, but who were actually too close. This daughter's staying home from school, and staying up late, was a response to her mother's need for companionship. What was indicated was not an increase in the mother's executive functioning, which would have increased the involvement of an already overinvolved dyad, but a distancing, helping each of them develop more interaction with their own peer groups.

In summary, the structural family therapist challenges the way people relate to each other, controlling and being controlled by one another. He helps people realize that they are parts of a whole, changing the grammar by which they punctuate reality in such a way that the possibility of alternatives becomes apparent. The therapist has to be in the system, functioning in proximity, but he must also maintain distance so he can challenge, unbalance, and stress. Above all, he must be able to respect people's idiosyncracies, and work with them within their own values toward their own goals. He must know his own biases and make them so explicit that neither he nor the family members become controlled by them.

Substantiating Data

Family therapy yields many dramatic sessions, filled with material of enormous anecdotal interest. But one of the problems of psychiatry is that data remain at the anecdotal level, humanly fascinating and significant, but of limited generalizability. The only possibility of joining the art of therapy to the science of therapy is to look at the results of therapeutic approaches over time with a number of cases large enough to be significant.

At the Philadelphia Child Guidance Clinic we have worked intensively with one patient population that presents a unique opportunity for the evaluation of therapy: children with psychosomatic illness. With this population, there is a concrete definition of improvement: symptom remission, as well as the more traditional soft data of psychiatry. This psychosomatic population is composed of children suffering from many different psychosomatic complaints though the major research concentration was on labile diabetics, intractable asthmatics, and anorectics. Table I shows that the effectiveness of structural family therapy is maintained in follow-up studies.[5]

Besides our follow-up studies in working with the brittle diabetics in the psychosomatic group, we have been able to develop a method for documenting the connections among the physiology of the child, his psychological constructs, and his family context. The following experiment was performed. The children along with their parents were seen for a stress interview. During this interview, the child and both parents had intravenous needles through which aliquots of blood were withdrawn at regular intervals. The interview was divided into four parts. During the first two parts, the child was outside of the room observing his parents through a one-way mirror. Following a baseline period in which the parents spoke about neutral topics with one of the investigators, the parents were asked in Period I to discuss problems in the family. In Period II, the interviewer entered and exacerbated stress by siding with one parent against the other. During Period III, the child came into the room. Part IV is a turnoff period in which the family relates alone in a room without interviewer, nurses, or one-way mirror being present.

In the first three periods we were able to study the behavior of the participant by analysis of the videotape, and the physiological response to stress by measuring the free fatty acid (FFA) in the blood of the family members.

The physiological evidence supported the hypothesis that the psychosomatic symptom plays a role in family homeostasis. . . . The FFA levels of the index child were plotted along with those of the parent whose arousal during the interview was most pronounced. Focus on Periods III and IV of the interview—the period of family conflict when the child was present and the recovery phase—revealed in the psychosomatic group a crossover phenomenon. The parent whose FFA indicated that he or she was emotionally aroused showed a decrease when the child was brought into the situation. In contrast, the child's FFA continued to rise when he or she was brought into the situation and did not return toward the baseline during the recovery period. The physiological measurement showed that the presence of the child decreased the parent's emotional arousal at the cost of a continued rise in the child's arousal, propelling him toward disease. The sustained arousal of FFA during the recovery period attested to the maintenance of the pattern in the face of unresolved family conflict.

In addition, the crossover phenomenon strongly supports the hypothesis that the illness plays a role in these families. Parental arousal can be alleviated by the participation of the child, but only at the expense of symptom maintenance.

Summary

In conclusion, family therapy is an effective approach. It is also economical. The time people are in therapy is shorter, hospitalization is reduced, and the psychological burden on the family and the financial burden on both family and institution are lightened. The economy of family therapy is not a matter of superficiality—ignoring the deep meanderings of the human situation. It is, rather, economy allied with effectiveness, and both are related to the fact that the therapist evokes the family's own healing and supportive capacities. In the process of change, family members become cotherapists, eliciting and reinforcing the more competent and appropriate segments of the behavioral repertoire of their own family. Family therapy utilizes therapists as enablers of self-healing, and awakens people's capacity to help themselves.

Notes

1. **S. Minuchin**, *Families and Family Therapy* (Cambridge, Mass.: Harvard University Press, 1974).

2. **S. Minuchin, B. Montalvo, B. G. Guerney, B. L. Rosman, and F. Schumer**, *Families of the Slums: An Exploration of Their Structure and Treatment* (New York: Basic Books, Inc., 1967).

3. **S. Minuchin and P. Minuchin**, "The Child in Context: A Systems Approach to Growth and Treatment," in *Raising Children in Modern America: Problems and Prospective Solutions*, ed. N. Talbot (Boston: Little, Brown, 1975).

4. **S. Minuchin, B. L. Rosman, and L. Baker**, *Psychosomatic Families: Anorexia Nervosa in Context* (Cambridge, Mass.: Harvard University Press, 1978).

5. **B. L. Rosman**, "Family Therapy for Psychosomatic Children," paper presented at annual meeting of American Academy of Psychosomatic Medicine, Atlanta, Georgia, November 17, 1978.

Table I
Outcome Results—Psychosomatic Studies

Median Age (Range)	Presenting Problems	Median Family Therapy in Months (Range)	Median Follow-Up in Years (Range)	Outcome:	Medical*	Psycho-social[†]
Psychosomatic-Diabetics						
13½ (10–18)	Severe, relapsing ketoacidosis N=11	8 (3–15) (2 dropped treatment)	4½ (2–9)	Recovered Fair Unimproved	88% 12% 0	83% 17% 0
	Chronic acetonuria and/or extreme instability in diabetic control N=9					
Anorectics						
14½ (9–21)	Median weight loss 30% N=53	6 (2–16) (3 dropped treatment)	2½ (1½–7)	Recovered Fair Unimproved	86% 4% 10%	86% 4% 10%
Asthmatics						
11 (7–17)	Severe attacks, regular steroid therapy N=10	8 (2–22)	3 (1–7)	Recovered Fair Unimproved	82% 12% 6%	88% 12% 0
	Intractable illness, steroid dependency N=7					

*MEDICAL ASSESSMENT

Diabetes	*Recovered:*	No hospital admissions for ketoacidosis; stabilization of diabetic control within average or "normal" limits.
	Fair:	Marked reduction in number of hospital admissions and/or more stable diabetic control; some symptoms persist.
Anorexia	*Recovered:*	Eating patterns normal; body weight stabilized within normal limits for height and age.
	Fair:	Weight gain but continuing effects of illness (borderline weight, obesity, occasional vomiting).
	Unimproved:	Little or no change or relapsed.
Asthma	*Recovered:*	Little or no school days lost; mild to moderate attacks with occasional or regular use of bronchodilator only.
	Fair:	Weeks of school lost; prolonged and severe attacks; still some use of steroids but symptomatic improvement.
	Unimproved:	More than 50% school loss with need for special schooling; persistent symptoms; dependent on regular steroid therapy.

[†]PSYCHOSOCIAL ASSESSMENT

	Recovered:	Satisfactory adjustment in family, school or work, and social and peer relationships.
	Fair:	Adjustment in one or another of these areas unsatisfactory.
	Unimproved:	Little or no change or relapsed.

This article originally appeared as Report III, Unit IV of *The American Family*, a continuing education service of Smith Kline and French Laboratories. Copyright 1980, SmithKline Corporation. Reproduced with permission.

Editors' Commentary

Groups in the School

Both for studying children in groups and for putting our knowledge of groups to work, the everyday groups in which children naturally gather in and around schools provide the ideal setting, because it is a "natural" setting (not one imposed by some form of clinical intervention). It is very important that teachers understand the structure, purposes, and form of the groups they work with daily.

The reader is referred to George Dennison's excellent book, *The Lives of Children*,[4] an account of one year at the experimental First Street School in a New York City slum. The book illustrates the intelligent and sensitive handling of children in their own groups, children of various races who had been cast out or considered unteachable by the city school system, although none was intellectually incapable and some were gifted. Mr. Dennison is a writer and teacher. His point of view and that of the First Street School derive somewhat from A. S. Neill's Summerhill, somewhat from Leo Tolstoy's rural experiment, but most of all from John Dewey's philosophy as Dewey originally intended it, not as it has been distorted by some of his earlier apostles and later critics.

The following excerpt, by special education teacher Eleanor Craig, is included because it represents a different kind of in-school therapeutic group.

4. **George Dennison,** *The Lives of Children* (New York: Random House, 1969).

P.S. Your Not Listening

Eleanor Craig

[An early session of a therapeutic school-group.]

"Mmm . . . sick."

"Where don't you feel well, Kevin?"

"Sick, mmm." His words were barely audible. "I'm homesick, that's what. She doesn't believe me."

I patted his back. "It's hard to come to school when you've been absent."

Suddenly he leaped up, darted into the closet, and closed the door on himself.

Douglas became alarmed. "Listen Kevin, we were having a good morning till you started messing up."

Kevin stuck his head out, then began to pull the door shut on his neck.

"Don't, don't!" Douglas yelled. "You're going to hurt yourself!"

"So what," Kevin answered flatly. "I want to."

"Make him stop, Mrs. Craig." Douglas pleaded. "He's wiping his sweat on us!"

Jonathan bounced in his chair. "Whooeee, he's blowin' his top! He's gonna blast off!"

Kevin's face was scarlet from the pressure on his neck. I rushed to the closet and yanked the door from his grasp. He crumpled to the floor gasping. Douglas began to whimper.

Eddie, scornful of Douglas' concern, mocked, "You worried about that tomato face? That crazy tomato face is your friend!"

"See what you've done?" Douglas sobbed. "You bum!" He bolted across the room. "You've embarrassed me! Eddie thinks I've got nutty friends. He thinks I taught you to be nuts!" He kicked Kevin in the stomach.

Kevin doubled up in pain, while Douglas went on his all-time rampage. Picking up a chair, he hurled it across the room. Two legs flew off as it cracked a section of blackboard. Coats and jackets were hurled out the window, followed by the wastebasket, papers, and workbooks. I tried to reach him, both physically and with words. He was grunting and snarling, upsetting desks and chairs, scattering papers everywhere.

He grabbed a new tin of chalk from the closet and dumped it, sawdust and all, on Kevin, yelling. "I don't care if you get hurt! I don't care if you die!"

The chalk bounced off Kevin's motionless body. Sawdust filtered into his hair, his eyes and mouth. He gagged and spat.

I caught Douglas' wrist, but he kicked my ankle and ran, calling back. "Shut up, shut up, shut up . . . ." I pursued him to the door and watched him zigzag down the hall, ripping everything off the bulletin boards on both sides as he ran.

Luckily an intercom had just been installed. Miss Silverstein's secretary answered sweetly.

"Doris quick! Tell Miss Silverstein [school principal] that Douglas is somewhere in the building, and we need the nurse immediately for Kevin."

"Hmm? Really? My gosh. Oh, okay."

Seconds later, Miss Silverstein and Mrs. Rogers, the nurse, rushed in, visibly distressed by the havoc in the hall. Our room looked like the aftermath of a tornado.

Kevin had recovered enough to howl. Eddie was prancing around, holding the broken chair aloft. "That boog did it! He broke school property! Now who's a punk?"

Jonathan, having taken cover under his desk, was grunting suspiciously. He zapped the nurse and principal with his invisible atomic gun. "Pow—bam—got ya—you're dead!"

Mrs. Rogers went to Kevin. Eyeing me accusingly, she demanded, "What happened to him?"

"Douglas kicked him in the stomach."

"My God! He could have a rupture!" The nurse, in her late forties, was a tall, heavy-set woman, capable but formidable. Effortlessly, she scooped up the limp child. Chalk and sawdust rained from both of them. "This whole setup just babies kids, lets them get away with murder. In a bigger class they wouldn't dare behave this way. Four kids in a room, a waste of time and money! Just spoiling them, that's what I say."

Her words came with such vehemence that I realized she had felt this way from the beginning. I thought of the innocent classmates these children had victimized previously, but it was no time to justify the program.

She stormed out, Kevin draped limply in her arms. . . .

[A later session in the same therapeutic school group.]

"I had a disturbing conversation yesterday," Ceil [school psychiatric social worker] was saying before school on Friday. "Just as I was leaving the office, Eddie's mother called.

"She'd locked him in his room for the day and gone to modeling school. A policeman was waiting inside when she got home. One of the neighbors had seen Eddie climb out his bedroom window onto the roof. Afraid he'd fall, she called the police. But he just stood there exposing himself. The officer said he wouldn't file a juvenile report, but threatened Mrs. Conte with child-abuse charges if she locked him up again. Can you believe, she doesn't see anything wrong with that? She's just furious at the boy for getting her in trouble."

"Oh, God, that's so discouraging, Ceil," I said. I was facing the window. The bus had turned into the driveway.

"I thought about him for hours." Ceil picked up her briefcase. "At least we know, now, more of what's going on. Maybe we'll have to face an unpleasant decision. As long as he's in that home, Eddie may never be better."

"They're here." I heard the door open. "What's your schedule?"

"Send him in at nine. I'd like to see him first."

"Okay. I'm anxious to talk to you after school," I said.

"Right, but we'll have to cut it short. Don't forget the reception for our new boss at four in the Administration Building. Have a good day."

Seeing Eddie come down the hall, I knew his two-day absence had served no purpose. Rather than helping him understand that disruptive behavior was unacceptable, it had increased his need to act out. We had to find an alternative to exclusion for children whose problems were aggravated at home.

Eddie was already provoking Douglas, crisscrossing in front of him, impeding his progress. "I'll bite you anytime I want! My teeth are good weapons. I bite my sister, too."

"Use them again and you'll be swallowing them." Douglas held up his lunchbox menacingly. They stopped, ready to fight, a few feet from our room.

"Good morning, Doug," I called. "Take a look at the new puzzle on your desk." Hand on his back, I guided him in. "And Eddie, I'm glad you're back." I directed him straight ahead with the other hand. "Mrs. Black wants to see you first today."

While Eddie was with Ceil, the rest of the class did creative writing. More and more, our mornings were passing peacefully and productively. Even rewards, stars, prizes, and privileges were less urgently sought. The feeling of success, the satisfaction when work was well done was becoming a goal in itself.

But Eddie's return an hour later interrupted the day's progress. "You're not telling me what to do! I'm not sitting down!" he yelled as he jogged in.

"You're standing up?" I said.

"That's right! So would you if you got whipped like me. I hate getting whipped. It doesn't do any good. I'll just do it all over. Next time I get locked in I'm gonna make a bomb. I'll blow up the stinkin' house. Then I'll get out."

"Whoo-ee! You'll get out in a hundred pieces!" Jonathan now was much more aware of the other children. Though he had not yet learned to converse, he made occasional comments.

"Here's your folder." I handed it to Eddie. "Where are you going to stand?"

With a red crayon he scrawled "fuck you" across the cover.

"Psst!" Kevin stage-whispered to Douglas. "What'd your grandmother say about that mad dog bitin' you?"

Eddie turned pale. He clutched the folder to his chest and watched Douglas anxiously.

"I wouldn't tell who did it." Douglas rubbed his bandaged wound. "I may be mean, but I'm not that mean."

Eddie sagged with relief. He looked around, headed for the windowsill, placed his folder there and opened it. He stood as he wrote. After a brief silence, he turned toward the group. "Hey Doug, wanna have a race? See who's done first?"

"I would've, but you've been takin' too much sweat out on me. It's just 'cause you hate dark skin, right?"

"Naw! It's 'cause I didn't used t' like ya. But now I do."

"Okay," said Doug cautiously. "Ready, get set, go!"

Kevin was irked at being excluded from the competition.

"Let's hide the punk's lunch" he said to Douglas.

"No thanks." Douglas kept working.

Within an hour he was raising his fist in a victorious gesture. "I'm winning! I'm winning!"

From Eddie's vantage at the window he could see that Douglas' last assignment, tracing the human body from his science book, was almost completed.

Eddie threw his pencil down. His voice was high-pitched, whiny. "You big bragger! Just because I don't feel like bragging!"

Too pleased with himself to be offended, Douglas said, "I'm sorry, I was conscientious of braggin'."

Julie handed Eddie his pencil, which had rolled under her chair. As if pleading his case, he

said to her, "He's makin' me nervous! It's not nice to brag, ya know."

"You're doin' good, Eddie." Julie glanced at his work and returned to her own, cutting sandpaper versions of those troublesome letters b, p, and d.

Then Douglas, with a side glance at Eddie, shouted with enthusiasm, "I'm losing! I'm losing!"

"Liar! You liar!" Eddie threw his papers and books across the room. "You know you were winning!"

"Think, Eddie." I stayed beside Jonathan, hoping the incident would go no further. "Why would Douglas say he was losing?"

"Because I've got manners," Douglas interposed. With both hands in the pockets of his ragged jeans, he walked confidently toward the window. "Just take five minutes off, Mrs. Craig. I can handle this."

"Thanks, anyway," I said. "Only one teacher to a room."

Forgetting his sore bottom, Eddie boosted himself onto the windowsill, away from Douglas, who was addressing him. "You better start respecting your elders, kid. I say I'm losing, I'm losing. Don't forget who's already nine."

Feeling threatened, Eddie knew only one response. He crouched, readying himself to jump down on Douglas.

"If you say you lost, Doug," I spoke loudly, "that means Eddie gets first choice for the afternoon."

"I take woodworking." Eddie abandoned the attack.

"Uh-uh," Kevin muttered under his breath. "That's what I choose."

"S-S-S. Pow-pow." Jonathan rocked back and forth in his seat.

"We use words, Jonathan. Remember?" I said. "What's the trouble?"

"I don't know any word beginning with S. Pow-pow." He held up the anagram.

"Easy." Douglas turned away from Eddie. "Psychological. Like disturbed children. And it's psychological how black people and white people treat each other. Don't ya hear the S?"

Jonathan rummaged through a mound of letters and produced S-I-K-O-L-O.

"Still," Douglas looked out the window, "white people might get black themselves if they stayed in the sun too long."

Julie was listening thoughtfully. "Or a beautiful brown like you," she said.

"Gee, thanks. I never heard such a complimentary thing about my skin." He lifted his desktop and poked through the contents. "How about havin' my eraser?"

Julie didn't reach for it. "Maybe my mother

would like it." Her eyes were downcast. "She's mad at me, but I'm not sure why."

"Why don't you think about yourself?" He tossed it on her desk.

"I don't like to." She toyed with the eraser. "It makes me feel sad."

Kevin nodded. "Me too," he said softly.

She smiled at him. "You're like me."

The blush began at his neck and spread to the roots of his hair. . . .

[A much later session of the same therapeutic school group.]

The night before, Ellie had been in the kitchen until after ten decorating brownies with blue and white peace symbols for a class sale. Now, with silent acknowledgment to her I proposed a bake sale for our class.

"Cool. Me and my grandmother'll make raisin cookies."

From that day on, my wish for group activities was realized. Even Jonathan worked on the posters that were proudly distributed to every class. Excitement mounted. Central School had never had a bake sale. Other children came to our room to ask about it.

Arithmetic time was devoted to making price signs. Debates were held on which class should come in first. Douglas, of course, opted for the oldest. Julie argued. "The little kids won't buy as much. Let them choose before everything's gone." Surprisingly, she won unanimously. Even Douglas was swayed.

I sent notes home, explaining the purpose of our sale and thanking parents in advance for their cooperation.

When the great day came, Julie dragged in a carton containing a hundred cellophane bags of popcorn. Kevin's mother drove him and delivered a chocolate sheet cake, cut into fifty servings. Mr. Brenner took Eddie to the store en route to school. He purchased twenty double packages of cream-filled cupcakes, each of which he sliced in quarters. Douglas ceremoniously removed the covers from the two shoe boxes he'd carried. Both were filled to the brim with plump golden raisin cookies.

Jonathan came empty-handed.

"You're the only one who forgot," Julie scolded.

"You bum!" Eddie said.

Jonathan sought solace with his paper friend, but both were relegated to a corner in preparation for the customers. The merchants stood behind double desks, on which they spread the goods. There was a hectic scramble to sort out price tags, and a frantic search for the magic marker when

Douglas insisted that none of the prepared cards indicated the true worth of his cookies.

"Ten cents each," he insisted.

"For one cookie?" said Eddie. "You're flaky."

"I'm chargin' five cents for my cake," said Kevin.

"Five cents is fair for everything," Julie decreed.

"Now listen," Douglas thrust a cookie in her face, "these have eggs and margarine and genuine raisins. Do you know how long it takes one single grape to become a raisin?"

"They're beautiful," I said, "but if you charge too much, kids won't be able to afford them."

"Okay, okay, five cents." He held up his hands in resignation. But for five cents they're not getting raisins."

At nine-fifteen the first graders filed into our room. At the same time, Jonathan's mother appeared and left a tray of candied apples. Julie quickly arranged a desk for Jonathan, who with his paper ghost was recalled from the corner. He and his silent partner sold every apple.

Douglas did not participate. He'd moved his wares to the "office," where he stood with his back to the class.

By the time the second graders arrived, he, too, was in business—a mound of crumbling de-raisined cookies on one desk, tiny piles of raisins on the other, both products labeled "5¢ Each."

The last group of sixth graders left at eleven-thirty. By now the room was a shambles, desks and floor littered with waxed paper, crumbs, candy-apple sticks, and mashed popcorn. But from the beginning the event was a social success. Children who were reluctant to enter our room, having heard who-knows-what about its occupants, found it not only safe but perhaps even enviable.

"Hey, you got only five kids and all this audio-visual jazz?" one sixth grader said admiringly.

"You're lucky, getting to have a cake sale," a little girl told Julie.

I was delighted with the effect of such recognition, particularly on Kevin and Jonathan. As the morning progressed they changed from mumbling self-effacing boys to confident salesmen, enjoying positions of authority.

Miss Silverstein was our last customer. She bought everyone's leftovers and lingered to hear Douglas announce the final tally. Eleven dollars and thirty cents, all but one dollar in small change.

"Boss!" Douglas said. "That's a lotta bread!"

"Will you bring it to the hospital today," Julie asked me, "and tell 'em it's from us?"

"Better yet," Miss Silverstein paused in the doorway, "I'll call now and let their office know how hard you worked.". . .

[The final session of the same therapeutic school group: Tuesday, June 18; the last day of school.]

At first, Douglas and Julie had asked about Kevin often, but this past week they had been spending the entire day with their new classes. I was receiving glowing reports from Mrs. Tefft and Miss Flynn. Both children would return to their neighborhood schools in September.

All morning Eddie and Jonathan helped me carry books to the storeroom, collect paints and crayons, and take down papers and charts. Until today, Eddie had seemed almost relieved about going to Green Valley, but now, knowing that he'd soon be on his way, he was edgy and apprehensive.

"It's your fault, isn't it?" he asked, continuing to sweep the floor. "You're the one who kicked me out."

"You know that's not true, Eddie. You understand why that school's a better place for you."

"Sure!" He threw down the broom. "Because you're so selfish and critical. Admit it, goddamnit! You don't think I'm good enough, but you're keeping that crazy fatso."

Jonathan had improved to the point of caring when he'd been insulted. He stopped polishing his desk and sat back pensively. "I never call you names."

"I'll call you anything I want. Freak. Bastard. Bum." Eddie began circling Jonathan's desk.

"Come on, Eddie." I shook my head. I wanted this one day to be pleasant for all. "Anyone can say those words, but what does it prove? Think about the things you've said you liked at Green Valley, and stop feeling angry at Jonathan and me."

"Don't worry!" he shrieked. "I'm glad—glad to get outta this stinkin' place."

School was closing early, and the bus was due at noon. At eleven, Douglas and Julie returned to clean out their desks. When they were done, I served cookies and punch at the reading table. We ate together for the last time, conscious that this whole year together would soon be a memory. I looked at each child.

Douglas gulped the drink and held his cup for more. "I miss my ole buddy Kevin today."

"I'm gonna miss everybody." Julie nibbled her cookie. She edged her chair until it was touching mine.

"I'll miss you all too. But I'll be seeing your new teachers next year, so I'll get to hear about you."

Eddie ate cookie after cookie but said nothing.

Douglas slammed his fist against the table. "Don't make bad predictions, Mrs. Craig. I'll always be loyal to Central. You sound like we'll never even visit here again."

"Visiting's not the same Douglas." Julie looked out the window. "We won't even know the kids."

Douglas stopped eating. "I guess I'll never get to play under the new lights in the gym." He sounded gloomy.

Jonathan smiled at me for the very first time. "I'm glad I don't have to worry about missing that."

Julie put both hands on her hips. "Just because you're getting retarded doesn't mean it's good to stay back."

"Now, Julie," I said. "You know that Jonathan is not really staying back. He's—"

"The bus is here! The bus is here!" Eddie leaped up, knocking over his cup of punch. "Quick! I gotta do something." He grabbed a paper, ran into the closet, and closed the door. He was out in a minute and dropped the paper in his desk. "There, I left ya a note."

Pleased, I went to speak to him, but he dashed by me and out of the room.

Julie threw away her cup and napkin, then flung herself at me, her arms clutching my waist.

"Happy vacation, Julie." I hugged her. She was quivering. "You go ahead to the bus. I'll be out to say good-bye."

That left Jonathan and Douglas, still at the table. "C'mon," Douglas was leaning toward Jonathan. "Make one last goofy sound like you always used ta."

"Heck no!" Jonathan stood up and pushed in his chair. "Are you crazy? Do you think I wanna be in this class forever?"

While they were getting ready, I couldn't resist a peek at Eddie's message. Raising his desktop, I picked up the crumpled note and unfolded it slowly.

He had blown his nose all over the paper.

Sickened and discouraged, I walked to the door behind Jonathan and Douglas. Ceil must have driven over to say good-bye, I thought, seeing her standing beside Julie. Eddie was already in a rear seat by a raised window. Not wanting his upsetting note to be our last communication, I went to the bus and spoke through the opening.

"I got your note, Eddie. Someday you won't feel so angry. Come back and see me." I barely removed my hand before he slammed the window.

Julie kissed Ceil and me. Jonathan allowed us each a brief hug and hurried onto the bus.

Squinting in the sun's glare, Douglas extended his hand. "Well, it's been nice knowin' ya."

I clasped his hand in both of mine and looked into his expressionless face. It was hardest to say good-bye to Douglas, perhaps because he'd been the first and always so unpredictable. "Have a wonderful summer, Doug."

"Summa? Oh, God! Oh, God! Not summa! It's

summeRRR. Can't ya hear the R?" He shook his head, hopped on the bus, and shouted out toward Ceil. "Help her, Mrs. Black. She still can't speak our language!"

The driver closed the door.

Ceil and I stood waving. I struggled to maintain a smile and call out a last good-bye, but my throat was hopelessly jammed.

Eddie was crouching. Only the tip of his head visible. Julie blew an abundance of kisses. Douglas,

leaning out perilously, waved both arms in a slow crisscross pattern. Jonathan didn't wave. But through the window I could see him mouthing "good-bye, good-bye" until the bus turned the corner.

From *P.S. Your Not Listening* by Eleanor Craig, pp. 66–67, 144–147, 170–177, 211–214. Copyright © 1972, by Eleanor Craig. Reprinted by permission of the Harold Matson Company, Inc.

Editors' Commentary

Drugs in Therapy

Although drug therapy may be used with the school program or any other special therapeutic interventions (individual, group, or family), it may be eschewed as an interference in the child's growth, learning, or ultimate cure. It should never be used without thorough diagnosis, constant monitoring and evaluation, and direct supervision and recommendation of a medical doctor. It cannot work, even under the best circumstances, without the parent's or surrogate parent's collaboration.

The use of medicinal drugs in the treatment of children's emotional disturbances is a controversial subject. Some believe they are tremendously helpful; others are fearful of their use. Both sides have their points. The answers depend, obviously, not only on the child and the drug but also on the doctor and what he or she intends to accomplish. It is important to work with the child, the family, and the school to make sure that use of the drug will not be too alarming or special a matter for the child to handle. The meaning of the drug to the child, the way in which he or she understands it, is also important. Leon Eisenberg, author of the next article, is one of the most authoritative physicians working with disturbed children. He combines the mental health point of view with a vast pharmacological knowledge.

The Role of Drugs in Treating Disturbed Children

Leon Eisenberg

Few topics of discussion generate more heat and less light than the proper role of drugs in treating disturbed children. At one extreme are those physicians who argue that meaningful treatment is possible only by using the insights provided by psychotherapy—that drugs, if they function as more than placebos, do so only as chemical straight jackets for troublesome children—and that their use serves to delay recognition of the real psychopathology in the family. At the other extreme are those physicians who consider drugs the agents of choice because drugs attack disturbed function at

the physiologic level, the place at which they believe the ultimate pathology lies. Partisans of this viewpoint usually also deride psychotherapy as an insubstantial metaphysical occupation, hardly worthy of the honorable calling of a physician. The controversy engages the passions of psychologists, social workers, and teachers, as well as parents. The first law of psychopharmacology might be formulated to state: the certainty with which convictions are held tends to vary inversely with the depth of the knowledge on which they are based.

There is as yet no universal and completely

validated theory of human behavior that would permit a confident prediction of the utility of drugs. Even if we had such a theory the final decision would remain an empirical one. If an agent works well, then a physician, whatever his theoretical persuasion, will be a fool not to use it. For an empiricist, the relevant question becomes: What are the facts?

Experimental Principles

First, it is necessary to consider how the "facts" are obtained. If we wish to know whether aspirin lowers fever we need first of all accurate thermometers to measure fever. Then, we need a group of febrile patients to study. Next, since we know that fever is usually a transitory rather than a permanent condition, we need an experimental design that permits us to discriminate between a drug effect and a "natural" return of the patient's temperature to normal levels. This might be accomplished by having matched groups of patients, one treated by aspirin and one untreated, or perhaps one treated by aspirin and one treated by a second drug. But hold! What does the word "matched" mean in this context?

We know before we start the experiment that the fevers of a cold, of pneumonia, of malignancy, and of brain injury differ from one another in their mechanisms, duration, and susceptibility to modification. Furthermore, the course of the same disease differs in young and older patients; also, if other treatments are administered, these may influence the course of the fever.

Thus, a proper experimental design will require that the control and experimental patient groups be equivalent on those variables known to influence the phenomenon under study: in this case, the variables include diagnosis, age, other treatments, and other factors such as severity of condition and duration of illness. Moreover, we have to assume that other variables not known at the time of the study may be important. Since we cannot match patients on unknown factors, we attempt to take this into account by the random assignment of patients to one or the other group.

With these elementary conditions fulfilled, we must now include a sufficiently large and representative sample of patients to permit the meaning of any obtained differences between groups to be subjected to statistical analyses. These are simply mathematical procedures that enable us to determine how often the observed difference might be likely to arise by chance alone.

Again, the word "representative" requires attention. If we are to have any confidence that our treatment is useful for certain diseases, then we need to be reasonably sure that our sample is representative of patients with the diseases under study. For example, if they were all adults, we would not know whether the findings would hold true for children—indeed, for aspirin we would get quite different results.

Perhaps this simple model will illustrate the ingredients of a well-planned drug study: specification of the phenomenon to be studied; accurate instruments to measure the phenomenon; control for subject variables likely to influence outcome; random assignment to treatment groups; numbers sufficient to permit statistical analysis of findings; and a representative study population.

Effects of Expectation

But we have thus far not considered a major element in drug studies particularly relevant in psychopharmacology—the psychological effect of administering medication upon both the patient and the physician. We have all had the experience, when ill, of beginning to feel better once the doctor arrived, even before treatment began. Countless studies have demonstrated, both with objective signs (blood pressure, heart rate, skin lesions, and so forth) as well as with subjective symptoms (depression, anxiety, pain), that the expectation of a beneficial effect is often in itself sufficient to cause striking improvement.

When the medication is given to a child, it may influence him psychologically in one of two ways or both: (1) directly through his own expectations; (2) indirectly through altered parental behavior generated by anticipation of change in the child. Also, the physician or technician who judges the response may read into it results in keeping with the expected outcome. This is not "cheating"; the bias is usually outside the observer's awareness. Consequently, special precautions are necessary to keep from the patient and the doctor knowledge of the medication the patient is taking. This is done by giving a placebo, an inert substance made to resemble closely the active drug. The record of which patient is getting the drug and which the placebo is kept coded and is not revealed until all results have been scored. Such an experiment is termed "double blind." . . .

Principles of Drug Treatment

Our observations have led us to the following principles:

1. *Drugs can be useful agents in managing pediatric psychiatric disorders when chosen appropriately and ap-*

plied with discrimination. They can control symptoms not readily managed by other means and can facilitate psychotherapy by allaying symptoms that disrupt learning. If they are not the panaceas portrayed in advertisements, neither are they the poisons claimed by their foes.

2. *Skill in using drugs requires knowledge of their pharmacologic properties and sensitivity to their psychologic significance.*[1] Every drug study reveals the potency of placebo effects—benefits occurring from relationship with physician and from positive expectations of patients. These effects can be used to potentiate pharmacologic results by recognizing that the prescription of medication is an important communication to the patient and his family; contrariwise, they can have a negative impact if the physician regards drugs solely as weapons to impose control or as measures of desperation.

3. *No drug should be employed without firm indications for its use, without careful control of the patient, and without due precautions against toxicity.* With any potent drug toxicity is inevitable; to justify its use the severity of the condition and the likelihood of benefit must outweigh the possible toxicity. Toxicity studies on adults cannot be safely extrapolated to children because of differences in the immature and developing organism; clinical decisions must be based on data from pediatric studies.

4. *An old drug is to be preferred to a new drug unless evidence of superiority for the latter is clear.* This principle of pharmacologic conservatism is based upon the fact that unexpected toxicity from a new agent may be apparent only after prolonged experience with it. This is not pharmacologic nihilism. Drugs can make a decisive difference in treatment, but their very potency commends us not to use them lightly.

5. *Drugs should be used no longer than necessary.* Dosage should be reduced periodically, with the goal of ending treatment if symptoms do not return on lower dosage.

6. *Dosage must be individualized.* Each person is metabolically unique. Undertreatment as well as overtreatment can result in erroneous conclusions about unsuitability of a particular medication for a particular patient.

7. *The use of drugs does not relieve a physician of responsibility for seeking to identify and eliminate the factors causing or aggravating the psychiatric disorder.* All currently available psychopharmacologic agents treat symptoms not diseases. Symptomatic relief is not to be disparaged. But to prescribe drugs for a child whose symptoms stem from correctable social, familial, biological, or psychological disturbance without attempting to alter the factors causing the symptoms is a disservice to the child.

There is no assumption here that psychotherapy is necessarily any more of a specific than drug therapy. It, too, has symptomatic and nonspecific effects; exacting proof of its efficiency remains to be provided. It, too, can act as an anodyne if not accompanied by searching efforts to correct the untoward life stresses acting upon the youngster. The justification for psychotherapy appears to lie in its possibilities for modifying learned unhealthy behavior patterns. However, the patient may become accessible to psychotherapy only after the acuteness of his symptoms has been diminished by pharmacologic methods. It should be emphasized that control of symptoms by drugs is not an end in itself; symptom control provides a climate in which the patient can learn new and more effective patterns for coping with his environment.

Drugs have a definite but limited role in the treatment of disturbed behavior. Medical evaluation of new drugs seems to follow a time sequence characterized by: early enthusiasm, growing criticism and awareness of toxicity, premature calls for discard, and final sobriety with moderate agreement on indications and dangers. Drugs are neither the passport to a brave new world nor the gateway to hell. With thoughtful selection, careful regulation of dosage, and close scrutiny for toxicity, they add a significant element to a total plan of patient care.

Note

1. **B. Fish**, Drug Theory in Child Psychiatry: Psychological Aspects. *Comprehensive Psychiatry* (February 1960 and August 1960).

From Leon Eisenberg, "The Role of Drugs in Treating Disturbed Children," *Children*, Vol. 2, No. 4, 1964, pp. 167–173, U.S. Department of Health, Education, and Welfare.

4

What Kinds of Schools
and Programs Are Provided?

Editors' Commentary

Once a child is identified as having learning and behavior problems, a modified educational program is usually recommended. The major problem confronting the schools is not formulating such a recommendation but carrying it out. Finding the right educational and therapeutic program for a child is a search even Sherlock Holmes would find difficult. The choice of an appropriate placement is affected by the professional standards and functions of the special education placement team and the social influences of race, money, and parental status. New attempts to rectify these biases by the legal action of Public Law 94–142, with parents having power of final approval, should have a marked influence on the kinds and quantity of special education services available for troubled children. Over the next decade we shall have an opportunity to evaluate the effectiveness of this law in guaranteeing the rights of all handicapped pupils to quality education.

In the first article of this chapter, Evelyn Deno suggests a strategy for increasing the school's capacity to integrate exceptional pupils into the mainstream of education by redefining the responsibilities of both special education and regular education. The Cascade System of Special Education service is designed to provide flexible but sequential levels of help and structure.

Strategies for Improvement of Educational Opportunities
for Handicapped Children

Evelyn Deno

One's view of the educational scene is unavoidably colored by personal experiences encountered in trying to deal with educational systems, whether this experience was accrued as a consumer of the system or as a professional trying to improve it. The view from my position is that education is a single continuum on which all children have a place where they should be educated as individuals rather than as parts of systems. The primary educational goal, to me, is to increase the educational mainstream's capacity to accommodate to differences in the individual characteristics that children bring to school learning-tasks. The burden of achieving this goal, consequently, rests with those of us who are concerned with the training of teachers for the classroom. . . .

The Relation of Regular and Special Education

A first-order conviction born out of my experience as a teacher, child psychologist, special education administrator, and consumer of the literature in the field is that whatever distinctions can be made between regular education and special education are mainly organizational and not substantive, that is, the manner in which learning experiences need to be presented is the main basis of distinction. Whatever learning principles apply to handicapped children apply to all children and end goals are the same in their most essential aspects.

Useless amounts of time and energy are wasted in trying to define for all time and all places what differentiates "regular" and "special" education when the definitional effort addresses to anything other than who is to be responsible for providing what *services*. It is my impression that administrators responsible for implementing whatever is "special" about special education seldom are confused on this point. They are well aware that what is "special" about special education is the delivery system and not the fundamental content of what is to be delivered or the purposes of delivery. Regular educators and academicians seem less certain.

Some special educators find unacceptable the distinction of their responsibility on the basis of the outside capabilities of the regular system. They cringe at the thought of defining their responsibilities as those that regular education rejects or fails to perform. They prefer to rest their identities as special educators on what they perceive to be more positive professional grounds.

This lack of understanding and agreement on boundaries of responsibility is one of the central difficulties standing in the way of better articulation between regular and special education services. In my opinion, *better coordination of regular and special education services is a primary need of our time if we hope to improve education for handicapped children.* . . .

The special education field must direct whatever forces it can muster to helping the regular system achieve the necessary understanding and tangible resources to become maximally accommodative to the needs of children who show different learning styles and, at the same time, to insure that specialized education facilities and appropriate treatment options will be available for those residual children who genuinely need special circumstances and methods outside mainstream provisions to maximize their learning. Special education has to organize itself for a double-pronged approach: direct service to children who cannot reasonably be accommodated in the educational mainstream and, working hand in hand with regular education, the development of mainstream technology and implementation mechanisms to improve the total enterprise. Regular educators cannot afford to ignore the richness of technology and curriculum opportunities emergent in mainstream education.

On this assumption, I recommend that we envision educational services on the kind of service continuum illustrated in Figure 1. The tapered design is used to indicate the considerable difference in the numbers of children anticipated at the different levels and to call attention to the fact that the system itself serves as a diagnostic filter. The most specialized facilities are likely to be needed by the fewest children on a long-term basis. Actual work with children provides the best diagnosis if it is thoughtfully conducted.

This organizational model can be applied to the development of special education services for all types of disability. It assumes that there will always be some children who require the help of specialists. It assumes that the characteristics of children who fall out of mainstream provisions will change continuously as mainstream provisions, medical practice, and social conditions change, because learning problems are presumed to be the product of the interaction between the child and the kind of "education" impinging on him at home, on the streets, and in school. Where regular education responsibilities should end and special education's should begin is definable only in terms of the individual case in its particular situation. Under such conditions role conflict is inevitable. What is needed is will and mechanisms to solve the problem of who should do what, not tighter role-boundary definitions.

The cascade model assumes that children are seldom all able or all handicapped. They more frequently present their teachers with a marble cake of aptitudes and dysfunctions that cannot be adequately described by categorical classification of

Figure 1. The Cascade System of Special Education Service

Level I	Children in regular classes, including those "handicapped" able to get along with regular class accommodations with or without medical or counseling supportive therapies	"out-patient" services (assignment of pupils governed by the school system)
Level II	Regular class attendance plus supplementary instruction	
Level III	Part-time Special Class	
Level IV	Full-time Special Class	
Level V	Special Stations	
Level VI	Homebound	
Level VII	Instruction in hospital or domiciled settings "Noneducational" service (medical and welfare care and supervision)	"in-patient" programs (assignment of children to facilities governed by health or welfare agencies)

children on a "he is or he isn't" basis. The organizational model recognizes that children need to be programmed individually, that the only fundamentally meaningful class, for educational purposes, contains an N of one.

This conception provides language and pictures relations in a way that may help to clarify some of the problems to be expected in trying to blend regular and special education services.

A monograph published and distributed through the University of Minnesota, Department of Audio-Visual Extension, 1971. Reprinted by permission.

Editors' Commentary

The selection of articles to represent each of the levels of service was a difficult process. In the first place, many of the services and strategies proposed at one level are also used at a higher level of service. An example is the crisis/resource teacher. Second, we wanted to show programs that were successful with different ages, groups, problems, and theories. Third, we identified many outstanding and innovative programs at each level. As a result, our selection cannot present the range of programs in each level. Rather, it offers a superior example within each level of service.

Level I programs give ongoing support to the classroom teacher attempting to mainstream educationally handicapped pupils. This can be accomplished by providing a consultant. In the past, school psychologists and mental health clinicians have played the consultant role successfully. In many schools the function has been assigned to the school-based special educator. In the next article, Mark Montgomery explains the complexity of the consultant's role and the skills this educator must have in order to listen, learn, and help teachers become more objective and responsive to the needs of these pupils.

The Special Educator as Consultant: Some Strategies

Mark D. Montgomery

I've got this kid who . . . How many times have you heard sentences beginning like that? A thousand? Usually, it's in the hall or the teachers' lounge. You're trying to get yourself prepared, or composed, or relaxed, and one of the regular classroom teachers in your school comes over and begins with, "I've got this kid who . . ." Sometimes it seems like an imposition on your time, but you try to give some help anyway. All this is nothing new. What *is* new is that you, the special educator, are going to be asked to do more and more of this type of thing—more and more consultation with regular teachers.

Why Me?

Good question. After all, there you were just a few years ago: responsible for a class of 15 kids in the old mimeograph room at the end of the hall. Nobody bothered you. Nobody cared. Maybe you were able to "mainstream" your kids into lunch or physical education. Maybe not.

Now, all of a sudden, you are a resource room teacher (whatever that means) and your kids are *really* mainstreamed—into reading, math, spelling, or science. New laws have been written adding constraints and responsibilities to your job. One of the new responsibilities is to work with those regular classroom teachers whom you hardly know outside of the teachers' lounge. Not only that, but you are expected to get them to do the right thing by kids with whom they would rather not have to deal at all. So asking, "Why me?" is understandable.

There are three good reasons for you, the special educator, to act as consultant to regular teachers on learning/behavior problems. First, new laws (e.g., Public Law 94–142) have mandated placement of "handicapped" children in the "least restrictive environment," which could, and often does, mean the regular classroom. And, while teachers are technically responsible for the mainstreamed student, they are supposed to get some kind of help. Direct intervention (e.g., tutoring) is a time consuming and, therefore, expensive process. Furthermore, the effectiveness of this kind of service has been seriously questioned (Dunn, 1968; Gallagher, 1972; Lilly, 1970). Consultation, an indirect service, has a "ripple effect." That is, by helping just one teacher do a better job, you are improving the programs of all the children in the classroom, something you would find difficult to do directly. So, from a cost benefit standpoint, more and more consultation seems to be in order.

A second reason for your doing consultation is that about one third of all school age children are experiencing some kind of difficulty in school (Swift & Spivack, 1975). That means in an elementary school of 500, 150 to 200 kids need more than they are currently getting from their school experience. Obviously, you cannot give them all that they need directly. What you *can* do is help the teachers in your school deal more effectively with the problems in their classes—which is what consultation is all about. By providing this kind of indirect service, you are helping not only the individuals about whom the teacher is immediately concerned, but all the other children in that class. And, while the effects of consultation may not be as measurable as, say, tutoring a dozen kids in reading, the "ripple effect" makes it a more effective proposition in the long run.

A third argument for consultation is that your job as a resource teacher puts you in a unique position in the school—one that is particularly well suited to working with other teachers. Writers have pointed to several factors that make consultation work. For instance, consultation is more effective when it is a collaborative undertaking, rather than a relationship between an "expert" and a "nonexpert" (Dinkmeyer & Carlson, 1973). Also, consultation works better when it is a continuing, long term relationship, rather than a once a month visit from a school psychologist or supervisor (Moed & Muhich, 1972). You probably have these things working for you already; that is, you are seen as an equal, as a permanent member of the faculty. Here are a few tips on harnessing your position for consultation in the school.

Being an Expert Is Not So Smart

A lot of special educators are frustrated doctors. We like to be able to give advice, prescribe cures. It makes us feel good to be "experts," to know The Answer. We tend to use impressive terms like *hyperkinesis, dyspraxia,* and *strephasymbolia* not for what they communicate about the student, but for what they communicate about ourselves: that we are, in fact, a special breed of teacher.

We often feel that we are the only ones who really understand the nature and needs of the exceptional child (after all we took a course with just that title!). We see the regular teacher as unacceptable for "our" special kids. While these feelings are all too justified, they are rarely very productive. By thinking of yourself as the only hope for the special child you are building a barrier between your program and the rest of the school. Furthermore, by helping regular teachers abdicate their responsibility you are keeping them from growing, from expanding their capabilities in needed directions.

Remember this: they are not *your* kids. They are the responsibility of their teacher. So, if Mrs. Smith has Johnny for reading, Johnny is her responsibility, whether he is retarded, learning disabled, or speech impaired. Your responsibility is to help Mrs. Smith do *her* job better, by offering her suggestions or assistance. Don't let Mrs. Smith make you feel that she is doing you a favor by "taking one of your kids."

You are neither the expert who is going to tell Mrs. Smith what to do, nor her aide, helping her by doing her job for her. You need to foster a cooperative relationship with the regular teacher, where you can function as two equals, each bringing your unique skills and perspective to the situation.

Curb your natural tendency to tell Mrs. Smith how she should teach Johnny. Nobody likes unsolicited advice. For that matter, nobody listens to unsolicited advice. Wait for Mrs. Smith to feel a need, and to ask for help. Only then will she appreciate and benefit from it. Of course you can help her feel a need for help by being in her room a lot, asking about the situation, or suggesting to the principal that something needs to be done about Johnny. But wait to be asked for your advice.

It's What You Don't Say That Counts

Let's assume that you have developed a nice cooperative relationship with Mrs. Smith, and that she does ask you what to do with Johnny. It's your move. What do you do? You tell her what to do with Johnny, right? Wrong! Snap answers are never appropriate. If you're wrong you've embarrassed yourself. If you're right you've embarrassed Mrs. Smith, who may have been struggling with the problem for months. What's more, even if you are right, it's unlikely that Mrs. Smith will take your ideas seriously unless she feels that you have taken the time to gather information and give thoughtful consideration to the problem.

The first rule for consultants is to *listen.* It seems like a simple notion, but it usually marks the difference between an effective and an ineffective helper. Being a good listener is not just polite, it's smart. By giving Mrs. Smith a chance to talk freely about the problem you are doing two positive things: helping her relieve her anxiety about the situation, thereby making her more receptive to your ideas, and gathering valuable information— her view of the problem.

So practice listening—not the passive, polite, waiting for your turn kind—but active, concerned, therapeutic listening.

If Everybody Likes What You're Doing, You're Probably Doing It Wrong

Change hurts. It's a more or less painful experience for everyone involved. If you, as a consultant, are doing anything worthwhile, you are causing change—in the way Mrs. Smith teaches reading, in her attitude toward "kids like Johnny," in the atmosphere in her classroom, or in her relationship to her class.

So, expect a certain amount of discomfort. Expect teachers to get upset with you from time to time, to tell you to mind your own business, to try to avoid you. Don't consider it an indication of failure. Just the opposite! If you have established the right kind of relationship with her, Mrs. Smith's occasional negative behavior is probably a sign of growth, which always involves anxiety and uncertainty.

Systems resist change. Like giant oysters they try to smooth down or expel irritants. Successful consultant/change agents know just how irritating to be—enough to stimulate change, but not enough to be kicked out of school. School faculties are very good at smoothing out your rough edges. They want you to go along, not to rock the boat. "After all," they say, "we're a team. We all have to pitch in." This often means "helping" teachers to abdicate their responsibility to kids who represent problems to them.

Be on alert for attempts to get you to do things

for the convenience of the system, rather than for the benefit of the children. Don't let Mrs. Smith tell you that she will not teach Johnny because she doesn't have time. (You'll hear this one at least twice a day!) Help her to find time, to realize that it is her responsibility to teach Johnny unless she has a contract that allows her to teach only the kids she wants to, and to see that by expanding her skills now, she will do a better job with her whole class, and with other "problem learners" that she might have in coming years.

A Teacher's Classroom Is Her Castle

One of the surest ways to get the average teacher uptight is to invade her sanctuary—her classroom. Whatever your reason for being there, your presence invites her anxiety or even hostility. The problem is that you, as a consultant, need to see how her class works, how she manages her time, how the kids respond to her instructions, many things that can only be reliably observed in person. So how do you get the information you need without causing (or experiencing) undue discomfort?

Keep in mind four things regarding classroom observation. First, Mrs. Smith's reaction to your presence is natural. Everybody gets anxious when someone is looking over his shoulder. This is especially true in schools, where, typically, classroom visitors are there to evaluate the teacher. Second, be as unobtrusive as possible. Don't get too involved with helping or talking to the kids. Take a seat and disappear as much as possible. Third, make a point to talk to the teacher after your visit, and stress your *positive* reactions to her teaching. Finally, make visits often enough to acclimate Mrs. Smith and the kids to your presence. The more you are around, the less threatening you'll be.

Everything Broken Doesn't Have to Be Fixed

A few years ago I took my car to the shop for routine maintenance. About noon the mechanic called me at work to tell me that the left turn signal was broken and it would cost ten dollars to have it fixed. I thanked him for calling and explained that, while the turn signal did not blink on and off automatically, it did blink each time I depressed the lever. So, as long as I was willing to move the lever up and down (and I was) the blinking effect was normal. Thus, I concluded, there was no need to fix the turn signal. "But," came his unruffled reply, "it's broken." I went on patiently, "I don't mind

operating the lever manually, so there is no problem. And since there's no problem, there's nothing to be fixed." "But," he repeated, "it's broken."

It's easy for us to fall into a "fix it" mentality. Whenever we diagnose a "hyper-something," or an "a-something," or (heaven forbid!) a "dys-something," we feel duty bound to treat it, to bring it up to manufacturer's specifications. Often, in our blind pursuit of normalcy, we overlook the fact that no *problem* exists, except in our own heads. Johnny reads with his book turned sideways, or kneels instead of sitting on his chair, or wears his jacket in class. Do we "fix" him or let him be? Before we can answer that question realistically we must ask, "Is it a problem for Johnny—or for *us?*" Does it hamper Johnny's learning, or do we see it as a problem because of our own preoccupation with things being normal, with Johnny acting like everyone else?

In dealing with teachers who bring you problems, use caution. Make sure that a problem, not just a difference, exists. Don't waste your energy, the teacher's time, and the child's self concept fixing something that doesn't need to be fixed.

Having said that, let me add: If a teacher sees a problem, you can bet that a problem exists. A contradiction? Nothing of the sort. If Mrs. Smith sees Johnny as a problem, then whether or not *Johnny* turns out to be a problem, something is probably wrong with the relationship between him and Mrs. Smith, or with Mrs. Smith herself, or with the school's expectations of Johnny. Look at some of these areas for the problem.

Three Final Suggestions

First, take yourself seriously. Consultation is a real job. It can provide your school with an invaluable service if it is undertaken conscientiously. Second, look and listen. Input comes before output. Watch what's going on in your school. Listen to the concerns of the teachers. Third, learn. There is a lot to know, both about the nature of learning and behavior problems, and about the process of consultation.

References

Dinkmeyer, D., & Carlson, J. *Consulting: Facilitating human potential and change processes.* New York: Merrill, 1973.

Dunn, L. M. Special education for the mildly retarded—Is much of it justifiable? *Exceptional Children*, 1968, 35(1), 5–22.

Gallagher, J. J. The special education contract for mildly handicapped children. *Exceptional Children*, 1972, 39, 527–535.

Lilly, M. S. Special education: A teapot in a tempest. *Exceptional Children*, 1970, 37(1), 43–49.

Moed, G., & Muhich, D. E. Some problems and parameters of mental health consultation. *Community Mental Health Journal*, 1972, 8, 232–239.

Swift, M. S., & Spivack, G. *Alternative teaching strategies*. Champaign IL: Research Press, 1975.

Editors' Commentary

The crisis/resource teacher typifies Level II and III services to emotionally disturbed pupils. Crisis/resource teachers are trained in remedial education and behavioral management. They provide direct, immediate help to individual pupils who are unable to cope with the usual classroom demands. Many children who are referred to a special class could be taught and managed in a regular class if such a teacher were available to provide them with temporary support and control. The crisis/resource teacher must work closely with classroom teachers and supportive services and make referrals for diagnostic and intensive help. The next article, by William Morse, explores this special education role, ranging from crisis intervention to ongoing part-time special group placement.

The Crisis or Helping Teacher

William C. Morse

Development of the Concept

There is both a theoretical and practical background to the role of the crisis or helping teacher. First, as to the theoretical matter. At a time of problematic behavior it has been the general practice in schools to wait until a youngster "cools down" or until the migrating specialist comes to deal with a problem. This has serious limitations when one considers the nature of children. While there are times when a child stores up and retains incidents over a long period of time, much of the time they exist in a brief time module, responding to conditions of the moment. Time serves as a sponge, absorbing especially the reality which does not fit with the needs of the pupil. A burst of anger may be replaced by quite a different tone by the time someone gets to the incident. Adults spend a great deal of effort reconstituting the situation, but it seldom goes far beyond a simulation—except for the adult.

Now some schools are crisis prone: in fact there are those which seem to move from one crisis to the next with hardly a pause. But the traditional response to the crisis is usually a dictatorial confrontation, often with a strong emotional reaction on the part of the adult. To expect the behavior changes which are implied is akin to belief in magic. Those who have had the most extensive training in child behavior and management are usually the most remote from the action. Crises are often a condition where schools are least effective.

But crises can be considered a resource for helping youngsters. Caplan has proposed that intervention is most effective at the time of crisis. The theory of crisis intervention is not a surface substitute for dynamic understanding. Characteristically, the efforts of the on-the-line workers have been relegated to a second level importance. Such personnel have been given the responsibility for stemming the immediate tide as a sort of stopgap process, while those with deep involvement have assumed the responsibility for the real corrective influence. Crisis intervention concepts permit no split between what has to be done on a managerial basis and the most significant interaction with children.

The importance of all of this for contemporary mental health ideology is as follows. Studies of life histories show that those making successful adjustments differ from those who make unsuccessful adjustments less in the degree of stress they have faced than in how adequately they learned to cope with that stress. Thus, two case histories can be identical as far as the potential genesis of pathology is concerned, but one turns out reasonably well-adjusted while the other does not. Corrective influence and good mental health are the result of satisfactory solutions to the life crises. The proper intervention provided at the time of a crisis is significant teaching.

This is not to say that people are always particularly "teachable" at a time of a crisis, in the sense that they stand there awaiting help to learn how to cope with a particular situation. It merely means that at that time of crisis a person is in turmoil and seeks some resolution. The object of crisis intervention is to assist with coping action which will have long term value. The Harvard group which has dealt with this problem has studied overwhelming crisis situations such as accidents, bereavement, and other catastrophic life events. Caplan states that during such a period a person is more susceptible to being influenced by others than in times of relative psychological equilibrium.[1]

With the spread of the concept of crisis intervention, particularly using life space interviewing, adults must take care not to consider every incident as a profound life experience for extensive intervention. Particularly with youngsters, that which seems a crisis to adults may not be that at all. It should be clear that the less the individual himself feels the sense of crisis or press, the less likely will the event fit this system.

This brings us to a psychological definition of crisis. An event with a great deal of explosiveness is not necessarily a significant crisis if it is unrelated to the child's abiding problem. The selection of a particular event for potential crisis intervention requires just as much sophistication as does any interpretation in traditional therapy. Bloom has provided help on the problem of definition.[2] Is the crisis in the eye of the "crisee" or just in the eye of the beholder? Is it sensed by the child or only the teacher? Many so-called crisis situations may have no meaning as far as the primary individual is concerned. It is a crisis to the external consumer of

the behavior. Many interventions fail because they are posed with an inadequate awareness of this fact. Events which are crises to adults are often satisfying, ego-building, and gratifying to pupils. Stated in simple terms, a crisis occurs when the child's coping capacity is overloaded. This may be generated by external conditions such as confronting of difficult academic or behavioral tasks. Or a crisis may be a consequence of internal perceptions, distorted or accurate. The coping failure is of such severity that the child cannot be helped by the typical, mild supporting tactics which teachers use day in and day out. Thus, a crisis is a psychological duress which may or may not be accompanied by overt signs.

Caplan states that a crisis is a relatively sudden onset of disequilibrium in a child.[3] The disequilibrium is acute enough to be differentiated from previous functioning. These become turning points for personality consolidation and there is a relative saturation of negative feelings such as anxiety, depression, anger, shame, and guilt not contingent with what one expects. These are states of turmoil. Caplan points out that many children who are facing an identity crisis will have a period of this type but are not necessarily emotionally disturbed unless this develops into a chronic negative pattern. He also differentiates between developmental and accidental crises. The developmental crises are transitional periods which one anticipates for both normal and disturbed children. For example, the third grade and beginning of school are significant periods. The onset of adolescence constitutes a developmental crisis period. These conditions are precipitated by loss of basic support or some threat or a challenge which puts heightened demands on an individual. Caplan sees these as pathways leading to increased or decreased capacity to cope with one's environment.

We should be wary of the idea that children are always more *easily* influenced at a time of crisis, at least by the adult who is attempting an intervention. In a state of heightened emotion, an individual is more prone to search for cues from some aspect of his inner or outer environment to solve his dilemma. He may take his directive from another child who provides a pattern of what to do about a stress situation. The point is that during this extreme crisis period he is in a labile state.

It is obvious that crisis teaching requires the person who provides the help to be available at the time of the crisis. As a matter of fact, it has been found that the inability of a teacher of disturbed children to resolve chronic crises by providing reasonable coping assistance results in growth stalemate. The important point, from Caplan's view, is that a small force acting for a short time during the period of acute crisis can produce more pronounced impact for change than would otherwise be possible. This is the most central concept of the whole procedure. Of course, interventions are not only verbal but also include manipulation of all aspects of the environment. One uses the emotional potency of the situation to help the child understand what he is feeling and what can be done. When you let a child "cool-down," the impetus for change often cools too. In fact, many helpers spend a good deal of time in regenerating the problem so that it can be discussed. It is even sometimes necessary to actually create a crisis in order to have effective material to deal with, even though the child was a continual problem in a classroom, but at a lower level of intensity.

We have examined the theory of crisis intervention. Now for a look at the practical considerations. Teachers have observed the following. A disturbed child is not in difficulty 100 percent of the time. In fact many of them handle the classroom, most of the time, in an adequate fashion. Also, when a youngster is in the process of falling apart, he needs more adult investment, a fact well known to the classroom teacher. Most often the assistance he needs is too extensive to provide. When there is time it is often too late. In the school setting, the child with problems does not come in neat behavior or academic packages. It is frequently necessary to move back and forth in both arenas to help. A personality specialist is one thing; a remedial tutor another; but both are needed. Further, influence attempts not directed toward helping the pupil with the school reality may be fine, but not what a return to the classroom requires. Most of all, teachers want a teacher type person always available as a back up resource. Itinerant workers are not enough. Furthermore, with the increased pressures being put on schools, with an effort to do something more with the failing pupil, with the resistance to separation of problems in special classes, and with stress involved in integration, teachers want help, not advice, and direct assistance rather than consultation. This led to the design called the crisis teacher.

Style and Service

While schools use such space as is available for the helping teacher, the preferred situation is a small classroom divided so that two individual children or two small groups can be worked with at the same time. To the usual remedial art and game resources are added the "hardware"—typewriter, language master, and tape recorders are typical. Some teachers have found teaching machines a real asset.

The helping teacher works both in the emotional and academic life of the pupil. As a special teacher for disturbed pupils, the training includes an intermeshing of both aspects. At one time, the child may be too upset to work on an academic task and a variety of means will be used to begin business. Life space interviewing may work; sometimes a child has to wait himself out for a while. He may draw, type on a note what he can't speak. Usually conversation can be started. It is a complex matter to decide when and what issues are reasonable to approach. Where the trail goes depends upon the nature of the problem. It may be that the presenting issue is a clear academic problem—"how to divide big numbers." Not at once, but over a period of time, every effort is made to get at such underlying factors as are needed to help the child adjust. But the child is seen as a unified total with academic and emotional spheres all as one. This does not imply that probing needs to be done when academic failure is a major source and can be approached directly. The teacher is not wed to any theoretical approach except the total problem-solving approach involved in situational analysis. One examines the nature of the child, the life space press and access points. The self-concept and self-esteem of the child may give leads to the proper interventions. What are the gratification channels available? While there may be elaborate conclusions of what should be done, there is the reality problem of deciding what *can* be done. Interventions in any part of the internal system by life space interviews, remedial help, planning, and so forth will be developed. It may mean writing a contract to support an inadequate ego or teaching study skills. It may mean an attempt to change the regular teacher's handling, a peer discussion, or a design with parents—not always done exclusively by the crisis teacher of course. One goes as far as finding a big brother for identification. Plans may include groups of children, as in the case of sixth grade children assisting first grade ones—none of them being good readers. There is a search for any natural resources which can be utilized.

The term "crisis teacher" was soon replaced with "helping teacher" for several reasons. Schools do not favor being stigmatized as crisis institutions and indeed should not be. Also, helping is the more favored activity. Further, handling crises smacked too much of after the fact, while prevention was the intent. The actual stress-producing conditions cannot be ignored. In addition, there was the issue of what does a crisis teacher do between crises? This implies that a crisis must always be a visible upset in the system. This is not the truth: a youngster may slip into a depressed state when he feels no hope, and he is certainly a case needing help. Further, there are many children who are achieving far below any reasonable expectation. Often reading assistance has not been effective because the problem is motivational and not tutorial. In short, there is enough individualization work to do in any school to employ the full effort of a teacher when there is no uproar.

This helping teacher must really know curriculum at the school level served, must be steeped in remedial teaching techniques, and must be skilled in life space interviewing. Since each school is unique, the modus operandi will fit the specific needs of a given school. However, there are several generalizations which may serve as guidelines.

The helping teacher has the most direct relationship with the child and his regular teacher. Referral procedures are the responsibility of the total staff. When a teacher feels that a pupil cannot be helped through the regular classroom alone, it may be because his behavior is disturbing to others or because he is failing in his own efforts to cope with tasks. One does not await a complicated diagnosis or parental permission because the pupil is not, in the usual sense, a special case. His behavior "in situ" provokes the referral. When possible, plans are worked out in advance with the regular teacher. When not, the regular teacher may take the pupil directly to the crisis teacher and present the reality situation in a nonrejecting, nonmoralistic but frank manner. This special service is not a dumping ground or a discard heap. Rather, the two teachers discuss sympathetically the educational complexity at hand. Cues relative to the pupil's attitude about the referral are faced directly and the crisis teacher goes over possible goals. The pupil returns to the classroom, after an episode, only when he is deemed intact and ready: it may be soon, or it may take days. The referral back procedure involves the same teacher team work, and the fact of an integrated effort is made clear to the pupil.

Pupils come and go, sometimes on a regular basis as seems advisable but often on an episodic basis when specific pressure accumulates. Of course, at times the special teacher may be working with more than one pupil. As crisis demands decrease, there are always those less demonstrative problem children to be given individual help.

As indicated, the work which goes on during the special session is determined by the pupil's problem. Children seldom compartmentalize their relationships or their quandaries. Home, school, and play are intermixed. General attitudes and school work motivation come in confused combinations. Consequently, the teacher has to take a broad humanistic approach in crisis teaching. The interaction may take on characteristics of a "man to man," a parental surrogate, or a counselor, as well as the general teacher role. Free of large group responsibilities, immediate achievement goals, and time restrictions, this teacher can operate with a new flexibility. Perhaps it will be individualized tutoring, an informal talk, a diversionary activity, or an intensive life space interview session around the feelings and tension evidenced in the pupil. In short, what is done is what any teacher would wish to do were it possible to determine action by the needs of the child rather than respond to a large group process in the classroom.

The difficulty may turn out to be a learning frustration, an interpersonal conflict, or an internal feeling. As the crisis teacher sizes up the situation, plans are made for immediate and long-term steps. This teacher may get the outpouring of the child's inner conflict and must be prepared to handle whatever the child brings as well as refer special problems to other services. At times several children may be involved, and group work is called into play.

It is particularly important that the child learns he will be listened to and that his problem will be considered, even to the point of initiating joint sessions with his regular teacher to discuss conditions. There are few of the "secrets" and confidentialities which some professional workers make much of at the expense of the exchange of necessary information among parties involved with the pupil's school problem. While it is obvious that this takes utmost skill and sensitivity, it should also be clear that co-equal members of a staff can be open with the child, and no professional worker is "handling" another. All too soon we are faced with the fact that the total staff, with all the insight it can muster, will still not be able to influence the lives of some of these children at any more than a surface level. Problems may stem from the family or outside influences beyond school reach. On the other hand, if we can help a pupil meet what are for him reasonable social and academic school expectations, this is itself a worthwhile goal, although other problems remain.

The teacher's role with teacher peers has come to be an aspect with great significance. Most school consultation depends for its momentum on the expert (often from the outside) relating to a person asking for help. The consultant is seldom in the setting all the time and has limited knowledge of all that goes on there. This enables the teacher to take or leave advice, and to protect himself by various means if the implied dependency role with the consultant is not acceptable.

There is another style of consultation, mutual problem-solving, which Ruth Newman (among others) has clarified. Production of viable solutions is the test, rather than implied expertise. This is the stance the crisis teacher takes with colleagues. When the focus is on mutual collaboration to help the child, many of the role conflicts disappear. But this is a most difficult part of the work. Seldom can an effective remedial effort be staged unless the two teachers work in concert. Skill in problem-solving style consultation is thus one requirement for the helping teacher.

A word should be added about the type of effort planned for the child. Most workers develop facility with one technique over another, but the approach must be kept flexible. Interventions should be relevant to the problem, whether they involve changing certain conditions (or stimuli, rewards, etc.) in the life space or are directed to insight or relationship. Whatever is done should be done on the basis of prescription to fit the nature of the child's problem and the access to change, from operant to classical therapy.

Relationship to Other Specialists

Some of the helping teacher's clientele will already have been studied intensively by specialists. Other pupils will be new and present baffling questions to the crisis teacher and staff. Here, specific data on classroom behavior, psychological study, visiting teacher investigation, or material from a psychiatric examination may be in order. Perhaps it will become evident that the pupil's needs are for individual case work or family contact which can be best done by the visiting teacher or counselor. Since these specialists participate in the planning, trial decisions are the product of mutual discussion. The sharing of cases becomes the sharing of a problem-solving venture. In this way, the school principal, specialist, crisis teacher, and classroom teacher work as a team: possessiveness and contention are luxuries schools cannot afford.

The phrase "diagnosis on the hoof" has been used to differentiate this type of diagnosis from the studies done to categorize children. The set is, what can we do to help the pupil? What more do we need to know to help? This is in reverse of using diagnosis as a substitute for planning and remedial effort. Often we already know more of what is needed than we can seem to do. When the reverse is true and we need information to determine practice, this must be provided. While the crisis teacher is the functional entrée to the educational system in a given school, this does not imply

that all the requisite information or skills could possibly reside in this individual. Many others will be needed, but they should not be brought in on a hit-or-miss, sporadic basis. When the crisis teacher monitors and integrates the effort, the experts are required to produce more than theory. Now there is a resident worker to follow up on ideas and to test the contribution. Actually, this changes the whole role of external consultation.

Relationship to the Milieu at Large

Two things are frequently missing in a problem saturated educational milieu. Little overall effort is being put in for preventative mental health. Defensive, protective police and authoritative repression become the stance because "school must keep order." Here the crisis teacher serves as a mental health influence on the school at large through turning attention to causes and restorative possibilities, even including changes in the school system itself. There is dedication to reducing the abrasion of daily contacts in the school through the use of any viable procedure. While a particular child is in focus, the whole system is really under analysis. This scrutiny, while indirect, is an important change possibility. Change built on solving problems is more penetrating than preachment.

The second general milieu function is that of ombudsman or advocate. In many distressed schools the perception of depersonalization is acute. Youth feel they are handled without concern for their individuality. While no crisis teacher can be cast in a role of solving all the difficulties, the able ones have developed skills in bringing the estranged parties to discuss matters without fear of loss of face. Again, the overall life space interviewing approach has been useful. This is the psychological alternative to the legalistic approach which is accelerating at a rapid pace. Exclusions spawn lawsuits, particularly as the deprived learn of their rights. As racial incidents become more explosive, some nonauthoritative bringing together of the contending factions is necessary. In a small way, the crisis teacher sometimes serves this function.

Thus the crisis teacher can be effective only to the degree that his effort is part of a total school milieu dedicated to the maximum understanding and help of the deviant child. Case conference and strategy planning meetings are held with the total school staff. Some planning for particular children can be done on a sub-group basis. The orienting principle is this: all of the adults who deal with the pupil share in constructing the plan and evolving the strategy. Many times school management failure is a consequence of inadequate communication and time to work this out is required. Just another specialist alone will not make the necessary impact on the school environment. Also, regardless of what is accomplished in the special work, the real purpose is to assist the child to function as adequately as possible back in the regular classroom setting. The classroom teacher continues to spend most of the many hours with the pupil and any plan will have to encompass these times as well as that time the child spends with the crisis teacher. Therefore all adults must be aware of the dynamics and think through the most appropriate management procedures. Frequently, after an encouraging start, an improvement plateau is reached and new plans must be evolved based upon a more complete understanding of the pupil and how he reacts.

It is particularly important to have someone looking at the totality of the problem and alert to introducing new techniques which are appropriate to the matter at hand.

Evaluation

Efforts are currently underway to study the nature of the crisis or helping teacher program. Like everything else which is introduced to the educational complex, it soon is made to serve diverse purposes and is distorted to the will of the administrator or inclination of the practitioner. There should be some knowledge concerning the variety of patterns and the perimeters of utility of such a service.[4] The various roles and time spent in particular functions are under study.

Some general information on the program in Ann Arbor gives an indication.

Most children who participated in this program in one school between 1961 and 1964 received aid for seven to nine months, although some were involved for much shorter periods while others required help for ten to twenty months. During the three-year period, twenty-four children in the first through sixth grades were seen on a regular basis.

Of these, 12 students participated for more than one year. The fraction of the 24 derived from each grade was: first grade, 8.3 percent; second grade, 16.7 percent; third grade, 4.2 percent; fourth grade, 8.3 percent; fifth grade, 16.7 percent; sixth grade, 45.8 percent. These data show that the major effort was directed toward children in the upper grades. This policy was established to help children who would soon have to meet the demands of secondary school, and to determine the effectiveness of the program in intensive short term application with children who required the most help.

Since its inception, the greatest pressure has been to service the more seriously disturbed, older children, despite the belief that the most effective and efficient use of

this service would involve younger children, where the cycle resulting in underachievement is not yet firmly established. Although sex was not a factor in the selection process, only 2 of the 24 were female.

Assistance was offered in all phases of the academic curriculum. However, the record shows that the greatest need was in reading and arithmetic. Help was also offered in the following subjects, listed in approximate order of decreasing priority: spelling, language and writing, penmanship, book reports, social studies, oral reports, and science.

While the program is basically oriented toward improving attitudes and motivation, objective appraisals of such changes are unavailable. Nevertheless, subjective evaluation by independent observers, including classroom teachers, guidance counselors, etc., leads to the conclusion that the program has achieved these goals in many cases.

The average rate of gain in achievement for the twenty-four students was $+2.3$ in reading and $+1.6$ in arithmetic, with a range of $-.9$ to 5.0 in reading and $+.5$ to 5.0 in arithmetic (an expected gain is $+1.0$). Many of the pupils were two years or more retarded at the start, which conditions the meaning of this.

The report concludes with a review of the problems. In a population of 500 children in this instance, only about half of the underachievers were usually the more seriously disturbed. Time was too short for productive relationships in some cases. So much was dependent on the nature of the regular classroom teacher, and not all were receptive. Were changes temporary or permanent? The prognosis for junior high of those with deep-rooted problems was limited. In a more recent review of children going on to junior high, only three of ten were considered ready, but such predictions are notoriously poor.

On the other hand, based upon the current scene, many pupils in the Ann Arbor group appeared to be on the road to success.

The following positive results were achieved: (a) A healthy, and generally fruitful relationship was established with almost all of the children. Even where it appeared that no measurable gains were made, this was the first time that many of these children experienced society's concern for their welfare. (b) Most of the group became more highly motivated, exhibited less anti-social behavior, and advanced significantly in their academic work. (c) Some of them learned to adjust to highly unfavorable home environments. (d) Negative experiences, such as crisis, were used to strengthen the child's resources so that he learned to meet future crises in a positive manner. (e) Many more children were involved than could be accommodated in a segregated classroom. For example, all crisis children in the school were included. (f) The mental health problems of the school were defined as a result of the process of evaluating the students in each class for the program. Other plans were made for students who needed assistance, but who could not be accommodated in this program. (g) An ancillary, but important, benefit was the immediate, on-the-spot assistance that the program offered to the classroom teacher. Furthermore, the total staff, and particularly the classroom teacher, accepted and promoted the concept that each child be treated as an individual within the framework of his present and potential abilities.

In another system, intensive interviews were conducted with a random sample of the pupils involved in a system-wide elementary program. It included thirteen boys and eight girls. Each child was rated by the teacher, evaluated by the helping teacher and the interviewer, and given a self-concept and card sort scale on his attitudes.

The interviews included discussion of the problems the pupil felt he had, what the helping teacher did, what (if any) changes took place, and parent attitude. The youngsters were most open. Boys saw their problem as mostly behavior—fighting and the like; while girls saw mostly academic difficulties. Many feared they would fail. Their views coincided with the perceptions of the conditions by the helping teachers. Most of the pupils had serious difficulties, several having failed at least once and others being diagnosed as almost hopeless by the psychiatrist. They spoke of their sibling hostilities, parental problems, school discouragement, and lack of hope. They felt they were getting aid in academics and could give specifics relative to behavior control. All but two said the help was useful. In only a few instances was any direct work done with parents.

On the Coopersmith self-concept scale, the averages for self, social, and school were all at the thirtieth percentile or lower. Some individuals were at the very bottom of the scale.

On the level of moral development or value internalization (after Peck and Havighurst, *The Psychology of Character Development*) this group of pupils is rated lower than most other disturbed populations. These pupils were more anxious about school, had lower morale about school, saw themselves more as troublemakers, and felt their adult relationships were negative more so than other groups of disturbed children in school or hospital programs. They did perceive themselves as more adequate in peer relationships than those in other groups, however. The lower the anxiety, the higher the self-esteem.

The teachers rated pupil progress greater in social adjustment than in school achievement. Self-esteem was rated improved. Of course, they started so low that even with improvement there was still a long way to go.

Several pupils were seen as making no changes at all. Improvement is indicated in pupil feelings of being able to cope with school and interpersonal relationships.

The problem of evaluation is most complex, and these efforts are hardly a start. The hope is to first study what the child needs and then to indicate the prescription. Evaluation has to include relevance of what is done. Further, improvements may be washed out by subsequent in or out of school difficulties. Children seldom get the continued support they are supposed to need.

Further, whatever we do as planned, known intervention may be infinitesimal compared to what happens elsewhere. It is easy to credit or debit a program with impact when in actuality we do not know really what was significant to the child in his life. This difficulty is common in all types of evaluative effort. But it is still essential that external indices of success or failure and the pupil's internal perceptions be codified and data assembled on new and traditional programs of intervention.

Notes

1. **G. Caplan,** *Prevention of Mental Disorders in Children* (New York: Basic Books, 1961).

2. **R. Bloom,** "Definitional Aspects of a Crisis Concept," *Journal of Consulting Psychology,* **27:** 6 (1963), 498–502.

3. **G. Caplan,** "Opportunities for School Psychologists in the Primary Prevention," *Mental Hygiene,* **47:** 4 (1963), 525–539.

4. Some descriptive material on practice with particular cases has been made available. ("The 'Crisis' or 'Helping Teacher' in the Public School: Theory and Practice," Special Education Committee, School of Education, University of Michigan, 1966.)

Editors' Commentary

Level IV programs represent special class placement for disturbed pupils with mainstreaming in selected subject areas where the children show strength. Most state departments of education have set clear standards and conditions for these classes. The teachers must be certified in special education, have an aide, and take no more than ten pupils in a class. Some states and school systems also mandate remedial and clinical resources. These classes are a far cry from the programs of the early sixties, when teachers who had severe psychological problems were excluded from teaching in regular classes but assigned to classes for socially maladjusted students. The operating theory then seemed to be: "You have to be one to teach one." In the next article, Valerie Slattery describes a very innovative public school program for autistic children. Before 1970, the majority of these pupils were excluded from public schools and placed in state institutions. Their behavior tends to be extremely provocative, frustrating, and primitive, and they therefore demand unusual teacher maturity and system support.

"That's Good Smiling": A Public School Class for Autistic Children
Valerie G. Slattery

Violent temper tantrums, screaming, tears—all for no apparent reason. A time bomb set at unpredictable times. He flaps his hands, positions them in bizarre postures, and stares endlessly at them. Objects lined up in a precise manner must not be disturbed or chaos ensues. Staring off into space—laughing or vocalizing faintly with bizarre sounds. He spins objects endlessly or twirls string. He bangs his head. He bites his arm. Yet he does not cry from pain. He sits and picks at material for hours. He does not talk, and, when he does, the pattern is distorted or he parrots what you have just said. He is physically beautiful—almost glass-like. Why does he partake in such behaviors? How do you break through the barrier to teach such a child? What do you teach him? Why do you teach him? Can he learn? As a teacher of autistic children, I constantly ask myself these questions.

Perhaps the answer is coming. There is a new awareness of the strange and tragic developmental disability of autism. There are, sadly, few educational services and still fewer appropriate services. With the impetus of Public Law 94–142, educational services for autistic children have increased, but these children continue to be grouped with the educable mentally retarded, trainable mentally retarded, and multiply handicapped children. Not only is this an inappropriate placement for and disservice to autistic children, but it is also quite a

hardship on the teacher. It is hard enough to teach ten to twelve multiply handicapped children adequately without the added emotional stress of an autistic child.

There are few public school systems exclusively for the autistic or autistic-like student. The Fairfax County (Virginia) Public Schools opened their first classes for autistic children in the winter of 1972. The children in this program are selected by a special education screening committee. Most children have at one time been diagnosed as autistic based on behavior and communication difficulties that are typical of this disorder.

Being part of a public school system, the program is hampered by many restrictions and much red tape. Nonetheless, great flexibility is provided for each teacher. The teacher is the core of the program. She or he designs and structures the classroom. Not only the children's day but also their environment is structured. Each classroom is divided into specific areas: group language area, individual session room, small group instruction areas, playroom, time-out room, and places for independent work. Teachers have found that dividing the room provides a physical structure, cuts down on visual stimulation and distraction, and helps the children understand a daily sequence of times and places. Each class consists of four children, a teacher, and an instructional aide. The teacher is solely responsible for assessing the children's skills and developing the curriculum. She or he plans an individual educational and behavioral program for each child and sees to it that goals and objectives are met. The teacher must be able to recognize and understand the problems of these children. A most important requisite is the ability to strike a delicate balance between discipline, which is necessary, and understanding and warmth.

The teacher devises a behavioral hierarchy for each child to decrease inappropriate behaviors and increase desirable social ones. Great caution is exercised in choosing the intervention technique to decrease inappropriate behaviors. Turning away, ignoring, and removing a desired object are commonly used. For severe behaviors, such as biting, slapping, or having tantrums, a loud "NO" may be used or the child may be placed in the time-out room, which removes him or her from the positive reinforcers of the classroom. Positive reinforcement is a must throughout the day. For children with a low level of functioning, reinforcement is immediate and primary, while it may be more delayed and abstract for those functioning at higher levels. The teacher must be creative in devising activities for the children and devising backup programs if the initial venture does not work. She or he needs to be able to perceive process step by step and, if a more advanced program does not work, have the flexibility to go back to a more basic activity in a smooth transition.

Often a teacher has to back up until there is nowhere left to go. Imagine a nonverbal six-year-old autistic boy. He screams and has tantrums for no apparent reason. He bites his fingers or arms until welts and bruises discolor them. Day in and day out you attempt to elicit speech, but fail. Your tension and frustration increase; despair sets in. Another approach—another failure. You read more research, searching for new techniques. His mother calls you at home: "When will Todd talk? What are you teaching him anyway?" You feel more frustration and emotional stress. Your only release of stress is daily talks with the other teachers in the program. This sharing of ideas, feelings, frustrations, and the joys of progress takes place among colleagues daily.

Since the etiology of autism is not known at present, for educational purposes little emphasis is placed on this aspect. A developmental model is accepted for dealing with the problems of uneven developmental patterns and distortions of perception. The program is primarily designed to help each student develop self-awareness and awareness of the environment. The major thrust is on acquisition of communication skills and behavior management.

The autistic program also has a strong, consistent home component, designed to give the parents much needed support and information. One of the major goals is to increase the parents' understanding of their child's needs. "What do I do when my child screams violently in the grocery store?" "How will I know when he is sick, if he can't tell me?" "She won't eat anything except pretzels and baby food." "When will she talk?" "Why does he bite the back of his hand?" These are real questions asked by parents. Each is difficult to answer. The teacher must be optimistic yet avoid creating a false sense of hope.

Autistic children may experience difficulty communicating their emotional needs and reactions because they lack communication skills. It is quite plausible that they view situations differently because of distortions in their perceptions. The program emphasizes that the children *do* experience a wide range of feelings, although these may be almost impossible to interpret because of the children's deficiencies in language and behavior patterns. The emotional needs and feelings must be carefully considered when methods are planned.

Teachers need to have emotional stability to give ongoing support to these trying and troubled children. They cannot give in to frustration over the children's slow progress or become upset at sudden screams or purposeless laughter. They must pursue a steady, day-by-day course, aiming not only to improve the children's skills slowly but also to give them something of the pleasures of normal life—for example, trips to the zoo or the swimming pool. All the frustration, anguish, and stress felt by the teacher are worth the joy when a child makes a slight step forward.

You prepare for the day when you will not have to reward each rare smile with the words, "That's good smiling." You must believe in your heart that someday these autistic children will be smiling on their own.

Editors' Commentary

Level V represents special school and/or center placement for pupils with severe emotional problems. These pupils need the professional services of an interdisciplinary team: usually a social worker, a therapist, and various remedial teachers. In this placement, intervention usually is focused on the family as well as the pupil. Fortunately, there is a growing number of outstanding day treatment programs, including public school programs at the Rose School in Washington, D.C.; Carl Fenichel's League School in New York City; Mary Wood's Rutland Center in Atlanta; and Peter Knoblock's Jowonia: The Learning Place, in Syracuse, New York.

In the next article, Ron Laneve describes the Mark Twain Public School for severely disturbed children in Montgomery County, Maryland. This is probably the most comprehensive, attractive, well-designed, creative, and successful school in the country. It is very clear that the citizens, board of education, and educators of the county cared enough to provide a first-rate center for troubled children. This outstanding program can serve as a model to all public school systems.

Mark Twain School: A Special Public School

Ron Laneve
The Mark Twain Staff

All students who attend Mark Twain School are identified as being seriously emotionally disturbed and are therefore covered under Public Law 94–142 and section 504 of the Rehabilitation Act of 1973. The term *seriously emotionally disturbed* means a condition exhibiting one or more of the following characteristics over a long period of time and to a marked degree that adversely affects the student's educational performance:

An inability to learn that cannot be explained by intellectual, sensory, or health factors;

An inability to build or maintain satisfactory interpersonal relationships with peers and teachers;

Inappropriate types of behavior or feelings under normal circumstances;

A general pervasive mood of unhappiness or depression;

A tendency to develop physical symptoms or fears associated with personal or school problems.

The term includes children who are schizophrenic or autistic. It does not generally include children who are socially maladjusted, unless a determina-

tion has been made that they are seriously emotionally disturbed.

The Montgomery County school system, which serves 108,000 students, is divided into five administrative areas. When a student's needs cannot be met with the resources provided by the regular schools, that pupil is placed in one of the Montgomery County alternative centers. The alternative centers provide programs for students who are moderately retarded, who are seriously emotionally disturbed, and who have learning disabilities.

Mark Twain is one of the alternative centers. Students from all regions of the county are placed at Mark Twain by the Admissions, Review, and Dismissal Committee if their complex behavioral and emotional problems make it impossible for them to attain success in a regular school program. The school provides an intense individualized educational program for 310 students. The goal is to enable the student to return to the regular Montgomery County schools with the academic and social/interpersonal skills needed to achieve success with less support.

Approximately 40 percent of the students are involved in therapy, and many of their families are also in therapy. In the past few years, the number of students from single-parent families has significantly increased; it is now approximately 55 percent of the students. These students get only limited support, assistance, and guidance at home. Many of the parents of Mark Twain students have unique, complex, severe, and profound problems in their own personal lives, in addition to the stresses and demands of having a child who is severely emotionally disturbed. All Mark Twain students suffer from the "invisible" handicap—emotional disturbance. The students' inability to handle their emotions results in immature, irresponsible behavior, and frequently they are rejected by school, community, and family. As a result the students may resort to sadistic or masochistic behavior. Many have attempted suicide. One is alleged to have taken the lives of two people.

Mark Twain School opened in February 1972. Before the first students arrived, a six-month institute was held to train staff members. During the institute, the staff developed and planned the program to be provided for the students. The present cost of educating a student at Mark Twain is approximately $5,000 per year.

The facility consists of three separate "schools within a school"—Lower School, Middle School, and Upper School. The building also houses Talented Readers Enrichment Activity Team (TREAT) programs, the Instructional Resources Center (library), and learning laboratories for industrial arts, home arts, music, drama, and art, and a complete physical education facility (gymnasium, weight training room, tennis courts, and swimming pool). The schools are connected by corridors, but the instructional space for each school is separate.

The students are served in six different programs.

Lower School. The Lower School serves one hundred students in grades 6, 7, and 8. It is staffed by a coordinator, two crisis support teachers, twelve teacher/advisers, a full-time physical education teacher, two special education aides, and a school secretary.

Middle School. The Middle School has ninety students in grades 7, 8, and 9, and is coordinated by the assistant principal. There are two crisis support teachers, ten teacher/advisers, a full-time physical education teacher, two special education aides, and a school secretary.

Upper School. The Upper School has fifty students in grades 9, 10, 11, and 12. It is staffed with a coordinator, a crisis support teacher, six teacher/advisers, a full-time physical education teacher, a special education aide, and a school secretary.

TOSSPro. The Out-of-School School Program (TOSSPro) has ten students in grades 9 through 12. This program provides special experiential learning activities outside of the school environment for students whose needs cannot be met in a classroom. One coordinator, one teacher, and one special education aide make up the program staff.

Junior and Senior High School Satellite Centers. In addition to the students who attend the Mark Twain School, fifty students are enrolled in either the junior or the senior high school satellite center. Since a student can attend Mark Twain for a maximum of only two years, placement in a satellite center provides continued support for some students during their transition back into a regular school program. The satellite centers are located in Montgomery County junior and senior high schools. They provide the student with a regular school environment and continued additional support. Each satellite center is staffed with a coordinator, two teacher/advisers, and two aides.

Instructional Media Center. Class assignments frequently require the use of the resources in the IMC. The IMC staff—two resources teachers and a part-time media specialist—assists students in locating appropriate materials and finding pertinent information. Encyclopedias, dictionaries, books, other publications, and filmstrips on a wide range of topics and reading levels are located and cataloged by topic in the IMC. The materials are displayed in a way that encourages students to pick them up.

The videotape recording system (VTRS) is in the IMC. Teacher/advisers use the system to present videotaped material to classes to complement instructional activities; to observe, record, and evaluate their teaching methods; and to record student behavior.

Teacher/advisers offer a visit to the IMC as a reward for students who have completed academic tasks. There are comfortable chairs in the IMC for pleasure reading or working on a puzzle. New educational and high-interest films (on snakes or motorcycles, for example) are continuously available to students. The atmosphere in the IMC is quiet, unhurried, and restful, yet the staff closely supervises the students and encourages them to complete tasks.

The Teacher/Adviser

The heart of Mark Twain School is the teacher/adviser (TA). Each TA is responsible for ten or twelve students. The TA is the student's advocate, helper, counselor, confidant, and *teacher.*

TAs meet three to five times per week with their students in small groups to discuss problems the students may be having in or out of school. The groups, led by the TAs, help Mark Twain students gain social skills and identify appropriate alternatives for solving problems. The TA groups also develop close peer relationships and student leadership skills. Group discussions enable students to hear how their peers view the problems they are experiencing.

A teacher/adviser could be called a case manager, teacher, friend, and confronter. Students at Mark Twain School will not tell outsiders about the beautiful facility—the swimming pool or the fully air conditioned and carpeted buildings—the closed-circuit television system, or the computer-based math instructional system. They will talk about the help provided by their teacher/advisers. As one student put it, "My teacher/adviser is the only person that I have ever felt that really understood me. Not only does he understand me, I feel that I could tell him anything about how I am feeling or what I am thinking. My teacher/adviser will keep the important part of what I say and let the rest fade away." The responsibility of a teacher/adviser extends far beyond the duties assigned to classroom teachers.

The TA role is demanding. Excellent teaching, counseling, and group leadership skills are required. TAs must also have the desire, ability, and training to work with parents. The teacher/adviser's responsibilities are:

Entry and orientation of students

Plans and provides for student orientation and entry to the Mark Twain program.

Uses information in cumulative folders and other school records.

Designs and develops student programs based on assessment data.

Plans for evaluation of student progress toward objectives.

Coordinates and disseminates information to staff.

Implementation and monitoring of individual program in IEP

Identifies pertinent data from cumulative folder, records, and referrals, for incorporation into individual education plan (IEP).

Assists in formulating affective and cognitive objectives.

Assists in setting priorities among objectives for student.

Assists in identifying criteria for attainment of IEP objectives.

Selects specific instructional techniques and programs for students.

TA activities

Counsels student groups toward improved understanding of self and others.

Leads groups of students in discussions regarding academic, social, and behavior problems.

Assesses group process and group dynamics.

Establishes, promotes, and supports appropriate group behavior.

Participates comfortably in conversations with students.

Individual counseling

Counsels students, using a variety of techniques.

Communicates understanding of feelings.

Interacts with students about areas of concern and disagreement.

Gives and receives constructive feedback.

Demonstrates student advocacy by establishing, promoting, and supporting appropriate group and individual behavior.

Reporting student progress

Consults with therapists or other outside resources.

Interpolates pertinent data.

Conducts parent and/or family conferences.

Communicates effectively with staff members and parents on an ongoing basis.

Return and follow-up support for students

Assists in identifying appropriate school environments for returning students.

Uses appropriate resources to help students with transition.

Coordinates school planning for students who are leaving.

Establishes communication with receiving school.

Completes reports on returning students.

Follows up students' circumstances in September.

Serves as resource for ongoing support.

Teacher/advisers also play a major role in designing and implementing Mark Twain parent programs, under the direction of a social worker. The parent program uses a wide range of activities to help parents understand the Mark Twain program and to encourage their support of the students and the staff. When possible, both parents are required to attend the four reporting conferences held each year. Teacher/advisers also maintain constant communication with the parents by telephone. The social worker plans "Family Nights" at the school—occasions when the entire family can come to use the swimming pool, gymnasium, tennis courts, and other recreational facilities. The social worker also plans programs to help parents understand reality therapy, parent effectiveness training, assertiveness, and other skills that can improve interactions between students and their parents, help the parents to understand the Mark Twain program, and make the parents part of the total effort. As stated by one of the teacher/advisers, "Our job is frequently to teach parents to be parents—to make them feel that they have the power and the ability to modify behavior and to play a key role in the student's development and success at school."

In addition to the teacher/advisers, the professional staff includes a psychologist, a social worker, a diagnostic-prescriptive teacher, a media specialist, a principal, and two liaison teachers who support the students after they leave Mark Twain and return to a regular school.

The Montgomery County Health Department helps to meet the needs of Mark Twain students by allocating a full-time nurse and aide and a half-time medical adviser and consulting psychiatrist to the school.

Behavior Management

The school philosophy is best expressed by the statement, "We never give up on a kid." The staff realizes that a student is placed at Mark Twain because of failure in a regular school environment. We can't give up, and we can't use methods that have already failed to help a student modify inappropriate school behaviors.

The methods and techniques used to manage a student's behavior are described in the IEP. The first step in managing a student's behavior is to place the student properly in one of the six Mark Twain programs. The allocation of resources is based on the student's need for supervision and structure. As a student develops mature and responsible behavior, fewer resources are provided, and privileges and freedoms are increased. Students who need a high degree of structure, supervision, and consistency in their programs are usually placed in self-contained classrooms with a teacher–student ratio of one to five. Some students are placed in semi-self-contained classrooms, while some are in larger classes (ten to fifteen students) that receive instruction from four or five teachers during the school day. Other students are placed in TOSSPro or one of the two satellite centers.

The staff is eclectic in its approach to behavior management and draws from a wide variety of methods and techniques to help students modify inappropriate behavior and develop coping skills. Staff members must first become involved with the students to let the students know they care about them. Next the staff deals with the present behavior—what the student is doing right now. Staff members attempt to make the student aware of his or her present behavior while avoiding any reference to the past. The staff emphasizes behavior, not feelings. After the student is aware of the present behavior, he or she is asked to evaluate it. The student might be asked, "Is what you are doing right now helping you achieve your goal?" Then the staff works with students to formulate alternatives that the student can achieve within a short span of time and that give the student opportunities for success. The next step is the most important: The staff member obtains a commitment from the student and sets up a way to check back with the student. This follow-up provides positive reinforcement and helps the student to accept responsibility. When the student agrees to a commitment, a contract is usually written.

One of the most difficult phases of this system occurs when the student fails to meet the commitment. Three principles are generally agreed on:

(1) The staff accepts no excuses. It is important not to let the student make excuses for not meeting the commitment. All individuals can rationalize and justify almost anything if given the opportunity.

(2) There is no punishment. Many educators have difficulty relinquishing the right to punish. However, when punishment is administered, it removes responsibility for the behavior from the student. Natural consequences are used, however, and the students are constantly reminded that they are responsible for themselves and their behavior. This takes staff time, energy, and *consistency*.

(3) The staff never gives up. Never is a long time. When we say we never give up, what we really mean is that we will keep trying longer than the students think we will.

The Mark Twain program is designed to make the students feel responsible for their own behavior and feel a sense of power. Psychiatrists tell us that individuals who are in a state of severe depression or seriously emotionally disturbed feel powerless. They feel they cannot effect change. It follows logically that these individuals do not have the power to take responsibility for their behavior.

Staff members attempt to provide students with alternative choices (for example, "You may sit down, or you must leave the room"). They also give students opportunities to express their feelings appropriately about any situation. "Time-out" of a program is frequently used when students are disruptive or are a danger to themselves or others. Students are placed in time-out rooms away from the instructional area. Conversely, students who complete their assignments and maintain appropriate behavior are rewarded with free time to participate in leisure activities of their choosing.

When students are completely out of control or are a danger to themselves or others, physical restraint is used. When this occurs, the staff tries to make sure the student has an opportunity to modify the behavior before restraint is imposed. To encourage the student to modify the behavior without restraint, many staff members may be called to the area. They give the student the message that they will use as much power and force as is necessary. If an individual in a confrontation with a student must initiate physical restraint, as soon as the student is under the control of the staff, this person is sent away from the area so that the student can be calmed down. Each physical restraint is followed by notification to the parents and another counseling session with the student.

Suspension is also used as a behavior management technique, but, because the Mark Twain students have long histories of suspensions, it is used only as a last resort or when a student needs an extremely clear and strong message from the school.

Students who maintain appropriate behavior receive rewards ranging from free time within the program, to special trips and experiences provided by the staff, to rewards from the parents that have been arranged by the teacher/advisers and are a part of the student's contract.

Special Programs

During the past several years, emphasis has been placed on developing alternative educational opportunities for students. The Mark Twain program includes many special instructional alternatives.

The arts teachers use art, drama, home economics, industrial arts, and music to enhance learning and to help students develop new skills. Various activities in the arts program involve body movement and manipulation of objects. Fre-

quently, success in the arts program has a positive effect on a student's willingness to attempt academic tasks. The students are expected to carry out tasks and to behave appropriately in the arts program just as in other classes. The arts teachers have close contact with the academic instructional teams to keep goals and strategies consistent for each student.

Many students who refuse to participate in reading programs take an active part in the Talented Readers Enrichment Activity Team program (TREAT). This program capitalizes on individual student interest to motivate students. After the student has identified an area of interest, he or she sets about making a slide-tape presentation to be shown to other students and parents. The teacher helps the student obtain resources and reading materials to develop the content of the presentation. Students gain skills in photography, writing scripts, and basic research methods to produce their presentations.

A computer-based method of tracking students in the accomplishment of basic mathematic skills was implemented during the 1977–1978 school year. This program provides information when the students enter Mark Twain and facilitates their return to the regular Montgomery County Public School program. The student's record of progress is maintained by the computer and can be recalled at any time by using the student's identification number.

Under a special education student aide program, some Mark Twain students are employed by the Montgomery County Board of Education. These students undergo the hiring procedures experienced by other county school employees and receive a nominal wage for supervised work in one of the county schools.

Some students in grades 9 through 12 have the opportunity to attend one or two classes in a nearby high school as a part of their regular Mark Twain program. Their transportation is provided by county school bus. One Mark Twain staff member is assigned to the high school to facilitate this program and provide the needed support. Participation in these classes enriches the students' school programs and gives them experience in "regular" classrooms.

An Outward Bound program offers students in grades 7 through 9 a three-week experience in a regular middle school or junior high school to prepare them to return to their regular school in the fall.

Mark Twain students have the opportunity to participate in outdoor education—camping, hiking, environmental, and life skills. Outdoor activities are also emphasized in the Mark Twain instructional program. Through these activities students develop group skills and learn to depend on one another. Tasks are shared among group members, and each person plays an important role in making the group successful.

In 1980, an Experience-Based Career Education program will be implemented to give students an opportunity to work in the community. From this experience they can gain an understanding and awareness of the world of work. The students will not be paid for their work, but it will reinforce the knowledge and skills they have developed in school. In addition, the program will allow students to develop relationships with the adults outside the school who organize and supervise their work.

Editors' Commentary

Level VII represents residential placement for emotionally disturbed pupils. Residential placement is the last and most extreme alternative for helping troubled children. To remove a child from family and community to a new setting creates innumerable psychological and logistic problems for the family and the child. The justification for such a move is that it will protect the child from destroying self and others by providing a supportive, predictable environment designed to meet the disturbed individual's personal needs. The goal of residential treatment is to develop a unity of approach, understanding, management, and reeducation. A representative list of residential programs illustrates the contrasts within this general framework:

1. A state hospital, e.g., St. Elizabeth's, Washington, D.C.

2. A state psychiatric treatment center, e.g., Hawthorne Children's Center, Northville, Michigan

3. A private children's psychiatric center, e.g., Menninger Clinic, Topeka, Kansas

4. A residential treatment school, e.g., Grove School, Madison, Connecticut

5. A therapeutic boarding school, e.g., Cumberland House Re-Ed School, Nashville, Tennessee

6. Therapeutic camping, e.g., Wilderness Camp, Hope Center for Youth, Dallas, Texas

7. Group homes, e.g., F.L.O.C., Washington, D.C.

It is reasonable to expect that the intensity, duration, and cost of residential programs will increase with the severity of the children's problems. Concurrently, the staff must devote more time and skill to support services for the child. Unfortunately, this has not been the case. Just as one can't tell a book by its cover, one can't assess the quality of a residential program by its brochure. Some programs for the most severely handicapped receive the least effort and support from their funding agencies. Some special educators are convinced that all state institutions for children should be closed, because they are dehumanizing and depreciating.

Although some institutions are destructive to the well-being of children, other institutions provide children with the humanistic care, support, and skills they could not receive in the community or a mental health center. The next article illustrates how a new five-day-a-week residential center, TREES, has developed multiple treatment programs, from behavior modification to group therapy.

TREES: A Five-Day Residential Alternative School for Emotionally Disturbed Adolescents

Charles M. Heuchert
Daniel Morrisey
Stephen R. Jackson

TREES (Therapeutic Residential Experience for Emotional Stability) is an alternative school sponsored by Augusta County, Virginia, and jointly funded by federal (Title VI–B) and state (Vocational Education Department) resources. This project is a unique response designed to meet the very special needs of a group of primarily emotionally disturbed adolescents who were withdrawing from or disrupting the regular education programs and failing to achieve their academic potential. Many of these students would qualify for institutionalization on the basis of their lack of ability to function within the limits of a normal special program.

TREES gives these students a five-day-per-week residential school that is an alternative to the demands of the regular school program. It uses a psychoeducational therapeutic model in a minimally restrictive environment, to engage students in self-actualization and learning problem-solving skills without losing contact with their academic and vocational education.

The emotional stability of the students is developed by:

1. Removing them from a failure situation in the school.

2. Placing them in a summer-camp-type environment with a structured social order and involving them in a psychoeducational program.

3. Providing their families with parenting skills to support the child's personality development and achievement in regular school.

4. Returning the children to regular programs in their home schools with follow-up services.

The project serves as both a diagnostic and a treatment center. All students are considered in a diagnostic status until they are continued in the program, referred to other psychotherapeutic services, or returned to their home schools with specific management recommendations.

The therapeutic program of preinstitutional care explores the psychodynamics of the students' interaction with each other and the staff through group and individual counseling, value clarification sessions, and activities on and off campus, ranging from Outward-Bound style excursions to attendance at local cultural events. The extent and variety of these activities is a direct result of the school's location at a summer camp facility in foothills of the Blue Ridge Mountains and its proximity to the University of Virginia in Charlottesville. The accommodations include winterized cabins, an infirmary, offices, a dining hall, a swimming pool, tennis courts, athletic fields, a pavilion, and horseback riding facilities.

The academic/vocational education program is operated on a continuum of structures ranging from individual tutoring to formal group lessons, depending on the specific needs of a student. Individual education programs (IEPs) are designed for these students based on information from the student's psychotherapist, house parent, previous teacher at the home school, placement committee, and project special education teachers. These resources provide a total plan for the educational, social, and psychological rehabilitation of the student that could not be offered, or delivered, by any local school system.

Parent/Family Participation

A significant component of the project is parent/family participation in the program. Because the students return home every weekend, their families maintain contact with and responsibility for them. In addition, the students are able to keep up their social contacts, and this enhances their smooth transition to the home school eventually.

The following parent services are available:

1. Preview of the program and a visit to the site before the child is admitted.

2. Contract agreement on the educational and behavioral plan for the child.

3. Observation of the child in the program with recommendations about parent–child relationships at home.

4. Evaluation of family interaction patterns, with

appropriate short-term counseling for those who want it.

5. Group instruction on child development, management techniques, behavior modification, parenting skills, and realistic expectations for the child.

6. Evaluation of the child's program by the parents.

7. Follow-up services to the parents by the school division's pupil services team.

8. Individual and group parent visits to the site when they are mutually beneficial.

University Involvement

The University of Virginia participates indirectly in the TREES project by supplying masters and doctoral level psychology and special education interns. A number of the house parents and volunteers are university students. In addition, the project's educational and psychological consultants are university faculty members.

School Program

The basic educational objectives are to prepare an individual school program and not to move the student further away from a typical school model than is necessary. The time spent in academic and prevocational classrooms and in interest activities varies for each student. The school schedule is divided into periods, like that of a regular school; however, within that structure programs differ individually.

The following daily schedule varies on Monday when the students arrive at 10:15 A.M. and on Friday when they leave at 1:30 P.M.:

7:00 A.M.	Arise
7:45 A.M.	Breakfast
8:45 A.M.	Classes begin Periods I, II, and III
12:00 P.M.	Lunch
1:00 P.M.	Classes resume Period IV
1:55 P.M.	Activity period
4:00 P.M.	Free time, special interests, sports
5:30 P.M.	Supper
6:30 P.M.	On-grounds activities or field trips: study time, planned recreational activities, university special events, psychotherapeutic sessions
10:00 P.M.	Bedtime

The school program offers six hours of daily instruction in English, language arts, math, science, social studies, general living skills, general shop, and home economics. The educational component is geared to remedy academic deficits through the use of individual instruction and innovative teaching strategies and materials. Progressing at their own rates, students earn credits toward high school graduation, study for the general education diploma, develop prevocational skills, or work on independent living skills.

Each day following lunch, students meet to choose their activity for the 1:55 activity period. Some of their options are:

Gardening
Education games
Value clarification sessions
Nature hikes
Videotaping, drama
Greenhouse
Solar oven
Storage shed construction
Making snacks
Physical education

Billiards	Ice skating
Fishing	Table tennis
Bowling	Volleyball
Softball	Horseback riding
Swimming	Roller skating

Field trips
Ecology projects
Auto mechanics

Students Served

1. All students meet the Virginia description of those who are seriously emotionally disturbed.

2. These students cannot be maintained in a self-contained education classroom or other special education placement offered by the regular school system.

3. Students must be able to live at home and be managed by their parent or guardian on weekends.

4. Students must need to be placed at TREES for at least one school semester.

5. Students must not require confinement and must not be a constant physical threat to themselves or others.

6. Students must have normal general health.

The students' academic abilities range from early elementary levels to twelfth grade level in reading and mathematics. The average academic gain during a stay of about two semesters is over two years (as measured by the Key Math, Peabody Individual Achievement Test, and Woodcock Reading Mastery Tests).

Teachers

Two teachers holding degrees in special education with endorsement in emotional disturbance teach the basic academic subjects. The prevocational program is taught by two trained vocational education teachers. Comparing her TREES teaching assignment to a special education resource room teaching assignment in the public schools, the head teacher listed the following advantages at TREES:

Closer and more supportive interaction with fellow staff

More freedom in academic design

Freer and more varied activities for teaching

Less administrative interference

Less confining building structures

Peaceful setting encourages calmness

Rule enforcement is simplified

Teacher is known more as a human being

More innovative and creative curriculum opportunities

Easier to manage students' reward/punishment system

Easier communication

A community feeling

More supplies and materials

An open setting

More consultant support in education and psychology

Students and teachers have a larger voice in the learning constructs

Greater input and responsibility for the program

Feels more effective than a resource teacher

There are disadvantages also:

Lack sufficient planning time

Eight hours with students

No substitute teachers

Draining due to intensity of input and involvement in much counseling

When students do well, they leave; don't have a chance to enjoy the "changed" student

The students also voiced their opinions on the advantages and disadvantages of being placed at TREES. The following is their list, composed during a typical rap session:

Advantages

Academic work is easier

More individual help

Get away from parents

More food

Many activities—swimming, bowling, roller skating, movies, etc.

Swimming pool

Get away from family pressures

Better grades

Apprenticeship program

Disadvantages

Away from friends 5 days a week

Can't raise hell around town

Can't party as much

Too few girls

Can't have cigarette lighters

No high school sports to watch

Can't go home in evenings

Always being watched

No privacy

No reclining chairs

No pets of our own

People don't understand what TREES is— get teased

Psychological Component

A general description of the students' troublesome behavior includes:

1. Severe acting out or withdrawal

2. Refusal to attend school

3. Disruptive behavior when attending school

4. Serious difficulty establishing and maintaining satisfactory interpersonal relationships with peers and adults

The dynamics underlying these behaviors suggest several things:

1.   There is a large discrepancy between the student's realistic view of self (as seen by others) and the idealized self (how the individual would like to be). Often the resultant feeling is negative and stressful.

2.   Most students want to feel better about themselves; the issue is developing appropriate coping strategies and means to feel better about self. As an example, many use behavior such as fighting and bragging to compensate for their feelings of inadequacy. Instead of gaining peer admiration, which would help them feel better about themselves, however, they alienate peers by this strategy.

3.   The feeling of powerlessness is prevalent. Most of the students have little sense of their impact on others. Their acting out and violence, as Rollo May (1972) astutely points out, stems from feeling powerless, not powerful. They don't know that their words, facial expressions, eye contact, and sharing of feelings affect others. They are often reminded of their powerlessness by their circumstances, and they are quick to engage in power struggles with adults in an effort to affirm their power.

Another means by which students seek to feel better about themselves is by trying to be heroes. Ernest Becker (1973) indicates that this strategy is used by people in general. He aptly states (p. 251), "the problem of mental illness is one of not knowing what kind of heroics one is practicing or not being able—once one does know—to broaden one's heroics from their crippling narrowness."

To some extent two traditional classifications of emotional disturbances help to differentiate the two ends of the continuum.

1.   Character disorders, in which the symptoms are consistent with the person's image of self and are not felt by the disturbed person to be a problem. The students' symptoms, such as acting out or withdrawing, are primarily a problem for others (parents and teachers). The motivation to change is limited.

2.   Neurotic disorders, in which the symptoms cause the disturbed person to suffer and motivate that person to change.

The Therapeutic Psychoeducational Model

The model for TREES is based on the brief therapy model of Watzlawick, Weakland, and Fisch (1974), and it shares an important assumption with the psychosituational model of Bersoff and Grieger (1971). The locus of the problem is not assumed to reside in the student. Hence, removing the student from the family system and the regular school system and altering various contingencies may be the major interventions needed. The student as a total person is viewed as separate from the behaviors and learned coping strategies. In line with the theory of Albert Ellis (1973), TREES therapy emphasizes helping students to avoid globally rating themselves as total persons while learning to rate their behaviors (coping strategies) and to decide which are effective. Coupled with this is the notion that the coping strategy is learned and hence may be unlearned.

Individual and Group Interaction

The intervention is designed to alter coping strategies, not the total person. The students' means are to be changed, not their ends. Basically the staff and the students agree on the ends from the outset—namely feeling better about themselves and their lives. This notion may not be made explicit, however, because the students do not readily admit feeling bad about themselves.

The paradox of accepting and helping students to accept their current views of themselves is used (Watzlawick, Weakland, and Fisch, 1974). What the student presents is accepted. For example, one student claimed he had no problems, and he was validated as being okay. In order to return to regular school, he needed to do some things differently but not change himself. This subtle semantic difference has an impact on helping the students feel good enough about themselves to change their coping strategies. An individual therapy plan is developed for each student, with input from both student and parents. The emphasis again is not on changing self but on changing behaviors the student and the parents would like to see changed.

It is important to take what the students present as their own perception of the problem and start at that point. For example, if a boy states, "The principal is a jerk," the way to guide this boy is to accept his comment to some degree. These students have rarely had their perceptions validated at home or at school. A staff member and the student might develop a strategy for dealing with the principal. The student might treat the principal differently with the goal of changing the principal's behavior, e.g., stopping the principal from "hassling" the student. Once "hassling" is defined concretely and the criteria that indicate change—that the principal is not hassling the student—are specified concretely, the student learns to deal more effectively with authority figures. This approach uses the student's defensiveness and resistance, which are expressed as "I'm right, and the principal isn't." Rather than argue about who is blameworthy, the staff member accepts the picture as the student presents it and does not discuss it much. This boy needs the message that he is okay, to counter the message told to him throughout his life that he is no good or deficient.

The psychologist in this therapy model not only engages in individual or group intervention but also plays other roles.

1. Consultation as a systems or community analyst is often required. Periodically, the psychologist needs to perform an ecological assessment, i.e., an assessment of the functioning of the various subgroups (administrators, teachers, students, and house parents). Following the assessment, the psychologist may need to plan and implement an intervention aimed at a systems change for the total residential community. This might entail a community meeting of all the subgroups. In addition, the psychologist may meet separately with each subgroup. The focus is primarily on facilitating communication between the various subgroups. Seeing that the needs of each subgroup are met allows the community as a whole to function smoothly.

2. At times family interventions are necessary. Students and their parents may need help in improving their communication. However, generally the parent education groups ensure that the home environment supports the work being done at the school.

A large portion of the therapy uses the environment by making interventions *in situ*. When students come into conflict with their peers or staff members, the psychologist can seize the opportunity to intervene as quickly as possible, on the spot. The *in situ* approach reduces the artificiality of "office hours" and directs the student's motivation for change while he or she is still embroiled in a stressful situation. Playing basketball gives students an ideal opportunity to come in contact with the frustrations of defeat, competition, rejection, and so on. The therapist can clarify the feeling and provide the student with ways of dealing effectively with the stress. For those students who are motivated, structured one-hour weekly sessions may be used as an adjunct to the ongoing situational therapy.

In summary, a variety of techniques may be used in this brief therapy model. Although behavior is emphasized and concrete changes are the goal, gestalt therapy techniques, dream therapy, and occasionally behavior contracts are used. Behavior modification may be applied, but only as one of many methods that is effective. The goal is to change the students' coping strategies so that they can ultimately return to the regular school milieu.

References

Becker, E. *The Denial of Death.* New York: Free Press, 1973.

Bersoff, D., and Grieger, R. "An Interview Model for the Psychosituational Assessment of Children's Behavior." *American Journal of Orthopsychiatry* 41 (1971): 483–493.

Deno, E. "Special Education as a Developmental Capital." *Exceptional Children* 37 (1970): 235.

Ellis, A. "Psychotherapy and the Value of a Human Being." In *Humanistic Psychotherapy: A Rational-Motive Approach,* ed. A. Ellis. New York: McGraw-Hill, 1973.

May, R. *Power and Innocence: A Search for the Sources of Violence.* New York: Dell, 1972.

Watzlawick, P.; Weakland, J.; and Fisch, R. *Change: Principles of Problem Formation and Resolution.* New York: W. W. Norton, 1974.

Editors' Commentary

While the cascade of services goes from the least restrictive school program to the most restrictive, students must be able to move in both directions, according to their needs. Unfortunately, little attention and even less research have gone into studying the psychological and procedural problems of returning a pupil from a higher level to a lower level of help. This complicated process has been left to professional chance. The next article describes a project dedicated to helping adolescent pupils in residential care to return to their communities with protection and planning.

Project Aftercare: Follow-up to Residential Treatment

Elaine H. Harding
James Bellew
Larry W. Penwell

Introduction

Phil G., the handsome son of well-educated parents living in a suburban Cincinnati neighborhood, began experiencing problems in his early teens. By the time he was fifteen, Phil was underachieving in school and frequently suspended for fighting or provoking disruption. He was a heavy drug and alcohol user. At home, Phil was willfully disobedient, noncommunicative, and belligerent. He threw temper tantrums and damaged family property. Antagonistic to peers as well as to adults, he had few friends.

Phil's acting out and defiance of authority led to his placement at Children's Home of Cincinnati, a residential treatment center for emotionally disturbed and delinquent adolescents. During his stay in the treatment program, Phil learned to separate his own problems from those of his parents. He made great strides in identifying his emotional needs and finding acceptable ways of fulfilling them. Upon his discharge from the cottage program, Phil was described as "experiencing only normal adolescent conflicts with his parents." However, both Phil and his parents expressed some anxiety over his return to the neighborhood and their home. The family members still had difficulty communicating with one another, and it seemed likely that problems might again develop. Phil and his family were referred to Project Aftercare.

The following is a description and discussion of a program at the Children's Home of Cincinnati designed to assist children leaving the residential treatment center to return to the community.[1] While the effectiveness of this new program cannot yet be evaluated, it deserves description as one agency's attempt to reduce the likelihood that former residents will need further institutionalization by increasing their socialization and adaptiveness.

Purpose of the Program

The Children's Home Aftercare Program extends comprehensive services to the child and the family following the child's discharge from residential treatment. The primary purpose of the services is to solidify the gains made by the child during residential treatment. The Aftercare team, made up of a social worker, a special educator, and a community services worker, assists the newly discharged child to become reintegrated into the family, resume an educational program, and begin to use recreational and social resources in the community. Because comprehensive, intensive home and community services are extended to children and families on an outpatient, postinstitutional basis, the length of the child's institutional placement may be shortened.

The Children's Home Residential Treatment Center discharges approximately forty children each year. Before the present Aftercare program was developed, follow-up services were provided in a rather unplanned, unsystematized, informal fashion. Some children were given postinstitutional services by the original referring agency; some maintained occasional contact with a residential center staff person; others had no one. Concern about what happened to children when they left the treatment center led to a 1976 follow-up study of former residents. The study confirmed that children leaving residential care fared poorly following discharge, even if they had made significant gains while residents. According to the study, "nearly all continued to have problems in school, at home, and/or in the community. These youngsters displayed a need for continued service and guidance after their discharge."[2]

A further quote from the study clearly notes the need for the type of aftercare program that was later developed and is currently serving up to twenty-five children.

[Study] data suggest certain service implications for youngsters discharged from Children's Home. There is a need for more systematic and thorough planning prior to and following discharge in order to facilitate the transition from Children's Home to post-placement living. A comprehensive aftercare program which assists in education planning, coordinating community resources, and provides continued family counseling would facilitate the youngster's discharge and subsequent adjustment.[3]

The local county welfare department officials also recognized the need for such a program and encouraged its development, since many of the children served are wards of the welfare department and in need of specialized services.

Certainly there are pecuniary as well as humanitarian reasons for extending Aftercare services to children and families. Large amounts of public and private funds are expended so that children may receive rehabilitation services. The 1975 per diem cost per child in residential treatment at Children's Home was $50.03; the 1976 cost was $60.25. This large outlay of funds—this investment in children—may be lost if treatment is not followed by intensive social and educational services.

The Aftercare Team

The project team consists of three professionals, each delivering services in an area of concern and expertise. Nothing may describe Project Aftercare as well as a discussion of the roles of the project personnel, as they perform individually and in concert as an interdisciplinary team.

The Role of the Family Worker

The problems of troubled adolescents are viewed by Aftercare staff members as symptoms or manifestations of family dysfunction. When a child's problems and behavior reach a point where the child is removed from the home and placed institutionally, family pathology is clearly indicated. Although significant gains may be made by child and family during the child's stay in residential treatment, not all the child's and the family's problems can be resolved during this time. In addition, the returning adolescent and the family face a new set of potential difficulties as the family equilibrium that was established during the youngster's absence is disturbed. Family stress may result from structural changes in patterns of relating within the family. Too often there is a gradual erosion of earlier treatment gains and an insidious resumption of destructive relationships and problem-causing behaviors.

It is the responsibility of the Aftercare social worker to concentrate on the entire family's functioning: patterns of interacting and ways of relating; the way in which family members communicate with one another; their mutual needs satisfaction; and other pragmatic family management concerns.

The social worker performs several roles in areas of administration, supervision, and direct services to children and families. This staff member is responsible to the agency's executive director for the overall operation and coordination of the Aftercare program. He or she supervises the

Aftercare staff, serves as a team leader, and conducts family counseling sessions. This article, however, focuses on the social worker's role of providing direct counseling to families of children in Aftercare.

The social worker first meets the child and the family several weeks before the child's planned discharge date. Even before this initial meeting the Aftercare social worker meets with the social worker from the cottage where the child is in residence to discuss child and family. The Aftercare social worker also reviews the child's case record.

The cottage social worker is present at the first family meeting with the Aftercare social worker. This is supportive to the family and conveys a sense of orderly and planned transition for child and family from one program to another within the same agency. At this initial meeting the social worker explains the Aftercare services, encourages full family involvement, and develops an initial impression of the child's and the family's anxieties about the client's return home. The social worker uses the session to allow each family member to verbalize his or her concerns; to explore with the family the possible feelings and problems that may arise; and to set the tone that will be used for addressing issues in subsequent family sessions. Essentially these intrafamilial issues will deal with parent–child, parent–parent, and child–sibling relationships. Effective communication—clear, open, honest, direct, and feeling communication—allows family members to focus on recognizing their individual needs, finding ways of meeting their needs, and understanding what others in the family want and need from each other. Family and child are alerted to the fact that all may experience a "honeymoon" period following the child's return home. They are also cautioned that this period may be short-lived.

The social worker and the family agree on a plan for family counseling—usually weekly sessions of approximately an hour. The frequency of these sessions may be reduced in proportion to the progress made, until counseling is no longer needed.

While the focus is on the total family, and total family participation is emphasized, there are times when the social worker may conclude that a particular relationship within the family requires special attention. For example, the primary impaired relationship within the family constellation may be between mother and son. In this case, the mother and the son would be asked to come alone to the next counseling session. Sometimes the weakest relationship in the family is between the parents. To strengthen this relationship, marital counseling may be provided; this is important, for the parents are the architects or foundation of the family structure. It is the aim of the social worker to engage the family in ongoing counseling in order to resolve stresses and problems that led to the child's referral to institutional care.

In addition to counseling, more concrete services are sometimes provided to aid family adjustment. Some parents are incapable of performing their parental roles and responsibilities adequately, not because of deep pathology, but because they lack parenting skills. When this is the case, the social worker may focus on educating them on sound parenting principles. More tangible services are provided some families. Financial assistance is available, for example, to help defray the cost of tuition, clothing, music lessons, or recreational activities.

If, as is sometimes the case, a child simply is not adjusting at home, if the family is making no progress, and if the situation continues to deteriorate until the child's physical and/or psychological well-being is jeopardized, the social worker must begin to consider removing the child from the destructive home environment.

In summary, the team social worker must use his or her own skills to the fullest, recognize and fully use the skills of fellow team members, and blend these skills into a service program that will build upon existing strengths of the child and the family so that both may more nearly achieve their full potentials.

The Role of the Educator

The child referred to Aftercare often is still dysfunctional to some degree in academic or behavioral areas or both. Frequently learning and school behavioral problems are a source of family friction, with parents setting demanding standards of performance and siblings offering critical comment. When a problem student leaves the residential school to enter a public school whose staff is unaware of special needs and possible difficulties, conflict becomes more likely, arises sooner, is sharper, and may have more disastrous consequences for the child. Serving the needs of the client in educational settings becomes the responsibility of the special project teacher.

The preferred qualifications for the Aftercare teacher are:

1. Certification in either vocational education, special education (especially behavior disorders or learning disabilities), or a related area;

2. Classroom experience with troubled adolescents;

3. Knowledge of community educational and vocational resources; and

4. Ability to work as a member of an interdisciplinary team.

Broadly stated, it is the responsibility of the project teacher to function as a team member in meeting the goals of Aftercare. In this capacity, five major types of duties are performed:

1. Academic and/or vocational assessment and planning;

2. Educational counseling with client and parents;

3. Assistance with placement into programs;

4. Liaison between the community educational or vocational programs and the project; and

5. Coordinating educational and related services to the client with the community school or vocational training agency.

Planning for the educational or vocational program after discharge begins with referral from the residential treatment program, which may include suggestions for the direction of the planning. During the initial, transitional, meeting between treatment staff, Aftercare staff, and the family, the client and the parents are informed about the educational services available. An interview between the client and the educator brings out helpful information about the child's ambitions, interests, attitudes, and plans. The educator contacts teachers in the residential school for input on the student's academic and behavioral strengths and weaknesses. The educator also examines school records and the child's final educational assessment. Eliciting the parents' expectations for the child's schooling can reveal goals, doubts, anxieties, and the extent to which parents are capable of dealing with the schools.

If the child and the parents have no placement in mind, or if the placement is unrealistic, the teacher may investigate available alternatives and plan a visit with the family for educational counseling. Ideally, the educator makes a recommendation while offering several program choices.

The suitability of placement alternatives frequently depends on the diversity of opportunities. The range of educational services varies considerably from community to community, and it is affected by factors such as the socioeconomic level of the area, the number of students requiring special help, and the orientation of students toward vocational versus college preparation. Project Aftercare clients have been considered for the following types of programs:

Public school

comprehensive track

college preparatory track

special education classes for educable mentally retarded (EMR), learning disabled (LD), behavior disordered (BD)

prevocational

Parochial school

Job Corps educational and vocational training

Following a decision, the student is enrolled in the program. This process is simplest if the student is entering the public school to which he or she would normally be assigned. Attendance elsewhere in the public school system, or in a special or vocational program, may require application to the program, an interview, obtaining a transfer and bus pass, or referral for testing. Attendance at a private or parochial school may call for negotiations about tuition and a more complex enrollment process. The student in need of vocational training who has no interest in an educational program may be referred to BVR for assessment, counseling, and training.

The educator's liaison activities may begin when the placement possibilities are being explored. At the time of enrollment, or shortly thereafter, the educator contacts the counselor at the junior high or high school to arrange the student's schedule, based on the student's skill level and interest. Through the counselor, the educator may meet with the receiving teachers to give them selective background information about the child, describe Aftercare services and the role of the Project Aftercare teacher, and share information about the student—his or her academic skills level and learning style, and the types of discipline or handling to which he or she best responds. In gathering these data, the educator's past classroom experience tells him or her what kinds of information are likely to be useful in a school setting. This type of meeting frequently engages the interest and sympathies of receiving teachers. The project educator is thus an advocate for the student as well as a resource for the teachers, who may require support, suggestions, or simply an opportunity to ventilate from time to time. Continued contact is maintained through conferences with the counselor and the teachers and through "classroom ob-

servation sheets" requested from teachers periodically. The educator sees the student periodically as well. The frequency of the educator's school and student contacts, after initial placement, may differ for each client. The parents may be involved in normal parent–teacher interchanges, but the Aftercare educator usually seeks feedback on the student's progress at more frequent intervals. The Aftercare teacher may coordinate parent conferences, visits, or other contacts in the interest of the student's positive adjustment. Should the student require support to increase attendance or tutoring to maintain grades, the Aftercare educator is responsible for coordinating efforts to these ends.

In summary, the educator on the Project Aftercare team deals with a school and its staff as needed, in a flexible plan to enhance the opportunity for a client's successful educational adjustment.

The Role of the Community Services Worker

The children served by Project Aftercare face a multitude of problems when they return to their homes. Placement in the residential treatment center may establish, for the parents as well as for the child, that he or she was the problem. Even if these children come to understand that they are not entirely the cause of the family's problems, they may suffer from depleted feelings of self-worth. Parents may support this by making the child the scapegoat when he or she returns home. The community services worker meets with the child in an attempt to rebuild his or her self-concept and rearrange the personal environment, replacing poor influences with growth-oriented ones.

The qualifications for the community worker in the project are:

1. College degree in social work or a related field;

2. Experience in serving troubled adolescents;

3. Knowledge of community resources; and

4. Ability to function as a team member.

The responsibilities include seeking out and involving the youth in appropriate community programs and activities; providing recreational, social, and cultural enrichment opportunities for the child; engaging the child in a caring relationship while providing an appropriate role model; and serving as an advocate for the child in the home and the neighborhood. The community services worker fulfills these responsibilities in various ways with each child.

During the referral process, residential treatment personnel share information about the child with the community worker. During initial contacts, the worker evaluates the child further in three essential areas: innate abilities, interests, and ambitions. The community worker may find it necessary to resolve inconsistencies between the child's interests and ambitions and his or her aptitudes. The worker may even have to generate the interest or the ambition within a child. Through activities, clients are encouraged to explore aspects of themselves that may figure into their life plans. The activities include attendance at cultural attractions, sporting events, and artistic or crafts experiences, participation in physically demanding sports and recreational games, and exploration of vocational possibilities. These activities are initiated by a statement from the child: "I'd like to . . ."

The available resources vary from community to community. In some areas, the child may join planned group activities under close professional supervision at a community recreation center. The community worker may be able to stimulate recreation counselors to take an interest in the child, encouraging them to become agents in the child's resocialization. In some areas, the schools are the only resource for activities, and the worker may try to motivate the child to participate in extracurricular activities. In some cases, the worker may enroll the child in private music, art, or karate classes, giving the child a new form of expression for experiences.

Many of the activities involve the community worker in a one-to-one setting with the child. In some circumstances, the local Big Brothers and Big Sisters organization provides volunteers who are matched with children and meet on a regular basis. The worker's relationship with the child, the one-to-one activities, and the supervised group activities help to rebuild the child's self-concept and restructure behavior patterns. The child may rely heavily on these supports as well as on the strengths developed while in residential treatment as he or she deals with the environment.

One gauge of the child's progress is the type of activities chosen. As the youngster feels able to risk ego-threatening activities, the community worker introduces more challenging occupations. The child experiences the freedom to fail and the pleasure of success.

The community services worker may also play a role in helping the youth find work. Again, the approach must vary according to the characteristics of the child and the nature of the community. In some areas federally funded job programs supply employment for adolescents who meet financial and other criteria. The work counselors in such programs may be of great help in making the child's experience both meaningful and therapeutic. If the child cannot qualify for such programs, the community worker must provide motivation, help the child compile a list of potential employers, and aid in the search. The worker has the difficult job of supporting the child when he or she must deal with being turned down for a job.

When a client obtains employment, the worker may act as an advocate and counselor for the youth on the job. This can be delicate work; in some cases the child's background may jeopardize the position. In the best of circumstances, however, the community worker generates the employer's sincere interest in the child.

In summary, the community worker uses an eclectic approach in functioning as a counselor, role model, problem solver, court liaison, and youth advocate in the Aftercare Program. It is the ultimate goal of the community worker to help each child come to grips with his or her own reality and carve from that reality a future.

Team Work

Aftercare staff members are required to work not only as independent professionals in their specific disciplines but also as members of an interdisciplinary team. The weekly team meeting, central to the functioning of Project Aftercare, is the forum to which each professional brings insights and experiences with the child, and the source from which each takes a plan for further service. The team forms a holistic picture of the child's functioning in the environment as individual members share information on family dynamics, the child's progress in school, and community involvement.

Value of the Program

Project Aftercare has a valuable position as an integral part of Children's Home services. The program has provided a bridge between residential treatment and home/community living, demonstrating that, with adequate, comprehensive services, troubled adolescents can adjust favorably in family settings. As part of the same agency that provides residential treatment, Project Aftercare spares clients the awkwardness or frustration of transition to another organization.

This aid can decrease the time children spend in a residential setting, thereby decreasing the likelihood of reinstitutionalization. The development of a viable program supported by substantial funds has lent weight to the agency's stated commitment to return youths as quickly as possible to the least restrictive alternative placements.

Members of Project Aftercare, working with graduates of the treatment programs, find themselves in a unique position to offer feedback to the residential center. Such feedback may eventually result in improvement of services to clients for residential treatment.

This multidisciplinary approach to aftercare services need not be restricted to this particular type of agency or client. Aftercare may be fruitfully used in settings as diverse as prisons, halfway houses, institutions for the retarded, and youth training centers—in short, in any setting from which clients may be going out alone.

Notes

1.   The Children's Home of Cincinnati is a private, nonsectarian, multiple-service child welfare agency.

2.   **D. A. Cook and D. F. Clapp,** *Residential Treatment Center: Follow-up of Former Residents* (Cincinnati: Children's Home of Cincinnati, 1976), p. 19.

3.   *Ibid.,* p. 22.

5

How Can We
Manage These Children?

Editors' Commentary

The therapeutic management of emotionally disturbed pupils requires a complex set of teacher behaviors that need clarification and elaboration. It is the most demanding, difficult, complex, and challenging part of being a special educator, and this ability is prerequisite to effective classroom instruction and learning. With specific training and supervision, management can be learned and internalized as a way of living rather than a bag of tricks. Therapeutic management involves dynamic understanding of the psychosocial forces coming from the pupil, the groups, the social atmosphere, the physical setting, the learning task, the instructional method, and the various school, family and community norms. All of these forces are processed through the teacher, who has responsibility for developing, maintaining, and enforcing minimal behavioral values, standards, and limits.

The first problem is: whose standards and what limits? Many pupils are justified in opposing how they are treated and what code they are expected to accept. Often, when the rules are examined, they support adult comfort and convenience and a host of arbitrary issues. Yet therapeutic management must reflect the basic human values in our society: fair play, the protection of nonexploitive interpersonal behavior, the right to self-esteem, respect for property, respect for the community, etc. Therapeutic management means teaching, modeling, and respecting these values in all interpersonal relationships, although they are rarely put into full practice in our society.

There can be no therapeutic management in a punitive, repressive setting. Unfortunately, most adults punish children when the adults "have had it." Frequently, the intervention is not done to teach but to relieve adult anger, rage, or confusion. Redl, Glasser, and Dreikurs[1] have made it clear that reality should be the basis of intervention rather than adult authoritarianism, whims, or righteousness about a given state of order.

One of the most important and least understood aspects of therapeutic management is that it is based on the relationship between the teacher and the pupil as much as on the specific strategies a teacher may use. This is why we say that all significant learning evolves and revolves around the teacher. This relationship is extremely complex be-

---

1. **William Glasser,** *Reality Therapy* (New York: Harper and Row, 1965).

cause each teacher must struggle with his or her history to get in touch with feelings and conditions that will allow him or her to experience empathy with certain pupils, tolerance towards others, and disgust, anger, and rejection towards still others. No teacher has a symptom-free history or the capacity and the skills to work therapeutically with all the pupils assigned to the classroom. The "great teacher syndrome" is an educational fantasy. All teachers carry their history with them, including some unfinished psychological problems, attitudes, and prejudices.

This is why some special educators relate to aggressive pupils more comfortably than to dependent, anxious pupils. Some teachers can accept the confusion and infantile behavior of autistic pupils, while other teachers would perceive their behavior as annoying and repulsive. As a result the same management techniques used by these two teachers on the same pupil could have significantly different outcomes. This is why we accept behavior modification as *a* technique and not *the* technique: it is relationships that are most important to learning.

Once teachers understand that their mental health is an important part of therapeutic management, they can focus on what the pupil is doing that will cause them to perpetuate or intensify the pupil's emotional problems. In plain language, it is the teacher's task to make sure that the child does not fulfill the prophecy that the teacher is here to hurt, depreciate, and fail him or her. This concept is one of our training principles: *A pupil in stress can create in teachers the pupil's own feelings and, if they are not trained, the pupil's own behavior.* This is why an untrained teacher who is not basically aggressive can end up being counteraggressive and tell a pupil, "You said you won't do it and I'm telling you you *will* do it!" It is fascinating and alarming to know that emotionally disturbed pupils can get teachers to take on the disturbed personality aspects and behaviors during emotional conflict. This is why this chapter focuses first on the teacher and second on specific classroom strategies—ranging from stress reduction techniques to group life space interviewing, and from the use of punishment to the positive use of parents.

The first selections deal with the teacher as the source of the teacher–pupil relationship: (1) the teacher relating to different types of emotionally disturbed children, (2) the teacher's own problem, and (3) the teacher's image of his job. The first article by Long and Newman does not attempt to define the teacher's job, nor the teacher's complex role, nor the teaching process per se, but rather attempts to give a picture of the teacher confronting a class of disturbed children. The authors look at the demands made on a teacher, reactions to these demands, and the consequent effect on the children.

The Teacher and His Mental Health

Nicholas J. Long
Ruth G. Newman

Considering the contradictory concepts included under the image of a good teacher, it is little wonder that a teacher is confused about his role. Confusion is often a step on the road to mental health, but it never is, in itself, mentally healthy. At this moment, many teachers seem to be caught in a trap of confusion, not knowing which way is out. It would help them on their journey to define

mental health in a most specific sense. For there is no question that a teacher's mental health is of primary importance. His influence over the developing personalities of the children in his charge is a basic determinant of the future he creates, and there are subtle as well as obvious reasons for his influence—more of that later. But let it be emphasized that it is a bad mistake to define mental health as the same for all people. Mental health is a statistical average to which everyone ought to try to conform, not as a norm; it is the quality of mind, body, and attitude that, on the whole, usually leads a person to feel reasonably comfortable—that quality which frees him to use whatever capabilities he has much of the time and which leaves him open and sensitive to what is going on around him instead of needing to defend his own structure.

Mental health does *not* mean, as so many of the statements in education textbooks and lectures imply, that every teacher must mold himself into a pattern of smiling, calm, responsive patience, and have no quirks and no off-beat notions. As a matter of fact, some of the best teachers in the past, as in the present, are, in other realms of life, considered eccentric or painfully shy (see *Goodbye, Mr. Chips*). But in the classroom, "odd ball" or not, many of these people seem to be able to marshal all their resources. Their pupils often love them and/or learn from them. It is not necessary to come off a mental health assembly line to be a good teacher. It is no more necessary (or possible) for teachers to be alike than for individual children to be alike. Uniformity is not the goal for which to strive. It is, rather, to see that teachers like teaching (most of the time), because when one likes doing something one is apt to be fairly good at it; to see that they get pleasure from the children they teach—not all of them, but most of them; that they feel satisfied enough with their work and their lives so that they can view their own successes and failures with some objectivity; and that they feel hopeful enough to keep the capacity to learn and grow, and are comfortable enough to ask for help and to use it.

Human Beings and Teachers

Focusing then on this specific definition, one may agree with that theme mentioned more than any other in all the literature concerned with the mental health needs of teachers, namely, that teachers are human beings. This would seem a self-evident statement, yet the very fact that it is stated so often implies that in practice it is not so accepted or acceptable a tenet after all. Unquestionably, the insistence of the culture that its teachers, like its ministers and its psychiatrists, be better than everyone else contributes to the contradictory notions concerning a teacher's right to be human.

Common sense, intuitive understanding, and artist's insight, along with present-day contributions from psychology, sociology, anthropology, and psychiatry, have informed us that human beings have a good many feelings they are not proud of and that our culture frowns upon. People feel

anger. They feel fear. They feel hate. They feel these things when they are threatened (and indeed they would not have survived as a species had they not experienced these feelings). Being a somewhat more complicated species than other animals, and being more adept at manipulating their environment to fit their needs, they are not so frequently threatened by the enmity of nature as they are by forces inherent in the culture: by approval and disapproval, by need for love and ego enhancement, by need for control, adequacy, and self-regard, for belonging, and for nourishment and warmth of a psychological as well as physiological kind.

This being true of human beings in general, how does the teacher's humanness especially affect his job, and what particular threats does the teacher experience more than, or different from, those of people in other occupations? How can these threats which determine his behavior affect the children he teaches?

Well, take the simple fact that teachers deal with children of all ages and that children, having not been around the earth as long as the teachers, are more primitively organized. They have not yet learned to hide, to control, and to repress their feelings (and considerable mental health time is spent worrying about ways to help them use their feelings and not repress them in unhealthy fashions). Children, directly or indirectly, cry out their needs; perhaps they cannot define them, or place them correctly, or even do anything useful about them, but they make demands one way or another. The teacher must meet those demands, not only of one child, not only of many children, but of groups of children. He must meet these demands or divert them and at the same time teach subject matter. He must do this every day—even when he and his spouse have had a devastating fight the night before; even when he is worried sick about the fact that his own child has been moping about the house and has developed a stutter; even when his mother has become ill and has moved in on him. Even when he has not slept all night worrying over the unpaid bills and comes to school only corporeally, Mary will still need the extra attention she does not get at home before she can start in to work; Bill will still need to be set straight and quieted down before he can launch on algebra problems; Warren will need a hand on the shoulder to bring him back from outer space into earthly contact; and that group of devils in the back row will have to be brought into line.

If these management tasks are not done with some humor, warmth, firm quietness, or cheer, they will not work; and if they do not work, the class will collapse, and it will be one of those days in which everyone would better have stayed home in the first place. To be sure, this is not too different from any businessman in any office, except that children are more obviously demanding and they react more readily to the first signs of irritation, disquiet, or panic. Their reactions are less clothed behind social masks, so that their fear, disturbance, or counteranger is more immediately transferred back to the teacher, who in turn reacts as threatened organisms usually do, with fear or with flight, or, in the exceptional case of someone aware of his feelings, with an ability to see what is occurring and to put a behavioral thumb in the already leaky dike and start afresh.

A Teacher's Self-Awareness

The ability to perceive what is going on outside oneself is no small matter and does not fall naturally like the gentle rain from heaven. It is precisely that ability which is built in by successful psychotherapy and allied techniques. It is what psychotherapy and mental health are about.

This psychological premise is based on the well-documented assumption that the human being is influenced by a multitude of forces from within and from without. A person can afford to be aware of some of these forces, but, because of his culture, his upbringing, his individual personal experiences, and his picture of himself, he cannot afford to be aware of other forces. These latter forces are at least as powerful as those of which he *is* aware, and they may lead him to do all sorts of things which he himself may well not approve of. Moreover, since he cannot accept these things as part of himself, he can have no notion whatsoever of the effect of these actions on people around him, for good or for evil. For example, he probably does not realize that something about Joe in his class reminds him of his brother, Phil, whose very existence made his life utterly miserable all the years of his childhood, and that, without knowing it, he is quite unable to speak to Joe without irritation or to be aware of what *this* boy really is asking for. He may be equally unaware of the fact that the kids in the class are right when they accuse him of playing favorites. He may not know all the times he quite unconsciously smiles benignly at Margaret, how extra patient he is with all her questions and her need for special help. If someone should comment on his treatment of Margaret, he would ask, "Is this not good teaching?" Without special insight, he will never relate the fact that dependent Margaret is most appealing to him because he himself had always longed for someone to answer his dependent needs. He cannot afford to be aware that Margaret has become unpopular with her class because of the favoritism he has shown.

In a different context, Jules Henry[1] has reported a study in which teachers of middle-class children have been observed over long periods of time, their techniques of management noted, and their own self-report of their styles of operation recorded. Two cases out of many were specifically cited in which both teachers thought of themselves as strict disciplinarians. One teacher was quite unaware of the reassuring physical touches she continually gave to a child the minute he began to get out of bounds or the second he needed some extra push, and thus she controlled her class in a manner quite unknown to her. The other teacher was equally unaware of the number of times she pleaded with the children to do what they were asked, because she so needed their assistance. These two teachers would have been just as unaware that they used these techniques out of school with their sweethearts, their mates, their own children, or the clerks at stores with whom they dealt. They had no notion of how they actually went about the business of relating to people. Each had created a picture of herself, as all people do, having little to do with observable reality.

Actually, many of the things that teachers, along with other human beings, do unconsciously are helpful and useful things. Simply because they are done unconsciously does not mean they are bad. It is curious the amount of distrust people have of their unconscious. It is as if they began, as early as possible, to bury all the things they did not like—their hate, their fear, their anger—and in so doing, they managed to forget that not only these qualities but other feelings have been buried there as well. All those feelings are closeted in their unconscious which, from infancy on up, have made them uncomfortable, have hurt them, or have left them open to attack or criticism. Often these feelings are affection, warmth, tenderness, humor, sympathy, non-conformity, creativity. Frequently, when they have succeeded in locking the skeleton in the closet, they forget that in that very same closet lie their jewels and warmest or loveliest clothes. Teachers who receive more than the usual share of criticism from so many sources tend to be more vulnerable and therefore more fearful of letting their unconscious feelings come to the surface.

The Teacher's Personality Structure

Although there are many teachers who have a natural self-awareness and an inborn talent enabling them to see what really is occurring, there is no one who cannot use additional tools to be able to better see and to better evaluate his own actions. There is no one who does not have shutters in his mind that go down when a particularly threatening experience occurs. What is threatening for one person may be entirely different for another. The way the shutters go down may also be quite different. This is what is meant by the patterns of defense talked of in psychiatry: repression, denial, projection, rationalization, displacement, identification, and the rest. What a person does when his defenses are set into motion may be quite different too. He may greet the threat with flight, with withdrawal, with despair, with increased energy, with extra control, with rigidity, with hostility, with tears, with illness, with laughter, or with sarcasm. These methods of behavior are not lost on the children he teaches, regardless of what the teacher *thinks* he is teaching. Johnny *may* learn arithmetic, but he *surely* learns that Miss J. quickly changes the subject when he says something in a loud voice. In other words, the child learns patterns of behavior more surely than he learns academic subject matter. The younger the child, the deeper the learning.

Of course the child learns his patterns of behavior from home first and foremost. But the school is the child's first venture into a foreign society. It generates in him some new pressures, sets alien standards, and arouses strain in him. Moreover, he spends a large part of his waking life with the teacher—in most cases a larger part than he spends with his parents.

So, if it is an accepted premise that children identify with meaningful adults and that their growth is determined by those people with whom they identify, it is clear that the teacher's ways of reacting are of utmost importance. Furthermore, although it would be nice to think that the child only identifies with the best part of adults, this is not necessarily the case. Since the teacher is in authority and appears to have power, and a child invariably seeks strength or support for his own helplessness, he will identify with, or try to be on the side of, strength; therefore, he may well identify with the more unpleasant parts of a teacher, the very parts, as a matter of fact, that the teacher may have kept out of his own awareness. Or the child, finding a teacher displeasing or too weak to help, may negatively identify. That is to say, if the emotional tone of the teacher has been, in a direct or an indirect way, threatening or non-need-fulfilling, the child may adopt a reverse image and try to become just those things the teacher is not. Thus, what a teacher is, who he is, and how he reacts to the hundred million situations, crises, and interactions that occur in class everyday are the child's armory of knowledge of the outside world.

From these he learns how the whole world works and how one copes with anxieties and drives.

Fundamentally, it is not that a teacher is or is not a human being that is at question; it is what kind of humanness he exhibits and how his breed of humanness can be most effectively used in the classroom. The very humanity of teachers makes saintly behavior impossible. No human is always cheerful, patient, and carefree. Moreover, it is not such a good thing to be constantly euphoric. Indeed, if the teacher consistently represses his anger, the children may become increasingly convinced that their own angry and hostile feelings are unique and singularly evil.

Repressed, unaware, unusefully-directed rage and hostility, whether experienced by teacher or child, cannot forever be denied. It comes popping out, at most inappropriate moments, much too much, much too distorted, much too ineffective, much too overwhelming. Or else it appears in physical symptoms such as stomach aches, asthma, headaches, or dizziness. It may appear in nonlearning, in tics, in pretense and indirection, in lying, stealing, or truancy. The more we know about emotional health, the clearer it is that a teacher who gets angry appropriately is apt to be far less harmful to his class than a teacher who is generally irritable. A teacher who can face his own hostility toward a school task, or even toward the behavior of an annoying child, is likely to be one who can warmly take a child's sorrow or dilemma to heart. A teacher who is aware of his own vanity can laugh at himself and is likely to be able to keep the facts of school life in proportion. A teacher who knows he has acted crabby all the morning, because of a squabble at home, can pull himself together and keep the squabble where it belongs. He can proceed to make something more pleasant for the rest of the day. The teacher with awareness knows that, when too many people have been sent to detention hall that week, something may well be wrong not with the class but with himself. . . .

The Straws That Break the Teacher's Back

What first appears in applying informed personal services is the variety of things teachers find particularly frustrating in their classrooms. Ask a teacher to report honestly what most drives him to distraction: sometimes it is the big things like overcrowdedness, or having no time to do a job; sometimes it is the personal idiosyncrasies that make life unbearable. There is no use in placing a hierarchy of importance on the gripes. As anyone knows, a spilled glass of orange juice at breakfast can, at a given moment, be just as upsetting as not receiving a pay raise. It is possible for both kinds of events to be devastating for the time being, or to be met and handled in proportion when awareness and support are available.

Below are some examples of teachers' frustrations as they expressed them. They represent the kinds of frustrations which carefully planned in-service or consultative programs try to meet, in an an Androcles and the Lion kind of way, by seeing them as thorns which can, temporarily or permanently, cripple the teacher and keep him from performing, and can consequently hold back the child. A truly good consultative service to teachers could be of help, regardless of which of the following complaints one chooses.

Overcrowding is experienced with a sense of helplessness by some teachers:

In our school district during the past school term there was an overflow of children in our school causing most of the classes to have from 39 to 45 children. There was a constant assignment of new children from other schools in the city as well as from surrounding areas. This impact was felt tremendously in the school program and its operation to accomplish certain goals. As for me, this kind of "bargin'-in" (that was my inner feeling) of from one to two children each week was quite frustrating, as my concern in meeting individual differences was thwarted and my anticipated goals seemed out of reach. I found myself unconsciously resenting the fact that the child was sent to my room, and I became quite peeved if he did not have command of the skills expected of a second grader, for this meant that my job was to take time to help him if I could or at least to provide opportunities to expose him to the skills. I was not even willing to take him where he was and to work from that point, as that would take time, and time was what I didn't have, especially since time had already been sacrificed to register, enroll, and welcome him to the class.

I dread going to school these days—210 children a day, about 40 kids in a class. They tell me a new school is being planned to take up all the kids from the new housing settlement, but until then just try to teach English to 180 kids: the slow ones, the fast ones, the noisy ones. I thought you were supposed to know the kids you teach. I hardly know most of their names, let alone what they need from me. I love English. I have theories about teaching it. All that's been scrapped. Now I'm lucky to simply follow the prescribed dull study plan. I feel I'm not doing a thing for these kids. I'd give my soul for five classes of 20 children each!

I teach kindergarten. Once was, when I had a nice small 16 in a class group. Now I have two sessions: 50 in the morning, 42 in the afternoon, a volunteer parent helper for each class—when they show up. By the end of the day I feel as if I have the D.T.'s, with hundreds of moppets instead of pink elephants passing by. They call this teaching? Not in any child development course I ever had.

Special rules of personal and social behavior, as well as extra and menial chores and low salaries imposed on teachers, are often bitterly resented:

Then there is the "universal" frustration, not so much of salary (although everyone agrees that we are grossly under-paid) as of the benevolences I must cater to. I honestly hold in high esteem the virtues of the YMCA, YWCA, Boy Scouts, Girl Scouts, Red Cross, United Fund, and professional organizations, but somehow they seem to lose their flavor when I am aware that I must join in order to be considered a "good, cooperative" teacher. How nice it would be to join these wonderful organizations simply because I want to join them by choice only!

In the community in which I reside, teachers are somewhat expected to be "saints." This notion, to me, is ridiculous, for teachers, like everyone else, are human. It struck me as funny when I was interviewed for this particular position that the principal mentioned rather pointedly that this area had many people who drank in it, but that pressure was put on to get rid of any teacher who did so. He suggested that if I drank, not to drink in this area.

It would be nice to go into school in the morning and just teach and not have to be collecting money, taking attendance, playing nurse, and trying to discipline those who do not respond to the classroom role. It is difficult to be satisfied with doing just half a job all the time. It is difficult to realize that we cannot be 100 per cent effective but have to settle for much less. It is difficult for me to adjust to this situation as I am more of a perfectionist and like to get the best results all the time.

I hate to quit because I like to teach, but like it or not, I have to resign. My wife is expecting our second child and can no longer work. Since our first child is ill the doctor's bills and living expenses are just too much. I am overtired, tired trying to meet expenses by working at the post office in the Christmas rush and in a factory during summer times. I've been offered a job in an insurance company and, like it or not, I've got to take it. You've got to be rich to afford to teach if you've got a family.

The policy of administration is sometimes felt by teachers to be so outrageous (whether right or wrong) that their total teaching attitudes are affected:

To teach under an administration which focuses its attention upon creating benevolent public relations, even at the expense of school standards, seems to be my outstanding frustration. How is it possible for a high school principal to condone a student's laziness, slowness, and apparent lack of interest in subject matter, in a conference among the child's parents, the child, the teacher involved, and himself, and to state explicitly that possibly the reason for the child's failure was due to the lack of motivation and severity of grading done by the teacher. Mary, the student concerned, was a high school senior. She had failed sophomore and junior English and she was retaking both of these courses during her senior year as she needed both to graduate. Miss T. had Mary for sophomore English. She passed Mary because, as Miss T. said to me, "You can't fight city hall." I did not pass Mary, but when she graduated, she had no record on her permanent record of a failure in junior English. She had instead a "C."

The procedure of giving a contract for eight or nine months seems to have a decidedly negative effect upon the teacher. The implication read into the action is that the employer doesn't trust his judgment and has little faith in the training and prior experience of the applicant—that there is so much possibility that the teacher will be unsatisfactory that he cannot afford to hire her for a longer period than a year at a time. The result is an undermining of the teacher's performance, self-confidence, and feeling of security.

Most permanently established teachers would not have been asked to take such a teaching load, but many principals feel that they can ask a beginning teacher to accept almost any situation. This is a particularly hard thing to do, because a beginning teacher needs all of the help and encouragement that she can get, and even in the most pleasant situation will have many problems to cope with anyway. I feel that for a teacher, especially a teacher in her first year of teaching, to be so totally out of her teaching field is an injustice not only to the teacher but to the students.

The emotionally disturbed child in the classroom often generates despair and helplessness in the teacher:

There is a child in the classroom who suffers from an emotional problem. He is withdrawn, sensitive, and nervous—a condition which I know results from his home environment—a broken home, rejection, poverty, etc. I try to work with this child, give him projects that will display his self-worth, encourage him to join in the play activities of other children, give him extra "slaps on the back" for work well done, etc. All of this I do in the limited time the child is in school and under my jurisdiction. After school he goes home, back into the same surroundings that have caused him to be emotionally disturbed in the first place. My work, seemingly, becomes undone; the child enters the classroom the next day in the same condition as he entered the day before. I know the mind, soul, or body cannot be cured in one day, but as this chain of events goes on and on each day, I cannot help but sense a feeling of failure and helplessness.

Suzy was sent to me as an incorrigible seven-year-old who followed no rules, fought with all children, and caused constant room disturbance. She had an I.Q. of 78 on the Kuhlmann-Anderson and 79 on the Stanford-Binet. She was hostile, and yet on the first day of school she threw herself on me, nearly suffocating me with an embrace. Inquiring into her background, I found she lived in a house with seven or eight adults and as many children, seemingly all related, yet no definite relationship could be determined. I could not find out where the father was or even if he were living. Three women claimed to be her mother, but none would talk to me about her. Each said that her grandmother was responsible for her and she went to work at three in the afternoon and worked all night. I was never able to contact the grandmother. The frustration came about because I could find no one who seemed to care enough about Suzy to talk about her or try to help her. During the year I worked on the theory that if I loved her enough, she in turn would feel more secure and want to conform. I felt both I.Q. scores were invalid, because Suzy could think and reason. She was quite capable of finding information and presenting it when she desired.

I can't stop worrying about one little girl in my first grade. She behaves so peculiarly. She doesn't talk most of the time, though she can talk. She answers the other children and me with animal sounds. She hides under chairs like a dog and barks at people. She even bit one little boy. She draws pictures of dogs and insists on eating her lunch on all fours. I've talked to her mother, who is frantic about her behavior, but they have no money to see a psychiatrist. She's been on a clinic waiting list for six months, and I've had the child up for Special Service to test her for three months. In the meantime, the class all laugh at her, and she just gets worse, and I don't know what to do.

Parents are often experienced by teachers as an impossible cross to bear, whether this is because of the teacher's own unresolved feelings about his parents or whether the parents actually *are* obstructionists:

As a teacher, I try to give all the love, energy, consideration, and understanding to each pupil that I possibly can. To have a parent question my attention to another child over his makes me quite frustrated, baffled, and thwarted. If only parents would understand that some pupils require more attention than others and that it is not that the teacher is partial in any respect.

The most frustrating thing I've encountered has been parental attitude. Some, and I must say generally speaking it's the mothers, feel as though their children are bordering on genius. When the mothers classify their dear offsprings as such, the teacher shouldn't expect them to do such trivial things as study a lesson or do a class assignment, but should give the child superior grades in subject matters and satisfactory for attitude.

I have a parent who calls me every night to complain about her child's behavior. At first I tried to be nice and tell her what to do, but nothing is enough. Can't she see I have a right to my evenings, and can't she handle her own child? But I can't seem to cut her off, and I feel helpless to do anything. I've told the principal, and he doesn't seem interested in helping me. "Oh, she'll stop," says he. But when?

Interpersonal relations with staff, where there are differences of opinion of approach or personality conflicts, can be of determining importance to a teacher:

Although students may have difficulty in other subjects, social studies presents quite a problem to several of my students. I believe it is because it involves a great deal of reading and comprehension. Extra time is needed to give those students help who are having difficulty mastering social studies. But what is most frustrating to me is the fact that many of our teachers frown on me for giving special help to students because the teachers feel that the administration will require them to help with special problems also. Then too, some teachers have accused me of trying to impress the administrators because I give some special help.

The school was more of the traditional type, and, although I did try many new ideas and techniques, I found that I began following a somewhat "middle-of-the-road" position. Rather than actually teaching according to the way I had planned, I began to lean more and more to the type of teaching which was customary in the school system. There was not any real pressure from my critic teacher or from the superintendent, who was a personal friend, but I somehow felt that my efforts pleased them more when I followed the line of "traditional" teaching. At the same time, I felt that I was not doing a good job when I did not follow the practices which I had studied in my methods classes. Discipline

seemed to be the main objection to the newer methods. Whenever the boys and girls were working on their committees and the room was "noisy," I noticed that I worried about distracting the other rooms nearby. I even began to question the worth of my opinion. I sometimes felt that the older teachers humored me in conversations when I voiced my approval of modern methods and theory. This was not always the case, but I occasionally detected an attitude of "You'll learn. You may think this way now, but wait until you've taught several years." Perhaps this is why I began my graduate work right away rather than beginning teaching as I had previously planned.

I could do my job all right if that sixth-grade teacher would stay out of my way. We have a school where the principal is with us two days a week and with another school three days. When she's not here, that bossy, nosey Mrs. D. just takes over, calls down my kids in the hall when they're not doing anything, criticizes my bulletin board, disciplines my children in front of me, and undermines my authority. The principal is so dependent on Mrs. D. that there's no use talking to her. Anything Mrs. D. does is fine!

Sometimes deeply experienced personal conflicts can overwhelm a teacher:

I do not like having things on my desk looked at or handled. My desk is verboten. There are always children who want to rifle the papers or just look. They do not want anything, it just seems to be something they do. It doesn't matter to me that I never have anything on my desk that I do not want anyone to see or handle, I just don't want anyone to bother anything that is there. Inside, I have the feeling of "It's mine—hands off!" I know that this is silly, but I feel it strongly. The same feeling carries over to my personal things at home. I want them left alone.

When I may be about to come to a climax in a science experiment, or in the explanation of a transitive passive verb, or have all the attention of every eye and am about to express the punch line, there comes a knock at the door. I may as well answer it, because all hope of competing with that unknown factor of "Who's at the door?" is to no avail. Upon answering, I am handed a clarinet by a mother who says, "Would you please give this to Jeanne? She forgot she had band today." About that time I feel like a plugged-up volcano unable to blow the proverbial top.

If I were to name frustrations, they would come not from teaching but from the fact that I find my family is shorted. I find myself, at the end of the day, weary physically and mentally, often unable to cope with home demands. I will give a short answer to those at home, whereas at school I would weigh my words and answer with a smile. Meeting the needs of two sons, age 15 and 6, and a husband who is far from well could be a full-time job in itself. I feel frustrated in that I have little enthusiasm and patience to give at home after a full day of being enthusiastic and patient with a room full of children.

The other area of frustration is a difficult one to explain and also to admit. When I entered teaching, I had no intention of making it a career. I had hoped eventually to marry and raise my own family. After four years of teaching, I realized I would not meet many eligible men in the classroom. I realized I had to make a choice as to the type of career I wanted for myself. I knew that teaching was the one in which I would feel the happiest and gain the most satisfaction. I am going into guidance and counseling. I like working with people and think I have a reasonable amount of understanding of them. However, at times I feel very unloved and unwanted. I know this is going to hinder my working relationship in some cases. I can remember during my first two years of teaching that I threw myself whole-heartedly into helping students with extracurricular activities. I know I was looking for their appreciation and affection as an outcome of my work. But in most cases the students forgot about my help and enjoyed the activities themselves, letting me sit on the side and watch. How does a single person manage to fill this need for love and affection without becoming the embittered old maid that is often used as a stereotype for teachers? I feel this is an important problem with me. I know the solution cannot come in a short time, nor can anyone else solve it but myself. I would like some suggestions as to possible solutions.

I know one should not dislike a child, but there is one in my class who so offends me that it spoils my whole day. She is sloppy and fat. Her hair is stringy and unkempt. She sits sulky and slumped in her chair, never shows any pleasure in anything, answers in a fresh way, if at all. I know she must have a hard time at home, and I bend over backward trying to be nice. But at the end of the day, I am exhausted from the effort. I even dream about her nights.

As different as these personally recounted examples of frustrations are, there is not one of them that could not be to some degree alleviated by on-the-spot, psychologically sophisticated supervision, consultation, or whatever is called the process of airing one's difficulties, looking at them honestly with an informed and sympathetic person, and being helped not to deny them or let them grow to giant size but to perceive them in a fresh context. Whether by new pathways of communica-

tion, or by a reshuffling of the way one sees things, or by simply getting the jumble of enraging feelings into a framework of words, or by a sense of human support, *something* can grow out of this process for the teacher and the pupils. But this can only be effected when the school and the teachers are openly hospitable to this kind of help, and when the help itself becomes, with increased experience, the kind a teacher asks for. To be of use, it cannot be poured down the throat like medicine; to be nourishing, it must be sipped slowly like the good wine that it can be. . . .

The Disturbed and Disturbing Child in the Classroom

Another of the classroom teacher's common frustrations is the disturbed and disturbing child. Any teacher with the slightest grasp on reality knows full well he will have some difficult children in his class. The course of education, like that of true love, does not run smooth.

But it is true that even *difficulty* is a term that should have *normal* in front of it. There are some children far too sick to be in a regular class. They may be without impulse-control, or their behavior may be bizarre, or they may be withdrawn to the extent of being unreachable. Increasingly, special attention is being given and special provision being made for such children. But where is the severity of their disability first discovered? Rarely in the home. Rarely in the doctor's office. Mostly, severe emotional disturbance is first diagnosed in the classroom.

This means that a teacher—certainly a teacher of the early grades—has to live with, and try to teach, the child who is too ill to be lived with or too ill to be taught. Such a child disrupts the class, demands constant attention, and fills the teacher with a sense of failure and confusion, to say nothing of rage and sometimes of terror or revulsion. All of this causes him to feel guilty as well as inadequate. With the waiting lists of children on special services as long as they are, it is the rule, not the exception, that sees this child in the classroom for months before diagnosis, and longer before replacement. In the meantime, child, class, and teacher are often badly harmed. A growing awareness of this condition indicates the possibility, through teacher training, of earlier diagnosis, a better use of consultation, and increased skills for the teacher to help him recognize and deal with these disturbances on an emergency basis. (The emergency often lasts the whole school year!)

Merely relaying to the teacher the fact that he cannot hope to teach this child and that it is not his fault that the child behaves or feels as he does or learns poorly, is sometimes enough to improve matters. Just knowing this often relieves the teacher, and the child's behavior relaxes in direct proportion to the lessened tension of the teacher. But teaching such children is no easy matter.

Ask any psychiatrist how anxiety-provoking it is to be around very ill people. The teacher is in this spot daily; his anxiety rises sky-high just at a time when he is also forced to deal with his usual load of problems and tasks, and his anxiety makes him less able to do so. Again, to play variations on our theme, the teacher's self-awareness may make all the difference between his survival in school and his collapse, just as it may determine the way a class will survive or the amount of damage the sick child experiences.

Some teachers—often the best motivated— court trouble by becoming over-involved in the child and then feeling rejected and angry when their efforts fail. For some, particular symptoms are too evocative of repressed impulses or hidden childhood experiences of their own. Often, a child placed with a different (not necessarily a better) teacher fares better. Each teacher can take certain kinds of abnormalities and has his own personal aversions, the causes of which may be hidden from his awareness.

To make matters for contemporary teachers even more threatening, the notion of disturbance is even more complex than it used to be. There are, of course, the usual (though difficult on sight to distinguish) characters who are basically healthy but temporarily disturbed over a situation arising at home or at school with which they cannot cope, one which sets them into behavior very like the most disturbed child. The Johnny who throws a book at Peter may be a disturbed child or he may be suffering from an overload of criticism from Papa at the breakfast table. The act is a disturbed and disturbing one, but it can mean anything on the continuum from health to illness.

There are those with disturbances which are indeed very serious and severe but which are not too disturbing to the teacher in the classroom unless he is more than averagely conscientious: these are the too quiet, book-buried, non-social, shy and fearful children, whom teachers are learning increasingly to note, but who do not disrupt class activities as a rule, do not set an entire group into panic or mayhem, and therefore are not so quickly noticed by the teacher.

But in addition, a new phenomenon of disturbance has come to school and makes for a serious fraction of irritation for the class and the teacher.

These are children who may not be intrinsically as emotionally flooded as some of the others mentioned, but they are disturbed and most surely are disturbing. They make up the increasing group of lower-class and upper-middle-class children who, in a world much more mobile and less rooted than heretofore, have parents who move from place to place on jobs or who are looking for jobs. These children sometimes come from immigrant families (such as constitute a severe educational challenge in large cities like New York), or sometimes from indigent farm or unskilled labor families whose work is seasonal, or from military service people who move from post to post, or from the families of highly skilled young engineers or businessmen whose companies move them back and forth to branch offices in many states. These children have lacked the security of a place and a constant in their lives; they tend to make thin and superficial relationships, to be either desperate followers in order to belong, or desperate leaders in order to shine and to make a mark while the brief candle of their stay burns brightly. Often they make up the gangs and the cliques and the socially worrisome element. Teachers have not yet found ways, other than by trial and error, of dealing with this phenomenon. They have not learned how to relate to these children, how to motivate them for long-term goals or long-term relationships. The very task of doing so, when one thinks about it psychodynamically, borders on the impossible. For these children have learned the hard way not to invest too much in relationships that are bound to change, not to count too much on any way of life when next month or next year the way of life will have to be quite different. Being basically healthy animals, they have learned to adapt superficially to everything in some way or other, and they convey an impenetrable wall when a teacher tries to help them invest themselves emotionally in work, in projects, or in relationships. This problem has just begun to be recognized as a severely frustrating aspect of teaching today.

Reasons behind Choosing Teaching as a Profession

From all that has been said so far, the reader must be beginning to feel as swamped with helplessness as the teachers themselves feel with some of their classes. Why, one begins to ask, would anyone choose teaching for a profession? It is a good question and has been the subject of some study. A teacher's reasons for choosing the profession often underlie the last frustration to be discussed here.

What does a teacher hope to derive from teaching? What conscious and unconscious forces may lead to his decision to become a teacher?

Some teachers take to teaching out of a sense of mission or dedication: it is a way to make the world, which often does not look so good, better for the future. This can coexist with many other reasons.

Some teachers fall into teaching. They begin with other fields, find other experiences unsavory, or feel they cannot succeed in them. A job of teaching is open and they attempt it.

Despite the pitiful salaries teachers have always been paid, there are people who feel more secure working on state, county, or city salaries than in business—a teacher's salary, though low, seems reasonably certain. But since low salaries are the rule, the teaching field has become increasingly attractive to many married women. These people often can supplement a limited income by teaching. They can buy the extras at home, or they can contribute to the necessities without the full burden of having to support a family on a teacher's salary. Education schools these days have more and more students who are middle-aged and have children past the toddler stage themselves. For these people, the economic strain tends to be less, but the strain of filling two full-time jobs, teaching and family life, often brings with it its own frustration.

A man or woman may take up teaching because a teacher has been so important in his own development. When he was in school, a particular teacher may have made a great difference in his life, may indeed have become someone to pattern himself on. Some people, contrariwise, take up teaching because of their own school sufferings and because they remember with chagrin and bitterness the poor teaching to which they were exposed, and they resolve to live life over for themselves through others, and this time to do it right. Some people seem to get along beautifully and comfortably with young people of different ages, but they may do very poorly, feel awkward, out of place, and inadequate in adult groups. Such people often make excellent teachers, especially of the very young (though they are frequently the ones who have the most trouble with the parents of the children they teach). These people may be reliving what was a real or a fantasied happier time of their lives. They may be educational Peter Pans and find it necessary to ally themselves with the young folks against the adults. Many of these people, though by no means all, often find it difficult to deal with the authorities in school. They are still carrying on childhood or adolescent rebellions.

Some people are much happier without people. They fall in love with subject matter, with mathematics, or physics, or ancient history. They may have discovered that real, present-day life is simply too much, that relationships demand a closeness that is too frightening; high school or college teaching allows them to legitimately drown themselves in their subject. They are often very skilled in their subject matter, and show a passion and love, when involved in content, that may well be inspiring to some of their like-minded students. These teachers are practically never the ones who find satisfaction in relating to the children in their classes, either as a group or as individuals, unless they find someone who is the budding image of themselves or who seems to be as interested in falling in love with that particular subject matter as they themselves are. These teachers (and some of them are very gifted, if one accepts their limitations) are virtually never interested in the psychology of children or interpersonal relations.

The fact that a teacher may have all sorts of reasons he does not recognize for choosing his profession does not differentiate him from anyone else. It is, again, part of his humanness. The same kinds of reasons, or equally unconscious ones, may impel a person to become a nurse, a doctor, an engineer, a bus driver, an executive, a secretary, a salesman, a plumber, a cattle raiser, a lawyer, or a fireman. The crucial difference for the teacher is that, because he must constantly deal with children and cannot avoid having an important effect on them, he, more than most of his fellow human beings, must be *aware* of the possible reasons for his choice of profession.

Redl and Wattenberg[2] have made a list of 15 of the more commonly stated reasons people tend to go into teaching.

1. Status
2. Family pressure
3. Love for subject field
4. Identification with a former teacher
5. Love of children
6. Fun in teaching
7. Helping to build a better world
8. Self-sacrifice for an ideal
9. Correcting the shortcomings of one's own past
10. Reliving childhood patterns
11. Desire for affection
12. Need for security
13. Halfway house to other ambition

14. Need for power and group leadership

15. Guaranteed superiority

In the discussion above, merely some of these factors have been mentioned. One might not only discuss the rest but add many more. The fact is that people's motives are rarely, if ever, single-purposed, and most people make these decisions on many counts, on a series of personal, rational, irrational, and coincidental factors. Moreover, the reasons a person gives himself for doing something are nearly always the reasons his own self-image can tolerate. People have a great stake in hiding from themselves other reasons, perhaps just as strong or even stronger, which they do not want to face. A teacher afraid of his own aggression may be quite unable to see that he went into teaching not only for love of subject matter but just as much because he had a need for power unfulfilled in other areas. A teacher who takes great pride in his independent, controlled handling of life may not be able to recognize his loneliness and his need for affection as a driving motive. To restate the theme as a coda, the awareness mentioned earlier comes back into the picture again; for the more aware a teacher is of the hidden, as well as the obvious, reasons for teaching, the more fully will he be able to do his job and face its frustrations; for he will be more aware of the areas of satisfaction from which he derives pleasure and will not need to feel so resentful that he is not getting what he intended to get when he took his teaching certificate. Through awareness, he will have either given up impossible goals and substitute more realistic ones, or he will have found ways to reach the goals unanswered by his job in other areas of his life. . . .

Notes

1. **Jules Henry,** "The Problem of Spontaneity, Initiative and Creativity in Suburban Classrooms," *American Journal of Orthopsychiatry,* **29** (April 1963), 266–279.

2. **Fritz Redl and William W. Wattenberg,** *Mental Hygiene in Teaching* (New York: Harcourt, Brace and Co., 1959), pp. 479–482.

From Nicholas J. Long and Ruth G. Newman, "The Teacher and His Mental Health," *The Teacher's Handling of Children in Conflict,* Bulletin of School of Education, Indiana University (July 1961), pp. 5–26. Reprinted by permission of School of Education, Indiana University.

Editors' Commentary

Stress and Coping

For years teachers have been reporting that certain emotionally disturbed pupils can get them to say and do things that they do not want to say or do. One mild-mannered teacher expressed this problem with feeling: "Each night I promise myself that I will not lose my temper with Peter, but by 11 A.M., after he has done all his passive-aggressive tricks on me, i.e., not remembering what I said, not hearing the instructions, always diddling around with a smirk on his face, I want to kill the little bastard!"

To understand this painful interaction, Nicholas Long has developed a model called the conflict cycle. In Long's view the transaction between pupil and teacher follows a circular process in which the attitudes, feelings, and behaviors of the teacher are influenced by the attitudes, feelings, and behaviors of the pupil. During a stressful incident, this circular process becomes a conflict cycle, creating additional problems for both pupil and teacher. In other words, this negative interplay is extremely difficult to interrupt once it begins. For example, we know that children under stress are emotional, not rational, beings. They behave out of feelings, not by thinking. They protect themselves from physical and psychological pain by becoming defensive, primitive, and regressive. If the teacher reacts to these behaviors impulsively or with righteous indignation and believes that the pupils should be taught a lesson, a "power struggle" develops in which understanding and helping disappear and "winning" becomes the only acceptable outcome for the teacher.

In the next article, Long and his coauthor Betsy Duffner elaborate this basic model, changing it to a stress or coping cycle. Their description of the nature of stress, the dynamics of the stress cycle, and the specific skills and techniques a teacher needs to reduce stress and promote coping skills, is clinically sound and professionally helpful to every teacher who must struggle with distressed pupils.

The Stress Cycle or the Coping Cycle? The Impact of Home and School Stresses on Pupils' Classroom Behavior

Nicholas J. Long
Betsy Duffner

For decades, educational psychologists have been studying how learning in the classroom can be improved. This has led to numerous research findings about how specific teacher behaviors, instructional methods, curriculum programs, group dynamics, and audiovisual equipment can be used to motivate pupils. For many educators, these studies have resulted in the simple axiom: "If teachers can teach, pupils can learn!" While we affirm that competent teachers and positive teaching techniques are important, learning is more complex and broader than what takes place in the classroom. Each pupil comes to class with a unique history, attitudes, values, and current life stresses. What pupils experience at home and in their neighborhoods can have profound impacts on their ability to learn in the classroom. For some pupils, these daily nonschool experiences increase their motivation for classroom learning, while for other pupils these experiences interfere significantly with their ability to concentrate and learn. In any case, it is no longer tenable to separate arbitrarily the pupils' school environment from the rest of their lives. What happens at home and in the community influences what happens in the classroom. It is this dynamic interaction that needs to be described. Special educators need to be more aware of the pupils' home and community lives. They need to understand how these forces affect a pupil's feelings of adequacy and success in school. They need to know what they can do to understand and assist their pupils during times of overwhelming life stresses.

This article focuses on the pupil's home and school environments and answers the following questions:

1.   What is stress?
2.   How does stress manifest itself?

3.   What are the various types of stress?
4.   How does stress lead to the pupil–teacher stress cycle?
5.   What can teachers do during times of stress to promote coping skills and the coping cycle?

What Is Stress?

Stress is defined as a personal and subjective reaction to a specific life event, causing the individual to experience a physiological and psychological feeling of discomfort. Stress can be experienced in response not only to real situations but also to anticipated and imagined ones.

Stress is not intrinsically either good or bad. As educators we must help pupils view stress as a normal, natural, and accepted fact of life. The usefulness of stress, however, depends on its *frequency*, *intensity*, and *duration*. If all stress were eliminated, pupils would become lackadaisical and passive. Too much stress overwhelms them, causing psychological panic and thinking disorders. However, the right combination of stress and comfort motivates pupils to new levels of creativity and problem-solving activities. The ability to master stress builds pupils' feelings of competence, success, and self-esteem.

How Does Stress Manifest Itself?

Although stress was first studied as a medical problem in the early twenties, researchers are just beginning to understand how it functions and what impact it has on the mental health of individuals. First there is a single basic biological response to a stressful incident. This response is automatic, unconscious, and very predictable. Stress prepares the body for action. It does this by releasing a series of hormones into the bloodstream that activate the autonomic nervous system. This sytem controls the involuntary muscles that alter the blood pressure, respiration, and digestive systems. Anthropologically, stress has functioned as a personal alarm system enabling a person to survive an attack. During this stress state, all bodily senses are intensified. The person has an abundance of energy, creating increased levels of strength, agility, and endurance. The person can either attack a foe with new ferocity or escape by running great distances without tiring. In either case, for primitive humans stress served a very useful, specific, and important purpose. In many cases it was the basis of their survival.

However, in today's complex society there are many rules against attacking others or running away. Pupils must learn to control what their bodies are urging them to express. Pupils must learn how to cope with this state of stress instead of acting it out. Since self-control takes considerable skill and maturity, and is a difficult task even for adults, we can expect that even "normal" children and adolescents will break down and act inappropriately at times.

If this interpretation of human behavior is true for the average pupil who has been protected from chronic life stresses, what about the few pupils who have been flooded by stress and have developed emotional problems? For these pupils even the normal life stresses can become overwhelming. Many of these pupils are woefully lacking in coping skills. In fact, they perceive themselves as incapable, defective, or victimized by stress. They feel the only solution for them is to escape from the situation as quickly as possible. The behaviors they choose may include aggressive outbursts, such as throwing objects, cursing, or threatening others. Or they may adopt withdrawal/defeat behaviors, such as giving up, sobbing, staring into space, refusal to talk, inattention, and passivity. In any case, these classroom behaviors take their toll on the emotional energies of both pupil and teacher. A mutual wear-and-tear occurs when pupils are overwhelmed by stress. This is why teachers who are responsible for helping these pupils need to know about the sources of stress.

What Are the Various Types of Stress?

Pupil stress can be classified in the following four categories:

1. Developmental stress
2. Economic stress
3. Psychological stress
4. Reality stress

Developmental stress refers to stress arising from all the normal developmental crises or stages from birth to death. For example, to be born is stressful. To be weaned from the breast or bottle is stressful. To be toilet-trained is stressful. To leave parents and home for teacher and school is stressful. Learning to read is stressful. Learning to understand basic sex differences between boys and girls is stressful. Learning to be part of a group is stressful. For adolescents, there are numerous developmental stresses: watching one's body change, becoming independent, developing personal values as opposed to group values, understanding the excitement and confusion of one's own and others' sexuality, developing career courses, graduating from high school, etc. Each of these developmental events is stressful and predictable. They arise for all pupils, regardless of race, color, creed, or socioeconomic level.

Economic stress is felt by millions of families in our society who are living on the brink of economic disaster. Not all of these families come from the slums, ghettos, or disadvantaged groups. Many striving middle-class families are living beyond their financial resources and have extended their credit line to the breaking point. Also financial worries are created by extended labor strikes. In one year we observed aerospace workers, coal miners, auto workers, and teachers on strike for over three months, causing considerable family stress and problems.

For the chronically poor, economic stress shows itself in poor diet and food; poor health habits; greater susceptibility to illness; lack of acceptable clothes; lack of privacy; lack of sleep; lack of opportunity to participate in social and school-related activities; greater parent exhaustion and conflict; parent models of joblessness and helplessness; social isolation from the mainstream of society; and a sense of being different from the group.

Psychological stress consists of a conscious and deliberate attempt by individuals, groups, and institutions to systematically and consistently destroy the worth of the individual. For example, many pupils are told that they are unwanted, that they are the source of their parents' problems, that life would be better if they were not around, that they spoil the family and neighborhood because of their demands and behaviors. They are told that they are stupid, dumb, infantile, inconsiderate, ungrateful, and totally useless to themselves and others. For some pupils the stress does not come from open rejection but from trying to meet unrealistic standards. Pupils are told they must be perfect to be loved. Whatever they do is not good enough. They must be smarter, more responsible, more mature socially, and more loving than they are capable of showing. For other pupils, the psychological stress is related to specific adults who are socially maladjusted, for example, the seductive, pleasure-seeking parent who frequently stimulates the pupil's sexual awareness and fantasy by showing excessive attention to and interest in sexual topics and fun. The psychotic parent, who is suffering from a major mental illness, is not capable of carrying out adult responsibilities. In homes with psychotic parents, simple issues become distorted, creating a tense atmosphere for everyone in the family. The alcoholic or drug-abusing parent creates a home where there is little consistency, where children never know if the parent will be available to care and relate to them or whether the parent will expose them to shame or terror—from exhibitionism, to physical and sexual abuse, to desertion, to suicide.

Other pupils must deal with the overprotective parent, the retarded parent, the moralistic parent, and the depressed parent. Moreover, any parent, sibling, relative, or significant friend who is disturbed will have a profound effect on the pupil's emotional development and ability to focus his or her remaining energies on classroom learning.

Reality stress arises from all the unplanned events that frustrate the personal goals of a pupil. These frustrations happen spontaneously, rather than from an organized attempt to defeat the pupil. But they happen with such frequency for a few pupils that the students begin to believe the world and all the people in it are against them. For example: (1) A boy looks forward to wearing his favorite sweater only to discover that his brother wore it yesterday and spilled syrup on it. (2) A girl lends her algebra book to a friend who forgets to bring it to school the next day. (3) Two classmates are fooling around in class. One pushes the other into a third girl's desk tearing her English composition, which is due in a few minutes. (4) A teacher warns the class that the next pupil who talks will be given a detention. The pupil next to one boy whispers to a friend and the teacher points to the boy as the offender. (5) A teenage boy's dad lets him use the car to go to a basketball game. The boy goes to pick up his friends only to discover on the way to the game that the gas tank is empty. In other words, things go wrong, that should not go wrong. It is not anyone's fault, but the stress is very real, frequent, and intense.

For some pupils stress comes not from one source but from multiple sources. For example, a boy may have the normal developmental stress of a final exam. That evening his parents have a violent argument, and he is unable to study or sleep. On the way to school he is scapegoated by a hostile group who call him various racial and ethnic names. As he enters the classroom a friend greets him by slapping him on the back, causing his glasses to fall off and break. Finally, the teacher announces a new school policy that no exam can be taken over, regardless of the circumstances.

When teachers understand these multiple cycles of stress, they are more willing to help pupils develop new coping skills rather than *blame the students for their misfortunes.*

This is a major change in thinking for most pupils and teachers. Our personal history has taught us that when goals are frustrated or something goes wrong, someone is to blame. For example, teachers find it easier to criticize pupils and parents for not trying, being careless, and being irresponsible, rather than understanding what is blocking or interfering with this pupil's ability to learn in the classroom. Simultaneously, pupils find it easier to attack the educational system, teachers, parents, peers, and rules for their failures than to understand what is overwhelming them.

The Stress Cycle

Our goal is to develop a no-fault stress program, like no-fault auto insurance, in which the focus is on understanding, supporting, and teaching new skills to the injured party. To accomplish this, Dr. Long has developed the concept of a stress cycle. This model can help teachers understand how the negative cycle of stress functions, and how children under stress frequently create their feelings and at times their behavior in teachers. This stress cycle is illustrated in figure 1.

1. Stressful Incident. The cycle begins with a pupil experiencing a stressful incident from a developmental, economic, psychological, and/or reality source.

2. Feelings. Many pupils, unfortunately, are taught that certain feelings are bad and unacceptable and that "healthy" children should not have these feelings. Pupils who have these unacceptable feelings must find ways of getting rid of them by denying them, by giving them to others, or by reorganizing them so that they are acted out in disguised forms. Since all feelings are natural, intrinsic parts of the human being experiencing them, *it is our goal that everyone should learn to own his or her*

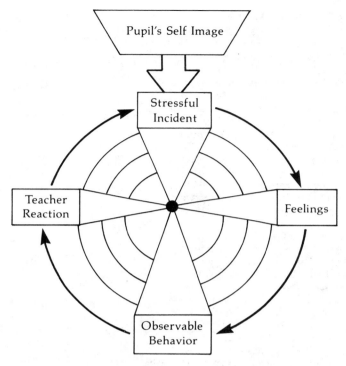

Figure 1. The Pupil's Stress Cycle

feelings. While feelings give meaning and excitement to life, there is a difference between having feelings and being had by our feelings. Pupils need to distinguish between their feelings and their behavior. For example, it is healthy to feel anger when we have been psychologically depreciated or cruelly discriminated against, but it is not acceptable to assault the person inflicting the insult. It is healthy to experience fear when someone threatens to hurt us or abuse us but it is not helpful to encourage the threat to happen. It is very healthy to experience intense feelings of sadness, when someone we love dies or moves away, but not healthy to withdraw from all relationships. It is healthy to feel guilty when we behave in a way that we know is unacceptable, but it is not useful to act out so that others will punish us. It is normal to experience anxiety when we are anticipating a new experience or new relationship, but it is not healthy to handle this anxiety by alcohol or drug abuse. It is normal to feel happiness when we are in love but it is not helpful to express blatant sexual feelings in front of others. The existence and importance of these feelings are incontestable. The debatable question is how they are to be expressed in behavior.

3. Observable Behavior. When pupils react to feelings of stress by expressing them directly or by defending against them, they usually create additional problems for themselves in their school environment. For example, hitting, running away, becoming ill, stealing, teasing, lying, becoming hyperactive, fighting, using drugs, becoming inattentive, and withdrawing cause pupils to have difficulty with teachers, peers, learning, and school rules. When a young man dumps his feelings of hostility toward his mother on his teacher, an inevitable teacher–pupil problem develops. When a pupil becomes depressed because her mother is having a baby, the pupil may not be able to complete her assignments, and a learning problem emerges. Accepting this interpretation of behavior, the problems pupils cause in school are not always the causes of their problems. More accurately, the problems pupils cause in school are the result of the ways they have learned to cope with their feelings of stress.

4. Teacher Reaction. One of the amazing concepts of interpersonal relationships is that a pupil in stress can actually create in others the stressed feelings and at times, the pupil's behavior. For example, an aggressive pupil can quickly bring out hostile feelings and counteraggressive behaviors in others. A hyperactive pupil can make others feel anxious and act in impulsive, irrational ways. Likewise, a detached pupil frequently gets others to feel depressed and to ignore him or her. If teachers are unaware of this natural reaction, the inappropriate pupil behavior will become automatically reinforced and perpetuated by the teacher's reaction. The phrase, "Do unto others as you would have others do unto you" is an accurate but unfortunate psychological consequence of this negative stress cycle.

For example, the negative feedback a young woman receives from a teacher simply supports her original view of herself and her world, increasing intense feelings, which the pupil then shows in even more unacceptable and primitive ways. When this happens, the teacher becomes more angry and disgusted by the pupil. Consequently, the teacher reacts further in a negative, punitive way, which the pupil perceives as more rejection, intensifying her stress, feelings, and behavior. The stress cycle continues until an intense *power struggle* develops between teacher and pupil. When this happens, logic, caring, and compassion are lost, and the only goal is to win the power struggle. The teacher sees the pupil as the source of the problem and tells her to "shape up," to improve her attitude and behavior. If she doesn't, the teacher labels her as disturbed, delinquent, dangerous, and disgusting. The pupil is usually suspended, transferred, or referred to special education.

What is important to remember is that there are no winners when the stress cycle reaches the level of the power struggle. This cycle cannot be broken by asking immature children to act maturely during intense states of stress. If change is going to happen, then the adult must accept responsibility for acting in a mature, professional manner. This means understanding how children in stress can incite concerned, reasonable, and dedicated educators to act in impulsive, dispassionate, and rejecting ways. This problem becomes more complex when the source of the stress is in the child's home environment, frequently outside the teacher's awareness and knowledge. In these cases, the teacher needs even greater diagnostic awareness. Here is an example of how the stress cycle functions and ends up as a power struggle between the pupil and teacher:

Example 1: The Stress Cycle

Joe is a sixteen-year-old of average intelligence, who has had chronic but minor behavior problems in the classroom.

Stress 1	Joe breaks up with his girlfriend.
Feelings	Anger and inadequacy.
Behavior	Did not turn in English assignment. Said it was a stupid assignment anyway.
Teacher reaction	Surprised by his attitude. Tells him he knows better than to act like this, etc.
Stress 2	Feels psychological stress: Teacher picking on him.
Feelings	More anger.
Behavior	"Why do you always pick on the boys in this class and not the girls?"
Teacher reaction	"I do not. Besides, that is not the issue . . ."
Stress 3	Continued psychological stress.
Feelings	Anger, with pleasure.
Behavior	"Yes you do, and you don't even know you do it. Ask the class."
Teacher reaction	"What I do know is that you are getting yourself into trouble if you don't settle down."
Stress 4	More psychological stress
Feelings	More anger.
Behavior	"I don't care what you do, it means nothing to me."
Teacher reaction	"If you don't care, then you'd better not stay in class and mess it up for the others."
Stress 5	More psychological stress.
Feelings	Intense anger.
Behavior	"It's a pleasure to get out of this damn class." Walks out of the class and slams the door.
Teacher reaction	Yells, "Don't you slam that door!"

In this example we can see how the pupil escalated the problem into a power struggle and how he was successful in getting his female teacher to reject him as his girlfriend had. He never was aware that the source of his difficulty was the rejection by his girlfriend. Instead, he projected these feelings on the teacher and ended up blaming her for his school troubles.

Coping Strategies for Teachers

The dynamics of the stress cycle illustrate how students in stress create their feelings and behaviors in others, and how the student's hope for help from the school environment frequently ends up in an intense and destructive power struggle with the authorities. Once teachers understand these concepts and are no longer reacting to the student's defensive and defeating behaviors, the teachers become psychologically ready to help their students cope with stress. The next set of questions to ask are:

1. What coping skills do teachers need to learn?

2. How can these coping skills be used in an educational setting?

All Help Is Useful

Let's assume that any degree of help is useful to a student in stress. Some teachers feel that a student's problems are so severe, complicated and long-standing that their efforts to help are useless and hopeless. One teacher expressed this concern openly, "I am willing to help Carl, but I feel it's like building sand castles that are washed away by the nightly tide of his home and community struggles. What I do doesn't seem to make a difference. He needs much more than the school or I can provide. After all, I have only a limited amount of time and skill."

While this attitude is understandable, it overlooks several significant factors that are intrinsic to any helping relationship:

1. When students are in stress, they need to believe that there is some hope to their life situations. Even if the hope is marginal and temporary, students can experience from the adult some personal acceptance that does not blame them for their circumstances or magnify the severity of their problems.

2. Every successful experience a student has with an adult, no matter how small, is important. While a teacher's help may not be enough to "turn the student around," or make a significant difference

his or her life, it does create and establish a basic trust of adults. It is an experience that cannot be taken away. Perhaps next semester or next year another adult will be able to build on this foundation, making it possible for the student to make significant changes and to compensate for his or her life problems.

3. Psychological conditions at home and in the community change with time. Nothing remains static or fixed. Crises in the family or community do become resolved or at least tolerable. If students can be helped *not to complicate* their lives by creating new problems, then they can find relief when the stress in this "other environment" diminishes.

Given these factors, teachers can use the eight strategies presented next for helping students cope with stress.

Teacher Strategy One: Forming a Helping Adult Relationship

In helping students cope with stress, teachers need to look beyond the surface explanation of behavior and to focus on the feelings causing the behavior. How students feel often determines the way they perceive and behave in school. Many pupils under stress try to hide their feelings by withdrawing from activities, or becoming hyperactive, or exploding in anger. To help these children, a teacher must make the initial contact, reaching out and decoding the student's behavior. This is not always a simple task. Many students who need help and support begin by refusing or ignoring the teacher's effort to help. However, we know that if a student can share thoughts and experiences with someone and have that adult understand and accept the problem, the exchange will result in a new feeling of emotional support and direction. In this kind of relation, student and teacher move toward each other. They talk and listen to each other. They open up. The student begins to share concerns and fears. To make this helping process happen, the teacher must be able to empathize with the student. She or he must be able to enter the student's world in such a way as to encourage the student to trust the adult. The teacher must develop the skill to see beyond what the student is saying and to decode how the student's verbal and nonverbal ways of communicating can provide cues to the real source of pain and stress. To do this, the teacher must understand the psychology of nonverbal communication, verbal communication, and labeling and accepting feelings.

Nonverbal Communication. The more we observe students in stress, the more we listen to what they tell us without words. We learn to respond to their body language. We become acutely aware of the messages they send with their eyes, muscles, skin temperature, breathing pattern, and body movement. Many students learn early in life that if they express negative feelings and words, adults react in anger. They also learn that the spoken word can be held against them as self-incriminating evidence. To avoid this problem, they learn to say one thing with words, while their bodies express a different sentiment.

Verbal Communication. When students are under stress, their language is often used to mislead, hide, and protect their real feelings. Consequently teachers must learn to pay more attention to *how* the students are speaking than *what* they are saying. By listening to the flow and tone of the words, a teacher can "hear" them in terms of feelings such as anger, fear, sadness, ambivalence, or happiness. For example, a student may say, "Get out of here and leave me alone!" while trying to communicate a feeling of, "Please don't go; I need your help but I'm afraid to ask, since you might reject me or tell me I'm acting silly or immature."

Labeling and Accepting Feelings. After a teacher listens to students and learns to trust the authenticity of nonverbal communications, the teacher is ready to label the student's feelings. Based on what the teacher perceives and feels, she or he can say to a child in stress, "You look sad today, can I help you?" or "You look really upset. Can you talk to me about it?" or "I have a feeling that you are worried about something. Did anything happen on the way to school today?" As you reach out and share the student's inner life with honesty, reflecting the unspoken feelings and words, a meaningful relationship develops. The next step, accepting the student's feeling, is far more complex than labeling the feelings. The teacher needs to support the student's feelings as a genuine and healthy expression of interpersonal struggles. The teacher must indicate that the feelings the student has toward school, home, society, and the world are legitimate to the student and that no one should argue with their existence. For example, the teacher can say, "It's okay to feel sad when you lose something," or "I know you're angry with Larry, but I can't let you hit him back." In many cases, the teacher can drain off the student's feelings by allowing him or her to express them through words, as in the following exchange:

BILLY: *I would like to punch him out!*
TEACHER: *I know you're really angry. You really hate his teasing.*
BILLY: *Boy, he makes me mad.*

The student needs the chance to run through all the complaints of injustice or disappointment that he or she is feeling without fear of adult retaliation or rejection.

Offering a helping relationship to pupils means developing the skills of listening to, labeling, and accepting feelings. During this process students can discharge their pent-up feelings in a safe, nondestructive manner. As these feelings are expressed, the students are in a better position to evaluate the situation and to put their lives in proper perspective.

There are some serious pitfalls in helping students, however. The teacher must not rush to the student's rescue, take over the student's responsibilities, and plan a logical and clear solution for him or her. The helping relationship is based on the following four ethical considerations:

1. The helping teacher is sympathetic but insists that the pupil has some responsibility for improving the situation. The helping adult does not convey a message of pity for the child. This feedback simply reinforces the child's feeling of being gypped and encourages him or her to act out, to take what he or she feels entitled to in any manner available. Instead, the teacher helps the child focus on the questions: "What can you do to make the matter better?" What can you do that will make the situation worse?"

2. The helping teacher accepts the student's problem in a matter-of-fact way, indicating that the student is not stupid for having this problem. The teacher accepts the problem as part of the normal process of becoming an adult.

3. The helping teacher positively reinforces all attempts by the pupil to improve the situation, even if the efforts were not successful.

4. The helping teacher can be trusted to keep all conversations confidential. The teacher must serve as an advocate and protect the pupil's rights.

Teacher Strategy Two: Lowering School Pressure

While teachers cannot control what happens to the student in the "other environment," they can control what happens in the classroom. One significant way teachers can reduce student stress is by lowering academic requirements, standards, and deadlines temporarily. They can tell a boy that he has enough on his mind right now and not to worry about the term paper, book report, or exam next Friday. Once the crisis is over, the teacher will help him catch up, but right now it is important for him to understand his feelings and situation. This strategy is like providing the student with an academic aspirin that will temporarily take away the academic aches and pains. However, it is important not to take away the student's total responsibility for learning or classroom assignments. Students must be expected to turn in any assignments they can complete during the crisis, but they need not feel they will fail if the assignment is late or at a lower level of competence. This strategy is an obvious one, but it is used all too infrequently by classroom teachers.

Teacher Strategy Three: Redirecting Feelings into Acceptable Behavior

Just as people have found a way of channeling the potentially destructive force of a rapidly flowing river into electrical power that can increase their personal comfort and productivity, students can be taught new and diverse ways of expressing intense, explosive thoughts and feelings as socially approved behavior. This strategy for coping with stress not only relieves physical and psychological tensions but also develops personal and social skills. Aggressive, sexual, fearful, and sad feelings can be directed into school activities such as art, sports, dance, manual arts, literature, drama, and creative writing.

It is important to stress that this strategy does not *deny* or *block* the feelings but rather uses the feelings as a source of motivation and power. For example, the teacher or coach may say, "Okay team, now that you are mad, let's go out and get a touchdown!" "You know, Cathy, maybe it would help you to spend some time in the art room on the kickwheel. You might feel better if you could put some of your energy into throwing a few pots." "I think Mr. Donnelli needs some help in the auditorium with the light fixtures. Maybe if you would work with him for some time this morning you'd feel like you've accomplished something. I know when I feel confused, helping someone else always makes me feel like I have a little more control over things."

Teacher Strategy Four: Accepting Disappointment and Failure

Disappointment and failure are natural and inevitable conditions of interpersonal and family life, and little can be done to prevent students from experiencing frustration by others. However, it is important for teachers to help students learn that their stress is not due to their *badness* or *inadequacy*. Many times the focus is to help students develop a greater capacity for enduring upsetting or disappointing life events without falling apart. This can be promoted by teaching students to accept a normal amount of hostility from others.

Unfortunately, many middle-class students have an unrealistic expectation that people should be nice, kind, sympathetic, courteous, and fair. When they experience an action of rejection, a lack of confidence, and/or a blast of verbal abuse, they may perceive it as a personal offense instead of accepting it as a reasonable amount of hostility that people must learn to expect from each other. If the student does not overreact to this behavior, the stress cycle can be stopped. Teachers can help students to expect some negative feelings from all relationships, even those with their closest friends.

Another meaningful way of coping with stress is to accept defeat. "I know it's really hard to lose after you've worked so hard to win. You've been practicing that speech every afternoon, and we all thought you were excellent at the contest on Saturday. I know how much you wanted to win, and I know you feel bad. But I also know you learned a lot about contests and you'll never have to go through your 'first one' ever again. Next time you'll be a veteran and not so afraid of the unknown. You really did get something from that experience." The teacher must give the student the message: "You have done everything possible to improve your situation but right now you are going to have to live with it. You are a fine person and need to be proud of your skills. It will be difficult at times, but I believe you have the strength to tolerate it."

Teacher Strategy Five: Completing One Task at a Time

When too many stresses and responsibilities build up, the collective view becomes gigantic, and many students panic into a state of helplessness and frozen behavior. They feel as if they've been handed a ball of string tangled in a hundred knots and told to straighten it out in sixty seconds. Where can they begin? The task seems impossible! After a few attempts, they sink into total hopelessness. A helpful strategy is to assist the student to reduce the task to a manageable unit of work. Just as a thousand-mile trip must begin with one small step, the skill of coping involves selecting one concrete task and completing it within a day. This single action generates new energy, hope, and productivity. It reflects the basic law of inertia: A body in motion stays in motion, while a body at rest stays at rest.

The teacher may say: "Right now it seems as if you have a lot of problems that you're dealing with. Sometimes when you have so many things to think about it's hard to know where to start. You might feel that it's just too much—they can't all be solved at once. You're right! It helps to start with one area and work on that one alone for awhile, until it's cleared up. Then you'll start to feel a little better and get the energy to move on to the next. We all need to feel we have control over our lives. Doing one task at a time gives us order and a sense of control. Let's begin by doing one task that you can complete by tomorrow."

Teacher Strategy Six: Reducing Stress by Helping Less Fortunate Students

Opportunities to wallow in feelings of self-pity, grief, and anger are available to everyone. Many middle-class students have little appreciation of the multiple pains of life, and they can overreact to normal developmental stresses—failing an exam, being rejected by a girlfriend or boyfriend, not being selected for a team, etc.—as if these were disasters rather than disappointments. These students can derive many benefits from helping less fortunate and younger students:

1. The experiences force the students to realize that there are others whose problems are more complex and stressful than their own. When they observe the coping skills of these students, the helping students may see their own problems diminish in size and importance.

2. The process of helping others enhances the helper's feelings of self-worth while concurrently diminishing the need for self-depreciation.

3. The process of helping pushes the helper to focus on the present and future rather than analyzing the past.

A teacher may say, "You know, Richard, I think it's sort of hard for you to understand that life isn't always exactly the way you'd like it to be. I know you'd like everything to work out and be pleasant. I think it would be an interesting experience for you to get to know Peter in Mrs. Kellogg's classroom. He's younger than you and needs some help in reading. Since his illness he has fallen a month behind in his English assignments. Maybe you could spend a half hour with him a couple of times a week. I know that he will appreciate it. You might help him figure out how to catch up."

Teacher Strategy Seven: Separating from the Setting

One of humanity's basic survival mechanisms is flight. When stress becomes a huge red alarm, one way of coping is to leave the stressful environment temporarily. To withdraw to a more supportive environment to rest, play, and think, alone or with others, is a useful technique. The notion that a person can be "too close to the trees to see the forest" is applicable. It is our belief that physical distance between the stressful setting and the student frequently provides the needed psychological condition for problem solving. Free from the pressures of the situation, the student is better able to think through the situation.

"Sometimes, Sherry, it makes good sense to get some time away from a problem to regain a little strength. Didn't you tell me your Girl Scout troop was planning a backpacking trip? Maybe a few days away from all the concerns you have, would give you a break from the chaos. You might even have a better picture of the situation at home when you come back."

"You know, Andy, maybe it's a good time for you to visit your grandfather for the weekend. You've been talking about how long it's been since you two visited together. I bet a few days at the lake would not only give you a chance to visit with him but also give you some energy to deal with these problems here. I think everyone needs time away from what seem like overwhelming problems to restore themselves a little. Sometimes a little distance from the problem brings you closer to a solution."

Teacher Strategy Eight: Helping the Student Seek Professional Help

When stress becomes chronic and overwhelming, teachers are in the right position to refer a student for psychological services or to encourage a parent to seek professional mental health assistance for the child. All too often, parents and children who are unhappy and dissatisfied with life perceive asking for professional help as an obvious sign of personal weakness and inferiority. They become ashamed of needing help and spend their time denying and avoiding the problem situation. Teachers can be helpful by reflecting the view that the decision to call the local community mental health center or a private psychotherapist is painful but takes personal courage, maturity, and insight. The teacher can stress the parents' conviction their child should be helped to feel more comfortable with self and the world.

Initially, students are anxious about going to therapy, but once they learn that the therapy sessions are confidential, the fear subsides and the students begin the process of discovering the support, catharsis, and power of therapy. It is the most loving gift a parent can give a child and one that a teacher can support.

The Coping Cycle

The next example illustrates how the stress cycle can be changed into a coping cycle when teachers decode their pupils' problems, label and accept their feelings, and find ways for the students to give expression to these feelings in socially approved ways in school.

Example 2: The Coping Cycle

Mary is a nine-year-old student in the fourth grade. She attends a resource room one hour per day for remedial reading. She is an anxious, frightened girl with obvious feelings of inferiority. Her parents are getting divorced, and her mother will be moving the children to a small town.

Stress 1	Mary is upset by the divorce and the tension in the home. She is also angry about leaving her friends and activities, and she is worried about living in a "small stupid town."
Feelings	Depression and anger.
Behavior	Sullenness. Inability to concentrate on classroom assignments. Withdrawal from activities and friends.
Teacher reaction	Notices recent change in behavior (unaware of the family problem). Begins to decode behavior. "You are looking quite sad today, is something troubling you?"
Stress 2	Psychological stress: Mary thinks, "Why is she meddling into my life?"
Feelings	Irritation.
Behavior	"I'm fine. I'm okay. There is nothing wrong!"
Teacher reaction	"I hear your words, but your body tells me something else. Perhaps this is not the time to talk about it." Teacher backs off to give pupil some comfort.

Next Day

Stress 3	Developmental stress: Mary thinks, "Perhaps she can help me."
Feelings	Depressed, detached.
Behavior	Cannot complete assignment.
Teacher reaction	"When someone I know as well as you starts staring into space and looking sad, then my eyes tell me that you are troubled by something."
Coping Cycle 1	Begins to feel teacher can be trusted.
Feelings	Sad but feeling adult support.
Behavior	Tells the teacher about the divorce, her mother's plans to move, etc.
Teacher reaction	(Decodes) "It's painful and difficult. It must be upsetting. Most important, it is normal to have these feelings of sadness and anger. It's okay." (In addition, the teacher must talk about the difficulty of leaving friends and activities and the anxiety about going to a new place.)
Coping Cycle 2	Feels emotional support.
Feelings	Appreciation for being understood by the teacher.
Behavior	"I still find it hard to study."
Teacher reaction	"I understand that, but now that we have talked about it, I think that you will be able to concentrate more. Before you leave, Mary, we will arrange for you to get everyone's home addresses. Perhaps you can take some photos and write a story about this school. When you're settled in your new school, please write us a letter and tell us all about it."

In this example, the teacher was able to avoid the power struggle and to help the pupil cope with her separation problems in a more positive way in school. This is our goal.

Summary

Stressful home, school, and community experiences can influence a pupil's ability to learn and behave appropriately in the classroom. Teachers can use stress, however, to teach coping skills and concepts, such as:

1. Stress is a natural and acceptable part of life.

2. Stress is not necessarily good or bad; the effect of it depends on the frequency, intensity, and duration.

3. Some pupils experience multiple stresses—developmental, economic, psychological, and reality stresses.

4. During stress some pupils become flooded by their feelings and behave inappropriately.

5. During stress, some pupils are unable to help themselves and will respond negatively to adult help and support.

6. During stress, pupils can create their own feelings in teachers and, if the teachers are not well trained, also their behaviors.

7. If the stress cycle follows its normal pattern, the stressful incident will end up as an intense power struggle between teacher and pupil.

8. When a power struggle develops, neither pupil nor teacher is a winner.

9. To change this stress cycle to a coping cycle, teachers must have the ability to:

   a. be in touch with their feelings;

   b. recognize that these feelings originally came from the pupil;

c. verbalize their own feelings;

d. decode the pupil's feelings;

e. support the pupil's feelings but not the pupil's inappropriate behavior;

f. show how coping with a difficult situation leads to feelings of competence, success, and pride;

g. demonstrate a feeling of hope and not helplessness about life;

h. reduce stress by lowering school standards;

i. reduce stress by redirecting the pupil's feelings into acceptable behavior;

j. reduce stress by helping the pupil to accept disappointment and failure;

k. reduce stress by helping the pupil to complete one task at a time;

l. reduce stress by having the pupil help less fortunate students;

m. reduce stress by separating the pupil from the setting; and

n. reduce stress by having the pupil seek professional help.

Editors' Commentary

The next article, by Stanley Fagen, is an elaboration of how teachers can teach troubled pupils to cope with frustration in terms of modifying their goals, trying new paths to the goals, and identifying positives in self. This article is an excellent example of how to break down a general psychological concept like frustration into understandable and specific instructional skills.

Adaptive Frustration Management

Stanley A. Fagen

Adaptive frustration management can be characterized as having three major facets: (1) attitudes and perceptions associated with the goal-thwarting or frustrating experience, (2) coping behaviors available to the individual, following the frustration, and, (3) tolerance for experiencing frustration

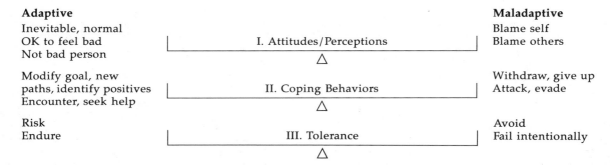

Adaptive		Maladaptive
Inevitable, normal		Blame self
OK to feel bad	I. Attitudes/Perceptions	Blame others
Not bad person	△	
Modify goal, new		Withdraw, give up
paths, identify positives	II. Coping Behaviors	Attack, evade
Encounter, seek help	△	
Risk		Avoid
Endure	III. Tolerance	Fail intentionally
	△	

Figure 1. Three Facets of Adaptive Frustration Management

(Fagen, Long and Stevens, 1975, ch. 11). Figure 1 depicts the three facets of adaptive frustration management.

Attitudes and Perceptions

A primary frustration reaction for many young children is either rage or helplessness. As children grow older, they learn to attach words and ideas to their experience with the result that others or self are seen as at fault. The blaming others perception is often a correlate of aggressive, acting out behavior, whereas blaming self is associated with inhibited, withdrawn behavior.

Blaming self or blaming others are not necessarily mutually exclusive. To the contrary, the two perceptions or attitudes are frequently dynamically related to one another, as when hating others is used as a defense against the pain of hating oneself. Such a relationship is depicted by Sanford and Comstock (1971):

> The disposition of destructiveness is not inborn but is generated out of experience and learning in a social environment . . . Fundamentally, its source is inner conflict, which leads to a need to get rid of what is all too human in oneself. If this badness is felt to be located in the self, a person may become self-destructive; but, often, he may ascribe the badness to other people . . . (p. 331)

Unfortunately, much of our social learning and modeling emphasizes placing blame for not achieving goals. Parents and teachers constantly criticize children for "not trying," "being careless," "being stupid," etc. Or, parents blame teachers, teachers blame parents, and so on. Children are taught that someone *must* be at fault when frustration occurs, and, of course, they become experts in blaming by the time they reach 2nd and 3rd grade.

It is possible, however, to reeducate youngsters so as to promote adaptive perceptions of frustration. This can be accomplished by helping students to acknowledge their upset feelings without reinforcing faultfinding. Helpful comments might be: "I know you're really upset about it," "Things like this happen a lot. I got angry when all those PA announcements came on when I was talking," "Look, you tried darn hard and have a right to feel bad. But you're all right." Positive teaching points are those which (a) share or empathize with the student's feelings, (b) confirm the normalcy of feeling bad, (c) support the worth of the student despite the failure to reach the goal, and, (d) foster appreciation for the necessity or inevitability of frustration. As students begin to regard thwarting of their wants as acceptable, rather than as a time for depreciating someone, they are able to assimilate the experience into their lives and move on to further efforts.

Coping Behaviors

Children with serious emotional problems are usually woefully lacking in resources for coping with stress. Perceiving themselves as incapable, defective, or victimized, there is little left to do but escape from the situation as quickly as possible. Escape routes may take the attacking–evading form of loud outbursts, throwing things, cursing, or running away. Or, they may follow withdrawal–defeat behaviors, such as giving up, sobbing, staring into space, shrinking into a corner, or refusing to talk. Each frustration can precipitate a crisis in self-esteem, trust, and peer relations, since emotional controls are likely to be marginal and perceptual distortions are prevalent.

To promote adaptive coping behaviors for these students, the teacher must first have a firm hold on coping resources within self. The abruptness and explosiveness of the child present a tremendous challenge to the teacher's own capacity to maintain self-control. It is natural for the child's teacher to experience intense counter-aggression, helplessness, or discouragement. Thus, the teacher must quickly process the child's distress and cope adaptively with his or her own frustration before being able to help the child. In other words, positive coping behaviors must first be internalized on the part of the teacher if the child is to be successfully taught new alternatives.

Given that frustration must occur, the question becomes how to cope with it effectively. Effective coping is defined as "behavior which promotes positive change in self or environment, i.e., change which maintains or heightens self-esteem, prospects for successful striving towards constructive goals, or understanding and helpfulness between self and others" (Fagen and Hill, 1977, p. 179).

Two major strategies are available for adaptively coping with frustration experiences: (1) self or internal change, and (2) environmental or external change. That is, the frustration may be managed by modifying one's own personal behavior or by seeking assistance from another person(s).

1. Self (Internal) Change

Three basic classes of behavior are available within the self (internal) change strategy, namely: (a) modifying goals, (b) trying new paths to the goal, and, (c) identifying positives in self.

Modifying Goals. It is not possible or desirable to set goals in advance for which success is assured. Sensitive teachers strive to prescribe learner goals or objectives which represent a "reasonable challenge," necessitating a "stretch" upwards for the student. Often, the student attains the desired objective and consequently gains in personal satisfaction and esteem. Just as often, however, the student falls short of the goal as a result of ability limitations or uncontrollable natural obstacles (e.g., space, time, physical, or communication). The exact same factors pertain to the teacher's own goal setting for self. In fact, when one considers the teacher–student relationship, it becomes evident that, for the conscientious teacher, any student frustration is in some way a teacher frustration, as well.

In falling short of an initial goal, a person may choose to modify this goal in one of several ways: (a) *select a partial* or *sub-goal* and recognize that progress has occurred. For example, a student is striving to obtain an A by answering 10 problems correctly. After a good try, he correctly answers only 7 and earns a C. The student can revise his goal of 10, bring it to 7, and reflect on the fact that 7 correct was better than he had done previously; (b) *clarify and prioritize the goal importance.* The stu-

dent could decide that getting an A was not as important as improving in a different subject. Conversely, the student might be helped to recognize that achieving an A means a great deal to him and, therefore, that additional time and effort may be necessary to accomplish the goal. Developing a plan for attaining this end would follow as a next step toward positively coping with the initial frustration; (c) *postpone or cancel the goal.* It is important to understand that some goals may need to be postponed or canceled. Teachers, like students, usually are simultaneously engaged in multiple goal-seeking. At any given point in time a teacher may be struggling to accomplish a host of tasks, such as: formulating a lesson plan, arranging the room, doing some reading on a particular subject, consulting with a colleague, calling a parent, completing some forms, preparing for a PTA meeting, grading class papers, etc. To the extent that all goals are given equal importance within a narrow time span, futility and frustration must result.

Trying New Paths to the Goal. Another technique for coping with frustration is to maintain the desired goal but alter the method used to reach the goal, i.e., find a new way around the obstacle. This coping mechanism requires an openness to alternative and unfamiliar actions. Emotionally handicapped youth are known, however, for their lack of behavioral freedom and for their tendency to employ a restricted and inflexible range of reactions, particularly in times of stress. Introduction of possibilities for new paths to a goal must occur in the context of an empathic and trusting relationship. In addition, students must know the potential risks or gains from using a new path.

For example, John constantly sought to achieve a prominent place in his peer group. To accomplish this he yelled out, came late, interrupted others, and boasted about his deeds. Through conferencing with John, it became evident that new paths were available. John agreed to try gaining group importance by praising others and offering help to the group if it were requested. He was surprised to learn that other students came to notice and accept him far more when he was supportive than aggressive.

New paths can be explored and tried through various supportive strategies such as life space interviewing, e.g., "new tool-salesmanship" (Redl, 1959), training in behavior principles to increase acceptance by others (Graubard and Rosenberg, 1974), and peer group counseling (Berg and Johnson, 1971). Regardless of the strategy used for identifying a new path, it is important to create a relaxed optimism about trying out something new.

Follow-up support will be necessary to provide for further adjustments or modifications to the new paths.

Identifying Positives in Self. Reactions to the experience of frustration frequently include temporary declines in self-evaluation (cf. Diggory, 1966). For example, the child who wants to read aloud but cannot has an immediate feeling of stupidity; the teenager who asks a girl for a date and is turned down has an immediate feeling of unattractiveness; the teacher who wants to command class respect but finds noise, disorder, and backtalk has an immediate feeling of incompetence.

Frustration experiences signal times when one's own real self is apt to be lower than one's ideal self, and thus represent low points in self-esteem. The more important the goal that is thwarted, the greater the blow to self-esteem. Adaptive coping requires that these blows to self-esteem be absorbed and shaken off so that renewal of esteem can take place. On the other hand, maladaptive coping means a prolonged focussing on preoccupation with one's deficiencies, making it extremely difficult to strive or risk again.

Identifying positives in self may enable one to break free of negative self-messages and get back in touch with the "OK" core of one's existence. To reexperience own positives, exercises or activities may be employed which: (a) focus on existing strengths and sources of pride, (b) demonstrate that failure in one goal does not mean total inadequacy, (c) strengthen appreciation for own best efforts, and (d) reaffirm interests and desires for enjoyment in other life areas.

Students may be helped to see positives despite the wound to self-esteem through such means as how others view their strengths ("strength bombardment"), having the opportunity to use a strong skill, hearing appreciation for the real effort, and encouragement to enjoy a satisfying personal interest or pursuit.

2. Environmental (External) Change

In addition to the possibilities for coping by self-change, frustration can be effectively resolved by seeking to effect change or help from the environment. Two basic classes of coping behavior may promote environmental change: (1) encountering the frustration source, and (2) seeking help and assistance.

Encountering the Source. The term "encountering" is intended to mean the direct sharing of one's own thoughts and feelings with the person(s) viewed as responsible for presenting an obstacle to reaching one's goal. Encountering requires that the individual experiencing frustration must first take ownership of his or her own feelings by accepting and identifying these feelings by sending a clear "I message" to the intended receiver (Gordon, 1971). In its purest form the encountering "I message" describes both a strong existing feeling and the reason for this feeling. For example, "I am mad because you did not call on me," "I feel good because you smiled at me," "I feel like quitting because the work is too hard for me." These "I messages" are in marked contrast to communications which blame others for the discomfort one feels. Examples of "you-blaming" messages are: "You are being unfair," "You're always telling us what to do," "I'm disgusted because you're so dumb."

Encountering the source of frustration is the first step in creating a meaningful and constructive dialogue, which hopefully can lead to a more mutual fulfillment of wants and goals. Preparing a student or staff member to effectively execute the first step, however, does not assure a constructive resolution of differences. All too often we have seen how receivers are unable to accept the genuineness or forcefulness of the "I message" and become threatened. Many times, staff have lacked the communication skills to constructively respond to students. In effect, encountering the source of frustration may result in additional frustration which then needs to be handled through seeking help, or self-change strategies.

Emotionally disturbed children have a great deal of difficulty encountering others constructively. Some may attack with very clear expressions of emotion, verbal or otherwise. Others may be totally unable to acknowledge their own feelings. Almost all such students will be reluctant to risk learning to encounter others due to their anxiety about possible harm from emotional release (whether that potential harm is attributed to own explosiveness or to another's reaction).

A gradual, continuous process of emotional reeducation is essential for these students. Teachers with excellent communications and counseling skills can, through patient and trusting relationships, promote the development of encountering skills for students with emotional problems (Fagen and Guedalia, 1977). We have found that the model of sending effective "I messages" can, to a large extent, be regarded as a criterion for emotional growth and development. That is, as students learn to encounter others constructively they are also overcoming their emotional problems.

Seeking Help and Assistance. As obvious as this method of coping appears to be, far too many youngsters avoid its use. Invariably in every classroom there are a few students who create disruptions as a behavior equivalent for getting help. For example, the student who bothers others when he cannot understand the task directions; the student who destroys or damages objects when the fine motor demands exceed his tolerance level; the student who daydreams when she's not sure what to do next. The sensitive teacher can spot these students. Through caring inquiry into their concerns or feelings, the teacher can usually identify the point at which a student needs help. As long as the teacher does not make the child feel infantile or inadequate for needing help, it is usually a simple matter to arrange a means for the child to signal the need for help or assistance. Signals have included such things as: raising one's hand, clasping hands on desk and looking up, tugging at an ear, sitting in a rocking chair, and going to a "help station."

Class norms will greatly influence the ease with which students seek help. Classes which have developed an acceptance and appreciation for differences will display open sharing of help. One very successful mainstreaming program has a motto: "It is dumb not to get help."

Tolerance

Once children believe that they have resources for accepting and coping with frustration, it is possible to build their tolerance level for frustration by promoting awareness of the multiple, natural obstacles which occur during their daily experiences. Everyday obstacles may be *physical* (e.g., a wall, a person in the way, a desk), *temporal* (e.g., lack of time to finish a task), *interpersonal or communications* (e.g., speaking too low, not listening), or *cognitive* (e.g., complex instructions, high level vocabulary words).

Teachers need not feel guilty about the presence of such obstacles in the classroom, since it is impossible to create an obstacle-free environment. However, the teacher should be alert for these obstacles and be ready to positively reinforce students for their willingness to endure or persist in the face of these obstacles. The opportunities for such reinforcement are unlimited. A few illustrations are: "Good Sally. You were able to wait until they got out of your way"; "I'm pleased that you did not get upset when Roger bumped into your desk"; "Thank you for repeating your question. I was distracted"; "Children, you were so good about stopping your drawings this morning that we will have a special game this afternoon."

Mastery activities can be conducted in the classroom to demonstrate the students' ability to tolerate frustrating situations. Thus, activities can be arranged which expose the students to a variety of obstacles. The shared aspect of facing common frustrations, as well as a game-like format, promote an atmosphere in which children can feel challenged without being threatened.

Summary

This paper is based on the fact that stress is a fundamental aspect of living. As Selye (1975) has found, "wear and tear" of the body is constantly occurring and determines the rate of aging. As long as people continue to strive towards fulfillment of goals, we are vulnerable to experiences of frustration and concomitant emotional drain. Adaptive management of frustration can minimize emotional wear and tear and thus prolong the quality and enjoyment of life. On the other hand, maladaptive responses to frustration will prolong emotional agitation and the maintenance of self-defeating reactions of helplessness/self-blame and rage/blaming others.

Adaptive frustration management can be taught and learned—to teacher trainers first, next to teachers, and then to children. Three major facets of frustration management have been sequentially presented: (1) attitudes/perceptions, (2) coping behaviors, and (3) tolerance. Concepts and general teaching strategies have been described with the hope that a total perspective for managing frustration will facilitate teacher development. It is envisioned that teachers of emotionally disturbed children will need to provide leadership for regular teachers in helping students to constructively manage disturbing negative emotions—emotions which so normally and inevitably result from caring enough to try.

References

Berg, Robert, and Johnson, James. *Group Counseling: A Sourcebook of Theory and Practice.* Fort Worth, Texas: American Continental, 1971.

Diggory, James. *Self-Evaluation: Concepts and Studies.* New York: John Wiley, 1966.

Fagen, Stanley, and Guedalia, Leonard. *Individual and Group Counseling: A Competency-Based Manual for In-Service Training.* Washington, D.C.: Psychoeducational Resources, 1977.

Fagen, Stanley, and Hill, Jeffery. *Behavior Management: A Competency-Based Manual for In-Service Training.* Washington, D.C.: Psychoeducational Resources, 1977.

Fagen, Stanley; Long, Nicholas; and Stevens, Donald. *Teaching Children Self-Control: Preventing Emotional and Learning Problems in the Elementary School.* Columbus, Ohio: Charles Merrill, 1975.

Gordon, Thomas. *Parent Effectiveness Training.* New York: Peter Wyden, 1971.

Graubard, Paul, and Rosenberg, Harry. *Classrooms that Work: Prescriptions for Change.* New York: Dutton, 1974.

Redl, Fritz, "The Concept of the Life Space Interview." American Journal of Orthopsychiatry, 29, 1959, 1–18.

Sanford, Nevitt, and Comstock, Craig. *Sanctions for Evil: Sources of Social Destructiveness.* San Francisco: Jossey-Bass, 1971.

Selye, Hans. "The Stress of Life." In *Human Life Cycle,* edited by W. C. Sze, pp. 589–598. New York: Jason Aronson, 1975.

Excerpted from a paper published in *Proceedings of a Conference on Preparing Teachers to Foster Personal Growth in Emotionally Disturbed Students,* Advanced Institute for Trainers of Teachers for Seriously Emotionally Disturbed Children: University of Minnesota, May 29–31, 1977. Used here by permission of the author.

Editors' Commentary

When a pupil teases others, falls out of the chair, makes funny sounds, swears, refuses to complete an assignment, etc. the teacher needs some additional techniques that have been field-tested. In the next article, Nicholas Long and Ruth Newman apply Fritz Redl's four-notched scale[2] to classroom management. These techniques are not new, but they are well organized here to be helpful to teachers. The article highlights nine therapeutic reasons for interfering with pupil behavior and twelve teacher strategies for stopping, modifying, or redirecting inappropriate behavior.

2. **Fritz Redl,** training notes, Child Research Branch, National Institute of Mental Health, Bethesda, Maryland, 1957.

Managing Surface Behavior of Children in School

Nicholas J. Long
Ruth G. Newman

There are four major alternatives to handling behavior. They are: permitting, tolerating, interfering, and preventive planning. Redl emphasizes that no one of these alternatives is better than any of the others. The task is to find the right combination of techniques for each child.

Permitting Behavior

Most rules in a school are made to inhibit and regulate the impulsive behavior of children. During the day, they are told in many ways to stop, slow down, and control their behavior. No one would argue against the importance of these rules in a group setting. If it is important for children to know what they cannot do, it is equally important for children to know that they can do. For example, children should be told that it is permissible to run, shout, and scream on the playground, to be messy when they are fingerpainting, to have some degree of movement within the classroom, to go to the lavatory when necessary, to show some freedom of expression in their creative works, and to express an opposing view without being ridiculed or chastised. Children are reassured when they know in advance that their activities will not meet with adult frowns, shouts, or physical interference. More important, the sanctioning of behavior by adults eliminates much of the children's unnecessary testing of limits. A teacher who permits children to leave their desks and go to the book corner after they have finished the assignment should make this privilege clear. Then a child does not have to sneak a book and feel guilty about it or feel victorious about squeezing more freedom from the teacher than the child thinks he would expect.

Tolerating Behavior

A lot of classroom behavior must be tolerated, but children should have no reason to believe that teachers approve or sanction it. The more common basic assumptions behind tolerating behavior are (1) learner's leeway, (2) behavior that reflects a developmental stage, and (3) behavior that is symptomatic of a disease.

1.   *Learner's leeway.* Whenever a child is learning a new concept, experimenting with ideas, or trying to win status in the group, the teacher should expect that the child will make mistakes. He should not expect that the child will do it perfectly. For example, many sensitive teachers tell their class that they are not going to be upset when children err in trying to master new academic and social skills. With some groups, the more mistakes they make, i.e., on an arithmetic assignment, the easier it is for the teacher to help them clarify their misunderstandings. This was found to be true in the following incident:

I have noticed that Carole (third grader) became very upset if she made a mistake on an assignment. The children were writing to a railroad company for some free material, but they did not know how to address an envelope. I went to the board and showed them the proper form and asked them to practice. In a little while I noticed that Carole had her head on her desk. When I asked her what was the matter, she said that she couldn't do it and that she already had made three mistakes. I asked her to show me her work. (She had misspelled one word, did not capitalize one of the words, and had the return address crowded up on the upper left-hand corner.) I told Carole that these are the kinds of mistakes that many boys and girls make and that I did not expect her or any of the other children to do it perfectly the first three or four times that they tried. With this encouragement, she started again.

Sometimes it is helpful to talk about "good mistakes" versus "poor mistakes." A good mistake is made when a pupil's answer reflects some personal logic. A poor mistake is one which rests on impulsive behavior with no semblance of logic.

2.   *Behavior that reflects a developmental stage.* Some behavior is age typical and will change as the child becomes more mature. Any attempt on the part of the teacher to alter or inhibit this behavior results in such negligible changes that it usually is not worth the inevitable fight. For example, children in the early grades are impulse-ridden and motor-oriented. Every kindergarten teacher knows this and has accepted the fact that very little can be done about it except tolerate it. This state of tolerance should not be confused with sanctioning it or permitting wild behavior. Another example is that children in the late third or early fourth grade, caught between group pressure and allegiance to the teacher, are notorious for tattling; e.g., "Miss Jones, Johnny hit Mary," or "Johnny pulled a leaf off your flower when you were in the hall." Other illustrations of age-typical behavior are the unscrubbed, unhygienic appearance of the preadolescent boy, the primping of sixth-grade girls, the secrets of preadolescent girls, and the sex language and behavior of adolescent boys. A classroom example of age-typical behavior is presented below:

At noon, several fifth-grade girls came bursting into the room relating a story about the fifth-grade boys. The boys had discovered several pictures of nude women which were hidden in a bush on the playground. In small groups, they were examining the pictures in detail when a few of the fifth-grade girls "worked their way in" to see what was taking place. The girls screamed and found their way to my room. They related the story; then the bell rang.

The boys entered (without pictures), as though nothing had happened. Silence prevailed. They knew that I knew. Finally, I asked one of the boys where the pictures were. He explained that they had hidden them in the bushes and planned to secure them after school for more detailed study. I asked another of the boys to bring the pictures into the room. This he did and I, without looking, threw them in the wastebasket.

Then we discussed the situation, emphasizing the value of good literature. The children themselves brought out the idea that such material was available at all newsstands and that anyone could buy it; however, the individual who is attempting to be a good citizen will by-pass such trash. Even the curious boys agreed with the majority viewpoint.

The pictures remained in the wastebasket until after school. Several students sought me out at the teacher's desk, casting glances at the wastebasket all the while. Others, whom I had never seen before, entered the room and quickly left upon finding me there.

Next morning the wastebasket was empty; the pictures were gone. I didn't see them again until I entered the boiler room, where they were on the wall—property of the school janitor.

3. *Behavior that is symptomatic of an illness.* When a child has a respiratory infection, the chances are that he will cough in class and that the symptom (coughing) will continue until the child is well. This cause and effect relationship is accepted among teachers; however, when a child who is emotionally disturbed shows the symptoms of his illness, such as recurring temper tantrums, fights, and irrational fears, the child is likely to be unpopular with his classmates, his teacher, and even with himself. A psychologically oriented teacher realizes that, when a child suffers from emotional problems, the symptoms are rarely conscious forms of meanness but are simply an explainable outlet for his intrapsychic conflicts. For example:

Some of the things that Martha did were fighting, tearing up other children's property, walking the floor constantly, tearing pages out of her book, name calling, and spitting. Although Martha makes me angry and caused all of us many problems, I feel we have grown a little in understanding that we all have problems and that the class is simply not divided into good and bad, accepted and unaccepted. Martha's behavior has improved during the year and, if I did anything to help it, I was doing it with kindness, firmness, and accepting her as an individual, rather than judging her on the basis of her actions.

Interfering with Behavior

While the psychologically trained teacher is aware of long-range goals and is sensitive to the child's core problems, the teacher still has to handle the spontaneous behavior that occurs in the classroom. Some behavior has to be stopped if the classroom learning is to take place. A child cannot continue to act out all of his feelings. The task is to find ways of interfering with the behavior so that it does not disrupt the group greatly but still may be helpful to the particular child. Redl and Wineman in *The Aggressive Child* have listed 21 specific influence techniques that they have been able to identify in their work with aggressive boys. Twelve of these techniques will be developed as they apply to the positive management of children by the classroom teacher.

Before suggesting ways of intervening, the question of when a teacher should intervene needs to be considered. While this question cannot be settled without considering many variables, school psychologists have observed that too many teachers never set limits or intervene until they are choked with counter-aggressive feelings toward a child. When this happens, the teacher is likely to intervene in a way which is unhygienic and too severe. On the other hand, teachers have not been given any guidelines to help them with this difficult problem. They are not really sure whether they should interfere in a particular bit of behavior. Once again Redl gives us the direction and suggests the following criteria for intervention.

1. *Reality dangers.* Adults are usually more reality-oriented than children and have had more practice predicting the consequences of certain acts. If children are playing some crazy game, fighting, or playing with matches so that it looks as if they might injure themselves, then the teacher moves in and stops the behavior.

2. *Psychological protection.* Just as the adult protects the child from being physically hurt, he also should protect the child from psychological injury. If a group of boys is ganging up on a child, or scapegoating him, or using derogatory racial nicknames, then the teacher should intervene. The teacher does not support or condone this behavior and the values it reflects.

3. *Protection against too much excitement.* Sometimes a teacher intervenes in order to avoid the development of too much excitement, anxiety, and guilt in children. For example, if a game is getting out of hand and continues another 10 minutes, the children may lose control, mess up, and feel very unhappy about their behavior later. Once again, the teacher should intervene to stop this cycle from developing.

4. *Protection of property.* This is almost too obvious to mention, but sometimes it is easy to overlook. Children are not allowed to destroy or damage the school property, equipment, or building. When the teacher sees this, he moves in quickly and stops it. But at no time does he give the impression so common in our society that property is more important than people. Protecting property protects people.

5. *Protection of an on-going program.* Once a class is motivated in a particular task and the children have an investment in its outcome, it is not fair to have it ruined by one child who is having some difficulty. In this case, the teacher intervenes and asks this child to leave or to move next to him in

order to insure that the enjoyment, satisfaction, and learning of the group are unimpaired.

6. *Protection against negative contagion.* When a teacher is aware that tension is mounting in the classroom and a child with high social power begins tapping his desk with his pencil, the teacher might ask him to stop in order to prevent this behavior from spreading to the other students and disrupting the entire lesson.

7. *Highlighting a value area or school policy.* There are times when a teacher interferes in some behavior not because it is dangerous or disturbing but because he wishes to illustrate a school policy or rule which may lie slightly below the surface of the behavior. For example, he might want to illustrate why it is impossible for everyone to be first in line, or to point out how a misunderstanding develops when there is no intent to lie or to distort a situation. The focus is on poor communication.

8. *Avoiding conflict with the outside world.* The outside world in school can mean neighboring classrooms or the public. It is certainly justifiable to expect more control on the part of your children when they are attending an assembly or are on a trip than when they are in their classroom.

9. *Protecting a teacher's inner comfort.* Inner comfort is not the first thing to be considered by a teacher. If it is, he is in the wrong profession. For example, if a certain type of behavior makes a teacher feel exceptionally uncomfortable, the behavior may not need to be totally inhibited, but the teacher may have to learn to be more comfortable with it, whether he likes it or not.

It would be foolish, however, for a teacher, given limits of human endurance, to put himself in a situation in which he is abused constantly or serves as a punching bag for the class. This would not be healthy for anyone. The problem is to distinguish between behavior which is developmental or momentarily cathartic and behavior that is pathological in origin. Once a teacher recognizes his personal idiosyncrasies and realizes that he is overreacting to the behavior, in the long run, he might better stop the behavior than do nothing and inwardly reject the child.

It is obvious that a teacher does not consciously work through all these hygienic steps before deciding to stop a behavior. However, the nine points listed above can serve as a guide or reference point against which one can examine his actions. What makes this whole process challenging and complicated is that the child behaves in a way which, according to the proposed list, ought to be stopped but under certain psycho-physical conditions the teacher does not stop it. After all, life is flexible and usually cannot be condensed into an orderly list of psychological procedures.

What are some of the counter indications against interfering, assuming that the behavior is not dangerous? (1) The fuss that it would create at this time is not worth it! The group confusion that is certain to follow might disguise the real purpose of the interference. In such a case it might be better to wait for another time. There is a written guaranty that it will come. (2) The teacher decides to wait until the behavior deviates to the point where it is obvious not only to the child but also to the entire group. This way the child's typical defenses, such as projection, i.e., "You're always picking on me," or "I never get a fair deal," are clearly inappropriate. (3) The teacher is in too good a mood today. He cannot work up enough genuine concern to impress the child and/or the group with the seriousness of the child's behavior. While this feeling is a common one, it should not be the barometer for intervention.

Before returning to the discussion on how to stop inappropriate behavior, there is a need to impress upon the readers that the following techniques are designed to help a teacher maintain the surface behavior of children over some rough spots. They only are stop-gap methods and do not substitute for a well-designed program or replace the teacher's knowledge of individual and group psychology.

The 12 influence techniques to be discussed are planned ignoring, signal interference, proximity control, interest boosting, tension decontaminator through humor, hurdle help, restricting the classroom program, support from routine, direct appeal, removal of seductive objects, antiseptic bouncing, and physical restraint.

1. *Planned ignoring.* Much of children's behavior carries its own limited power and will soon exhaust itself if it is not replenished, especially if the behavior is designed to "get the teacher's goat." Assuming that the behavior will not spread to others, it might be wise for the teacher to ignore the behavior and not feed into the child's need for secondary gratification. In the following example, the teacher is aware of the underlying meaning of the boy's behavior.

One technique that I find successful is to ignore disruptive behavior. It works most successfully with Frank. When he starts dropping his pencils, or tapping his feet, I know that it is a signal that I had better get over there in a few minutes and help him. I have found, however, that if I confront him with this behavior, he usually argues with me and causes additional problems.

In this example, the teacher responds to the motivation of the behavior and not to the manifestations of the behavior.

2. *Signal interference.* Teachers have developed a variety of signals that communicate to the child a feeling of disapproval and control. These nonverbal techniques include such things as eye contact, hand gestures, tapping or snapping fingers, coughing or clearing one's throat, facial frowns, and body postures. Such non-verbal techniques seem to be most effective at the beginning stages of misbehavior.

When a student is acting up in a mild way, I have found that a glance in his direction will usually stop the behavior temporarily. Usually I do not have to look at a child for a long time before he is aware that I am looking at him. I have also found that this technique is most helpful with those students who like me. Another signal that I have used is to stand up from my desk when there is a lot of whispering. I hasten to add that there are some children who would have me stand and look at them all day without it helping them control their behavior one bit.

3. *Proximity control.* Every teacher knows how effective it is to stand near a child who is having some difficulty. Just as a crying infant will stop crying when he is picked up by his mother, although the actual source of discomfort still exists, the early elementary child usually can control his impulses if he is close to the teacher. The teacher operates as a source of protection, strength, and identification. As one of the teachers explains:

One technique I have found helpful is to walk among the children. As I walk down the rows, I help the children having trouble with their work, or I give the bored ones something else to do. My closeness and help show that I am interested and concerned. It creates a better atmosphere and rapport and diminishes problems. I have found it very helpful and more effective than just standing behind the desk and telling them what to do. When I have a child who needs more than the usual help, I usually put his desk close to mine so that we are both aware of each other.

There are some children who not only need to have an adult close by but who also need the adult to touch them before they are able to control their impulses. This is done by having the teacher put his hand gently on the child's shoulder. This action should not be confused with the teacher who leaves five red marks after he has made physical contact with the child.

The advantages of these three techniques, planned ignoring, signal interference, and proximity control, are that they do not embarrass or even identify the child in the group. The teacher may use all three of these techniques while maintaining his classroom program.

4. *Interest boosting.* If a child's interest is waning and he is showing signs of restlessness, it is sometimes helpful for the teacher to show some genuine interest in the child's classroom assignment, asking whether problem 10 was very hard for him or mentioning his personal interest in athletics, cars, etc. Tapping a child's area of interest may help him mobilize his forces and view the teacher as a person whom he wants to please. One teacher described an experience with a child with whom he used this technique as follows:

Craig was crazy about dinosaurs. He read about them; he drew pictures of them; and he even had a plastic collection of them. As you can guess, Craig was a problem. He did not bother the boys or girls or defy me, but he would spend his class time either daydreaming or else drawing pictures of dinosaurs. I talked to him many times about this and he promised to stop, but the following day he was back at his drawings. I decided that if I could not fight him, perhaps I could join him in his interest. That night I spent the evening reading the Encyclopaedia Britannica. *The next day I told Craig that I was very interested in dinosaurs, too, and even had a course in college that studied them. Craig was somewhat skeptical of my comment, but after I mentioned some vital statistics about dinosaurs he was impressed that I was an expert in the field. Together we studied dinosaurs but structured the work so that it would only take place after he had completed his regular assignments.*

5. *Tension decontamination through humor.* There is nothing new about this technique. Everyone is aware of how a humorous comment is able to penetrate a tense and anxiety-producing situation. It clears the air and makes everyone feel more comfortable. The example below shows how one teacher used this technique to advantage.

I walked into my room after lunch period to find several pictures on the chalk board with "teacher" written under each one. I went to the board and picked up a piece of chalk, first looking at the pictures and then at the class. You could have heard a pin drop! Then I walked over to one of the pictures and said that this one looked the most like me but needed some more hair, which I added. Then I went to the next one and said that they had forgotten my glasses so I added them, on the next one I suggested adding a big nose, and on the last one a longer neck. By this time the class was almost in hysterics. Then, seeing that the children were having such a good time and that I could not get them settled easily, I passed out drawing paper and suggested that they draw a picture of the funniest person they could make. It is amazing how original these pictures were.

This example illustrates the phenomenon of group testing. The pictures were put on the board to test the vulnerability of the teacher. Some teachers would have reacted with sarcasm. They might have said that this was infantile behavior and not becoming a fifth-grade class. Other teachers might have given the class extra work or administered a group punishment, such as denial of recess or free time. However, this teacher demonstrated that she was secure, that a drawing could not cause her to regress or to become counter-aggressive, and that she could be counted on during stressful periods. Here is another excellent example of tension decontamination:

As soon as I entered the room two students who had remained in the room during the playground period informed me that Stella and Mary had a fight in the girls' restroom and were at present being seen by the principal. Since both of these girls are good pupils and are well liked by the class, I imagined that they and the class were wondering what I would do when the two girls returned to the room. Fifteen or 20 minutes elapsed before the girls returned. They entered and took their seats and the room became very quiet. I closed my book, looked at one of the girls and said in a rasping voice of a fight announcer, "And in this corner we have Stella, weighing 78 pounds." Everyone laughed. The tension vanished and we proceeded with our work.

Once again humor was used to communicate to the class that everything was all right, that there was no need to worry about it, and that the children could relax and return to their lessons.

6. *Hurdle lessons.* Disturbing behavior is not always the result of some inner problem. Sometimes the child is frustrated by the immediate classroom assignment. He does not understand the teacher's directions or is blocked by the second or third step in a complicated long-division problem. Instead of asking for help and exposing himself to the teacher's wrath for not paying attention or for exhibiting his educational inadequacies, the child is likely to establish contact with his neighbors, find some interesting trinket in his pocket, or draw on his desk. In other words, he is likely to translate his frustrations into motor behavior. The solution is to provide the child with the help he needs before the situation gets to this stage, as was done in the following example.

Sonya was very stubborn and usually persisted in not doing her work. After making an assignment, I would give the students some time to work on it in class. I would walk around the room and casually stop at Sonya's desk. Noting that she had not started, I would ask her some of her ideas and would suggest that she write those thoughts on paper. She could do the work and would do it if I explained it to her and personally got her interested in it. If I let her alone, she would usually sit and begin filing her nails or looking at the boy next to her who would become quite flushed. While this technique meant more work for me, it finally paid off because, as soon as she began working, she worked without assistance and began making passing grades.

7. *Restructuring the classroom program.* How much can a teacher deviate from his scheduled program and still feel he is meeting his "teaching responsibilities"? Another way of asking this question is, "Does the teacher control the program, or does the program control the teacher?" For example, some teachers feel compelled to follow their class schedule with no "ifs," "ands," or "buts." Otherwise, they feel they cannot hope to complete the assigned course of study. Besides, they feel children must learn not to be affected by every passing emotion. They must learn how to concentrate even under undesirable circumstances. Other teachers voice a different position. They feel that the complexity of life and the many extenuating forces make it impossible to follow a standardized course. The task is not so much to teach children as to provide the conditions under which learning can take place. Perhaps these are straw arguments and the question that needs to be raised is, "Does restructuring a program ever facilitate learning?" "If so, under what conditions?" This takes the task out of the realm of "either-or" arguments and places it in the teacher's ability to predict the tension level of the class in terms of feelings of irritability, boredom, or excitement. If the teacher feels that the class is tense but that the tension is decreasing, he may decide not to redesign his program. However, if he decides that the tension needs to be drained off, i.e., verbalized or channelized, before the class can involve itself in the next assignment, he may

change his program immediately. Two interesting examples are presented below:

Shortly before a grade school basketball tournament I was forced to cancel basketball practice for the evening. This met with much disapproval from the team members. The lesson for civics that day concerned labor strikes. As I walked into the classroom, I detected the basketball boys were signaling for everyone to remain silent. It looked as though they were going to have fine cooperation from the rest of the class. Seeming to be completely unaware of their intentions, I canceled our discussion period and proceeded to assign them the written work at the end of the chapter. This work, I explained, was necessary before we could discuss the chapter adequately. The period was spent in constructive work and avoided a head-on clash. Later I talked to the boys and explained why I had to cancel the practice.

The next example of restructuring illustrates how a teacher created an atmosphere of comfort and relaxation.

The children were just returning to the room after the recess period. Most of them were flushed and hot from exercise, and were a little irritable. They were complaining of the heat in the room, and many of them asked permission to get a drink of water as soon as the final recess bell rang. I felt it would be useless to begin our history study as scheduled. So I told all of the children to lay their heads upon their desks. I asked them to be very silent for one minute and to think of the coolest thing they could imagine during that time. Each child then told the class what he had been thinking. The whole procedure lasted roughly 10 minutes, and I felt that it was time well spent. The history period afterward went smoothly, the atmosphere within the room relaxed, and the children were receptive.

8. *Support from routine.* We all need structure. Some children need much more than other children before they can feel comfortable and secure. Without these guideposts for behavior, some children become anxious and hyper-active. This is especially true during unstructured time, when children are moved by every wind and breeze of classroom behavior. Most beginning junior high school children find themselves in this state during the first few weeks. One boy summarized his feelings by saying, "It's like one great big surprise. Each hour you go to another teacher and you don't know what's going to happen until it's too late." To help these children, a daily schedule or program should be provided, as this may allay some of their feelings of anxiety. They can predict what is expected of them and prepare themselves for the next activity. As one teacher says:

Each morning I outline the activities for the day with one "leading question." I find that this is helpful to some of the children. When they come into class, they start thinking about the activities we have planned, instead of waiting for me to announce them. This saves time and eliminates the majority of random behavior.

9. *Direct appeal to value areas.* One of the most frequent mistakes of an untrained teacher is that he feels he must intervene severely and drastically in order to demonstrate that he has control of the situation. We know that this is not desirable. Another alternative is to appeal to certain values that the students have internalized. The conflict is that some children have not internalized the same values that the teacher has internalized. For example, a teacher cannot appeal to the child's sense of fairness if the child feels he has been "gypped" out of something he has a right to possess. A partial list of some of the values that most teachers can appeal to includes: (a) An appeal to the relationship of the teacher with the child, i.e., "You are treating me as if I did something bad to you! Do you think I have been unfair to you?" (b) An appeal to reality consequences, i.e., "If you continue to talk, we will not have time to plan our party," "If you continue with this behavior, these are the things that will probably happen." In other words, the teacher tries to underline cause and effect behavior. (c) An appeal to the child's group code and awareness of peer reaction, i.e., "What do you think the other boys and girls will think of that idea?" or "If you continue to spoil their fun, you can't expect the other boys and girls to like you." (d) An appeal to the teacher's power of authority. Tell the children that as a teacher you cannot allow this behavior to continue and still want to take care of them. The trick is to learn how to say "no" without becoming angry, or how to say "yes" without feeling guilty.

10. *Removing seductive objects.* Teachers have learned that they cannot compete against such seductive items as a baseball in a group of boys or a picture of the latest crooner in a group of preadolescent girls. Either the objects have to be removed or teachers have to accept the disorganized state of the group. It is not entirely the children's fault. Certain objects have a magnetic appeal and elicit a particular kind of behavior from children. For example, if a child has a flashlight, it says "Turn me on"; if he has a ball, it says "Throw me"; if he has a magnifying glass, it says "Reflect the

sunlight"; if he has a whistle, it says "Toot me"; if he has a pea shooter, it says "Shoot me"; and so on. These objects feed into the child's impulse system, making it harder for children to control their behavior. One of the most exasperating experiences in a teacher's lifetime is to set up a science corner only to have it fingered to death in the first five minutes of bell time.

11. *Antiseptic bouncing.* When a child's behavior has reached a point where the teacher questions whether the child will respond to verbal controls, it is best to ask the child to leave the room for a few minutes—perhaps to get a drink, wash up, or deliver a message. This was done in the following situation.

I had only one occasion to use antiseptic bouncing. One morning during arithmetic study period I became aware of giggling in the back of the room. I looked up to see that Joyce had evidently thought of something hilariously funny. I tried signal interference, and, though she tried to stop, she succeeded only in choking and coughing. By now most of the children around her were aware of the circumstances and were smothering laughter, too. I hurriedly wrote a note to the secretary of the principal's office explaining that Joyce "had the giggles" and asked that she keep her waiting for a reply until she seemed settled down. I asked Joyce if she would mind delivering the message and waiting for an answer. I think she was grateful for the chance to leave the room. When she returned, she appeared to have everything controlled, as had the class, and things proceeded normally.

In antiseptic bouncing there is no intent of punishing the child but simply to protect and help him and/or the group to get over their feelings of anger, disappointment, uncontrollable laughter, hiccups, etc. Unfortunately, many schools do not have a place that would not connote punishment to which the classroom teacher can send a child. To send him to the principal where he sits on the mourner's bench is not very helpful and defeats the purpose of nonpunitive management. However, with staff planning, it is amazing what alternatives can be found.

12. *Physical restraint.* Once in a while a child will lose complete control and threaten to injure himself or others. In such emergencies, the child needs to be restrained physically. He should be held firmly but not roughly. Once again there is no indication of punishment, but only a sincere concern to protect the child from hurting anyone. If a feeling of protection is to be communicated, such techniques as shaking, hitting, or spanking him only make it harder for him to believe that the teacher

really wants to help him. Some teachers who are ignorant about psychodynamics feel that a child should be punished for such inappropriate and deviant behavior. However, if these same teachers ever had a chance to observe a child who has lost complete control over his impulses, they would soon realize how frightening and fearful this experience is for the child. These teachers would see the suffering and anguish these children go through. It is no game with them, but strikes at their basic feelings of survival.

The preferred physical hold is for the adult to cross the child's arms around his sides while the adult stands behind him holding on to the child's wrists. Occasionally it is necessary to hold a child on the floor in this position. There is no danger that the child can injure himself in this position although he might scream that you are hurting him, or causing him considerable physical pain. Many of the children who need this type of control, go through four different phases. First, the child fights being held and controlled. He becomes enraged and says and does things that are fed by feelings of frustration, hate and desperation. He may swear, bite, and carry on in a primitive way. Most teachers who are not used to being treated this way, find it difficult to absorb this much aggression without becoming frightened and/or counter-aggressive. While we can be sympathetic towards this teacher he must provide the child with non-aggressive handling that he needs during this crisis situation. A professional nurse doesn't take away a patient's antibiotics because he happens to vomit on her. Likewise, a teacher does not reject a child when he needs adult controls the most. The teacher's control system must take over for the child's until his controls are operating again.

During the first stage it is sometimes helpful for the teacher to tell the child softly that he is all right, that in a little while he is going to get over his angry feelings, and that he (the teacher) is going to take care of him and not let him hurt anyone or anything. Once the child realizes that he cannot break away and that he *is* being controlled, the rage usually turns to tears. This is phase two. At this point the child's defenses are down, his coat of toughness has vanished and his inadequacy and immaturity become evident. After this period the child usually becomes silent or asks to be let go, which is phase three. If the teacher thinks the child has control over his feelings and is not going to start the cycle all over again, the teacher should release his hold on the child. It must be emphasized that the teacher, not the child, makes the decision. One evidence that the child is gaining control over his impulses is that his language becomes more coherent and logical. If the child knows who he is, where he is, and what has happened, he is usually on his way up the ladder of integration. As he gains controls, the child usually has to save face, which is often accomplished by pulling away from the teacher or making a sly remark. This is phase four and usually a good sign that the child is ready to move on his own power. Next, the teacher may ask the child to go the washroom and clean up.

Occasionally, a child may have to be held in the classroom, but this should be avoided whenever possible. If it cannot be avoided, one of the students should get the principal immediately so that the child can be removed from the class. Later, the teacher *needs* to explain to the class and to the child exactly what has happened in order to counter any delusional interpretations of the teacher's behavior.

An important point to remember is that whenever a teacher holds a child and is able to control his own personal feelings of anxiety and aggression, the chances are that his relationship with this child will improve significantly. The message the child receives is: "I care enough about you to protect you from your own frightening impulses. The fact you had to be held is no point against you. I'm not angry, but pleased that you are feeling more comfortable and are in control of your emotions." This kind of support can only foster the child's feeling that the teacher is a person whom he can trust.

Preventive Planning

The fourth of Redl's four alternatives is preventive planning. Sometimes disruptive behavior can be avoided by developing a better school and classroom procedure. If a teacher always has difficulty during transitional periods, if there is undue conflict on the playground or in the corridors, the disturbing behavior cannot be attributed solely to "problem children"—perhaps the school program is inadequate. For example, if a teacher bores, fatigues, or regiments children into acting out, their behavior cannot be explained in terms of inner conflicts but simply in terms of a poor living design for healthy children. One teacher solved her problem as follows:

In a large elementary school in the heart of Detroit, the staff's major problem during the snowy months was snowballing. Although more teachers were scheduled for playground duty and the severity of the penalty was increased, the problem did not diminish. The children still threw snowballs, but they were much more clever about it. One teacher who was unhappy about additional playground duty suggested that they paint a huge circular target on the back brick wall of the two-story school and actually program more snowballing. After much discussion and apprehension, the idea was presented to the students. They thought it was a wonderful idea, so a student-faculty committee was appointed to draw up some rules and regulations. Once the target was drawn, the problem of snowballing was virtually eliminated. The children threw all their energy into hitting the bull's eye rather than one another. Some children would actually come to school early just so they could have the highest daily score. One teacher commented that many of the "problem children" were very active in this activity and threw themselves out by the time school began. He reported that they were even easier to teach. . . .

Abridged from Nicholas J. Long and Ruth G. Newman, "A Differential Approach to the Management of Surface Behavior of Children in School," *Teachers' Handling of Children in Conflict*, Bulletin of the School of Education, Indiana University, XXXVII (July 1961), 47–61. Reprinted by permission.

Editors' Commentary

Behavior Modification

In both clinical and classroom applications, behavioristic approaches have gone full cycle to find ways to manage undesired behavior. Teachers have always used contingencies, rewards and punishments, praise, and threats, but their use was so haphazard and unsophisticated that it took a psychological revolution to give these methods understanding and discipline. In this movement, like most movements, however, there were (and are) exaggerated claims, esoteric applications, ritualistic and mechanistic approaches, and cults. Children as human beings were ignored; strong aversive stimuli (shocks) and denial were practiced in the name of therapy. M & Ms, checkmarks, and chips became central teaching techniques in some instances.

Yet all of us know that various extrinsic rewards and restrictions are potent forces. We know that a prompt response to behavior is critical if we wish to influence. In short, while many behaviors are primarily a product of human motivation, others are responses to contingencies, and most of our behavior is a combination of both.

There are two questions that a teacher asks about the use of behavior modification: How does the behavioral emphasis fit with our short- and long-term goals regarding the kind of human beings we wish to raise? How can we design, whenever possible, implicit contingencies and rewards that are part of the natural setting rather than "tacked on"? This is not to deny that sometimes a specific contingency plan is the best stepping stone to further a youngster's growth or the only access we have.

The emphasis on behavior modification has inundated special education; there is no more popular topic in the literature. Of particular value is Thorp and Wetzel's[3] discussion of the natural environment as the base. Ferster[4] introduced this concept some time earlier.

The following article, by Deno, is an excellent overview of the field of behavior modification and includes a clear discussion of the differences between token economies, precision teaching, and contingency contracts.

3.   **Roland G. Thorp and Ralph J. Wetzel,** *Behavior Modification in the Natural Environment* (New York: Academic Press, 1969).

4.   **C. B. Ferster,** "Arbitrary and Natural Reinforcement," *Psychological Records* 17 (1967): 341–347.

Contingency Management in (Special) Education: Confusions and Clarifications

Stanley L. Deno

... Skinner's doctrine that organisms learn from interaction with their environment is important to us because it places a heavy responsibility on those of us who chose to intervene in the progress of human development. If behavior is in fact functionally related to changes in an individual's environment then responsibility must be accepted by those who deliberately intervene in human environments for the changes in behavior which occur in those environments. This means that when a child becomes more aggressive in an environment which we are managing that we are responsible for that increase in aggression. It also means that when behavior does not change in predicted directions that necessary environmental conditions have not been arranged to bring about the change. A child who is reading no better now than he was when we first began to care for him is *a child we have failed rather than a child who has failed.*

Performance contracting and accountability are clearly consistent with interventions based upon Skinnerian philosophy. To adopt such a position leaves us with little opportunity to explain away failure on the basis of inadequacies in a child.

The third doctrine is, perhaps, the most interesting to point out because it is surely the most offensive to us all. The notion that man is by nature an active organism which learns from interaction with its environment and is not by nature anything else must be not only unpleasant for most of us to consider for personal reasons but also unpleasant because it does violence to much of the psychology upon which many psychologists base their professional lives. This last doctrine says in effect that it is foolish to spend time creating grand explanations for behavior and its changes in terms of fictitious nonbehavioral states within an individual—whether those inner states be of mind or emotion. If we accept that all that man is and does is behavior then we can approach all human problems using the techniques of behavioral science. We treat "mental health" as a behavioral rather than a medical problem. As we shall see later, accepting this assumption does not require us to deny the existence of our "inner lives." It requires only that we treat these private events as behavior when we undertake to change them. The confusions surrounding this point are many, but a reading of Skinner on this point makes it patently clear that our understanding of behavior is incomplete without analysis of inner behavior.

It is well to remind ourselves here that we have very briefly considered three basic assumptions which can fairly be gleaned from the writings of B. F. Skinner, the leading spokesman for behaviorism. While it is interesting to speculate on the validity of these assumptions, what is important here is to recognize that these doctrines are the basis for a philosophy of human nature, and that they need not be embraced when one undertakes to analyze behavior in the manner practiced by Skinner and other behaviorists. One can, I think, practice the functional analysis of behavior without believing any of the doctrines enunciated above.

Functional Analysis

The functional analysis of behavior is an attempt to specify the *environmental variables* of which behavior is a function. The analysis is undertaken for the purposes of predicting and controlling individual behavior. Doing a functional analysis does not require that one believe that behavior and environmental events are all that exist. Nevertheless, it is helpful if one approaches problems of behavior change optimistic that solutions will be derived from changes in environmental variables. If we begin our explanations of behavior change by relying upon inner events that are not subject to environmental influence then we must become pessimistic about the possibility that solutions for changes in behavior can be systematically obtained through intervention programs.

The elements of the functional analysis of behavior are simple (see Figure 1): first of course there is behavior itself; second, there are the environmental events which precede behavior; third, there are the environmental events which follow behavior; and finally, there are the contingency relations among those three terms. The term "reinforcement contingency" has arisen from the fact that within a functional analysis behavior can be

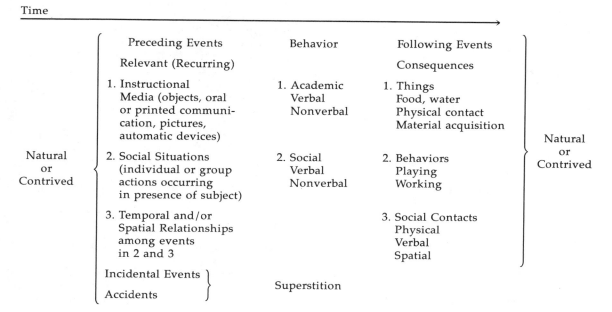

Figure 1. Functional Analysis

strengthened (reinforced) by changing the events which follow and are contingent upon the occurrence of that behavior.

While heavy emphasis has been given to the final two terms of the analysis (i.e., behavior and its contingent consequences) it would be well to remember that Skinner himself has said that "an adequate formulation of the interaction between an organism and its environment must always specify three things: (1) the occasion upon which a response occurs, (2) the response itself, and (3) the reinforcing consequences." (Skinner 1969, p. 13) The first term of the contingency (preceding, antecedent or discriminative stimulus events) is as much a part of the analysis as the second and third terms. Rarely are we concerned with strengthening or weakening behavior without regard for the occasion upon which that behavior occurs (the preceding events). In fact we cannot judge behavior as appropriate or inappropriate in a social system unless we know the situation (the preceding events) in which the behavior has occurred.

H. S. Terrace, in reviewing Skinner's latest book, *The Contingencies of Reinforcement: A Theoretical Analysis*, likens the functional utility of the three term contingency relation in the analysis of behavior to that of the cell in biology:

Indeed, just as the cell or the atom can each assume a variety of forms by changes in the nature of their components, so can the character of a discriminative operant [the relationship between the first two terms of the analysis] be modified by changes in the nature of the discriminative stimulus, the response, and the reinforcing consequences. Most readers are probably familiar with the variations that are possible with the reinforcement term. Reinforcement can be positive or negative, and, depending upon the schedule, reinforcement may follow only a small fraction of the responses that have been emitted. Less familiar are the ways in which the first two members can vary. Discriminative stimuli can derive from either the external or the internal environments. Likewise the response may be overt or covert. It is mainly from contingencies in which a stimulus from the internal environment controls either an overt or covert response that Skinner formulates the examples which encompass activities normally referred to as mental. Internal stimuli and covert responses are assumed to be potentially measurable in the same physical units applied to external stimuli and overt responses. (Terrace, 1970, p. 532)

That the functional analysis is an approach to understanding the controlling relations of all behavior regardless of its character and does not require the denial that covert behavioral events actually occur in the lives of individuals is evident

from Terrace's further discussion of Skinner's analysis.

Much of Skinner's analysis of the activities of the mind is directed at showing how awareness of feelings, of thoughts, or of the external world, results from contingencies of reinforcement. In chapters 6 and 8 of Contingencies *Skinner tries to show that private events can and should be conceptualized in much the same way in which we conceptualize conditioned overt behavior. Skinner is quite explicit about the amenability of private events to scientific analysis and about the validity of contingencies as the unit of analysis. "It is particularly important that a science of behavior face the problem of privacy . . . an adequate science of behavior must consider events taking place within the skin of the organism not as physiological mediators of behavior but as part of behavior itself . . . private and public events have the same kinds of physical dimensions. So far as we know, the same process of differential reinforcement is required if a child is to distinguish among the events occurring within his own skin. (Terrace, 1970, p. 532)*

A brief discussion of the functional analysis has been included here to distinguish it from the philosophy of human nature which was summarized previously. Hopefully, it can now be seen that while a philosophy of behaviorism requires belief in certain assumptions, the functional analytic approach which Skinner has used requires only that one be interested in ascertaining the specific preceding and following environmental events which function to strengthen or weaken a behavior. This approach to analysis does not require a belief in the implicit doctrines. It requires only that one be able to apply the three term contingency analysis to events in the behavioral world to determine the contingencies of reinforcement.

Motivation and Management Techniques in the Classroom

While it is true that:
    "Naming is not explaining" (The nominal fallacy)
It is also true that:
    "Explaining is not changing" (The word game)

First person: You behaviorists are all alike. You care only about what someone is doing, never why he is doing it. What about his real problems?!!

Second person: If I encountered a patient on a ward who spent most of his time smearing feces or walking in little circles I could do something to stop it—you couldn't!

[Quoted without reference.]

Professionals who have embraced the concepts and procedures of behavioral psychology have done so not out of philosophic or theoretic predispositions. They have done so because behavioral scientists have provided models not only for how behavior changes (i.e., explanations) but also for changing behavior. Explanations for a child's ineffective behavior in academic and social settings are of little value to the professional unless they lead directly to alternative procedures for increasing the effectiveness of behavior. Change procedures follow directly from operant conditioning and functional analysis.

Behavioral psychologists have recognized the professional educators' demand for change procedures and have developed what might be called "model systems for changing behavior" which incorporate essential procedures from both operant conditioning and functional analysis. These systems have been disseminated widely in education under the names "Token Economy," "Precision Teaching," and "Contingency Contracting." The salient features of these systems are summarized in Table 1.

Usually, when these systems are presented in teacher workshops, for practical reasons very little time is spent in laying a conceptual base for the system procedures. The systems seem "cookbooky." We will not attempt to provide the basis for each system here, but it should be understood that basis does exist. Unfortunately, learning only procedures without the conceptual basis probably limits the procedure's effectiveness and adaptability for the teacher. It is only when the systems are improperly adapted to the specific instructional setting that remarks such as "I tried behavior modification but it didn't work," or "Behavior modification is fine for some kids, but not all of them" make any sense at all. Failures in these cases are not failures of behavior modification systems; they are failures attributable to the manager's incomplete knowledge of the systems and their bases.

The System: Some Personal Observations

Precision Teaching. Of the three systems summarized in Table 1, precision teaching is the most tightly organized and managed. It is the brainchild of Ogden R. Lindsley of the University of Kansas, perhaps Skinner's best known student. The system is almost a pure application of the experimental methodology developed by Skinner. That methodology places special emphasis on continuous recording of the frequency (previously referred to as

Table 1. Three Common Systems for Managing Classroom Contingencies:
A Summary of Salient Features

Token Economies (Allyon)	Precision Teaching (Lindsley)	Contingency Contracting (Homme)
1. Desired changes in behavior are specified.	1. Behavior to be recorded is pinpointed (may be overt or covert).	1. Academic achievement is measured through formal or informal tests.
2. Effective reinforcers are identified and made potentially available.	2. Recorder and Charter are identified (may be behaver).	2. A sequence of daily task assignments is developed.
3. A medium of exchange (token, point, chip, star, etc.) is established.	3. Frequency of behavior is recorded on 6-cycle semilog graph paper (Behavior Research Co.).	3. A Reinforcing Event menu is constructed depicting potential reinforcers (usually high preference activities).
4. Tokens are made contingent on measured increments (frequency, duration, proportion) of behavior specified in objective.	4. Change in frequency described in terms of "multiplier" or "divisor."	4. Performance areas and RE areas are created.
5. Opportunities to exchange tokens for effective reinforcers are made available.	5. An instructional change is made (which may involve change in preceding or following events or both).	5. Contingency Contracts (a statement of how much time in the RE area completing each task will earn) are written for each child.
6. Records of behavior are maintained (usually time series records).	6. Effect of change observed on chart and calculated as change in "multiplier" or "divisor."	6. Contracts are presented to, and accepted by, each child.
	7. Charts are almost always "shared" by Charters.	7. Tasks are completed, checked, and access to RE area is made immediately available.

"rate") of a specific behavior. Recording procedures in precision teaching are highly developed and continuously modified. The materials and conventions of recording are rigidly adhered to by anyone calling himself a precision teacher. Learning to be a precision teacher involves learning to use the materials and conventions that Lindsley and his followers have developed and that they disseminate through one week institutes on precision teaching offered frequently in Kansas City. The Behavior Research Company of Kansas City publishes and distributes materials to be used by precision teachers. Records of precision teachers are fed back to a computer bank managed by Lindsley. These records are, hopefully, used to develop some scientific facts about behavior.

Although the system appears to be essentially a measurement system, implicit in the measurement procedures is the functional analysis of behavior specified in the first section of this paper. Precision teachers do not use the language of operant conditioning but rather a kind of jargon called "precise basic English" for communication purposes. Perhaps the most interesting recent development in precision teaching is the acceptance of recording what are referred to as "inners" (covert behaviors). It has become proper to count "urges," or "feelings" and to apply change procedures to inner behaviors as well as outer behaviors. This development in particular seems to hold greatest promise for promoting a rapprochement between behavioral and humanistic psychologists. At the same time, however, it tends to fractionate so-called behavior modifiers into different camps.

Contingency Contracting. Contingency contracting is a system developed by Lloyd Homme, another student of Skinner's, who for some time has applied the principles of operant conditioning and the procedures of functional analysis to education. Contingency contracting differs markedly in one respect from precision teaching. Measurements of student performance which are obtained are conventional achievement tests or subject matter tests. Although daily testing is required for contingency contracting, the system does not involve extensive daily recording of frequency of student behavior. The system is based primarily on what has become known as the Premack Principle, which states that if a high-frequency behavior is made contingent on the occurrence of a low-frequency behavior, the low-frequency behavior will increase in strength.

A contingency contract is written on the assumption that behavior on many academic tasks is lower than it is on nonacademic tasks or on academic games. Therefore, an open and explicit bargain is struck between the teacher and the student such that if a student successfully completes a certain unit of work (low-frequency behavior) then he will be able to engage in something else that he might enjoy more (high-frequency behavior). Contracts are carefully written and developed. Homme also encourages teachers to turn over to the student the writing of contracts, which involves both the setting of the task and the reinforcing event. Contingency contracting classrooms are characterized by intense high performance in academic areas and a great deal of movement between performance and reinforcing-event areas.

Token Economies. Token economies are probably the most widely used systems which incorporate the principles of operant conditioning and the procedures of functional analysis. In addition, they are probably the most widely criticized because they seem to involve "bribery," "commercialism," and use of the profit motive. This is unfortunate. For one thing, the "token" has its theoretical origins in the secondary or conditioned reinforcer, i.e., the token is an event which has acquired the power to strengthen behavior only because of its repeated pairings with other reinforcing events. In a token system it is used only as a temporary substitute for the "back-up" reinforcers, which cannot be made immediately available for practical reasons involved in classroom management. Unfortunately many people who have used token systems rely heavily on edible and tangible reinforcers to back up the tokens. It is *this* use of tangible reinforcers which is most susceptible to criticism. The fact that so many token systems have relied on tangible reinforcers suggests that the system managers were either not imaginative enough to use more acceptable back-up reinforcers, or that tangible reinforcers happen to be the most effective reinforcers in most of the systems which were established. Token systems can be effectively used in cooperation with students for mutual benefit, can serve as an excellent device for teaching both academic and social behavior, and, in some ways, are more honest than the subtle manipulation systems we sometimes employ in our relationships with children.

If these short summaries of precision teaching, contingency contracting, and token economies do an injustice to the complexities of these systems, perhaps the brevity has made some of the features of each system more salient. Rather than attempting a more complete presentation (precluded by space limitations), following are general procedures for changing behavior (in that they apply to all behavior), which can serve as a basis for discussions about behavior change.

Procedures for Changing Behavior

Step 1. Specify the behavior to be changed. All that we do is behavior. In schools behavior is usually termed "academic" (e.g., adding single digit numbers, reading aloud, or writing simple sentences). Some behavior in school is "social" (e.g., talking aloud, leaving the seat, touching another student, or running in the halls). When you pinpoint a behavior begin your description with a gerund ("add*ing*," "read*ing*," "writ*ing*," "talk*ing*," "leav*ing*," and "touch*ing*"). You have adequately described a behavior when two people can independently *count* its occurrence and obtain the same total.

Behavior by itself is never right or wrong; *rules* make behavior (whether academic or social) appropriate or inappropriate.

Step 2. Record the frequency of its occurrence. Recording is necessary for precision and consistency. If you don't really need to know whether you are successful in changing the behavior you don't need to record. To be sure of success you must record.

To know whether or not behavior changes, it is first necessary to know what it is now. Our subjective judgments are almost always wrong. For that reason you should record a behavior for 4 or 5 days before you try to change it. If the amount of daily observation time changes, record the number of minutes elapsed during each observation period, and divide the number of occurrences of the behavior by the number of minutes observed.

Step 3. Change some conditions. Two sets of conditions can be changed:

1. Preceding events (discriminative stimuli or antecedent events): The directions or instructions you give to guide performance can be changed. These usually take the form of telling students what to do or how to do it but also include demon-

strations by yourself, another person, or pictures, manually or technologically. The *materials* or *situation* connected with the behavior can be changed (e.g., you can change a student's book, the number of problems he must work, the amount of time he has to work, his seat in the classroom, or when he does the assignment). *But be sure to continue recording the same behavior.*

2. Following events (consequences): Changing events which immediately *follow* behavior usually produces the biggest change in behavior. You could arrange for any event described below to immediately follow behavior: Doing something different (schoolwork, something social, going to another place—a room, outside, home, a more preferred activity); acquiring or losing something different (adult or peer attention, praise or disapproval, a material item—a toy, tablet, ball, money, food, book). In arranging for a change in an event which follows the behavior, you must assure that the event will occur *immediately* and *consistently.*

Step 4. Appraise. Once you make a change continue it for at least 2 or 3 observation periods and watch your daily record. If the frequency of the behavior doesn't begin to increase (or decrease) make another change. Continue this cycle if necessary.

References

McClellan, James. B. F. Skinner's philosophy of human nature. In B. P. Komisar and C. B. J. MacMillan (eds.) *Psychological Concepts in Education.* Chicago: Rand-McNally Co., 1967.

Skinner, B. F. *Contingencies of Reinforcement: A Theoretical Analysis.* New York: Appleton-Century-Crofts, 1969.

Terrace, H. H. Toward a doctrine of radical behaviorism. *Contemporary Psychology,* 1970, *15,* 531–535.

From a paper prepared for distribution at the Institute for College Instructors on Behavior Disorders in Children, August 1971. Used here by permission of the author.

Editors' Commentary

In the next article, Patricia Gallagher cautions readers about the cultlike adherence to behavior modification principles and techniques that can develop. She writes about the need for more discriminating use of behavior modification and describes twelve specific conditions in which it should be avoided. Finally, she concludes, behavior modification is a management technique that promotes positive social behavior if it is used with sensitivity.

Behavior Modification? Caution!

Patricia A. Gallagher

The successful application of behavior modification techniques in special and regular classrooms has been documented in the literature; furthermore, many classroom teachers and education consultants are enthusiasts of these modification techniques. While the success of behavior modification in school settings cannot be denied, there are situations which indicate that other intervention procedures should be used; and situations which indicate that a more discriminate use of behavior modification should be considered.

It may be very worthwhile to consider and analyze the following classroom conditions and students' behavior before embarking on a behavior modification program:

Avoid using behavior modification when a student is learning a new activity through experiences which may normally be labeled inappropriate. Andy was finger painting. Finger paint was on his paper, arms, face, clothing, table, and floor. The messy behavior could easily become a target for behavior modification; however, Andy was a seven-year-old child who had spent a year and a half in a special class. He had a history of being upset if he were in a situation that required contact with materials which could lead to getting his skin or clothing "dirty." He refused to use finger paint, clay, or chalk. If there were sand or lint on his clothing, he would frantically brush it off. He would not paste unless he could use a paste brush; nor would he lick gummed paper or postage stamps. Although the teacher substituted alternate ways for Andy to complete "dirty" tasks, she frequently encouraged him to engage in tactile media activities. Furthermore, Andy could observe the other students' pleasure in these activities. Andy was currently experiencing a developmental activity, "messiness," by exploring and enjoying tactile media. A behavior modification program designed to reduce messiness was not appropriate, since Andy needed the opportunity to be messy without *any* contingencies imposed.

Avoid using behavior modification when another intervention technique is more direct. Phyllis, a second-grade student, frequently complained of "imaginary" aches and pains. Her whines "turned off" the students and the teacher. The teacher could use behavior modification to decrease the whines; however, she decided on a simple, direct approach. The teacher had a private discussion with Phyllis and pointed out that many of Phyllis' poor peer interactions were a result of her complaints. (Children are frequently short-sighted regarding their behaviors which affect others.) Shortly after the discussion, a noticeable change in Phyllis' behavior began. Her complaints decreased, and her peer interaction increased.

Avoid using behavior modification when a study of other behaviors in the student has not been made. During mid-October, an eight-year-old blind child, Norma, was described as being very unhappy and "crying at the drop of a hat." She frustrated easily, became easily upset, and clung to the teacher whenever they were in the hall, playground, and lunchroom. The crying could be a target response for behavior modification; however, the teacher was hesitant. She suspected that there might be other variables contributing to the child's crying and general mood of unhappiness. In reviewing Norma's behavior during her ten months at the school, the teacher recalled that Norma had been injured in an automobile accident the previous year. The accident occurred in November during the Thanksgiving Holidays. As a result of the accident, Norma had lost her sight. Norma was enrolled in a special class two months after the accident and hospitalization. In class she did not display any overt reaction to the trauma. She seemed to adjust well to her new school, children, and to her blindness. Ten months later, however, Norma was displaying behavior associated with depression. In discussing her behavior with several professional people, it appeared that Norma was going through a period of depression which frequently follows an individual's reaction to the loss of a sense or an extremity. She did not need to have her crying modified; rather, she needed counseling and some supportive adult help in a variety of situations. Her teacher provided additional emotional and physical support in the classroom, and an adult with whom Norma had confidence was available for counseling sessions. Norma gradually expressed her reactions to the accident and hospital trauma, and regained her emotional stability.

A second example will also illustrate this point. An adolescent girl, Vicki, was always late to her first-hour math class. When she arrived at school, she did not go immediately to her classroom. She stopped in the restroom to take care of her personal appearance. The math teacher was concerned about the student's tardy behavior and planned to modify it. She discovered, however, that Vicki was responsible for taking care of the younger children in her motherless family. It was necessary for her to dress, feed, and walk the younger children to school. After these tasks were accomplished, Vicki was able to go to her own school. She was concerned about her physical appearance, especially after a busy morning, so she took time to groom herself. This time added to her tardiness. After studying the situation, the teacher terminated her behavior modification planning and arranged for Vicki's first hour to be a study hall, with the math coming later in the day. If portions of the study hour were missed, the student could make up the time independently.

Avoid using behavior modification when the positive traits of a student cannot be discerned. Students with behavioral disorders frequently elicit negative reactions from others. Often these students exhibit a number of inappropriate behaviors which tend to obfuscate positive behaviors which they have. If a teacher cannot see the student's positive traits, it is best to avoid a behavior modification program. The program may focus on the negative behaviors, thus emphasizing the negative aspects of the student. For example, a teacher described one of her students, Mike, as the student who ran away, threw toys, pinched other children, screamed, never used Kleenex when he had a runny nose, and couldn't tie his shoes. When asked to describe Mike's positive behaviors, she replied, "He can't do anything right." The educational consultant suggested that the teacher select one of the negative behaviors, for example, "pinch other children," and look at the opposite behavior, "does not pinch; keeps hands away from other children." The teacher could give positive reinforcement during periods of time when the student refrained from pinching. Thus, a modification program could accent the positive. Further discussion revealed that the teacher could not discern any of Mike's positive behaviors, nor could she accept the positive approach to behavior modification.

Avoid using behavior modification when there is opposition to a change in the target behavior by other individuals involved in the student's life. Behavior modification may be the most appropriate technique to use to change a student's behavior; however, if the building principal, supervisor, student's parents, peers, siblings, or other teachers are opposed to changing the target behavior, behavior modification should not be used. Placing the student in a potential conflict situation should be avoided. For example, Matt, a fifth grader, was frequently involved in playground fist fights. The teacher had initially planned a modification program designed to decrease the fighting; however, after a parent conference she decided to delay the behavior modification project until she could gain parental support. She discussed the plan with Matt's parents; however, Matt's father adamantly supported Matt's playground aggression. "My kid is a good fighter." "He isn't going to let the other guys beat him up." After the conference, the teacher decided to delay the modification plan and initiated an interim strategy which placed Matt "working out" in the gym during the recess period.

Avoid using behavior modification until an over-all academic program and its goals have been planned. A six-year-old boy, Joey, shouted for the teacher's attention. The educational consultant was concerned with Joey's shouts, and suggested that the teacher use behavior modification to reduce the shouting. The teacher replied that behavior modification was not necessary because she had current goals for this child, the least of which was shouting for teacher attention. She discussed Joey's behaviors with the consultant when he first entered a special class. Joey had daily petit mal seizures, no self-identification, and many tantrums. His language skills were at the two-year level. He was physically abusive to the teacher, and ran away whenever he had the opportunity. His left arm had atrophied from lack of use. (There was no medical evidence to explain this atrophy.) A year later Joey began to recognize himself as a person; he could carry on conversations with adults at a four-year-old language level; he had developed a sense of humor; tantrums were rarely seen; and he ceased running away. He was no longer physically or verbally abusive to his teachers; but he did shout for the teacher's assistance, and was occasionally flippant. He used empty threats periodically. The teacher described her current goals for Joey: (1) complete activities with emphasis on using the left arm; (2) work independently on a task for ten minutes; (3) participate in the language development program for twenty minutes; (4) accept guidance and help from others when it was necessary; and (5) learn how to interact with children. The teacher felt these major goals were much more important behaviors to develop before shouting was modified. She did not want to overwhelm Joey with too many demands.

Avoid using behavior modification if a student is physically ill. An ongoing modification program was designed to help Larry achieve a specific level of accuracy on his papers. When this level was achieved, Larry would receive his reinforcer, the opportunity to pick up absence slips. While he recuperated from a cold and the flu, the behavior modification was temporarily halted, as Larry was neither up to par nor able to concentrate on his work. When Larry felt better, the modification program was reinstated.

Avoid using behavior modification if consistency in the plan can't be accomplished. Once the stimulus, response, contingency, and reinforcer have been planned, it would be most unwise for a teacher to embark upon a modification program if there could not be consistency in carrying it out. A modification program designed to increase Henry's independent seat-work time was planned. If Henry could respond appropriately for fifteen minutes, he would have five minutes free time. A kitchen timer was set for the fifteen-minute work period; however, the teacher, busily engaged in working with other students, did not always hear the timer ring. Consequently, Henry was inconsistently reinforced, and his seat-work behavior improved minimally.

Avoid using behavior modification if support from other individuals is necessary and cannot be obtained. Ernest, a sixth-grade student, frequently teased his peers, who responded by angry shouts. The teacher and building principal decided that Ernest would have a "ten-minute time-out period" for each episode of teasing. Time out was defined as removal from classroom and time spent sitting on a chair in the principal's office. After the behavior modification program was initiated, it was observed that Ernest's "time outs" increased. The teacher discovered that Ernest enjoyed the ten minutes, because he frequently sat in the principal's outer office where he could observe much staff activity and the operation of the ditto machine. The principal wasn't able to follow the plan to have Ernest sit in his office.

Avoid using behavior modification until the behavior to be modified can be accurately identified. A teacher was concerned and agitated about a visually handicapped girl, Glenda, who was dependent. Dependency was initially described as, "The girl will not walk alone between the change of classes. She is dependent on others for mobility." After defining dependency, which the teacher indicated occurred "all the time," she decided to modify it; however, another teacher encouraged her to take baseline data on the behavioral description to obtain a premodification frequency count, but more importantly to determine if she had pinpointed the target behavior. Further observation and a baseline recording revealed that in four days Glenda had 17 between-class changes. During these 17 class changes, she walked alone two times, and began walking alone 15 times until her close friend, Kay, told her to wait so they could walk together. A baseline recording designed to pinpoint the behavior revealed that the teacher's initial behavioral description was partially erroneous, because Glenda did initiate independence in walking to classes. Her independent mobility was interrupted by a friend who wanted to socialize with her on the way to other classes. If the teacher had not pinpointed that target behavior, the wrong behavior would have been modified.

Avoid using behavior modification until the student is ready to engage in the target behavior. Bob, a shy fifth-grade boy who rarely interacted with his peers, was beginning to show interest in them; however, he did not engage in their activities. He had initiated some interaction with his teacher. A future modification program designed to have Bob interact with his peers was anticipated, but it was not initiated at the time when Bob was just beginning to approach adults.

Avoid using behavior modification if the curriculum materials have not been evaluated. As the beginning school weeks elapsed, Tracy, a third-grade transfer student, was described by her teacher as being "hyperactive," "having a poor attention span," and "not completing assignments." Another third-grade teacher described two of her transfer students as having similar problems. Reinforcers selected and arranged in a modification program designed to change the students' inappropriate behaviors were seriously considered. Referral to a school psychologist was also considered. The third-grade teachers discussed the students' behaviors and possible solutions with an education consultant who suggested that they reexamine their curriculum and student expectations. Subsequently, the third-grade teachers discovered that these transfer students could not read cursive writing, a subject taught in third grade in their former school and in second grade in the current school. The board lessons and assignment directions were done in cursive writing; and the children, struggling to respond to the stimuli, developed inappropriate behaviors. A typical modification program focusing on the application of reinforcers contingent upon specific behavioral changes would be in error. A modification program emphasizing a change in the curriculum stimuli, cursive written directions, was designed to bring about desirable academic changes in the students. Board lessons and assignments were written in manuscript, and peer tutoring sessions involving cursive lessons were conducted.

Students, particularly those who have academic and/or social problems, need to be understood before techniques can be implemented to bring about desirable changes. If children are "listened to," then teachers can be judicious in their selection of intervention procedures. If behavior modification is used without careful consideration and analysis of environmental conditions and students' developmental behaviors, it can have deleterious effects on students. Behavior modification accompanied by sensitivity, however, can bring about successful experiences which can enhance a student's growth.

Reprinted from *Academic Therapy*, Spring 1976, pp. 357–363. Used with permission.

Editors' Commentary
Punishment

In considering management, "punishment" has been almost synonymous with "discipline." The next article shows a theoretical and a practical view of this common theme and broadens the significance of the word "punishment." Perhaps the key to understanding a dynamic approach to punishment is concentrating on what the experience means to the child, not what it means to the adult (a basic distinction between the operant and dynamic approaches). We cannot take for granted how a child will experience our efforts. Particularly important is the matter of timing, which Redl develops at some length.

The Concept of Punishment
Fritz Redl

Professional Use of the Word "Punishment"

As educators or clinicians, our behavior toward children deserves the name "punishment" only if it is done with a *clearcut goal to help the child.* Thus, it is always a means to an end, and is always employed for the sake of the basic welfare and growth needs of the individuals involved. Whether the actual punishment administered under this policy was correct or helpful; or whether it was stupid, mistaken, wrongly handled; or whether it backfired in its intended effect, is not the point here, as we try to *define* our terms.

It is equally obvious that the use of punishment implies an attempt to produce an experience for the child which is *unpleasant.* It is based on the assumption that sometimes the affliction of an unpleasant experience may mobilize "something" in a child that gets him to think or change his behavior, a change which, without such a "boost" from without, would not have occurred. Tying those two aspects of punishment as viewed in the tool cabinet of the professional educator or clinician together, we might arrive at the following definition, which I think serves our purpose for the time being.

I refer by the term "punishment" to: *a planful attempt by the adult to influence either the behavior or the long-range development of a child or a group of children, for their own benefit, by exposing them to an unpleasant experience.*

The inclusion of the statement that it has to be a "planful attempt, guided by the benefit of the children as a goal," excludes all simple outcropping of adult sadism, bad temper, or personal vengefulness, as well as the use of the child as a prop to assuage one's own anxiety. The statement that all punishment aims at using the production of an "unpleasant" experience in the child marks this intervention technique as different from others. It also raises the crucial question which underlies all speculations about the wisdom of punishment as a tool in a given case: Just what is there to the underlying assumption that producing an unpleasant experience in a child is going to help him rally better to reason and control than he was able to before? For this is obviously the *only assumption* on the basis of which any educational or clinical use of punishment makes any sense at all.

Analysis of the Punishment Experience

"You can lead a horse to water, but you can't make him drink." This age-old saying is rather trite, but many a punishment discussion I have been in would have benefited if this had been written in bold script on the blackboard before it started. For what counts most in punishment is not what we do to *the child*, but *what the child does with the experience to which we have exposed him.* To make a long story short, *this is what must happen within the child if things go well:*

1. *The child experiences the displeasure* to which we expose him. This "displeasure" can be the loss of a privilege or pleasure he took for granted, or the exposure to something that is unpleasant or even "painful" in some way or other. Or both. For instance, I can take away his dessert, I can sock him one, or I can insist that he stay in his room while he hears the others playing outside.

2. Whether the displeasure be in the form of frustration or pain on some level, it is bound to produce an *upsurge of anger* in the child. This anger may not be conscious, nor does it have to be strong. But it is normal for the human to react to frustration or pain with an upsurge of fury.

3. The child clearly perceives—at least after the first few moments, the difference between the *source of his predicament* and *the real causes.* The source of his predicament is obviously the adult who inflicted the punishment, or the institution which made him do so. The cause for his predicament, however, is equally obviously *his own previous misbehavior,* for without it the adult would not have imposed the punishment to begin with.

4. The child now directs the anger produced in him by his predicament, not against the source of his trouble but at its cause: *he gets mad at himself* and realizes he would have avoided all this had he only shown more impulse control and wisdom in his actions to begin with.

5. He does however, not only get a little "mad at himself," but he *transforms* this self-directed aggression into *energy that can be used* for his own benefit. By "transforms" we refer to a process by which what was originally personalized fury or self-hatred can be changed into neutralized energy, now available for a multitude of more sublimated ends.

6. He uses this energy, drawn from his fury about his predicament, for two purposes: (a) he forces himself to regret what he did; (b) he forces himself into a sort of "New Year's resolution": "I'll sure not be dumb enough to get myself into a situation like this next time."

7. In a future temptation of somewhat similar kind, he can make use of the image left from the previous incident, and can mobilize self-control power before the act. The previous punishment experience has helped him, not only toward better insight, but also left him with increased energies for temptation resistance.

These, basically, are the steps every child goes through each time a punishment experience to which he was exposed is "handled well" by him— even though these steps are, of course, not really experienced clearly in the process. They are the *condition* for a constructive use of a punishment experience by a child.

How do we know if this can work? It would be easy, with the above outline in hand like a "map," to predict exactly just what could go wrong with the way a child handles his punishment experience, and what conditions must be met within a given punishment plan to make a successful ending most likely. It would be easy—but it would take an estimated 80 pages to do it, so let's skip it for the time being. Let's select what seem to me the five most crucial items in this picture—leaving a dozen or so just about as crucial ones unmentioned for now:

1. From what we know about the child, is the specific *form of displeasure* which we selected for a

given punishment situation likely to be used by him as an incentive for concern, or is it either going to roll off him without impact, or throw him into a tizzy of irrational response?

Examples. Some children prefer to sit in their room and masturbate anyway, rather than participate in a competitive game with dubious results for them. Sending such a child to his room won't even be experienced as punishment, no matter what *name* we may want to give the procedure. *Or:* A really good moral masochist *loves* to feel sorry for himself and nurse his grudge against the world, which has "done him wrong." Most punishments, for him, do not hold much displeasure, and what little they hold he turns around into self-pitying delight or juicy gratification of a perverted need. *Or:* Being sent back to stay in one's room as punishment for some misdeed or other, might, in itself, be a good "displeasure dose" to rattle a given child into more thoughtful self-appraisal. Only—we sent him back while his neighborhood gang was just coming to pick him up for a ball game, and the things we said while we sent him back would be likely to make any self-respecting and emancipation-hungry teenager cringe with unconquerable shame. *Or:* Some children are "allergic" to being alone in a small room. Being sent into one for punishment would produce unbearable panic in them. They are allergic to this type of experience, so you can't use it on them no matter how well they may have "deserved it."

2. From what we know about the child—is he going to be able to *differentiate between "source" and "cause" for his predicament* under the impact of the specific punishment experience which I have provided for him? If the answer to that is no, then you had better save yourself the trouble. Your punishment won't work, and whatever momentary benefit you draw from it will be badly outweighed by the negative side-effects.

Examples. Very little children do not have such discrimination well developed yet. A small child, bumping his head against the table, is likely to turn around and hit the table in revenge for "what it did to him." He is incapable of differentiating the source of his trouble (the contact with the table) from its cause (his own clumsy movement, and not looking where he was going). Some older children regress to that level under the *impact of displeasure or pain.* If that is so, punishment has no chance to help. *Or:* Some people are quite capable of making such distinctions, but they don't want to make them. It is much more gratifying to hate the

cop who gave one the ticket than to admit one wasn't driving as one should have. Especially children who are still in the grip of a concerted effort to view the adult as hostile and to deny their own participation in the events of their lives, will construe any experience of displeasure as a "personalized wrong coming from a hateful opponent" rather than consider it a challenge to revise their own style of life. As long as they are in that stage, even the most clearcut form of punishment is going to backfire.

3. From what we know about the child—is he going to be able to *turn his aggression in the right direction,* under the impact of the punishment experience? By the "right direction" we mean, of course, toward that part of himself that made him misbehave, instead of toward the punishing adult, the institution, the world at large, God, or the Universe—or the child in the upper bunk.

Example. Some children are quite capable of knowing and admitting that they were in the wrong and "deserved what they got." Yet, their ego is still totally incapable of coping with any amount of frustration or aggression in a constructive way. Thus, even when correctly mad at themselves, they will have to pour their fury at the people and things around them, or they simply explode into an orgy of diffuse and frantic aggression-discharge. This is especially true for our hyperaggressive child: even at the stage when they begin to feel guilty for what they did, as we hoped they eventually would, they still have not developed enough ego skills to cope with guilt feelings adequately. So, even though they know they are at fault themselves, their aggression still is poured toward the world outside them. As long as that is true, even otherwise well planned "punishments" are of no avail.

4. From what we know about the child—is he capable of sifting and transforming the anger we produced in him through our punishment, into the type of energy that can be used for increased insight and self-control? Among all the puzzles, this is probably the most serious one. For, even if the child gets correctly mad at himself instead of at me the administrator of punishment, or at the institution and its laws, the crucial question still remains: what is he going to do with the fury he now directs against himself? For the fact that aggression is turned against ourselves alone is not enough. It depends very much on just what we do with the aggression we turn against ourselves. Unless the "sifting and transforming gland" for internalized

aggression functions well, a child is not going to benefit from punishment received. By "sifting" and "transforming" I am referring to two separate tasks: by "sifting" I mean that the child's ego must be able to decide just how much should be discharged as a waste product. Some children, for instance, discharge all of it as a waste product—none of it sticks and is internalized. Others can't allow themselves any "waste product discharge," so the full brunt of their anger is turned against themselves, which means they are *flooded with much too much repentance, discouragement and self-accusation.* The normal child has glands which operate well that way: punished by an adult he can vent some of his anger by mumbling under his breath or slamming that door, some of it by a quickly produced "revenge fantasy against the punishing adult," some of it by diffuse discharge motions, such as, restless pacing of his room, rough manipulating of a ball, etc.—*and only the right amount is then sent to the transformer* to be turned into internalized energy for self-insight and self-control.

Examples. Some children *know* that they are to blame but if the punishment, pain, or frustration, or their already existing proclivity toward guilt feelings is too strong, they simply get *paralyzed* by their repentance and regret, drift into orgies of self-accusation, or they end up feeling no good, incapable of ever amounting to anything, or not worthy of the adult's love or their own self-confidence.

In that case, all the previous steps of punishment worked well, for they *should* have admitted they were wrong, as they did, they should have got "mad" at their own bad behavior, as they did. *Only,* they *did so too much,* and in a totally ineffective way. For simply being mad at oneself is no good, unless one has the energy for doing something about it. *Or:* Some children get angry at themselves, as they should, but they puff out this anger in waste motion rather than in an increase of energy available for self-control. That means they punish themselves by slip actions and "accidents," by losing their favorite toy, breaking their prize possession, but they cannot use their self-anger for the purpose of more impulse control. No matter how "repentant" they seemed to be in their immediate reaction to the punishment, they are as helpless as they were before at the next onslaught of temptation. Whenever things are wrong with the sifting and transforming machinery in the child's ego, a punishment experience cannot be benefited from.

5.   From what we know about the child, is his ego in good enough shape to cope with the complica-

tions of the "time" element in punishment? In my estimate, the misfiring of punishments which were otherwise well designed because of this very factor of timing is the most serious trouble source in educational as well as clinical practice. I guess I had better lay this one out a little more in detail. By "time element" I refer, here, to three entirely different issues—all of them, however, equally crucial to the constructive use of punishment by a child.

a. The time relationship between punishment experience and offense. Public opinion is wildly confused on this issue. It either assumes that the two should be in high proximity—or else the child forgets what he is punished for—or that they should be far apart—so that the basic issue has time to sink in, and the adult has enough time to check on guilt, on issues of justice, and to get his machinery in motion. As is frequently the case, there is a kernel of truth in both extremes, but neither of them is *it.* The reality of the situation is more complex than either theory would like to have it.

In life with our hyperaggressive children we have learned that there is great importance to the issue of timing, but whether proximity or distance is of the essence depends on many items in each case. Talking about punishment: some children's awareness that they did something wrong—or even what they did—evaporates so fast that the act of punishment hits them after it is entirely evaporated. Then, the displeasure felt during the punishment experience makes little sense, it is likely to be perceived as rank meanness of an irritable adult rather than as punishment one has "deserved" for something one "did." On the other hand, some children's "offenses" were entangled in so many issues, soaked with so much affect, anger, confusion, delusion, etc., that no punishment experience can have much chance to do its trick, unless that confusion is disentangled first. Knowing this much about the ego of a child will make it clear that certain forms of punishment that create complications in the time relationship between punishment experience and offense are by that very fact counterindicated.

b. The timing of exposure to the punishment experience is of crucial concern. Some of our children, for instance, might well "understand" that they deserved to be sent to their room, and might be able to "take" that part of it without distortion of the real facts, at least on occasion. The question to be asked next, however, is clearly: What will they do with themselves while exposed to the punishment condition, such as staying in their room, paying back for a damaged item out of their pocket money, or staying home while others go on a fishing trip, etc.?

Many children's egos are not in shape enough to take the time exposure involved in a given punishment. In such cases, this specific form of punishment is counterindicated, no matter how good it may look from all other angles.

Public opinion, unfortunately, is caught in a hopeless confusion on this item, too, which causes no end of trouble even in professional discussions on the issue. Namely, public opinion has assumed a fixed relationship between length of exposure and seriousness of offense. Thus, for a little offense in the swimming pool, one might assume that a child should be sent to his room maybe for just 5 minutes. For a bigger offense, maybe it would be "fair" if he were told to stay out of activities for 2 days. Well, it may be "fair" all right, but what effect will it actually produce? As long as Johnny sits there watching the other youngsters splash around happily while he is sulking about his predicament, but still under the impression that he "had it coming" because of the freshness of the memory of what he did, all may be fine for a while. The moment the self-perception of what he did is evaporated, though, the experience assumes an entirely different shape. From then on it is not: "too bad I had to get myself into this trouble," but, "see, that bastard waterfront guy lets all these other kids have their fun, it's only me that doesn't get a break, hell with *him*."

In short, the psychological weight of a time issue has to be weighed with psychological scales, not with judiciary ones, and the psychology of timing belongs among the trickiest issues I can think of.

c. By "timing" we sometimes refer to the fact that the real test of the efficacy of a punishment lies in the question whether a child can make use of what he learned from it in the next temptation situation. Thus, its major effect is hoped for from its impact on the future event. This however, means no less than the question of whether a child can, at all, learn from experience, especially from an unpleasant one. And, beyond this, whether he can not only "learn" a lesson from the experience, but whether his ego can supply him with the necessary control energies to make use of what he learned when the next crucial moment comes around. It ought to be clear by now that this is quite a lot to be expected, and I can't help being amazed time and again, that adults are so naive to believe that a few strong punishments do not result in long-term improvement. The question whether a given child has it in him to "learn" from

a given punishment experience is an important one to estimate correctly. For punishment, contrary to popular fantasies, does not teach a thing unless the recipient is in any shape to do the learning. In the case of children with severe ego disturbances, it is clear that this is one of the reasons why one would not expect much help from the punishment department. The ability to tie up a well interpreted experience from one's past with an equally clearly perceived experience from the present, and on top of that mobilize just the right quantity of energy for self-control and send it into just the right control-direction—this is obviously a task which a messy ego is likely to flunk. Yet—the use of punishment now makes little sense, unless we have some expectation that its impact can be utilized at some moment in the future tense.

About this issue of the "time element"—we want to assess just how well a child is likely to do in all three aspects of the time issues: Can he take the time relationship between a given offense and a given punishment without getting confused; can his ego sustain him for the *duration* of the punishment experience with all the specifics a given case involves; and is there a chance for some *future usability* of the experience to which we expose him now. If the answer to this is no, punishment isn't worth the effort you put into planning and suffering through it, to say nothing of the complications in the lives of children.

d. Punishment and the problem of in-situational and post-situational support. At this point, I hear you moaning: "Are you trying to tell us that punishment is as complicated as all that? What ever happened to the idea that it was a 'simple' technique, sort of clearcut and very concrete, and much more 'definite' than most of the other intervention techniques we talked so much about?" The answer to that is: Yes. That's exactly what I am trying to convey. The idea that punishment is a simple, clearcut technique belongs in the chapter of optical illusions. What the *adult* does in an act of punishment may be as simple and clearcut as a kick in the pants. What the kid does with this experience and how he reacts to it is anything but simple and clearcut. It involves the most sensitive and vital organs of his psychological organism, as I have just tried to show. In this respect, punishment is much more comparable to a case of surgical intervention than to what you see happen when the guy at the delicatessen slices that salami for you with a sharp knife.

Unfortunately, I have to make it even more complicated, especially when we think of punishment in relation to a disturbed child. The prevalent thinking of the layman still puts most of his effort into finding the "best" form of punishment, having the educator impose it on the child—and from here on in he expects the effect to be sort of automatic.

Fortunately, we already know better than that. We know that even a well planned play experience for a child may need constant support during the time when the child is supposed to be exposed to it, or may need some post-situational followup. This principle, again, is not new. Remember the time spent not only on figuring what game should be selected in the evening, but also on just how we give the children the support they need to live through the game successfully once it gets under way? Remember how important we felt it was not only to physically hold a child when that becomes necessary, but to help him get through this experience without misinterpreting it? Remember how important it was to stick around all through their tantrums, even after we didn't have to hold them anymore, just so we can catch that moment when the child needs or is ready for some activity he can hang onto and pull himself together again?

All this is as true of "punishments" as it is of other experiences in our children's lives. Thus, our responsibility is not ended with the decision to send that child to his room, or to tell him he has to pay part of the damage he has done to the other boy's toy for the next two paydays. The safeguarding of the right *effect* of a punishment experience is a job that continues as long as that experience lasts, and the real help to make sense out of it all often occurs much later in a post-situational exploitation of the kid's reaction to it. Whenever we figure on any kind of punishment for our children, therefore, it is important to plan just as much for in-situational and post-situational support, as it is to decide what kind of punishment should be tried to begin with. Even a well designed punishment will backfire badly if for some reason we are not able to give the child the support he needs going through it, without distortions, and "learn" from it what we wanted him to learn. With the act of punishment our work with the child on this issue does not end. It only begins. . . . If you ever thought of using punishment in some situations because it "saves trouble" or makes things work more simply, you'd better give that daydream up in a hurry.

Loose Ends for Sale

The "analysis of the punishment experience" which I just presented was not meant to be a photograph; only a map. It makes no pretense of answering your question of just what to do. It only tries to

point out a few salient points you will run into if you get into this terrain. . . .

Next, I would like to brush lightly past a few issues that I remember having come up in our staff discussions.

The usage of the term punishment being as loose as it is, we often discuss under the same label situations where we demand that a child "make up" for a hurt he has inflicted, or a damage he has caused. The form this takes may vary. We may insist that he at least "apologize" or show he is sorry; we may want him to clear up the mess he has caused and which inconveniences the other boy in his cabin or room; we may demand partial payment for damage done, etc. I personally do not like to see these arrangements thrown into the same pot as punishments, for they have only a small part of the process in common with them. But I won't quibble about words at the moment. Suffice it to remember that such procedures are actually much more rituals for the restitution of the individual into the grace of the group or of his victim, including an attempt to help him come to peace with himself. The following are the *three major goals* one has in mind when using this technique:

1. We may want to help the child get the taste of some *consequences* of his behavior, and at the same time offer him a way to *do something about it* that is more or less apt to re-instate the status quo.

2. By giving the child a chance to "make up for it," we also help him to reduce his guilt feelings and to restitute the previous relationship between him and the person or group against which he has offended.

3. We also make it easier for the victim of the kid's misbehavior—be it individual or group—to "forgive him," to terminate their own state of wrath against him, and to stop whatever revenge measure they in turn might have in mind. We sort of offer the victimized kid or group a pound of his psychological flesh as a premium for their "forgetting" what he had done to them.

It must be obvious by now, that this technique may have a number of great advantages and may well be used at times to restitute what had been disturbed, which may be a great relief for all concerned. It is also clear, of course, that this only would work where the child has some guilt about what he had done to begin with, where he is clearly aware and admitting that he was in the wrong, is basically ready to wish it hadn't happened, and is himself relieved at the idea of having it all "repaired." The major danger of the technique lies with the case of a child who not only has few guilt feelings, but defends himself against the development of such by a system of "pay as you go" arrangements. Offering this type of child too many opportunities to "pay off for what he did" is inviting his exploitation of this technique to feed his own resistance against real insight and awareness of right and wrong. Great care must be taken in those cases where such "restitutional arrange-ments" seem feasible, that the youngster gets all the help he needs to interpret his own "making up" correctly, and that we make no mistakes in the nature and duration of the restitutional rituals we may choose. . . .

From Fritz Redl, an original article presented at the American Orthopsychiatric Association meeting, 1959, pp. 9–44.

Editors' Commentary

Life Space Interviewing

How does a teacher intervene in a crisis or other problem situation? Changes in the situation or tasks may be used to manage the classroom, but many times external manipulation of conditions is not sufficient. Human beings are verbal, and words can be cues to action. Children use a verbal system as part of the way they organize their world. Thus, teachers naturally use verbal interplay as an intervention strategy.

Prejudiced adults conclude that deprived children lack verbal skill, and they do not encourage these children to use language as a means of control. Yet the children demonstrate astonishing verbal expression in creative poetry and writing. Pupils influenced by strong inner feelings or perceptions about their situation need to explore, clarify, and reassess their reactions verbally.

Most of us have little sophistication in interviewing children. We either moralize, antagonize, or allow ourselves to be overwhelmed by their negative verbal responses. These adult reactions only inflame the student and complicate the situation, making a supportive and insightful encounter more difficult to manage. Redl was the pioneer in recognizing that special skills were needed to deal with children in crisis. He described the need to interview the student in his environment rather than to take the student to the adult's office for a "chat." He pinpointed the psychodynamic goals of the various interviews, helping the interviewer realize that the same behaviors may need to be treated with very different interview strategies. For example, a student may hit another pupil because of his misperception of reality, the joy and rewards of being aggressive, his attempts to make friends (right attitude but wrong behavior), being set up by another friend, or being flooded by guilt and seeking punishment. According to the interviewer's assessment of the situation, he or she will decide how to handle the crisis and how the student can learn from it.

The Concept of the Life Space Interview

Fritz Redl

It is our contention that life space interviewing plays an important part in the lives of all children. All adults in an educational role in children's lives find themselves in many situations which could correctly be thus labeled.

It is our contention that the life space interview assumes a mediating role between the child and what life holds for him, which becomes just as important as the interviewing that goes on within the pressurized cabin.

It is our contention that in work with seriously disturbed children, even if they are not exposed to the special type of pressurized cabin therapy over and beyond their exposure to milieu therapy, the strategically wise use and technically correct handling of the life space interviews held with the children are of foremost clinical importance.

It is our contention that even where children are exposed to clear-cut pressurized cabin therapy, for special therapy of one phase of their problem, the wisdom of strategy and technique used by their natural home or school life personnel in mediating life experiences for them is of major strategic relevance in its own right.

It is, before all, our contention that what goes on in a life space interview, even though held with the child by somebody not his therapist, in the stricter interpretation of the term, involves as subtle and important issues of strategy and technique as the decisions the psychoanalyst has to make during the course of a therapeutic hour.

It is our contention, last and not least, that any application of total life milieu therapy as supportive to individual therapy, or undertaken in its own right, will stand or fall with the wisdom and skill with which the protectors, teachers, and interpreters in the children's lives carry out their life space interview tasks.

It is for this reason that we shall try to subject some of the occurrences during the process of a life space interview to the same type of scrutiny that psychiatric therapy techniques have for a long time been exposed to in our technical seminars. By the way, one more word about the *term:*

What we have in mind when we say "life space interview" is the same thing as what my staff, my friends, and my coworkers, while I still lived in Detroit, referred to under the name of *marginal interview.* The reasons for the change in terms are many, and seem to me so strong that they outweigh the equally obvious disadvantages of the switch in name. When I, and many of us in the same type of work, started talking about the marginal interview, it was pretty clear, out of our own context of operation and to us personally, what we felt it was "marginal" to. We meant, at first, the type of therapylike interview that a child may need around an incident of stealing from the "kitty" in his club group, but which would be held right around the event itself by the group worker in charge of that club, rather than by the child's therapist—even though the material around the incident would probably later be getting into therapy, too.

So—it was "marginal" in two ways: marginal in terms of the rest of the life events around which it was arranged; and marginal in terms of the overall job expectation of a group leader, who uses casework or therapy technique even while functioning in his group leader role.

Since I moved into the operation of our residential treatment design[1] within a huge hospital setting, the term "marginal" has lost the clarity of its meaning entirely, besides other disadvantages which the low-status sound of the word "marginal" seems to assume for many people.

In changing to the term "life space interview," we apologize for the possible confusion that might be created because we are using the term here with an entirely different meaning from the one Kurt Lewin had in mind. In spite of this disadvantage, we feel that the term is at least frank in its emphasis on the major characteristics of this type of interview we have in mind: In contrast to the interviewing done in a considerable detachment from direct involvement in the here and now of Johnny's life, such as the psychoanalytic play therapy interview, the life space interview is closely built around the child's direct life experience in connection with the issues which become the interview focus. Most of the time, it is held by a person who is perceived by the child to be part of his "natural habitat or life space," with some pretty clear role and power-influence in his daily living, as contrasted to the therapist to whom one is sent for "long-range treatment." We are fully aware that none of the similarities or differences implied here are truly characteristic for the two operations; in fact, to find similarities and differences is the goal, not the starting point for our research. For the time being, and until someone with more imagination and linguistic know-how gives us a better clue, we think the term is as good, or bad, as any we could think of to connote what we have in mind. . . .

Goals and Tasks of the Life Space Interview

First, I want to select for discussion two major categories of goals and tasks for life space interviewing: (a) Clinical Exploitation of Life Events; and (b) Emotional First Aid on the Spot. The difference between these two categories does not lie in the nature of the event around which the need for the life space interview arose—we shall in the future refer to this event as the "issue"—but in our decision as to what we want to do with it; it is also defined, of course, by the question as to just what the situation itself allows.

Let's assume that a group of children are just about ready to go out on that excursion they have anticipated with eagerness for quite a while. Let's assume there is, due to our fault, somewhat more delay at the door because of a last-minute search for lost shoes, footballs, etc., so that irritability mounts in the gang that is already assembled and raring to go. Let's further assume that in the ensuing melee of irritated bickering two of our youngsters get into a flare-up, which ends up with Johnny's getting socked more vehemently than he can take, furiously running back to his room, cursing his tormentor and the world at large, all educators in particular, swearing that he will "never go on no trip no more in his whole life." We find him just about to soak himself in a pleasurable bath of self-pity, nursing his grudge against people in general and adding up new evidence for his theory that life is no good, people are mean "so-and-so's" anyway, and that autistic daydreaming is the only safe way out.

Well, most of us would feel that somebody ought to move into this situation. The staff member who tries to involve the sulking child in a marginal interview at this time has a choice of doing either of two things:

He may want to be with John in his misery, and to assist the child in disentangling the complicated web of emotions in which he is so hopelessly caught, simply in order to "get him over it" right now and here, to get him back into his previous enjoyment-anticipating mood. This situation seems to be quite comparable to the concept of "first aid"; the organism is capable of taking care of a wound produced by a minor cut, but it might be wise to help it.

On the other hand, depending on how much time there is and how Johnny reacts to the adult's interview strategy, the adult may suddenly find that this opportunity gives him a long-hoped-for chance to help John to come to grips with an issue in his life which we so far have had little possibility to bring to his awareness. Thus, he may forget about his intention of getting John back to his original cheerful excursion-anticipating mood; he may even give in to his sulky insistence that he "wasn't going to go nohow," but he may decide to use this special opportunity to start on an interpretational job. He may begin to tie this event up for John with many similar previous ones, and thus hope to help him see how John really "asks for it" many times, even though he has no idea that he

does so, and how his irritably rude provocation or lashing out at other children often gets people infuriated, or whatever the special version of this perennial theme may be. In short, half an hour later our interviewer may be driving after the rest of the group with a somewhat sadder but wiser companion at his side, or he may at least have laid the groundwork for some such insight to sink in at a future opportunity, or to be picked up by his "therapist" at a later opportunity in case John happens also to be "in individual therapy" of the more classical style.

By the way, most of the time we can't be sure before an interview under which of the two goal categories it will eventually have to be listed, for we may in the middle of an interview find good enough reason for a switch from the original intent with which we entered the scene.

This differentiation between "Emotional First Aid on the Spot" on the one hand, and "Clinical Exploitation of Life Events" on the other, however, still leaves us with two rather comprehensive categories before us. I feel that the practitioners among you would like it better if we broke those wider concepts down into smaller units and thus brought them closer to the observational scene.

The Clinical Exploitation of Life Events

Our attempts at pulling out of a life experience, in which a given child is involved, whatever clinical gain might be drawn from it for our long-range treatment goal, may assume some of the following special forms:

Reality Rub-in. The trouble with some of our youngsters, among other things, is that they are *socially nearsighted.* They can't read the meaning of an event in which they get involved, unless we use huge script for them and underline it all in glaring colors besides. Others are caught in such a well-woven *system of near to delusional misinterpretation of life* that even glaring contradictions in actual fact are glided over by their eyes unless their view is arrested and focused on them from time to time. More fascinating even, are the youngsters whose preconscious perception of the full reality is all right, but who have such well-oiled ego skills in alibi-ing to their own conscience, and rationalizing to any outside monitor's arguments, that the picture of a situation that can be discussed with them is already hopelessly repainted by the time we get there. It is perhaps not necessary to add how important it is, strategically speaking, that such children have some of this "reality rub-in" interviewing done right then and there, and preferably by persons who themselves were on the scene or are at least known to be thoroughly familiar with it.

Symptom Estrangement. In contrast to their more clearly neurotic contemporaries, our children's egos have, in part at least, become subservient to the pathological mechanisms they have developed. They have learned well how to benefit from their symptoms through secondary gain, and are therefore in no way inclined to accept the idea that something is wrong with them or that they need help. A large part of the "preparatory" task at least, without successful completion of which the magics of the more classical forms of individual therapy are rather lost on these children, consists in alienating their ego from their symptoms. Hopeful that there must be somewhere a nonpathology-swallowed part of their ego functions waiting for a chance to speak up, we use many of their life situations to try to pile up evidence that their pathology really doesn't pay, or that they pay too heavily for what meager secondary gain they draw from it, or that the glee they are after can be much more regularly and reliably drawn from other forms of problem-solving or pursuit of life and happiness. By the way, the assumption in all this is *not* that one can simply argue such children through well-placed life space strategy into letting go of their symptoms; part of the job needs to be tackled, in addition, by many other means. However, we can *enlist* part of their insight into helping their ego want to liberate itself from the load of their pathology. To make it possible for them, even after they want to, to shuffle off the unconscious coils of their neuroses, is an issue in its own right. We also ought to remember at this point how important it is that symptom estrangement be pursued consistently by all the staff all the way down the line. It would do little good to *talk* in interviews about the inappropriateness of their symptomatic actions, if the social reality in which they live made it too hard for them to let go of those very symptoms. Our action definitely has to be well attuned to our words in this task more than in any other.

Massaging Numb Value-Areas. No matter how close to psychopathic our children may sometimes look, we haven't found one of them yet who didn't have lots of potential areas of value appeal lying within him. But while the arm is still there, circulation has stopped. Value sensitivity in a child still needs to be *used*, and something has to be done to get circulation going again. Admitting value

sensitivity, just like admitting hunger for love, is quite face-losing for our youngsters. There are, however, in most youngsters some value areas which are more tax-exempt from peer group shame than others. For instance, even at a time when our youngsters would rather be seen dead than overconforming and sweet, the appeal to certain codes of "fairness" within their fight-provocation ritual is quite acceptable to them. Thus, in order to ready the ground for "value arguments" altogether, the pulling out of issues of fairness or similar values from the debris of their daily life events may pay off handsomely in the end

New-Tool Salesmanship. Even the most classicism-conscious therapists confess from time to time that they spend quite some effort helping a youngster see that there are other defenses than the ones he is using, and that doing this may at least partially widen the youngster's adaptational skills. The therapist, however, who operates in the "pressurized cabin" of a long-range classical style individual therapy design cannot afford to waste too much of his effort in this direction, or he would puncture the pressure-safe walls he has spent so much time building up to begin with. So, as soon as the potential to use such mechanisms has been liberated in individual therapy, the adults who "live" with those children can begin to use many of their life experiences to help them draw from them the vision of a much wider range of potential reaction to the same mess. Even the seemingly simple recognition that seeking out an adult to talk it over with is so much more reasonable than to lash out at nothing in wild fury may need to be worked at hard for a long stretch of time with some of the children I have in mind.

The life space interview offers a chance to leave the more general level of propaganda for better adjustment tools, and to become quite specific in the demonstration of the all too obvious inadequacy of the special tool previously chosen by the child. In this respect we feel the same advantage that the salesman may feel who, besides having leaflets to distribute, is given the opportunity to demonstrate.

Manipulation of the Boundaries of the Self. From time to time one invariably runs into a child who combines with the rest of his explosive acting-out type of borderline aggressive pathology, a peculiar helplessness toward a process we like to refer to as *group psychological suction*. Quite vulnerable to even mild contagion sparks, he is often discovered by an exceptionally brilliant manipulator of group psychological currents, and then easily drifts into the pathetic role of the perennial "sucker" of an exploitation-happy subclique.

The life space interview, of course, offers a strategic opportunity to begin to move in on this. To illustrate what we mean by this concept of "manipulation of the boundaries of the self"—and leaving out all the details as to life space strategy employed in the case—the following example may serve:

Several months ago, we felt that the time was ripe to "move in" on the problems of one of our youngsters around "group psychological suction" described above, so we decided to exploit incidents of this sort, wherever they might happen, through an increased use of "life space interviews." We felt good when eventually the following incident occurred one day in school: Two boys of the subclique that enjoyed exploiting this youngster were hard at work to get him to "act up" for them. This time their wiles didn't seem to get them anywhere; in fact, in the process of accomplishing their job they got out of hand themselves and got themselves "bounced." They were hardly out of the room when the youngster in question turned to the teacher, with a relieved look on his face, and declared, "Gee, am I glad I didn't get sucked into this one."

Many of our children are more ready than one would assume at first sight to expand their concept of the wider boundaries of their self into including other people, benign adults, their group, or the whole institution to which they feel a sense of belonging, and so on. In an entirely different direction, again, we may want to use life incidents to help youngsters with the problem of acceptance of their self, or of hitherto split-off parts of it. Anything that educators describe under terms such as "encouragement," "inculcating a feeling of worthfulness and pride," and anything that betrays confused attitudes of the children toward their "self" in the form of despondency coupled with megalomanic illusions, etc., might well be grouped under this heading.

In summary, we should underline the implication that these five goals for the use of the life space interview were meant to be illustrative rather than system binding. In all the instances we have raised so far, the real *goal* of what the life space interviewer did was the clinical exploitation of a given life event. It meant making use of a momentary life experience in order to draw out of it something that might be of use for our long-range therapeutic goals.

Emotional First Aid on the Spot

While children are exposed to therapeutic long-range work on their basic pathology, it is important to remember that they are still forced to live with their symptoms until they finally can shed them, and that child development is also still going on. For, while it is true that our children are sick enough to deserve the term "patients," we must never forget that child patients are still *growing youngsters*. This means that the adult, who accompanies them during the various phases of their growth, is also needed as an *aid on the spot* in those adjustment demands of daily life that they cannot well manage on their own. It is our contention that this in itself is an important enough task to deserve special technical attention, and that the opportunity for such "aid in conflict" includes the situations which we term "life space interview." The emphasis here lies in the fact that emotional first aid in itself is a perfectly valid reason for a carefully planned life space interview, even if this special issue around which the interview is built promises no long-range gain in the same way in which we described it in the previous section. As illustration of the goal which a given life space interview may set itself, we should like to enumerate again five randomly assembled subcategories:

Drain-off of Frustration Acidity. Even normal children experience easily as something quite infuriating the interruption of the pleasurable exploit in which they happened to be engaged. This is especially unfortunate with our type of child who has such low frustration tolerance, for he is over-aggressive and hostility-projective to begin with. It is here that the life space interview has an opportunity to serve as an over-all hygienic device. In sympathetic communication with the child about his anger or justified disgust at the discomfort of having been interrupted, we can drain off the surplus of intervention-produced hostility, and thus avoid its being added to the original reservoir of hate. Such situations offer themselves especially when something has gone wrong with a planned enterprise, or if the mere need to maintain a schedule may force interruption.

Support for the Management of Panic, Fury, and Guilt. The trouble with many children is not only that they *have* more feelings of anxiety, panic, shame, guilt, fury than they should or than the normal child would experience, but also that they don't know what to do with such states of mind when they get into them. We have already

complained, in *Children Who Hate*, about how difficult it is to help such children to react correctly
even if they do feel guilty when they should. It is
important, then, that the adult intervene and give
first aid as well as therapeutic support whenever
heavier quantities of such emotions hit the child or
the group. In our own over-all strategy plan, for
instance, we consider it important that an adult always stay with the child, no matter how severe his
tantrum attack may become. The knowledge that
we are just as interested in protecting him from his
own exaggerated wishes, as from the bad intent of
other people, has been found quite ego supportive
in the long run. By being with the child right after
the excitement of a blowup abates, the adult can
often help the child "put things back into focus
and proportion" again. He can also aid him in the
return to the common course of activities or social
life of the day without the sour after-taste of
unresolved hurt.

*Communication Maintenance in Moments of
Relationship Decay.* There is one reaction of our
children to experiences of emotional turmoil
which we fear more than any other they may happen to produce—and that is, the total breakoff of
all communication with us and full-fledged retreat
into an autistic world of fantasy into which we are
not allowed to penetrate. We get scared, because
with children at the borderline of psychotic withdrawal from any and all reality this weapon of defense against help from us is the most efficient one.

It is used especially frequently when events
force us to a clear-cut form of intervention in a
youngster's behavior, the nature of which seems, at
first sight, to offer an especially "clear-cut" point of
argument or interpretation to the child. Yet, at this
very moment he is liable to drop all relationships
with us, and thereby makes us quite helpless in our
attempt to offer sympathy, explanation, or support.
Often, for instance, after a particularly vicious
attack upon another child, a youngster will mis-
perceive the motives for the intervention of a protective and battle-interrupting adult to such a
degree that he interprets even the most well handled interruption of the fight as rude and hostile
"betrayal." To this he reacts with such resentment
that the breakdown of all previously established
relationships with that adult seems imminent. It is
important that this process be stopped right then
and there and that we prevent the *next step* in the
youngster's defensive maneuver, namely, the withdrawal of all communication and the total flight
into autistic daydreams. Often, in such a moment,
it is obvious that nothing we could do would make

any impact on the hopelessly misconceived image
in the youngster's mind. However, our attempt to
involve the youngster in some form of communication may prevent the next level of retreat from us
right then and there. So we surrender any plan to
"talk to the point," but simply try to keep communication flowing between child and adult, no matter on what theme and no matter how trivial or far
removed it may be from the issue at hand.

Regulation of Behavioral and Social Traffic.
This specific task of the life space interview doesn't
look like much, and we have become painfully
aware that people have a tendency to consider it
too "superficial" and undignified to be included in
items as status-high as the discussion of "interview
techniques." Yet, our respect for the clinical importance of our service as *social and behavioral traffic
cops* has gone up, if anything, over the last ten
years. The issue itself is simple enough and doesn't
need much explaining. The performance of the
task, however, may get so difficult that it is easily
comparable to the most delicate problems that
might emerge in individual therapy of either children or adults.

The facts of the situation are these: The children know, of course, what over-all policies,
routines, rules of the game of social interaction are
in vogue in a given place. Only, no matter how
well they "know," to *remember* the relevance of a
given issue for a given life situation is a separate
task, and to muster enough ego force at the moment to subject impulsivity to the dictates of an
internalized concept of rules is still another. Thus,
the service they need becomes very similar to the
job the traffic cop, when functioning at his best,
would perform for adults, and even the most law-
abiding ones amongst us may need such help from
time to time. He reminds us of the basic rules again
or warns us of the special vicissitudes of the next
stretch. He may point out to us where we deviate
dangerously even though we happen to be lucky
this time. Since people do not necessarily learn
even from dramatic experience, unless they are
aided by a benign and accepted guide, it may be
important to go, in a subsequent session, through a
stretch of behavioral confusion and to use it for
reinforcement of our overall awareness of the implications of life. Since our children are especially
allergic to moralizing or preaching or lecturing of
any kind, it would not do to offer them a condensed handbook of behavioral guidelines. It is
important to subdivide that phase of their social
learning into a number of aids *given on the spot*
when needed most.

For example: we have a clear-cut policy on our ward about the child's going to our school sessions, and about the reasons for this, as well as the course of events which will take place if a child gets himself "bounced" for the time being. We have spent great effort to have everybody live this policy consistently so that the unanimous attitude of all adults involved could serve as an additional nonverbal reinforcer of the basic design. Yet, in order for all this to become meaningful and finally incorporated and perceived as part of the overall structure of "life in this place" for our children, it took hundreds of situations of life space interview surrounding school events.

Umpire Services—in Decision Crises as Well as in Cases of Loaded Transactions. The children often need us for another function, which may sound simple though the need for it may be empathic and desperate: to *umpire.* This umpiring role in which we see ourselves put may be a strictly internal one. It sort of assumes the flavor of our helping them decide between the dictates of their "worser or their better selves." For those instances, our role resembles that of a good friend whom we took along shopping—hoping he would help us maintain more vision and balance in the weighing of passionate desire versus economic reason than we ourselves might be capable of in the moment of decision-making. However, we wouldn't want to restrict this term to its more subtle, internal use. We envision it to go all the way from the actual umpiring of a fight or dispute, of a quarrel about the game rules in case of conflict or confusion, to the management of "loaded transactions" in their social life. Into the last category fall many complicated arrangements about swapping, borrowing, trading, etc., the secondary backwash from which may be too clinically serious to be left to chance at a particular phase. Many such situations, by the way, offer wonderful opportunities to do some "clinical exploitation of life events." But, even if nothing else is obtained in a given incident of this kind, the hygienic regulation and the emotionally clean umpiring of internal or external dispute is a perfectly legitimate and a most delicate clinical job in its own right.

Summarizing all this, we should like to emphasize what we tried to imply all along: All these "goals"—the strategic exploitation type, as well as the moment-geared emotional first-aid ones—may be combined sometimes in one and the same interview, and we shall often see ourselves switch goals in midstream. We probably need not even add that the type of goal we set ourselves at a give time in our project would also be strongly influenced by

the phase the children find themselves in in their individual therapy, and of course, just where they are in their movement from sickness to mental health. In fact, the "stepping up" as well as the "laying off" in respect to selecting special issues for life space interview or for purposely leaving such materials untouched is in itself an important part of the overall coordination of individual therapy and the other aspects of our therapeutic attack on the pathology of a given child.

Speculations about Strategy and Technique

The importance of a clinically highly sophisticated concept of *strategy and technique* in regard to the life space interview is taken for granted in this discussion by now. That this short symposium cannot hope to do more than open up the issues and point at the need for more organized research seems equally obvious. In view of this, it may seem most advisable to concentrate on one of the core problems of all discussions on strategy and technique, namely, the question of *indications and counterindications;* and to draw attention to some of the most urgent aspects that need further elaboration soon. If we say "indications and counterindications," by the way, we mean to refer to both: indications and counterindications for the *holding* of a life space interview to begin with, as well as indications and counterindications for a specific *technique* or for the establishing or abandoning of a specific strategic move. The question "Should I keep my mouth shut or should I interpret this dream right now?" which is an issue so familiar to us from discussions of individual therapy, has its full analogy in the orbit of life space interview work.

The following criteria seem to turn up most often in our discussions of technique:

Central Theme Relevance. By this we mean the impact of overall strategy in a given therapeutic phase on the question of just what situations I would move in on and what issues I would select for life space interview pick-up. It would not do to surround the children with such a barricade of attempts to exploit their life experiences for clinical gains that it would disturb the natural flavor of child life that needs to be maintained; and too much first aid would contain the danger of over-dependency or adult intervention oppressedness that we certainly want to avoid. As an example for this: At certain stretches we would purposely keep away from "talking" too much about our previously quoted youngster's proneness to allow himself to be played for a sucker. It is only after certain overall therapeutic lines have emerged that we decide in unison that such incidents should from now on be exploited more fully. It was felt, at that particular time, that the child's individual therapist would welcome such supportive rub-in from without.

Ego Proximity and Issue Clarity. The first of these two is an old standby, well known from clinical discussions in classical psychoanalytic work. One simply does not sail interpretatively into material that is at the time so "deeply repressed" that bothering it would only unnecessarily increase resistance or lead to marginal problems in other areas. On the other hand, material of high ego-proximity had better be handled directly, else the child might think we are too dumb or too disinterested to notice what he himself has figured out long since on his own. The same issue remains, of course, an important criterion in life space interview work.

The item of *issue clarity* is a more intricate one and becomes especially complex because of the rapidity with which things move on the behavioral scene of children's lives and because of the many factors that may crowd themselves into the picture. Just one brief illustration of what we are trying to point out:

Johnny has just attacked another youngster viciously, really undeservedly. The other child's surprise and the whole situation are so crystal clear that this time we are sure that even our insight-defensive Johnny will have to let us show him how he really asked for it all— so, here we stand, our clinical appetite whetted while we watch the fight. But—wham—a third child interferes. He happened to run by, couldn't resist the temptation of getting into the brawl, and he is a youngster Johnny has a lot of hostile feeling about anyway. Before anybody quite knows what has happened, Johnny receives from that interfering youngster a blow much too heavy and unfair for anybody's fight ritual, and so, of course, Johnny leaves the scene howling with fury, pain, and shame about losing face. Obviously, we had better assist Johnny in his predicament, but the idea of using this life space interview for a push in the direction of Johnny's self-insight into the provocativeness of his behavior seems downright ridiculous at this point.

Role Compatibility. Children who live in an institutional setting do not react to individual people as "persons" only. There is also a direct impact brought to bear on them from the very "role" they perceive a particular adult to be in. This issue has long been obscured by the all too generalized as- sumption that the personal relationship between child and adults is the only thing that counts. To illustrate this point:

When a camp counselor finds her whole cabin up on the roof where they know they shouldn't be, she may have trouble getting them down no matter how much the children may all love her. I, as the camp director walking in on that scene, may find it much easier to get them off the roof; in fact they may climb down as soon as they see me coming along. This does not mean that they have a less good relationship to their counselor or a better one to me. It simply means a difference in their role expectation. The counselor for them is seen in the role of the group leader, which heavily contains the flavor of the one who plans happy experiences with them. It is true that on the margin of this role they do know that the adult counselor also has certain "overgroup-demanded" regulations to identify herself with and to enforce. However, that part of her role—and for the sake of a happy camp experience we hope so—is less sharply in focus than the program-identified one. In fact, if that counselor got too fussy or too indignant about the youngsters' not responding immediately, or used the argument of the overall camp regulations against her gang too fast, this would create resentment and a loss of subsequent relationship for a while. The role of the camp director, no matter how cordial individual feelings toward him may be, is much more clearly loaded with the expectation that it is his job to secure overall coordination of many people's interests. The children would therefore expect the director to make a demand for them to get off that roof, and would not hold it as much against him that he does interfere with the pleasure of the moment or considers the whole camp more important than "Cabin 7" at this time.

The compatibility of the major role of a given adult with the role he is forced into by the life space interview is an important strategic consideration. In our present operation, for example, we felt, during the first year or so, that it was quite important that the role of the *counselor* be rather sharply set off from that of the *ward boss*, the *teacher*, the *therapist*. . . . During that phase it also seemed important for us to protect the counselor from too many unnecessary displaced hostilities, since she has enough to do to handle those that would naturally come her way. In short: During that period of time we felt it important that all requests for going home or for special prolonged week-end visits, etc., were steered to the psychiatrist, who was seen as the ward boss by the children. The transference character of many of these requests and the terrific ambivalence of the children about them, thrown on top of all the aggression manipulation a counselor has to cope with anyway in her daily play life with the child, would have increased the ensuing confusion. The arrangement we created allowed the ward boss to absorb some of the extra frustration acidity unavoidably generated during such interviews, while the counselor was, so to say, "taken off that hook." At the same time, however, we did feel that the counselor is the most natural person to assist the child in *first aid* interviews around his concern about home, mother's not turning up for a visit, etc.

Mood Manageability—The Child's and Our Own. With due respect to all the clinical ambition any staff member can have about managing his own mood, there is a limit beyond which he cannot be forced any further. Such limits need to be recognized. Oversimplifying the issue for purposes of abbreviation:

If I work for an hour in order to get the children finally in shape to be quite reasonable and have a good stretch of quite happy and unusually well modulated play with me, I can't possibly act concerned enough if one of them does something that needs a more serious "reality rub-in" for good measure. This is especially the case where we allow a child to play his "cute antics" for the service of everybody's entertainment, and where he suddenly begins to go too far. Even a serious talk with someone who quite visibly found the same antics cute two minutes ago will not have the same strategic chance as a talk with one who was not involved in the original scene.

The item of mood manageability is, of course, an even more difficult one as far as the mood of the children is concerned. The issue may be clear enough, and the event beautifully designed to draw some learning out of it. If the youngster in the meantime gets overexcited, bored, tired, or grouchy, the best laid-out issue would be hopelessly lost and we had better look for another occasion for the same job.

Issues around Timing. One of the great strategic advantages of the life space interview is the very flexibility in timing that it offers us. We don't have to hope that the child will remember from Friday noon until his therapy hour next Wednesday what was happening just now. We can talk with him *right now*. Or, having watched the event itself that led to a messy incident, we can quite carefully calculate how long it will take the youngster to cool off enough in order to be accessible to some reasonable communication with him, and move in on him at that very calculated time. Or we

may even see to it that he gets enough emotional first aid from us or from our colleagues so that he can be brought into a state where some insight-focused discussion with him is possible at last. One of the most frequent dilemmas that aggressive and explosive children force us into is the fear of waiting too long to talk about something, because we know how fast they forget, as opposed to the need to let some cooling off take place, lest the interview itself get shot through with the aggression debris left over from the original scene. Sometimes external things happen and the "time" aspect may often work against us. I shall never forget the painful experience several years ago in which I finally had succeeded in working a bunch of quite recalcitrant delinquents into a mood conducive to my talking with them about an issue they didn't want to face. Just then the swimming bell put a rude end to my efforts. To keep them one minute longer while they heard and saw everybody else running down to their beloved free swim would have made shambles out of my carefully built up role as interpreter of the rules of life.

The Impact of Terrain and of Props. Both the life space interview and the more classical styles of individual therapy believe in the importance of terrain and props. In the long-range therapy, after we have figured out the most goal-supportive arrangements, the problem of terrain and props loses its importance because it can easily be held constant or can at least be kept under predictable control. While the most favorable terrain is always the one in which both partners feel most comfortable, in life space interviewing the terrain may be terrifically varied, and neither it nor the selection of props is often within our power.

In fact, more often than not, terrain as well as props are on the side of the child's resistance, rather than on our side. This is, of course, especially true when we move in on a situation involving extreme behavioral conflict.

For the child, the most comfortable place may be the one behind his most belligerently cathected defenses. From bathtub to toy cabinet, from roof or treetop to "under the couch," his choice of terrain seems endless. In all cases the problem of what emotional charge the surrounding props may suddenly assume remains of high technical relevance. Besides what is going on between the two people, what is going on between *them and space and props* can become of great relevance.

In summary, the choice of a given technique must be (1) dependent on the specific goal we have in mind (2) within a given setting (3) with a specific type of child (4) in a given phase of his therapeutic movement.[2] There is no "odd" or "bad" technique in itself. The very procedure that "made" one situation all by itself may be the source of a mess-up in another, or may have remained irrelevant in a third. However, this reminder, while disappointing, would not be too hard to take, for we have learned that lesson from the development of concepts of strategy and techniques for the psychiatric interview long ago. Rather than relearn it, we simply need to remember the difference between a pseudoscientific technical trick-bag, and a more complex, but infinitely more realistic concept of multiple-item conditioned choice of criteria for the selection of strategy as well as of techniques.

Notes

1. Whenever in illustrations the "children on our ward" are mentioned, this refers to the following setting: Closed Ward within the premises of the National Institutes of Health, a large research hospital. The children referred to here: a carefully selected group of six boys ranging in age from eight to ten years at the time of intake, chosen as representative of "borderline" disturbances commonly referred to as "explosive acting-out type of child." They are children of normal IQ, however, and are expected to be free from traceable physical pathology, characterized in their behavior by a rather extreme volume of aggression, extreme forms of reckless destruction, and loaded with an amazing array of learning disturbances and charac-

ter disorders to boot. The ward on which the children lived was staffed and operated more along the lines of a camping program, with the hospital as a base, but not ultimate limit for the activities. At the time of the presentation of this material, the movement of the children into a newly constructed open residence was imminent. The treatment and research goals of the operation included the study of the impact of intensive individual psychotherapy (four hours per child per week), of observations in our own school setting (individual tutoring as well as group school), and exposure to "milieu therapy" in their life on the ward.

2. Many illustrations used in this paper need to be understood as limited by the specific conditions under which the observations were made. For their full evaluation, a detailed description of the overall program and ward policies for the clinical management of the children and for the guidance of staff behavior would have to be added here. It is, therefore, expected that most of our illustrations will have to be read with this reservation in mind. While literal translation into practice with other children in different settings is not intended, we do imply emphatically that the basic principles we are trying to illustrate here should hold for a wide variety of designs.

Abridged from Fritz Redl, "The Concept of the Life Space Interview," *American Journal of Orthopsychiatry*, XXIX, January 1959, 1–18. Copyright © 1959, the American Orthopsychiatric Association, Inc. Reprinted by permission.

Editors' Commentary

Life space interviewing should not be linked with crises alone. Rather it is an appropriate style of teacher–pupil interaction to deal with many issues. Although the process evolved as a control technique, it is now more generally applied. In the following article by Morse, more or less extreme cases are used for illustration, but other, less stringent, problems can also be appropriate opportunities for using it. Redl's article gives the psychological elements of life space interviewing. Morse gives steps and stages that teachers can use to organize interviews. In LSI training programs, discussion and study of actual interview tapes enable the supervisor to help teachers use the technique effectively. Without supervised practice, it is difficult to lean any new skill. However, a conceptual system helps teachers practice talking with children in the format of life space interviewing. No one would go through the "steps" in sequence, or even use them all in the same interview. But they provide nodal points in thinking about the process as a model of interaction. This article should be read with Redl's theory article, which preceded it.

Worksheet on Life Space Interviewing for Teachers

William C. Morse

A major problem for teachers is how to talk or counsel effectively with pupils and groups of pupils, whether it be for the purpose of exploring a general attitude, a motivational complex, or a control and management problem with mild or severe implications.

These conditions are apparent: (1) teachers cannot adopt a counselor's role, be it psychoanalytic or non-directive; (2) it is not possible to refer all "working through of problems" to persons outside the classroom; (3) it is not adequate to continue an outmoded moralistic approach or some equally unsophisticated and undynamic method.

Any model worthy of teaching as a profession must embody the deepest understanding of individual and group dynamics. But it must be focused on practice suited to the "firing line" operation of teaching rather than the consultation room. There is considerable disagreement about the role of a teacher, but no one will argue that the profession is sorely in need of new methods for assisting in the socialization processes and for dealing with the increasingly complex and frustrating behavior that pupils bring to the school. Whatever we do should be based on the generic nature of the educative process and the legitimate responsibility of the school. The concept of LSI is geared to these propositions.

Several theoretical developments have produced the present theoretical stance.

1. The concept of milieu as developed by Lewin and Redl. The application to the school implies an awareness of the total psycho-social system of a school.

2. The concept of Life Space Interviewing by Redl is designed to work with behavior "in situ."

3. The concept of crisis intervention by Caplan and others makes it clear that active intervention in times of stress is a most productive teaching opportunity.

4. The concept of differential diagnosis and strategic planning emphasizes going beyond the symptom and applying a variety of stratagems.

5. The concept of coping skills gives a rationale to the newer methodology as a means for teaching the pupil-needed ego skills. There is no belief that this alone will always be sufficient, but it is implied that without such new skills, much traditional therapy pays a low dividend.

6. The empathic relationship which the teacher generates underlies any "technique," and is more imposing in its impact than is method per se.

The following steps are not meant as a formal series, for there will be a great deal of flexibility in the development of any situation. Teachers seldom can conduct an extensive sequence at one interview, but the process can still be seen in its entire scope.

It should be noted that the goals differ significantly. In depth work, the expectation is for long-term gradual emergence of a more healthy personality, with possible regression followed by integration and eventual independence. In LSI, the hope is for a degree of behavioral compliance accompanied by life space relief, fostering adjustment. Marginal behavior then, may be all one expects. Traditionally, teachers act as if they expect to induce an immediate character change by exterior verbal exchange.

I. Instigating Condition

Goal. In LSI, a specific incident (or series) calling for interference starts off the interview, but not as a moral issue, which is the traditional approach. The choice of proper timing and selection of an incident is critical. Many times it is preferable to allow certain incidents to pass by until one worthy of exploration occurs. There is usually a need for some "on the spot" managerial involvement. In LSI, direct use is made of milieu reality events. Choice of time and place of handling is selected to enforce or mitigate.

Process. One first works to obtain the individual (or group) perception of the state of affairs. While this is partly a matter of permitting catharsis and ventilation, it is basically the mode of establishing relationship by emphasizing your real interest in the child's perceptions rather than in your opinions. It is a matter of psychological truth rather than legal truth to which the adult is sensitive. To listen is to accept: it requires empathic feeling. Frequently the interviewer will be faced with resistance that demands tact and skill to penetrate. You end up with his perceptions, and you have already begun to size up the dynamics of the situation.

II. Testing for Depth and Spread

Goal. Some events are, to the child, isolated incidents. Others stand for something more extensive: "I always get caught," or "I can never do anything." To what is this event attached as the child sees it? One drops many issues that seem to have no significant attachments since to the child these have little meaning. On the other hand, if what happened is a symbol of life for the child, it deserves minute attention.

Process. What is the basic central issue involved? Is this symptomatic of general life experience? Is it attached to some deep personality aspect? ("Do teachers always pick on you?" "Are all the others leaving you out?" "You always get caught, others don't?") What is the psychological factor underlying the behavioral episode and the reason for the depth of reaction?

III. Content Clarification

Goal. It should be noted that here the content focus is very different from the traditional approach where there is an emphasis on standardized morality and surface compliance. Nor is the concern with the fantasy, conscious and unconscious content through dreams, early conflicts, and so on as would take place in depth counseling. Nor is the emphasis only on feeling, as in the less directive efforts. It is on what happened in sequence, descriptive at this level and without implied judgment.

Process. The teacher explores what went on: the reality is reconstructed with attached feelings and impulses recognized. It is accepted in a nonvaluative way, although pupils already know we have values in ourselves. We are interested in the world as the pupil perceives it—not in the "reality" world as we would see it at this juncture.

IV. Enhancing a Feeling of Acceptance

Goal. In truth, the way we conduct the interview is the only way we can cultivate a feeling of acceptance in the relationship with a child. Some have limited capacity to respond, but many find a really concerned, listening adult a new experience. We do not aim for a deep transference as in therapy. We aim to be seen as an understanding, helpful teacher-counselor, a role most pupils already anticipate for us.

In classical therapeutic work, significant transference is anticipated. In traditional teaching, the adult-teacher role is one of authority, paternalistic or autocratic. In LSI it is empathic, with a deep involvement in understanding. This consists of non-interpretive utilization of basic conscious or unconscious motivations. It requires a non-defensive, assured reasonableness. It is permissive in the sense of recognizing "the right to be heard," not in condoning behavior unsuited to the setting, such as hitting or destroying. The adult accepts that behavior is caused, that change is slow and hard, that motivations must be understood—but on the ego level. Any portion of positive potential is nurtured in contrast to exclusive attention to the pathology.

Process. Obviously it is not only what is done, but also how the basic tone is established, the acceptance, the ability one has to help the pupil while maintaining the adult role. This is a most complex condition but one many teachers can accomplish. It requires essentially non-interpretive responding to deeper feelings, which sometimes the pupil does not consciously recognize in himself. The significant aspect is to deal with the feelings behind the defense, not counter-attack the defense itself.

V. Avoiding Early Imposition of Value Judgments

Goal. We aim to put understanding before judgment. Traditionally, teachers appeal to a value system, use threats, admonition, exhortations, and denial of impulses.

In the depth process, transference, resistance, interpretations, insight, identification, and acceptance of impulses (interpretations of unconscious material), high verbal permissiveness, acting out are interpreted. Play therapy and projective devices may be employed in the quest of the "diseased" and deepest level of difficulty. Obviously these methods are suited to the traditional therapeutic settings and not to the classroom.

Process. In LSI, the perception of the pupil is accepted as a perception, but other perceptions are explored, too. The implications of his view are realistically contemplated in a non-punitive manner. The emphasis is on behavior and methods of coping with his problem in a more satisfactory way. Ego level interpretations may be given only on the basis of the overt data and, ideally, are acknowledged by the pupil in the life setting. Impulse control is studied, support planned, hurdle help provided, and coping skills "taught." Implications of the present behavior are faced in actuality, not as a threat. Arguments over "right" and "wrong" behavior imply the pupil does not know right from wrong, which is usually not the case, and a challenge often sets off a secondary adult–child contention. If no real (rather than abstract) violation of the rights of others has taken place, it may be impossible to find an appeal to the child anyway.

VI. Exploring the Internal Mechanics for "Change" Possibilities

Goal. The goal here is to find what superego values or fragments are relevant in the pupil's perception of events. It is a matter of presence of guilt and anxiety *vs.* just being caught. The pupil must be free to express antisocial values. Group-related guilt reduction must be explored.

The ending of this phase moves toward "What should be done about it?" Many issues resolve themselves at this point: on the other hand there may be extensive resistance which has to be handled over a long series of contacts.

Process. Essentially we ask, what will help the pupil with this problem as he sees it? How can I help, or who can help? Here we get important diagnostic cues regarding his self-concept and goals as well as rationalizations. We see something of his hope or despair, his belief in "instant change." Frequently there is again resistance and denial. The worker can clarify the reality of assumptions which the pupil makes, without judgmental overtones, always looking for evidence to consider.

VII. The Two Resolution Phases

Goal. In the traditional work of teachers, surface compliance is usually demanded for whatever it is worth. In depth work, the anticipation is for eventual transfer to life situations with the expectation that sometimes things get worse in the action arena for a time. In LSI, one cannot expect great changes or even any improvement at times. The whole environment of life milieu is utilized for any relief or alterations it may have to offer. This may mean mitigation of given critical conditions, or planning and building in some support in

the milieu. The limited outcome may be evidence that something more intensive in the way of help may eventually be needed—deep therapy, institutional treatment, or whatever the condition reveals. There is no supposition that, in all cases, even a tolerable situation will result. While LSI has the long view, it has to operate in the immediate, so in a sense it requires a bifocal view of events. What can we do to prevent a repetition of this behavior?

Process. (a) *Presenting the "Adult" View.* If the problem has not worked itself out to some reasonable next step, the adult at this stage begins to inject reality factors in an objective way: implications of behavior, standards, expectations. Reality limits are explained in a non-moralistic way. Why some attention must be given to the behavior is covered, but not vindictively. It may be a matter of basic social behavior or the nature of school and its inherent demands or the implications of nonconformity. Considerable skill is needed here to avoid the typical moralistic stance. At the same time adult responsibility must be acknowledged, and the nature of the real world frankly examined.

Process. (b) *Working Through to a Solution—Strategic Planning.* The reality demands are clarified and some reasonable first-step plan is developed. What is going to happen or will happen the next time? Here is where the sanctions, freedom restrictions, need for more intensive help, the special assistance, and behavior contingencies are discussed. It is essential that the plan be one which can be carried out, whether it be removal, a talk with parents, or a discussion with a third party. Thus, we are led again back to the milieu and its potentials. A pupil should be left with a feeling of milieu solidarity and support for him in his dilemma, rather than permissiveness or escapism. Vague and severe threats have no place whatsoever. Discussion of extensive and obviously not-to-happen consequences of continued limit breaking serve only to confuse the issue. On the other hand, there should be no hiding or reluctance to examine what may actually have to take place. We have to help him feel we are non-hostile and that we have hopes of really helping him cope with the difficulty. Since many pupils feel they must test any stated plan, no nonworkable program should be risked. That is, no plan is envisioned which [it] will not be possible to conduct if the pupil needs to test it out. Here needed specialists are worked into the design and all of the school's resources are reviewed for potential help. It well may be that LSI and other methods will work in unison when the program is a very complex one.

Worksheet on Conceptual Variations in Interview Designs with Children

	Psychodynamic	Life Space or Reality	Traditional
1. Instigating condition	General personality problem, long-term, not responding to supportive and growth correctional effort	Specific incident (or series) of behavior usually calling for "on the spot" managerial interference	Both implied but interpreted as moral issue
2. Goal	Long-term expectations of gradual emergence of more healthy personality, possible regression followed by integration and eventual independence	Degree of behavioral compliance accompanied by life space relief fostering adjustment	Induce an immediate character change, exterior change
3. Setting	Office isolation away from immediate life pressures, formal setting, sequence timed	Direct use of milieu reality aspects; choice of time, place to enforce or mitigate as needed	Isolated, integrated, frequent use of group or setting for pressure
4. Relationship	Classical transference resistance inter-personal relationship	Emphatic, child identified role by adult	Adult role of authority; paternalistic, autocratic
5. Content	Conscious and unconscious, fantasy, early conflicts, projection, focus on feeling, impulse exploration	What went on, reality exploration, reconstruction with attached feelings, impulses, recognized, accepted	Emphasis on the standard morality interpretation of event
6. Processes	Transference, resistance, interpretations, insight, identification, acceptance of impulses (interpretations of unconscious material), high verbal permissiveness, acting out interpreted	Causal behavior "accepted," clinical exploitation of LS events, ego-level interpretation, impulse-control balance critical, support given, explanations fostered, ego support, hurdle help, "skills" depicted, behavior implications faced	Appeal to value system, threats, admonition, exhortations, denial of impulses
7. Resolution	Eventual transfer to life situations	Support and milieu planning to mitigate critical conditions	Surface compliance or rejection

References

Bandura, Albert. Social Reinforcement and Behavior Change—Symposium, 1962. *Am. Jo. Ortho.*, 33:4, July 1963.

Caldwell, Bettye M., Leonard Hersher, Earle Lipton, and others. Mother–Infant Interaction in Monomatric and Polymatric Families. *Am. Jo. Ortho.*, 33:4, July 1963.

Caplan, G. Mental Health Consultation in Schools. Milbank Memorial Fund Proceedings, 1955 Annual Conference.

Caplan, G. (ed.) *Prevention of Mental Disorders in Children.* New York: Basic Books, 1961.

Dean, S. J. Treatment of the Reluctant Client, *Am. Psych.*, 13:11, November 1959, pp. 627–630.

Dittman, A. T. and H. L. Kitchener. L.S.I. and Individual Play Therapy, *Am. Jo. Ortho.*, 29:1, January 1959, pp. 19–26.

Kitchener, Howard L. The Life Space Interview in the Differentiation of School in Residential Treatment. *Am. Jo. Ortho.*, 33:4, July 1963.

Krasner, Leonard. Reinforcement, Verbal Behavior, and Psychotherapy. *Am. Jo. Ortho.*, 33:4, July 1963.

Lindsley, Ogden R. Experimental Analysis of Social Reinforcement: Terms and Methods. *Am. Jo. Ortho.*, 33:4, July 1963.

Long, Nicholas J. Some Problems in Teaching Life Space Interviewing Techniques to Graduate Students in Education in a Large Class at Indiana University. *Am. Jo. Ortho.*, 33:4, July 1963.

Morse, William C. Working Paper: Training Teachers in Life Space Interviewing. *Am. Jo. Ortho.*, 33:4, July 1963.

Morse, W. C. and E. R. Small. Group Life Space Interviewing in a Therapeutic Camp. *Am. Jo. Ortho.*, 29:1, January 1959, pp. 27–44.

Murphey, Elizabeth B., Earle Silber, George Coehlho, and others. Development of Autonomy and Parent–Child Interaction in Case Adolescence. *Am. Jo. Ortho.*, 33:4, July 1963.

Newman, Ruth G. The School-Centered Life Space Interview as Illustrated by Extreme Threat of School Issues. *Am. Jo. Ortho.*, 33:4, July 1963.

Redl, Fritz. Strategy and Techniques of the Life Space Interview. *Am. Jo. Ortho.*, 29:1, January 1959, pp. 1–18.

Redl, Fritz. The School Centered Life Space Interview. Washington, D.C.: School Research Program, Washington School of Psychiatry, 1963.

Redl, Fritz. The Concept of Therapeutic Milieu. *Am. Jo. Ortho.*, 29:4, October 1959, pp. 721–727.

Editors' Commentary

Parent Participation

Within the Bureau of Education for the Handicapped, parent education has become a new funding priority for the Division of Personnel Preparation (DPP). Public Law 94–142 outlines the minimum requirements for parent–teacher interaction. It is clear that parents of handicapped pupils will in the future play a more significant and central role in their children's programs than they have in the past. In the next article, Gwen Brown describes this new frontier and the skills teachers need to have to work with parents of emotionally disturbed pupils.

Parents in the Classroom

Gwen Brown

Through the last two decades, parents have effectively organized, demonstrated, and lobbied to obtain an appropriate education for handicapped children. Despite the enormous gains made for children, public school doors remained closed to many parents when it comes to policy making. Schools have assumed the sole authority in decisions about testing, placing, and educating children, and parents rarely were consulted or given information until after the decisions were made (Nazzaro, 1976). The new Education for the Handicapped Act, Public Law 94–142, however, revolutionizes the role of parents in the educational process. As local education agencies implement the law, special and regular educators find themselves in closer contact with parents of handicapped children. Unfortunately, this contact does not always result in closeness and affection.

Who Are These Parents?

For many years, teachers carried a fantasized image of "parents." Adjectives easily associated with it were "troublesome," "hostile," "passive," "neurotic," "uninformed," "meddling," or "uninterested." It is little wonder that so many parent education programs developed by the schools failed to interest or meet the needs of large numbers of parents.

Today teachers are learning that parents are not a homogeneous group; rather they come to the school with all the variety of the population as a whole (Kroth and Brown, 1978). In addition to the variables of ethnicity, religion, education, and income, a wide variety of attitudes, values, and child-rearing practices must be taken into account when planning a parent-involvement program (Bridge, 1976). Some parents come to the school with years of experience and great sophistication in special education, parent organizations, and educational planning and behavior management; others have never heard of an IEP or considered themselves important teachers for their children.

While parents of handicapped children are a diverse group, most share intense feelings of disappointment with their child beyond that typically experienced by parents of nonhandicapped children. In their struggle to find help for their child, they too often have found ignorance, rejection, or indifference among members of the medical and educational establishments. After going through the typical stages of denial, guilt, and a search for services, many parents turn their frustrations into militance and a demand for social action. When this happens, parents frequently are labeled uncooperative by educators, and they experience the pain of a power struggle in which there are no winners.

Generally, parents of children with behavior disorders have not successfully organized themselves for mutual support and social action, as have parents of other types of special education children. (Parents of autistic children are an exception—they have organized.) Guilt, a sense of personal failure, and family disorganization have kept many parents from reaching out successfully for support from others. Especially if a biological basis for the child's disturbing behavior is not evident, parents often are overwhelmed with their own sense of inadequacy and are too embarrassed to ask for help from others. In some cases, parents repeat unsuccessful behavior patterns, developed from stressful experiences in their own childhoods, not only in dealing with the child, but also in relating to the school. When interacting with such parents, teachers need to be firm and patient and to step out of the way of hostility, just as they would when dealing with a student exhibiting inappropriate behavior patterns. Teachers should never make the mistake, however, of presuming that, because the child displays inappropriate behavior patterns, the parents also will present inappropriate and self-defeating behaviors. On the contrary, many parents of children with behavior disorders are models of successful life functioning and good mental health.

A final characteristic of these parents that is worth mentioning is that they, like all other parents, have a wealth of information and skills that they can share. Parent education programs will fall short of their potential unless teachers encourage the parents to share these with the schools and with each other. Parent involvement is likely to be least effective when teachers do all the teaching.

Setting Up Programs

Parent involvement can take many forms, ranging from the once or twice a year IEP conference, to extensive parent education groups and classroom participation. At a minimum, teachers conduct early IEP conferences with all children receiving special education services. If conducted properly, early individual meetings with parents can prevent or reduce problems of attendance, discipline, and dropping out and can improve grades and appropriate home–school contacts (Duncan and Fitzgerald, 1969). If not conducted with skill and sensitivity, of course, the conference can lead to lawsuits and/or a deterioration of the child's performance. The following books may help teachers conduct conferences that foster satisfying home–school relationships and improve the child's performance:

Barach, Ray J. *The Parent Teacher Partnership.* Reston, Va.: Council for Exceptional Children, 1969.

D'Evelyn, Katherine E. *Individual Parent Teacher Conference.* New York: Bureau of Publishers, Teachers College, Columbia University, 1963.

Garett, Annette. *Interviewing: Its Principles and Methods.* New York: Family Service Association of America, 1942.

Kelly, E. J. *Parent–Teacher Interaction—a Special Education Perspective.* Seattle: Special Child Publications, 1974.

Kroth, Roger. *Communicating with Parents of Exceptional Children.* Denver: Love Publishing Co., 1975.

Kroth, R. L., and Simpson, R. *Parent Conferences as a Teaching Strategy.* Denver: Love Publishing Co., 1977.

An educational package entitled, *Conference Time for Teachers and Parents: A Filmstrip for Teachers,* developed in 1972 by the National Education Association, may be helpful to both parents and teachers. It includes a filmstrip to help parents learn effective conferencing strategies.

After considering available time and resources, teachers can determine whether they will stop at the IEP conference or develop a more extensive parent-involvement program. In developing parent programs, teachers must consider the characteristics of the families involved. Before informally assessing interests, teachers can brainstorm to develop lists of possible avenues for program development. Following are three lists that may get teachers started in their thinking. The lists are broken into informational, social, and skill area needs. While only ten items are listed in each area, many other interest items will emerge as the particular characteristics of the children and families involved are determined. The lists teachers develop in these three areas can help them in informally assessing parents or families and in developing individual educational programs specifically suited to their interests and needs.

Typical Informational Questions Parents May Have

1. What happens at an "I.E.P." conference?

2. What are my rights and responsibilities under the law?

3. How do you see my child's problem in relationship to normal development?

4. How is my child progressing academically? Socially? How can I support this development?

5. What is the prescriptive/diagnostic procedure all about?

6. What other community resources are available to my child? Library materials? Medical services? Camps? Child care?

7. Are there other parents in the community who can be of help to me? Parent organizations? Civic groups?

8. How do I handle siblings' reactions to the child's behavior?

9. How do I talk to neighbors and relatives about the child's behavior?

10. How can I use the home environment and resources to their best advantage for the child and my family? Budgeting? Nutrition? Inexpensive materials to stimulate learning? Reinforcing home and school behavior?

Skills with Which Many Parents Want Help

1. Actively listening to their children.

2. Communicating warmth, acceptance, and positive regard to their children.

3. Accepting the children's feelings, but not necessarily their behaviors. Saying no firmly, but with positive regard. Assisting the children in releasing their emotions at appropriate times and not acting them out inappropriately against others.

4. Behavior management, including observation, pinpointing target behavior, charting, reinforcing, and time out.

5. Involving other family members in the children's programs.

6. Working with professionals, including school personnel, to get services for their children.

7. Tutoring their children in academic areas.

8. Stepping out of the stress cycle.

9. Communicating their own feelings and needs to others, including their children.

10. Handling their own frustrations, anger, and despair appropriately.

Typical Personal and Social Needs Parents May Have

1. To be listened to.

2. To have both positive and negative feelings accepted.

3. To be respected as competent individuals who can take a strong role in helping their children.

4. To hear from other parents going through similar kinds of experiences.

5. To have time away from the child, now and then.

6. To be appreciated for what is going well with their children and in their own lives.

7. To feel free of guilt and the blaming attitudes of others.

8. To feel some optimism and hopefulness about the future.

9. To have supportive relationships and recognition for their successes in trying to implement new strategies in their homes and with their children.

10. To have a major role in the decision-making process about their own programs as well as their children's.

Once the particular needs and interests of the families are established, teachers can set up parent programs in much the same way as they set up programs for their students. Good educational programming strategies work for young people and adults alike. The following steps are recommended in developing parent-involvement programs that really work:

1. Meet around the child's successes, rather than simply at times of crisis. Help parents see what is going well. Avoid blaming parents for the child's difficulties.

2. Involve parents in the decision making as much as possible. Offer some options about what is to be covered in the parent program.

3. Determine and use to advantage the skills and information of parents, relatives, neighbors, and siblings.

4. Accept feelings, although not necessarily all behaviors. Firm direction may be needed at times.

5. When engaging parents in child behavior change projects or in child tutoring be very specific about what they are to do; limit the number of things that they try to do at any one time; check frequently to see how they are doing; adjust plans when necessary; and reinforce the parents' behavior frequently!

6. When holding conferences or meetings with parents, have information ready to share; be ready to hear what the parents have to share; and expect to develop a cooperative relationship.

7. When holding conferences with parents, do not overwhelm them with the presence of large numbers of professionals.

8. Be flexible in program planning. For ideas, read, read, read! Parent articles are springing up in all the leading psychology and education journals. *Exceptional Child Education Resources*, published by the Council for Exceptional Children, contains relevant articles.

9. Be sure to maintain realistic optimism and a positive attitude toward the future.

10. Use mistakes to advantage whenever possible. Learn from them; never let them stand in the way of trying again. This may be hard at times, but it can be done. Most of the time it will be fun.

Resources That May Be Helpful to Parents

Although the books, kits, filmstrips, and other resources available to parents are too numerous to discuss extensively in this article, some of particular interest can be mentioned. First, a recent annotated bibliography that is helpful to both teachers and parents is, "Help for Parents of Handicapped Children," compiled by the Eastern Pennsylvania Regional Resource Center for Special Education, King of Prussia, Pennsylvania 19406. Second, the journal *Exceptional Parent* may be of interest to parents and to those developing parent education programs. Finally, parents having difficulty locating resources in their communities can write to Closer Look, National Information Center for the Handicapped, P.O. Box 1492, Washington, D.C. 20013. This federally funded center provides a national information retrieval service available to parents who are unable to find the help they need locally.

References

Bridge, R. G. "Parent Participation in School Innovations." *Teachers College Record* 77 (1976): 366–384.

Brown, G. B., and Palmer, E. J. "A National Review of BEH Funded Personnel Preparation Programs in the Area of Emotional Disturbance." *Exceptional Children* 44 (1977): 168–175.

Duncan, L. W., and Fitzgerald, P. W. "Increasing the Parent–Child Communication through Counselor–Parent Conferences." *Personnel and Guidance Journal*, 27 (1969): 514–517.

Kroth, R., and Brown, G. B. "Welcoming in the Parents." *School Media Quarterly*, June 1978, p. 72.

Nazzaro, J. "Comprehensive Assessment for Educational Planning." In *Public Policy and the Education of Exceptional Children*, edited by F. J. Weintraub; A. Abeson; J. Ballard; and M. L. LaVor. Reston, Virginia: Council for Exceptional Children, 1976.

Editors' Commentary

Summary

Therapeutic management is a very complex topic, taking us from specialized techniques and whole classroom designs to the community and family influences. Teachers who have unusual difficulty in control will need training to unravel the causes and trace the ramifications.

Part of the problem of management is manpower—the right person doing the right thing at the right time. The ratio of adults to disturbed youngsters seldom approaches that needed. We look in vain for enough therapists, for enough support personnel, or for smaller class sizes. We are going to turn more and more to new staffing patterns in the classroom, where extra hands count most. Aides, assistants, parent helpers, and older youths can contribute one-to-one help for certain very disturbed children in the early stages of their education. Such help will be required for adequate control.

Therapeutic management means helping pupils find themselves and regulate their own behavior more adequately. We seek to teach basic socialization in some cases, a sense of inner belief and security in others. These goals will not be reached without considerable human investment. To keep order is not an adequate goal for management.

6

How Can We
Teach These Children?

I tray to tell the truth
and not lie but my problem is that
I can't seem to remember anything or
that I'm just not <u>listening</u>. I understand that already but I don't know
why I just start listening or just
start remembering. Most people think
that sounds easy to do, but I wonder why
I can't start doing that. Not listening
and not remembering has just about
got me in trouble everytime I've been
in trouble since I've been alive (and
take my word for it I've been in a lot of
<u>trouble</u>!) I don't mean I've only been
in trouble at school but at home
too. When I was in first grade
I got strait A's and I've gotten worse
every year until now <u>unexceptable!</u>
I think I would be happier if I could
finish my work and relax. I wish

I could just dump every paper out of my binder and start out fresh. And see the change. I bet it would be a good one chances are they'd be good changes (90% to 10%). I'd have better holiday's weekends and even in and out of school.

Editors' Commentary

Just as the invisible quality of air can affect our physical well-being, the invisible quality of classroom instruction can affect the emotional well-being of pupils. Silberman,[1] in his book *Crisis in the Classroom*, gives a gloomy view of public education as organized around the theme of mindlessness and hopelessness. When people think "clean air smells funny," this is because clean air is an unusual occurrence. Creative teaching in the classroom is also an unusual occurrence. This view is supported by the high school dropout rate, which has reached 40 percent in some urban schools. In addition, 20 percent of the school population is not learning at a rate commensurate with intellectual ability. For pupils who lack the linguistic, cognitive, and affective skills necessary for school success, the standard instructional methods available in the classroom cannot reduce the pain of failure. In time, these pupils become immune to the curriculum, give up attempts to achieve, and avoid help from others.

When these pupils are referred to our special education classes because of learning or behavior problems, we must be careful not to let our specific goals (such as helping them catch up in basic academic areas, or mainstreaming them in a regular classroom) distract us from our primary goal of "helping pupils learn how to learn." Biber[2] reminds us that the purpose of schooling goes beyond teaching specific skills and facts; it is related to the unseen but essential four goals of education: (1) development of sensitivity to the world around us; (2) development of techniques and attitudes for learning by discovery; (3) development of cognitive power and intellectual mastery; (4) development of synthesis in learning through symbolic expression. These educational goals are even more important for children with learning and behavior problems. They need specially trained teachers, teaching strategies and instructional materials to help them overcome their resistance to learning how to learn.

This section is devoted to the methods of teaching these pupils—the "specialness" of special instruction. Is special instruction the same as regular teaching except that the teacher has fewer pupils and more time, or is it different as, say, a workhorse is different from a racehorse? We think it is different. We feel special instruction takes more than good "horse sense" and a stable mind—these help, but they are not enough.

1. **Charles E. Silberman,** *Crisis in the Classroom: The Remaking of American Education* (New York: Vintage Books, 1971).

2. **Barbara Biber,** "Integration of Mental Health Principles in the School Setting," in *Prevention of Mental Disorders*, ed. Gerald Caplan (New York: Basic Books, 1961).

The act of special teaching is independent of the act of special learning. Special teaching hinges on understanding how the learner processes the material received; in other words, the unique conditions of the learner determine the effectiveness of the teaching. For example, a boy who considers geography totally irrelevant to his personal life makes a teacher's geography lesson ineffective (at least for himself); a girl who is fearful of hurting people because of her own aggressive drives learns very little from the experience of dissecting a frog; a pupil with a visual motor dysfunction may become sullen and hostile when asked to complete a three-dimensional drawing assignment. An understanding of individual differences, interests, and abilities is essential in changing teaching into the desired act—learning. In addition, special teaching means blending cognitive and affective components of living and learning so that troubled pupils may experience school as a vital, exciting, and growth-facilitating environment.

Through flexible, skillful use of the right lessons, materials, and teaching methods, the teacher slowly engages the learner. Curriculum and methodology become the instruments of the teacher who, with a virtuoso performance, can soothe, nurture, and excite a new-found appreciation and love for education. Great pains must be taken to ensure the curriculum's relevance to the learner; materials and content are potential sources for enhancing the pupil's self-esteem. Without doubt, the teacher's development of personal competence and the ability to teach in a relevant, challenging way are indispensable to this process.

We feel there is no panacea, no single model or theory, for reeducating emotionally disturbed children. The needs of children go beyond present models. That is why we are suggesting the label "psychoeducational approach" to include all the psychological and educational strategies of helping emotionally troubled pupils.

The Psychoeducational Approach

The term *psychoeducational* has been viewed as a theory, a method, and a viewpoint. Fagen's[3] position is that the psychoeducational approach postulates a circular, interacting relationship between thoughts and feelings, in which cognitive experience and emotional experience affect each other simultaneously. A pupil who cannot learn to read develops intensely adverse emotional behaviors, just as a pupil with severe anxiety about performance on tests experiences difficulty in comprehending the written words of the test.

To give this concept some substance, the following operating principles and beliefs are considered basic to the psychoeducational approach:

1. Cognitive and affective processes are in continuous interaction.

2. Accepting the existence of mental illness, our task is to describe the pupil in terms of functioning skills that highlight areas of strength and pinpoint areas of weakness for remediation.

3. The psychoeducational process involves creating a special environment so that initially each pupil can function successfully at his or her present level.

4. Given this specialized environment, each pupil is taught that he or she has the capacity and resources to function appropriately and successfully.

5. Understanding how each pupil perceives, feels, thinks, and behaves in this setting facilitates educational conditions for optimal behavioral change.

---

3. **Stanley A. Fagen,** "A Psychoeducational Approach to Specifying and Measuring Competencies of Personnel Working with Disturbance in Schools" (Paper presented at The Council for Exceptional Children, April 23, 1971).

6. There are no special times during the school day. Everything that happens to, with, for, and against the pupil is important and can have therapeutic value.

7. Emotionally troubled pupils have learned a vulnerability to many normal developmental tasks and relationships such as competition, sharing, testing, closeness, etc. As teachers, we are responsible for awareness of these areas and for modifying our behavior in appropriate fashion.

8. Emotionally disturbed pupils behave in immature ways during periods of stress. They will lie, fight, run away, regress, and deny the most obvious realities. We can anticipate immature behavior from children in conflict; our hope for change is to expect mature behavior from adults.

9. Pupils in conflict can create their feelings and behaviors in others: aggressive pupils can create counteraggressive behaviors in others; hyperactive children can create hyperactivity in others; withdrawn pupils can get other children and adults to ignore them;

Table 1. Facilitating Conditions in a Psychoeducational Environment

Source of Change	Focus of Learner's Transaction	Facilitating Conditions
Learner–teacher	Person(s) responsible for interacting with learner to effect positive change	Reality orientation; flexibility; respect; emphatic understanding; support; protective limits; consistency; appreciation of feelings; positive modeling and expectations; involvement
Learner–curriculum	Tasks, materials, and problems planned for mastery	Reasonable challenge; relevance; relatedness; self-direction; meaningful choices; feedback
Learner–peer group	Other students interacting with learner on regular basis	Mutual respect and sharing; openness; cooperation; appreciation of differences; balanced groupings; stability; support; feedback
Learner–school system	Rules, attitudes, values, and people organized to support teacher, curriculum, and students	Cooperation; interdependence; openness; mutual respect and sharing; clarity of responsibilities and policies; self-renewal; orderly change mechanisms; participatory decision making; appropriate consequences for deviant behavior; positive modeling and expectations
Learner–learner	Self-awareness of personal responsibility for self-control and direction	Identification with positive adult; life space interviews; therapy

passive-aggressive pupils are effective in getting others to carry their angry feelings for days. If these children succeed in getting the adult to act out their feelings and behavior, they succeed in perpetuating their self-fulfilling prophecies of life, which in turn reinforce their defenses against change.

10.   Emotionally troubled children have learned to associate adult intervention with adult rejection. One staff goal is to reinterpret adult intervention as an act of protection rather than hostility. Pupils must be told over and over again that adults are here to protect them from real dangers, contagion, psychological depreciation, etc.

11.   We are here to listen to what the pupils say, to focus on what they are feeling.

12.   We are to expect and accept a normal amount of hostility and disappointment from pupils and colleagues.

13.   Pupils' home and community lives are an important source of health that must be considered by any remedial process. However, if all attempts fail, the school becomes an island of support for pupils.

14.   We must demonstrate that fairness is treating children differently. Although group rules are necessary for organizational purposes, individual expectations are necessary for growth and change.

15.   Crises are excellent times for teachers to teach and for pupils to learn.

16.   Behavioral limits can be a form of love, i.e., physical restraint can be a therapeutic act of caring for and protecting pupils.

17.   Teaching pupils social and academic skills enhances their capacity to cope with a stressful environment.

18.   Pupils learn through a process of unconscious identification with significant adults in their lives. This means the teacher's personal appearance, attitudes, and behavior are important factors in teaching, which must be evaluated continuously.

Translation of the above principles into a supportive psychoeducational environment provides a means by which the multiple transactions of a pupil's life space can be studied. In table 1 Fagen[4] conceptualizes this learning environment by outlining sources of change, focuses of the learner's transaction, and facilitating conditions.

In the next article, Sally Smith, a leader in the field of learning disability, has compiled a list of typical academic problems that special educators must be able to diagnose and remedy. While this list is not meant to be comprehensive, it does illustrate the wide range of learning problems a pupil can have in one subject area. In addition, there seem to be a growing number of pupils who have academic problems in all areas—reading, spelling, math, science, etc. For these pupils, the task of motivating and teaching is complex and frustrating. It demands a comprehensive and integrated reeducation program that goes beyond a tutoring program.

To make matters even more difficult, it is our experience that approximately 40 percent of the pupils labeled emotionally disturbed also have underlying learning disabilities. Unfortunately, many of these pupils are so adept at hiding or denying their learning problems by acting up or running away, that they are untestable and invalidate the standard diagnostic tests. As a result, the teacher does not have adequate assessment information for planning and frequently ends up feeling confused and ambivalent about how to begin the reeducation process.

---

4.   **Stanley A. Fagen,** "Psychoeducational Management and Self Control," Chapter 9, pp. 235–272 in *Special Education for Adolescents,* edited by D. Cullinan and M. Epstein (Columbus, Ohio: Charles E. Merrill, 1979).

Typical Academic Problems of Learning-Disabled Children

Sally L. Smith

Some Typical Reading Problems

1. Confuses b and d, reads bog for dog and often confuses b, d, p, q.

2. Confuses the order of letters in words—reads was for saw.

3. Doesn't look carefully at the details in a word, guesses from the first letter: reads farm for front.

4. Loses his place on a page when reading, sometimes in the middle of a line or at the end of the line.

5. Can't remember common words taught from one day to the next; knows them one day not the next. Most frequently forgets abstract words: us, were, says.

6. If he doesn't know a word, he has no systematic way to figure it out. Guesses or says "I don't know."

7. Reads without expression and ignores punctuation. The mechanics of reading are so hard for him that he has no awareness of the ideas expressed by the written symbols.

8. Reads very slowly, and reading tires the child greatly.

9. Omits words or adds words to a sentence, attempting to make meaning out of the symbols he has trouble decoding.

10. Reads word by word, struggling with almost each one of them.

Some Typical Language Problems

1. Cannot state something in an organized, cogent way. Tends to muddle, starts in middle of an idea. Cannot organize words properly into a question.

2. Has trouble following directions, particularly long sequences of them.

3. Doesn't enjoy being read to. But does like looking at pictures in book.

4. Becomes distracted in class when instruction is presented orally. Learns from watching, not listening.

5. Very literal. Misses inferences, subtleties, nuances, innuendoes.

6. Poor sense of humor, doesn't understand jokes, puns, sarcasm.

7. Trouble with abstract words. Defines words by their concrete attributes or function.

8. Rigidity of word meanings, can't deal with multiple meaning.

9. Can't tell a story in sequence or summarize, can only recount isolated and highly detailed facts about an experience.

10. Forgets names of things that he knows, has to describe them (word-finding problem). Later, when not under pressure, will recall the word he wanted to say.

Some Typical Spelling Problems

1. Writes b for d and vice versa.

2. Transposes the order of letters, spells was, s-a-w or the, h-t-e.

3. Doesn't hear the sequence of sounds in a word and writes isolated parts of it; writes amil for animal.

4. Has no memory for common words that are not regularly spelled. May try to spell them phonetically, writes sez for says.

5. Does not hear fine differences in words, writes pin for pen.

6. Has trouble with consonants, writes wif for with.

7. Often disguises poor spelling ability with consciously messy handwriting.

8. In sentence writing, uses no capitals and no punctuation.

9. Leaves words out of sentences, can't express himself in complete written sentences.

10. Avoids writing whenever possible, at nearly any expense, because it is so difficult and so demanding.

Some Typical Handwriting Problems

1. Holds pencil awkwardly, too tightly, inefficiently. Gets easily tired by writing.

2. Can't write without lined paper. Spacing is poor. Leaves no space between words. Leaves no margins.

3. Writes letters backwards.

4. Mixes lower case letters with capitals. Memory for the forms of letters is poor, so he uses whichever form he can remember.

5. Letters are written above and below the line. No size consistency.

6. Writes in very large hand, can't control pencil enough to write small.

7. Holds pencil too tightly and writes very small. Can't relax hand and pencil. Also hides poor spelling.

8. Process of writing is incredibly slow. Takes 5 minutes to write a sentence. Perfectionistic tendencies—each letter must be perfectly formed.

9. Can't remember how to form letters, uses his own way. Draws letters inefficiently.

10. Erases often and writes over the same letter several times.

Some Typical Arithmetic Problems

1. Counts on his fingers.

2. Cannot commit multiplication facts to memory.

3. Reverses two place numbers—13 becomes 31. Also reverses 5 to $\bar{c}$, etc.

4. Doesn't understand place value.

5. May solve addition and even multiplication problems by counting on fingers, but cannot subtract, which is the reverse operation.

6. Subtracts smaller number in a column from larger number. In the problem $25 - 7$, he subtracts the 5 from the 7 simply because the 5 is smaller, not seeing the 5 as representing 15, thus he arrives at the answer $25 - 7 = 22$.

7. Often understands concepts but can't do it in written symbolic form with paper and pencil.

8. On the other hand, sometimes a child can do rote arithmetic on paper, but it has no meaning and he can't solve problems in daily life, such as making change for a dollar.

9. Can't remember sequence of steps to multiply or divide, has trouble switching from one process to another, such as dividing and subtracting in long division.

10. Solves problems left to right instead of right to left.

Some Typical Thinking Problems

1. Has a hard time sticking to the main point, brings up irrelevant, extraneous points.

2. Doesn't grasp cause–effect relationships. Rarely uses the word "because." Doesn't anticipate and evaluate.

3. Rigidity of thought. A word can have only one meaning. Or knows $5 + 7 = 12$ but can't answer $12 = 5 + ?$. Or knows $8 \times 7 = 56$ but can't reverse gears and solve $56 \div 8 = ?$.

4. Has trouble seeing similarities and differences. Has trouble understanding relationships.

5. Doesn't see patterns. All words have to be memorized as he can't see spelling patterns; all multiplication facts have to be memorized one by one (that's why he gives up) instead of seeing patterns that simplify the task. He doesn't group ideas together to form patterns of thought.

6. Poor memory. Can't remember names of people or places. Also trouble with faces. Reasoning often gets sidetracked because of poor memory.

7. Doesn't organize the facts and concepts he does have and thus can't mobilize them to solve problems, to predict or foresee consequences.

8. Can't categorize or classify. Each experience is an isolated event. Doesn't summarize. Can't generalize from the concrete to the abstract.

9. Doesn't transfer learning from one lesson to another. Has to relearn each concept from scratch.

10. Understands concepts too narrowly or too broadly. All 4-legged animals are dogs. Only black and white cats (like his own cat) are cats. Or he may call all cats Puff, the name of his own cat.

Some Typical School Problems

1. Erratic. Inconsistent. Unpredictable. Appears to be lazy. Good days, off days. Forgets what was

learned yesterday. But without reteaching, he may remember it 2 days hence.

2. Poor attention span—no sustained focus.

3. Works very slowly—never finishes work in allotted time. Or works carelessly, finishing in half the expected time. Feels need to hurry, without thinking.

4. Poorly organized. Desk a mess. Always losing his coat or lunch.

5. Late to class, lingers after class.

6. Loses homework, or hands it in late and sloppily done. Doesn't understand or forgets assignments.

7. No study skills—doesn't know how to organize work, how to plan in regard to deadlines, how to organize time.

8. Low frustration tolerance. Gives up easily, or explodes.

9. Freezes when asked to perform on demand. When he volunteers information, he can tell what he knows; in responding to questions, he appears dull and ignorant.

10. Can't plan free time. Daydreams, acts silly, or repeats same activity over and over when given free choices.

Reprinted by permission of the author.

Editors' Commentary

Academic improvement does not take place by chance or magic but by carefully planned, structured, sequential learning experiences. Emotionally disturbed pupils should not be allowed to choose their curriculum or daily assignments. It is the teacher's responsibility to decide what is appropriate for the pupil to learn and the teaching condition under which that pupil is most likely to succeed. This means the teacher needs to have clear short-term and long-term goals for each pupil in the classroom. With the advent of Public Law 94–142, all handicapped pupils are required to have an IEP (individual education plan) developed for them before their placement in any special program. In the next article, Naslund and Werner present an IEP on a pupil who has serious emotional problems. When an IEP accurately describes the strengths and weaknesses of the pupil, it becomes the essential reeducation guide, providing the teacher and/or interdisciplinary team with structure and direction.

Writing an Individual Education Plan (IEP) for a Child with Emotional and Behavior Problems

Shellie R. Naslund
Anthony R. Werner

The IEP is divided into two parts. The first, "Part A: The Total Service Plan," is developed by the Child Study Team (CST) at an IEP conference. The CST is made up of various school personnel (teacher, counselor, psychologist, social worker, psychiatrist, placement specialist); the child's parents or guardians; if desired, their legal representative; and, if possible, the child. The purpose of Part A is:

1. To describe the child's strengths and weaknesses and thus identify the critical factors impeding his or her capacity to learn in the regular classroom;

2.   To determine whether or not special education intervention is necessary;

3.   To describe the characteristics of the ideal special education program for the child.

The completed Part A becomes the working document that is used as the basis for selecting the most appropriate placement for the student. Included in Part A is a comprehensive profile of the student's strengths and weaknesses, identification of the critical long-term goals for the student, the short-term program goals, the services and resources needed to achieve the goals, and the school persons responsible for providing the services described in the program. Part A also has room for comments on the child's learning style, recommendations for placement, the review dates for the CST, and the required signatures of the CST members.

Once the most appropriate program for the child is selected, the IEP Part A accompanies the child to that placement. It is then used as a guide for developing the specific program for the child. "Part B: The Implementation Plan" is developed by the staff at the new placement in response to the goal statements defined by the CST in Part A. It includes the specific behavioral objectives, learning activities, methods of evaluation, review date, and summary of the child's performance in relation to the behavioral objectives. As the child meets the performance criterion of each performance objective, additional objectives are added. In this regard, the document defines the sequential learning program designed to advance the child from the present level of functioning to the level defined in the long-term goal statement.

The Behavioral Description of the Child

Joey is a nine-year-old boy. One of Joey's present problems is his inability to control his impulses. He becomes angry and he hits. He sees something interesting across the room and he runs to it. When he thinks he knows an answer to a problem the teacher has put on the board, he shouts instead of raising his hand or giving others a chance to speak. Joey acts before he thinks and often finds himself in trouble without knowing how he got there.

Joey's self-esteem is low. He is used to being scolded or told that he is bad. He has now begun to believe that this is true, and he acts accordingly. He tries to do things "right," but things usually turn out "wrong." When this happens, Joey be-

comes discouraged, frustrated, angry, and sad. He usually avoids completing his assignments by tearing his paper or starting a fight with a child who "got in his way." Frequently, he simply refuses to begin the work and saves himself from one more painful failure experience.

Joey doesn't know how to make friends. He tries to get people to like him, but he usually ends up in some kind of argument or becomes excluded from the group.

Joey can talk. In fact, one of the first goals set for Joey was for him to be able to control his use of language and speak at appropriate times. But when he gets angry or anxious about a situation, his words become bottled up. He explodes, he shouts, and he cries; he loses his capacity to reason to himself or others. He thus fails to understand the dynamics of the situation, and his problems intensify.

Joey has trouble reading. Sometimes he just doesn't have the patience to practice all those words. In writing, his paper always looks messy or somehow becomes torn before the writing practice is complete. As for math, his problems never come out right. By the time he has learned to add, the rest of the class is subtracting. He gets further and further behind.

Joey's Individual Education Program (IEP)

It may be deduced from the above narrative that Joey is in need of a therapeutic program that will provide adequate support and structure to allow Joey to continue learning. He will need a program that can provide small group instruction, supporting adults who can intervene in crisis situations, and the additional support of psychological and family counseling services. Part A of Joey's IEP arrives at these recommendations.

Part A accompanies Joey to his new special education placement. A program must now be designed to meet the three main goals given priority in Part A of the IEP. This becomes the task of the personnel at Joey's new placement. The performance objectives and the descriptions of learning activities that will be used to achieve each goal of Part A are written onto a Part B form. For each goal statement of Part A, therefore, a corresponding Part B section must be written.

Part A of Joey's IEP indicates that he requires classroom activities that minimize anxiety. Specific tasks that trigger his resistance behavior must be avoided. He needs activities that are fun, that are

INDIVIDUAL EDUCATION PROGRAM

PART A Total Service Plan

CHILD STUDY TEAM

(1)   Identifyng Information

Name of Student   Joey   Birthdate   January 1, 1970

Age   9.0   School   Class

(2)   Hours/Days per week in mainstream
Hours/Days per week in regular and/or
    adaptive Physical Education

(3)   Special Notations   Joey was referred from the public school setting

for acting out and disruptive classroom behavior and lack of

academic progress.

---

(4)   STUDENT'S PROFILE

Academic Achievement

Reading: 1.5 Gates MacKillop: Exhibits extreme fear of failure when presented with reading tasks; refuses to attempt assignments, becomes explosive.

Math: 2.0 Key Math: Can add and subtract but has difficulty transferring concepts and refuses work.

Language Development

Communication 7.0 Vineland: Deficit in language development possibly related to underdeveloped reading and writing skills. Has difficulty with oral communication in stress. Is unable to label feelings or communicate with words when anxious and thus resorts to physical actions.

Psychomotor Skills

Fine motor skills underdeveloped. Can reproduce letters but becomes

(5)   ANNUAL LONG-TERM GOALS IN ORDER OF PRIORITY

1.   Joey will increase reading and arithmetic skills by six or more months.

2.   Joey will interact in a socially acceptable manner with both peers and adults.

3.   Joey will gain more control over his impulses.

(4)   STUDENT'S PROFILE (con't)

Psychomotor Skills (con't)

frustrated with writing tasks.
Lacks cursive writing skills.
Gross motor skills underdeveloped
for age. Appears clumsy and awkward
on playground. Frequently ends up
fighting with peers during play
activities.

Social Adaptation

Social Age Equivalent of 7 years-
Vineland. Has difficulty getting
along with others in both structured and unstructured activities.
Has poor control over impulses
which interferes with ability to
share or take turns in games. Most
social activities result in arguments or angry withdrawals.

Self-Help Skills

Age appropriate for basic tasks.
Tends to overindulge compulsively
in cookies and sweets. Lacks impulse control and knowledge of
proper dietary and hygiene requirements.

Prevocational/Vocational Skills

Age appropriate at present. Tends
to idolize heroes who are powerful
either physically (Superman) or
monetarily (doctors, actors, or the
president). A growing disparity
exists between accumulating hero
images and academic skill development. Intervention here should be
cautionary as it may affect his
already low self-esteem.

Other

Mother is receptive to receiving
assistance in further development
of parenting techniques such as
limit setting.

(5)   ANNUAL LONG-TERM GOALS IN
ORDER OF PRIORITY (con't)

PART A

Name of Student JOEY   Birthdate Jan. 1, 1970

Age   9   School _____ Class _____

(6) Short-Term Instructional Goals (incl. a time period)	(7) Services and Resources	(8) Person(s) Responsible for Imple-Mentation
1. A program will be provided to include: a. daily remedial reading sessions (1 year) b. classroom instruction in reading using a language experience approach (4 mo)	Special Ed Program Remedial Reading Program	Classroom teacher Remedial Reading tutor
2. A sequential, individual program in cursive handwriting will be implemented. (6 mo)	Special Education Program	Classroom teacher
3. A program will be provided to include small group classroom instruction in math using manipulatives and game reinforcement activities. (1 year)	same as above	same as above
4. Using behavior management techniques, a program will be implemented to help Joey follow classroom rules and participate in academic activities. (2 mo)	Special Ed Program Crisis Program Psychological Services	Classroom teacher Crisis teacher School psychologist
5. A program will be implemented to help Joey improve interpersonal relationships with peers and adults.	same as above Group Psychotherapy	same as above Psychiatrist
6. A program will be implemented to extend school support services into the home. (1 year)	Family Services	Social worker

PART A

Name of Student   JOEY_____   Birthdate _____

Age _____ School _____   Class _____

(6) Short-Term Instructional Goals (incl. a time period)	(7) Services and Resources	(8) Person(s) Responsible for Implementation

7. A program will be provided to facilitate development of inner controls and problem solving skills through use of:
  a. crisis intervention
  b. controlled group activities in affective education
  c. individual psychotherapy
    (1 year)
	Crisis Program Special Ed Program Psychological Services	Crisis teacher Classroom teacher School psychologist Psychiatrist

(9)   Interim Review Date(s) by CST   June, 1979
      Annual Review Date by CST _____ January, 1980

(10)   Comments and Recommendations: Special Education Program Placement
      Observed Learning Style: Requires small group or individual learning setting, with use of multisensory and language experience activities. Game reinforcement recommended.

(11)   Recommendations and Justification for Placement: It is recommended that Joey be placed full time in a therapeutic day treatment program that provides intensive academic remediation, has small classes, and provides psychotherapy and family counseling services.

(12)   Date of Child Study Team (CST) Meeting(s) January, 1979
      Persons Present -
      Name/Position (print or type)   Signature(s)

_____   _____

_____   _____

_____   _____

Chairman: _____

INDIVIDUAL EDUCATION PROGRAM

PART B Individual Implementation Plan

IMPLEMENTERS

Complete this sheet for each goal statement.

(13) Identifying Information

Name of Student ___JOEY___ Birthdate _January 1, 1970_

Age _9.0_ School _____ Class/Teacher(s) _____

Date of Entry into Program _January, 1979_____

Information from Total Service Plan

Goal Statement: _#1 Joey will increase reading and arithmetic_

_skills by six or more months._____

_____

Current performance level as related to goal statement: _____

Reading: 1.5 Gates MacKillop_____

Math: 2.0 Key Math_____

Responsible Staff _Classroom teacher_____

Hours/days per week _____

(14) Behavioral Objectives	(15) Date Started	Date Ended
Given a signal from the teacher, Joey will participate in classroom reading activities.	January, 1979	
Given problems in arithmetic, Joey will compute and write the answers without argument or resistance.		
Given cursive writing sheets, Joey will trace them without tearing the paper.		

PART B

Name of Student ___JOEY___   Date of Birth ___January 1, 1970___

Age ___9.0___   School _____   Class _____

(16) Learning Activities (Methods, Materials, Media)	(17) Method of Evaluation	(18) Interim Review Dates Performance Summary
Give Joey comic strip sections from the paper. Have him sequence the section, create a story, and create a dialogue for the characters. Give Joey cursive writing sheets with his name and other familiar words written on them in pencil. Have him trace over the words in brightly colored marking pens. Organize a math game such as Addition Bingo to play at the end of math class time. Joey may participate after completion of a reasonable number of arithmetic problems or after participating well in an arithmetic lesson.	Informal teacher evaluation and observation	March, 1979

(19) Additional Comments and Recommendations: Testing and formal evaluation not recommended at this time as it would conflict with goal of minimizing anxiety reaction to academic tasks.

PAGE 2

INDIVIDUAL EDUCATION PROGRAM

PART B Individual Implementation Plan

IMPLEMENTERS

Complete this sheet for each goal statement.

(13)   Identifying Information

Name of Student ___JOEY___ Birthdate ___January 1, 1970___

Age __9.0__ School _____ Class/Teacher(s) _____

Date of Entry into Program ___January, 1979___

Information from Total Service Plan

Goal Statement: ___#2 Joey will interact in a socially acceptable___

___manner with both peers and adults.___

Current performance level as related to goal statement: ___Social___

___age equivalent--7 years. Has difficulty getting along with others.___

___in both structured and unstructured activities. Frequently gets___

___into arguments or withdraws from peers.___

Responsible Staff ___Classroom teacher, physical ed. instructor___
Hours/days per week _____

(14) Behavioral Objectives	(15) Date Started	Date Ended
Given classroom teaching situation, Joey will participate in class discussions without arguing or verbally interrupting classmates.	January, 1979	
Given structured and supervised play activities, Joey will be able to participate at recess without fighting with peers.	January, 1979	

PART B

Name of Student __JOEY_____   Date of Birth __January 1, 1970__

Age __9.0_____ School _____   Class _____

(16) Learning Activities (Methods, Materials, Media)	(17) Method of Evaluation	(18) Interim Review Dates Performance Summary
Discuss the need to raise hand before speaking and listening to others. Draw up contract where Joey will receive credit each time he raises his hand before speaking out.	Informal teacher observations and graphing of contract progress achievements.	March, 1979
Have group choose game in which all can participate at recess. Review rules, anticipate where problems might occur, and talk over best way of handling the difficulties. Work into contract credit for each recess period Joey completes without a fight or each time he verbally works through a problem with a peer.		February, 1979
Conduct daily class meetings to review the day's events and the interactions the students have had with one another. Restate positive interactions. Encourage students to suggest alternatives for actions that caused problems.		June, 1979

(19) Additional Comments and Recommendations: _____

_____

_____

_____

_____

INDIVIDUAL EDUCATION PROGRAM

PART B Individual Implementation Plan

IMPLEMENTERS

Complete this sheet for each goal statement.

(13)   Identifying Information

Name of Student   <u>JOEY</u>   Birthdate <u>January 1, 1970</u>

Age <u>9.0</u> School <u>   </u>   Class/Teacher(s) <u>   </u>

Date of Entry into Program <u>January, 1979</u>

      <u>Information from Total Service Plan</u>

Goal Statement: <u>#3 Joey will gain more control over his impulses.</u>

<u> </u>

<u> </u>

Current performance level as related to goal statement: <u>Social age</u>

<u>equivalent--7 years. Has poor control over impulses. Frequently</u>

<u>fights with peers. Is unable to label feelings or communicate with</u>
words when anxious and resorts to physical actions.

Responsible Staff <u>Classroom teacher, crisis teacher,</u>

Hours/days per week <u>   psychotherapist, counselor   </u>

(14) Behavioral Objectives	(15) Date Started	Date Ended
Given cue from teacher, Joey will ask for time out when angry before aggressive action occurs.	January, 1979	
Given regularly scheduled therapy sessions, Joey will attend weekly.	January, 1979	
Given a program of crisis intervention, Joey will be able to label his feelings verbally, describe the process that led to the feeling, and suggest problem-solving alternatives.	January, 1979	

PART B

Name of Student __JOEY_____   Date of Birth __January 1, 1970__

Age __9.0_____   School _____   Class _____

(16) Learning Activities (Methods, Materials, Media)	(17) Method of Evaluation	(18) Interim Review Dates Performance Summary
Arrange for crisis teacher to visit class and spend unstructured time playing games or talking with Joey to facilitate development of trusting relationship.	Collaborative meetings and team consultation; teacher observation	June, 1979
Crisis teacher will use LSI techniques to aid Joey in identifying feelings, developing coping and problem solving skills. Conduct daily class meetings where the children can discuss daily events and their resulting feelings.		

(19) Additional Comments and Recommendations: _____

_____

_____

_____

_____

PAGE 2

nonthreatening, and that provide successful learning experiences.

Preceding are the implementation plans (Part B) designed to correspond to each goal statement of Part A.

Summary

The above example shows how an Individualized Education Program may be written for a child who is serviced by a special education program because of emotional and behavior disorders. The behaviors and goals that might have been included are innumerable. Each IEP written is as different as the child it describes. What is important is that the goals match the needs of the child. For these special children, if the IEP is to serve as an effective, working tool for both teacher and child, it must include affective and behavioral descriptions and goals.

Editors' Commentary

In the next article, Cheney and Morse present an overview of the therapeutic value of school and the various curriculums used to help disturbed pupils deal with the academic, interpersonal, and intrapsychic dimensions of learning. Kauffman,[5] a devoted behaviorist, explained this process with feeling when he wrote that the education of disturbed children requires a curriculum that will teach them how work is accomplished, play is learned, love is felt, and fun is enjoyed—by the child and the teacher. This is the essence and the outcome of any therapeutic curriculum.

5. **James M. Kauffman,** *Characteristics of Children's Behavior Disorders* (Columbus, Ohio: Charles E. Merrill, 1977).

Psychodynamic Intervention

Carol Cheney
William C. Morse

The school can regulate the degree of comfort vs. stress in many ways: through the careful selection of material, through gradation of steps to assure success, and through ending demands for "perfection." School is a place of work and creativity and of fun and play. The social context of school provides a laboratory for peer and authority corrective role learning for the scapegoat or bully. There are so many reality factors that direct interpretation is a natural expectation. There are peer and adult models available. Competition can be mitigated, cooperation enhanced through educational methodology, if one so chooses. There is bibliotherapy and a vast array of cognitive-curricular approaches. A unique blend of cognitive-affective synthesis can be undertaken systematically. Any environment with such potentials has at once the power to be corrective or destructive. A youngster can find a new target for hate and fear, or new and useful things to do and people to care about. The capacity for utilizing the potential of the school resources for mental health ends requires special education insight as well as flexibility to do what is needed.

The school, from this viewpoint, provides special people who do therapeutic teaching (dealing with the affective-cognitive mix) rather than just remedial teaching. The individualization can include peer and lay parent surrogates, such as proposed in the Teaching Moms concept (Donahue and Nichtern, 1965; Fenichel, 1966). Therapeutic personnel, however, lay or professional, do not become so because assigned a role. One's concern would be with the identification image provided by the person. There should be people available who can help when you are in crisis, or to speak to when you need special help with your "internal curriculum." Crisis intervention as a mental health teaching process has been described by Caplan (1964). Such school resources are especially important for disturbed youngsters (Newman, 1967).

School can even provide help for the child's life in many ways which have long-term implications. We can see in the school normal activities which are similar to established therapies: recreation, work, relationship, group, identification, achievement, music, art, dance, and even Slavson's activity group (Slavson, 1943). If they can become special therapies, the school can use them as therapeutic tools.

The therapeutic consequences of active involvement and participation are facilitated by experiences which are intrinsically appealing to the child's normal interests and curiosity. A study by Kounin et al. (1966) has demonstrated that in the classroom a high level of "seatwork variety change" produces an increase in appropriate behavior in both normal and disturbed children. Thus a situation which minimizes boredom and maximizes involvement can improve overall pupil behavior. The open classroom, when it is guided by a perceptive teacher, can embody a high therapeutic potential (Knoblock, 1973; Dennison, 1969). Since the psychodynamic position anticipates interaction, this is not a proposal for laissez faire or for converting the class into a classical clinic type setting (Berkowitz and Rothman, 1960).

One cannot discuss the school situation without touching on the issue of stress, particularly the almost universally experienced test-anxiety (Sarason et al., 1960). One hopes, of course, for the temporary and eventual total elimination of tests, with the substitution of better methods of feedback and evaluation. Many alienated delinquents and deprived children find it impossible to cope with failure induced by present practices. As Kohl (1969) points out, however, nearly all children must deal at some point with batteries of standardized tests, often with baffling coded answer sheets and unfamiliar types of questions. As Glasser (1969) says, schools should be without failure. But until test taking is not a survival skill, special education hopes to gradually, over a period, acclimate the pupil to the harsh reality, starting with possible tasks and no failure. Since mainstreaming is a

goal, and since school success is critical to that goal, the matter cannot be ignored. Kohl thus undertook to teach his Harlem youngsters *how* to take the tests that determined such important things as their class placement, their IQ ratings, etc. As students took practice tests and discussed how tests were structured, "their anxiety decreased to a manageable level, and therefore they were able to apply things they had discovered in their own thinking, reading, and writing to situations that arose in the test" (Kohl, 1969, p. 340). After their short introduction to test-taking, students' reading scores jumped one to three years over scores they had achieved a few months earlier.

Curricular Approaches as Interventions

Among the basic considerations for curricular approaches to emotional disturbances which Rhodes (1963) outlines are:

1.   The child should have new experiences in relation to his old problems.

2.   The child should be surrounded with new opportunities which will call up such positive motives as adventure, achievement, exploration, and discovery.

3.   Learning should be active and involve sensory input through as many channels as possible.

4.   Activities should center on those goals which the child values most.

5.   The child should be encouraged to reflect back on experiences and consider what meaning they hold for him.

In addition to such specific educational interventions as indicated above, there have been suggestions for a restorative curriculum which capitalizes on the latent self-corrective capacities of the disturbed child to enhance emotional growth and mental health. Insight and understanding of emotional problems do not always have to be gained within the highly individualized learning context of counseling or individual psychotherapy. Personal discovery can be made through the curricular context as well. The curricular approaches to mental health vary greatly in their focus, from establishment of basic learning skills to fostering awareness of the child's feelings and needs.

In their experimental study Minuchin et al. (1967) used ten sequential lessons to develop basic skills needed for learning and communication. The subjects of their lessons included:

listening

implications of noise

staying on the topic

taking turns, sharing in communication

telling a simple story

building up a longer story

asking cogent and relevant questions

categorizing and classifying information

role-playing

Several curricular approaches focus more specifically on the child as an emotional being. Such curricula reflect several basic beliefs:

1. It is both unrealistic and undesirable to try to eliminate the child's emotional involvements from the classroom.

2. Children learn best when the subject matter is relevant to their experiences and interests.

3. As Weinstein and Fantini write, "unless knowledge is related to an affective state in the learner, the likelihood that it will influence behavior is limited" (Weinstein and Fantini, 1970, p. 28).

Although these curricula were not specifically designed for use with emotionally disturbed children, these basic concepts (as well as many of the specific techniques within each curriculum) conform closely to Rhodes' criteria for work with the disturbed. The point here is, the psychodynamic approach does not favor an antiseptic, exclusively cognitive or skill-oriented educational experience, for either normal or disturbed children. The fact is that most classrooms for the disturbed already have a surplus of unexploited emotional experiences. The curricular programs which have been developed to exploit experiences are thus very relevant to teaching the disturbed child.

Several curricula and textbooks reflect these concerns explicitly. Jones (1968) discusses "Man, A Course of Study," a curriculum developed from the ideas of Jerome Bruner. The subject matter of this social studies curriculum is man's nature—his universal characteristics and his differences from culture to culture. Much use is made of realistic films and stories depicting important aspects of the lives of men in other cultures. Attention is paid to the cognitive content which they contain. Jones suggests equal time for the affective responses aroused. Materials include allusions to such emo-

tion-laden subjects as the selenecide and infanticide practiced by the Netsilik, the relative values of being male or female, and pictures of the bloody killing of a seal. The subjects presented in the program have been chosen for their relevance to the developmental tasks of childhood, and the relationship between emotions and subject matter is reciprocal. Subject matter should be chosen for its relevance to the child's emotional concerns, and the child's emotional involvement facilitates his work with the subject matter. An example of the interrelation is presented in the discussion of family life in Iraq presented below:

Student: "We don't have the whole family living with us like they do."
Student: "The girls there can't get married until the grandfather dies. That's different from us."
Student: "I agree with Sylvia. My whole family doesn't live together."
Student: "Here it's different about the boys and girls. Here girls learn faster and are smarter, and the mother enjoys having girls around because the boys are just rough."
Student: "I disagree. Boys do just as much around the house as girls."
Student: "Sometimes men can sew better than women. Also the chefs in restaurants are usually men."
Student: "Boys and men are built more rugged."
Teacher: "Therefore?"
Student: "I read a book about the frontier days. When the mother and father died the son worked all his life to help the sisters and brothers grow up and get educated."
Student: "Boys don't change the baby's diapers."
Student: "In Puerto Rico I had to work in the fields and the girls could stay home."
Student: "Mrs. Jackson, I want to defend my statement. Because it is less work to hunt and fish than it is to prepare the food, so the woman works harder."
Student: "Men have stronger constitutions than ladies."
Teacher: "Therefore?"
Student: "If it weren't for ladies, men wouldn't even be born."
Student: "How come they say 'It's a woman's world?'"
Student: "I disagree with the girls who say that girls are better, because if you put a girl in a cage with a bear, she would just cry." (Jones, 1968, pp. 167–168)

In the course of the discussion such important concepts as biological and individual differences, division of labor, and the human life cycle are elicited; identity problems and the loaded issue of sex roles are discussed. Such an encounter reflects the usefulness of incorporating the child's emotional involvements into the process of his education.

The approach of Weinstein and Fantini (1970), whose curriculum of affect was originally developed to address the needs of the underprivileged child, is very similar. They place a strong emphasis on identification of the child's personal concerns, which they group into three broad classes: self-image, disconnectedness, and control over one's life. To the psychodynamic psychologist, these are the very things which confound the child with problems, "the intrinsic drives that motivate behavior" (Weinstein and Fantini, 1970, p. 24). Education must speak effectively to these concerns in order to function. Among the techniques which have integrated the affective and the cognitive realms are:

1. *Creating situations which arouse the pupil's emotional involvement.*
A new unit on revolution, for example, was begun by a new teacher who immediately began to forcefully order all blue-eyed children out of the room. The anger aroused prompted a lively discussion of justice, protest, etc. (Weinstein and Fantini, 1970, p. 60).

2. *"One-way glasses."*
Pupils practice seeing specific persons through "glasses" which are colored "curious," "things-aren't-really-that-bad," "suspicious," "gloomy," and so on (Weinstein and Fantini, 1970, pp. 70–90).

3. *Procedures to identify pupil concerns.*
The Faraway Island.
Students are asked to describe the six people they would choose to accompany them to a secluded island.
Ten Years from Now.
Children are asked to speculate about what they will be doing in ten years. This situation often provides an excellent opportunity for clarification of reality factors.
Time Capsule.
The class selects pictures and songs and makes a tape recording to depict what they think is significant about their lives.

4. *Games.*
Games were devised by the Western Behavioral Science Institute to help students develop their view of self and increase their self-esteem. Examples are presented below:
"Complain, Gripe and Moan."
Each child gets coupons labeled "home," "school," and "block." There are booths of the same names where the children "spend" their coupons to complain about each of these aspects of their lives.

"Spies from Xenon."
Children are designated spies from "Xenon" and directed to report back what makes earth children mad, afraid, strong or happy.
"Amnesia."
An adult appears, dazed. He reports being hit and losing his memory. Through an elaborate earphone arrangement, the children tell him what has been happening and help him reconstruct his memory.
"Mirror."
The child is directed to "stand up in front of that mirror, look right at yourself, and say something nice to yourself" (Weinstein and Fantini, 1970, p. 191).

The goals of the curriculum developed by Raths, Harmin, and Simon (1966) are closely related to those we have discussed. Their approach has grown out of the feeling

that the pace and complexity of modern life has so exacerbated the problem of deciding what is good and what is right and what is worthy and what is desirable that large numbers of children are finding it increasingly bewildering, even overwhelming, to decide what is worth valuing, what is worth one's time and energy (Raths et al., 1966, p. 7).

Their curriculum thus focuses on the problem of *value formulation and clarification.* Their emphasis is on the *child's* own exploration of alternatives, on consideration of goals, and on behavior consistent with his choices; no one tells him what is best.

The mechanisms which Raths *et al.* have developed to achieve these goals include:

1. *Value clarification responses.*
This technique consists of responding to statements made by the child in such a way that he must clarify his feelings or attitudes to himself and his teacher. Raths et al. (1966, pp. 56–67) enumerate thirty "clarifying responses" such as "How did you feel when that happened?" "Did you have to choose that; was it a free choice?" "What other possibilities are there?" "Do you do anything about that idea?" and "What do you have to assume for things to work out that way?" Appropriate use of such value clarifications requires sensitivity to those situations and statements which suggest unstated values. Raths et al. (1966, pp. 65–72) list five statement topics which lend themselves to value clarification: attitudes, aspirations, purposes, interests, and activities.

2. *Value sheets.*
These are lists of value-related questions which are prompted by a provocative statement or reading.

3. *Role-playing.*

4. Contrived incident.

The teacher contrives a situation to "shock [his] students into an awareness of what they are for and against" (Raths et al., 1966, p. 123).

5. Open-ended questions.

6. Public interviews.

The teacher interviews one of the pupils "publicly" on some emotionally-charged question such as "What do you hate about your sister?" (Raths et al., 1966, p. 143).

7. Action projects.

Students participate in projects which actualize the values and goals they have been discussing.

In addition to these proposals, there have also been textbooks developed to strengthen the child's emotional health, self-concept, etc. Limbacher's *Dimensions of Personality* series is designed to help the child learn to "accept himself, others, and their society" (Limbacher, 1969, p. v). The texts contain lessons focusing on self-awareness ("Getting to Know Myself," "Knowing I'm Alive," "My Mirrors"), feelings ("When I Cried for Help," "My Feelings are Real"), and other people ("How Different are We?").

Bruck's "Guidance" series (Bruck, 1968–1970) shares a similar emphasis. The series consists of "workbooks" [sic!] each of which presents the child with provocative reading material, specific questions raised by its content, and suggestions for discussion topics. The child is presented with suggestions for action related to the lesson, and asked to choose one of those presented or develop his own plan. Later, he returns to the lesson to reflect on how effectively he has fulfilled his plan. The hope is that the teacher will use these as stimulants rather than as workbooks.

Jones' point was that regular curricular experiences have enough emotional stuff, and these can be approached naturally as part of the total cognitive-affective binding together of ideas. With disturbed youngsters there is the life of the class itself, which is laden with emotionally charged "curriculum." These matters should not be handled with repression, authoritarianism, or rule fixation. Here is where the class converts to a social-emotional laboratory, giving the time needed to penetrate events. It may take additional personnel to help, and the Reality Interview or Life Space Interview is the technique (this is discussed elsewhere). It is mentioned here to point out that curriculum is life, as well as "books."

The implications of this section of intervention techniques are clear. One deals with the affective aspects in the educational context, which of course means that teachers must be as well trained in these procedures as in other mental health techniques. Mental health implies the proper bonding, synthesis and integration of the thinking and the feeling components of the individual. The school, being a microcosm of life, offers a wide variety of opportunities for unwinding tangled lives, and for providing new images to be integrated into troubled personalities.

References

Berkowitz, P., and Rothman, E. *The Disturbed Child: Recognition and Psychoeducational Therapy in the Classroom.* New York: New York University Press, 1960.

Bruck, C. M. *Guidance Series for the Elementary School: Focus—Grade 8, Search—Grade 6.* New York: The Bruce Publishing Company, 1968–1970.

Caplan, G. *Principles of Preventive Psychiatry.* New York: Basic Books, 1964.

Dennison, G. *The Lives of Children: The Story of the First Street School.* New York: Vintage Books, 1969.

Donahue, G. T., and Nichtern, S. *Teaching the Troubled Child.* New York: The Free Press, 1965.

Fenichel, C. "Mama or M. A.? The 'Teacher-Mom' Program Evaluated." *Journal of Special Education* 1 (1966): 45–51.

Glasser, W. *Reality Therapy.* New York: Harper and Row, 1965.

Glasser, W. *Schools Without Failure.* New York: Harper and Row, 1969.

Jones, R. M. *Fantasy and Feeling in Education.* New York: New York University Press, 1968.

Knoblock, P. "Open Education for Emotionally Disturbed Children." *Exceptional Children* 39 (1973): 358–366.

Kohl, H. "A Harlem Class Writes." *In Radical School Reform,* edited by B. Gross and R. Gross. New York: Simon and Schuster, 1969.

Kounin, J. S.; Friesen, W. V.; and Norton, A. E. "Managing Emotionally Disturbed Children in Regular Classroom." *Journal of Educational Psychology* 57 (1966): 1–13.

Limbacher, W. J. *Dimensions of Personality: Here I Am.* Dayton: George A. Pflaum, 1969.

Minuchin, S.; Chamberlain, P.; and Graubard, P. "A Project to Teach Learning Skills to Disturbed Delinquent Children." *American Journal of Orthopsychiatry* 37 (1967): 558–567.

Newman, R. G. *Psychological Consultation in the Schools.* New York: Basic Books, 1967.

Raths, L. E.; Harmin, M.; and Simon, S. B. *Values and Teaching.* Columbus, Ohio: Charles E. Merrill, 1966.

Rhodes, W. C. "Curriculum and Disordered Behavior." *Exceptional Children* 30 (1963): 61–66.

Sarason, S. B. *The Culture of the School and the Problem of Change.* Boston: Allyn and Bacon, 1971.

Sarason, Seymour B. et al. *Anxiety in Elementary School Children.* New York: John Wiley & Sons, 1960.

Slavson, S. R. *An Introduction to Group Therapy.* New York: International Press, 1943.

Weinstein, G., and Fantini, M. D. *Toward Humanistic Education: A Curriculum of Affect.* New York: Praeger Publishers, 1970.

From William Rhodes and Michael Tracey, eds., *A Study of Child Variance,* vol. 2, Interventions Conceptual Project in Emotional Disturbance, Ann Arbor, Mi.: University of Michigan, 1972.

Editors' Commentary

Teachers report that the initial adjustment from home to school during the first fifteen minutes of class is extremely important and can set the atmosphere for the entire day. For example, some pupils enter the classroom loaded with angry, fearful, or sad feelings that were caused at home, on the bus, or on the playground. Hay and his staff have systematically reviewed the multiple problems that occurred during this brief period in their Junior Guidance classes in New York City.

Their report reflects the cooperative efforts of more than 200 teachers of emotionally disturbed children and offers the beginning teacher specific methods that have been proved effective in practical use.

Good Morning, Boys and Girls

Louis Hay
Gloria Lee

Who Are Our Children?

John enters the room like a bomb. He flings the door open and crosses the room in two or three leaps, vaulting over a desk or two on the way. He proclaims to the group that he has had several fights on the way to school and has beaten one or two boys. He seems wound up like a coiled spring. . . .

Vanessa comes into the room dragging her feet. She pulls her books along the floor behind her. She goes directly to her desk and sits in a forlorn fashion, slumped in her seat. . . .

Henry is late. He slips furtively into the room. He hides his books in the closet, gathers together some art materials, and begins working—yet fully dressed in his outer clothing. . . .

Harold is late every morning. He does not come into the classroom but stands by the side of the door. His shirt is unbuttoned, his shoes unlaced, he wears one sock. His hands are in his pockets holding up his pants because he has no belt. Sporadically, he kicks the wall. . . .

Each morning the emotional bridge from the world of the home to the world of the school must be built anew by each child with the help of the teacher. She helps the child view himself as an accepted individual. For children in Junior Guidance Classes this marks the most significant transition of the day, calling for a rallying and redirecting of psychic energies from the focus of the home to that of the school.

In schools where classes line up in the yard, children of Junior Guidance Classes should proceed directly, singly or with classmates, to their rooms. Each child of this population of troubled children has his own physiological and psychological tolerance for non-mobility. Lining them up invites inevitable disturbances.

Where Have They Been?

At the close of each school day a disturbed child returns home, often reluctantly, to the source of his major conflict. Here the drama that fostered his patterns of maladjustment is re-enacted. This may be a parent–child or a parental conflict or sibling rivalry in which the child becomes a pawn. Peer pressure may also augment dissension. Meal time and bed time are crucial periods with nighttime bringing nightmares instead of tranquility. There may be simple neglect with no breakfast, or little nurturing provisions or over-insistence upon eating. The morning views another occasion for a new round of conflicts at breakfast. For most of our children the home represents an arena of painful experiences in which anxiety and anger mount and aggression or withdrawal is used as a defense. In either case, the price is a loss of self-confidence as well as a loss of trust of the adults. It is left to the teacher each morning to help recreate an atmosphere of security.

The morning period should be a quiet one in both tempo and substance. Problems can emanate from the class structure as well as the materials which lead to a high level of activity or stimulation. Competitiveness should be avoided. This should be a time in which children can be alone if they need to be; can move freely; can obtain needed nourishment; can find constructive release opportunities and can test wholesome social relationships. This kind of atmosphere helps children to move into the day's activities gradually.

How Can the Teacher Help?

The opening period of the day is a time when the teacher is vitally needed by her pupils. She must be available and active. She reveals her *respect* for the children by providing the materials and the opportunities for activities which are fitted to the needs and interests of the children.

The teacher also sets the stage and defines this time by the materials which she makes available and by the activities she allows, encourages and suggests. She is faced with the problems of how

and when to help the child who needs adult direction in getting started; how and when to involve the child who flits about interrupting the activities of other children; and how and when to introduce new materials.

The teacher is active in the following ways:

1. She observes carefully each child as he enters the room. She uses this morning observation as a comparative basis for noting daily differences in clothing, tempo, mobility, physical well being, etc. She participates most actively during the first period by observing "inner movement" through nonverbal communication.

2. She gives each child some sign of welcome and continued interest.

3. She looks at each child individually to sense which children will need that little bit of extra support this day.

4. She is available to answer questions and mediate controversies.

5. She moves in temporarily to support a faltering group activity.

6. She listens to accounts of experiences from individual children.

7. She interests a child who is at "loose ends" in an activity.

The art of encouraging a child toward initiative without making him dependent on the continued presence of the starter is invaluable in a Junior Guidance classroom. It is therefore extremely important that this period be set within a carefully planned but flexible framework. It must not be a haphazard one.

What Kinds of Activities Can Be Planned?

Early morning projects should be nonthreatening and gratifying. They should not depend upon teacher direction. It may be possible to have an ongoing activity that is carried on only during the first period. The last period of the day can serve as a link with the first period of the next day.

Suggested activities for younger children:

1. Individual scrapbooks (These pupil-made scrapbooks may be no more than three or four pages.)

2. Personal story books, written and illustrated by the children

3. Water painting on blackboard (mop should be available)

4.   Surprise box (a large box, decorated, containing enough activities for the whole class)

5.   Listening to phonograph or radio (child may be able to assume responsibility for operation of machine)

6.   Salt, coarse (for pouring)

7.   Writing on blackboard

8.   Sorting materials (arithmetic chips for color, kinds of beans, kinds of beads, etc.)

9.   Table blocks

10. Small finger puppets

11. Dominoes

12. Trays of different materials

   a. Two or three toy cars and a box for a garage

   b. A little bath tub and small plastic doll and water (in limited amount) for bathing doll

   c. Pieces of very small furniture

   d. Science materials

13. Easel painting

14. Sewing and knitting (horse reins, etc.)

15. Special art materials (felt pens, colored pencils)

16. Looking at magazines

17. Puzzles

18. Housekeeping activities

   a. Watering plants

   b. Straightening block shelf

19. Stringing (beads, cut-up straws, macaroni, buttons)

20. A shelf of special books available only during the first period. This supply of books should be changed periodically.

Older children can be helped to a positive carryover from the previous day through helpful classroom discussion.

Suggested activities for older children:

1.   Special interests (scrapbooks, collections)

2.   Science materials and projects (dry cells, magnets, old clocks or radio to take apart and put together, microscope)

3.   Knitting, weaving and sewing, particularly for girls

4.   Class projects (class newspaper with use of typewriter, writing letters)

5.   Mailbox (for communication among children in class and teacher)

6.   Small scale construction (e.g., models)

7.   Listening to phonograph or radio, with child or children assuming responsibility for operation of machine

8.   Making articles for a younger class (Word Lotto game, Go Fish cards)

9.   Special jobs for the teachers or for the class

10. Sorting (making picture files, collating xerographed worksheets for the class)

11. Notes on the bulletin board to the class or to individual children telling them about something special available that day or suggesting a particular activity

12. Browsing through newspapers and magazines.

Suggested activities for individual children who pose special problems:

1.   Finger painting

2.   Surprise bag for an individual child (two or three small toys)

3.   Care of a doll

4.   Printing set

5.   Miniature slide viewer

6.   Easily assembled construction games such as "Mr. Potato Head"

7.   Follow-the-dot books

Some of the activities mentioned previously, such as stringing, sorting, or using the phonograph for quiet records, prove soothing to distraught children.

Additional Guidelines

1.   Seasonal change should be considered.

2.   This is not a work period with floor blocks, wood working, etc. Activities that require a long period of time and self-investment should be bypassed.

3.   One cannot talk of meeting the needs of children in Junior Guidance Classes at the beginning of the day without planning for the availability of food at this time. Children who are hungry cannot turn their attention to the world around them except in anger. A tray of sandwiches saved from the previous day, a few boxes of dry cereal, some slices of bread and jelly or some cookies are signs of welcome which these children cannot mistake.

4.   The sharing of food is also a natural way for bringing the class together at the close of the morning period. How much easier it is to look

ahead to the rest of the day while sipping from a container of milk, or a cup of hot cocoa, and feeling good about being in this place.

5.   This is a time for children to renew their relationships, to talk and play together, to exchange experiences and feelings.

6.   At all times opportunities for individual differences should be respected. One child may enter, sit down and not participate in any activities. Whether he is accessible for some direction from the teacher may vary from child to child and at different times with the same child. Doing "nothing" may be doing much.

A paper by Louis Hay and Gloria Lee, with the assistance of Shirley Cohen, Hellie Jones, Lottie Rania, and Judy Schmidt. Reprinted by permission of Louis Hay.

Editors' Commentary
Strategies for Specific Skills

The U.S. Office of Education has proclaimed that reading is not a personal *privilege* that can be given or denied, but a *right* that society must guarantee all children. Whether the child's problem is immaturity, retardation, poor instruction, deprivation, neurological deficit, emotional disturbance, brain injury, learning disabilities, or all of these, the difficulty of teaching that child to read is enormous. Over 10 percent of the school population has reading problems severe enough to require special instruction. Although numerous remedial methods (kinesthetic, phonetic, visual, and auditory) are available to the classroom teacher, there seems to be a consensus among experts regarding the process of teaching. This process includes (1) breaking a lesson down into tiny sequential steps; (2) maintaining clarity and simplicity of structure; (3) using repetition; (4) selecting materials carefully designed to eliminate remedial deficits; and (5) developing highly motivating activities centered on the pupil's level of interest and ability. Fagen, Long, and Stevens[6] have outlined these instructional steps in greater detail.

1.   *Start at or below functional level.* Always try to proceed from a point that the child can handle. Work up to harder tasks gradually, and avoid presenting tasks that cannot be simplified or modified when necessary.

2.   *Increase difficulty by small steps.* Try not to force big jumps in skill development unless the child's readiness and self-esteem are sufficient. Usually it is best to proceed by gradually increasing difficulty, building harder requirements on top of earlier accomplishments.

3.   *Place teaching tasks in a developmental sequence.* Attempt to organize tasks so that high-order skills follow on development of more elementary skills. Break complex tasks into separate components and order them sequentially (for example, kicking a ball requires left-right discrimination, balancing on one foot, freedom to move).

4.   *Provide positive feedback.* Be sure to indicate through praise, gesture, pictures, charts, videotape, or some other method that progress is being made. Do not overdo praise so that it sounds artificial or untrue, but use it freely. Frequently remind the child of gains made since the start—often this offsets discouragement during plateau phases.

5.   *Strengthen by repetition.* Return to earlier tasks often during the year, and always repeat the last few tasks performed at a prior session.

6.   *Show appreciation for real effort.* Of critical importance is offering recognition for effort rather than the more usual practice of recognizing results. Work at converting

6.   **S. Fagen, N. Long, and D. Stevens,** *Teaching Children Self-Control in the Classroom* (Columbus, Ohio: Charles E. Merrill, 1975).

appraisal methods so that success is defined relative to the child's baseline level and the progress made. Appreciation for goal achievement is also important, but praise given for that should not be at the expense of praise for real effort.

7. *Enhance value of skill area.* Unless the particular skill being taught is perceived as valuable by the child, meaningful change is not likely. The enhancement of value is therefore a *sine qua non* for effective teaching.

8. *Maintain flexibility and enjoyment.* The planned program is never sacrosanct and should be subject to modification at any time. Combat boredom, fatigue, and restlessness with appealing educational games that may or may not have teaching value. A change of scenery by interesting trips, walks, or outdoor activities can be beneficial—and these excursions may be used as rewards for hard work.

9. *Prepare for real life transfer of training.* Keep in mind that learning tasks are not ends in themselves but gateways to satisfactions in everyday life. Transfer can be optimized by extending and generalizing the learning tasks to as many everyday activities as possible.

10. *Plan short, frequent, regular training sessions.* Hold teaching sessions at the same time and place, daily if possible, and for periods of no more than one half hour. Sharp, energetic, complete attempts at a few tasks in a short session are better than half-hearted, apathetic tries at many.

In the next article, Stiles describes the complex process of teaching a pupil who is resistant to remedial learning. Note the fusion between the author's interpersonal skills in avoiding a power struggle with Roger and her outstanding and precise remedial techniques. This blend of skills can effectively overcome a "hard-core" remedial pupil like Roger, who has successfully defended himself from failure in the past by attacking the teacher's personality (e.g., "You are a stupid, ugly woman"), the teaching techniques (e.g., "You don't even know how to teach"), and the usefulness of the content (e.g., "This is baby stuff. It's silly. Only an asshole would find this interesting").

A Strategy for Teaching Remedial Reading: I'm Not Gonna Read and You Can't Make Me!

Claudia Stiles

This is a story of Roger, an eight-year-old nonreader who slowly emerged from a world of confusion and despair into the promising world of communication and reading. Roger is a boy of average intellectual abilities who was unable to learn through conventional classroom instruction. His history of failure throughout the first and second grades left him with feelings of bewilderment, frustration, and hopelessness. He saw himself as somehow damaged and strangely different, for he was painfully aware that he was unable to learn like other children. He was extremely wary of risking himself to the reading process again and was filled with hostility and fear at the prospect. Unfortunately, his condition is not unlike that of most children who are referred to remedial reading specialists.

Roger was referred to our psychoeducational system by the public schools because of poor academic progress and disruptive classroom behavior. His behavior was characterized by impulsiveness, distraction, anxiety toward change, aggression, and manipulative tactics. His home environment was highly unstable and unpredictable. His mother's immediate concerns centered on his inability to cope with the recent death of his father, his enuresis, nightmares, and his open expressions of hostility toward adults and peers. Through a process of assessment and consultation, we learned that Roger's learning problems were partially due to auditory and visual perceptual problems—both areas are integrally related to the reading process. At this point, because of the complexity of his learning and behavioral problems, it was difficult to isolate the factors which were mutually interfering.

Without delay I began to formulate plans for his remediation. Each of our sessions would be diagnostic, with each day's lesson carefully built on the previous one.

When I explained to Roger that I would be his new reading teacher and that I was there to help him learn, he considered that possibility for a few minutes and responded defiantly, "Whatta ya mean, just the two of us?"

"Yes," I explained. "We will work together for thirty minutes, three days a week."

"When?" he asked cautiously.

I took him into my office and showed him the schedule posted on the wall. He found his name and I explained the hours to him. "Where are we gonna be?" he wanted to know.

We walked down the hall and into one of the reading rooms, which he acknowledged with outrage, "There's nothin' *in* here!"

This was a fairly accurate statement, for the room contained only two small desks and two chairs. "Well, we might add some of our own things later," I explained. Of course, the design was intentional. A learning environment free of auditory and visual distractions is a necessity for children with learning problems. It is also a way of clearly focusing attention on learning and minimizing behavior which interferes with that single goal.

He walked around the room, looked into an empty closet, and announced, "I'm not gonna read and you can't make me!"

"I agree Roger. But I also hope you know that *reading is difficult! It is not easy.* If it were easy you could do it by yourself. This is why you have a special tutor. I promise, however, not to force you to read, and will stop when you feel it is too upsetting for you—how about that?"

With an incredulous look on his face he declared, "Well, I might come and I might not!" And with that he vanished into his classroom.

After administering the Gates McKillop Reading Diagnostic Test, I discovered that Roger knew at least six of the initial consonant sounds. I would therefore begin on familiar terrain. For our first lesson I laid out an assortment of enticing little objects on the desk, all of which began with the intial consonant sound of hard *c* with which he was familiar: a cat, a small calendar, a can, and a cup. On entering the room he announced, "I'm not gonna read today!"

"That's right," I quietly assured him, "we aren't going to read today. We are going to do other things." Although this was slightly reassuring, he was not yet ready to sit down and start working. As I began to rearrange the objects, he slipped into his chair asking, "Whatta ya doin' with those toys?"

"Well, I'm thinking of something that begins with *c* (giving the hard *c* sound, not the letter name) and you can pour hot chocolate into it," I said.

His face lit up, and with a hint of superiority he said, "Oh I know that, it's the cup."

We proceeded in this vein, taking turns guessing objects and focusing attention on the initial consonant sound. I then presented him with a beautiful flocked copy of the letter *c* from the *Alphabet Box*. He traced the letter with his index and middle finger, and then with a pencil he wrote the letter *c* on the paper I provided for him. Roger's fine motor skills were above average and would serve as excellent reinforcement for acquiring other skills.

I began to add other objects representing the initial consonant sounds that he knew, carefully selecting those that were aurally and visually dissimilar (*c, m, p, f*) so as to avoid the possibility of confusion and to assure success. We followed this procedure for the three remaining consonant sounds, and he was exuberant over his success in handling this task.

I presented him with a colorful, new, spiral notebook and suggested that we make it his book for all the things he knew. This felt good to him, and he asked if he could write his name on it. It would become his consonant dictionary and would be the first step toward helping him develop independence. If he did not know or forgot something, he would at least know where and how to look it up for himself without teacher intervention. It was also through this method of providing a resource and a record of his growing skills that he would learn to trust me to never ask him to do any task that he was unable to do. I had already cut several pages with tabs for locating four of the consonant sounds he knew, and from a selection of pictures, he chose the appropriate one for each page (see Figure 1).

With these tasks completed, we terminated the first of our many reading sessions.

"Is that all we're gonna' do?" he asked.

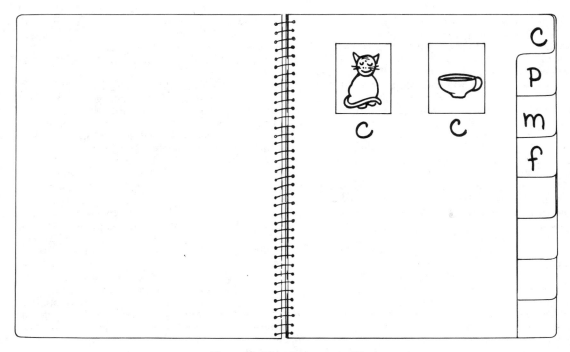

Figure 1. The Consonant Dictionary

"That's it!" I replied and off he went.

Roger had not developed any new skills on our first day of remedial reading, but we had both learned a lot about each other and the path that lay ahead of us.

We continued in this way for the next few lessons, sometimes substituting pictures for the objects used earlier and often eliminating pictures altogether as a riddle-game activity. To further strengthen his visual memory, we varied the activity by arranging the pictures, removing one and then taking turns recalling the missing picture and its initial sound.

He was also pleased with the inclusion of the Consonant Race Game. A convenient method of constructing games for flexibility and storage is to use the back of file folders. The board pattern is marked off for the basic game pattern and a plastic see-through pocket is placed across the top so that different patterns can be utilized for different children's needs (see Figure 2).

We took turns drawing from a stack of picture cards, and then we placed them into the corresponding column depending on their initial consonant sound. The first one who completed a row won ten points and an extra turn. I often included

picture cards starred for extra points he could earn by writing the letter which represented the corresponding sound or thinking of another word that began with the same consonant sound. Another valuable and favorite game activity became the Consonant Go Fish Game.

The sequence for learning each consonant sound was first auditory discrimination, then vocal, and then association of the sound with its visual symbol. Helpful guidelines for establishing a learning sequence are:

1. Can he hear it in isolation?

2. Can he hear it in words?

3. Can he pronounce it himself?

4. Can he associate it with the proper symbol?

5. Can he blend it with other sounds to read words?

6. Can he blend it with other sounds to write words?

7. Can he use it rapidly (automatically)?

So far Roger was only able to apply skills through step 4. His ability to use initial consonant sounds would provide him with his first real word-

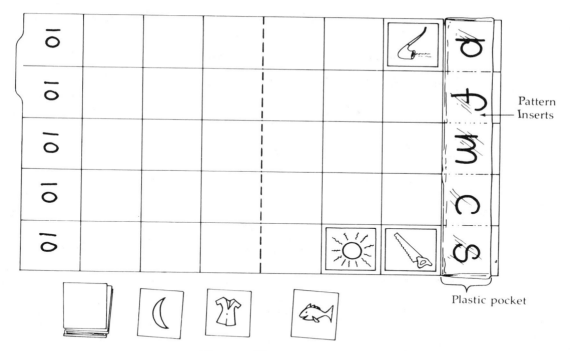

Figure 2. The Consonant Race Game

attack skill. I was careful at this time to avoid consonant blends and digraphs such as *cl, br, st, ch;* these would come later.

Throughout these first few lessons I hesitated to begin work on sight words because of Roger's anxieties and fear about "reading." A very important part of each lesson, however, was spent in my reading the simple Dr. Seuss books to him. I moved my finger along under the words as I read and provided him ample opportunities to furnish the predictable rhyming words and occasionally, to note the familiar, initial, consonant sounds in relationship to recurring words.

It was through this positive introduction to books within a trusting and friendly atmosphere that I hoped to whittle away at Roger's resistance and fear of books and the reading process. Words were becoming friendly things and they were communicating. They were providing us the opportunity for sharing enjoyable moments together as pupil and reading teacher.

We continued to practice correct script forms for each of the sounds he was learning, and he was able to learn the letter names as well.

During our first lesson together, I had noted his confusion in discriminating and writing the letter *p*, inverting and confusing the sound and visual symbol with the letter *b*. The *p, b,* and *d* confusion is typical of many children with visual-perceptual and directional confusions. At the beginning of our second session I presented him with a card on which was printed the letter *p* subtly disguised as a clown, but in such a way as to avoid distorting its essential shape and form (see Figure 3).

Counting on Roger's proclivity toward rhyme and rhythm, we traced over the *p* as we recited together, "*p* is a clown, his leg hangs down." He repeated this rhyme several times, advancing from the card to "invisible" wall-writing, and then to a magic marker on a plastic see-through sheet, which provided an easy flow of movement without restriction. He was delighted with this idea and wanted to take it to his classroom. Of course, I supported this suggestion, knowing that it could serve as a valuable reminder whenever he needed it.

Another simple technique worked well with Roger: the bat–ball idea developed by Mary Mitchell of the Kingsbury Center. Through the use of a miniature bat and ball, tracing, and visual imagery, a child learns to discriminate first the bat (the line) and then the ball (the circle). Both of the words,

Figure 3. P Is a Clown, His Leg Hangs Down

"bat" and "ball," reinforce the consonant sound and the correct sequence utilized in writing the letter (see Figure 4).

The effectiveness of any similar technique is the degree to which it is successful in separating out *one* of the mutually interfering elements so that the pupil can develop a sure base for discriminating differences. It is equally important for the teacher to provide many opportunities for drill and easy accessibility to visual reminders.

We continued to work through a process of tiny sequential steps. For at least five or six minutes of each lesson, I concentrated on our consonant ritual. I would give him a sound and he would write the letter, or I would reverse the procedure and give him a letter name. He would write it and then give me the sound. Through similar kinds of drill and the reinforcement of games and varied activities, Roger was slowly but surely learning upper and lower script forms, sounds, and letter names. As we began to accumulate many pages, I mounted them into book form, and he was quite proud of the menagerie of brilliant bird, butterfly, and shimmering star stickers that adorned each page as recognition of his good work.

"Now I have two books," he said. "But they aren't real books," he hastily reminded me. In his own way he was letting me know that the prospect of reading books was still highly anxiety-provoking. Learning to read also had other frightening implications for Roger. It represented growing up, becoming independent and accepting responsibility; he was still unwilling to risk himself.

I was amused and highly encouraged one day when, after completing one of these pages, he announced, "I don't think I'll have a bird sticker today. Just write *delicious* on that page up there at the top." (It is important to mention at this point that Roger was a child with insatiable needs for oral gratification, still at the developmental stage of equating food with love, attention, and rewards.) Without hesitation I wrote d e l i c i o u s across the top of the page, and he promptly drew a big juicy hamburger next to it. He then looked carefully at the word, noted its initial sound, and with his finger moved along under the word as we had done with the Dr. Seuss stories, synchronizing without error the *d* and *l* sounds of the word. Perhaps this assimilation of the middle consonant *l* was purely coincidental, but there was no denying his ability to relate the initial sound with the appropriate visual symbol and then the whole word. So this became one of his very first sight words— we were on our way.

With the acquisition of initial consonant sounds Roger possessed a reliable word-attack skill, and he had vividly shown me that he was ready to use it. I made plans for presenting the carefully controlled preprimer level vocabulary in the first of the Bank Street Readers Series, *In the City*. Through the use of many games, work sheets, and related activities, he would learn the twenty-eight words needed to read his first book.

As he entered the room for our next session, he was excited by the huge picture which I had

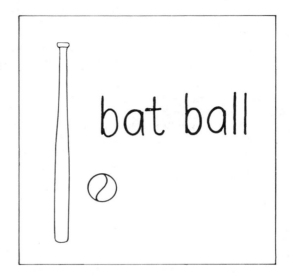

Figure 4. First the Bat and Then the Ball

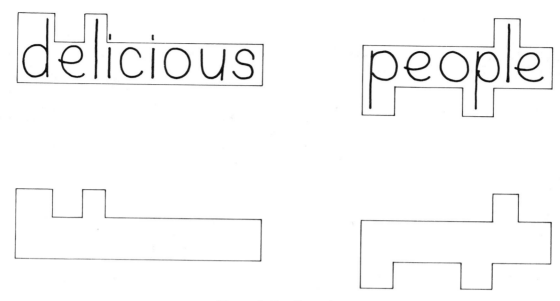

Figure 5. Configuration

taped to the wall of our room. It was a brightly colored illustration of life in a city: full of streets, buildings, parks, rivers, modes of transportation, and people engaged in a wide variety of activities. We spent a lot of time discussing the picture, locating activities, and identifying buildings by their unique characteristics (a post office flag, a school building, the capitol dome, etc.). We even pretended to devise routes of travel for getting from one place to another. I then presented him with a card on which was clearly printed the word "people."

Instructional Note. I did not choose the word "city" for his first sight word since the soft *c* sound was inconsistent with all that he had learned up to this point. He would learn to deal with exceptions and inconsistencies later.

We then discussed the various kinds of people in the picture and the activities in which they were involved. I provided him smaller copies of the word, and he taped them to the various groups of people pictured throughout the city.

Roger then traced the word, following the VAKT (Visual-Auditory-Kinesthetic-Tactile) procedures.[1] I presented him with a large copy of the word written in crayon so as to provide a distinct tactile stimulus. He traced over the word three times with his index and middle fingers, repeating the whole word as he did so. He did *not* spell the

word, but pronounced it as he traced it. In this fashion he could develop a "feel" for the gestalt of the word, not its separate parts as in spelling. I removed the word and he then wrote the word in "invisible" writing on his desk. He was successful at this, so I gave him a pencil with which he could write the word without looking at the original copy. He checked his copy against the master copy and was quite pleased with his efforts. We then compared its configuration with his other known word, "delicious," cutting around the two words so that they appeared clearly dissimilar in length and shape (see Figure 5).

He was now learning that he could also rely on configuration in discriminating words. Through picture associations, tracing, configuration, and initial consonant sounds, Roger slowly began to accumulate other sight words: *many, go, street, houses, in, city, the.* I began to make little books for him with pictures he could label with appropriate words, phrases, or sentences (see Figure 6).

He was happily content with his collection of little teacher-made books. they were simple, short, and nonthreatening. They weren't "real books."

During this time we continued our work on the remaining consonant sounds and began the first short vowel sound, *a.* He learned the isolated sound of short *a* by association with the visual clue, an apple. The other vowels would be added as he was ready (see Figure 7). Here again was another simple but valuable resource for helping Roger develop independence.

The phonetic blending process was extremely difficult for Roger, but by using the *Structural Reading Series*, he began to make slow but steady progress. With this method the emphasis is on avoiding the risk of distorted sounds through the blending process of isolated letters, such as *b - a - t*, by relating the initial consonant with the vowel and then the ending: *ba - t, pa - n, pa - l*. He used the structural reading dominoes (with words divided in this manner) to build words, followed by writing and spelling tasks, and the reading of short vowel words in context and in games. In this manner Roger was learning to blend words phonetically through a sequence of related sounds and symbols. Because he was able to learn well through multisensory approaches, we also utilized gross motor and kinesthetic skills. I placed enlarged copies of short *a* words on the board. Standing in front of each word, he would blend the words as he moved his hand along under the letters, utilizing his arm, hand, and shoulder muscles to "feel" the visual and auditory left-to-right sequencing

process. This procedure also helped him to establish the beginnings and endings of words, aurally and visually (see Figure 8).

With the acquisition of phonetic words and sight words he was able to read many simple sentences. He was proud of his growing collection of little books made of construction paper and brightly colored pictures. Through short, simple sentence structures he was learning to rely on context as another way of learning words. A regular activity of our reading lesson became the Sentence Cube Game (see Figure 9).

I made three cardboard cubes with words or phrases on each side that could be changed as his vocabulary increased. We would take turns rolling the cubes and then arranging them to form a sentence. This required discerning capital letters at the beginning and punctuation marks at the end of sentences. Points were printed on each side of the cube, and if the words on the sides which were rolled face up formed a sensible and complete sentence, those points were accumulated toward the winning score of 20. He delighted in the absurdities that often occurred (such as "Three cats can

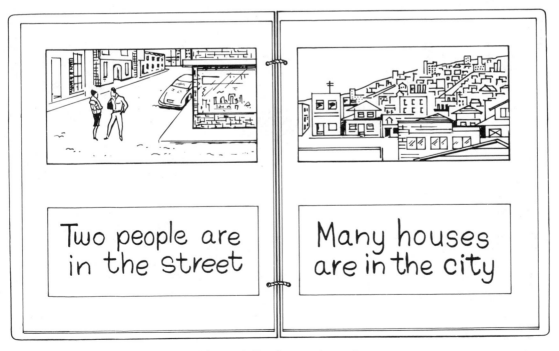

Figure 6. Teacher-Made Books

Figure 7. Short Vowel Reminder

spotting and reading friendly and familiar words on every page.

"Hey, slow down!" I laughed. "Let's go back to the beginning and see what this is all about."

An excellent procedure in remedial reading sessions is for teacher and pupil to share the reading. The child, as he listens to the teacher read portions of the story, and as he follows along silently, picks up the appropriate use of expressions, inflections, punctuation, and pacing. But that was not to be the case today. Roger was in control of the situation and my offers to read a page or two were refused with a hasty "No, no let me do it. I can do it." And so he did, from the beginning to the end. The other activities which I had foolishly planned for the day were immediately scrapped. Nothing could follow that act.

He was eager to show his new book to his teachers and classmates, so we rushed downstairs to share the exciting news. His classroom teachers had been awaiting this event for weeks, but they were full of "surprised" exclamation over his accomplishment. Upstairs, for future lessons, were three more supplementaries which contained the same controlled vocabulary as *In the City*, but it would be a day or two before Roger was ready to part with his very first reading book.

Roger and I had completed thirty-five remedial reading sessions together. His progress had been slow and often painful, and I was frequently discouraged by the many problems that interfered with his ability to learn. But I made every effort along the way to avoid communicating to Roger that sense of frustration which is so familiar to all remedial reading teachers. Roger would continue to confuse look alike words for many months to come; the assimilation of each short vowel sound would continue to be a difficult process; he would continue to forget without constant review and reinforcement. Many more months of structured remedial reading sessions would be required before he could begin to function independently. Roger had only begun his venture into the world of reading, but he was armed now with a few reliable skills and a growing sense of confidence and achievement.

Reluctant readers are easily discouraged and quickly lose interest if they are not provided access to a multitude of high-interest, low-level reading books. It is important that every remedial reading department be equipped with books which meet these requirements. The children with whom I have worked, from six to twelve years of age, have found great pleasure and satisfaction in the following list of old favorites. Most of these series begin

work in the store."), his joy undiluted by his gaining no points for arranging these silly sentences.

After months of carefully structured remedial reading sessions, the eventful day arrived. He had learned all of the sight words needed to read the entire book, *In the City*. I was still a bit unsure of his reaction to such an expectation, but the groundwork had been laid and he had gained not only the necessary skills but increased confidence in himself and his ability to learn.

As he slipped into his chair, he spotted the book lying on his desk. "What's that? Are ya gonna read that to me today?" he asked.

"Oh, I might. Why don't we look at the pictures first," I suggested.

That suited him fine and he opened the book. Immediately he spotted "One Two Three."

"Hey, I know that: One Two Three," he shouted. Then he began to race through the book,

Figure 8. Reinforcement of the Phonetic Blending Process

with books at the preprimer level (and gradually progress through third-grade reading levels).

The *Moonbeam Series,* Benefic Press

The *Sailor Jack Series,* Benefic Press

The *Tom Logan Series,* Benefic Press

The *American Adventure Series,* Harper and Row

Sounds of Language Readers by Bill Martin, Jr., Holt, Rinehart and Winston, Inc. (preprimer through sixth grade)

The Scott Foresman Reading Systems (preprimer through sixth grade)

The *Jim Forest Readers,* Field Educational Publications

The Wildlife Adventure Series, Field Educational Publications

World Traveler, Open Court Publishing Co. (a popular monthly with selected simplified articles from National Geographic, written at about third grade level)

Note

1. **Grace M. Fernald,** *Remedial Techniques in the Basic School Subjects* (New York and London: McGraw-Hill Book Co., 1943).

References

Bank Street Reading Series. New York: The Macmillan Company, 1972.

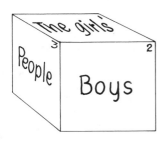 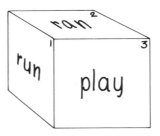 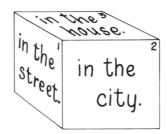

Figure 9. The Sentence Cube Game

Consonant Go Fish Game. 2d Series, The Kingsbury Center for Remedial Education, 2138 Bancroft Place, N.W., Washington, D.C., 1971.

Flocked Alphabet Card Set. Keystone Industrial Park, Scranton, Pa.: Harper and Row, 1969.

Gates, Arthur I., and McKillop, Anne S. *Gates-McKillop Reading Diagnostic Tests,* New York: Teachers College Press, 1962.

Stern, Catherine; Gould, Toni S.; Stern, Margaret B.; and Gartler, Marion. *Structural Reading Series.* Westminster, Md.: Random House–Singer Company, 1966.

Editors' Commentary

Except for children with specific learning dysfunctions in the visual motor area of integration or syntax functioning, writing is a natural expression of thinking and feeling. It should flow with richness and excitement as a pupil moves from concrete to abstract levels of thinking. Instead, there is a general attitude among high school students that a written assignment is equivalent to staying home on a weekend with parents—it's sheer pain!

Many educators are concerned about this attitude and wonder what happens to change the first grader's free and easy experiential story-writing skills into the ninth grader's dread of weekly English composition. Many critics feel the source of this problem is the teacher's overconcern with and emphasis on correct style, proper grammar, and neat handwriting. It is suggested that the fear of writing in imperfect form is so powerful that it discourages pupils from writing anything unless under direct adult pressure. Other critics feel that in our society writing is a "female skill" and consequently not masculine enough for boys to assume. This problem is compounded when it comes to teaching emotionally troubled pupils, who are notoriously resistant to writing. In the next article, d'Alelio demonstrates his ingenuity in motivating a group of severely disturbed pupils to enjoy the pleasure of creative writing. His use of fairy tales, with all their rich fantasy, is an excellent strategy for engaging pupils in writing assignments.

A Strategy for Teaching Remedial Language Arts: Creative Writing

William A. d'Alelio

Many pupils referred to a special class have had negative experiences in writing, and the teacher who attempts to teach creative writing in a typical fashion will encounter a wall of passive resistance or overt refusal. This article illustrates how I overcame my group's initial resistance to creative writing and shares some of the techniques which proved effective in freeing them from enough of their fears to enjoy writing.

One of the basic prerequisites for teaching language arts through creative writing is that your class must enjoy literature. In other language arts areas, a pupil must be able to read a word before he can write it, or recognize a word when he hears it before he can use the word as part of his spoken vocabulary. In creative writing, the teacher must provide his class with ample opportunity to listen to different forms of literature and to discuss them before he asks the class to write. A selection of fairy tales, poetry, short stories, and tall tales should be enthusiastically read to the group.

I found it useful to begin with fairy tales, because they afford a variety of universal themes and are a good source of high-interest material for class discussion. An example of such discussion follows:

Teacher: "When the ogre found he had accidentally let the boy and girl escape, what do you think he was feeling?"

Student: "He was probably real mad and wanted to get them, and lock them up again, and make sure they would never get away again."

Teacher: "What do you think he'll do now?"

Student: "He might get out his magic mirror to find out where they went, or he might just go out and look for them."

A discussion of this sort can center around any of the four elements that contribute to the success or failure of a story: theme, plot, character development, and style. I found it easiest to engage group discussion of the plot before trying to deal with the other elements.

From a pupil's point of view, a good plot involves plenty of action and many obstacles for the hero to overcome. A story with a lively plot also provides the teacher with many opportunities to break for discussion just as the plot is reaching a climax, thus allowing the children to test the rules of sequential story-line development and to explore the many possibilities of action within a story.

Another advantage of using fairy tales for a group's initial exposure to literature is the characteristic clarity of the story lines. A group can learn the basic structure of a well-written story by analyzing the plot development of fairy tales they have heard in class. The clearest method for teaching the progression of a story line is to chart a story's development on the format in Figure 1. The diagram can be placed on the board, and a story with which the class is familiar can be analyzed by the teacher as an example.

The next step is to have the group analyze another story with less assistance from the teacher. The diagramed stories can be transformed into a mural, with art work by the class and captions by the teacher. An outgrowth of this technique is to provide the class with a partially filled-in diagram and ask the class to make up a story to match the outline.

Once a group is comfortable with discussing plot line, they can be introduced to character de-

velopment. Character development, in this context, means: Do the children like certain characters in the story and dislike others, and how did the author describe the major characters to make them likable, foolish, scary, etc.? Group discussion is, once again, one of the primary tools for the exploration of character development. The group can be encouraged to discuss the characters of a story through questions such as: "Why do you suppose anyone would want to go into a valley where they knew a dragon lived?" "Do you think all witches were bad?" "What kinds of things did they do?" Questions of this kind can involve a group in a serious discussion of the characters without the inevitable turn-off of "Who did you like best in this story, children?" Open-ended discussion of characters also lays the groundwork for discussion of how an author lets us get to know his characters as individuals. Group discussions can eventually lead to such questions as: "When the story says 'the prince lived happily ever after,' what do you think he was doing?" "Can you make a guess what a guy like him would be doing from what we know he did in the story?" "What was he like?"

When a group has reached this degree of sophistication in discussing stories, they are ready to move into the areas of style and theme. A good group project is to list descriptive words to fit different characters in a story. An excellent format for this type of listing is a comparison of a good character and an evil one, such as the following:

OGRE	PRINCE	WIZARD	FOOL
ugly	handsome	aged	young
short	tall	clever	sleepy
fat	kind	grey-haired	dressed in
mean	friendly	sly and crafty	funny clothes
dangerous		powerful	stupid and silly
		good or evil	weak
			harmless

This exercise should be done at the board with the teacher in the role of secretary facilitator rather than active director. (Children will tend to rely on the teacher for "right" answers to this type of exercise unless they are given support to feel their contributions are of merit in and of themselves.) The teacher should try to foster an understanding of classification and descriptive language through comments such as, "An ogre is ugly; we need a word to describe the way a prince looks."

Once children develop an appreciation of literature, they will desire to participate more actively in group projects, such as the listing exercise suggested above. This involvement often starts with a request to draw pictures of characters from

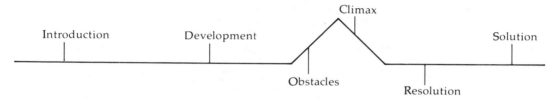

Figure 1. Story Development Format

the fairy tales, poems, and stories that have been read to the class. The desire to draw pictures of characters can be used as a method to encourage students to start their own written work. A suggestion is for the class to draw pictures of two characters listed for a certain day. The pictures can be drawn on ditto masters and collected. When run off, the pictures can be bound into a folder, with the list of descriptive words as a first page. A page listing the illustrators and their illustrations is an excellent idea as well. Write a sentence to label the picture. Soon, children can be encouraged to make their own "books" by writing lists of descriptive words about characters of their own choice, and illustrating the lists. Another variation of this activity which works well is having pupils label their illustrations with the name of the characters, a sentence describing what he is doing, or, at a higher level of development, two or three lines describing what he is like.

Moving into the area of style seems like a difficult task at first glance. This is particularly true when one is working with children who have no great love of language because of their own fear of failure. Again I broke through the initial resistance to stylistic analysis by exposing children to literature before asking them to write lists of characters' attributes. They began to use phrases to describe characters rather than the single adjectives they were using before. A discussion with the group about the advantages of using phrases rather than single words led them to the realization that language is based on chunks of meaning, rather than on single words held together by a capital letter at the beginning of a sentence and a period at the end.

Once a group has reached this realization, there are a number of activities that a teacher can use to reinforce language analysis. One of the first activities we used was an offshoot of the adjective listing. A character was described with adjectives, and the class was then asked to find phrases to re-

place the adjectives on the board. The format is as follows:

Chauncy the Crocodile

Chauncy is a crocodile who is

green: *the color of grass*
crafty: *always on his guard*
dangerous: *never to be trusted*
lazy: *usually asleep*
scaly: *covered with a coat of armor*

This activity can be adapted for adverbial clauses as well: "Chauncy runs quickly—as fast as the wind." Once the group begins to get the hang of this type of phrasing, they can be introduced to the general use of phrasing in sentences.

Using short selections the teacher has read orally to the class, the group can look for ways sentences can be broken down into meaningful phrases. This can be done by putting the sentences on the board without punctuation and asking the class to decide where the natural breaks occur. The following is an example of the type of sentence which is most useful for this type of exercise:

Harry went out to the garage and got into his car he thought about his basketball game the whole time as he drove to the gym

Another useful exercise for teaching phrasing is to pass out telegram messages typed on yellow paper, without punctuation, and have the group try to decipher the meaning.

dear Steve it was so good to
get your letter last Wednesday
I will be coming to visit your
school this week and hope to see
you then call to let me know where
I can reach you

One advantage of this technique is that it allows the teacher to adjust the reading level of each message while exposing an entire group to the concept of phrasing. Phrasing, for its own sake, will not hold the interest of a class for long—nor should it. It is one of the prerequisite skills for creative writing, not an end in itself. When the teacher anticipates his class has had enough of phrasing, he should be prepared to give them some exciting applied uses of the skill. Three such activities are sentence reduction, sentence transformation, and rearranging sentences.

Sentence reduction is an activity in which each pupil can be made to feel as powerful as a professional editor and as precise as a master detective. A complex sentence with many modifying phrases and clauses is placed on the blackboard and read to the group. The children are asked to figure out the sentence's main idea by crossing out descriptive phrases and language.

> *One day, Happy, the hippopotamus, who was used to eating and eating and eating, looked in his food trough and saw, to his surprise, that he had no food!*

This sentence can be reduced so that it reads as follows:

> *Happy saw he had no food!*

It would be unusual for a class to reduce a sentence to such a bare minimum on the first attempt, but with practice almost any group can become quite proficient and get a great deal of enjoyment out of reducing sentences of this sort. It is truly exciting to see a group of pupils who previously were not interested in the structure of language working with enthusiasm on a task such as this. Don't push them to make more deletions than they can with comfort. With my group, I found that the process of sentence reduction is developmental and that once a class becomes comfortable with it they will really learn how much of our written language is descriptive rather than purely functional.

There is another variation of sentence reduction which bears noting. When a class begins to show a high level of proficiency at reducing sentences, they can begin to work the process in reverse: They can expand sentences rather than reduce them. The teacher would tell the class he has some sentences which he has already reduced, and which he would like to put back in their longer form with the group's help. A sentence such as "Carl was angry" is written on the board with a list of adjectives and descriptive phrases:

Carl _____

    who didn't like to wake up
    the sleepy rhinoceros

was angry _____!

    who didn't know any better
    when Teddy
    outside his cage
    blew a trumpet

The class then suggests where the phrases fit to make the best sentence. As the class begins to show skill at this type of exercise, more of the phrases can be left up to their imagination. This exercise leads nicely into the next technique, sentence transformation.

Sentence transformation is similar to sentence reduction in that the class is provided with stimulus sentences on the blackboard. In this instance, their output is oral and kids enjoy it. The group's task is to maintain the given structure of several sentences while altering their content. A passage such as:

> *Who was it that was gliding? It was Wendell, the brown-winged bat!*

is placed in the following format:

> *Who was it that was gliding?*
>
>   *flying*
>   *soaring*
>   *hovering*
>   *swimming*
>
> *It was Wendell the brown winged bat!*
>   *Franklin   blue   speckled fish!*

Questions are asked, such as: "What if you didn't want to use the word, 'gliding'? What other word could you use?" The children's suggestions are then listed in the column under the word "gliding," and the sentence is read with the substitution of new words. By offering a word which entails a different activity, such as swimming, the teacher can draw attention to the interrelatedness of the two sentences (see diagram above). This activity also provides a good format for introducing such concepts as verb agreement within phrases. "When the first sentence is phrased in the present tense, what happens to the second sentence?" "Who *is* it that *is* gliding?" "It *is* . . . etc." A class can become so proficient at this activity that it can produce an entire family of sentences from one stimulus sentence. As with the lists of character descriptions, the different sentence patterns produced by the class can be put into book form. (New sentence families can be added easily if the book is a looseleaf.) Children can be encouraged to illustrate some of their favorite sentences.

One of the techniques frequently used by skilled creative writers is the rearranging of sentence order. An example of this technique is found below:

From the top of the bridge,
the river below is a piece of sky,
until you drop a stone in it.

Teaching this skill to children is a challenging process, and yet, if they have mastered the other phrasing skills, they can learn it rapidly. Two techniques prove effective in introducing the concept of sentence rearrangement: the first I call scrambling, the second unscrambling. I found it worked best to have pupils unscramble sentences before trying to scramble them. A sentence arranged in an unusual order is placed on the board. The class is asked to underline the phrases which make up the sentence and then rearrange the sentence in a more traditional order. An illustration of this technique, using the sample sentence above:

      (3)   *(1)*
From the top of the bridge,   *the river below is a*
                      (2)
piece of sky   *until you drop a stone in it.*

When the numbered phrases are read in their traditional order, they read:

The river below is a piece of sky, until you drop a stone in it from the top of the bridge.

Scrambling is similar to unscrambling in that the first stage involves breaking down the sentence into its component phrases. After a sentence has been broken down, the group can experiment with the various invented combinations from the root sentence. The sentence, "If you think about it carefully, Harry is the kind of person you want as a friend," will yield the sentence, "Harry is the kind of person you want as a friend, if you think about it carefully." When two sentences constructed from the same phrases are read with their natural inflections, it provides a class with a real sense of the significance of sentence order. It is a rare pupil who, hearing the two sentences above read aloud, fails to realize that the second sentence is none too kind to Harry!

The fourth area of literary analysis that can help overcome the fear of writing is theme. Most children will begin to notice basic similarities among the stories and fairy tales which have been read to them over a period of time. Through discussion of theme children come to understand that writing is merely a way of putting concerns and feelings down on paper. Understanding the nature of literary themes can best be developed through group discussion of stories after a class has been exposed to several different themes in two or three different stories. The class should be able to sort out the "scary" stories from the "fun" or "sad" ones. Pupils should be encouraged to discuss their ideas about why writers choose certain subjects, such as the need to overcome obstacles, find love, grow up, etc. They can also be asked their opinions on why sometimes characters who seem to be monsters, frogs, etc., turn out to be good figures, or why many small or weak heroes are the only ones who can kill giants or release people from spells. There are no "right" answers to these issues; they should be seen as an opportunity for pupils to decide what themes they like best and to start exploring what types of actions are appropriate to their favorite themes. At this point many pupils have acquired enough confidence to start their own writing.

There are two general styles of teaching writing: native expression and stimulus-response. The first method has been used by Sylvia Ashton Warner, Kenneth Koch, and Roger Landrum. The basis of this technique is the belief that children, unless inhibited by a fear of failure, are able to produce excellent written work, given an opportunity to do so. Warner and Koch believe in writing assignments that reflect a pupil's interests. Warner asks her class to decide on three words a day they want to learn and then has the class make up a story incorporating the new words. Her concept is that pupils will spontaneously evolve into writers as they begin to sense the security of writing within a group, and that they will soon start to write on their own. She also feels that children will develop into excellent writers without any need for adult intervention in terms of style, once they have begun the process of writing for enjoyment.

Koch's beliefs are similar to Warner's, except that he feels children should be encouraged to explore their natural writing style through individual writing assignments such as "Wish" or "Lie" poems. These consist of personal wishes or lies that each child uses as the basis for each poem:

I wish I had a magic helicopter
I wish I had a long red train
I wish I had a . . . , etc.
                              or

I ate 1,000 pancakes for breakfast
I swam across the ocean before lunch . . . , etc.

This basic technique is modified by specifying conditions that must be met in each poem (e.g., each line must be a wish that involves a color). Like Warner's techniques Koch's teaching style is used only to start a pupil writing; the goal is to stop influencing the child's writing as quickly as possible.

Landrum differs from Koch and Warner in method, but not in theory. He tries to engage a pupil in creative writing by getting him to dictate a story into a tape recorder during a one-to-one interview situation. The dictated story is then transcribed and read back to the child. In this way, the child is introduced to his own stories in print and becomes motivated to start writing on his own. Pupils reluctant to tell a story are interviewed about what they are doing in school or at home, and through skillful probing are led to develop their responses into a story.

The stimulus-response style of teaching writing has been with us for many years in one form or another. The class essay about summer vacation is an example of this method through which many of us suffered. Fortunately, many excellent teachers (Ruth Carlson, Mauree Applegate, and Walter Petty) have provided other examples of how to use this method creatively. Their ideas range from having pupils react to and write about art masterpieces, such as the paintings of Vincent Van Gogh, to having children collect objects while on a walk, and write a history of the object's life. These teachers believe in the importance of structured style development, and include in their books many suggestions for improving children's writing styles.

Because children in a special education setting have varied learning rates and styles, these teachers' techniques work with some children and fail with others. If a child is having consistent difficulty writing in the native experience style, it may be because he is easily disorganized and so needs the structure of a stimulus-response model. The inverse is also true—a child who is too rigid and too concerned with writing the "right" thing to get anything written at all needs the open-endedness and acceptance of a native-expression teaching style.

The most important thing to realize about teaching creative writing, especially to children who have been rejected and who have an extremely low self-concept, is something which is easy to lose sight of: Behind all of the resistance which you may face initially when you institute creative writing as part of your curriculum, the children *want* to be able to express themselves. The pupils want to be able to write and when they find that they can trust you to help them do it, you and your class will be starting on one of the most exciting and mutually rewarding experiences you can share.

One of my greatest rewards last year was this piece of writing from a twelve-year-old student whose initial response to writing was, "I ain't gonna do none of that shit!"

> *Shout*
> As I sleep
> with my eyes opened
> out of the dark
> I hear a N O I S E
> with my eyes
> but looking around the
> room I only hear
> the silence of
> dark. As I wipe
> the cold sweat
> from my brow.

References

Arbuthnot, May Hill. *Children and Books.* Glenview, Ill.: Scott Foresman and Co., 1964.

Carlson, Ruth Kearney. *Sparkling Words.* Geneva, Ill.: Paladin House Publishers, 1973.

Koch, Kenneth. *Wishes, Lies, and Dreams.* New York: Vintage, 1970.

Martin, Bill. *Sounds of Mystery.* New York: Holt, Rinehart, and Winston, 1967.

Editors' Commentary

The knowledge that many emotionally troubled pupils are reading two or more years below their mental age has motivated private educational companies to develop numerous remedial reading programs. Although Huber[7] has reported that low-achieving, emotionally disturbed elementary pupils have even greater deficiencies in arithmetic than reading, there is not the parallel interest in remedial mathematics programs.

Interestingly, emotionally disturbed pupils seem to have more difficulty with subtraction and division than with addition and multiplication. Proponents of psychoanalytic theory suggest that subtraction and division are mathematical processes that "take things away" or "cut them into smaller parts." For deprived and disturbed pupils, the symbolism of these processes creates feelings of sibling rivalry (losing to others) and castration anxiety (losing what little one has left). These interpretations may be true—they at least caution teachers about the symbolic meaning of numbers and mathematical processes—but they have not yet led to positive solutions. Perhaps some additional interpretations of mathematics learning problems will develop as special educators turn to experimental designs for remedial programs.

Because so few remedial programs in mathematics are available, some basic programs are briefly summarized below:

1. *The Primary Math Skills Improvement Program* (Special Education Materials, New York) consists of forty prerecorded tapes that involve highly motivating, individualized exercises, reinforcing fundamental skills in sets, subtraction, multiplication, division, and place value.

2. *Key Math,* by Dr. Austin Connally et al. (American Guidance Service, Inc., Minnesota), is an individual diagnostic arithmetic test with excellent visual materials. The test covers fourteen skill areas and can be used successfully with pupils who also have difficulties in reading.

3. *The A B C of Math* (Math Shop, Watertown, Massachusetts) is a complete curriculum series with unusually good manipulative materials such as multi-link cubes, logiblocs, and 3-D numbers.

4. *The Cuisenaire Rods* (Cuisenaire Company of America, Inc., New York) is the oldest and most frequently used technique of remedial mathematics. The method is concrete, precise, and simple. For most pupils, this is a new way of thinking and feeling about math. All special educators should be skilled in this particular technique.

5. *Math Readiness,* by Dr. Lola May (McGraw-Hill, Early Learning Division, Pennsylvania), is an individualized taped program using an audio and visual approach to instruction. Although it is designed for the primary-age pupil, it can be modified for older pupils who need to begin with basic concepts such as big, bigger, and biggest, right, left, etc.

In the following article, Rose Alpher describes her strategy for teaching pupils with severe mathematical disabilities. Her approach reflects the best of original, exciting, and personal methods of remotivating reluctant learners. A historical approach to mathematics leaves children with a greater appreciation of the world and knowledge that most pupils in regular classes never receive. It is teaching strategies like this one that make special education special.

---

7. **Franz Huber,** "Achievers and Non-Achievers Among Severely Disturbed Children" (Ph.D. dissertation, University of Michigan, 1964).

A Strategy for Teaching Remedial Mathematics: If I Had $1,000,000 . . .

Rose W. Alpher

Most school curricula manage to strip mathematics of its cultural content, leaving a bare skeleton of technicalities which manage to repel both normal and troubled students. To undo some of this antipathy toward mathematics, my initial remedial approach is to use a historical method that shows the evolution of mathematical concepts. This strategy brings a fresh outlook and a new interest to mathematics.

By allowing pupils to discover through reading graphically illustrated material and trips to the museum, or library, a comparison of Egyptian mathematics with Babylonian or Greek mathematics is first developed. The sole purpose of this historical look is for the pupils to feel an identity, a kinship with early civilizations. The excitement begins when the pupil discovers that the human race, even in its earliest stage of development, was endowed with a "number sense." This number sense permitted early man to realize that something had changed in a small collection of objects when one object was removed or added.

To expand this theme, considerable time is spent with a group of four to six remedial pupils in whimsical speculation. For example, I might ask: "What if we had no number names; how could we report how many pupils are in school? How could we determine how many books we have, or how many chairs we need around the lunch table or in the movie?" Frequently, the pupils answer with primitive methods: "one chair for Larry, one for Tommy, one for Mike, one for Teddy," or by making lines on a piece of paper. Soon they mention counting on fingers, which is my signal to review man's early method of matching persons with sticks or cutting notches in a stick of wood. It is most important at this beginning stage of remediation not to hurry the lessons; they must be relaxed and unthreatening. The pupils must believe they do not have to learn to add, multiply, or do anything else on a deadline contract. This arrangement relieves the pupil of immediate anxiety because he is still not motivated to learn math.

Another nonthreatening example of numeration is the Roman system. Because pupils are not expected to use it seriously, it can become an enjoyable and familiar system, a nice way of decoding the numbers occasionally found on buildings, in books, and as chapter headings. Of course, I do not expect them to solve math problems using Roman numerals. If, however, the teacher writes the Roman numerals on a chart, leaves it up within view, and from time to time gives them a decoding problem (for example, the Romans wrote 28 as XXVIII, 145 as CXLV, and 1974 as MCMLXXIV), interest is maintained. The pupil's ability to decode and solve a few of his own problems gives him pleasure and immediate gratification. More importantly, a triangular relationship among teacher, pupils, and numbers is built. This relationship is extended further by introducing graphic illustration of the Egyptian system of numeration as shown below:

Number	Symbol	Resembles
1	/	Stroke
10	∩	Heel bone
100	℥	Coiled rope
1,000	⚘	Lotus flower

Number	Symbol	Resembles
10,000	⌐	Bent reed
100,000	⌒	Fish
1,000,000	⚹	Astonished man

The Egyptians could write 25 as /////∩∩ or ∩∩///// (Because order made no difference, the ones could come before the tens, hundreds, or thousands.) The pupils are asked to suggest how the Egyptians might have written, let's say, 2,115. The various correct answers might be:

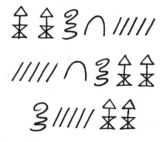

Again, the fun of playing with symbols becomes appealing to the pupils. They remain unthreatened by them, and they are still learning basic arithmetic. This method also can adopt the aura of a fairy tale, or a fantasy of long ago.

At this point, I begin to present our system of numeration. I help them discover the Hindu-Arabic system, complete with the symbols: 0, 1, 2, 3, 4, 5, 6, 7, 8, 9, and 10. For example, I begin by asking them to write Hindu-Arabic numerals for Egyptian symbols:

1. $\cap\cap//$ = 22.

2. $\mathcal{Z}\mathcal{Z}\mathcal{Z}\mathcal{Z}$ = 400.

3. $\mathcal{Z}\cap\cap\cap\cap\cap$ = 150.

Then, I reverse the process and ask them to write Egyptian symbols for Arabic numerals.

For this task I begin simple addition:

5	8
6	2
7	6
3	4

The transitional step in acquiring mathematical skills is the mastering of addition; the pupils are told that all they have to learn is how to add. Through examples, they begin to see that multiplication, subtraction, and division are multiple addition. With constant examples I insist on additive subtraction, i.e., 9 and how many is 15, not 15 minus 9. The transfer to standard division and multiplication occurs spontaneously as confidence increases.

Games are introduced which not only include division, fractions, estimating, and rounding out numbers, but also increase the spirit of working together, sharing knowledge, and learning to take some risk. An example of this kind of game is to (1) provide a small bag of M & M's; (2) allow the students to examine the bag, take a small handful, and estimate how many are in their hands, how many are in the bag; (3) give them the cost of the candy; and (4) have them figure out how much per piece. Thus, math sessions become centered around activities; much more interest is generated. One can actually feel the pupils' enthusiasm. They begin to understand concepts and acquire skills. They begin to explore and initiate many of their own ideas (one can see them measuring floors, desks, wallboards, the playground) by which they can demonstrate that they understand the meaning behind the symbol and can use this knowledge in a practical way.

With the functional knowledge of basic mathematical skills, curiosity returns and numbers can be used to expand their life. "What would you do if you had $100, $1,000, or $1,000,000?" becomes an understandable and entertaining question. Whether math is used for dreaming or reality, it's a tool that helps a pupil bring order to a complex world, security at a shopping center, and excitement to his inner life.

Editors' Commentary

Most pupils look forward to physical education and recess periods because, like candy, they are the sweet times of the school day. They are chances to relax, play, have fun, fool around, release tension, and relate to friends instead of to books and assigned lessons. Play provides children with vast educational experiences in social learning and physical cognitive skills. An average ten-year-old pupil is a master of numerous individual and group games: checkers, booby trap, Monopoly, fish, old maid, gin, twenty-one, slap, freeze tag, hide-and-seek, steal-the-bacon, drop-the-hankie, baseball, football, basketball, kickball, etc. Games teach children the important lesson that it is impossible to be first, best, and strongest all the time when playing with peers. The natural feelings of competition, frustration, joy, and disappointment that are a part of winning or losing a game provide meaningful opportunities for children to learn how to cope with strong feelings.

Unfortunately, emotionally troubled pupils frequently do not know how to play. They never internalize the rules or develop the skills to be successful at games. What is more important, they usually cannot discriminate between a disappointment and a disaster. For them, play is not a therapeutic activity facilitating growth but another painful conflict area. It is not uncommon for teachers to exclude these children from the playground because of the problems they create for others. There is little recognition that this decision to remove them from their peer group prevents them from learning the skills they need if they are ever to play with others. This practice is similar to telling a starving child he will not be fed until his hunger pangs go away. In special education, play is an important basic means; it should not be taken away or used as an enticement as if it were a dessert.

Research in this area is grossly neglected. One of the original studies, directed by Gump and Sutton-Smith[8] in 1955, examined how the social interaction among emotionally disturbed children was significantly different between two camp activities, swimming and crafts. They concluded that the activity itself was the important factor in determining the amount of aggression the campers exhibited. This means the type of programming for disturbed children becomes a significant factor. Each game carries its hidden psychodynamics. Significant group forces operate when the teacher selects dodge ball (in which the group plays against individuals) as opposed to tag (in which an individual is after the group). Some of the specific variables to consider in a game are: the amount of body contact (football); body mobility (statues vs. tag); the complexity of rules and the skill requirements (chess, Monopoly, checkers); the degree of luck (dice and spinner games); the use of space (kickball); the duration of the game (war); the use of props (balls, rackets); role-taking factors (quarterback, pitcher, "it"); and the degree of "horsing around" the game can tolerate (Mother-may-I vs. darts). Unless the teacher knows how a particular game can affect the frustration level of a group or an individual, he or she may inadvertently contribute to program breakdown and group chaos.

In the following article, Huber translates these concerns for the classroom teacher by describing the four sources of conflict that occur during play. He also offers guidelines for the constructive use of games and sports for troubled children. This article focuses on the skills teachers need to help aggressive pupils control themselves and withdrawn pupils become more active, by encouraging cooperative rather than competitive play.

8. **Paul Gump and Bryan Sutton-Smith,** "Activity Setting and Social Interaction: A Field Study," *American Journal of Orthopsychiatry* XXV: 4 (1955).

A Strategy for Teaching Cooperative Games: Let's Put Back the Fun in Games for Disturbed Children

Franz Huber

Ms. Smith breathed an audible sigh of relief. Jimmy, the last of the twelve-member, all-boy "academic-social adjustment class" had just passed reluctantly through the door for the twenty-minute recess. Not to play with the others, of course, but to brood and sulk and probably fantasize about what he could do if he had his older brother's ability. Jimmy was so puny and awkward he could barely make foot contact with the spinning, twisting ball so sadistically propelled by Robert, who automatically had taken over the coveted pitcher position. Perhaps Robert was not the most skilled player, but he certainly was the most dominant—overtly so outside of the classroom, and covertly in Ms. Smith's presence. With a look or a threatening gesture he could engender fear and acquiescence in the others. How he was able to buffalo the other boys she didn't quite understand, but didn't he intimidate even her at times?

She could just imagine what was going on out there, for it happened just about the same way every day, whether she went out with them or sent the part-time aide as she did this time. Neither could do much from the sidelines anyway except interact with the stragglers, observe the rest, and be prepared for the anger, resentment, recriminations, hurts, and smoldering hostility after everyone returned to the classroom.

Because her "class" had a separate, later time from any of the other grades, one of them always had to go out. Too many vociferous complaints from teachers, children, and parents about "those kids" had accumulated—their bad language and interfering behavior. From the intense yelling she was now hearing, the customary dispute of someone being either "out" or "safe" was probably occurring outside. Depending on the location, first base or home plate, these disputes were either settled by individual flare-ups with the toughest boy winning out, or, in a team-against-team conflagration, with Robert's team usually emerging the victor. Then, defenseless Jordie would either drop an easy flyball or let the ball slither through his legs for a home run. How she agonized over Jordie! He was always the recipient of the group's most vehement abuse. Whenever anything went wrong, whether Jordie did it intentionally or unintentionally, or was even involved, he could elicit the group's wrath. He would end up crying and pretending he was oblivious to any peer communication for the next few days. Then he would try again but usually end up in a similar situation.

He wasn't the only scapegoat. Any of the five boys on the lower end of the totem pole could hold that title. Many times she had seen abuse passed on from one child to another, right down the chain. John, a very intelligent but highly manipulative boy, would sometimes be on the receiving end, but generally he was able to turn things around so one of the less sophisticated boys would get it. John had the knack of working things out to suit himself. Yesterday, for instance, contrary to the rules, he convinced everyone that on a force play at third the runner had to be tagged. She knew she should have stepped in as a final arbitrator, but then she wasn't quite sure of the rules herself.

What was probably the worst for her was the reactions of the losers and the winners as they returned from the playground—she could spot them immediately by the way they held their heads. She remembered one authority on play who wrote that children aged ten to twelve weren't that competitive unless made so by adults. That might be true of some kids but not hers. The losers were so dejected, they were unconsolable and spent a good part of the day berating themselves, while the winners, with every taunt and gesture, made sure to remind them of their inadequacies. Or, she would let them stay out ten minutes longer than regulation—there'd be hell to pay, not only from the principal but from her own chaotic group when they came in. As she blew the whistle signaling their return, she wondered which was worse: remaining inside as she did and spending the whole time conjuring up the probable, or being beaten down by experiencing the actual. Did it matter? She still had the same mess to deal with!

It is well-known that disturbed children have major difficulties playing games and sports. It is less well-accepted that normal children and even adults evidence similar problems. What distinguishes the three groups is not so much a qualitative measure of the different kinds of problems that occur, but a quantitative measure of degree, frequency, duration, minimum provocation, and level of incapacitation. In other words, disturbed children react to common frustrations of games and sports (1) with extreme intensity of emotional response, (2) with high frequency, (3) with such long duration that the emotional behaviors pyramid, (4) to such slight provocation that it's barely detectable by the outside observer, and (5) with such a level of incapacitation that it makes it impossible for them to recoup sufficiently for continued participation in the activity. Normal children and adults react with more subdued responses to similar provocation. These exacerbated responses by emotionally disturbed children produce unmanageable trauma for teachers, recreational therapists, or aides, who attempt to have a relaxing time playing games.

Four factors can be identified as sources of conflict: (1) problems that reside primarily in the individual; (2) problems that stem primarily from peer interaction; (3) problems that reside primarily within the structure and organization of the activity; (4) problems that stem primarily from the supervising adult.

The Individual

In most instances, games and sports call for varying degrees of aggression, which should emerge in the form of controlled aggression. This is beyond the usual capability of many disturbed children. They show either too much aggression, resulting in verbal and physical attacks, or too little aggression, producing ineffectuality, defenselessness, and flight. Both responses can be frightening states for the disturbed child.

Closely allied to aggression is the winning and losing syndrome. Winning or losing graciously involves a great deal of understanding and tact. Disturbed children, especially, have not developed the affective skills to accomplish this task. Winning for some signifies complete vanquishment of an opponent; losing involves considerable self-abjection and self-devaluation.

Many disturbed children also do not have the requisite physical skills needed for participation in games and sports with their age mates. Dribbling a basketball, kicking a soccer ball, hitting a softball, all require considerable practice regardless of the inherent physical coordination of the individual. Without sufficient opportunity and sustained practice, these advanced physical skills can rarely be obtained. Consequently, few children enjoy participation in activities which highlight their weaknesses. For many children, it is safer not to play than to try and fail.

Peer Interaction

Peer interaction during latency age is rarely supportive. Peer rivalry is a common phenomenon and eventually produces a status hierarchy within the group. This status hierarchy fluctuates to some extent with the specific activity, but because most games and sports rely on similar skills, the hierarchy remains relatively stable. Lower-status members suffer considerable scapegoating, with displacement of feelings and projection of blame heaped on their least buoyant shoulders. As each child's main goal is to maintain his place within the hierarchy, there is little cognizance of another's plight. Looking through another's eyes and realizing his problems, much less acting to minimize another's pain, is an unattainable task for most children, especially disturbed children. Giving even partial credit to another for a good attempt, or supporting someone in need, is a rare occurrence. This makes it doubly hard for the ineffectual child to win the peer support needed to continue participation or at least bear the moment's inadequacies.

Structure and Organization of the Activity

The structure and organization of specific games and sports should be analyzed to determine their inherent potential for promoting satisfactory or unsatisfactory participant interaction. Most games and sports vary significantly in the general level of frustration. Consider the contrast between softball and soccer. In softball a significant percentage of enforced waiting time is often frustrating: waiting interminably for a flyball in the outfield positions (and when the ball does come chances are it will be out of reach), waiting for three outs to get to bat, waiting for one's turn at bat while other team members bat, waiting for the pitcher to pitch the ball. In soccer, a child has more control over his own destiny. He can go after the ball or not; he can be in the thick of the scuffling or choose to remain on the perimeter. His intensity of participation is governed by his own momentary inclinations, and he is not subjected to forced inactivity. Soccer tends to minimize the frustration induced by inactivity; softball tends to intensify it.

Certain games and activities overemphasize competition, whereas, with slight restructuring, cooperative elements can be accentuated. Take the game "Horse" played on a basketball court with three players. The first player shoots any shot from any position on the court. If the child makes the shot, the next player must duplicate the shot; if he misses he receives an "H." For every miss another letter is added until the word H-o-r-s-e is completely spelled out, and that player is eliminated. (Games in which players are eliminated are doubly hazardous for disturbed children. They must not only suffer through feelings generated by elimination, but early elimination substantially reduces practice time for those with the greatest need. Consider the usual elimination pattern in even a simple game like "Simon Says.")

A slight variation in the Horse game can easily make it a cooperative effort. Choose any word, a longer one preferably, and for every shot made by any of the participants a letter is generated until the total word is spelled out. This transforms the game into a cooperative endeavor with no one eliminated and all receiving equal amounts of practice.

Games and sports can also be analyzed by the degree of focus on the individual participants. High individual-focus games accentuate the crucialness of how a player responds at a particular point in time. A centerfielder either catches or drops the flyball; all players' eyes focus on that event, and this one play might determine hero or goat status. Tag, with only one child "It," is also a high-focus situation. If more than one child is "It," however, the degree of focus is lessened. Soccer is probably a much lower focus game than softball or kickball because of its complexity and the high probability of chance or fluke occurrences. This reduces the crucial responses for each player. Generally, disturbed children have a higher possibility of surviving low-focus games than those with high focus.

The Supervising Adult

The presence or absence of a supervising adult is of major consequence in predicting the emotional outcomes of games and sports involving disturbed children. Admittedly, presence alone is not sufficiently important to assure any degree of comfort, but, at the minimum, major conflicts can be resolved without the whole activity being jeopardized. Absence of the adult allows for such chaotic conditions that the required mopping-up procedures permeate all subsequent activities. Many teachers feel reluctant to give up precious "free time" or "recuperative time" by providing even minimum supervision for play periods. In the case of disturbed children, this is definitely a short-sighted view. Teachers do not realize how much they can contribute to making games and sports a worthwhile activity.

Guidelines for Constructive Use of Games and Sports for Disturbed Children

The following guidelines apply to any adult with responsibility for supervising normal children or disturbed children engaged in the whole spectrum of games, sports, and activities, both indoors and outdoors. Capability in this role becomes the crucial variable in determining beneficial utilization of these play activities.

1. *Active participation and "umpire services."* Two roles which place the adult in a strategic and highly influential position are active participant and "umpire." (In the active participant role the adult often serves simultaneously as umpire.) As an active participant the adult can control, at least to some extent, the outcome of the game so that extreme imbalances in scores don't occur and can assess and ameliorate the players' frustration levels by controlling play of the game at crucial times. Although this may come under the heading of manipulation, it is necessary if games are to become a constructive experience for disturbed children. If done skillfully, the adult's control can be practically imperceptible.

Active participation also enables the adult to include children who would otherwise be overlooked by peers before or during the game. In basketball, for instance, few high-proficiency players ever pass the ball to low-proficiency players. Thus, even if willingly on the court, low-proficiency players can be substantially eliminated from play. The adult active participant can assist the low-proficiency player by providing him, for example, with a clear shot or an open pass.

The umpire role is vital for maintaining the game. The umpire must be decisive, judicious, and sensitive to each individual's tolerance level. Decisions that could go either way can be guided by the spirit of the moment, depending on the vulnerability of the children. The umpire's knowledge of the game, his prestige in the eyes of the players, and his judicious decisions based on awareness of the total situation make the role a strong supportive factor in constructive play.

2. *Control of negative peer interaction.* The adult maximizes his opportunities to curtail negative peer interaction by being an active participant. Negative peer interaction feeds on itself—one hostile comment frequently leads to another. Scapegoating gains strength in direct proportion to the number of children on the attack. The best control

of this destructive form of interaction can be attained by catching it in its incipient stages. At the right time comments such as "Let's play the game," "Good effort," "Tough luck," "He tried," "Aw, come on, we'll get 'em," "Here we go," serve as tolerance builders and diversionary tactics. Quick resumption of play sets up required alternative responses and doesn't allow the disturbed child to work himself into a lather.

The reinforcement of any positive social behavior is also effective. One school went so far as to videotape kids during play and then replay for them individually scenes in which they displayed supportive, helpful, empathetic behaviors to others. The same effect can be more gradually attained through verbal reinforcement of appropriate interactions if the adult is alert to these behaviors. Values, too, need to be reinforced. When kids say "That was a good game," "Who cares who won or lost, " "It was a close game," "Everyone had fun," the values inherent in these comments need supporting.

3. *Modeling behavior.* An active way of precipitating prosocial comments, behaviors, and values in disturbed children is to deliberately model these for them. The adult participant's attitude, demeanor, and reactions should serve as an example of behavior worth imitating. When the adult gives credit even for a partial attempt, when he minimizes the player's errors, when he supports all participants and not just certain members, these behaviors are likely to be modeled by the children. The adult, by placing himself in the same position as the players, exerts tremendous influence on the whole tenor of the game through his exemplary behavior and his sensitivity to the individual participant's problems, needs, and pressure points.

4. *Building physical coordination and skill.* Many disturbed children are deficient in physical strength, coordination, and the physical skills needed for many games and sports, but these attributes can be developed in most youngsters. One pudgy, weak, and uncoordinated fourth-grader, isolated from play because of nonexistent ball-handling skills, became a respectable team member in four months. He was put on an exercise schedule consisting of push-ups, sit-ups, squat thrusts, kneebends, running in place, and isometrics. A high school student coached him in ball-handling skills: catching, throwing, kicking, etc. His physical strength improved considerably. At first he couldn't even begin to accomplish a push-up, but by the end of four months he could do four or five legitimate ones using his arms alone and with his body straight.

His game skills improved to such an extent, he was no longer ashamed to play with the others and they began to accept him. His posture, walk, and whole physical manner changed with his newfound control and appreciation of his body. With effort, similar results can be obtained with any group of youngsters. One teacher ingeniously provided six exercise stations throughout the classroom which she used for "activity breaks" whenever the group became restless or needed a diversion. After ten minutes of exercise the boys would return, somewhat more contentedly, to their academic tasks.

5. *Planning, play, discussion.* The constructive use of games and sports can be facilitated by adequate planning and preparation before actual play and by discussion and wrap-up afterwards. Planning involves a decision about the game to be played, a review and clarification of the rules, a review of good sportsmanship, and a review of how the players can make it more fun for everybody. This kind of preparation can forestall many problems. After play, a brief wrap-up session combined with quiet rest can provide the transition to other school tasks. The teacher may utilize this time to highlight various aspects of the activity or to commend various members for their play, behavior, or good sportsmanship. Focus should generally be positive rather than a continuation of arguments, conflicts, etc., unless there is an issue that definitely needs resolution.

6. *Modification of games.* Most games and sports can be modified to achieve different purposes. Games are not immutable—they can be changed in whatever way predicates constructive outcomes. Although the majority of games emphasize competition between individuals or teams, most games can be restructured to minimize the competitive elements and highlight the cooperative spirit among the players. Following are some examples of restructuring to make them more serviceable for constructive use.

a. *Simon Says.* This game can be played without the noxious elimination of players who miss a direction and thereby receive no further practice in the activity. By not being eliminated, the competitive factor between children is reduced, as well as the competition between teacher and child. If the competitive element needs to be reintroduced, the primary competition can be between the teacher and the total group: seeing how many can or can't be caught at any one time. The teacher will invariably lose, which isn't necessarily bad for the children's morale.

b. *Kickball and softball.* These games are usually organized by teams, with three outs indicating a team change from "at bat" to "field." Often one team is stronger and they remain at bat so long there's little time left for the other team. Futility and frustration galore! If each player has one time at bat in rotation, however, and then automatically the other team comes up to bat, every child has an equal turn at bat and the frustration of three outs is avoided. Runs may still be counted. Another variation allows all players three hits or kicks, running out only the last one. All players rotate through all positions, with the only competition being how far each player hits or kicks.

c. *Volleyball.* Volleyball can be a great cooperative game. With one team on either side of the net they can attempt to keep the ball in play as long as possible without it touching the ground; the challenge is to get higher and higher numerical counts. This form of volleyball is even more fun without a net. Three to ten players stand in relatively close proximity; one player taps the ball in the air with everyone attempting to maintain it there, but no player may tap the ball twice in succession. The higher the counts the more exciting the game gets. It's good for all age levels and gets everyone involved in a cooperative effort.

d. *Dodgeball.* This can be a very aggressive game for children—actually striking someone with a ball is overt aggression and repugnant to some children. To some extent, this can be controlled by the ball's softness. Occasionally, the game is prolonged by the group's inability to get a few agile players remaining in the center "out." This complication can be easily remedied, however, by making the circle smaller or giving the participants one or two more balls to throw. This will get them "out" in a hurry. With unskilled players in the center, limit the action to one ball and keep the circle large. This will result in better apparent performance by these children. These two factors—size of circle and number of balls—allow almost complete control of the game by the adult according to whatever intent he has in mind.

e. *"It" games.* "It" games should always start with a strong runner as "It," rather than a slower child who is unable to catch anyone. Also, the cumulative version (all participants caught become "It" until the last child is caught) makes for a more exciting game, brings forth maximum participation, and enables the slower runners to catch the speedier players at times.

"I got it" is a good variation highlighting the fastest runners. Anyone tagging "It" becomes the one who's "got it" and is chased by the group. This game always involves the group against one individual and rarely is the group unsuccessful. Of primary importance in "It" games is the designation of a circumscribed area for play. Otherwise, "It" can run off with the game.

f. *Soccer.* Soccer is a good all-around game for the preadolescent age group. It has good running activity, some physical contact, beginnings of teamwork, low-focus and chance occurrences, and quick shifts in offensive and defensive situations that keep the excitement level high. In addition, all children can participate regardless of the level of skill, and all can contribute something to the team. In soccer it is almost impossible for any player to be regarded as a liability. The necessity for umpire services is paramount in this game because of the inherent tendency to use the hands to control the ball. This becomes the one drawback for players forced to get along without these services. It is a pity soccer is not played more in this country because it has so much to offer children.

In conclusion, games and sports can be fun for disturbed children if they are sufficiently supervised, monitored, and controlled by adults, preferably in active participation. Leaving disturbed children alone to work things out for themselves is an overwhelming assignment and usually results in chaos. The adult must be constantly aware of the psychological aspects of the game and the best ways to ameliorate the negative impact on each child.

Many games and sports need adult restructuring to form the best possible circumstances for play. A perceptive analysis of each game or sport is essential in understanding the effects of these activities on children. It is then possible for any adult to respond with creativity and ingenuity in restructuring these activities to facilitate constructive and worthwhile outcomes for disturbed children.

Editors' Commentary

For years physical education has not been considered an important component of special education. In many programs, no distinction is made between physical education and recess or free time. In fact, many teachers use this period as a contingency management technique to reinforce academic assignments ("As soon as you complete your math lesson you can go outside and have your free time").

At Rose School, a therapeutic day-treatment program for severely disturbed pupils in Washington, D.C., the physical education program is not something to earn but a basic part of the reeducation curriculum, as important as remedial reading, psychotherapy, and classroom activities. In the following article, William Daniels, a recreational specialist, describes how his schoolwide tumbling group, the Leaping Lizards, provides its members with physical skills, group identity, and a sense of personal pride. Daniels's teaching strategies are so successful and his group so competent, that the Leaping Lizards are requested to give special tumbling exhibitions at regular public schools each year. These are the same pupils who were so disturbed and deviant in their public schools that they had to be referred to the Rose School for special placement. Now they can return to their public schools briefly as stars, not scapegoats.

Tumbling is an excellent medium for teaching positive skills to emotionally disturbed pupils in very clear, concrete ways.

Tumbling My Way to Success

William D. Daniels, Jr.

Ladies and Gentlemen, and Pupils of the Blockview Elementary School, I am proud to present the exciting and talented Rose School Leaping Lizards Tumbling Team. This team consists of seven boys and three girls from ages six to twelve. For weeks they have developed tumbling acts which they will now perform to the Disco Beat of Saturday Night Fever. *Let's give them a hand.*

As the music begins the children come onto the stage, circle the mat completely, and in sequence perform a basic forward roll, tucking their chins to their chests and pushing themselves over with their feet until they reach the end of the mat. After each Lizard has performed the forward roll, they line up in single file, face the audience, and bow. At the clap of the instructor's hands, the group forms two rows; those in the back then step between their partner's legs and lift their partners up onto their shoulders. The partners who have

been lifted then put their hands on their hips to put the finishing touch onto the stunt. After each student performs this stunt, they move back into their original positions and bow to the crowd's applause. The Lizards are now waiting to perform individually.

The first one is Joe. He walks to the mat and does a log roll. Kathy then executes a forward roll and handstand in sequence. Next comes Tony's stunt. With Joe's assistance, he does a two-handed dive, followed by a forward roll. The music is still blaring and the audience is impressed. Milton, Rob, and Claudia then go out to perform their combination stunt, diving through a headstand. While Joe is in an open-leg headstand position, Milton leaps off of both feet and dives through Joe's legs. Both Tom and Jerry perform the same dive and roll stunt. Sylvia, Bill, and Norman are the last to perform a combination exercise—a dive over two sitting bodies.

After everyone has returned to the team, Claudia and Kathy trot back onto the mat and assume a prone position. Each student then jogs out onto the mat and does a two-handed dive (over Claudia and Kathy), going into a forward roll, and then stands to take a bow. After all have performed this exercise, they return to the side of the stage and prepare for the final stunt. Joe, the line leader, trots out onto the stage, circles the mat once, and comes to a stop. The music is turned down. As the students are standing, with their hands at their sides and smiles on their faces, Joe walks to the front of the stage and says: "Ladies and Gentlemen, I would like to introduce the Leaping Lizards of the Rose School." He then introduces each member. As he gives the name, the individual does a small forward roll, stands, and takes a bow. After the team is introduced, Joe does a forward roll himself, and all of the other students call his name out. The music is then turned back up and Joe leads the children around the mat. To complete the act, they jog off the stage waving to the crowd's applause. As the audience continues to clap, the Lizards come back for a final bow or curtsy.

The Therapeutic Benefits of a Tumbling Team

One of the most rewarding experiences for an emotionally disturbed child is to feel that he or she belongs to (and is accepted by) a group. Because of their disabilities, many such children are reluctant to join a group or even to participate in play activities, and consequently it is essential that these children learn both to play and to share in play. Definite, understandable, and attainable goals should be set for each child in each activity—whether the activity is individual or group-oriented. The developmental approach, incorporating sequential learning stages, is especially helpful. With specific guidelines or steps to follow, even the most awkward child can be made to feel part of the group, can experience success, and can begin to develop a positive self-image. When these children see that peers recognize and appreciate their contributions, they naturally want to continue to participate. Children who only a few weeks before shied away from participation can become active and even eager members of the group. Danny, who swore to me that he could not do a dive over someone sitting on a mat, is a good example. He offered two basic reasons: first, he was afraid (of failure, embarrassment, etc.), and second, he felt he was too fat to

jump the necessary height. I devised a plan in which, over a period of four weeks, I placed balls of different sizes in front of him, and Danny gradually advanced to the point where he could easily and confidently jump the required height. Indeed, Danny went on to begin practicing a dive over two children—a feat he accomplished in half the time it took for him to acquire the confidence to perform the first exercise.

Tumbling is a particularly beneficial group activity for these children. Like other sports, it offers the children an opportunity to improve their basic motor skills and body movements, to develop a sense of rhythm and grace, to become better coordinated and more flexible, and to learn body control. Unlike many other sports (e.g., football and basketball), however, tumbling does not contain the kind of physical contact that intimidates many children. In addition, tumbling within the framework of a team allows the child to develop both individually and as a part of the group. From an emotional standpoint, tumbling brings out an improvement of self-image and an increase in self-respect, and it fosters a sense of identity. Many other activities could be equally beneficial, but, because tumbling does not call for any exceptional physical skills, I have found it particularly useful. The key, however, is for the program to be tightly structured—allowing the children to feel that this, unlike most of their other daily activities, has a definite purpose.

Tangible signs of reward, such as plaques or medals, have added significance for these children. When they receive such signs of commendation, they see that their contributions to the group have been both successful and necessary, and they often feel impelled to try even harder and face new challenges. Similarly, uniforms (matching T-shirts with each member's name inscribed on the back) add color and excitement to the activity and help foster the child's sense of being part of a group that he or she can be proud of. It is essential for these children to come to consider tumbling an important part of their daily routine. The program, because of its tight structure, gives them a routine within which they can watch themselves develop; they see their own improvement and become aware of their own potential.

Through the tumbling program, these children begin to develop a sense of identity and self-worth. The Leaping Lizards of the Rose School were enthusiastic after their performance at the Blockview School. As the audience continued to applaud after the show, many of the children came up to me and asked if they could put on another performance. Joe, who was always seen as being one of the clumsiest members, said: "Did you see my log roll? Wasn't it great?" Their happiness showed on their faces. They knew both that they had put on a good show and that they belonged to a team. They knew that they, individually and as a team, were important.

Editors' Commentary
Teaching Self-Control

Although we need to maintain and improve our present remedial services for handicapped children, most future resources should be devoted to primary prevention programs. As special educators, we must change from a crisis "firefighting" educational service to a "fireproofing" service. Unfortunately, fireproofing is less glamorous than firefighting, but it is our only real hope for preventing another ten million children from being overwhelmed by the future demands of society. The first step in establishing primary prevention programs was accomplished in 1973, when the Council of Exceptional Children amended its policy statement to read, "The first level of service and concern of C.E.C. will be the promotion of positive, cognitive, and affective psychomotor skills in all children that will prevent and/or reduce the frequency of handicapping behaviors." This change in priorities will take some time before it influences training and research activities in special education. At present only a few programs attempt to translate psychological and social skills into an educational curriculum for classroom teachers. Goldstein's[9] social learning curriculum was developed to facilitate social relationships in the classroom. The program involved a ten-phase curriculum to be used primarily with slow-learning pupils in special education. The sections on recognizing and reacting to emotion and getting along with others appeared to be most applicable in teaching young emotionally disturbed children.

Developing Understanding of Self and Others (DUSO) by Dinkmeyer[10] is a comprehensive, multi-instructional curriculum program for pupils in kindergarten through fourth grade. Based on affective education and developmental guidance principles, the program's primary goals are to develop positive self-image and value clarifications. Each lower and upper primary program is organized around eight specific themes, such as "understanding feelings" or "responsible choice-making." This program is rapidly gaining the attention and interest of many school districts, because it can be offered to an entire class rather than just special students.

A more cognitive approach to prevention is Schwarrock and Wrenn's The Coping With Series, which consists of twenty-three books for our contemporary society.[11] Using the books as a basis for group discussion, the classroom teacher can drain off and clarify many of the normal developmental problems of adolescence. Books such as Do I Know the Me Others See, and Parents Can Be a Problem stimulate high interest among adolescent pupils.

In 1972 an experimental study was conducted to investigate the impact of the self-control curriculum on observable classroom behavior, school adjustment, and academic

9.   Herbert Goldstein, Social Learning Curriculum (Charles E. Merrill, 1974).

10.   Don Dinkmeyer, DUSO (Circle Pines, Minn.: American Guidance Service, Inc., 1973).

11.   Shirley Schwarrock and Gilbert C. Wrenn, The Coping With Series (Circle Pines, Minn.: American Guidance Service, 1973).

achievement. The study sample consisted of 159 second-grade pupils attending three inner-city elementary schools in Washington, D.C. One experimental control class was selected in each school. Analysis of the data found the self-control curriculum was significantly related to improved school adjustment, with a significant trend toward improvement in observed classroom behavior. Although the data showed no impact on academic achievement, the classroom teachers felt the lessons and approach were useful in increasing their level of teacher satisfaction in the classroom. This program was at best a pilot study. The results, however, were so encouraging that active refinement of the curriculum and additional field-testing of the program are in progress. Although they are still in their infancy, primary prevention programs may become a major focus in special education in the future.

In the following article, Fagen and Long present their self-control curriculum. Based on years of development and research, their study outlined the following necessary conditions for any primary prevention programs for children. The program should:

1. Be available to all children
2. Begin as early as possible in the child's development
3. Focus on the concept of health rather than illness or pathology
4. Be educationally focused
5. Emphasize normal adult–peer–self interactions
6. Be functional to the teacher
7. Be intrinsically pleasant and satisfying to children
8. Be inexpensive enough to be applied on a mass basis
9. Increase or strengthen skills for effectively coping with the stresses of living

---

A Psychoeducational Curriculum Approach to Teaching Self-Control

Stanley A. Fagen
Nicholas J. Long

For the past ten years we have been striving to find ways to prevent and reduce emotional and behavioral disorders in schools. Like many others, we have been concerned about the persisting, inflexible, and generalized nature of problem behavior. We are now convinced that a critical measure of educational accomplishment is our collective ability to foster self-control in children.

This article presents an approach to developing skills for self-control. Our main premise is that the concept of self-control provides a positive alternative to behavioral or emotional disorder, one that can be translated into direct classroom instruction for preventive and remedial purposes.

The Self-Control Curriculum Model

A major conclusion of the 1970 White House Conference on Children (1971, p. 125) addressed the strong need for curricula to teach self-control:

We are further finding that curricula which help a child deal with his feelings and emotions, which teach principles of self control, and which help the child cope with the pressures and frustrations of an industrial society are desperately needed yet almost totally lacking.

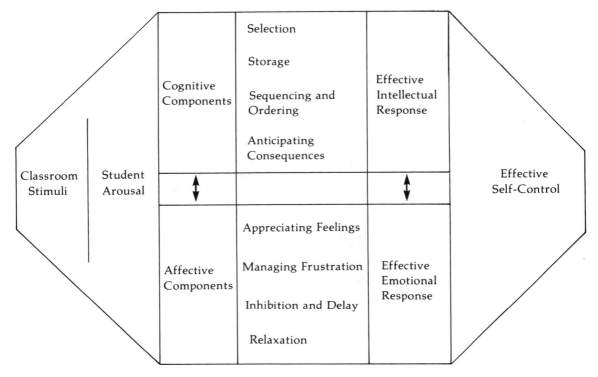

Figure 1. Self-Control as an Integration of Cognitive and Affective Skills

Our own experiences in public and private schools strongly confirmed this conclusion, and from 1968 through 1973 we developed a curriculum to promote direct classroom instruction in basic enabling skills for self-control (Fagen, Long, and Stevens, 1975). Through a process of classroom observation and analysis of disruptive behavior, in both special and regular school settings, we identified a core set of eight skill clusters that constitute basic parameters of self-control:

Selection—ability to perceive incoming information accurately.

Storage—ability to retain the information received.

Sequencing and ordering—ability to organize actions on the basis of a planned order.

Anticipating consequences—ability to relate actions to expected outcomes.

Appreciating feelings—ability to identify and constructively use affective experience.

Managing frustration—ability to cope with external obstacles that produce stress.

Inhibition and delay—ability to postpone or restrain action tendencies.

Relaxation—ability to reduce internal tension.

Each skill cluster subsumes several interrelated functions. The first four rely more heavily on intellectual or cognitive development, while the last four are more related to emotional or affective development. However, affect and intellect may interact across all areas. For example, *storage* pertains to memory processes, traditionally regarded as a cognitive ability, but memory may be disrupted by anxiety or emotional stress even to the point of amnesia. *Appreciating feelings*, on the other hand, clearly aims at affective experience but at the same time requires retention of verbal concepts (e.g., sadness, joy, resentment) if feeling states are to be correctly identified. Our contention is that cognitive performance is enhanced by the mastery of affective experience, which is likely to be enhanced by intellectual mastery.

By creating opportunities for balance and interaction between cognitive and affective events, the self-control curriculum adheres to a psychoeducational approach. As stated by Fagen, Long, and Stevens (1975, p. 56):

The basic function of a psychoeducational curriculum is to provide for planned learning situations which stimulate two major personal developments: constructive expression of affective experience, and integration of facts and feelings. Such a curriculum must include clear statements of teacher goals (which can be translated into learner objectives), specific learning activities, and a variety of teaching strategies for building interest and self-esteem.

The psychoeducational nature of the present self-control curriculum is fully evident from the following:

1. Cognitive and affective skills are given equal opportunities for development, as illustrated by Figure 1.

2. Teaching-learning experiences are structured to assure constructive expression and management of feelings. For example, students are taught to use words instead of striking out physically, to state

Table 1. Overview of Self-Control Curriculum Areas and Units

Area	Unit	Number of Learning Tasks	
Selection	1. Focusing and concentrating	9	
	2. Mastering figure-ground discrimination	4	
	3. Mastering distractions and interference	3	
	4. Processing complex patterns	3	
			(19)
Storage	1. Visual memory	11	
	2. Auditory memory	12	
			(23)
Sequencing and ordering	1. Time orientation	8	
	2. Auditory and visual sequencing	7	
	3. Sequential planning	8	
			(23)
Anticipating consequences	1. Developing alternatives	11	
	2. Evaluating consequences	7	
			(18)
Appreciating feelings	1. Identifying and accepting feelings	7	
	2. Developing positive feelings	8	
	3. Managing feelings	10	
	4. Reinterpreting feeling events	4	
			(29)
Managing frustration	1. Accepting feelings of frustration	2	
	2. Building coping resources	9	
	3. Tolerating frustration	22	
			(33)
Inhibition and delay	1. Controlling actions	13	
	2. Developing partial goals	5	
			(18)
Relaxation	1. Body relaxation	5	
	2. Thought relaxation	5	
	3. Movement relaxation	3	
			(13)

their own feelings without hurting someone else, and to replace negative and blaming reactions with positive coping techniques.

3. Curriculum activities are presented through instructional methods and sequences that promote affective comfort and involvement in association with new cognitive learning. For example, in teaching sequencing and ordering skills, a series of individual and group games are suggested to help the students' orientation and control in relation to time. Sequencing and ordering skills are then further expanded via units that develop the ability to arrange or reproduce several parts of a total action (auditory and visual sequencing) and plan and organize discrete steps or parts of an overall process (sequential planning).

The self-control curriculum consists of eight areas, corresponding to the eight skill clusters that promote the students' capacity to direct and regulate their personal behavior flexibly and realistically. Each curriculum area contains an introduction, including a statement of rationale, a description of units and goals, and recommended learning tasks. The introduction summarizes research documenting the importance of the skill area and states expectations for the teacher to establish with students. The description of each unit specifies teaching goals for that unit. Recommended learning tasks include the necessary instructions, procedures, and materials for each task. Table 1 provides an overview of the eight curriculum areas and their related units.

Three basic options are available in applying the self-control curriculum to a primary prevention program:

Option 1. The curriculum can be taught in one school year (eight months). Approximately one month should be spent in each curriculum area.

Option 2. The entire curriculum can be taught in one semester and then repeated (recycled) in the second semester. Approximately two weeks should be spent on each curriculum area. Or the entire curriculum can be taught in the first semester, spending approximately two weeks on each curriculum area, and the teacher can select special areas for the second semester, spending varying amounts of time on each, depending on the further needs of the class and the discretion of the teacher.

Option 3. Any curriculum area can be taught any time of the year, depending on the needs

or weaknesses of the class. The amount of time spent on any curriculum area is left to the teacher's discretion.

Our experience to date indicates that options 1 and 2 are best reserved for early elementary levels. Option 3 appears more appropriate for intermediate elementary and secondary levels. In option 3, instruction can be tailored to the identified needs of the group and the teacher.

Diagnostic-Prescriptive Intervention

The self-control curriculum may be employed within a diagnostic-prescriptive procedure, as well as for purposes of primary prevention. The following actual incidents illustrate the kinds of specific weaknesses in self-control that students with behavior disorders exhibit:

Tim: From Impulse to Antics

The second grade teacher is conducting a language experience lesson with her class, using photographs to reinforce a story on wildlife. Suddenly, Tim jumps out of his seat and begins talking like Donald Duck. He continues walking about the room, making animal noises, and flapping his hands, in a manner more like that of a three-year-old.

The teacher asks Tim to sit down but he continues to talk like Donald Duck. By now the rest of the class is laughing and copying Tim's performance. Within seconds, the teacher stops her lesson.

Analysis of Tim's Problem

Tim needs to learn to inhibit and delay impulses toward immediate expression, and to anticipate the consequences of his behavior.

Inhibition and delay: The teacher can help Tim learn to control his actions by presenting tasks that require increasing degrees of inhibition and self-regulation (Unit 1, Controlling Actions). For example, Tim can be taught to keep silent in the presence of distractions, to start and stop on signal, and to resist acting until the appropriate time.

Anticipating consequences: Tim's ability to evaluate choices of action in terms of their influence on others can be improved (Unit 2, Evaluating Consequences). Teaching activities can be used that promote awareness of behaviors that cause social approval, disapproval or embarrassment.

John: From Upset to Attack

John is a large ten-year-old boy with a reputation for physically acting out against other children. One day, the class is hard at work on a science project. Thus far the students have been surprisingly attentive. All of a sudden someone screams loudly. Larry, a thin, little boy with glasses, has been smacked in the face by John. The other children become very excited and noisy. One girl runs out of the classroom. Larry's nose begins to bleed. John is cursing violently and is about to grab Larry again, when the teacher intervenes and directs him out of the room.

In the corridor John says: "That little bastard better stop giving me the finger sign or I'll break all of his fingers."

Analysis of John's Problem

John needs to learn to manage negative feelings without being destructive, and to express feelings through words, not just raw physical outbursts.

Managing frustration: John can be taught to understand that upsetting feelings occur when one's needs are thwarted and that strength can be shown by enduring frustration, as well as by saying how you feel about being upset (Unit 1, Accepting Feelings of Frustration; Unit 2, Building Coping Resources; Unit 3, Tolerating Frustration). For example, the teacher may present situations where John can hear about and share with others experiences that "bug" people his age and how negative emotions can be handled without hurting himself or others.

Appreciating feelings: The teacher can assist John in recognizing when he is getting angry and using verbal or nonverbal signals to allow for "cooling off" (Unit 1, Identifying and Accepting Feelings). For example, role-playing may be used to give John practice in expressing himself acceptably when he is feeling mad (by writing notes, stating an "I-message," getting a drink of water, etc.).

Mary: From Anxiety to Avoidance

All pupils in the sixth grade class have begun their independent English work. The assignments have been individualized to meet each student's level of skill and style of learning. Each student is expected to answer 90 percent correctly. Mary, a very anxious, dependent student, begins to complain: "It's too hard, I just can't get going."

The teacher reads the instructions to her but within minutes Mary raises her hand for more help. When the teacher comes over, Mary says: "I can't remember what I wanted to ask you." The teacher leaves and in a little while observes that Mary is drawing rows of dots across her paper.

Analysis of Mary's Problem

Mary needs to learn to be more relaxed in situations where she has to perform on her own, and to take time for organizing a plan to proceed.

Relaxation: With help, Mary can be taught to reduce her levels of tension through body and thought exercises (Unit 1, Body Relaxation; Unit 2, Thought Relaxation). For example, Mary can learn to tense and relax muscles in face and arms, and to imagine pleasant scenes before starting a difficult or anxiety-producing task.

Sequencing and ordering: Teachers can help the student to divide an assignment into a series of manageable parts (Unit 3, Sequential Planning). For example, Mary can be given opportunities to write or draw plans for accomplishing an action such as writing a report, making a poster, or baking a cake.

References

Dupont, H.; Gardner, O.; and Brody, D. *Toward Affective Development.* Circle Pines, Minn.: American Guidance Service, 1974.

Educational Research Council of America. *Program in Mental Health and Human Behavior: Understanding Human Behavior.* Cleveland: Educational Research Council, 1972.

Fagen, S. A., and Hill, J. M. *Behavior Management: A Competency-Based Manual for In-Service Training.* Washington, D.C. Psychoeducational Resources, 1977.

Fagen, S. A., and Long, N. J. "Teaching Children Self-Control: A New Responsibility for Teachers." *Focus on Exceptional Children* 7 (1976): 1–12.

Fagen, S. A.; Long, N. J.; and Stevens, D. J. *Teaching Children Self-Control: Preventing Emotional and Learning Problems in the Elementary School.* Columbus, Ohio: Charles E. Merrill, 1975.

Kauffman, J. M. *Characteristics of Children's Behavior Disorders.* Columbus, Ohio: Charles E. Merrill, 1977.

Long, N.; Fagen, S.; and Stevens, D. *A Psychoeducational Screening System for Identifying Resourceful, Marginal, and Vulnerable Pupils in the Primary Grades.* Washington, D.C.: Psychoeducational Resources, 1971.

Meichenbaum, D. "Toward a Cognitive Theory of Self-Control." In *Consciousness and Self-Regulation: Advances in Research,* edited by G. Schwartz and D. Shapiro. New York: Plenum, 1976.

Palomares, U., and Logan, B. *A Curriculum on Conflict Management: Practical Methods for Helping Children Explore Creative Alternatives in Dealing with*

Conflict. La Mesa, Calif.: Human Development Institute, 1975.

Polsgrove, L. "Self-Control: An Overview of Concepts and Methods for Child Training." Proceedings of a Conference on Preparing Teachers to Foster Personal Growth in Emotionally Disturbed Children, pp. 29–55. Advanced Institute for Trainers of Teachers for Seriously Emotionally Disturbed Children, University of Minnesota, May 29–31, 1977.

Ross, D., and Ross, R. *The Pacemaker Primary Curriculum.* Belmont, Calif.: Fearon, 1974.

Stevens, D. "The Self-Control Curriculum Project, 1972–1973." Report to the Eugene and Agnes Meyer Foundation, Washington, D.C., 1973.

Thoresen, C. E., and Mahoney, M. J. *Behavioral Self-Control.* New York: Holt, Rinehart & Winston, 1974.

Vaden, T. B. "An Evaluation of a Psychoeducational Approach to the Concept of Self-Control." Doctoral dissertation, University of Virginia, 1972.

White House Conference on Children. "Confronting Myths of Education." *Report of Forum 8,* pp. 121–142. Washington, D.C.: U.S. Government Printing Office, 1971.

This article is based on material from *Teaching Children Self-Control: Preventing Emotional and Learning Problems in the Elementary School* by S. A. Fagen, N. J. Long, and D. J. Stevens. Copyright 1975 by Charles E. Merrill Publishing Company. Reprinted by permission.

Editors' Commentary

Summary

Much of the present educational and mental health effort has been directed toward managing, understanding, or treating the maladaptive behavior of children with identifiable problems. It is time to pay at least an equal amount of attention to developing the positive skills that will *prevent* learning and behavioral problems. This article presented a brief overview of a specialized psychoeducational curriculum that can be taught by the regular classroom teacher in the same way reading or any other basic skill is taught.

The self-control curriculum is a positive approach to learning the inner controls that are essential to the goals of our democratic society. Current social realities demand that public schools assume a greater responsibility in this area. By 1980, primary prevention programs in elementary schools will be integrated into the regular school curriculum. The self-control curriculum is a prototype of what will be developed in the future for classroom teachers.

No single theory, discipline, or profession owns the specialized field of teaching emotionally disturbed children. Although specific research and refinement of theoretical models will continue, the next phase will be a movement to integrate diverse points of view. After all, the common denominator of all these strategies is their commitment to find more effective ways of correcting learning and behavior problems. In recent years, the relationship between an individual's developmental disabilities and emotional disturbances has been ascertained. Advances in the analysis of pupils' strengths and weaknesses have prompted remedial education programs rather than institutionalization and psychotherapy for pupils with serious learning problems.

Sensitive and skillful understanding and handling of primary emotional problems is needed, of course, but remedial education is also an important tool for altering self-defeating life patterns. Prompt, knowledgeable identification of learning inadequacies, combined with a plan for corrective teaching, can prevent secondary emotional disorders. Furthermore, remedial strategies in the hands of an emotionally attuned teacher can alter the vicious cycles of inappropriate behavior associated primarily with emotional factors.

There is no magic, no one cure, no shortcut in teaching emotionally disturbed children. The task demands ongoing analysis of pupils' strengths and weaknesses, coupled with an appreciation and diagnosis of the different styles of learning and teaching that are effective in particular situations.

7

How Can We
Mainstream These Children?

Editors' Commentary

Mainstreaming as a Concept

In one professional lifetime the theory of education of the emotionally disturbed child seems to have undergone a complete cycle; in reality the changes have been less than complete. We started with mainstreaming or exclusion. For the most part the deviant pupil was in the regular classes without special provision. Of course there were informally designated "special" teachers and "special" classes who could handle the acting out pupils while the depressed and withdrawn pupils languished. When students were excluded and sent to the rare psychiatric hospital, this was done to cure them so that they could eventually come back to school and be taught. Or if they were sent to a school for delinquents, rudimentary education was a program component on the books and sometimes practiced. The effort to get separate but equal attention for disturbed children resulted in special classes in schools and educational programs in institutions. They were to be taught by teachers who had special training, since this was considered the sine qua non of ability to help such children. In the mental health institutions, schools often functioned apart from the psychological treatment. Therapy was the primary medium and schools secondary, often with little liaison. Public schools often had (and have) pupils who got no mental health intervention.

According to federal statistics, separated school programs for the disturbed never reached more than 20 percent of those who needed such assistance. In some locales, there was no program. Provision for adolescents was rare. So, there was never anywhere near a complete program of special isolated services. These pupils were in the mainstream for the most part. Little thought was given to whether the school was the source of the problem or the recipient, or whether education was the key intervention or not. In many programs the blanket thesis was that education could cure all, by itself, through traditional educational practices, with remedial tutoring. In fact, examination of what was going on in so-called special education reveals that it was special only in the smallness of the groups—often ten students instead of the usual twenty-five. Of course there has always been a core of educators who saw the special classes as a way to offer different and more complete help, to fuse education and mental health in the group life, and to develop programs that related to community services. And there were institutions that evolved to a milieu approach.

Gradually recognition grew that there were many potentially deleterious effects of placing disturbed pupils (often in the least humanistic manner possible) in special (negatively different) settings with programs that fell short of their needs. The studies used to push the movement for special programs did not focus on the quality of programs. When this aspect did receive attention, separate but equal facilities were rejected as being unfair and unequal. We then embarked on what U.S. Commissioner of Education Boyer has aptly called a courageous move to fulfill the dream of full opportunity:

while administrators are finding some inconveniences perhaps in coming to terms with the laws, that does not, in my view, begin to match the inconveniences, the frustrations, and the heartaches that for years have been generated by the failure to have a fair and open educational opportunity for children who had special handicaps.[1]

So we have come full circle to the concept of keeping these children in the education mainstream. But it can be a spiral upward rather than a return to square one. That depends upon our ingenuity, psychological sophistication, and program design. First, we now recognize that not all pupils, and certainly not all the time, are to be in the mainstream. There still must be a range of services available to meet the needs of a range of disturbed children. Second, there is to be an Individual Education Plan (IEP) for each special education pupil, with accountability. Third, we have to find ways to blend regular and special education, keeping the support services attuned to the needs. This means a change in some of the sacred educational cows, especially of the secondary schools. But mainstreaming is the law of the land and an ideal of which we can be proud. Implementing it will touch every teacher in the United States—no mean impact and no minor task. This chapter covers a few of the numerous issues involved in the new development.

The Law

Public Law 94–142 is both misunderstood and misinterpreted. It does not mandate mainstreaming—certainly not for all special pupils—although a few analysts have asserted that it does. Such a position can be taken only by a person who is not being held accountable for mainstreaming programs and who has no concern for the pupils' welfare. In fact, the zero reject concept means that all children are to have access to free public education; this does not necessarily mean in the mainstream. What the law does say is that all children have an inalienable right to public education in the least restrictive environment commensurate with the best possible education. Nor does the law say all children must be in regular settings 100 percent of the time, or that no special supportive services are required. The first two articles that follow digest the essential legal points about mainstreaming. It is interesting to note that the federal request for identification of all handicapped children in each state between the ages of five and seventeen requires that the number not exceed 12 percent of the total school population. The section of the law on IEPs is perhaps the most crucial in terms of teacher implementation. It is broad in scope, including the vocational sphere as well as the academic.

1. Quoted in "A Conversation with Ernest L. Boyer on Exceptional Children's Education," *Exceptional Children*, Vol. 44 (May 1978), p. 570.

Public Law 94–142 and Section 504: What They Say about Rights and Protections

Joseph Ballard
Jeffrey Zettel

Basic Thrust, Objectives, and Target Populations

What is P. L. 94-142?

P. L. 94–142, the Education for All Handicapped Children Act, is legislation passed by the United States Congress and signed into law by President Gerald R. Ford on November 29, 1975. The "94" indicates that this law was passed by the 94th Congress. The "142" indicates that this law was the 142nd law passed by that session of the Congress to be signed into law by the President.

What are the purposes of P. L. 94-142?

P. L. 94–142 can be said to have four major purposes:

Guarantee the availability of special education programming to handicapped children and youth who require it.

Assure fairness and appropriateness in decision making with regard to providing special education to handicapped children and youth.

Establish clear management and auditing requirements and procedures regarding special education at all levels of government.

Financially assist the efforts of state and local government through the use of federal funds (refer to Section 3 of the Act).

What is Section 504?

Section 504 is a basic civil rights provision with respect to terminating discrimination against America's handicapped citizens. Section 504 was enacted through the legislative vehicle P. L. 93–112, the Vocational Rehabilitation Act Amendments of 1973. Though Section 504 is brief in actual language, its implications are far reaching. The statute reads:

No otherwise qualified handicapped individual in the United States shall, solely by reason of his handicap, be excluded from the participation in, be denied the benefits of, or be subjected to discrimination under any program or activity receiving Federal financial assistance.

To whom do P. L. 94-142 and Section 504 apply?

P. L. 94–142 applies to all handicapped children who require special education and related services, ages 3 to 21 inclusive. Section 504 applies to all handicapped Americans regardless of age. Section 504 therefore applies to all handicapped children ages 3 to 21 with respect to their public education both from the standpoint of the guarantee of an appropriate special education and from the standpoint of sheer regular program accessibility. Close coordination has thus been maintained between the provisions of P. L. 94–142 and those of the Section 504 regulations (refer to Section 611 of P. L. 94–142 and background statement of the Section 504 regulation).

What is the relationship of P. L. 94-142 to the older federal Education of the Handicapped Act (EHA)?

P. L. 94–142 is a complete revision of only Part B of the Education of the Handicapped Act. Part B was formerly that portion of EHA addressing the basic state grant program. The other components of the Act (Parts A–E) remain substantially unchanged and continue in operation. Parenthetically, all programs under the aegis of the EHA, including the P. L. 94–142 revision of Part B, are administered through the Bureau of Education for the Handicapped under the US Office of Education.

Was there a forerunner to P. L. 94-142?

Many of the major provisions of P. L. 94–142, such as the guarantee of due process procedures and the assurance of education in the least restrictive environment, were required in an earlier federal law—P. L. 93–380, the Education Amendments of 1974 (enacted August 21, 1974). P. L. 94–142 was enacted approximately one year and three months later, on November 29, 1975.

How are handicapped children defined for purposes of this Act?

Handicapped children are defined by the Act as children who are:

mentally retarded, hard of hearing, deaf, orthopedically impaired, other health impaired, speech impaired, visually handicapped, seriously emotionally disturbed, or children with specific learning disabilities who by reason thereof require special education and related services.

This definition establishes ... two pronged criteria for determining child eligibility under the Act. The first is whether the child actually has one or more of the disabilities listed in the above definition. The second is whether the child requires special education and related services. Not all children who have a disability require special education; many are able and should attend school without any program modification (refer to Section 4 of the Act).

If a child has one or more of the disabilities listed in the preceding definition and also requires special education and related services, how does P. L. 94-142 define special education?

Special education is defined in P. L. 94–142 as:

specially designed instruction, at no cost to parents or guardians, to meet the unique needs of a handicapped child, including classroom instruction, instruction in physical education, home instruction, and instruction in hospitals and institutions.

The key phrase in the above definition of special education is "specially designed instruction ... to meet the unique needs of a handicapped child." Reemphasized, special education, according to statutory definition, is defined as being "special" and involving only instruction that is designed and directed to meet the unique needs of a handicapped child. For many children therefore, special education will not be the totality of their education. Furthermore, this definition clearly implies that special education proceeds from the basic goals and expected outcomes of general education. Thus, intervention with a child does not occur because he or she is mentally retarded but because he or she has a unique educational need that requires specially designed instruction (refer to Section 4(a)(16) of the Act).

How are related services defined in P. L. 94-142?

Equally important to understand is the concept of related services that are defined in the Act as:

transportation, and such developmental, corrective, and other supportive services (including speech pathology and audiology, psychological services, physical and occupational therapy, recreation, and medical and counseling services, except that such medical services shall be for diagnostic and evaluation purposes only) as may be required to assist a handicapped child to benefit from special education, and includes the early identification and assessment of handicapping conditions in children.

The key phrase here is "as required to assist the handicapped child to benefit from special education." This leads to a clear progression: a child is handicapped because he or she requires special education and related services; special education is the specially designed instruction to meet the child's unique needs; and related services are those additional services necessary in order for the child to benefit from special educational instruction (refer to Section 4(a)(17) of the Act).

Rights and Protections
A Free Appropriate Education

What is the fundamental requirement of P. L. 94-142, from which all other requirements of this Act stem?

P. L. 94–142 requires that every state and its localities, if they are to continue to receive funds under this Act, must make available a free appropriate public education for all handicapped children aged 3 to 18 by the beginning of the school year (September 1) in 1978 and further orders the availability of such education to all children aged 3 to 21 by September 1, 1980 (refer to Section 3(c) of the Act).

What about preschool and young adults under P. L. 94-142?

For children in the 3 to 5 and 18 to 21 age ranges, however, this mandate does not apply if such a requirement is inconsistent with state law or practice or any court decree. Refer to regulations for further expatiation of this provision (refer to Section 612 (2)(B) of the Act).

What does Section 504 say regarding the right to an education?

Section 504 makes essentially the same requirement. However, the 504 regulation says "shall provide." P. L. 94–142 says "a free appropriate public education *will be available.*"

The 504 regulation does not refer to specific age groups per se. Instead, it refers to "public elementary and secondary education," and, therefore, the traditional school age population. With respect to that school age population, the 504 regulation accedes to the September 1, 1978, date of P. L. 94–142 as the final and absolute deadline for the provision of a free appropriate public education. However, the Section 504 regulation also precedes that requirement with the phrase *"at the earliest practicable time* but in no event later than September 1, 1978." (Refer to #84.33(d) of the 504 regulation.)

What is required with respect to preschool and young adult programs under Section 504?

The 504 regulation appears simply to say that preschool and adult education programs will not discriminate on the basis of handicap, and further that such program accessibility is to take effect immediately. On the other hand, P. L. 94–142, as previously noted, explicitly states that there shall be available a free appropriate public education for children ages 3 through 5 and youth ages 18 through 21 unless such requirement is inconsistent with state law or practice or the order of any court. Again, P. L. 94–142 does not require such availability until September 1, 1978 (refer to #84.38 of the 504 regulation).

Since Section 504 and P. L. 94–142 are making, in essence, the same fundamental requirement of a free, appropriate public education, are federal monies authorized under Section 504 as they are under P. L. 94–142?

No. Section 504 is a civil rights statute, like Title VI of the Civil Rights Act of 1965 (race) and Title IX of the Education Amendments of 1972 (sex).

Must there be compliance with the fundamental requirement of P. L. 94–142 (as reiterated in Section 504 regulations) if P. L. 94–142 is not "fully funded"?

It is most important to note that compliance with this baseline guarantee of the availability of a free, appropriate public education is in no way dependent upon whether this Act receives appropriations at the top authorized ceilings, or in other words, is "fully funded." If a state accepts money under this Act, regardless of the amount of actual appropriations, it must comply with the aforementioned stipulation.

What does "free" education, as required in both P. L. 94–142 and Section 504, mean?

"Free" means the provision of education and related services at no cost to the handicapped person or to his or her parents or guardian, except for those largely incidental fees that are imposed on nonhandicapped persons or their parents or guardian (refer to #84.33(c)(1) of the 504 regulation).

What if a public placement is made in a public or private residential program?

If both the school and parents jointly agree that the most appropriate educational placement for the child is in a public or private residential facility, then such a program placement, including nonmedical care as well as room and board, shall be provided at no cost to the person or his or her parents or guardian (refer to #84.33(c)(3) of the 504 regulation).

Does "free" mean that no private funds can be used?

No. Private funds are not prohibited. To reiterate: there must be no cost to the handicapped person or to his or her parents or guardian.

What does "appropriate" education mean?

"Appropriate" is not defined as such, but rather receives its definition for each child through the mechanism of the written individualized education program (IEP) as required by P. L. 94–142. Therefore, what is agreed to by all parties becomes in fact the "appropriate" educational program for the particular child.

Individualized Education Programs

What are the basic concepts of the IEP?

The term *individualized education program* itself conveys important concepts that need to be specified. First, *individualized* means that the IEP must be addressed to the educational needs of a single child rather than a class or group of children. Second, *education* means that the IEP is limited to those elements of the child's education that are more specifically special education and related services as defined by the Act. Third, *program* means that the IEP is a statement of what will actually be provided to the child, as distinct from a plan that provides guidelines from which a program must subsequently be developed.

What are the basic components of an IEP?

The Act contains a specific definition describing the components of an IEP as:

a written statement for each handicapped child developed in any meeting by a representative of the local education agency or an intermediate educational unit who shall be qualified to provide, or supervise the provision of, specifically designed instruction to meet the unique needs of handicapped children, the teacher, the parents or guardian of such child, and whenever appropriate, such child, which statement shall include (A) a statement of the present levels of educational performance of such child, (B) a statement of annual goals, including short-term instructional objectives, (C) a statement of the specific educational anticipated duration of such services, and appropriate objective criteria and evaluation procedures and schedules for determining, on at least an annual basis, whether instructional objectives are being achieved.

(Refer to Section 4(a)(19) of the Act.)

May others be involved in the development of an IEP?

Good practice suggests that others frequently be involved. However, the law only requires four persons be involved (i.e., the parents or guardians, the teacher or teachers of the child, a representative of the local educational agency or intermediate unit who is qualified to provide or supervise the provision of special education, and whenever appropriate, the child). If a related service person will be providing services, then it seems to make sense that they be as involved as the teacher. Also, good practice indicates that parents often want to bring an additional person familiar with the child to the meeting.

Who must be provided an IEP?

Each state and local educational agency shall insure than an IEP is provided for each handicapped child who is receiving or will receive special education, regardless of what institution or agency provides or will provide special education to the child: (a) The state educational agency shall insure that each local educational agency establishes and implements an IEP for each handicapped child; (b) The state educational agency shall require each public agency which provides special

education or related services to a handicapped child to establish policies and procedures for developing, implementing, reviewing, maintaining, and evaluating an IEP for that child.

What must local and intermediate education agencies do regarding IEP's?

Each local educational agency shall develop or revise, whichever is appropriate, an IEP for every handicapped child at the beginning of the school year and review and if appropriate revise its provisions periodically but not less than annually.

Each local educational agency is responsible for initiating and conducting meetings for developing, reviewing, and revising a child's IEP.

For a handicapped child who is receiving special education, a meeting must be held early enough so that the IEP is developed (or revised, as appropriate) by the beginning of the next school year.

For a handicapped child who is not receiving special education, a meeting must be held within 30 days of a determination that the child is handicapped, or that the child will receive special education.

(Refer to Section 614(a)(5) of the Act.)

Do the IEP requirements apply to children in private schools and facilities?

Yes. The state educational agency shall insure that an IEP is developed, maintained, and evaluated for each child placed in a private school by the state educational agency or a local educational agency. The agency that places or refers a child shall insure that provision is made for a representative from the private school (which may be the child's teacher) to participate in each meeting. If the private school representative cannot attend a meeting, the agency shall use other methods to insure participation by the private school, including individual or conference telephone calls (refer to Section 613(a)(4)(B) of the Act).

Is the IEP an instructional plan?

No. The IEP is a management tool that is designed to assure that, when a child requires special education, the special education designed for that child is appropriate to his or her special learning needs and that the special education designed is actually delivered and monitored. An instructional plan reflects good educational practice by outlining the specifics necessary to effectively intervene in instruction. Documenting instructional plans is *not* mandated as part of the IEP requirements.

What procedures should education agencies follow to involve parents in the development of their child's IEP?

Each local educational agency shall take steps to insure that one or both of the parents of the handicapped child are present at each meeting or are afforded the opportunity to participate, including scheduling the meeting at a mutually agreed on time and place.

If neither parent can attend, the local educational agency shall use other methods to insure parent participation, including individual or conference telephone calls.

A meeting may be conducted without a parent in attendance if the local educational agency is unable to convince the parents that they should attend. In this case the local educational agency must have a record of its attempts to arrange a mutually agreed on time and place such as: (a) Detailed records of telephone calls made or attempted and the results of those calls, (b) copies of correspondence sent to the parents and any responses received, and (c) detailed records of visits made to the parent's home or place of employment and the results of those visits.

The local educational agency shall take whatever action is necessary to insure that the parent understands the proceedings at a meeting, including arranging for an interpreter for parents who are deaf or whose native language is other than English.

When must handicapped children be guaranteed the IEP?

For handicapped children counted under the fiscal funding formula of P. L. 94–142, not later than the beginning of school year 1977–1978.

For all handicapped children in each state, regardless of the delivering agency, not later than the beginning of school year 1978–1979.

What does Section 504 say with respect to the IEP?

As just discussed, P. L. 94–142 requires the development and maintenance of individualized written education programs for all children. The 504 regulation cites the IEP as "one means" of meeting the standard of a free appropriate public education (refer to #84.33(b)(2) of the 504 regulation).

Least Restrictive Educational Environment

P. L. 94-142 requires that handicapped children receive a free appropriate public education in the least restrictive educational environment. What does this mean?

It is critical to note what this provision *is not:*

It is not a provision for mainstreaming. In fact, the word is never used.

It does not mandate that all handicapped children will be educated in the regular classroom.

It does not abolish any particular educational environment, for instance, educational programming in a residential setting.

It is equally critical to note what this provision *does* mandate:

Education with nonhandicapped children will be the governing objective "to the maximum extent appropriate."

The IEP will be the management tool toward achievement of the maximum least restrictive environment and therefore shall be applied within the framework of meeting the "unique needs" of each child.

The IEP document(s) must clearly "show cause" if and when one moves from least restrictive to more restrictive. The statute states that the following component must be included in the written statement accompanying the IEP "and the extent to which such child will be able to participate in regular educational programs."

(Refer to Section 612(5)(B) of the Act.)

Correspondingly, what does the Section 504 regulation say with respect to least restrictive educational environment?

The language of the 504 regulation is, in most important respects, nearly identical to the least restrictive statute in P. L. 94–142. There remains one notable distinction, however. The 504 regulation would seem to consider the "nearest placement to home" as an additional determinant of instructional placement in the least restrictive environment (refer to #84.34(a) of the 504 regulation).

Procedural Safeguards

Under P. L. 94-142, what happens if there is a failure to agree with respect to what constitutes an appropriate education for a particular child?

States must guarantee procedural safeguard mechanisms for children and their parents or guardians. Those provisions of previously existing law (P. L. 93-380, the Education Amendments of 1974) toward the guarantee of due process rights are further refined in P. L. 94-142, and their scope is substantially enlarged.

Basically, the state education agency must guarantee the maintenance of full due process procedures for all handicapped children within the state and their parents or guardian with respect to all matters of identification, evaluation, and educational placement whether it be the initiation or change of such placement, or the refusal to initiate or change. Interested individuals are strongly urged to read Section 615 of the Act ("Procedural Safeguards") in its entirety.

It should be observed that the P. L. 94-142 refinements take effect in the first year under the new formula, that is, fiscal 1978 (school year 1977-1978). In the meantime, those basic features of due process as authorized in the prior Act (P. L. 93-380) must be maintained by the states.

It should be further noted that, when the parents or guardian of a child are not known, are unavailable, or when the child is a legal ward of the state, the state education agency, local education agency, or intermediate education agency (as appropriate) must assign an individual to act as a *surrogate* for the child in all due process proceedings. Moreover, such assigned individual may not be an employee of the state educational agency, local educational agency, or intermediate educational unit *involved in* the education or care of the particular child (refer to Section 615 of the Act).

Does the Section 504 regulation also require the maintenance of a procedural safeguards mechanism?

Yes. However, though most of the major principles of due process embodied in P. L. 94-142 are clearly present in the 504 regulation, *all* of the stipulations of P. L. 94-142 are treated only as "one means" of due process compliance under Section 504 (refer to #84.36 of the 504 regulation).

What does P. L. 94-142 say with respect to assessment of children?

P. L. 94-142 carries a provision that seeks to guarantee against assessment with respect to the question of a handicapping condition when such assessment procedures are racially or culturally discriminatory. The statute does not provide a comprehensive procedure of remedy with respect to potential discrimination but does make two clear and important stipulations in the direction of remedy:

"Such materials and procedures shall be provided in the child's native language or mode of communication."

"No single procedure shall be the sole criterion for determining an appropriate educational program for a child."

The provision, in effect, orders that assessment procedures be multi-factored, multi-sourced, and carried out by qualified personnel. The regulations governing this provision should therefore be carefully reviewed (refer to Section 612(5)(C) of the Act).

What does the Section 504 regulation say with respect to the assessment of children?

The objectives of Section 504 and P. L. 94-142 are identical on this matter, and the regulatory language for both statutes is also identical (refer to #84.35 of the 504 regulation).

What does P. L. 94-142 say with respect to the confidentiality of data and information?

P. L. 94-142 contains a provision that addresses the question of abuses and potential abuses in school system record keeping with respect to handicapped children and their parents. P. L. 94-142, as did the prior P. L. 93-380, simply orders a remedy and does not go beyond. The governing statutes for this provision are contained in the larger "Family Educational Rights and Privacy Act" (often referred to as the "Buckley Amendments" after the author, US Senator James Buckley of New York). That measure sets forth both the access rights and privacy rights with respect to personal school records for all of the nation's children and youth, and their parents.

Thus, readers should study the Act itself (contained in P. L. 93–380), the accompanying regulations for the "Buckley Amendments," and the modest addendums to those provisions contained in the regulations for P. L. 94–142 (refer to Section 617(c) and Section 612(2)(D) of the Act).

What then, in summary, are the rights and protections of P. L. 94–142 (which, for the most part, are also affirmed in Section 504) that must be guaranteed?

P. L. 94–142 makes a number of critical stipulations that must be adhered to by *both* the state and its local and intermediate educational agencies:

Assurance of the availability of a free, appropriate public education for all handicapped children, such guarantee of availability no later than certain specified dates.

Assurance of the maintenance of an individualized education program for all handicapped children.

A guarantee of complete due procedural safeguards.

The assurance of regular parent or guardian consultation.

Assurance of special education being provided to all handicapped children in the "least restrictive" environment.

Assurance of nondiscriminatory testing and evaluation.

A guarantee of policies and procedures to protect the confidentiality of data and information.

Assurance of an effective policy guaranteeing the right of all handicapped children to a free, appropriate public education *at no cost* to parents or guardian.

Assurance of a surrogate to act for any child when parents or guardians are either unknown or unavailable or when such child is a legal ward of the state.

It is most important to observe that an official, written document containing all of these assurances is now required (in the form of an application) of *every* school district receiving its federal entitlement under P. L. 94–142. Correspondingly, such a public document also exists at the state level in the form of the annual state plan, which must be submitted to the US Commissioner.

Reprinted from *Exceptional Children* 44 (1977): 177–185, by permission of The Council for Exceptional Children. Copyright 1977 by The Council for Exceptional Children.

Editors' Commentary

Implementation

The next article deals with the overall psychology of mainstreaming emotionally impaired children. The evaluation of effectiveness is related to the actual experience we provide the pupil—mainstream or special facility—compared with what the youngster needs. Deficiencies may be in terms of appropriateness and/or in terms of quality.

The Psychology of Mainstreaming Socio-emotionally Disturbed Children

William C. Morse

The concept and promise of mainstreaming for the socio-emotionally disturbed can be considered from diverse viewpoints. Historically it is nothing new: old style mainstreaming was once the total program and still is all that has been provided for many special education pupils. Politically, mainstreaming has been a popular approach and is envisioned as a way to serve more with less during this period of acute financial stress. A pupil is hardly special except for brief encounters and this has already led to the idea that reimbursement should be on a piecework basis—the child being special only when not in the mainstream. Administratively, mainstreaming might look simple at first glance, and consultation avoids the accountability and responsibility which accompany direct service to children. In many districts the teachers and their unions are not yet aware of the meaning of the new design. Regular teachers themselves frequently express dismay when they learn of the new obligations and extended accountability they have inherited.

Mainstreaming is usually combined with mandatory legislation giving parents and advocates a new power base for participation in getting service for children in need. Special education professionals range in opinion about mainstreaming from seeing it as a loss of financial and operational control to helping children to the dawn of the new day when special education is about to direct and reform the total educational establishment. Whether the specialists will actually increase or decrease their influence is still an interesting speculation. Philosophically we cannot forget that whatever actually happens in given circumstances, mainstreaming is the hope for a more humane and concerned special education. The guilt for our past sins and the cultural revolution leads us to know we must learn to do better. . . .

But attention to these matters does not allow us to avoid the central purpose of it all. The psychological study of mainstreaming focuses on one issue: how well does this process provide the actual experiences which the socio-emotionally deviant pupil needs? This psychological examination starts with the definition of our special education pupils. The socio-emotionally disturbed pupils are those, who by virtue of the dissonance pervading their inner and outer life space, have a need for more intense and more sophisticated professional investment than do their normal peers. The simple fact is, if there is no need for this special input, the youngster should not be considered a special education pupil. The unsimple fact is, if he has special needs, we have not yet begun the proper examination of how we can actually provide the help. The preoccupation with the various mechanics of the delivery of service is better suited to milk distribution than to providing mental health. It puts emphasis more on the conceptual efficiency of a system than on the profound complications inherent

in re-raising a child who is in the midst of his own unique constellation of stress. This is a psychological problem.

Exploring the Psychological Nature of our Task

We may begin our psychological exploration by reminding ourselves of an assumption. This assumption is that most of our subset population of special education, in contrast to other areas, can be restored and made whole. This goal of normality or recoverability sets off a chain of accountability expectations seldom recognized. Some have a goal of more than normality for these deviant pupils: they anticipate a high level of self-actualization. There is also the confounding aspect that the child's normal developmental growth is destined to produce periods of relative stress and relief within and without. This flux must be separated from long-term directional change. Since in many states special education resources are not legally available for prevention or crisis, the problem has to reach a proven "bad" level before it is "good" enough to be serviced. Without the continua of mental health service, the uncategorized child or adolescent is left to his own devices since he is not ours. We speak of alternative plans for such special program mismatches, but we forget that the intensity of help required may be equal, though presumably for a shorter time span.

But there are other matters: From the ecological point of view espoused by Rhodes (1970), we know we must be equally concerned with the child's nature and milieu factors. This expands the universe of both assessment and interventions. Again, since socio-emotional problems are seldom found in a pristine state, we should be involved with the welfare of special pupils who may "belong" to some other label, though they may have an overlay of emotional difficulty. Finally, we are given to ignore the fact that many of the socio-emotional problems are not born of the educational enterprise (though some are and others may be exacerbated by the school). But the necessary interventions may not be primarily educational in the usual school sense. It is not uncommon to see special programs for socio-emotionally impaired pupils which do not have even a remote mental health component.

It is necessary to devote brief attention to the children included before moving to specific psychological aspects of mainstreaming. Though special education has persisted in picking and choosing what it would consider, there are three syndromes which are included. Since these have been described in detail (Morse in Cruickshank and Johnson 1975 and Morse 1975), we need only to make it clear that we are not speaking of minor or temporary defections of behavior where cures are simple and even instant. While the fact is that the individual profile overrides any general pattern, the meaning of the child's specific symptoms rests in the pattern. Regardless of how the impairments were generated or the theories about recovery, there are three general states of serious impairment. The first overall pattern stems from an incapacitating struggle between impulse and control. At a conscious or unconscious level there will be evidence of subjective distress, anxiety, and guilt. Such children may act out or be depressed and are usually plagued by severely damaged self-esteem. A second category, which has often been ignored by special education, consists of children and youth who are growing up with serious defects in socialization. These are the value-deficient (as contrasted with value-different) children who are growing up without acquiring an age-appropriate concern for others. This pattern is probably the most rapidly growing group; we also see an increasing number of girls who evidence this dilemma. As the primary socialization factors in society have become less effective, there are more and more desperate children with no trust and no caring, who live on their impulses. They are damaged both by blunted feelings for others and by their limitations in using symbols, or reading (King 1975 and 1976). Third, special education is responsible for the severely disabled children who have profound communication difficulties, acute relationship distortions, and difficulty coping with even a simplified environment. They seem to have no interest in others and live immersed in their own preoccupations; their play produces neither the normal exploration nor the satisfaction found in the normal youngster. While many hold that both psychotic and autistic children have a limited future, we must increase our efforts to help.

Mainstreaming must be put in the context of the psychological nature of those children in the above syndromes. This raises two central considerations. One is that the idiosyncratic nature of each child determines the specific intervention of choice. The behavior patterns which help us think and plan cannot be a substitute for individualization of the work. Just as each child is individual, conversely, there is no mainstream entity. We made that mistake when we created the fiction of a hypothetical special class. We even talked about special classes as if the name delineated a given

psychological substance. Let us not make the mistake again. There are as many mainstreams as there are youngsters mainstreamed. Each has a unique set of intervention resources and strictures.

We turn now to a brief examination of the two parts of the puzzle—the children and the mainstream place. What is in the search for the degree of match? At best, we know very little about the children we would serve. Our lack of skill in understanding them has driven us to tests and devices, to meetings and consultations. Anything but the child! It is of much concern to find psychological tests now being given and interpreted by untrained personnel. It is of equal concern to find new unproven devices spawned at every turn. If we have enough scales to depend upon, there is no need to test our human understanding, which is what clinical skill was all about. It would be refreshing to ask, in the midst of the reports of data collected about the child, if the real child would please stand up. Of course he usually could not stand up because he is not really here. We are all busy trying to reconstruct him from examining his artifacts which we have collected. He has become an archeological discovery, known from his remains and not his person. And if he did stand up, would we recognize him? Diagnosis has become the blind foursome who, as the story goes, described their knowledge of the elephant. When we look at the evidence from discussions about disturbed children, we learn as much about the perceiver as the perceived.

The crux of the issue of mainstreaming lies in differential knowledge about the needs of a pupil. There seems to be an illusion that severity is the index of placement. "Mild cases" (whatever they are) can be mainstreamed, while severe ones never can be, or so we are told. Anyone who has tried to work with an ego-intact, value-deviant delinquent in a classroom might decide to try very different and more seriously impaired in the classroom the next time. We have as yet worked out no system for determining who can be helped where.

Since anyone's behavior is always a consequence of a given ratio of the internal and external condition, we can no longer focus on either just the child or just the environment. The diagnostic search is conducted to discover (Morse 1974) which intervention is relevant in the particular child-environment ratio. There is also the danger of the "greenhouse" phenomenon: an environment which exactly meets the needs of the deviant child may create an instant elimination of his reactive behavior, but is this a cure? Some believe that, if the environment is unprovoking, the given child will heal himself. Other times we anticipate that any correctional influence will take time to prepare for the later transplanting out of the greenhouse. Developmental growth counts for something, but we often wonder how much.

On the other hand, mainstreaming might result in a necessary confrontation revealing the child's inability to cope successfully. The problem can then be dealt with realistically. Teaching socio-emotionally impaired children presents a unique and continual challenge whether the pupil is in a special setting or in the mainstream. We want him to work up to his ability, but we do not want to push him beyond his coping capacity. We try to work at the very cutting edge of his cognitive and affective potential. This requires that teachers neither over- nor undersupport the youngster. This is a continual clinical judgment. If we require too little, the child is robbed of his ability to function on his own. If we give too little, we undersupport the need. If we give too much, the child remains dependent on the "helper."

Probably the most significant thing we can hope for in mainstreaming is innovation in the ability to infuse school with interventions (new and old) rather than the illusion of an automatic great stride forward based on the geography of where we put the problem. Often the old classes for the emotionally disturbed did very little for the "statistical average" pupil, but did help some a great deal. It was also clear that special classes so called were often really not special at all. . . . At other times and for particular pupils and their families the special class added insult to original injury. Then the task became one of getting the child to quit fighting the delivery system, never getting to his basic problem for which the placement was made. We have yet to study the persons for whom the class is useful versus those for whom it is not. Mainstreaming does not eliminate intervention problems; it just presents a new set of variables—a set, we hope, that can be better managed if we use it for the right youngsters.

Partly because of our educational myopia, we have had a tendency to overlook the psychological needs of the child. As it is put, the diagnosis must be educationally relevant. It can be that and still not relevant to the child we are trying to help. It may be heretical to say that every socio-emotionally disturbed child may not be a special education problem. Of course they must have schooling, and to say that rescue will not come from special education does not mean we should not provide special education. Many of the easy educationally based cures written about are children whose behavior

was a consequence of direct educational insult. These are reversible through educational interventions alone if caught soon enough. Not so with the many children who are casualties of massive family and societal destructiveness. The potential for restoration and compensatory support for these children is a matter of a life support system and not a class or a regular classroom alone. The educator who advocates going it alone in such instances will find the well-meaning effort of excellent teachers consumed in the too little which is provided.

With the diminution of multi-disciplined involvement and the ascendance of educational responsibility, we have unwittingly boxed ourselves in. The socio-emotionally disturbed child may not respond to special education. While the school often generates or acerbates a condition, education may be the *major* intervention channel, *one* of the channels, or it may be a *low power* involvement.

Educational Programs in Perspective

As we examine what is necessary to help a youngster toward a reasonable personal and social life, we have to ask to what degree the total milieu must be controlled and what specialization must be infused in the milieu if we are to be successful. We have to ask what must happen to give the child a new lease on life.

Will changes be necessary in the family and community, or will a change in how the child perceives and responds to the conditions be sufficient? Will minor changes in the child's behavior heal an interactive pattern (Henry 1971)? The work of Love (1974) suggests non-traditional, school-related methods for altering families on the ego level, which may be enough. If one can adjust the curriculum and method and by this end the child's problem, that is one thing. Experience with severe value deviancy raises questions about even a total milieu (unless it is highly sophisticated) ever providing what is needed.

When the change is made from providing a program to providing a sufficient program, the situation will be vastly different. To some of us educational accountability has become an excuse by the community for providing for the needs of emotionally and socially deviant children. A school program takes over just a part of life, but it can be made to look as though it cares for all of the child's needs so we can avoid the programs required for a total effort.

The generic problem of providing for the real psychological needs of the child does not change with a special provision or mainstreaming. We never mastered meeting the needs in special classes which is one reason for the mainstream mania. Sometimes, related to the special class, the most incisive experiences were on the bus trips and not in the actual classes at all—so little did we attend to the psychological realities. There are public school programs which have incorporated group therapy, individual therapy, and family interventions. There are those for adolescents which engage in work "therapy" but these are the exception to the rule. Even when resources of the work experience type are available to mainstream adolescents, members of our group are frequently rejected as misfits.

In planning interventions we have been very naive, ignoring the complexity of socio-emotional disturbance. Always we look for a short cut. There are three generalizations which have emerged in my own thinking with regard to this. The first generalization is that the child is a dynamic organism who fortunately often remolds what is done to him to fit his problem even if it is a poor choice. It follows then that there is no one magic way to assist a child. This lack of specificity results in the sometimes success by a wide variety of interventions and, at the same time, the never perfect success by any one mode—be it curriculum or psychotherapy, neither or both. Finkel (1976) lists twenty-two currently practiced approaches to psychotherapy along with six principal group therapies. This listing is really a restricted classical listing of therapy and those of us who have followed Redl see the therapeutic *potential* of many, many more approaches (Morse and Cheney 1972), most of which can be incorporated into the school experience. Many are emphasized in this volume. Can we professionals live long enough to get over focusing on the delivery mechanic rather than the pupil's problem? If we do begin to appreciate the wide variety of interventions which may be effective, we next realize that our ability to predict which one is appropriate for which youngster is often low. In a way this is because "help" is in the eyes of the helpee, not the helper. It is often indirect rather than direct, and has a quality of the consumer's perception about it.

A second generalization comes from the observation that pilot programs often cannot be considered as pilots at all. The successful model in many cases simply does not transfer. This may be because what is effective in obtaining positive results may not be the thing to which people attribute the change. The Hawthorne effect, zest, deeper human commitment, the hope engendered and caring (ex-

pressed in diverse ways to be sure), the emotion of initial surge vs. the grinding long term hauls—things of this nature may be involved. Thus it seems that the covert psychological conditions underlying help may override the overt elements described.

Third, the impatience for instant change looms large. It is possible that this violates the essential nature of child growth, development, and especially remediation. One could almost say if there is instant or rapid change there was either no real problem in the first place or else the new behavior is superficial. Yet impatience about change makes for much false expectation. What we should be concerned with is life stream as a psychological process and what we talk about is mainstreaming as an educational process. The degree to which the mainstreaming mode of instant pressing out of plastic objects in this society has been embraced by the child raisers is an indication of the shallow understanding of children which pervades our work.

The goal then should be to assess (we can no longer talk much about diagnosis) the dissonance in the person and place system as Rhodes has said and then apply the best possible psychological interventions.

Analyzing the Psychological Resources in the Mainstream

Kendall (1971) was one of the first to discuss the psychological realities of mainstreaming, and he based much of his point of view on the fact that "school systems are notoriously resistant to fundamental change." The questions he raises have to do with the nature of mainstream resources for the special child. These range from curriculum to attitudes, and not one of them is subject to easy control. We can focus on this matter by examining the three main sources of psychological input in the mainstream: the adults, the peers, and the tasks. The utility of mainstreaming has to do with what these immediate sources produce and what the child requires for both maintenance and improvement. The impact must not only be hygienic; it must be restorative. . . .

The Teacher's Input

It is well known that training and ability have only a low correlation. There are regular teachers who are able to interact usefully with socio-emotionally disturbed children though they never took a course, do not know the terms, and could not describe what they do. But there are also limits (of the initiated and uninitiated as well) in capacity to be psychologically helpful. In mainstreaming we had better seek out the natural human resources in teachers rather than take on the task of making over the whole profession. For example, children who need structure and an adult with a sense of authority should not be put in a classroom where the native style of that teacher does not embody such resources. The consequence of expecting the mainstream agents to generate a scarce or absent psychological input will lead only to defeat. Of course the fact that a pupil is sustained by a teacher does not always mean that there will be any automatic growth to absorb the problem which the child has. When we expect that the teacher or some resource adult will have to help the youngster with profound distortions of feelings, additional skills are needed in the mainstream. Can the teacher counsel in depth with the pupil? Does the teacher have the ability to dissociate counter transference responses? We know that trained and untrained alike falter (King 1976) in handling aggressive behavior which is a major component. Can the teacher referee the psychological games and avoid the traps children play with adults and peers (Newman 1974)? By any stretch of the imagination, can the teacher be a figure to fill the void in the child's identification pattern? From this viewpoint, we must consider the proper use of the native adult resources in the mainstream for the necessary psychological input. Sometimes there will be resources enough and other times not enough.

The Peer Climate

Classroom groups differ significantly in their mental health resource index. There are stable, resilient groups which absorb and diminish the output of a deviant child. Some go further and reach out in an empathic way to help a troubled child. Other groups have such a low margin or are already saturated with problems, whether designated as special education or not, that a precarious, marginal balance can be destroyed with an addition in the mainstream. There are groups with a frustration quotient so high that scapegoating is the order of the day. Other groups have so little reservoir of peer liking that there is no relationship to offer a new pupil. Fearful groups may be traumatized by the behavior of some youngsters. The dynamics of class size in itself are little considered in mainstreaming. The huge class sizes invoked to solve budget problems determine the time teachers have to invest in each pupil. What one pupil gets extra another pupil misses, and sooner or later the majority of the children (or the parents) are going to catch on and object. The

"value of learning to live with different children" may not be adequate compensation. At present, the movement to employ aides, get and train volunteers, and other modes to add to the ratio of adult investment is in need of a great deal of study.

It is our observation that the current social disorganization is producing a significant group of children without a primary group experience needed to establish basic trust and a sense of self identity. The usual classroom secondary group will not be enough: in fact such a child will attempt to use the classroom in ways destined to failure. Or to take another problem, current role identification problems of girls are producing an increasing number of failures which will need a more intensive relationship than is possible in many classrooms. If we are going to provide what is needed, we will have to find ways of breaking down the group size without putting expectations on regular classroom teachers which will drive them to further distraction. Let alone solving this problem, a good many in special education do not even recognize it. Behavior repression is not the solution for such deprived children.

While the school is a group work agency our own studies suggest that even in special classes there is little group work done. Since we know the group is often a more powerful agent than the adult, it is axiomatic that we must either select groups with the necessary qualities to provide what the mainstreamed special child needs or work through the group conditions which are counterindicated. This is seldom accomplished by consultation since group work itself is a very complicated process.

The research on how normal children in general respond to deviance has only begun—to say nothing of what might happen in any given classroom due to the idiosyncratic conditions. In a replication of earlier work by Kalter and Marsden, Hoffman (1976) has found that elementary age children can distinguish levels of pathology in described peers but their liking and disliking are independent of the level. Degree of disturbance does not always signify the degree of rejection. It is the disruptive or threatening character of the behavior which upsets the normal peer group. Regressive and immature behavior is often the most threatening. Gold (1958) has found four main dimensions in positive peer evaluation: expertness, physical attractiveness and prowess, social-emotional sensitivity, and skill and interests which are similar to peers. The very lack of these behaviors could be used to describe disturbed children. It is no wonder we have programs for these children which virtually "individualize out" any group involvement. The stark reality is that the peer culture can be a mainstream resource or disaster.

The Curricular Experience

To learn a fact or a skill can be therapeutic in itself. To see yourself as the slowest and lowest can be negative self-fulfillment. In an achievement-mad society—without special education protection—there are psychological messages all about. We have a right to ask, regarding mainstreaming, not only how much is the learning situation individualized but how much is the individualization accepted as a natural and inevitable condition. The careful scrutiny of many so-called open conditions indicates that to each his own is the way things are organized but if your "own" is to be low man on the totem pole, you have the curse. Providing psychological support for the child's state of accomplishment within the ethos of the typical classroom is the task.

There is a second part of the task factor in addition to the management of traditional curriculum elements. This is the affective educational enterprise. Since our special children are by definition having difficulty in the affective area, the utilization of affective education methodology becomes necessary. There are as many definitions of affective education as there are advocates, and as much confusion as direction in this field. Nonetheless, in mainstreaming a youngster, we need to attend to the breadth of the curriculum. In matter of fact, those few who appear to have the most impressive impact on the distraught child have moved so far from what a traditional classroom does that one has misgivings about finding the remedial environment in the typical regular or special education classroom. The bridge from the flexible special classroom to the typical regular classroom is a long one. The distance from the school-defined educational format to life-relevant programs for disturbed children may be too long to span. The few successful alternative schools may point the way. The degree to which these approaches have permeated the mainstream is also a question. One open elementary school (look—no inside walls at all!) absorbed all the problem kids who were able to just drift around in the low-pressure setting, but that is not special education accountability.

Conclusion

This book deals directly with the complications required to maximize the resources which can be generated in the mainstream. It is a truism that the very same generic elements constitute the conditions which create, acerbate, or restore. There are these adults, these peers, and these task experiences to consider. The psychological analysis of mainstreaming requires painstaking examination of what these elements produce relative to our best understanding of what is needed. It is necessary that we leave the fantasy world of decreeing arbitrary attributes and relevance to conditions whether they be the mainstream, the special class, or individual therapy. There should be many studies of "one special education boy's day" so that we begin to face up to the actual psychological transactions vis-à-vis the diagnostic prescription. Accountability is in the psychological substance of the experience. What must the socio-emotionally distraught child learn and where and how can it be provided? To speak of mainstreaming out of the psychological context can lead us astray.

References

Cruickshank, W. M., and Johnson, G. O., eds. *Education of Exceptional Children and Youth.* 3d ed. Englewood Cliffs, N.J.: Prentice-Hall, 1975.

Finkel, N. J. *Mental Illness and Health: Its Legacy, Tensions, and Changes.* New York: Macmillan, 1976.

Gold, M. "Power in the Classroom." *Sociometry* 21 (1958): 50–60.

Henry, J. *Pathways to Madness.* New York: Random House, 1971.

Hoffman, E. "Children's Perceptions of their Emotionally Disturbed Peers." Unpublished Ph.D. dissertation, University of Michigan, 1976.

Kendall, D. "Towards Integration." *Special Education in Canada* (November 1971): 3–16.

King, C. "The Ego and the Integration of Violence in Homicidal Youth." *American Journal of Orthopsychiatry* 45 (1975): 134–45.

———. "Counter-Transference and Counter-Experience in the Treatment of Violence Prone Youth." *American Journal of Orthopsychiatry* 46 (1) (1976).

Love, L. R., and Kaswan, J. W. *Troubled Children: Their Families, Schools, and Treatments.* New York: Wiley-Interscience, 1974.

Morse, W. C. "Concepts Related to Diagnosis of Emotionally Impaired." In *State of the Art: Diagnosis and Treatment.* Monograph, Office of Education, U.S. Dept. of HEW, Bureau of Education for Handicapped, Cont. No. OEC-0-9-25290-4539(608), 1974.

———. "The Education of Socially Maladjusted and Emotionally Disturbed Children." In *Education of Exceptional Children and Youth,* edited by W. M. Cruickshank and G. O. Johnson, 3d ed. Englewood Cliffs, N.J.: Prentice-Hall, 1975.

———. *The Seriously Disturbed: Psycho-Social Disorders of Childhood and Youth.* Report to Hawaii Special Education Department, 1975.

———, **and Cheney, C.** "Psychodynamic Interventions in Emotional Disturbance." In *A Study of Child Variance,* edited by W. C. Rhodes. Vol. 2: *Interventions.* Conceptual Project in Emotional Disturbance. Ann Arbor, Michigan: University of Michigan, Institute for the Study of Mental Retardation and Related Disabilities, 1972.

Newman, R. G. *Groups in Schools. A Book about Teachers, Parents, and Children.* New York: Simon and Schuster, 1974.

Rhodes, W. C. "A Community Participation Analysis of Emotional Disturbance." *Exceptional Children* 36 (1970): 309–14.

Reprinted from *Mainstreaming Emotionally Disturbed Children,* edited by A. J. Pappanikou and James L. Paul (Syracuse, N.Y.: Syracuse University Press, 1977), pp. 18–30. Used with permission.

Editors' Commentary

It has now become clear that several additional aspects need to be considered in implementing mainstreaming, especially in the secondary school. The following are necessary even when the most accepting teachers and healthy classroom groups are selected for mainstreaming:

1. School personnel have to analyze the interventions needed to really help the disturbed/disturbing youngster. Particularly when the problem stems from a family condition, if we provide no assistance to the family (e.g., the family members are inaccessible) or therapy to the youngster, why should we expect either mainstream or special classes to produce desired changes? When it is a school-induced problem, interventions by the school alone may be all that are needed.

2. Teachers don't want consultation—because they rarely know how to ask for what they want or get the help they are seeking by their questions. Instead they ask for actual curriculum materials, complete with the method to use in individualizing the classroom work. They seldom have time to make a separate plan for the disturbed youngster. If the pupil's work is more simplified than that of the rest of the class, this fact should not be blatant. The answer—individualization for all pupils—is not yet a reality.

3. Teachers want a plan for evaluation that is accepted by their peers. Grading is often where the disturbed child suffers the most acute hurt. In contrast, a task-achievement-based program can give youngsters flexible amounts of time to meet minimum standards.

4. Crisis support must be provided when the special student's behavior is detrimental to class conduct. There must be a teacher–pupil agreement on a rescue procedure without hostility and recrimination. See the article on the crisis teacher in Chapter 4. The regular teacher also wants consultation to be available on what is to be done and how to deal with peer problems.

5. A resource room for sustained support of certain students is a necessity. This is described in Chapter 4.

Many statements have touted the value of mainstreaming for both the handicapped and normal pupils. Yet the idea of propinquity as an automatic solution has to be abandoned. True, children *can* learn to help, *can* develop empathy, *can* get over their fears and antagonisms. But this happens only if the correct conditions for that learning are arranged. Otherwise, children scapegoated at home often find themselves in the same role in class—after all, they do have deficiencies in social skills. Children rejected by parents may be rejected by teachers. There is no magic in mainstreaming. Any opportunity for improvement also has the potential for negative change as well. Unfortunately, we have no large-scale systematic data on peers' views and the views of the children themselves. Such studies are now underway and will help us plan with more care.

Guralnick, author of the next article, has sensed the complications of integration. Since children's attitudes toward self and others develop early, it is reasonable to look at classroom interactions and see how peers can have a positive impact on handicapped pupils.

The Value of Integrating Handicapped and Nonhandicapped Preschool Children

Michael J. Guralnick

Presently, large numbers of handicapped and nonhandicapped preschool children are being integrated in various programs, including Head Start, day care, model demonstration projects, and even programs formerly limited to handicapped children. In part, the emphasis on integration at the preschool level is a downward extension of mainstreaming efforts for older children, and arises out of many of the same concerns.[19, 20] Although prominent among these are negative reactions to issues such as labeling and placement practices, as well as a general disenchantment with the outcomes of self-contained special education classes,[5, 7] a positively oriented rationale in support of the integration process can be identified.[6, 7, 31]

One aspect of this positive conception concerns the increased understanding and sensitivity to individual differences that nonhandicapped children, their parents, and their teachers can develop out of involvement with handicapped children; a host of important attitudinal processes are likely to be positively affected.

A second aspect concerns the benefits to teachers that can arise from the opportunity to observe a mixed group of children, especially at the preschool level; integrated classrooms provide teachers with a ready framework for gauging child behaviors within a developmental context.

The third aspect involves the potential benefits to handicapped children from observing and interacting with more advanced peers. This may take the form of increased frequency and complexity of verbalizations and higher quality of play as a result of specific modeling and peer reinforcement experiences, or more frequent positive interactions with others due to the existence of more appropriate social consequences from peers. Bricker and Bricker[6] have noted that:

The ways in which a non-delayed child plays with toys and other objects in the classroom and playground provide greater variation in the types of activity available than that provided by the more limited repertoires of the delayed youngsters. This modeling of object-relevant play may provide a better instructional medium than a teacher demonstrating the same activity directly, since both approximations to relevant use and greater variations in the use of objects are evident in the play behavior of the non-delayed child. (pp. 3–4)

This paper will explore the last aspect in detail, and will provide a conceptual and empirical framework relating to procedures that promote the development of handicapped preschool children as a direct result of their involvement with nonhandicapped peers. Certainly, information is needed to assist policy makers, program planners, and teachers in their decision making in this area. Unfortunately, research designed to identify the specific conditions *unique to the mainstreamed setting* that relate to the development of the handicapped child is very limited. As will be noted shortly, however, the few studies on integrating handicapped and nonhandicapped preschool children, as well as data extrapolated from a variety of related investigations, suggest that the critical component is not the simple presence of nonhandicapped children in the class, but the way in which interactions among these children are *systematically* guided or encouraged.

Planned Interactions

An excellent example of the need to organize the environment systematically in this regard can be found in a recent study on the reduction of social withdrawal using symbolic modeling. After identifying a number of socially withdrawn children, O'Connor[21] presented to half of them a film consisting of eleven scenes of peers interacting with each other in a very pleasant manner. After the showing of this film, peer interactions in the preschool increased markedly, while no change was detected in a control group which viewed an unrelated film. The question arises, however, as to why such an effect should occur, since the isolate child generally has available on a daily basis a large number of peer models playing happily. The answer seems to reside, as suggested above, in the systematic nature in which the scenes in the film were presented. As O'Connor[21] noted,

> The initial scenes involve very calm activities such as sharing a book or toy while two children are seated at a table. In the terminal scenes, as many as six children are shown gleefully tossing play equipment around the room. (p. 18)

Accordingly, mere exposure to appropriate models is often insufficient to obtain the desired effect.

Interestingly, in 1924, Mary Cover Jones[17] reported that the "method of social imitation" was highly successful in eliminating fear responses of very young children. This technique employed peers who modeled nonfearful behavior in a directed and controlled setting. As Jones noted,

> By the method of social imitation we allowed the subject to share, under controlled conditions, the social activity of a group of children especially chosen with a view to prestige effect. (p. 390)

A similar result supporting the need for planned interactions was obtained in a recent study[9] that evaluated the effects of integrating handicapped and nonhandicapped children on social play skills. Children were rated on a time-sampling basis, using a social play scale ranging from autistic-like and isolate play to cooperative play. After a variety of unsuccessful attempts to increase substantially the quality of the handicapped children's play, a group of nonhandicapped children were introduced into the play situation. Although the introduction of these children did improve the social play of the handicapped children to some extent, the change was not very substantial. Again, mere togetherness was not sufficient to produce the desired effect. However, when the teacher systematically structured the situation, using the nonhandicapped children to promote various interactions, a marked increase in the quality of play occurred.

Peers as Agents of Change

The studies described above are examples of procedures that employed peers as the primary agents of change in an educational or therapeutic program. In fact, a large number of studies have explored the roles peers play in the development, maintenance, and modification of behavioral patterns, especially their function as reinforcing agents.[14] One example can be found in the work of Solomon and Wahler,[24] who investigated peer interactions in a sixth-grade classroom. In this study, strong evidence was found indicating that peer reinforcement helped to maintain disruptive behaviors in the classroom. Of greater significance, instructions to nondisruptive peers to selectively reinforce socially appropriate behaviors and to ignore deviant behaviors resulted in a marked reduction of the disruptive ones.

Similarly, there have been a few demonstrations emphasizing nonhandicapped children as agents of change in promoting positive behavior in children classified as handicapped. In one, nonhandicapped primary grade children were paired with children classified as emotionally disturbed in a regular classroom setting.[8] Peers modeled appropriate behaviors and selectively reinforced only the appropriate behavior of these problem children. Although a multiple baseline design would have permitted some cause and effect statements,[12] a substantial reduction in deviant behavior did occur. Wagner,[26] in a review of the literature on children tutoring children, suggested that some benefits can be obtained with normal children assisting handicapped children, but there was little useful empirical data available. Hopefully, future research will determine if some of the dramatic effects found by Gartner, Kohler and Riessman[11] on cross-age tutoring can be obtained with peer tutoring among nonhandicapped and handicapped children.

In a series of experiments that have served as prototypes for some of our work, Wahler[27] conducted an experimental analysis of nonhandicapped preschoolers' interactions in free-field settings. A number of behaviors were identified that were correlated with high and low frequencies of contingent peer reinforcement. Peers were then instructed verbally and through role-playing exercises to attend selectively to certain classes of behavior. With this procedure, Wahler was able to modify the type and quality of play, speech to peers, and the passive and aggressive behaviors of various children.

Summarizing work of this sort, Hartup[14] stated that

... direct reinforcement from peers is a potent form of social influence during childhood. The effects of social influence are evident in very early childhood. In addition, very young children can serve effectively as the confederates of teachers and experimenters in bringing about behavior change through this medium. *(p. 429, emphasis added)*

Nonhandicapped Preschool Peers as Resources

Although programs in which handicapped and nonhandicapped preschool children have been integrated often report instances of positive changes in the handicapped children as a result of specific forms of peer interaction,[10] most of the observations have not been conducted in a systematic fashion. The preceding discussion does strongly suggest, however, that under properly arranged conditions such benefits can occur as a direct effect of integration activities. Consequently, as part of a more extensive project investigating the interactions of nonhandicapped and handicapped preschool children, we have attempted to identify some of these conditions and to provide a methodology that can be easily applied in a classroom setting. Two research studies on social and language development are described in the following sections.

Promoting Social Play

The general procedure was to select one handicapped child who did not play very effectively, and two nonhandicapped peers. Social play behavior was measured by the Parten[22] scale, which describes social play categories in terms of unoccupied, solitary, onlooker, parallel, associative, and cooperative play. This scale was utilized in a manner similar to that recently described by Wintre and Webster.[30] Accordingly, play behavior was measured on a time-sampling basis, with the handicapped child's play being rated for a ten-second interval followed by a five-second recording interval. Only one category rating was permitted per ten-second interval. Similarly, the existence of any positive verbalizations to peers by the handicapped child was recorded for each observa-

tion interval. Reliability was measured by having a second observer rate the same behaviors during at least fifteen percent of the sessions, and agreement by intervals never fell below 87%. All children were four- and five-year-old preschoolers. Both handicapped children participating in the social play study had relatively mild handicaps, one having an IQ of 58 and the other 78.

The play behavior of the handicapped child was measured in a group composed of two nonhandicapped children with three types of toys available. As Figure 1 indicates, during baseline the handicapped child spent virtually all of his time in solitary play. This was accomplished by either selecting a toy not used by the others or by vigorously preventing them from interacting with him when he was playing with a toy that was also of interest to them. We then attempted to determine if simple observation of the play of the nonhandicapped children, which was usually of the associative or cooperative type, would have any effect. Consequently, the handicapped child was asked to watch this play for the first five minutes of each fifteen-minute play period. This component was designed so the children played with each of the three different toys about the same amount of time to ensure modeling of all toys. As the figure indicates, this procedure had no effect.

The next step, then, was to provide separate training sessions, using role-playing and verbal descriptions to instruct the nonhandicapped children how to attend selectively to the handicapped child's appropriate behaviors and how to encourage him to interact with them. This procedure was followed prior to each play session as well. The toy most preferred by the handicapped child was selected as the context for the play behavior, and the nonhandicapped children were instructed to play only with that toy. The data in the figure for Toy A reflect the changes in the target child's play behavior. After a few sessions, his solitary play had been reduced markedly and he was engaging in very appropriate play behavior. To evaluate the degree of control exerted by this procedure, another toy was selected and the same procedure followed. The panel referred to as Toy B illustrates that this was successful, as was a final return to Toy A, again demonstrating control of appropriate play behaviors by peers. Notice also that the frequency of the child's positive verbalizations increased with the introduction of the peer reinforcement procedure and correlated with the increase in higher level play.

Figure 2 shows a similar result for an entirely different group of children. It should be noted that

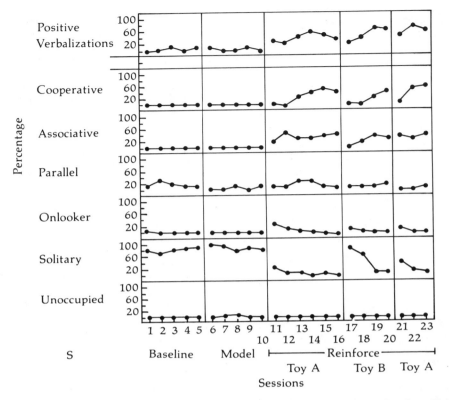

Figure 1. Changes in Social Play Behavior and Positive Verbalizations for One Child as a Result of Peer Modeling and Reinforcement

since these two groups were administered different numbers of peer modeling and reinforcement sessions, with change only occurring upon implementation of the reinforcement condition, this constituted a multiple baseline procedure as well as a replication.

The fact that modeling was not sufficient to produce any change in social play behavior suggests the following. First, it is possible that more basic social approach and interaction skills were not part of the handicapped children's repertoires and, consequently, even if the modeled play behaviors were transmitted, they would not be exhibited. Second, the modeling truly may not have been effective as presented here, perhaps being too complex or unsystematic. Of course, it is possible that modeling *per se* is not an effective way to communicate these skills, but this is quite unlikely. As Bandura[3] pointed out,

Indeed, research conducted within the framework of social learning theory shows that virtually all learning phenomena resulting from direct experience can occur on a vicarious basis by observing other people's behavior and its consequences for them. (p. 864)

Moreover, it should be noted that modeling of a more informal, dynamic, and interactive type than simple demonstration was actually an essential component of the process during the reinforcement conditions. Specifically, the nonhandicapped children often demonstrated a play activity and then encouraged the handicapped child to duplicate it. In any event, the peer reinforcement procedure as described here seems to be an effective means of developing social play behavior.

Promoting Language Usage

Another area in which nonhandicapped preschool peers can be an educational resource is that of language development. Since the frequency, length, and complexity of the nonhandicapped child's verbal behavior in social and academic interactions is generally greater than the handicapped child's, it may be possible to influence certain linguistic characteristics through peer modeling or reinforcement.

Accordingly, using a multiple baseline design, we investigated some of the parameters of peer influence on language behaviors with two children, one handicapped and the other not. The purpose here was to identify the conditions in which peer influence would be effective in modifying the verbal behavior of a mildly handicapped child who used brief and generally nondescriptive statements about common events. However, his linguistic competence far exceeded his usage.

In the initial part of this study the objective was to have the children describe the events in a complex picture using at least one *-ing* verb in conjunction with an appropriate subject (*e.g.,* boy running) to the request, "Tell me about this." Thirty pictures were selected, ten being used as untrained probe items and twenty as training pictures. All fifteen-minute sessions were tape-recorded, and re-

liability was assessed by having an independent rater score 20% of the tapes in terms of usage of the target speech form. Reliability always exceeded 95%.

Following testing of the probe items with the handicapped child, the nonhandicapped peer was introduced. Previously, this child had been trained to use the appropriate form of speech to these pictures and did so in all conditions at least 90% of the time. As illustrated in Figure 3 (looking only at the solid lines with circles), the target speech form was rarely used by the handicapped child during the initial probe. During modeling sessions, in which the children alternated in responding to the pictures, no feedback except non-evaluative comments and general encouragement was provided. Note that there was no change using this method. In the next step, verbal reinforcement was provided only to the nonhandicapped child. Appropriate sentences were followed by, "Good, you're saying it the right way." Again, non-evaluative

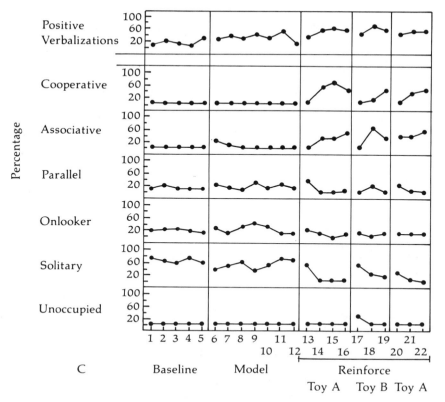

Figure 2. Changes in Social Play Behavior and Positive Verbalizations for a Second Child as a Result of Peer Modeling and Reinforcement

comments and general encouragement were given to the handicapped child. However, when the handicapped child produced at least six appropriate responses within the last ten trials, verbal reinforcement was provided to both children. As the panel labeled Model Plus Reinforcement of Peer indicates, this technique produced an increased usage of the target form, and it generalized to the probe items. Also note that no change occurred in the "negative" components of the multiple baseline (dotted lines with triangles). However, when this procedure was repeated in the second part of the study, with the child now required to describe one activity an agent was engaged in (positive) as well as one that he was not (negative), using the "not" term (*e.g.*, man not running), an increase in the negative usage did result.

Consequently, we can see that by simply reinforcing a specific class of verbalizations of a more advanced peer, an increase in the use of that class of verbalizations was observed in the handicapped child. As noted, it was not necessary to reinforce the handicapped child directly to obtain a marked change in frequency of usage, although that may be needed in other instances. Certainly, we will need to determine the characteristics of children for whom this procedure will be effective and Bandura and Harris[4] have suggested some conditions that should facilitate the modeling process in this area.

In addition, this procedure was used only for competencies (*i.e.*, comprehension of concepts and occasional appropriate usage) already existing in the child's repertoire, and it has been suggested that modeling procedures operate by remediating so-called production deficiencies in these circumstances.[28] If this analysis is correct, this technique should be of significant value since developmentally delayed children have great difficulty in using their language skills in the appropriate situations. Presumably, other more direct procedures, such as imitation training and selective reinforcement, would be needed for the acquisition of new grammatical forms.[29]

In any event, as Zimmerman and Rosenthal[32] pointed out in their recent comprehensive review, a wide range of cognitive and linguistic behaviors can be taught successfully through modeling, and the outcome is rule-like behaviors and not low level imitative skills. It remains to be seen how well and under what conditions these behaviors can be transmitted through peer modeling.

A Framework for Future Research

Conceptually, then, we can view other children as potential educational and therapeutic resources. Of course, we must be sure that the nonhandicapped children are provided with an appropriate educational environment as well, and carefully applied feedback and reinforcement can avoid imitation of less well developed or maladaptive behaviors. However, it is necessary to determine how to utilize these resources in the best pos-

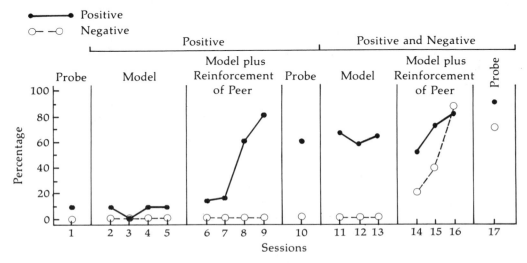

Figure 3. Changes in Language as a Result of Peer Modeling and Reinforcement of Peer

sible way in a manner similar to arranging other environmental events to promote certain goals.[18, 23]

The preceding discussion was intended to provide some direction for research and programming in this highly complex area. There are numerous other variables and factors, however, which play a significant role in this process; these are briefly noted below.

1. *Chronological age of the peer group.* This factor is important, since it is difficult to engage the cooperation of very young children (say, three-year-olds) in some of the more structured activities described. Nevertheless, other types of peer interaction activities of very young children may be of value to handicapped children. Indeed, a review of the infant and toddler literature[2] has suggested that

... the pace and course of infants' social, verbal, and motor development could be considerably accelerated if situations were structured in which peers were provided with the opportunities to learn from one another. (p. 14)

In addition, the use of more advanced handicapped children as models for those less skillful may be useful, but one would need to define carefully their developmental skills.

2. *Level of observational skills.* Some handicapped children may simply not benefit from certain forms of modeling if their observational skills are not sufficiently well developed. Of course, the influence of this factor relates to the systematic way in which modeling experiences are introduced (*e.g.,* complexity, salience, timing, etc.) and the provision of certain activities may even promote the development of these imitative skills.[2]

3. *Type of behavior.* It is quite possible that certain classes of behavior will be more susceptible to change through peer modeling and reinforcement than others (*e.g.,* social play as contrasted to language development). Factors such as salience, novelty, and "naturalness" of the modeled behaviors, among others, are certainly relevant here.

4. *Structure of the modeling context.* We do not know at this point the degree of structure needed to produce behavioral changes through modeling. Certainly, this will interact with many of the variables noted above and perhaps others, but I suspect that the difficulty of the behavior to be acquired will be an important factor here, as it is in other teaching situations.

5. *Grouping.* The characteristics of the handicapped children, the severity of their handicaps, and the proportions of these children integrated with their nonhandicapped peers are likely to be significant variables. Not only will these variables interact with the available resources in the classroom, but differences in performance may well emerge when a handicapped child participates in lessons composed primarily of nonhandicapped children, as compared to those occasions in which the proportions are more equally distributed. Again, this grouping factor is related to numerous others such as the ability of the staff effectively to generate the "many streams"[16] needed to individualize instruction properly and to establish an organizational structure for carrying out these instructional activities.[13]

6. *Characteristics of the models.* Relevant research has clearly suggested that the more competent the model, the more likely that an observer will imitate that model's behavior.[1, 25] Accordingly, the design of procedures to enhance and clarify the competence of specific behaviors of peer models should increase the value of the models as educational and therapeutic resources.[25] Other factors such as the history of peer interactions, their frequency of occurrence, and the rewarding aspects of the interactions will govern the effectiveness of modeling to some extent, but, as Hartup and Coates[15] have pointed out, the relationship even among these variables is quite complex.

This outline was not intended to be exhaustive but to highlight the nature of the variables involved and their potential interactions. It also may suggest a strategy for a systematic approach to the many interesting and important questions raised by this analysis.

Conclusions

Although movements such as mainstreaming, at any level, are subject to the vicissitudes of the social and political actions of major interest groups, it may be useful to bear in mind the suggestion here that the handicapped child may derive benefits of an educational and therapeutic nature from this process that are *not* available without the involvement of more advanced peers. However, in order for this to occur, a careful and systematic arrangement of events and activities is needed. Future research on mainstreaming and early childhood intervention, perhaps conducted within the framework and methodology outlined here, may provide us with a set of procedures and strategies that can be applied to further enhance the development of handicapped children.

References

1. **Akamatsu, T. and Thelen, M.** 1974. A review of the literature on observer characteristics and imitation. Devlpm. Psychol. 10:38–47.

2. **Apolloni, T. and Cooke, T.** 1975. Peer behavior conceptualized as a variable influencing infant and toddler development. Amer. J. Orthopsychiat. 45:4–17.

3. **Bandura, A.** 1974. Behavior theory and the models of man. Amer. Psychol. 29:859–869.

4. **Bandura, A. and Harris, M.** 1966. Modification of syntactic style. J. Exper. Child Psychol. 4:341–352.

5. **Birch, J.** 1974. Mainstreaming: Educable Mentally Retarded Children in Regular Classes. Council for Exceptional Children, Reston, Va.

6. **Bricker, D. and Bricker, W.** 1971. Toddler Research and Intervention Project Report: Year I. IMRID Behavioral Science Monograph No. 20, Institute on Mental Retardation and Intellectual Development, George Peabody College, Nashville, Tenn.

7. **Christopolos, F. and Renz, P.** 1969. A critical examination of special education programs. J. Spec. Educ. 3:371–379.

8. **Csapo, M.** 1972. Peer models reverse the "One bad apple spoils the barrel" theory. Teaching Except. Children 5:20–24.

9. **Devoney, R., Guralnick, M. and Rubin, H.** 1974. Integrating handicapped and nonhandicapped preschool children: effects on social play. Childhd. Educ. 50:360–364.

10. **Fine, S.** 1974. A high proportion of maladjusted preschool children in a group of normal preschoolers: results and implications. Canada's Ment. Hlth. 22:3–4.

11. **Gartner, A., Kohler, M. and Riessman, F.** 1971. Children Teach Children. Harper & Row, New York.

12. **Guralnick, M.** 1973. A research-service model for support of handicapped children. Except. Children 39:277–282.

13. **Guralnick, M.** 1975. Early classroom-based intervention and the role of organizational structure. Except. Children 42:25–31.

14. **Hartup, W.** 1970. Peer interaction and social organization. *In* Carmichael's Manual of Child Psychology, vol. II, P. Mussen, ed., John Wiley, New York.

15. **Hartup, W. and Coates, B.** 1967. Imitation of a peer as a function of reinforcement from the peer group and rewardingness of the model. Child Devlpm. 38:1003–1016.

16. **Hobbs, N.** 1975. The Futures of Children. Jossey-Bass, San Francisco.

17. **Jones, M.** 1924. The elimination of children's fears. J. Exper. Psychol. 7:383–390.

18. **Keogh, W., Miller, R. and Le Blanc, J.** 1973. The effects of antecedent stimuli upon a preschool child's peer interaction. Presented to the Society for Research in Child Development, Philadelphia.

19. **MacMillan, D.** 1973. Issues and trends in special education. Ment. Retard. 11:3–8.

20. **Martin, E.** 1974. Some thoughts on mainstreaming. Except. Children 41:150–153.

21. **O'Connor, R.** 1969. Modification of social withdrawal through symbolic modeling. J. Appl. Behav. Anal. 2:15–22.

22. **Parten, M.** 1932. Social participation among preschool children. J. Abnorm. Soc. Psychol. 27:243–269.

23. **Quilitch, H. and Risley, T.** 1973. The effects of play materials on social play. J. Appl. Behav. Anal. 6:573–578.

24. **Solomon, R. and Wahler, R.** 1973. Peer reinforcement control of classroom problem behavior. J. Appl. Behav. Anal. 6:49–56.

25. **Strichart, S.** 1974. Effects of competence and nurturance on imitation of nonretarded peers by retarded adolescents. Amer. J. Ment. Defic. 78:665–673.

26. **Wagner, P.** 1974. Children tutoring children. Ment. Retard. 12:52–55.

27. **Wahler, R.** 1967. Child–child interactions in free-field settings: Some experimental analyses. J. Exper. Child Psychol. 5:278–293.

28. **Whitehurst, G. T., Ironsmith, M. and Goldfein, M.** 1974. Selective imitation of the passive construction through modeling. J. Exper. Child Psychol. 17:288–302.

29. **Whitehurst, G. and Novak, G.** 1973. Modeling, imitation training, and the acquisition of sentence phrases. J. Exper. Child Psychol. 16:332–345.

30. **Wintre, M. and Webster, C.** 1974. A brief report on using a traditional social behavior scale with disturbed children. J. Appl. Behav. Anal. 7:345–348.

31. **Wynne, S., Ulfelder, L. and Dakof, G.** 1975. Mainstreaming and Early Childhood Education for Handicapped Children: Review and Implications. Final Report, Contract No. OEC–74–9056, Bureau of Education for the Handicapped.

32. **Zimmerman, B. and Rosenthal, T.** 1974. Observational learning of rule-governed behavior by children. Psychol. Bull. 81:29–42.

Reprinted from *American Journal of Orthopsychiatry* 46 (1976): 236–245. Based on a paper presented to the Council for Exceptional Children, Los Angeles, April 1975. Research was supported in part by grant OEG-0-74-0546, from the U.S. Office of Education, Bureau of Education for the Handicapped.

Editors' Commentary

Results of Mainstreaming

Like most social movements in our country, mainstreaming was the product of a set of conditions that pointed toward a new direction. Those conditions were indicated in the beginning of this chapter. The cycle of social movements includes legal sanction and mandates, which we have. Finances are usually inadequate, making cost an issue. In special education, where the money is partly federal, partly state, and more and more local, this has become a key issue. Then comes the struggle for money that is not mandated by the laws. Unless teachers and parents truly accept the principles of mainstreaming, there is a danger of sabotage of services and erection of paper programs. Court decisions will have to be implemented by skillful educators and accepting teachers: mainstreaming will not take place in court or the judge's chambers. The next article emphasizes the tasks ahead in changing educators' attitudes and then introducing new skills.

Mainstreaming: Affect or Effect

Edward E. Gickling

John T. Theobald

Regular teachers are now being required to mainstream mildly handicapped children at an unprecedented rate. This movement toward mainstreaming has resulted largely from the convictions of special educators who laud its praises. Mainstreaming is cited so frequently that one might mistakenly think it a magic elixir rather than a particular orientation toward supplying special education services for the majority of the mildly handicapped. It has been treated as if full participation in regular educational programs would overcome any adverse problems facing exceptional children.

At present the emphasis is clearly away from self-contained practices as the primary form of special education service. Instead the literature is filled with resource-room and resource-teaching articles indicative of a transitional stage approximating mainstreaming (Barksdale & Atkinson, 1971; Glavin, Quay, & Werry, 1971; Hammill & Wiederholt, 1972; Sabatino, 1971; Weiner, 1969; etc.). These transitional forms still represent pullout programs, however, leading Berry (1973) to advocate bypassing transitional stages and integrating the majority of the handicapped directly into regular education classrooms.

Neither the results of articles which were critical of mainstreaming (Franseth & Koury, 1966; Kolstoe, 1972; McKinnon, 1970; Roos, 1970; Vacc, 1968) nor the admission of methodological inadequacies within efficacy studies (Gallagher, 1967; Kirk, 1964; MacMillan, 1971; Nelson & Schmidt, 1971) has slowed down the mainstream movement. Interestingly, the most often quoted articles (Christopolos & Renz, 1969; Dunn, 1968; Johnson, 1962; Lilly, 1970) advocating alternatives to self-contained classrooms have not of themselves furnished original research to the data field. Instead they have been posited on a philosophical rather than a research foundation.

Thus the philosophical commitment to mainstreaming seems to have outraced its research support. In fact the only available option for public educators, as indicated by mandatory special education legislation, is to determine how best to meet the spirit of mainstreaming. In Tennessee, where the present study was conducted, state law (Public Chapter 839, House Bill 2053) mandated the education of handicapped children along with nonhandicapped children in regular classrooms.

If mainstreaming is to be the ultimate educational vehicle for the majority of exceptional children, then various factors which would restrict their full participation in regular education must be considered. An examination of the degree of communication between regular education and special education personnel and also the perceptions of both concerning the mainstream issue were seen as two fundamental factors which might restrict and vitiate mainstreaming. The basic purpose of this study was to investigate these two issues, more specifically to examine teacher and supervisor/administrator attitudes toward mainstreaming and toward the organizational mechanics used to prepare both regular and special education personnel to work together on behalf of a mainstreaming effort.

This study contrasted an earlier study by Shotel, Iano, and McGettigan (1972) which measured teacher attitude toward educating ED and EMR students through a resource-room/regular-class placement model in the following ways. First, it sampled an entire range of regular and special education personnel. The present study was contained among rural and urban populations and compared the responses of regular and special educators within these populations across elementary, secondary, and administrative positions. Second, unlike the Shotel et al. study, there was neither a disbandment of self-contained classes nor the absorption of ED and EMR students into regular classes as a condition for the study. Finally, in addition to assessing teacher competencies and exceptional children's needs, the study attempted to examine the needs of teachers themselves as reflected through their own perceptions about mainstreaming.

Procedure

Prior to the end of the 1973 academic year, 326 out of 400 teachers and supervisor/administrators in Tennessee from regular and special education responded to a 46-item questionnaire. In order to keep the responses anonymous, a triangular distribution and data collection arrangement was devised. This was accomplished by mailing a specified number of questionnaires identified only by a number and a special education or regular education designation to the central offices of the participating school districts. The central offices were instructed to randomly distribute the questionnaires to regular and special education personnel and to record the number of each questionnaire along with the name of its respondent on a separate list. After completing the questionnaire, the respondent was asked to mail the questionnaire back to the survey team in a return-addressed envelope— only the number of the questionnaire and the teaching designation were known to the survey team. After a 2-week waiting period, follow-up questionnaires specifying the delinquent number(s) and designation were mailed back to the various central offices for redistribution. Again the results were to be mailed to the survey team, bypassing each central office.

The survey sample consisted of approximately 5% of the regular education and 10% of the special education personnel of 14 participating school districts, or a ratio of three regular educators to every special educator. These participating districts were located in a 10-county area including and surrounding the metropolitan area of Knoxville, Tennessee. Sixty-four percent of the sample was from rural school systems representing communities of less than 10,000 population, and 36% was from urban systems exceeding 10,000 in population. Of the 326 respondents, 183 were regular-classroom teachers, 84 were special education teachers, and 47 and 12 were regular and special education supervisor/administrators respectively. The sample included regular teachers, guidance counselors, supervisors and administrators, homebound instructors, itinerant teachers, speech therapists, special education teachers, resource teachers, and separate day-school personnel. State agency personnel were not sampled, since this study concentrated upon a public education issue. The largest single body sampled (over 62%) was associated with elementary education. Over 90% of the respondents were certified to work within their present position, and 87% had had 3 or more years of service in education.

The initial portion of the questionnaire provided demographic information, while the remaining portion adhered to a "yes-no" format in an attempt to obtain a teacher's knowledge and attitude concerning present practices and trends within the field of special education. More specifically, the latter portion was designed to first elicit teacher attitudes toward (a) how the philosophy of equal educational opportunity applies to exceptional children and (b) their willingness to commit themselves to integrating exceptional children in their classrooms if assistance could be provided. Second, the questionnaire was designed to measure the organizational mechanics whereby teachers (a) were informed about exceptional children and (b) were made aware of and involved with the planning for exceptional children.

Since the information gathered from this questionnaire was descriptive, the survey team rejected a nonparametric statistical procedure to convey the results. Instead it was decided that a simple percentage presentation would best portray the practi-

cal significance of the data as well as allow for reflection by readers. It was the authors' hope that other special educators would ask similar questions to determine whether their own personnel were aware of present trends and programs within the field of special education and whether they had adequately communicated with regular educators to promote smooth integration of exceptional children into regular-classroom programs.

The percentage of "yes" responses for the various questionnaire items were reported in Tables 1–4. Each table contained questionnaire items specific to one of four areas of teacher attitude, commitment, knowledge, and involvement, with each item being reported across seven respondent categories. These categories consisted of the total number of personnel as represented by regular educa-

Table 1. Teacher Attitude toward Equal Educational Opportunity for Exceptional Children

Questionnaire Item	Percentage of "yes" responses per questionnaire item						
	Regular educ. N = 230	Special educ. N = 96	Sec. regular teachers N = 67	Sec. special teachers N = 25	Elem. regular teachers N = 122	Elem. special teachers N = 49	Elem. sup./ admin. N = 29
1. Being placed in a special education self-contained classroom restricts the chance for a student to fully participate in activities such as service organizations, clubs, sports, etc., normally available to regular classroom students.	48.2	66.3	50.7	68.0	47.1	75.5	48.3
2. If given a chance, special education students would participate in most school activities.	68.5	78.5	60.3	84.0	70.7	83.7	86.2
3. Public schools' philosophies and objectives are limited to the range of normal children.	68.8	58.5	62.7	56.5	69.7	64.6	67.9
4. Children placed in self-contained special education classes are more likely to be seen as different than if permitted to stay in regular classes.	61.3	73.0	56.5	66.7	62.7	81.3	69.0
5. A child is socially isolated from his peers when placed in a self-contained special education class.	56.4	71.4	49.3	72.0	61.5	72.9	67.9
6. Special education placement practices have been free of socioeconomic and racial discrimination.	29.4	41.9	36.4	26.1	23.9	41.3	34.5

tion, special education, secondary regular teachers, secondary special teachers, elementary regular teachers, elementary special teachers, and elementary regular supervisor/administrators. The two categories of regular and special education contained a combination of supervisor/administrative, consultant, and teaching personnel, whereas the other five categories were separate and discrete. Specific secondary regular education supervisor/administrators and secondary and elementary special education supervisor/administrators were not listed as separate categories; these personnel were represented in either the regular education or special education category; likewise, specific rural and urban categories were deleted because of overall agreements across the various questionnaire items.

The actual number of respondents cited on each of the seven categories merely represented the total number of participants in each category and should not be interpreted to mean the actual number of respondents per questionnaire item. Only "yes" and "no" responses were recorded; unanswered statements were omitted from the various tallies. Since some statements were not answered by all respondents, the resulting percentages were derived from a varying number of participants per each questionnaire item. Regardless of the variation in the number of respondents contributing to each percentage, the large majority of participants were teachers.

Results

Items 1, 4, and 5 on Table 1 showed that at least 66% of special education personnel felt that students placed in self-contained classrooms were more likely to be restricted from extracurricular activity, seen as different, and socially isolated than if permitted to remain in regular classrooms. Elementary special teachers expressed the highest agreement on these three issues, recording percentages of 75, 81, and 72 respectively. In contrast, approximately 50% of regular education personnel saw self-contained classroom placement as a restrictive force. These same approximations were maintained by secondary regular teachers, who saw students placed in self-contained classrooms as being socially isolated and different. Over 60% of the elementary teachers and supervisor/administrators also saw students in self-contained classes as different and socially isolated. The single highest percentage of overall agreement occurred on item 2, with a range of 60 to 86% concurring that special education students would participate in most school activities if given a chance.

According to item 3, the large percentage of respondents felt that public schools' philosophies and objectives were limited to a range of normal children, with special education responding slightly below regular education. Item 6 indicated that students representing economic and minority differences were also less likely to be considered normal. Approximately 60% of the special education personnel sample and 70% of the regular education sample agreed that special education placement practices had socioeconomic and racial overtones.

The results of teacher commitment toward integrating exceptional children into regular classrooms are shown in Table 2. Item 7 showed disparity between the perceptions of special educators about regular educators and the perceptions of regular educators about themselves: nearly a 20% discrepancy, with 30% of special education personnel indicating that regular classroom teachers feel imposed upon to help special education students, whereas nearly 50% of the regular educators voiced a similar sense of imposition. Concerning skills, however, less than 15% of the secondary and elementary teaching force felt that they had the skills to help exceptional children, as indicated by item 8.

A discrepancy also existed between the responses recorded on items 9 and 10. There was general agreement that special self-contained classes were not adequately providing academic services for the mildly handicapped, as indicated by item 9. However, approximately 60% of both regular and special educators felt that self-contained classes had proven to be more effective than regular classes for the mildly handicapped. Supervisor/administrators recorded the lowest percentage on this issue, while secondary regular teachers recorded the highest, or 45 and 72% respectively. There also appeared to be a residual preference of over 40% of all respondents for retaining self-contained classes in the future, as shown by item 15; however, this recommendation was not as strong as the future recommendation to use resource teachers. A comparison between items 14 and 15 indicated a future preference of two to one in favor of resource over self-contained procedures.

Even though over 60% of regular teachers felt that special education students were best served in self-contained settings, approximately 60% said that they would accept special education students into their classes if there was a movement away from self-contained classes for the mildly handicapped (see item 11). A higher percentage of com-

Table 2. Teacher Commitment toward Integrating Exceptional Children
into Regular Classrooms

Questionnaire Item	Percentage of "yes" responses per questionnaire item						
	Regular educ. N = 230	Special educ. N = 96	Sec. regular teachers N = 67	Sec. special teachers N = 25	Elem. regular teachers N = 122	Elem. special teachers N = 49	Elem. sup./ admin. N = 29
7. Under normal conditions the regular-classroom teacher feels imposed upon to help special education students.	48.9	31.0	47.1	30.4	48.7	31.1	46.4
8. The regular-classroom teacher feels he/she has the skills to help special education students.	15.2	10.5	14.7	13.6	12.8	10.9	18.5
9. Special self-contained classes seem to be adequately providing academic services for the mildly handicapped and do not need to be changed.	39.2	32.2	35.9	34.8	42.1	26.1	29.6
10. Special self-contained classes for the mildly handicapped have proved to be more effective than regular classes have been for these students.	62.1	59.3	72.1	62.5	58.2	53.1	44.8
11. If there was a movement away from self-contained special classes for the mildly handicapped, would regular-classroom teachers be willing to accept special education students into their classes?	59.3	47.5	57.8	54.5	64.5	54.5	70.4
12. The regular-classroom teacher would feel more comfortable if special education would assist in providing services in the regular classroom.	80.6	80.0	88.2	77.3	83.5	76.1	57.1
13. If time were available to work with special education personnel, regular-classroom teachers would take advantage of this opportunity.	95.3	91.6	97.7	91.3	94.6	90.7	93.1
14. In the future, I strongly recommend the use of resource rooms for mildly handicapped children.	85.8	82.0	90.2	88.0	82.7	77.1	82.1
15. In the future, I strongly recommend the use of self-contained classes for the mildly handicapped.	45.9	41.6	55.6	33.3	41.4	35.4	37.9

mitment by teachers was also noted, contingent upon special education making services and time available, as shown by items 12 and 13. Over 80% of the regular teachers indicated that they would feel more comfortable if special education were to assist them in their classrooms, and over 90% said that they would work with special education personnel if time were available.

Table 3 indicated that special education services were in most instances being provided by the 14 participating school district sample. The amount of service represented by item 16 approximated 90%. As part of the service component, however, less than 60% knew that the Tennessee State Board of Education (Public Chapter 839, 1972) had made provisions for moving away from self-contained classrooms. Only 70% of the supervisor/administrators were aware of the State Department's shifting emphasis, while only 33% of the secondary special teachers indicated such knowledge. Items 18

Table 3. Information-sharing Procedures to Inform Teachers about Exceptional Children

Questionnaire Item	Percentage of "yes" responses per questionnaire item						
	Regular educ. $N = 230$	Special educ. $N = 96$	Sec. regular teachers $N = 67$	Sec. special teachers $N = 25$	Elem. regular teachers $N = 122$	Elem. special teachers $N = 49$	Elem. sup./ admin. $N = 29$
16. Does your school system provide services for the handicapped?	91.5	94.3	89.9	90.9	92.4	93.6	89.7
17. Does the State Department of Education make any provision for moving away from self-contained classrooms for the mildly handicapped?	55.9	57.1	53.5	33.3	46.6	55.3	70.0
18. In school systems already providing special education, are plans being made to move away from self-contained classrooms for the mildly handicapped?	48.7	56.2	46.7	50.0	55.4	55.0	56.5
19. Do your school's future plans provide for a move away from self-contained classes for the mildly handicapped?	46.0	45.1	40.0	31.6	51.8	48.7	50.0
20. Has your school system started a program to inform the regular-classroom teachers about the services provided through special education?	35.2	26.5	19.4	27.3	34.2	15.2	48.3
21. Has your school system started a program to inform the regular-classroom teachers about the differences between mental retardation, behavior problems, learning disabilities, etc.?	30.1	22.9	16.9	19.0	28.7	13.0	40.7
22. In your school do regular and special teachers talk informally about special education problems?	81.6	75.6	76.6	76.2	84.5	77.1	85.2
23. I was not acquainted with most of the information asked for on the questionnaire.	51.0	23.5	60.6	20.0	55.9	20.0	16.0

and 19 also indicated the lack of unanimity on the part of educators to move away from self-contained classrooms for the mildly handicapped and toward resource-room services, either in terms of present or future program plans. Roughly 50% of those sampled were knowledgeable of such a move.

Item 22 demonstrated that the large percentage of regular and special teachers do talk informally about special education problems. However, their conversations did not reflect a strong mainstreaming posture, with 60% of regular secondary teachers and 56% of regular elementary teachers not being acquainted with most of the information contained in the questionnaire (see item 23).

According to teacher responses to items 20 and 21, less than 20% of regular secondary teachers, 35% of regular elementary teachers, 28% of secondary special teachers, and 16% of elementary special teachers acknowledged that their school systems were providing programs to inform them about exceptional children. Even elementary supervisor/administrators acknowledged a lack of organized activity, as shown by less than 50% indicating that organized information-sharing sessions were operating.

Table 4 indicated that self-contained and partially self-contained classes were the major instructional settings used to dispense special education services. Homebound and separate day-school programs were also well represented. Resource and itinerant means of instruction received the lowest overall percentages with respect to present types of special education services provided. In terms of the types of special education services proposed for the future, item 25 showed a fairly equal dispersion across self-contained classes, partially self-contained classes, resource-room teachers, itinerant teachers, and homebound programs. When comparing item 24 with item 25, there was a dramatic reduction in the use of self-contained and partially self-contained classes as proposed by future plans. This reduction was not offset, however, by gains in other types of special education services, as seen in item 25. It was noted that the use of resource and itinerant teachers did not show any appreciable increase from item 24 to item 25.

The organizational mechanics used to involve teachers in planning for special education students appeared to be limited. For example, item 26 ranged from a low of 54% for elementary special teachers to a high of 70% for elementary supervisor/administrators reporting formal meetings held concerning placement and reintegration procedures. Only 38% of all regular education personnel and 29% of all special education personnel indicated involvement in scheduled meetings for follow-up on behalf of special education students, as shown in item 27. Written reports and formal testing appeared to be the main source of follow-up. The infrequency with which follow-up was conducted, as well as the general lack of formal meeting times, would appear to restrict both communication and the mobility of the mildly handicapped into regular-classroom programs.

Discussion

When this questionnaire was administered, special education in Tennessee was in a state of transition. School systems were beginning to struggle with the interpretation of mandatory special education legislation as it applied to each school system's unique situation. Problems related to identifying students and students' needs were receiving the primary emphasis, while the procedural aspects of delivering services and holding formal inservice sessions about the needs of exceptional children lagged behind. In probable fact, if the questionnaire had been administered during the 1973–74 academic year, the responses might have been more in keeping with a mainstream posture, since inservice and training programs are now priorities for the sampled school systems.

Nevertheless, when the questionnaire was administered it appeared that the sampled population was undecided about the prospects of mainstreaming exceptional children. Even though the percentages on Table 1 indicated that most regular and special education personnel felt self-contained practices restricted and discriminated against exceptional children, Table 2 showed no overwhelming support on the part of either group to do away with self-contained classes for the mildly handicapped. Although academic dissatisfaction was expressed about self-contained classrooms, over 60% of the respondents indicated overall satisfaction with self-contained classes per se. These 60% felt that self-contained classes had proven to be more effective than regular classes for the mildly handicapped.

Since 60% expressed a bias favoring self-contained classes, only approximately 40% at the most could be considered strongly behind a mainstream approach, i.e., 40% of elementary regular teachers and 30% of secondary regular teachers. An additional 20% of the regular education respondents stated that they would be willing to accept the mildly handicapped into regular classrooms if there was a movement away from self-contained classes. However, once it was indicated that regular teachers would be given assistance in the form of

Table 4. Types of Services and Amount of Teacher Involvement in Planning
for Exceptional Children

Questionnaire Item	Percentage of "yes" responses per questionnaire item						
	Regular educ. N = 230	Special educ. N = 96	Sec. regular teachers N = 67	Sec. special teachers N = 25	Elem. regular teachers N = 122	Elem. special teachers N = 49	Elem. sup./ admin. N = 29
24. Types of special education services provided by your school system:							
Self-contained classes	73.3	83.7	59.7	79.2	80.7	83.7	69.0
Partially self-contained	41.0	54.3	47.1	54.2	31.9	38.8	69.0
Resource-room teachers	23.9	35.9	16.2	20.8	23.5	32.7	34.5
Itinerant teachers	24.8	43.5	16.2	20.8	24.4	32.7	34.5
Separate special education day schools	35.1	43.5	32.4	45.8	31.9	32.7	37.9
Homebound programs	62.6	84.8	50.8	87.5	57.1	81.6	75.9
25. Types of special education services proposed by your school system in the future:							
Self-contained classes	31.4	28.6	18.9	23.8	33.3	33.3	42.9
Partially self-contained	21.8	33.3	24.5	28.6	11.5	33.3	38.1
Resource-room teachers	26.3	34.9	22.6	28.6	26.9	42.4	42.9
Itinerant teachers	24.4	31.7	20.8	28.6	19.2	33.3	42.9
Separate special education day schools	16.0	11.1	11.3	9.5	12.8	9.1	23.8
Homebound programs	23.5	25.4	9.4	28.6	24.0	27.3	38.1
26. Are formal meetings arranged to communicate placement and reintegration of special education students within your school system?	66.0	63.6	62.3	68.0	66.0	54.2	70.4
27. In what way and how frequently is follow-up conducted as a result of meetings regarding the placement of special education students?							
Scheduled meetings	38.2	28.6	22.2	30.4	31.1	22.0	56.0
Written progress reports	51.5	49.4	41.7	52.2	54.1	39.0	48.0
Formal testings	61.0	67.5	66.7	65.2	60.8	73.2	52.0
No follow-up	9.8	10.9	13.3	10.5	9.7	11.4	4.5
Follow-up once each year	34.8	40.6	40.0	36.8	30.6	42.9	27.3
Follow-up every 6 months	8.0	7.8	10.0	10.5	9.7	0	4.5
Other means of follow-up	19.6	31.3	13.3	21.1	16.1	31.4	45.5

services and time available to work with special education personnel, there was almost unanimous agreement by regular teachers that they would make use of these opportunities if needed. This overwhelming willingness of regular educators to use special education assistance directly corresponds with regular educators' recognition of their own skill deficiencies in providing for the needs of special children. From an analysis of these results it appears that approximately 40% of the regular teachers were strongly opposed to mainstreaming, while a comparable percentage favored mainstreaming. An additional 20% were marginally committed in favor of mainstreaming if the situation arose.

The present authors contend that if mainstreaming is to be successful, teacher attitudes toward working with the mildly handicapped must be assessed. It is frightening to think that education in general, with its commitment to individualized instruction and the recognition of individual differences, might fail to recognize the individual preferences of its own practitioners. Does the concept of individualization also apply to teachers? Are all teachers equally willing to mainstream mildly handicapped children? The data would seem to indicate otherwise unless certain teacher attitudes change.

Further, a communication problem surrounding the mainstreaming issue was revealed by an examination of the actual organizational mechanics used to disseminate information about exceptional children and their educational services. Information about special education students and services should precede all other activities if mainstreaming is to become an effective means of helping the mildly handicapped. The adequacy of existing communication procedures is doubtful, since only 35% of regular education personnel indicated that attempts were being made to inform them about special children and their programs. Without informing and training regular educators about the limitations and assets of the mildly handicapped, special education may continue to see the negative attitudes of regular teachers strengthen (Shotel et al., 1972).

Perhaps poor overall communication on the part of special education has led regular education personnel to become hesitant about mainstreaming. With the inconsistent and infrequent follow-through demonstrated in the past by special education, regular education might conclude that inadequate follow-through by special education will continue. There would be hesitancy on the part of regular education teachers to integrate the mildly handicapped if they felt that there would be no or inadequate help from special education.

The admission by 60% of regular secondary teachers and 56% of regular elementary teachers that they were not acquainted with most of the information on the questionnaire may have adversely affected the various results. One might be tempted to interpret the questionnaire as invalid because of these high percentages. However, the lack of familiarity is again an indication that basic communication was not sufficiently provided to inform regular teachers about practices and programs for the mildly handicapped. Further evidence of inoperable or insufficient communication procedures was indicated by only approximately one-half of the respondents reporting knowledge of the State Department of Education provisions for moving toward mainstreaming.

An assessment of teacher attitude and information dissemination procedures would seem to be prerequisite to teaching the mildly handicapped in regular classes. Educators interested in mainstreaming would also do well to consider problems related to prescriptive teaching as regular and special education personnel begin to work more closely together (Joiner & Walizer, 1973). While special education's commitment to mainstreaming and its implementation is here, a critical review of its process thus far clearly indicates that past organizational patterns and procedures controlling educational services and attitudes of personnel in regular and special education must be jointly evaluated as a preliminary step to providing new services and making mainstreaming a reality. In effect, a needs-assessment relative to teacher attitude and program viability of the involved organizations appears appropriate at this time. Without a thorough understanding of each of these aspects, many mildly handicapped children who undergo the mainstreaming route may suffer because of teacher bias and the lack of a sufficient service-delivery model.

References

Barksdale, M. W., & Atkinson, A. P. A resource room approach to instruction for the educable mentally retarded. *Focus on Exceptional Children,* 1971, 3, 12–15.

Berry, K. E. *Models for mainstreaming.* San Rafael, Calif.: Dimensions Publishing Co., 1973.

Christopolos, G., & Renz, P. A. Critical examination of special education programs. *The Journal of Special Education,* 1969, 3, 371–379.

Dunn, L. M. Special education for the mildly retarded—Is much of it justifiable? *Exceptional Children,* 1968, 35, 5–22.

Franseth, J., & Koury, R. *Survey of research on grouping as related to pupil learning.* U.S. Department of Health, Education, and Welfare, 1966, No. 5. 220:20089.

Gallagher, J. J. New directions in special education. *Exceptional Children,* 1967, 33, 441–447.

Glavin, J. P., Quay, H. C., & Werry, J. S. Behavioral and academic gains of conduct problem children in different classroom settings. *Exceptional Children*, 1971, 37, 441–446.

Hammill, D. D., & Wiederholt, J. L. *The resource room: Rationale and implementation.* Philadelphia: Buttonwood Farms, Inc., 1972.

Johnson, G. O. Special education for the mentally handicapped—A paradox. *Exceptional Children*, 1962, 29, 62–69.

Joiner, L. M., & Walizer, M. H. Prescriptive instruction: Basic questions and issues. Paper delivered at a conference on Diagnostic and Prescriptive Education sponsored by the Minnesota State Department of Education, Minneapolis, May 10–11, 1973.

Kirk, S. A. Research in education. In H. A. Stevens & R. Heber (Eds.), *Mental retardation: A review of research.* Chicago: University of Chicago Press, 1964.

Kolstoe, O. P. Programs for the mildly retarded: A reply to critics. *Exceptional Children*, 1972, 39, 51–56.

Lilly, M. S. Special education: A teapot in a tempest. *Exceptional Children*, 1970, 37, 43–49.

MacMillan, D. L. Special education for the mildly retarded: Servant or savant. *Focus on Exceptional Children*, 1971, 2, 1–11.

McKinnon, A. J. Parents and pupil perceptions of special classes for emotionally disturbed children. *Exceptional Children*, 1970, 37, 302–303.

Nelson, C. C., & Schmidt, L. J. The question of the efficacy of special class. *Exceptional Children*, 1971, 37, 381–384.

Public Chapter 839, House Bill 2053 (substituted for Senate Bill 1906). General Assembly of The State of Tennessee, 1972.

Roos, P. Trends and Issues in special education for the mentally retarded. *Education and Training for the Mentally Retarded*, 1970, 5, 51–61.

Rules, regulations, and minimum standards. Tennessee State Board of Education, Nashville, 1972–1973.

Sabatino, D. A. An evaluation of resource rooms for children with learning disabilities. *Journal of Learning Disabilities*, 1971, 4, 84–93.

Shotel, J. R., Iano, R. P., & McGettigan, J. F. Teacher attitudes associated with the integration of handicapped children. *Exceptional Children*, 1972, 38, 677–683.

Vacc, N. A study of emotionally disturbed children in regular and special classes. *Exceptional Children*, 1968, 35, 197–204.

Weiner, L. H. An investigation of the effectiveness of resource rooms for children with specific learning disabilities. *Journal of Learning Disabilities*, 1969, 2, 223–229.

Reprinted from the *Journal of Special Education* 9 (1975): 318–328.

Editors' Commentary

In the following study, Jones and his colleagues do an essential first task: they set up criteria for evaluating mainstreaming. As they say, the early studies on which the movement based its decisions were seriously flawed.

Evaluating Mainstreaming Programs: Models, Caveats, Considerations, and Guidelines

Reginald L. Jones   *Samuel Guskin*
Jay Gottlieb   *Roland K. Yoshida*

It is becoming increasingly unpopular to make assumptions about the validity of an educational program, or even an idea, without amassing objective, systematically collected data bearing directly upon its value. (Zimiles, 1968, p. 547)

Programs for mainstreaming are being developed and implemented at a rapid rate. There was a similar, but longer, earlier period in special education history when self contained special classes were being developed and implemented. Unfortunately, the development of self contained special classes (particularly for the educable mentally retarded) was not accompanied by appropriate attention to the evaluation of program effectiveness—determining the soundness of underlying assumptions or the means by which program validity could be assessed. When careful attention was given to evaluation concerns (Guskin & Spicker, 1968; Kirk, 1964), special educators discovered that the evaluation designs were flawed in many respects and hence not really adequate to provide reliable data on program effectiveness. Sampling was often inadequate, instrumentation was weak, and there was little knowledge of what actually transpired in the classroom. Teacher background was seldom described, and there was only rare recognition that special class students—even in a single classification such as the educable mentally retarded—could not be considered an educationally homogeneous group.

Educators now have the benefit of critiques of previous efficacy studies and know their shortcomings, many of which must be avoided in the evaluation of mainstreaming programs. Moreover, the Education for All Handicapped Children Act (P. L. 94–142, 1975) and legislation at the state level make evaluation of special education programs mandatory. It is important, therefore, as new special education programs are developed and before implementation becomes finalized, that a variety of evaluation considerations be examined.

The present article is not intended to be the definitive treatise on the evaluation of mainstream programs, but the authors do hope to bring before the reader a variety of considerations which, if taken into account, can improve evaluation efforts. The article begins with a discussion of models for evaluating mainstream programs. Emphasis is given to the adequacy of the models (and studies) and the insights they yield for improved evaluation designs. This is followed by problems and issues in the evaluation of educational treatments in mainstream settings. The third section presents considerations relevant to developing and assessing measures that might be used to evaluate program impact, followed by a treatment of issues unique to evaluation of Public Law 94–142. Finally, a number of general considerations and a set of guidelines for developing or assessing mainstreaming evaluation activities are given.

Models for Evaluating Mainstreaming Programs

Perhaps the best place to begin a critical examination of the evaluation of mainstreaming programs is to ask whether these programs should be evaluated differently than any other educational or social program. To make this judgment requires both a clear view of what mainstreaming is and an understanding of common approaches to evaluation.

There are at least three broad concerns behind the mainstreaming movement: the removal of labels, desegregation, and more effective programing (Dunn, 1968). Some (e.g., Kaufman, Gottlieb, Agard, & Kukic, 1975) have attempted to incorporate these as well as other concerns into a comprehensive definition of the term *mainstreaming*. For purposes of further discussion, mainstreaming programs here will refer to programs that provide more instruction for more handicapped children in regular classes than previously: Further, the major intent of this change is to reduce the presumed stigma of labeling, to reduce the presumed social isolation, and, it is hoped, to increase the effectiveness of educational programing for handicapped children. It is essential, then, that models for evaluating mainstreaming programs incorporate these key features of the mainstreaming treatment and its anticipated outcomes.

General Strategies of Educational Program Evaluation

The general strategies that have been employed in educational program evaluation can be divided roughly into field research models and decision making models.

Field Research Models. Field research methods can be further subdivided into experimental and nonexperimental (or *ex post facto*) approaches. The former uses the model of the psychological experiment. A good illustration in the field of special education is the Illinois study of the efficacy of special classes for the educable mentally retarded (Goldstein, Moss, & Jordan, 1965). Children screened on IQ tests were randomly assigned to first grade or to special classes, and testing was carried out over a three year period to compare intellectual, academic, and nonacademic skills of the children in the two conditions.

An excellent example of evaluation using nonexperimental methods is the Equality of Educational Opportunity study carried out by Coleman and his colleagues (1966) to assess school desegregation effects. This large scale investigation used field survey and demographic methods drawn largely from sociology, along with verbal tests on children and teachers. Racial and socioeconomic status distributions in classes and schools were examined, as were the correlations of these and many other variables with the school achievement of children.

Within their own fields, each of these studies has stood out as far more significant and better methodologically than prior work. Nevertheless, they each have been seriously taken to task for inadequacies of sampling, data analysis, and interpretation of findings.

Decision Making Models. In contrast with those studies that evolved out of more traditional psychological and sociological research methods, the field of educational evaluation began in the 1960's to use terminology and methods derived from business and behavioral psychology in response to demands for accountability as a part of federal funding for new educational programs. The terminology included process and product evaluation (or the more elaborate Stufflebeam [1971] CIPP model, which assesses context and input as well as process and product), formative and summative evaluation, and discrepancy evaluation. The distinctive feature of these evaluation approaches is that they are concerned with providing information for decision making and often focus on specification of objectives, on providing feedback during the process of program development, and on describing the way in which programs have actually been implemented, as well as providing objective data on outcomes. Within the field of special education, these approaches have tended to be used in product (materials) evaluation (Thiagarajan, Semmel, & Semmel, 1974) and in descriptions of competency based teacher education programs (Semmel, Semmel, & Morrisey, 1976), though not to our knowledge in any major independent attempts at program evaluation.

Mainstreaming Evaluation Studies

The published or publicized evaluations of mainstreaming fall into two broad classes: large scale studies, involving many schools or school districts, and small scale studies, typically carried out in a single school or in a few classrooms.

Large Scale Studies. The large scale studies are illustrated by Project PRIME, carried out in Texas (Kaufman, Agard, & Semmel, 1978) and the California educable mentally retarded decertification study (Meyers, MacMillan, & Yoshida, 1975a). In addition to the large sample of schools employed in both studies, PRIME is distinctive for its collection of process data (i.e., systematic observation of teacher–pupil interaction) in every regular classroom in which handicapped children participated, in addition to an enormous number of input and output measures on all the teachers and children involved.

The California study was more modest, limiting itself to a more restricted number of input and outcome measures. These measures were selected for relevance to the objectives of the decertification procedures: reducing the racial and ethnic imbalance in special education and improving the achievement and adjustment of the previously labeled children.

Both large scale studies incorporated nonhandicapped regular class and handicapped special class comparison groups to help clarify the interpretation of their findings on "handicapped" children integrated into regular classes. However, in both studies, the special class group is not strictly comparable to the integrated group. Both studies also have in common a limited mode of conceptualization prior to data collection, primarily a specification of relevant variables rather than an attempt to conceptualize how the variables might operate (and interact) to affect outcomes. Both, and particularly PRIME, depend on extensive data analysis to unravel relationships. Both are limited in the availability of data prior to instituting program change. Yet, these studies provide—or are about to provide—more information on handicapped children in regular classes than has been accumulated in all previous research and evaluation on the topic.

Smaller Investigations. In contrast with these extensive studies, a number of smaller investigations have been carried out in single schools. The work of Gottlieb and his colleagues (Budoff & Gottlieb, 1976; Goodman, Gottlieb, & Harrison, 1972; Gottlieb & Budoff, 1973; Gottlieb, Gampel, & Budoff, 1975) provides a good illustration of what can be done in such situations. Although limited in sample size, they were able to arrange in at least one study that children be randomly assigned to integrated settings, and they were able to collect measures before and after integration in another case. They collected data on achievement, motivation, cognitive style, sociometric status, and observations of classroom peer interaction. Data analysis consisted largely of comparisons among groups. Among the more interesting findings was the fact that the observation and sociometric data provided opposite results: Observed interaction of educable mentally retarded children with peers was more positive in regular classes than in special classes, but peer acceptance of educable mentally retarded children by nonretarded children was less favorable when the children were integrated into regular classes. These latter data are consistent with the data that have thus far appeared in the large scale studies. Integrated handicapped children appear to adapt socially about as well as their nonhandicapped peers. Yet their popularity tends to be considerably below average.

Critique of Studies and Alternative Evaluation Strategies

Although the information from the mainstreaming studies has been well received and further findings are eagerly awaited, it is important to recognize their limitations when planning further evaluation studies. Perhaps the most significant weakness was the relative inattention to theory prior to collecting data. A disproportionate amount of time was spent in instrumentation, data analysis, and interpretation subsequent to data collection. Conceptualization appeared to be limited to a specification of relevant variables. Simple linear, additive relationships tended to be assumed. The complexities of relationships among variables were left to the computer to sort out.

What alternatives are there to these strategies? First of all, what theoretical formulations have promise? While it is certain that a number of promising formulations will derive from the report on Project PRIME, these conceptualizations will tend to be limited by the type of data to be interpreted. Instead, the authors would like to suggest frameworks uninfluenced by existing evaluation studies. One promising set of hypotheses has been proposed by Richer (1976). He was attempting to clarify what is called reference group theory in sociology by applying it to ability grouping. Given the enormous and conflicting body of literature on ability grouping (of which special classes and mainstreaming are special cases), any theoretical formulation that can provide some clarification of it should be promising for evaluating mainstreaming programs. A reference group is essentially any group, actual or imagined, that influences one's behavior. The influence is cognitive; that is, by the individual thinking of the group, the group influences the individual. There are two types of reference groups, normative and comparative. The normative reference group serves "as a source for [one's own] norms, attitudes, and values, while a comparative group is one serving as a standard of comparison for self appraisal" (Kelley, 1952, p. 412). Richer saw much of the debate over the advantages of ability grouping as revolving around whether for a low ability child in a heterogeneous class, the higher ability group will result in the low ability child comparing himself with the others

and perceiving himself as relatively deprived or responding to the higher ability group's norms and emulating them. The debate certainly sounds familiar, though with a different terminology.

Richer suggested that the ambiguity of findings on ability grouping is the result of a lack of identification of the classroom conditions most likely to influence reference group processes. For such processes to occur, the reference group must be salient, that is, visible and meaningful or prominent. This might be more likely to occur if teachers group the class into a small number of ability groupings and/or if the class is small. Even though visible, however, Richer pointed out that the high ability group may not be a meaningful reference group if it differs in too many other ways from the low ability child. However, meaningfulness of ability grouping may be increased if the teacher rewards the groups differentially.

Given the salience of the higher ability group, the choice of whether the group is taken as a comparative or normative reference group was seen by Richer to depend on the perceived possibility of upward mobility. The higher the perceived upward mobility, the greater the likelihood of the high ability group being taken as a normative reference group rather than a comparative one. The perception of mobility is least likely if grouping is by IQ rather than by achievement in specific subjects. "The more subgroups of different status a person belongs to, the more likely that low status in one group is rendered relatively unimportant" (Richer, 1976, p. 67).

This conceptualization raises a number of questions relevant to the assessment of mainstreaming programs: How salient are the special class, the resource room, and the regular class to the integrated child? How salient are subgroups within the regular class? How great is the association between ethnic background and grouping? Does the integrated child perceive that he or she becomes a real member of this higher ability group?

Aside from such general social-psychological theoretical formulations, a number of more limited conceptualizations could be of value. Certain critical factors tend to be ignored. Thus the period of time in regular and special classes is rarely taken into account. For example, should it be assumed that things change immediately upon entry into the regular class and remain constant over months or years, or is there adaptation? Perhaps the opposite occurs: Initial success is followed by depressed performance and self acceptance. Even when important factors are identified, overly simplified relationships are assumed. Curvilinear relationships need to be considered. For example, increasing the amount of supportive services received by a regular teacher may not continue to have favorable impact but may instead reach an optimal level after which it interferes with achievement and acceptance. Perhaps too much intrusion of special efforts begins to break up the structured efforts of the regular program and tends to set the child apart from others.

Finally, there is a need to deal more fully with the complexities of the individual case—the individual child, the individual school—perhaps using the qualitative methods of the anthropologist (e.g., Edgerton, 1975) or perhaps the quantitative methods of behaviorists (e.g., Herson & Barlow, 1976). Methods must then be developed for accumulating these complex data over individual cases in such a way that the resulting information is usable for decision making at the program level (e.g., Glass, 1976). It is necessary to know whether, overall, the program is relatively effective, but it is also necessary to know whether certain kinds of programs are more effective for certain kinds of children and school systems than for others.

To conclude, one of the greatest needs in future approaches to the evaluation of mainstreaming programs is to provide an adequate conceptualization of the processes involved. Both theory and methodology need to avoid the oversimplification of traditional educational research. The methodology needs to incorporate qualitative as well as quantitative procedures and intensive analysis of individual cases as well as methods for accumulating information over cases, school systems, and studies. Perhaps the best place to begin conceptualization and the development of methodology is with analyses of the nature of the mainstreaming treatment.

Evaluating Educational Treatments in Mainstreamed Settings

Instructional Time

The main thrust of mainstreamed education to date has concerned class placement. That is, mainstreaming has been defined by schools in terms of the amount of time a handicapped child spends in regular classes, for academic and/or nonacademic purposes. Although few data are available regarding the benefits that accrue to handicapped children who are placed in regular classes for differing amounts of time, the data that

do exist suggest that amount of time integrated per se has relatively little impact on the way other children feel about them (Gottlieb, 1975; Gottlieb & Baker, 1975). That is, children who are mainstreamed for approximately 10% of the school day do not differ significantly in social status from children who are mainstreamed for approximately 90% of the school day.

One reason for such apparently disappointing results could be that these studies did not consider the quality of educational treatments that were provided to the handicapped children when they were in the regular classes. It is to this theme—the manner in which handicapped children are instructionally integrated and the way that instructional integration is to be evaluated by teachers—that we now turn. The discussion will not focus on formal aspects of evaluating mainstreaming programs which necessitate appropriate statistical analyses but rather on more informal concerns which usually emerge when school personnel undertake self study or self evaluation of their school's programs.

Instructional Integration

Kaufman et al. (1975) wrote that instructional integration concerns the extent to which the handicapped child shares in the instructional environment of the regular class. In order for the handicapped child to share in the instruction that is offered in the regular class, at least three conditions must be satisfied. First, the handicapped child's educational needs must be compatible with the instruction that is offered to the nonhandicapped children. An illustration of a lack of compatibility is the situation where a handicapped child is assigned art work while classmates are engaged in reading lessons. The second condition that must exist for instructional integration to occur is for the regular class teacher to be willing to modify instructional practices to accommodate a child whose learning style or ability may be seriously discrepant from the remaining students in the class. The third facet of instructional integration is the need for a coordinated effort between the regular classroom teacher and the supportive personnel available in the school or district.

Educational treatments that are delivered under the rubric of mainstreamed education can be evaluated, then, with regard to the extent that they achieve the conditions just presented under the heading of instructional integration. Each element of instructional integration can then be considered in relation to the quality of the educational treatment that it was intended to achieve, and indexes regarding its successful implementation can be suggested.

Stating Goals and Objectives

Historically, one of the criticisms that has been levied against special education research has been its failure to specify the nature of the educational program that handicapped children receive. Although this criticism was originally voiced by Kirk (1964) in his comments regarding special classes, it is equally applicable with regard to handicapped children in mainstreamed settings. Before any evaluation of educational programs in mainstreamed settings is possible, there must be a clear statement about the academic goals and objectives that the handicapped child is expected to attain in the regular classroom. In the absence of such a statement there is little reason to expect that a meaningful educational program will be developed. Often, the primary goal in placing handicapped children in a regular class is not for academic purposes but to promote their social behavior by exposing them to appropriate peer models and/or by providing them with competitive situations that they ultimately must experience if they are to succeed as adults. While these are laudable goals for a handicapped child, they should be recognized for what they are: social goals, not academic goals. There is little reason to expect handicapped children to improve their academic competence if the primary purpose for mainstreaming them is to promote social competence. To summarize this point, an evaluation of mainstreamed educational treatments must begin by obtaining a clear statement on whether or not the purpose of placing the handicapped child in the regular class is to improve academic performance.

If it is established that a handicapped child is placed in a regular class for a specific academic purpose, the logical question that must be asked is whether the ongoing lessons are consonant with the stated goals. What active steps is the regular class teacher taking to facilitate the child's likelihood of accomplishing the goals that were established on the child's behalf? There is no simple answer to this question, because the material the teacher offers the handicapped child, or any child for that matter, depends on the type of classroom the teacher manages. However, although no precise data are available, data that do exist suggest that few regular teachers are taking the time to provide the handicapped child with special materials or teaching methods. Agard (1975), in a study of

several hundred regular classrooms, found that approximately 75% of regular class instruction occurred in large groups with the teacher standing front and center. Under such circumstances there is only a remote likelihood that the regular class teacher is providing anything "special" to the mainstreamed handicapped child. Therefore, a second consideration in evaluating programs for handicapped children is to obtain descriptive information regarding the content of academic activity that they are engaged in while in the regular classroom.

Assessing Teacher Willingness to Accommodate the Handicapped Child

The content that a handicapped child participates in is dictated in large part by the regular class teacher's willingness to tailor the class lessons to accommodate the individual needs of a handicapped child. This brings us to the second major aspect of instructional integration: willingness to modify instruction to accommodate the handicapped child.

Whether or not a teacher will provide an appropriate educational program for a handicapped child depends on a number of factors including the teacher's self perceived ability to teach a particular child, the extent to which the handicapped child deviates from the modal performance level of the children in the class, and the teacher's attitude toward that child.

Research evidence does exist to show that the overwhelming majority of regular class teachers feel that they are ill equipped to deal with handicapped children. As an example, Gickling and Theobald (1975) found that 85% of the regular education teachers they queried felt they lacked the necessary skills to teach exceptional children. These findings are consonant with Agard's (1975), who found that the majority of regular class teachers stood front and center and lectured to the class as a whole. In other words, these teachers were not doing anything extraordinary to accommodate the needs of exceptional children in their classes. The picture that develops regarding regular class teacher activity vis-à-vis exceptional children also conforms to data from more traditional attitude studies where regular class teachers' attitudes toward retarded children were negative and became increasingly more negative after a year's experience teaching them. This was shown, for instance, in the study conducted by Shotel, Iano, and McGettigan (1972). Overall, these studies indicate that regular class teachers harbor generally negative attitudes, and their instructional practices are not geared toward accommodating children whose ability levels and needs are widely discrepant from those of the majority of pupils in their classes. Therefore, a second point to consider when evaluating educational treatments is to identify precisely what the teacher is doing to tailor instructional strategies to accommodate handicapped children. Here, too, straightforward descriptive data will suffice.

Until now, the discussion has focused exclusively on the regular class teacher, but clearly this is only half the picture. It is obvious that an educational program for mainstreamed handicapped children requires the cooperation of regular and special education teachers. A substantial portion of handicapped children's academic instruction is obtained in resource rooms, which are most often staffed by trained special education teachers. One index of the effectiveness of an academic program for mainstreamed handicapped children is the extent to which regular and special class teachers interface and share responsibility for the child's educational program. Ideally, an articulated program involving coordination between regular and special class teachers evolves from regularly scheduled meetings in which the teachers discuss materials, methods that have been appropriate for the child, and, in general, the child's level of progress in the regular classroom. All too often the coordination between regular and special class teachers is conducted on a catch-as-catch-can basis, with the special education teacher discussing a particular child over lunch, sometimes; during a break, sometimes; or after school, sometimes. It is difficult to imagine an effective, well articulated program being developed from such haphazard meetings. This is less of a problem when the mainstreaming concept involves having the special education teacher assist the handicapped child directly in the regular classroom rather than in the resource room.

Monitoring Child Progress

Yet another concern when evaluating the effectiveness of mainstreamed education for a particular child is the steps that are routinely taken to monitor the child's progress. Once a program has been established for a child, how long will it be implemented before someone decides whether it is an appropriate program for that child? It is unreasonable to expect that a single educational plan is likely to be appropriate for all children all the time. But when is this decision made? And by whom? Evaluations of mainstreamed programs should consider whether there are any mecha-

nisms built into the system to decide whether the educational treatment is proving effective, by whatever criteria are valued by that school system.

The issue of what is being taught to a handicapped child is far more important than where it is being taught. A review of the literature on the effects of mainstreamed versus nonmainstreamed education on the academic performance of mentally retarded children suggests that there is little if any difference in the achievement gains made by these children regardless of their placement. There is tentative evidence, however, that instructional strategies can affect achievement of retarded children, as was demonstrated by Haring and Krug (1975). Unfortunately, despite the voluminous amount of prose on mainstreaming that has appeared in the published literature, pitifully few writings have discussed the merits of various approaches to mainstreaming while also presenting relevant data to support their assertions. In fact, empirical studies of mainstreaming, especially with regard to its impact on the academic achievement of handicapped children, have been few and far between. Federal legislation has mandated that handicapped children are to be educated in the least restrictive environment to the maximum extent feasible. It is difficult to imagine how the maximum extent feasible is going to be determined in the absence of empirical verification that the practices subsumed under the general rubric of mainstreaming are worthwhile insofar as they have a positive effect on handicapped children's educational performance. Thus, while it is critical that program evaluation provide data describing the type of treatment implemented, it is also essential that data be collected describing the consequence of the treatment.

Dependent Measures

If the true impact of mainstreaming is to be known, information will be needed from a variety of sources. Among more obvious data needs are those on student achievement and on attitudes of administrators, teachers, parents, and pupils. Data on school attendance rates, student adjustment and acceptance, and program cost-effectiveness will be needed as well. Ideally, such information should be obtained on nonmainstreamed pupils, since there has been concern that mainstreaming may impact negatively upon the adjustment and achievement of the regular class pupil. Some, including students, teachers, parents, and administrators, believe that the time teachers take to provide instruction to the mainstreamed student makes the teacher less accessible to regular students. Moreover, the classroom environment is thought to be less stimulating and demanding because of the presence of such students. Convincing data will need to be accumulated on such matters to allay the misgivings noted.

A description of certain dependent measures that ought to be included in mainstream evaluation reports is presented in Table 1, which also includes the measures' means of assessment.

There are a number of factors to be considered in using the measures described. First, concerning attitudinal measures, no scales of known validity and reliability have been developed for use with mainstreamed populations. There are a number of problems attendant to the use of such instruments, including the establishment of their validity.

A special problem is developing scales that are not so transparent that their purposes are easily detected, with the consequence that the respondents may manipulate their responses and thus distort the nature of their true attitudes. There are, however, problems that precede actual scale development and use. These concern the political realm and respondent protection from invasion of privacy. In the latter case, the rights of subjects to their own minds and thoughts may prohibit use of conventional attitudinal scales with students or with teachers and others (e.g., parents and school administrators). These same potential problems may impede the collection of data on student adjustment and social acceptance; the requirement that students reveal their likes and dislikes for their classmates will be unacceptable to many school administrators, parents, teachers, and the students themselves.

The requirement that students (and others) be protected from undue invasion of privacy will make it difficult to obtain some of the kinds of data needed for comprehensive evaluation of main-

stream programs. Little thought appears to have been given to alternative nonreactive methods of accumulating data on attitudes, acceptance, and adjustment, but the use of observational schemes and unobtrusive methods may prove beneficial and is recommended.

There are also special considerations in the use of achievement tests. The advantages of standardized achievement tests are well known: They have been developed on large numbers of children; they possess adequate reliability for group assessment; and they cover the range of objectives often found in many school programs. On the other hand, they have not typically included, in their standardization population, children who are candidates for mainstreaming. A consequence of this neglect is that attention may not have been given to the phrasing of questions, to format, or to other concerns that might make the test more useful for application to the mainstreamed student. Moreover, since most standardized achievement tests are designed to provide information about the performance of students in the vast middle range, the content is probably not valid or reliable for students outside that range.

Fortunately, the above problems are not as grave as was once believed to be the case. Yoshida (1976) and his associates (Meyers, MacMillan, & Yoshida, 1975a; Nystrom, Yoshida, Meyers, & MacMillan, 1977) have explored a variety of techniques for using conventional standardized tests with populations of exceptional children, including educable mentally retarded children returned to regular classes (Yoshida, 1976) and educationally handicapped children (Nystrom et al., 1977). The authors of these studies have demonstrated that through use of procedures such as out-of-level testing, in which standardized tests more appropriate to the student's level of functioning are adminis-

Table 1. Dependent Measures

Measure	Method of assessment
Student achievement	Standardized tests, locally constructed tests
Attitudes of administrators, teachers, parents	Attitude questionnaires, interviews, observations
Student adjustment	Observations, inventories, and questionnaires
Student acceptance	Sociometric methods, observations, inventories, and questionnaires
Cost effectiveness	Examination of expenditures in relationship to specified alternative objectives
School attendance	Attendance rolls

tered rather than those based on chronological age or grade placement, data on the mainstreamed child's level of achievement can be obtained. Thus, a mainstreamed child in the fifth grade may be given an achievement test appropriate for students in the second or third grade, the decision about appropriate level being made on the basis of teacher judgment and/or the student's past academic performance. The question that arises is whether or not the psychometric properties of the tests (e.g., reliability, validity, and the percentage of respondents scoring above chance levels) are affected by such testing procedures. Yoshida's (1976) work with educable mentally retarded students returned to regular classes indicated that these test properties are not affected at all, indicating that reliable information on student achievement may be obtained using the out-of-level procedure. It should be obvious that necessity for use of the out-of-level procedure suggests, *ipso facto*, that the mainstreamed child probably is not approximating grade level achievement expectations. If the child were, unmodified tests could be used.

Addressing similar concerns (i.e., modifying tests for use with the handicapped), Nystrom et al. (1977) investigated the effects of group size (testing in groups of two, four, or eight students) and group behavioral characteristics (behavior in testing situation) on the achievement scores of mainstreamed educationally handicapped students. They found no differences in test performance or frequency of disruptive behavior by group size under the experimental testing conditions as contrasted with the report that 63% of the students were unable to complete the testing in their regular classrooms. The small group method of administering achievement tests to educationally handicapped children is clearly the method of choice.

On the basis of their work with the administration of the Metropolitan Achievement Test (MAT) to a large population of decertified educable mentally retarded children, Meyers et al. (1975a) evolved a series of quite innovative procedures designed to

maximize motivation and test-wiseness of the examinees without sacrificing the standardization of the test proper. For example, students were told that they were not being evaluated for placement in any special program, were asked to respond to all questions even if they had only partial comprehension of specific questions, responded only in test booklets to eliminate errors due to unfamiliarity with separate answer sheets, were given extended rest periods to counter fatigue and frustration caused by a novel situation. Within the test proper, no suggested

procedure was modified; time limits for completing the subtests were followed strictly, test batteries were administered whenever possible on separate days, especially at the lower levels of the MAT. (p. 6)

Although experimental, the work of Meyers et al. has great promise for adapting standardized achievement tests with mainstreamed and other populations of handicapped children.

Racial and Socioeconomic Bias. The mainstream program evaluator also needs to be sensitive to the questions of potential racial and socioeconomic bias in cognitive tests. These questions revert, ultimately, to whether the tests are valid for the population(s) to which they are applied. Hilliard (1975) presented a list of "implicit assumptions" made by test users as a basis upon which tests are interpreted. Those relevant to present concerns include the following: (a) Each child understands the question being asked in the same way. (b) A child's cognitive function is observable only through the Anglo language and the Anglo value framework based upon Anglo experiences. (c) All people have the same experiences; therefore the same questions can be asked of everyone. A corollary assumption is: A question means the same thing in all environments. (d) A label or name for a cognitive component is a precise description of the whole component (Hilliard, 1975, p. 19). Obviously, these assumptions cannot be accepted for children from greatly different racial and socioeconomic backgrounds.

Evaluation within the Context of Public Law 94–142

Evaluation is a key feature of Public Law 94–142, the Education for All Handicapped Children Act. Section 618 of the Act is devoted specifically to evaluation. In this section the Commissioner of Education is enjoined to "measure and evaluate the impact of the program authorized . . . and the effectiveness of State efforts to assure the free appropriate public education of all handicapped children" (p. 63).

Many considerations relevant to evaluation of Public Law 94–142 have been given in preceding pages, particularly those related to the Act's requirement that the Commissioner of Education provide for the evaluation of programs and projects by developing effective methods and procedures of evaluation, the testing and validation of the methods and procedures, and the conduct of actual evaluation studies designed to test the effectiveness of the programs and projects. However, two of the specific major evaluation activities specified by the Act deserve special attention: (a) the requirement that the numbers of children being served and not served (The Numbers Game) be reported annually and (b) the requirement "that the Commissioner shall conduct a statistically valid survey for assessing the effectiveness of individualized education programs" (p. 65).

The Numbers Game

Public Law 94–142 requires federal, state, and district officials to provide data on the number of children served; that is, number of children mainstreamed, number removed from self contained special classes, decrease in the number of minority group children in self contained special classes, and so forth. While this information has its purposes and is among the easiest to obtain, it is also among the most useless, primarily because of issues that it does not address, for example, the appropriateness of the alternative educational placement and resulting improvement (or lack of it) in social adjustment, academic achievement, and other outcomes presumed to accompany mainstream placement. While various agencies will be required to provide such data in connection with the requirements of Public Law 94–142, deeper explorations of instructional practices, as suggested in earlier sections of this article, must be undertaken.

Evaluating the Individualized Education Program Concept

Evaluating the appropriateness of individualized education programs (IEP's) will be among the knottiest problems that evaluators of mainstream programs will face. This is true for programs designed to facilitate academic achievement, social growth and development, or both. Although there has been progress (Yoshida, 1976), questions about the availability of appropriate measures for assessing the accomplishments of students in special populations have not been entirely resolved (Jones, 1973, 1976).

The most critical problem, however, concerns the assumption that valid information is available on the growth and development of academic and social abilities of special populations, that something is known about the conditions under which such growth and development take place or about the upper level of growth of various kinds of achievement for different populations of mainstreamable and/or handicapped children. Regrettably, no such knowledge exists. It cannot be said with any certainty how much growth change can

be expected to occur in students with various profiles taught by method A or by method B, the answer to which is critical to assessing the adequacy of individualized education programs.

Further, Morrisey and Safer (1977), in addressing problems related to the evaluation of individualized education programs, noted:

> To measure program/IEP's effectiveness in terms of pupil change indicators (e.g. achievement) it would be necessary to confirm that what was prescribed was implemented, and that the variance which was observed/measured could be accounted for in terms of the implementation. This would be a particularly difficult change since IEP related activities will have varying correspondence to elements of the prescribed educational plan and take up varying amounts of the instructional day. These problems, coupled with the inherent difficulties in pretest/post-test methods of measuring/recording pupil performance, suggest that it may be methodologically difficult to assess IEP effectiveness in this way. Moreover, the precision and frequency of documentation that would be required to collect reliable and valid data, make the use of such methods prohibitive. Therefore it may be most desirable to consider multiple and varied measures of effectiveness—cost, resources, satisfaction, and pupil measures. At any rate, determining appropriate measures of effectiveness will be an initial and difficult task. (pp. 35–36)

It is true, but not enough, to say that more research is needed. Students are in classrooms now, and individualized education programs must be developed for them now. How, then, is evaluation of the effectiveness of IEP's to be made? The authors believe, given the current state of knowledge about relationships between instructional achievements and academic and social growth in populations of exceptional children, that IEP's can be evaluated only for their content appropriateness (face validity); that is, the assessment of experienced teachers about what is likely to work and what is not likely to work (with sensitivity to the need to monitor instructional activities constantly and to modify programs when changes are appropriate) seems to reflect the state of the art with respect to the evaluation of IEP's. It would be helpful if programs of research and development could be carried on alongside the ongoing instructional activity, but often this will not be possible, primarily because of limited personnel and fiscal resources. Some research and evaluation activity will be conducted, to be sure, but there would also seem to be great value in having a forum in which teachers and program developers could present the results

EVALUATION CONSIDERATIONS

1. Is the purpose of the evaluation described?
2. Is the reader given sufficient information to determine whether the evaluation is formative (i.e., for instructional improvement) or summative (i.e., a final program evaluation) or both?
3. Are the evaluation procedures and results clearly reported?
4. Is sufficient information provided to enable replication of the evaluation?
5. Are the evaluation procedures practical?
6. Is the intended audience specified?
7. Is there a description of the model(s) of mainstreaming employed, with sufficient data to permit an understanding of the kind of educational procedures followed?
8. Is information provided on the length of time that the mainstreaming model employed has been operational in the school(s) evaluated?
9. Is the number of hours of instructional integration given?
10. Are data given on school district location and size and on school and community characteristics?
11. Are the subjects, including regular classmates, described adequately (i.e., age, grade, sex, previous educational history, socioeconomic class, racial group membership)?
12. Are the means by which students are selected for mainstreaming described?
13. Is there information on whether the mainstreamed pupils were formerly enrolled in self contained special classes?
14. Is length of time the children were mainstreamed prior to evaluation activities given?
15. Are sample sizes adequate?
16. Was there reasonable sample stability during the evaluation period?
17. Is information on the experiential background of the teacher(s) provided?
18. Are evaluation instruments described?
19. Do the instruments possess satisfactory validity and reliability for the population of mainstreamed students involved in the evaluation?
20. Are statistical procedures appropriate?
21. Is attention given to the appropriateness of placement?
22. Is there assessment of instructional quality?
23. Is information provided on student achievement?
24. Is information provided on the attitudes of students, teachers, administrators, and parents?
25. Is information provided on student adjustment?
26. Is information provided on the social acceptance of the mainstreamed student?
27. Are data on the attendance rates of mainstreamed students presented?
28. Are cost-effectiveness data provided?
29. Is attention given to program impact on nonmainstreamed students?
30. Are political realities described and taken into account in program planning and program evaluation?
31. Are names and addresses of program planners and evaluators provided so that additional inquiries can be made?

Figure 1. Considerations for Preparing and Assessing Reports of
Mainstream Program Evaluation

of their experiences with various kinds of mainstream models and procedures, including their data and hunches about what seems to work and what does not.

Although conventional wisdom suggests that rigorous evaluation designs are necessary to determine the effectiveness of educational programs, teachers can play a critically important role in the evaluation of mainstreaming. It is the teachers, not the evaluators, who are in constant contact with the children, materials, and daily problems that arise. Whether or not mainstreaming will prove effective rests primarily in the hands of the teachers. The educational treatments they provide must at least be evaluated by them, however informally. There is nothing to be gained from ignoring this important source of information; moreover, teacher experiences and insights are likely to inform research and evaluation activities in a way that will make them much more useful than is presently the case.

Guidelines for Preparing and Appraising Mainstream Evaluation Reports

Most of the information on the evaluation of mainstream programs comes from unpublished studies. There would seem to be a critical need for a set of guidelines by which such reports can be appraised. Ideally, such guidelines should be followed by individuals preparing mainstream evaluation reports as well. To the extent that common guidelines are followed, it will also become possible to accumulate information from a large number of separate evaluation activities.

Evaluations are conducted for many purposes. Some evaluations are conducted for local use only, and others are intended to be generalized widely. In presenting guidelines herein, the authors are assuming that the evaluator intends to communicate the procedures and results to an audience wider than those having intimate involvement with the project. If this is the objective, reporting may need to be fuller than would be the case for strictly in-house reports. Evaluators who do not wish to provide complete data on populations, procedures, and so forth should keep their reports out of major dissemination channels (e.g., ERIC, *Exceptional Child Education Resources,* etc.) since partial and incomplete evaluation studies do more to confuse than to clarify.

It is obviously impossible to specify what ought to be included in each evaluation report, since report content will vary as a function of evaluation purposes and intended audience. Nevertheless, to give the reader a sense of the range of factors that ought to be considered in preparing or appraising mainstream evaluation reports, a fairly comprehensive set of evaluation guidelines for such work is presented in Figure 1. The authors recognize that the results of any single evaluation will rarely be reported in such detail.

Concluding Remarks

This article has attempted to present a variety of considerations related to the evaluation of

mainstreaming programs, and to set forth guidelines for the preparation and appraisal of mainstreaming evaluation reports. It should be apparent from the foregoing analyses that problems related to the evaluation of mainstreaming programs are not insurmountable. By giving early attention to matters addressed here, many pitfalls characterizing previous special education evaluation efforts can be avoided, and it will become possible to use evaluative procedures to improve instructional practices and, in time, to know the effectiveness of mainstreaming efforts.

References

Agard, J. A. *The classroom ecological structure: An approach to the specification of the treatment problem.* Paper presented at annual meeting of the American Educational Research Association, Washington, D.C., 1975.

Budoff, M., & Gottlieb, J. Special class EMR children mainstreamed: A study of an aptitude (learning potential) × treatment interaction. *American Journal of Mental Deficiency,* 1976, 81, 1–11.

Coleman, J. S., Campbell, E. Q., Hobson, C. J., MacPartland, J., Mood, A. M., Weinfield, F. D., & York, R. L. *Equality of educational opportunity.* Washington, D.C.: US Government Printing Office, 1966.

Dunn, L. M. Special education for the mildly retarded: Is much of it justifiable? *Exceptional Children,* 1968, 35, 5–22.

Edgerton, R. B. Issues related to the quality of life among mentally retarded persons. In M. J. Begab & S. A. Richardson (Eds.), *The mentally retarded society.* Baltimore: University Park Press, 1975.

Gickling, E. E., & Theobald, J. T. Mainstreaming: Affect or effect. *Journal of Special Education,* 1975, 9, 317–328.

Glass, G. V. Primary, secondary, and meta-analysis of research. *The Educational Researcher,* 1976, 10, 3–8.

Goldstein, H., Moss, J., & Jordan, J. *The efficacy of special class training on the development of mentally retarded children* (Cooperative Research Project No. 619). Washington, D.C.: US Office of Education, 1965.

Goodman, H., Gottlieb, J., & Harrison, R. H. Social acceptance of EMR children integrated into a nongraded elementary school. *American Journal of Mental Deficiency*, 1972, 77, 412–417.

Gottlieb, J. *Predictors of social status among mainstreamed mentally retarded pupils.* Paper presented at annual meeting of American Association on Mental Deficiency, Portland, 1975.

Gottlieb, J., & Baker, J. L. *The relationship between amount of time integrated and the sociometric status of retarded children.* Paper presented at annual meeting of American Educational Research Association, Washington, D.C., 1975.

Gottlieb, J., & Budoff, M. Social acceptability of retarded children in nongraded schools differing in architecture. *American Journal of Mental Deficiency*, 1973, 78, 15–19.

Gottlieb, J., Gampel, D. H., & Budoff, M. Classroom behaviors of retarded children before and after reintegration into regular classes. *Journal of Special Education*, 1975, 9, 307–315.

Guskin, S., & Spicker, H. Educational research in mental retardation. In N. R. Ellis (Ed.), *International review of research in mental retardation* (Vol. 3). New York: Academic Press, 1968.

Haring, N. G., & Krug, D. A. Placement in regular programs: Procedures and results. *Exceptional Children*, 1975, 41, 413–417.

Herson, M., & Barlow, D. H. *Single case experimental designs: Strategies for studying behavioral change.* Elmsford, NY: Pergamon, 1976.

Hilliard, A. The strengths and weaknesses of cognitive tests for young children. In J. D. Andrews (Ed.), *One child indivisible.* Washington, D.C.: National Association for the Education of Young Children, 1975.

Jones, R. L. Accountability in special education: Some problems. *Exceptional Children*, 1973, 39, 631–642.

Jones, R. L. Evaluating mainstream programs for minority children. In R. L. Jones (Ed.), *Mainstreaming and the minority child.* Reston, VA: The Council for Exceptional Children, 1976.

Kaufman, M., Agard, J. A., & Semmel, M. I. *Mainstreaming: Learners and their environment.* Bloomington: Indiana University Press, 1978.

Kaufman, M. J., Gottlieb, J., Agard, J. A., & Kukic, M. B. Mainstreaming: Toward an explication of the construct. *Focus on Exceptional Children*, 1975, 7, 1–12.

Kelley, H. Two functions of reference groups. In G. E. Swanson et al. (Eds.), *Readings in social psychology.* New York: Holt, 1952.

Kirk, S. A. Research in education. In H. Stevens & R. Heber (Eds.), *Mental retardation: A review of research.* Chicago: University of Chicago Press, 1964.

Meyers, C. E., MacMillan, D. L., & Yoshida, R. K. *Correlates of success in the transition of MR to regular class* (Final Report OEE 0-73-5263). Washington, D.C.: Bureau of Education for the Handicapped, 1975. (ERIC Document Reproduction Service No. ED 116 441) (a)

Meyers, C. E., MacMillan, D. L., & Yoshida, R. K. *Evaluation of special education programs.* Paper presented at the Second Annual Conference on Measurement and Evaluation, Los Angeles County Schools, Los Angeles, February 1975. (b)

Morrisey, P. A., & Safer, N. Implications for special education—The individualized education program. *Viewpoints*, 1977, 53, 31–38.

Nystrom, K., Yoshida, R. K., Meyers, C. E., & MacMillan, D. L. *Standardized achievement measurement with the mainstreamed educationally handicapped—Normalization or further segregation?* Unpublished paper, Neuropsychiatric Institute, Pacific State Research Group, Pomona, California, 1977.

Public Law 94–142, *Education for All Handicapped Children Act*, November 29, 1975.

Richer, S. Reference-group theory and ability grouping: A convergence of sociological theory and educational research. *Sociology of Education*, 1976, 49, 65–71.

Semmel, M. I., Semmel, D. S., & Morrisey, P. A. *Competency-based teacher education in special education: A review of research and training programs.* Bloomington: Center for Innovation in Teaching the Handicapped, Indiana University, 1976.

Shotel, J. R., Iano, R. P., & McGettigan, J. F. Teacher attitudes associated with the integration of handicapped children. *Exceptional Children*, 1972, 38, 677–683.

Stufflebeam, D. Relevance of the CIPP model for educational accountability. *Journal of Research and Development in Education*, 1971, 5, 19–25.

Thiagarajan, S., Semmel, D. S., & Semmel, M. I. *Instructional development for training teachers of exceptional children: A source book.* Reston, VA: The Council for Exceptional Children, 1974.

Yoshida, R. K. Out-of-level testing of special education students with a standardized achievement battery. *Journal of Educational Measurement*, 1976, *13*, 215–221.

Zimiles, H. An analysis of current issues in the evaluation of educational programs. In J. Hellmuth (Ed.), *The disadvantaged child* (Vol. 2). Seattle: Special Child Publications, 1968.

Reprinted from *Exceptional Children* 44 (1978): 588–601, by permission of The Council for Exceptional Children. Copyright 1978 by The Council for Exceptional Children.

Editors' Commentary

We have not dealt extensively with specific classroom methods for dealing with emotionally impaired youngsters in regular classrooms. The reason is that the individualization of curriculum and method has the same dynamics whether in mainstream or in special class. This process of individualizing education is taken up in detail elsewhere in this book, from understanding the specific problem behavior to implementing changes in method and content. While there is sometimes an automatic benefit to having the special child with normal students, this is often not enough. Since most special children also are behavior problems in the classroom, few spontaneous positive changes can be expected due to the dynamics of the group, teacher or curriculum. If left alone, these troubled pupils will continue their cycle of failure.

We are now embarked upon a crusade to make all teachers special education teachers, through pre- and in-service training. We sometimes forget the logistics problems these teachers face in class size and with groups which have negative feelings toward authority and learning. Paul, Turnbull, and Cruickshank[2] discuss thoroughly the efforts that must be undertaken to meet the resistance. They are among the few who see that it is not only teachers and school specialists but also parents, and the community who must be acclimated to the changes. There have been many efforts to change the schools: in fact, there is one at least every other year. As Silberman says, in *Crisis in the Classroom*,[3] they don't get far because they do not deal with the essential aspects of organization, the social role given to schools, the group nature of the operation, and the rigidity of the curriculum and methods. Let us not take the task lightly in implementing the new law.

It has frequently been said about mainstreaming, in Pogo's words, we have met the enemy and they are us. Change is never easy, and the magnitude of the implications of Public Law 94–142 is just beginning to be clear. All special educators have intensified responsibilities in communicating and helping the educational enterprise with the tasks of implementing the law. Special teachers will do their work in a variety of roles, but all educators must be prepared to play a part. Perhaps we may even be able to move from mainstream to life stream, where the whole community recognizes a responsibility for both exceptional children and exceptional adults.

2. **James L. Paul, Ann P. Turnbull, and William M. Cruickshank,** *Mainstreaming: A Practical Guide* (Syracuse, N.Y.: Syracuse University Press, 1977).

3. **Charles E. Silberman,** *Crisis in the Classroom* (New York: Random House, 1970).

8

The Measures of Success:
Evaluation and Innovation

Editors' Commentary

With the new legislative demand for free public education for all children in the *least restrictive environment* appropriate for their needs, with parent participation and vocational planning, the intent is to maximize integration into the mainstream but to have a spectrum of services available to fit a variety of pupil needs: mainstreaming with special education consultation and support; use of resource rooms; partially integrated classes; segregated classes; day schools; short- and long-term institutional care, followed by aftercare; and protected long-term provision for those who cannot move back into mainstream membership. All programs are to include the maximum educational components. As yet, few communities have the range of needed services or the right balance of provisions. And even when the services are available, there are other problems: How do we know which service is the least restrictive in terms of a given child's needs? If we could "know" what is best, could we persuade the parties involved to use that service? Judgments about needs and options are based on a series of "if/then" clauses. *If* the parents can change certain of their behaviors, *then* home would be best. *If* the child sees the long-run advantages of a given program, *then* that program would work out the best. *If* the mainstream teacher can adjust the work and the peers can be supportive, *then* a regular classroom is the placement of choice. There are more if/then clauses than certainty in special education.

It will soon be evident that the crux of the new special education is the individual education plan (IEP). Unfortunately the articulation of data collected, prognosis, specific interventions, and monitoring of interventions to determine efficacy is still in its infancy. Teachers are required to write an IEP for each special student. The goals may be stated in global terms (improve the self-concept) or specifics (add double digit columns). There are long bibliographies of goals from which the writers may select items. It is high time we became goal-oriented and specific, but that does not mean we now know how to articulate our information. At present, the burden of accountability is put on the teacher, when it should be on the total special education program. We are in danger of expecting teachers to perform the miracles we used to ascribe to therapists and magicians.

The task before us is clear: we must increase our psychological sophistication to match the surge in philosophical values. We have an opportunity to launch a new era in special education. But to prevent this from becoming only a paper or legal change we will have to develop new insights. Swift and Spivack[1] have done a masterful examination of the research on teaching disturbed pupils. They found there is a vast need for more knowledge on which to base practice. Studies that match personality traits and treatment styles would be very helpful. Cronbach and Snow[2] have dealt with one specific condition, anxiety, and variant treatments. The purpose of this chapter is to sharpen our wits about accountability by looking at some issues in evaluation.

On the subject of evaluative research, seldom does so little basic evidence so greatly influence direction. At present, evaluative research is required of almost every program. In general, the pressure for accountability has increased the production of psychologically fraudulent interpretations of research data, often with massive political implications (for example, the Headstart program funds were cut because of misleading research).

As MacMillan[3] has pointed out, problems of sample, nature of clientele, diagnosis, and teacher variables confound the issue. Early exploratory studies in one field on special education are continually offered as proof of intervention ineffectiveness in other areas. Thoughtful analyzers, however, are at last beginning to consider the vast complications in program evaluation. For example, Kendall[4] has given intensive thought to some basic concepts around segregated versus integrated special education. Among Kendall's eight variables to be considered in efficacy research are attitudes of teachers and children and the "goodness of fit" of the curriculum experience in both the integrated and the isolated setting. We know that the administrative format tells little, if anything, about the psychological experience of the individual child in either setting. A given psychological intervention cannot be evaluated apart from its prescriptive relationship to the problem it was intended to alleviate. Disturbed children are still given the available program, whether or not it is in tune with their needs. Although control groups may be an aid in evaluative research, they often provide further illusions, because no control group ever equals the experimental group in various significant dimensions. One simple observation should challenge glib acceptance of evaluative results: external interventions (from changing the child's teacher to family therapy) help certain children, and internal interventions (from "primal scream" to mechanical behavioristic approaches) appear to help other children, but no intervention yet devised "cures" every student.[5]

Even if a youngster has a given problem or set of problems and some type of "treatment" is provided, there are changes in his or her life other than the aspect under our surveillance. The part of life covered by planned intervention may range from less than .5 percent in many therapeutic efforts to close to 100 percent in residential milieus, where almost all waking hours are used for planned interventions. A close examination of the special class day often indicates that what actually takes place there has little relationship to the child's problem. The same is true of a series of therapy hours or tutoring sessions. Yet we evaluate this "therapeutic" experience as if it had the potency to effect great changes, even when it is not appropriate to the youngster's deep needs.

1. **Marshall S. Swift and George Spivack,** "Therapeutic Teaching: A Review of Teaching Methods for Behaviorally Troubled Children," *Journal of Special Education* 8 (1974): 259–288.

2. **Lee J. Cronbach and Richard E. Snow,** *Aptitude and Instructional Methods* (New York: Irvington Publishing Co., 1977), especially chap. 12.

3. **D. L. MacMillan,** "Special Education for the Mildly Retarded: Servant or Savant," *Focus on Exceptional Children* 2, no. 9 (1971): 1–11.

4. **D. Kendall,** "Toward Integration," *Special Education in Canada* (November 1971): 3–16.

5. **C. D. Catterall,** "Taxonomy of Prescriptive Interventions," *Journal of School Psychology* 8 (1970): 5–12.

Based on our own studies of evaluating interventions, we have adopted a research paradigm combining elements of behaviorist and case-study methods. The behaviorists taught us to look at the individual child and at precisely what is done to change him or her in specific ways. Case study involves a humanistic, dynamic view. Psychological technology is now available for dealing with single cases, the "N of 1."[6] Cases are combined for group analyses only when they present reasonably "identical" patterns of behavior that then can be related to a given psychological intervention. This is in contrast to the "shotgun" method, i.e., assuming we can unravel the nature of helping disturbed children (though each is a unique complex) by applying a common intervention. In group studies two supposedly similar groups are employed, an experimental (which gets the treatment) and a control (which gets nothing). If even small but statistically significant differences are found between the groups, due to large group size, the "significant" findings almost always cover up a more important result. Some children in each group improve and some in each group do not, regardless of the intervention and the significant group difference. Such assessments of the efficacy of interventions resemble weather reports with the probability of sunshine being just above chance. It may almost as well rain.

The "N of 1" paradigm for evaluating interventions follows this order: (1) gathering in-depth knowledge of the disturbed child to provide a sociopsychological assessment of the situation; (2) developing case-specific interventions directed to the child and/or environment; (3) acquiring evidence of the actual conduct of the intervention in its psychological substance; (4) monitoring possible unplanned positive and negative life-change events that may be more powerful and extensive than the planned interventions; (5) recognizing that the subject child may benefit from normal growth changes; (6) assessing the short-term outcomes and long-term follow-up. Unfortunately, we usually concentrate on evaluating what we do, whether it is relevant or not, rather than on finding specific relevant interventions. For example, in addition to evaluating the impact of the special class on disturbed children it is vitally important to find out and incorporate the impact of changes at home and elsewhere. One cannot assess the efficacy of the given intervention in an ecological vacuum. This is as true when a pupil *is* making progress as when he or she *is not*. A youngster who finds a peer pal, an adolescent who falls in love or gets a job, a family that overcomes poverty, a sibling who quits scapegoating—life is filled with fortuitous events that influence a child's life. Anyone recognizing the complications of children's lives should be hesitant to claim credit for a cure without knowing what has happened in both the external and the internal reality. Follow-up studies are particularly subject to these limitations, for they often assess the impact of a past program on the basis of the pupil's well-being in an entirely new set of conditions, after a return to the mainstream.

The effects of a special program often extend beyond the disturbed child, who may improve a little or not at all. Other youngsters who tried to adjust to that child's presence may now have growing room. A teacher who was formerly unable to meet the child's needs, may have a resurgence of resources for the others. Parents who were at the end of their endurance may now find relief that they are not called to school every other day. Perhaps the only value to the child personally will be a reduction in the continual conflict with a hostile environment. Or solving one problem may reveal a more serious deviation. The life space may be evaluated in many ways. Some changes may be for the better and others not.

The lack of generalizable conclusions should not be taken as depreciation of those who have done evaluation studies. Researchers have expended great energy over long periods of time; some have been willing to wait years to find results. Only the consum-

6. **W. C. Morse, J. Schnertfeger, and D. Golden,** *An Evaluative Approach to the Training of Teachers of Disturbed Preschool Children* (Ann Arbor: School of Education, University of Michigan, 1973).

ers who want instant answers and sure conclusions can ignore the equivocal aspects of the research.

The first article is a brief and insightful look ahead in the field of behavioral disorders.

Serving the Needs of Individuals with Behavior Disorders: An Interview with William C. Morse

[This selection was an interview article published by Exceptional Children *following William Morse's receipt of CEC's 1977 Wallin Award.]*

What would you view as the most significant development that has occurred in the area of behavior disorders during the last five years?

I would say that the biggest thing that has happened is the broadening of the concepts of intervention, that is, basically moving from a rather restrictive dynamic point of view to an inclusion of behavioristic and other learning approaches and to a greater appreciation of the ecological factors that tell us why some of the interventions that we try do not have long term permanence. I think this has probably been the biggest change in the way we have looked at things. We did not really have an ecological point of view before. Now we expect less to happen on the basis of how the individual changes and more on the basis of environmental input.

What new methods and techniques have proved to be successful in the education of behavior disordered students?

The main thing is the match of interventions with the type of the problem the youngster has. For example, if we take a child who has a serious neurotic conflict and apply only an external kind of measure of behavioristic approach, I think we are short changing that youngster. On the other hand, there are particular children with whom a behavioristic approach can be useful, such as in a child who has a value disorder or an attitudinal disposition that is alien to societal survival.

I see the main priority as matching the intervention with the type of problem the youngster has. We have to talk about the general personality style of the individual to decide what would be useful for that individual. We talk about individualizing the way we teach reading and everything else. It seems to me just as important to individualize and spot the method that might be used as well as the specific content that will alleviate the problem for an individual.

When we recognize that there are so many different ways to help a youngster, we focus on the specific intervention that will help a particular child. Some youngsters, for example, need a figure for identification; others may need success in school. We have to see the issues from the child's point of view and then use an appropriate technique. In my opinion, new methods and techniques are successful relative to our sophistication in diagnosing the child and his environment. The method does not predominate, the child predominates. This match is what I think we are coming to, which will make for more productive work with disturbed children and youth.

Which programs are currently productive and successful in the education of emotionally disturbed children?

What we have seen more than programs are particular people who have some charisma or some particular expertise. To give some examples, I think that Peter Knoblock is doing some interesting things at his alternative school, Jowonio; The Learning Place, in Syracuse, New York. There he is creating a mainstream type of intervention and relaxing the rigor and departmentalization of the academic setting. He has mostly normal children with a few disturbed kids all in a very small group with a considerable amount of adult input. This is quite expensive, but it is an example of somebody doing something innovative.

Nick Long's school in Washington, D.C., The Rose School, is another one where they are experimenting with various techniques. Certainly the whole development that Nick Hobbs started in Project Re Ed has been productive. His is a new approach that advocates working more with families and minimizing the institutional flavor.

I was impressed with some of the things that were going on when I visited England. They have what they call "The Mothers' Knee School" in which they attempt to replicate a family atmosphere in the school setting and help children find themselves through much less formal ways than we use. It isn't our concept of open education because they have some definite ideas about the kind of behavior they will accept and the kind of purposes they have. However, there is a great deal of attention to play and the use of activities to help children find themselves and establish their social relationships.

I also saw some work going on in one of the institutions in Scotland that impressed me. Again, however, it was an outgrowth of a particular person with unusual sensitivity. In this case, the individual had such a basic humanistic approach to things that he used a technique of discipline that would startle some of our people. If the youngster misbehaves and does something that violates the code, the adult who was in charge at that time sits down with the youngster and together they talk about what happened and why. The idea in this school about how to help children find themselves is to participate with them in their interaction far more intensively than most of our programs typify. The adult feels as responsible for the mistake as the youngster in the sense that the restoration to the institution is jointly performed by both the adult and the child. For example, if something gets broken, they have to repair it or do enough work to compensate for what it is going to cost. In other words, both of us together have a problem rather than you have the problem and I'm the adult overseeing your reparation.

Are you optimistic about the ability of our public schools generally to respond therapeutically to children?

Yes and no. There are promising things and then there are other things that make one wonder what's going on. First of all, we are in a tremendous financial bind in getting enough money to provide the resources. The things that I see on the positive side are definite new attitudes about what ought to happen, such as a more intense training for the teachers who are working in this area and a deepened expectation of using the schools with the maximum possibility.

The danger, as I see it, is the public school acting as if it can do everything alone, which it obviously can not. For many children, the school was not the source of the problem in the first place and they need other resources. I do not see enough examples where the community mental health people and the school are working together with the problems of the family and the child and are trying to deal realistically with the total life dilemma that many of the youngsters have. From that point of view, it seems a little discouraging in that there is not enough financial support to have the ancillary resources involved. There is a good example, however, in Montgomery County near Philadelphia, Pennsylvania, where the community mental health people, psychiatrists, and other professional workers come into the classroom and work with the teacher during group therapy. If the school does not try to go it alone and does expand its horizon, then we may have some promise.

I worry about vocational education because there is such a scarcity for many of our disturbed and learning disabled students. We find it very difficult to maintain those youngsters in the vocational program. I would say the public school has many more resources for these children than we have been able to use, but we have not developed ways to get the teachers off the hook while we mainstream these students. They have to be helped in some way or another to handle the grading problem when the students can not accomplish the work at the level expected of them. Teachers also have to have some agreement on what to do about behavior that is more deviant than that of the average child.

Until we find some way to resolve the problem of fear about classroom control breaking down and until we establish how we are going to help teachers with the grading or evaluation problems in high school, mainstreaming will be confounded.

You mention mainstreaming. There have been modifications suggested for the crisis resource model since its inception. Now that mainstreaming is in full force, what changing role do you see for the crisis model?

I think it has changed drastically. Special education was generic when we started out. That is, when a child had a problem, the question was not what category he or she was in. Rather, if a child was unable to function academically and emotionally in the classroom setting, an overgroup person, or crisis intervener, sat down and worked with that child through the affective and cognitive process. He or she helped the teacher to reabsorb that youngster and conferred with the teacher about what needed to be done outside the classroom and what could be done inside. As a matter of fact, sometimes when a crisis came up, the crisis intervener took over the rest of the teacher's classroom for a while so the teacher could deal with the individual having the crisis.

Now what has happened in general with the new mandate is that there is very little leeway in most cases to handle even a good proportion of the problems that come along. The child is supposed to be certified first and this is to protect the rights of the special child. The result is that a great deal of effort is spent to make sure we have certified, labeled, and categorized the youngster before he can get help. There are a lot of youngsters who are left out until they get bad enough that they can be certified, and this has become a painful experience. Many schools have no program to serve the group between normal children and certifiable children, children with less severe problems or, let's say, beginning problems.

The other problem is that with the effort to deinstitutionalize, we have many children in public schools that even good institutions can not manage. Hence, the intensity of the kind of problems that we are having in the schools increases the difficulty of using this type of resource. I think, however, that the idea of having an overgroup person for consultation certainly has viability and I hope that it will continue. I resist the kind of resource teacher who just consults and never works directly with students and hence does not provide the intensity of input for particular children that is necessary.

What are your views on open education and its relevance for educating disturbed children?

If it is guided by a masterful individual, open education probably has a great deal of promise for some disturbed children. We have been doing some studies of open education on our own and one of the big problems that we have found is that it means such different kinds of things in different places. If open education means more responsibility on the part of the youngster and the teacher to make individual plans, to use more informal ways of learning, to include other media besides the strictly academic, and to employ the group process, I would say all of these have a great deal of viability for certain aspects of special education. Again, the trouble is that we mix up the youngsters that we put in the open setting, and it is hard to individualize enough for 10 disturbed kids in a class, each of whom needs his or her own class. Some of these youngsters seem to need a great deal of rigorous limitation on what they can and can not do,

and that is not necessarily what they receive in an open setting. Again, the design ought to fit the youngster in his or her status of development, rather than fit some theory.

I would say that the main problem we have had in special education, particularly with all of the revolution, is that change has been based upon philosophical matters. The psychological reality has not been studied and sufficiently brought into the picture. Therefore, the question is not, should we have mainstreaming or should we have open schools. The germane question is, for what child is what design most appropriate? In some cases the mainstream or open education will help. In other cases a highly controlled initial stage may be necessary to get some kind of structure in the group. So I don't really believe that designs are in and of themselves good or bad. They are useful or not useful depending upon the skill of the teacher to individualize and the ability of the programs to fit the needs of the particular children. I personally prefer a program that gives more attention to human relationships and more concern about the social relationships of individuals.

Collective bargaining is growing more and more powerful. If teachers' unions succeed in writing reduced pupil loads into their contracts when behavior problem children are involved, what effect will this have on mainstreaming?

I think we have to start out with the fact that, at least in some schools, they have more problem students in regular classes than special education has. In addition to that, if you hear what some of our teachers are saying, "I'll take this one if you'll take these two who are more difficult than the one you're telling me about," the system is going to be overloaded.

There is a reservoir of willing educators out there if we don't overburden them. But what often happens is that the teacher who has the skill and interest is overloaded. We have to look at how many and what kind of students we put in each setting and what kind of support we can give that teacher. We've found that if we reward those teachers who are mainstreaming through some assistance, such as smaller loads or some type of additional resource, they feel that their efforts are worthwhile.

The point is that we can not do it cheaper. If we are trying to find a way not to pay for the added resource that we need, that is just impossible. The unions are beginning to realize this. They are also beginning to realize that mandated education without adequate financial backing means that the money is coming out of general education. Therefore, we have got to do a lot of interpreting to coordinate efforts because we have kept special education apart and now we are asking regular educators to take our children back. That revolution does not happen on a practical basis as fast as the ideology is conjectured. It's going to be a long, hard pull.

What priorities should be dealt with in inservicing the regular education teachers in order to improve their attitude about mainstreamed children?

I think we have to start with the basic training and ideology. We need to help teachers think through solutions to the problems that are acceptable in the code of the school in which they are working. I would prefer to find a cadre of positive people, which I know exists in our schools, who are willing to make a partnership with special educators. We should try to upgrade the willing workers before we attempt to take the teachers who have negative attitudes and reform or change their whole style of behavior. I doubt we're going to be able to do that.

The other side of it is to have a mandate about equal teacher behavior toward all pupils. In our own experience, if you are going to have a code like that, you have to provide a release valve. This is what the crisis intervener was and should be and in many cases still is. If things are not workable according to reasonable standards in your classroom, you do not have to be punitive. There must be another place for this child to go until some more permanent arrangement can be worked out.

We have to work together to figure out what is the reasonable and right way to treat that youngster and what are the rights of the teacher to conduct a class without having to deal with certain kinds of problems in a group situation. Those things have to be understood and I would prefer that our mainstream effort was psychologically more realistic and less traditionally oriented toward having meetings, conferences, and workshops that are supposed to change attitudes. I have little hope that changes are going to happen that way.

What kinds of training and experiences will be needed by crisis or helping teachers of the 1970's and 1980's?

We should select bright and empathic teachers to start with. They must be able to work with individual students, to work with small groups, and to deal with certain problems in the school system. They have to have some skills in diagnosis in these three areas so that they can understand what the issues are. They also have to have some skills in interventions and evaluation.

It's quite clear with the new legislation that crisis teachers need broader training particularly in learning disabilities and mental retardation because emotional disturbance occurs in packages with other anomalies. They need a lot more training in consultation and working with both teachers and systems to figure out how they can change some of these fundamental elements that cause or accelerate problems. They certainly need more supervised experience in working in these settings under professionals who have had enough experience so that they can point out to them the various aspects of the work. The more seriously disturbed and deviant students who are in schools of all kinds make extended inservice work imperative.

One of our mistakes was to think we could train crisis teachers after we put them in the field. Now we know we should start training before they go out, and then we should merge the training with supervised on the job experience. The real indepth work concerning their capabilities and skills comes after preservice training.

Finally, I think all of us who are trying to work in this difficult field of special education need constant available consultation and upgrading so that we can continue to grow.

How adequately are the teacher training programs preparing people to work with the behavior disordered population?

Basically, it seems to me, we give them a good start, but the survival rate is discouraging. I mean survival in two ways. First, when there are other jobs available, the turnover tends to be high. Second, maintaining a high level of professional work frequently disappears as soon as the teachers become acclimated into the profession. We know now that survival depends upon the ecological conditions under which people work, the expectations that are set, the kind of teaming that goes on, and the system's support efforts.

For many teachers, the first year is a year of agony and they go through a great trial. It is at that point that we need to help them. Sometimes it is not the teacher who is the problem. A judgment should be made not only on the basis of the program which includes the teachers and their skills, but also on the support that is given and the whole use of resources in the system. I think we have evaluated teachers when we should evaluate programs.

Are there some promising new directions or developments that you think the field of educating emotionally disturbed children should move toward?

I think that we have got to take the knowledge that we already have and put it to work in better order. We are going to have to do some research in this area to see just what directions we ought to take. For example, research with an "N of one" will be necessary to examine interventions. The focus will be on individual children rather than all these group studies and averages that we have been doing.

We'll also have to have a new style of research. The new direction should evolve from actual field studies. What is really happening to the children in the mainstream or in the special class or in an institution and in their life outside the school environment? We need to see what this is actually like. We need to actually look at the encounters that a child has and begin to examine what is happening to him. I think we would find many things happening that could not produce positive results. If we looked at the potential of a total resource bank of interventions and then at what actually is happening in the melee where we put the youngster, we might be able to understand a little bit better where we ought to concentrate for the future.

Are there any other crucial research questions that should be addressed if monies were available?

I would strongly concentrate on getting out there and seeing what is actually happening in the school environment, not investing in somebody's spectacular esoteric idea. What I really believe we have to do is to investigate how to apply what we already know and discover why we are not putting it together in a more workable fashion for some of these children. I suspect it will turn out that the kinds of things you would actually have to do to help families with problems or the resources you would need to help inner city kids find their way in the maze of life that they are confronted with are more demanding than we care to invest in at the present time. If we are really going to make an impact on some of the youngsters, we have to deal with their multiple problems.

Do you see the field entering into an area of humanistic behaviorism? In other words, is there a linking between behavior modification and psychodynamic theory rather than a bandwagon for each?

As I see it, humanism should not be put into that context because humanism represents a value system. I know there are humanistic psychologists and they do not separate their value system, their philosophy, their goals, and their attitudes from the means. But, of course, in all of us, values (philosophy) and processes (psychology) are all mixed up. The humanistic approach represents the basic attitudinal disposition we in special education should have toward human beings, a concern for their welfare. This approach says that the youngster or the person should be self determining to a large extent. Psychology is supposed to tell us how to go about developing those values in contrast with some others.

Actually, I would say the big movement is the blending relationship between the psychodynamic approach, which is the recognition of the inner life, the emotional life, the motivations, the goals, the aspirations, the drives, and needs that the individual has, and the behavioristic approach. This side has emphasized the external contingencies that are just as real as the internal ones, and it is always the mediation of these two that we have to deal with. The external reality, with its rewards and gratifications, is on the outside. What gets rewarded or gratified is on the inside.

The leaders in the field have finally gotten around to realizing that the human being behaves in a more diverse way than either of these positions alone. Both positions imply things about human nature and about learning. The psychodynamic position certainly has had to expand its horizons about human nature and how behaviors change, and I think the same thing is true in behaviorism. The reason teachers sometimes grab onto one of these positions is because somebody sells it to them as the solution to everything.

There is a synthesis in the air, but it seems to be starting pretty far at the top. The problem lies in the proper assimilation, a more complete knowledge of children, an awareness of the complexity of man, and a more astute understanding of how we use behavioristic or learning techniques. All of this is related to the issue of humanism because it focuses on the kind of person we want the child to be in the end. This should be uppermost in everyone's mind.

Reprinted from *Exceptional Children* 44 (1977): 155–164, by permission of The Council for Exceptional Children. Copyright 1977 by The Council for Exceptional Children.

Editors' Commentary

In the next article, Redl discusses some subtleties of improvement as an evaluation measure. Since help-giving is a dynamic interaction in Redl's view, any changes affect both the adult and the youngster. One of the particular values of this selection is its application of concepts to day-by-day intervention. It is evident that staff expectation does have an impact on outcomes. Hopes become self-fulfilling prophecy. This can be as true for prognosis-improvement ("he relates so well") as for prognosis-failure ("her diagnostic label is schizophrenic"). In this far-ranging article, Redl directs our attention to easily overlooked aspects of the improvement process we are to study in detail in this chapter.

Clinical Speculations on the Concept of Improvement

Fritz Redl

. . . Long ago, Freud made the casual remark that, if an especially brilliant patient uses obviously especially stupid arguments for his defense, then it is a sure sign that there is more to the resistance involved in this than meets the eye. If some people on our level of clinical endurance are thrown into frenzy by a process of "improvement"—the very thing we are actually working and living for day and night—then there must be angles to this that might well stand exploration beyond what we are aware of right now. . . .

Improvement—What Do We Really Mean?

If anything became clear to us . . . when we tried to come to grips with our collective improvement panic, it was the fact of multiple meanings with which this term is bandied about in discussion. This isn't much of a discovery, of course, but since the hesitation—or resistance—against coming to grips with this multiplicity of meaning seems to be very strong, it might help future discussants if we laid bare the major traps in concept formulation right here and now. When people argue about improvements the following four meanings seemed to be involved—and confused:

Meaning A. Improvement—Meaning a Specific Function in Mid-Air. Thus, one would hear claims that children can read better now than before, that they are able to stick to an assignment, to fulfillment of a task, that they can participate in a competitive game without being thrown by failure or success, so that they can now "allow themselves to learn" how to swim, paint, spell, or what have you. Such claims by the various disciplines involved in the cultivation of such skills would frequently be met by the therapists with an uneasy frown, a polite nod in the direction of the sister-discipline, followed by a hot debate as to whether this "really" constitutes improvement—but that one we shall come back to soon.

Meaning B. Improvement in Overall Mental Health. In this respect, staff would argue whether a given child is getting "better"—usually referring to a rather specific part of his well known pathology. Most frequently though this type of statement ends up in a list of "symptoms dropped," or in more hard to formulate statements about desirable attributes customarily described in our American Culture as signs of well being: less tense, more relaxed, freer to react to reality as it is, less "driven" by irrational impulse, etc. etc. etc.

Meaning C. Improvement from the Vantage Point of the Consumer. By this I mean all the adjustment demands which are made on a child by the surrounding universe, many of which have primarily to do with the comfort and taste buds of those who are on the receiving end of the line of child behavior. Thus one would find statements such as these: He is less rough on trips outside, sticks within rules better, is much quieter, has fewer tantrums and then they aren't quite so hard to live through; when in a sulk it doesn't take quite as long to get him out of it, etc. etc. etc.

Meaning D. Improvement as a "Human Being." Into this category fall a variety of statements which do not seem to be quite founded in either psychiatric theory or in any special educational creed, and frequently mark themselves quite clearly as different from strictly clinical statements. People get easily embarrassed while making them in the course of a case discussion, and frequently also apologize for them with the type of pride one usually displays when apologizing for something one really deems more important than what happens to be on the official agenda. Thus staff would refer to our children as "more lovable" than before, would insist that Bobby is more of a "Mensch" right now, and he seems to be a more "decent" human being, more responsive to overall expectations or just in terms of plain human charm.

Needless to emphasize—any one of these four different meanings may actually be contained in a given statement in mixture with the other three. . . .

The moral of the story that we want to lead up to today lies in the impact of the above described multiple connotations on staff discussion in an interdisciplinary team. The following chance observations may be of interest:

1. Individual staff members lose, under the impact of improvement panic, whatever level of *conceptual astuteness* they really possess, at least for the duration of a case conference. Thus you may find a therapist who knows very well that a given teacher who said that Bobby has improved in reading, does *not* for a moment delude herself that this might mean he is cured—you may find a therapist going, in spite of this knowledge, into a long harangue about "improvements" often really being in "the service of resistance" and so forth, which then in turn leads to a somewhat angered insistence by the teacher that skills do count also, after all.

2. Members of disciplines which have a reputation for being "clinically more sophisticated" than some others (Psychiatry versus Teaching, art therapy versus nursing, etc., as the case may be) have a tendency to get irritated beyond reason by even modest statements of improvement of part functions or skills, and on the whole pride themselves on a somewhat over-ostentatious pessimism—as though even the mention of improvements would throw them back into a lower status field. The representatives of more part-skill oriented disciplines have a tendency to hide their improvement observations, for fear of being deemed unpsychiatric or clinically too naive for words. The debate thus avoided usually breaks out in displaced areas of clinical or technical issues.

3. On a good team, members of the same discipline who meet the children in their daily life in different roles or at different times, have a tendency to hide their observations of improvements if their revelation might seem as though they took undue credit for them. Thus, in our case, a lot of quite clearcut improvements remained unmentioned for a while simply because a given counsellor was afraid his teammates might interpret his statements about Bobby's new relationship of trust as though it was meant to tell the others on the team how skillful the speaker was. Such is the price of good battle-morale after return to civilian life.

4. A frank discussion of these issues and an encouragement to record observed improvements, and never mind what they might *imply* brought about an increase in recording and observations offered, but the effect of such "medication" never lasts very long; it needs to be repeated more often than one might assume.

Improvement—How Do We Know It Is "Real"?

What people are most afraid and ashamed of, on a high-level interdisciplinary clinical team, is to appear overconfident, overoptimistic, too naive in one's expectation about human change, rash in one's claims and "too easily fooled." Working with child patients whose very pathology seems to lay traps for such weaknesses with special wile and skill, this "countersuspiciousness" of the adults in battle with the suspectness of child motivations seems to assume an even higher force.

In discussions, this theme usually comes up under the guise of questions, whether a given claim of improvement is "real" or not. Some of this way of putting it is actually only a concession to the amenities of middle class conduct—for you can't very well tell a teammate that he is a fool who doesn't know what he is talking about and sees improvements where there are none. Rather, one can concede the appearance of improved behavior claimed, as long as one shifts one's incredulity to the question of the substance it might hold.

In actuality, the question "but is it real" seemed, in our struggles at least, to cover six rather discrete issues that should be carefully kept apart:

1. Is it "real"—or is this only improved behavior, produced as a *defense* against treatment or change?

Example: The tough kid who becomes quite `goody-goody` after arrival for a few weeks, because he wants to stall for time to `size up the joint`.

The originally obstreperous youngster who suddenly becomes more amenable to adults because he has changed tactics: he takes revenge on them now by manipulating the behavior of his peers into anti-adult escapades behind the scenes.

2. Is it "real"—meaning, *is it ready for transfer?* In this respect, we do not doubt the appearance of improvement where it is claimed, but question whether it would stand up if situations were even slightly changed.

Example: Youngster suddenly opening up in a real friendship for one counsellor—does this mean he is reducing his hostile warfare against the adult world, or does he simply reserve this attitude to this one person alone, thus even reinforcing his warfare against the rest of the world.

Bobby shows more interest in activities on the Ward, gets involved in much more complex art projects there—does this mean now he is ready for prolonged interest spans in his work in school?

3. Is it "real"—meaning, *is it re-traumatization-proof?* What we really question in that case is not the clarity of improvement, but just how much of the old bad stuff could the youngster take without a relapse. It should be noted, by the way, that I have found many clinicians fall into the trap of General Public Opinion on this score. I find therapists blushing at the thought that somebody might come around a year—or two foster home placements—away from now and say: "See, I told you it wouldn't last"—irrespective of the questions whether the new breakdown wasn't perhaps due to totally unacceptable traumatization of the child. In no other field of medicine do I find people that trust less in their own domain. A cured pneumonia remains cured as far as the physician goes, and no-

body expects retraumatization proofness for the rest of the patient's life.

Example: Bobby has made tremendous strides in trust, is capable of accepting reprimands or even punishment if handled wisely and with proper care. But what will happen if he runs into a sadist of a teacher, a drunken fool of a foster-home parent, a stupid prediluvian practice of rule enforcement in a next institution?

4. Is it "real"—or rather, is the basis on which behavior rests `genuine`? In this frame of reference we do not really doubt the factualness of an improvement claim. What we wonder, however, is how much improved behavior or attitude flows out of real "personality change from within" or how far it is actually maintained only through unusual pressure from without.

Example: Some children suddenly get scared we might `abandon them` if they are too bad. Under the impact of that separation panic, their surface behavior seems to `improve`. However, does that mean that the `real problem` has been solved?

Under the impact of a momentary enthusiasm for a special project or a newly found adult friend, we find youngsters acting and promising way above their means. The way they act and feel during that phase is quite visibly an improvement over what we saw before—how solid, though, is the basis on which such improvements are erected?

5. Is it "real"—meaning: is this improvement worthwhile as measured against the *price we may pay?* This is especially true where our ambition may lead us to squeeze out of youngsters levels of operation which are developmentally premature, thus cramping the style of life they ought to have in order to complete their developmental phase at ease.

Example: A pre-adolescent who is trapped into displaying a lot of `Emily Post` adaptation to adult taste patterns as to how a little lady or little gentleman should act, thus missing the leeway for rough and tumble play which this age phase ought to have a large dose of.

An adolescent who is trapped into premature job or vocational ambitions thus becomes a much more `serious` youngster, while he is actually postponing an important shift in adolescent psychosexual growth in a much later phase, or forces himself into a compulsion-neurosis-like state of pseudo maturity.

6. Is is "real"—or are we just *having luck for a while?* Often our improvement statements are obvi-

ously well rooted, and we are sure we haven't done anything to force the children into a higher level of operation. Only—we soon discover that all that happened was that we had a special piece of luck. Sometimes, it just so happens we hit a day of unusual relaxedness for the program we had in mind, or one of those situations where a "positive mood" simply is in the air from the first waking hour on, or where a lucky surprise, an unusual event, sets the tone so well that even disturbed children, with that much supportive luck, can really *live above their means* for a while. Only, it would be premature to expect their continued function on that level, or to forget what price in regressive interludes we may have to be taxed for after a while.

Example: A skillfully designed school or play hour would often turn out unexpectedly well. Seduced by such luck, the adults may try to make such planning part of the regular and prolonged diet of the group. If premature, the result is a throwback or regression to, or beyond the original level, and the insight that the experience of such happily "improved reactions" was just a piece of unusual good luck.

By the way, this element of "living above their means" should not be ignored entirely. The ability to do so for certain stretches seems to be one of the safest signals of imminent ego change.

In summary—all those 6 interpretations of the question whether a given phenomenon of "improvements" is "real" or not, are valid issues in their own right. They need to be viewed separately, though, and confusion between them is among the most dreaded pitfalls in staff debate. *Observations* from our own "Improvement Panic phase" as to these issues:

1. In interdisciplinary team discussions, *disappointments* along the line of meaning No. 6 (is it "real," or did we just have luck for a while) and No. 2 (is it ready for transfer) seem hardest for the staff to take with grace. They frequently lead to "I told you so" debates rather than time spent on realistic re-appraisal of the scope of improvement exploitability, or they lead staff members to withdraw all their previous improvement statements, rather than to modify their degree of transferability at the time.

2. *Irrespective of realities* in the picture, *therapy staff* in the stricter sense of the term is inclined to suspect all program and school staff of overexploiting mild improvement cues beyond what the treatment traffic can bear; child care and teaching staff

has a tendency to suspect and accuse therapy staff of being "overfussy" and holding the kids back from experiences for which they would be quite ready.

3. Faced with *predictions* as forerunners of a widening scope of community contact of the child patients—partial, as before changing room, hospital school to community school, or total, as in the case of impending home, foster home, or after care placement—*all staff* tends to become panicky and ends up with predictions much more negative than they really thought the improvements themselves amount to. In short, trust in transfer power of improvement goes down, panic about retraumatization vulnerability goes up. In fact, sometimes it even looks as though we *hoped* or at least *expected* that the subsequent handling of the child will have to be traumatic in nature, for only then could we have an alibi for having thought him ready for discharge to begin with, in case it didn't work out.

Improvement—at What Cost?

In the preceding discussion we mentioned the case where we feel that improvements can be obtained at "too high" a price in terms of other areas of the child's life. Of course, such mistakes will have to be avoided. However—let's face it, all improvements give us a rough time, at least for a while. Of course we somehow know this, and in specific case discussions this problem is invariably raised. Yet, I do not find that literature has given enough emphasis to the very specific problem it constitutes for the child to run around with an improved personality in the same old stable, for the adult to live with a child who has improved program readiness, and for the institution which has to maintain a disease-protective atmosphere for some of its patients while others need to be put on the path to the way out.

In the following I shall try to list just a few of the thoughts that forced themselves upon us during those months of improvement panic.

Just What Does It Imply for the Child?

The ego of a child who allowed himself to "improve" while under our treatment and care—and let's forget for a moment just which of the aspects of "improvement" we may be talking about, the problem is there in all of them to some degree—has the following added complications to face, and will need a lot of resilience to bear the burden of improvement with courage:

1. *Extra elation and depression load.* Children of the type we are talking about remain, for a long time, quite incapable of dealing with even normal quantities of feelings of elation or depression, excitement or emptiness. Both throw them into frantic gesticulation of their ego instead of eliciting the usual coping mechanisms children have available for such events. Therefore, for a long stretch of time, the therapeutic team needs to avoid any planning that contains too much of a chance for either, and the adult has to substitute for coping mechanisms his controls from without, if either experience should hit the child too hard. Under the grip of improvements occurring within—even of partial ones, such a state of protectedness from elation or depression can no longer be maintained. Widening the scope of their experiences in areas where they are ready for it also implies the exposure to elation and triumph, of sudden insight into the distance between where they think they are and where they really are, and a sudden onslaught of depression. For all practical purposes then, an ego that is exposed to the right diet of challenging enough experiences to feel elations will also have to take in its stride accompanying accidents of depressions, and will have to be ready for both. Only—often enough the movement in skill or personality area where improved functioning can occur is not necessarily well timed with the development of such coping mechanisms. Result: the children's ego experiences more failures with coping with either than before, which makes life for and with those children more tumultuous than it had been while they were still in the grip of their old pathology.

2. *Increased problems in dealing with failure and success, criticism and praise, punishment and rewards.* For years we had to learn to avoid exposing our child patients to either of those, since the incapacity of their egos to cope with such experiences or educational techniques is among their primary characteristics. Astounding ingenuity had to be developed by staff to find a way of life in which to spare the children's ego the necessity for such coping, to find forms of child handling and child care which would substitute for the challenge such experiences and techniques involve.

With the emergence of new improvement potentials, this state of affairs, too, can no longer be maintained. Expanded exposure to life of more complexity makes use of such techniques unavoidable. Growing into normal life makes the learning of how to deal with such experiences paramount. Thus, hardly freed from the onslaught of their old pathological impulsivity, these children now have to practice new ego techniques in coping with the consequences of their widened area of potential functioning.

3. *Increase in newness panic and additional fear of loss of control.* More newness brings with it also an increase of the anxiety that goes with exposure to new situations—a liability from which we had to protect these children for quite a while. Exposure to trying themselves in situations of increased scope also implies their increased fear of loss of control, of being overridden by an onslaught of impulsivity. In fact, since these children along with the improved functioning also usually develop some level of increased insight into their selves, their own awareness that they *might* be suffering loss of self-control in a new situation also goes up. It seems paradoxical but is an important fact of clinical life that with improved movement toward mental health the self-perception of these children's actual weakness of internal controls becomes more *realistic*, which increase in internal realism, so to say, has in its wake a new wave of anxieties about loss of control. A chain reaction which probably poses one of the most delicate clinical policy problems of all.

4. *Fear of commitment, nostalgia for old pathology fun.* This phase of the improvement curve has been better documented in reports on individual therapy with children and adults than the others. It nevertheless introduces new challenges to meet in the children's daily lives. What we are referring to is the well documented fact that the emerging awareness of the healthier ego and what life in health implies, also brings with it the dawning idea of the price one pays for freedom and health, and the demands society—and oneself—is likely to make once one has left the dreary but relatively safe refuge of mental disease. Also—newly tasted gratifications are still wobbly, the secondary gain extorted from old pathology-geared gratification, while spurious, is at least safely predictable and well known. Thus, the "improvement prone" child travels a road more challenging, but also much emptier of the known, and much more unpredictable in terms of the nature of the gratifications to be expected as a reward.

5. *The diversion of improvements as bargaining tools with the world of adults.* Of all the pitfalls, this is probably the worst one, at least in therapy with the type of children we have in mind today. For, once improvement on several levels has been tasted, these children are not slow in detecting its terrific bargaining power over the adults on the behavioral scene. And once a given piece of improvement becomes a bargaining tool in the battle with

the surrounding universe, its *value, clinically speaking, has been nullified.* In fact, the improvement we produced, once it is in the service of such battle against change, is but an additional weapon in the child's hand. We shall talk about the problem of keeping staff from playing into the hands of this vicious and perverse process in a minute. At the moment what we are referring to is the tendency and skill of children on the way to health to bribe and blackmail their surroundings with that very issue of health itself. Only after they have improved enough, can they use regression as an efficient weapon for punishing their therapist or themselves. Only after they have shown considerable gains on several levels, can they successfully trap us into confusing surface improvements with real change, or taking their coins of more pleasing behavior as a sign of advancement rather than of the resistance it really is. The "promise" to be good—by word or deed, the "threat" to regress—by deed or word, are a new piece of agenda on the strategy discussion table during those phases in the children's clinical life.

6. *Estrangement from peer group and peer culture with all that this implies.* This phenomenon is most visible, of course, when some of the children move "faster" than others in the same subgroup, or if an individual's move out from under pathology happens more rapidly than the behavioral code of the peer group can keep step with. Since this is the more frequent situation anyway, we might list shortly what the problems of the "improving" child will be under those conditions:

a. Behavior which is rated as "improved" in the world of the therapy-success eager adult may have the opposite rating on the peer code scale, which still has strong natural power in their lives, and needs to retain such for quite a while to come. Thus, for instance, the ability "to ask for help rather than to lash out in wild destructive despair" is a clearcut improvement item on anybody's scale. For the kid who produces such behavior it easily contains the flavor of "sissiness," of "giving in" or "playing up to" the adults, of acting like a "teacher's pet."

b. Improvements in basic health issues invariably also are accompanied by changes in *taste.* Accepting sublimated gratifications for more primitive ones obviously creates a gap between the child now and the child before, and therefore between him and his less advanced playmates. Thus, we will find two phenomena in the wake of such moves: our improved youngster may become *contemptuous* of, or hostile to, those who still linger in their old rough, obviously crazy and uncomfortable pleasures and behavior, or he may become envious of them, developing nostalgic yearnings for the more simple life of yore. Experiences, by the way, which our youngsters may not yet be able to cope with, even at the time when their improvement in sublimation of their taste-buds already has taken place.

c. *Exposure to additional dare and group-loyalty tests. Ambivalence also toward this new image of self.* Groups don't like to let people go. In the organized adult crime gang, the punishment for estrangement is death. In kid groups it is ostracism or an endless chain of "loyalty tests." Thus, the changing child in the not yet changing group will find himself suspect of being a fifth columnist in the battle against adults, for the very "improvements" he has not yet learned how to savor. He will be exposed to a constant flow of "dares" to show that he is still O.K. in spite of that suddenly discovered eagerness to hold up his hand in class for contributions, to finish products adults are proud of, or his obviously gratifying use of his relationship to a therapist. Thus, our changing individual undergoes a new phase of group conflict at the very time when his first improvements need a chance to emerge.

7. *The turmoil of choice.* Improved personalities need a wider scope to operate in. The nourishment of improvement potentials invariably implies the increase of free choice. Thus, the very children who, during their sickness, had to be protected by the adult from being exposed to too exciting choice making, because their egos could never bear such a load, will now have to emerge into choice making on a stepped-up scale. Rather than have an adult stand behind them who can hold them when they make the wrong decision, they will have to be kept in a program that gives them a chance to be on their own, to make their own decision whether to behave or to misbehave, so that the consequences of such decisions can then be picked up in therapy or life-space interview work. No matter how closely supervised their overall life frame may remain, this withdrawing of the adult in tactful awe of the importance of an autonomous decision making process is the core of all treatment into health.

The result of this for the internal household of our children is obvious: wrong decisions have to be made. The ego will then be tempted to use its old alibi and projection techniques to ward off the insight-consequences that might have to be drawn from them. Our "Life Space Interview" records are bursting with colorful illustrations of just this very sort of thing. It is the clinical exploitation of life events—life events which are allowed to occur—that marks this phase of therapy, as against the protection from stress that marked the previous one. While this is the only safe way back into health, it isn't an easy one, and the casualties on this path are not less numerous than those on the previous treatment stretches.

All in all it should be clear by now that we are deeply impressed with the fact that real improvements—on any one of the counts we mentioned above—make additional demands on the child. This is especially true for settings in which the children under treatment live in a group with other child patients, while in part branching out into widened areas of school and community life. While the "group" may, under circumstances, support the way to health, it is also quite likely to try to block it. In either case, the "improving child" will be faced with frustrations and failures which are the result of the widened horizon of his experiential life and to which he would not have been exposed to begin with, had he not improved. Thus, the child's ego assumes, with each "improvement" step, also the challenge of managing more complex life situations, and a new batch of frustrations, anxieties, confusions and fears. Quite a job to perform until, finally, digested experiences of this sort can be turned, by the child, into a renewed concept of his self.

Improvement—What Is the Cost for the Clinical or Educational Adult?

To lump both of them together isn't really quite fair; for obviously the problems we have to face vis-à-vis the improvement issue will vary considerably in terms of the specific function we are expected to fulfill in the youngster's overall treatment scheme, and the specific role we have to play in his daily life. However—time is costly at this point, so let us oversimplify and abbreviate without too much apology and guilt:

1. *Coping with the temptation to over-expect and exploit.* Frankly, not all of the resistance of youngsters against our therapeutic wiles to bring about a change is just a function of their pathology. Even without its distorting influence, I can't blame some of them for being leery of being free to improve, for there is one instinct most powerful in all adults in this professional game—a terrific drive to hang onto whatever changes we finally seem to notice; and, while they hardly show us a finger of improvement, to grab the whole hand and try hard to pull them into a level of health they are far from ready for.

We all know that, but we haven't spent as much time learning to recognize our secret wishes in that direction as we have spent learning to know when we are liable to get angry and mad, frustrated or hostile, so we can take professional action against such feelings flooding our clinical gates.

The more skill-oriented professions have a natural tendency in that direction by the very nature of their job. But the therapist, in the stricter meaning of the term, isn't free of it either. It only shows in different ways. In fact, I have seen Bobby's therapist mad at his group worker for expecting the child to enjoy games or experiences still much too frightening to him, just because he had improved some, and yet would find the same therapist disappointed an hour later that a youngster who had been so capable of insight style therapy by now should suddenly return to a phase of non-verbal resistance against any and all interview work, and wondering what mistakes we had made. In short—one of the greatest internal problems of staff is that once they have smelled the flavor of a few moments of success, felt the relief in seeing irrational kids respond with normal reactions, they are liable to forget all they have learned through the years of severe pathology onslaught—or rather, to throw it out of the window as though the millennium had arrived.

2. *Bargain basement deals with the pseudo-normal child.* Worse than the temptation to over-expect and exploit improvement potentials is the temptation to fall into the trap of using their promises and "good behavior" or their verbal threats of regression for bargain deals which are clinically as destructive as anything could be. To make this point, which I consider the most important of all, safe against misinterpretation, a slight detour back into our pre-improvement policies seems justified.

The specific type of child patient on whose back, so to say, we discuss the whole improvement issue today, requires, during the first years of therapy, an avoidance of all *punishment* in the usual sense of the term. I cannot re-argue the reasons for this here.

The appearance of marked "improvements" seemed to confront us with the need to plan as carefully about our anxieties about optimism and hope as we had needed to plan about our dangers of hostility and despair. It is my impression that there was no automatic transfer from the principles that had guided us against the wrong reactions to the youngsters' "bad" behavior into the avoidance of the wrong handling of their promises to be "good." In the struggle with all this, the following directives resulted as a side piece to our original batch of training policies:

Whenever we are confronted with it, *we cannot afford* to make them feel our widening of their leeway for autonomy and expressional scope is "*reward*" or "*privilege.*"

a. If we did, this would only stir up their "make-a-deal" philosophy of life and seduce them into exploitational pseudo-promises and adjustments, and they would *escape the real issue* again.

b. They would not tie up the experience of Reward and Promise with either their own past behavior or with the future predicament anyway, so those rewards and privileges would only be considered a premium for symptom-disguise.

c. However—we must not be considered as being *indifferent* to their improved behavior and attitude. It is important to show them that we are happy about it, but not to the degree that the loss of such recognition would become something to be *constantly afraid of.*

d. Whenever we have to terminate temporarily a new scope in their autonomy and mobility, we must make sure they do not experience this as *punishment.* This must be interpreted quite similarly to our previous intervention policy; we just think you can't make it yet, that's all there is to it. Not whether they were good or bad, but *whether we know they are ready* for an experience is the criterion for them to have it. Thus, we must also protect them from their own *illusionary need to produce phoney or rash promises.* We have to protect them against unrealistic self-expectation just as we used to protect them against unrealistic feelings of defeat.

e. The attitude to be conveyed is: "We love you anyway, we shall do everything to help you 'make it,' whenever you enter a new area of widened autonomous decision making, or experiential tryout of new situations. However, we shall also protect you from trying more than we know you can handle, even if you get mad at us at the time. We are happy about every step forward you can make, but we don't want you to feel you have to produce improved behavior as a prize. We shall help you move at your own rate. On the other hand, the production of improved behavior as a coin for special privileges is out, in this outfit, too. It isn't necessary. What you get, you get because you need it, it is good for you and you are ready for it."

These are the only basic criteria on which the granting of special extensions in autonomy of decision making, and of experiential expansion, de-

pends. To convey such an attitude in the turmoil of daily events is not an easy task, but neither was the handling of negatively experienced interventions mentioned above. Only, staff is usually caught unawares for the latter, and the very fact these kids begin to look and act in many moments of their lives so much like plain ordinary normal kids easily fools us into the same type of bargain deals, or of institutionalized punishments or rewards that, with normal children, are known to work so well. In fact, the healthier these kids get, the harder it is to remain aware of the amount of clinical caution and clinical tact that still has to remain part and parcel of our treatment policy. In all those cases where we made bad mistakes along that line, and tried to rely on promises, threats, rewards, punishments, no matter how mild and wise, we were soon forced to regret it. And even then it was hard for us to realize that the only people we can afford to get mad at for such mistakes are ourselves, rather than the kids who "disappointed" our fond hopes.

3. *Improvement muteness because of a repressed desire to grow.* After so many months and years of hard labor without any reliable signs of success that could be trusted, it is hard to avoid a strong wish to brag about a real improvement, or to overtalk it in case conference or in luncheon gossip with the rest of the clinical crowd. Afraid that we might do so, and realizing that this would be misinterpreted by the rest of the gang as a rather prima-donnaish and conceited act, we often defended ourselves against our own narcissistic hopes by not admitting or noting actual improvements to begin with. Thus, one often sees children handled with much too little improvement leeway, thereby slowing up the possible clinical pace. And recordings, just when improvements of all sorts actually set in, become quite unreliable, a not inconsiderable deficit for an operation that is geared toward research.

4. *Renewed competitiveness among team members and distorted relationships to "the other field."* With the first "improvements" finally becoming undeniable, a new wave of competitiveness is likely to hit an otherwise already quite team-oriented staff. It seemed easier to love each other, and to respect the other guy's discipline, as long as we were all in the same boat of struggling with little visible success against overwhelming odds. Once improvement happens, our narcissistic investments are reinflamed. This may happen on a personal level— why should Bobby do this (showing reliable behavior when trusted with keys) for counsellor X when I know he would never have done that much

for me? It may also happen on the level of displacement into interdisciplinary issues: sure that teacher thinks she got Bobby to read. Little does she know that he would never have allowed himself to want to do so, unless I had opened it all up for him in that therapy hour the other day. To bring this new wave of potential staff conflict under control seems to be a more arduous task for all involved than to become aware of and cope with our feelings of frustration, aggression, and fear.

In summary—there seems to be a considerable implication of all this for the task of pre-service and in-service training of staff, and for the ongoing supervisory process on all levels. Without going into any of these details . . . , it may suffice to state that the clinical morale and astuteness of a given residential staff well developed for the original onslaught of pathology in the raw, may need considerable re-structuring, in order to be equally foolproof against the terrific onslaught of the first improvement wave.

Improvement—What Is the Cost to the Institution?

When child patients are treated in an institutional setting of any kind—and some of this even holds for the less enduring settings, such as outpatient therapy clubs—the phenomenon of improvement creates new tasks and new problems, which seem to me to deserve much more recognition than they have gained in the past. All too often do we design our institutional framework primarily for the "treatment" of a given disease entity or disturbance of some kind. Somehow we hope that within all this the patient will "get better" and finally be ready for discharge. Not enough do we often realize how the step by step impact of improvements which have already taken place may change the whole treatment need of individual or group, to the point where co-existence with the originally clinically correct pathology service design becomes a problem of first order. To mention but a few of the most obvious observations to the point:

1. *Danger to a real "treatment atmosphere" in favor of a system of institutionalized penalties and rewards, or of assessments of part achievements.* In a place where most kids have shed their worst primitiveness, it is quite possible to make demands, set standards, which give a smooth image of a well run place, with the kids on the health-proximity end of the line more or less setting the tone and representing the place to the world outside. As soon as this happens, regression becomes a luxury hard to afford, conformity to some standardized expectations be-

comes a real issue with the group of kids, even if the adults would retain clinical flexibility in their thoughts. Individualization, respect for special anxieties, oddities, and pathological blow-ups become something the institution is increasingly ashamed of. They blush if it happens, instead of taking pride in how wisely they handled it when it occurs. Even a clinically highly sophisticated setting may temporarily suffer such a *relapse into pre-clinical naiveté* just at the very moment when their first successes become clear to all. In our own experience, for instance, I had little trouble convincing even clinically not very sophisticated or highly trained staff of the impossibility of using punishments on kids who have obviously no sense of future or of past. When the children began to improve, I found myself forced to write long essays to reassure even the treatment staff of the difference between intervention and punishment, between normal children at home and child patients on a still closed or just opened ward. . . .

2. *The emergence of a system of "caste" and "outcast."* The adults may "understand" why Bobby is now ready for more leeway and less tight supervision, more trust with gadgets and less fussiness, and even Bobby may. But how will this affect the other children? For *them*, what I and the child know is simply a concession to his greater self-control looks like rank favoritism of the worst kind. Also, if the group "improves" in too uneven rates, it is unavoidable that some consider themselves quite excluded from "privileges" which the others seem to enjoy, and the concept of the "privileged character" can be as destructive in a treatment setting as in detention homes. Also, once the pressure of such a system of "privileges one enjoys after one has improved" and "absence of rights one is doomed to because one isn't trusted enough" becomes more or less institutionalized, it develops a suction power of its own with disastrous effects all around.

Only the constant vigilance of staff about their own motives, and the careful interpretation—by word or deed—of all events that might give rise to such suspicions to all children involved—including the group of "onlookers"—can safeguard an institution against this trap.

3. *Program distortion for the rest of the group.* Aside from these interpretational pitfalls, it also easily happens that the program diet which the less improved children get *actually* changes way beyond what is clinically wise. This change may occur in two directions: it may lead to a *pauperization* of the program for those who don't quite seem to be up to it yet. Staff may betray their annoyance with the

level of operation of the less improved, and too openly display their understandable gratification with the program for those who are more advanced and therefore more gratifying to work with. Or the change may lead to *stepped up demands* for all, with disastrous results for those who just cannot yet make it. In both cases an institution would lose its clinical value for some of the children, while increasing its fitness for those on top.

4. *Differentiation between "regression" and legitimate "improvement mess."* One of the hardest issues to interpret to outsiders, and occasionally to oneself, is the fact that improvement, in growing kids, of course does not mean the termination of problems or even of problem behavior. An adolescent, for instance, who spent his pre-adolescent years in a closed ward with a small group of also disturbed peers, and who is really "coming along well," will be *expected* to have to live through all the usual turmoil of adolescent awakening sexuality, of concern about peer status, of battle with home personnel about his newly discovered status of emancipated young man. Life with teenagers alone, no matter how normal, can be full of problems, and of problem behavior of considerable proportions. Why should "our kids" be an exception to this? And yet, we were very tempted to interpret their first steps into adolescent rebellion as just "regression to their old ways," to react to their normal adolescent overestimation of anything outside and devaluation of what they have at home, as though it simply meant "we never got anywhere, they are as hostile and hard to please as they were when they came." In fact, if your youngsters enter their adolescent phase just at the time when improvements set in and when their scope of activities is branching out into the community more and more, staff is likely to develop some sort of envy toward people outside, who seem to have an easier time with them, than the home base personnel. Yet any parent of any normal child is quite used to just that. The real problem, however, lies in the difficulty to *assess* correctly, even in our own domain, just what we have before us: regression or problem behavior which accompanies their coping with a new part of life. Research in this direction is practically nonexistent; its expansion way beyond its present state devoutly to be wished.

5. *Accepting the challenge of the calculated risk—and the public hatred in its wake.* It is hard but safe to run a place for the extremely sick. Nobody expects any better from you, as long as you keep them out of their hair. You, yourself, have a constant alibi in your vest pocket—in view of the enormous pathology that stares you in the face, even superhuman effort can't well be blamed for failing.

Once the children "improve," doubt rises, whether we couldn't do "more" for them, and indeed, ever more seems to be needed. To cater to the needs of an "improved" personality on the way back to health, however, is quite a different task from treating a bunch of incurables humanely and with some clinical hope. It involves an increased demand for *calculated risk*. For some institutions, such as mental hospitals for instance, this even constitutes a legal and administrative problem of considerable scope.

To use just one illustration for many: at a certain state in his development, Bobby could be trusted with the ward keys for a short trip down to the coke machine. In fact, he *needed* such trust experiences when half-way ready for them, for how can anybody develop autonomy on a leash? On the other hand, in a mental hospital such practice is strictly against the rule; lower status staff can well be fired for such a breach of rules. Or: Johnny and Max are now in need of partial independence from the group, and of an experience of behaving well, out of decency to the counselor who is "on." Result: this said counselor will of course give in to their requests to "go on up the creek a little for some more crabs while you are packing up, we will be back in five minutes, honest." If the counselor knows his children and their mood, and the clinical phase they are in, such a permission is a clinical *must*. Yet, he better not record the incident, for it is against all laws of the land. And of course, we don't even insist that this judgment was entirely right. We even hope the risk will misfire from time to time, for only such misfiring gives us the chance for the "clinical exploitation of a dramatic life event," which may shorten the child's treatment by months.

In the transition from a closed unit to open life in the community, the cost of the improvement of our children became even more painfully visible. For the public in general has little tolerance for a risk that misfires, no matter how well it was calculated, or how wisely exploited for the therapy of the child. In fact, this may well be one of the reasons why we still have so many closed wards or highly restrictive institutions, and so many fewer places where the "last stretch from sickness to health" could be taken. For, as our societal hatred of those who deal with the dangerous and the mentally sick is what it is known to be—who could take the risk of supporting that last stretch toward mental health, without losing his own?

Abridged from Fritz Redl, "Clinical Speculations on the Concept of Improvement," presented at the American Orthopsychiatric Association Meetings, 1959.

Editors' Commentary

The field of emotional disturbance is continually beset with overgeneralizations. One of these in current vogue is the matter of degrees of disturbance, as if one hypothesis were adequate for all psychological conditions. The behaviorists and interactionalists generally see personal flexibility as the issue of treatment. The biologically oriented practitioners lean toward a maturational expectation. Those who believe that an early psychological set in the first years of life will predict a child's future personality will be significantly influenced by those forces. In reading the following articles several related matters should be kept in mind: Certain behavior is obviously more biologically determined and other behavior less so. It is also apparent that any given intervention is helpful to certain children and not helpful to others. Thus, evaluation should concentrate on which children are helped and which are not, rather than on percentages of children helped. Lewis's article is a classic in the field, combining keen insight with a review of past studies. His concluding paragraph deserves special attention as a prelude to the studies that follow.

Continuity and Intervention in Emotional Disturbance: A Review

W. W. Lewis

The treatment procedures used in child guidance clinics are based implicitly on two hypotheses regarding the relationship between emotional disturbance in children and mental illness in adults. The first of these, which we will label the continuity hypothesis, is that emotional disturbance in a child is symptomatic of a continuing psychological process that may lead to adult mental illness. The second, which we will call the intervention hypothesis, is that therapeutic intervention enhances the child's present adjustment and thereby reduces the likelihood that he will experience serious mental problems later in life.

As working hypotheses, these presumed relationships have served us well in allocating our resources in the mental health field and in making operational decisions regarding when and to whom treatment should be offered. As hypotheses, however, they need to be examined from time to time in the light of accumulating evidence that may increase or decrease our confidence in the procedures we employ.

Levitt (1957a) published a review of outcome studies of psychotherapy with children which raised doubts about what we are calling the intervention hypothesis. While his conclusions are relevant to this review, and will be taken up in context, the evidence that will be considered in this paper is somewhat broader in scope than whether children improve more with psychotherapy or without it.

The continuity hypothesis can be translated into a prediction that children who have been identified as emotionally disturbed will have more problems of adjustment as adolescents and adults than children who have not been so identified.

There are two general types of studies that can help evaluate this prediction: retrospective studies of adult mental patients and followup studies of adults who had been seen diagnostically in child guidance clinics as children.

Similarly, the intervention hypothesis can be translated into a prediction that children who have received treatment for emotional disturbance will have fewer adjustment problems than emotionally disturbed children who have not received treatment. Two kinds of studies can help evaluate this prediction: outcomes of clinic treatment in terms of very general criteria, e.g., percent of children who were improved following treatment, and experimental studies designed to investigate more specific changes accompanying treatment.

The Continuity Hypothesis: Retrospective Studies

Retrospective studies generally employ a sample of adult mental patients whose childhood symptoms are reviewed through the case histories, questionnaires, and interviews with informants. Kasanin and Veo (1932), Bowman (1934), Friedlander (1945), and Wittman and Huffman (1945) have all followed this pattern in reporting a correlation between childhood problems and psychosis in adult life. A common conclusion in these studies is that adult psychotics have had visible signs of disordered behavior early in their lives and presumably could have been identified and treated long before they reached a stage of frank psychosis. Two alternative interpretations may be offered. One is that since the person making judgments of the quality and severity of the childhood symptoms knew that the subject was a hospitalized psychotic, a negative halo effect may have been created. The other interpretation is that there is no way of determining how many other children had similar problems but were not studied because they did not become psychotic later in their lives.

Bower, Shellhammer, Daily, and Bower (1960) attempted to eliminate the knowledge of outcome bias by obtaining descriptive ratings from former teachers of hospitalized schizophrenics without the teachers' awareness of their present status. Comparison of these ratings with those for a control group selected from the same high school classes indicated that the teachers had been aware to some extent of the prepsychotic students' deviant tendencies. That there may have been still other students in the same high school classes who had similar symptoms was not raised as a question.

A study by Birren (1944) attempted to eliminate both alternative interpretations by examining psychological reports of children referred to psychologists in a public school system and who later were committed to mental hospitals. Thirty-eight records of this kind were compared with a control sample of nonpsychotics who had been examined at the same time for similar problems. The test records did not reveal significant differences between the two groups of children and ". . . in none of the cases studied was there suspicion on the part of the examiner that the child examined had severe conflicts or would later become psychotic" (p. 93).

The Continuity Hypothesis: Adults Followup

Followup studies of adult adjustment status of an entire population of children who had been referred to child guidance clinics is a defensible way of establishing the correlation between developmental problems and mental illness. Two studies of this type have been reported, both designed to investigate the relationship between particular childhood problems and adult schizophrenia.

The association between withdrawing, internalized tension symptoms in children and adult schizophrenia was the focus of attention in a study of the adjustment of adults seen diagnostically at the Dallas Child Guidance Clinic 16 to 27 years ago. From case history materials, 54 former child patients were classified as internal reactors on the basis of comprehensive social history, one or more psychological examinations and a psychiatric interview. On the basis of followup interviews the authors concluded: ". . . they are on the whole getting along quite well. Approximately two-thirds are classified as satisfactorily adjusted and one-third as marginally adjusted. Only two of the 54 are considered to be sick, and only one of these is in a mental hospital . . . one has the impression that most of the people who we diagnosed as internal reactors turn out to be average, normal people in most respects" (Morris, Soroker, and Burress, 1954, p. 753). Another report on the same clinic population described the classification of case histories of 606 former child patients into three categories of symptoms—introverts, ambiverts, and extroverts. The names of 24 of these former patients were found in the files of mental institutions in Texas, presumably indicating a severe kind of mental illness during adulthood. Of the 164 persons whose records had been classified as introverted, only one was among the group of 24 hospitalized patients. "The results point to the conclusion that there is not adequate justification for the assertion that children who might be classified as introverts are more likely to develop schizophrenia ... introverted children may be least likely to develop neuropsychiatric disorders ... which would require hospitalization" (Michael, Morris, and Soroker, 1957, p. 337).

An even more ambitious followup study of former child patients is under way at the St. Louis Municipal Psychiatric Clinic. The subjects are 525 consecutive admissions 30 years prior to the beginning of the followup. In addition, one hundred problem-free control subjects were selected at random from public school records of the same time to match the former child patient group on sex, race, year of birth, and socioeconomic status. Adult social and psychiatric status of both the former patient group and the controls has been determined by a standardized interview with each subject and a search of public records. In summarizing present psychiatric status of the former child patients, 21 percent are in the no disease category. By comparison, 60 percent of the control group are placed in the no disease category (O'Neal and Robins, 1958b). In the former patient group ten percent received schizophrenic diagnoses as adults. In this group too, the withdrawing, internalizing symptoms in childhood problems seemed not to be prodromal of adult schizophrenia. None of the preschizophrenic children had been diagnosed as psychotic, although some suspicion had been expressed in three cases out of 28. Rather, the childhood symptoms of the schizophrenic group seemed best described as antisocial, along with a greater number of areas of disturbed functioning (O'Neal and Robins, 1958a). Comparisons of the former patient group with controls or variables other than present psychiatric status showed a higher rate of mortality in the patient group, a higher proportion who had moved away from the St. Louis area, and a higher proportion of arrests for serious crimes (Robins and O'Neal, 1958).

Continuity Hypothesis: Conclusions

The conclusion that can be drawn from both these child patient populations is similar in one important respect. It is the acting out, disturbing child who is likely to become seriously mentally ill as an adult, rather than the shy, withdrawn child. It is interesting to note in passing that in the much quoted Wickman study, comparing teachers' and clinicians' judgments about problem behavior in children, the teachers may have been better predic-

tors of adult psychiatric status than clinicians. These two studies give us different answers on the larger question—"Do problem children become mentally ill as adults?" The reason, undoubtedly, is the difference in criterion of adult status used in the two studies. When a more rigorous criterion of adult mental illness, admission to a mental hospital, is used in the Dallas Clinic followup, the answer is "no." When the criterion is "no psychiatric disease" determined by examination, as in the followup of the St. Louis patients, the answer is "yes, problem children do have a higher proportion of psychiatric difficulties as adults." The later conclusion is tempered somewhat by referring back to the proportion of control subjects in the St. Louis study who had been classified in the no disease category. They had been selected to provide a comparison with a healthy population, and subjects in whose school records there was any suggestion of problem behavior were not used for control purposes. In this group, who would presumably be somewhat freer of problems than a group selected entirely at random, almost one-half either received a specific psychiatric diagnosis, or their status is not sufficiently clear for them to receive the no disease label. The findings, therefore, seem to offer only mild support for the continuity hypothesis.

The Intervention Hypothesis: General Outcomes of Therapy

The effectiveness of therapeutic intervention on children's adjustment status has received attention in the literature for more than thirty years. In general, the question that has been asked in these studies is "How many of the children who were treated showed improvement in their presenting symptoms?" At the simplest level of investigation there is a statement of the percent of the treated children who were showing improvement at the time the case was closed. These studies can be summarized rather quickly by stating that improvement is usually noted in two-thirds to three-fourths of the treated cases regardless of the treatment setting, the professional discipline of therapist or the age of children treated (Allbright and Gambrell, 1938; Beaumont, 1945; Brown, 1947; Gibbs, 1945; Jacobsen, 1948; LaMore, 1941; Rotenberg, 1947). The most recent and comprehensive figure, based on reports of 994 clinics of cases closed during the year 1959, is 72 percent improvement (Norman, Rosen, and Bohn, 1962).

Conclusions based on the statement of the child's adjustment status at the termination of clinical treatment must be guarded since it may reflect simply the degree of optimism of the therapist at the time the case is closed. Followup studies of treated clinical cases by persons other than the clinic staff provide a somewhat more detached evaluation of the outcome of treatment. The usual format of followup studies is to select a sample of cases from a clinic's file and interview an informant, usually the child's mother, in order to assess the child's adjustment for a period of time after treatment is terminated. The assessment is then summarized as a dichotomous judgment in terms of improvement in presenting problems or adequacy of present adjustment as opposed to no improvement or poor adjustment. In studies ranging from one year to seven or eight years following treatment, the proportion of improvement reported is still mostly within the two-thirds to three-fourths range. Witmer and students (1933) reported 73 percent for a New York clinic, and a range of 60 percent to 84 percent in a study of 16 clinics (Witmer, 1935a, 1935b). Other reports of this kind give improvement figures of 76 percent (Hardcastle, 1934); 73 percent (Hubbard and Adams, 1936); 80 percent (Shirley, Baum, and Polsky, 1940); 63 percent (Cunningham, Westerman, and Fischhoff, 1956); and 71 percent (Rodriquez, Rodriquez, and Eisenberg, 1959).

Most of these studies have made an effort to relate factors other than treatment to successful adjustment at followup. However, none of them report a clear relationship with the length of treatment, whether or not the child finished treatment, the sex of the child, or his age at referral. Some evidence has been found for interaction effects between treatment and intelligence, initial diagnostic classification, and socioeconomic status of parents. One rather puzzling finding in the study by Shirley et al. (1940) was the lack of relationship between adjustment at close of treatment and adjustment at followup. Judging success in a dichotomous way, four of every ten children who were judged successful at the end of treatment were unsuccessful at followup, and four of every ten unsuccessful treatment cases were judged successful at followup. Unfortunately, the other studies did not report their data in a way that allowed for a comparison with this finding.

Effects of Intervention

The effects of intervention in treating children's problems can be more rigorously tested if the followup method includes a comparison group of children who have been identified as emotionally disturbed but who have received no treatment.

Levitt (1957a) touched off a spirited debate a few years ago by concluding that improvement rates among children who had been treated in child guidance clinics were no higher than improvement rates for children who had been on clinic waiting lists but had never been treated. Following the method used by Eysenck (1952), Levitt established a base line recovery rate of 72.5 percent from two followup studies of children who had been withdrawn from clinic waiting lists. He then presented data on outcome of clinical treatment with 7,987 children in which the percent improved was 73.3, not significantly different from the control figure. He went on to analyze the difference between reported improvement at the close of treatment and at followup. That the time since identification of a problem in a child might be a more important factor in his present adjustment than whether or not he had received treatment was the inference that Levitt drew from his comparison. Followup studies of longer duration tend to report higher rates of improvement than studies at the close of treatment.

Levitt's conclusion has been criticized on several grounds, but primarily on the appropriateness of defectors from clinic waiting lists as controls (Hood-Williams, 1960; Heinicke and Goldman, 1960). It has been suggested, for example, that the initial motivation for treatment is probably not as high, the problems are not as serious, or sudden improvement in symptoms occurred while the child's name was still on the waiting list. Levitt has countered these criticisms by showing that treated and defector child cases do not differ on 61 factors, including two clinical estimates of severity of disturbance and eight other factors related to symptoms (1957b, 1958a), and that in followup interviews with parents of defector cases only 13 percent attributed defection to improvement of the child's symptoms (1958b). On the other hand, a spontaneous recovery rate of 50 percent has been reported in a study by Morris and Soroker (1953).

Waiting List Defectors as Controls

Whatever the shortcomings in the use of waiting list defectors as controls in studying outcomes of child therapy, it is the only basis of comparison presently reported in the literature. The study by Witmer and Keller (1942) reported a followup study of children eight to 13 years after their clinic contact. In this group there were 85 children who had received treatment and 50 who had been seen only diagnostically. Improvement at followup was reported for 60 percent of the treated group and 78 percent of the untreated group. Lehrman, et al. (1949) also reported a comparison of adjustment of 196 children seen for treatment and 110 children seen only for diagnostic evaluation. A one year followup showed 75 percent of the treatment group with improved adjustment and 70 percent of the untreated group with improved adjustment. A five year followup study of 202 former clients of a child guidance clinic in England was reported in terms of mean ratings rather than percent improved. However, the comparison on ratings between treated cases and cases seen only diagnostically showed no significant differences (Barbour and Beefell, 1955). Levitt, Beiser, and Robertson (1959) studied the psychological adjustment of a sample of 579 cases, averaging about seven years after the termination of treatment. Controls were 427 waiting list defectors from the same period of time. Twenty-six outcome variables, including psychological tests, biographical data, self-evaluations and clinical judgments failed to show any significant differences in the psychological adjustment of the two groups. Levi and Ginott (1961) reported a 55 percent remission of symptoms rate in 314 children treated in a clinic, compared to 20 percent remissions in a group of 300 children whose parents had made application for treatment but had failed to complete the intake procedures.

These five studies, comparing more than one thousand treated children with more than one thousand children whose problems were not treated, are almost uniformly discouraging in evaluating the outcome of treatment in a child guidance facility. The Levi and Ginott study alone would encourage optimism, and it is interesting to note that the improvement figures reported in that study, both for the treated and for the untreated groups, depart markedly from figures reported in most other studies. Depending on how seriously one takes the question of the appropriateness of comparison with waiting list defectors, the evidence at least does not increase confidence in the intervention hypothesis. One might wish for an intake arrangement in clinics that would allow children to be randomly assigned to treatment and control groups, to help rule out the alternate explanations based on motivation and severity of symptoms in the waiting list defectors.

Cambridge-Somerville Youth Study

This kind of design was used in the Cambridge-Somerville Youth Study, a program designed to prevent juvenile delinquency. Pre-

delinquent boys were matched at the beginning of the study on age, intelligence, social, and emotional ratings and probability of developing delinquent behavior. One of each matched pair was randomly assigned to a treatment group, and received a case work counseling service for a period of six to eight years. By the criterion of preventing juvenile delinquency, measured by police and court records, there were no differences between the treatment and control groups either at the end of the study (Powers and Witmer, 1951), or at followup, ten years after the study was terminated (McCord, McCord, and Zola, 1959). Included in Witmer's evaluation of the program is a comparison of results using the same format as that generally used for comparison of clinic treatment and control cases. A terminal rating of adjustment was made from case records for each boy in the treatment group. A similar rating for 148 of the boys in the control group was made at the end of the study by an interview with the boys and their parents and by a questionnaire sent to their school. Comparison of the terminal adjustment for the 148 matched pairs of boys showed 71 percent of the treatment group receiving ratings of good or fairly good adjustment, and 74 percent of the control boys receiving similar ratings. The question of degree of disturbance would seem to be clearly answered in this study by the original matching of treatment and control subjects. The question that still may be raised is one of motivation for treatment. In the Cambridge-Somerville experiment none of the boys or their families sought treatment; the service was offered to them.

Studies of the general effectiveness of residential treatment for disturbed children have, to date, been carried out along the same lines as the evaluations of outpatient clinical treatment of children. Controls from a waiting list are not generally available as a comparison group. In most studies a gross report of general adjustment is given either at the termination of treatment or at some specified followup period. In a descriptive survey of 12 residential treatment centers for emotionally disturbed children, Reid and Hagan (1952) reported a general outcome figure for each of the institutions studied. The figures reported by each institution on successful treatment vary from 50 percent to 76 percent, with a cumulative average of about 68 percent for 519 children reported upon. The range is somewhat lower but the average is comparable to the figures reported for outpatient treatment of children. Hamilton, McKinley, Moorhead, and Wall (1961) report a two-thirds success rate at the close of residential treatment of 110 adolescent boys.

Other studies give followup information on children who have been treated in residential settings. Rosenthal and Pinsky (1936) reported a 63 percent success rate, Zick (1943) reported 63 percent, Johnson and Reid (1947) 74 percent, Benjamin and Weatherly (1947) 71 percent, and Rubin (1962) 67 percent. The only study of this general type that departs from the approximately two-thirds improved rate for residential treatment is a followup by Morris, Escoll, and Wexler (1956) in which the two-thirds rate was reported at termination of treatment, but by age 18, 21 percent of those who could be located were judged by interviews to be doing well. The rest showed varying degrees of poor adjustment.

The major informational value of the studies of outcome in residential treatment centers is that success is comparable, as far as gross judgments of outcome are concerned, to success with children treated in outpatient clinics. Since there have been no untreated controls employed in any of these studies, it is difficult to draw conclusions relevant to the intervention hypothesis, i.e., that children benefit more by treatment than they would by no treatment.

The Intervention Hypothesis: Predictions Based on Specific Variables

Some experimenters have approached the problem of outcome of clinical treatment by making predictions on variables more specific than whether or not a child improved. These studies have been conducted in nonclinic settings, sometimes with children who have not been referred as problem cases, but have been able to approximate a true experimental design more closely than studies whose intent is to evaluate outcome of clinical treatment. The pattern of reporting on brief play therapy experiences for children is to use questionnaires, ratings, and sociometrics as measures of direct consequences of play therapy, and measure of reading achievement as an indirect index of improvement in emotional adjustment.

Fleming and Snyder (1947) selected seven subjects, who had high scores on tests of maladjustment, for group therapy sessions followed by retest on the initial measures. It is difficult to conclude that the reported changes were a function of the group therapy experience, because of the tendency of extreme scores to show regression toward the mean on retesting. Nevertheless, the study established a pattern of using a nonclinic population of children, a non–waiting list control group, a prede-termined length of time for experimental intervention and direct measurement of criterion variables. Mehlman (1953) employed nondirective group play therapy with institutionalized familial defective children. Using personality test scores and behavior ratings as the criterion for change, the study found slightly more changes in the therapy group, compared to controls, on scales of the Haggerty, Olson, Wickman Behavior Ratings. Cox (1953) used an elaborate design to include age roles of children in an orphanage as one of the independent variables in a study of play therapy. His prediction that the older children in the group would show changes in sociometric measures as a function of play therapy was confirmed; personality measurements were in the predicted direction but did not achieve significance. In a study by Seeman, Barry, and Ellenwood (1956), an experimental design controlling for the effects of regression was used, by choosing both the experimental and control group from children with extreme scores on adjustment. Following individual play therapy sessions, the experimental group showed significant changes in reputation test scores, teacher ratings were in the predicted direction but not significant and, for aggressive children, there was a shift away from aggressive ratings. Dorfman (1958) approximated a clinic population in an experimental therapy group by using children referred by classroom teachers for help. The design included a wait control period for the experimental subjects, and matched no-therapy controls, and followup of both groups after one year. Scores from a personality test showed no change during the wait period for either group, improvement in the experimental group during therapy which was maintained, but not enhanced, during the one year followup. An adjustment score from a sentence completion test showed a similar pattern of change for both groups.

A different base line was used in reporting the outcomes of brief psychotherapy with children (Phillips and Johnson, 1954; Phillips, 1960). Disappearance of specific symptoms, present in each child on referral, was used as a criterion for change. Comparisons were made with the remission of symptoms in children treated by conventional child guidance methods, rather than a control group. The comparisons of specific symptom remission favor the brief treatment technique in all of the cases reported.

The use of reading achievement as an indirect indication of change attibutable to play therapy is based on the notion that reading is an extremely complex skill, and sensitive to interference from emotional maladjustment in children. Bills used an own-control design to investigate the effects of play therapy on the reading achievement of maladjusted retarded readers (1950a). Standardized intelligence and reading achievement tests were used to establish the degree of reading retardation and to measure change in reading skill. There was significantly more gain in reading scores during the therapy period, compared with the control period, and gains for some of the children continued through the followup. A second study by the same author (Bills, 1950b) tested a corollary hypothesis—that retarded readers who were not emotionally maladjusted would not improve in reading skills with play therapy. Fisher (1953) found improvement in reading ability in a group of boys receiving psychotherapy in addition to a remedial reading program, compared to other children in the same remedial reading program who did not receive psychotherapy. Seeman and Benner (1954) reported a mixed outcome among two groups of children randomly assigned to an experimental group exposed to a group therapy experience and a control group. Experimental children gained more on reading achievement, showed no difference on sociometric scores, and showed a trend that was not quite significant toward greater maladjustment on a personality test.

Studies in Special Program Settings

Three studies reported specific outcomes in treatment of children in residential settings. Rausch, Dittman, and Taylor (1959) used an observational technique to study the change in social interaction of hyperaggressive boys in a residential treatment center. While the pattern of interaction of these children with their peers did not undergo any change during the time of treatment, there was a significant change in their relationship to adults, a decrease in what the study referred to as hostile-dominant behavior. In their evaluation of New York's Wiltwick School for Boys, McCord and McCord (1956) reported a cross sectional comparison of Wiltwick boys with boys in a public reformatory on personality test scores. Differences included lower anxiety among Wiltwick boys, lower authoritarian tendencies, decrease in prejudices, more satisfaction with the world and with themselves, greater interest in constructive activities and a closer attachment to staff members. The only study approximating a pre-post design with experimental and control groups in a residential setting is reported by Weeks (1958), a comparison of boys at Highfields and boys in a public reformatory. No

control over assignment could be exercised, since administrative groupings had to be used, so the assumption of initial comparability of the two groups may be questioned. The dependent variables in the study were attitudes in regard to family, law and order, and outlook on life, measured by questionnaire. There was little evidence that either group of boys was able to change basic attitudes measured by the questionnaire in the direction of greater conformity to society's values; in fact some subgroups showed change in the reverse direction.

Only one study reported psychometric outcomes of a day school program for emotionally disturbed children. Haring and Phillips (1962) reported test data for a one year experiment with three groups of emotionally disturbed children in Arlington County, Virginia. Administrative groupings were used to study three methods of instruction. Group I received structured instruction, Group II were children left in ordinary classrooms, and Group III received permissive instruction. Behavior ratings by teachers and academic achievement test results were used in a pre-post design to assess change. Changes during the year on both variables clearly favored the structured method, and the authors concluded that the difference was a function of superiority of the method of instruction. Although gains on both dependent variables did favor the structured group, initial differences, especially between Groups I and III, raise serious doubts about the appropriateness of such a comparison. The administrative grouping resulted in large initial differences on all variables reported, age, achievement, and ratings of behavior. In spite of this weakness in design, it is encouraging that an experimental approach has been introduced into an educational setting and definitive criteria have been used to determine outcome in a program for emotionally disturbed children.

Summary

Two working hypotheses in clinical treatment of disturbed children have been examined in this review. The continuity hypothesis, that emotionally disturbed children will become mentally ill adults, has received only mild support. If one begins with mental patients and reviews their developmental history, he is likely to find a record of childhood problems. If one begins with a population of children identified as emotionally disturbed and follows the whole group to adulthood, the evidence is mixed. Neither of the two large scale followup studies was designed specifically to test the continuity hypothesis, so the conclusion must be guarded. The conclusion of the Dallas study is that it is hazardous to predict particular forms of adult mental illness from childhood symptoms, at least in the language we customarily use to talk about children's problems. In any event, only a small proportion of the total group of children became so disturbed as adults that they had to be admitted to a mental hospital. The St. Louis study, on the other hand, identified psychiatric problems in almost two-thirds of its former child patients, but very few of the problems identified could be called serious or incapacitating, and, as in the Dallas study, no accurate predictions could have been made on the basis of presenting symptoms in childhood. So far as the continuity hypothesis is concerned, we must at least conclude that it is incomplete. The extent to which a childhood predisposition to mental illness influences appearance of problems in adult life is not entirely clear, but it is apparently not a determining factor. In this perspective, Levitt's suggestion that time may be more important than treatment has more meaning. That some disturbed children will grow up to be disturbed adults is undoubtedly true, but many others will grow up to be ordinary adults with no more than their share of problems.

The second hypothesis of clinical treatment, that therapeutic intervention enhances the general adjustment status of disturbed children, has received even less support than the continuity hypothesis. The regularity with which the two-thirds to three-fourths improvement figure occurs in studies of disturbed children, regardless of treatment, suggests a widely shared bias that allows us to see all but the most obstreperous children as "better than they were."

The most convincing evidence for the effectiveness of intervention is in studies using criteria more specific than assessment of general adjustment. While some might argue that sociometric scores, questionnaires, and tests beg the real question of whether the child is better, the fact is that as outcome variables they reflect differential change while global judgments of improvement do not. One way of interpreting this difference, of course, is that as research tools, judgments about general adjustment are simply not as reliable as test scores or ratings on specific items of behavior. However, in the absence of compelling confirmation of the continuity hypothesis, we may need to re-examine what we hope to accomplish by intervention, rather than concluding that the evaluation of intervention is a hopeless undertaking. If we do not postulate a linear relationship between emotional disturbance in childhood and mental illness in

adulthood, the treatment of symptoms may be all we can realistically undertake. If we cannot aspire to reconstruction of personality that will have long range beneficial effects, we can modify disturbing behavior in specific ways in present social contexts. This more modest aspiration may not only be more realistic, but it may be all that is required of the child-helping professions in a society that is relatively open and provides a variety of opportunity systems in which a child can reconcile his personal needs with society's expectations of him.

References

Allbright, Sue, and Gambrell, Helen. Personality traits as criteria for the psychiatric treatment of adolescents. *Smith College Studies in Social Work*, 1938, 9, 1–26.

Barbour, R. F., and Beefell, C. J. The followup of a child guidance clinic population. *Journal of Mental Science*, 1955, 101, 794–809.

Beaumont, Arlene. Psychotherapy of children by social case workers. *Smith College Studies in Social Work*, 1945, 15, 259–286.

Benjamin, A., and Weatherly, H. E. Hospital treatment of emotionally disturbed children. *American Journal of Orthopsychiatry*, 1947, 17, 665–674.

Bills, R. E. Nondirective play therapy with retarded readers. *Journal of Consulting Psychology*, 1950a, 14, 140–149.

Bills, R. E. Play therapy with well-adjusted retarded readers. *Journal of Consulting Psychology*, 1950b, 14, 246–249.

Birren, J. E. Psychological examinations of children who later become psychotic. *Journal of Abnormal Social Psychology*, 1944, 39, 84–95.

Bower, E. M., Shellhammer, T. A., Daily, J. M., and Bower, M. *High school students who later become schizophrenic.* Sacramento, California: State Department of Education, 1960.

Bowman, K. M. A study of the pre-psychotic personality in certain psychoses. *American Journal of Orthopsychiatry*, 1934, 14, 28–35.

Brown, Marjorie. Adolescents treatable by a family agency. *Smith College Studies in Social Work*, 1947, 18, 37–67.

Cox, J. N. Sociometric status and individual treatment before and after play therapy. *Journal of Abnormal Social Psychology*, 1953, 48, 354–356.

Cunningham, J. M., Westerman, H. H., and Fischhoff, J. A follow-up study of patients seen in a psychiatric clinic for children. *American Journal of Orthopsychiatry*, 1956, 26, 602–612.

Dorfman, Elaine. Personality outcomes of client-centered child therapy. *Psychological Monograph*, 1958, 72 (Whole No. 456).

Eysenck, H. J. The effects of psychotherapy: an evaluation. *Journal of Consulting Psychology*, 1952, 16, 319–324.

Fisher, B. Group therapy with retarded readers. *Journal of Educational Psychology*, 1953, 44, 354–360.

Fleming, L., and Snyder, W. U. Social and personal changes following non-directive group play therapy. *American Journal of Orthopsychiatry*, 1947, 17, 101–116.

Friedlander, Dorothea. Personality development of twenty-seven children who later became psychotic. *Journal of Abnormal Social Psychology*, 1945, 40, 330–335.

Gibbs, J. M. Group play therapy. *British Journal of Medical Psychology*, 1945, 20, 244–254.

Hamilton, D. M., McKinley, R. A., Moorhead, H. H., and Wall, J. H. Results of mental hospital treatment of troubled youth. *American Journal of Psychiatry*, 1961, 117, 811–816.

Hardcastle, D. H. A follow-up study of 100 cases made for the Department of Psychological Medicine, Guy's Hospital. *Journal of Mental Science*, 1934, 80, 536–549.

Haring, N. G., and Phillips, E. L. *Educating emotionally disturbed children.* New York: McGraw-Hill Book Company, 1962.

Heinicke, C. M., and Goldman, A. Research on psychotherapy with children: a review and suggestions for further study. *American Journal of Orthopsychiatry*, 1960, 30, 483–494.

Hood-Williams, J. The results of psychotherapy with children: a re-evaluation. *Journal of Consulting Psychology*, 1960, 24, 84–88.

Hubbard, Ruth M., and Adams, Christine F. Factors affecting the success of child guidance treatment. *American Journal of Orthopsychiatry*, 1936, 6, 81–102.

Jacobsen, Virginia. Influential factors in the outcome of treatment of school phobia. *Smith College Studies in Social Work*, 1948, 18, 181–202.

Johnson, Lillian, and Reid, J. H. Evaluation of ten years' work with emotionally disturbed children. *Ryther Child Center Monograph*, 1947, IV.

Kasanin, J., and Veo, L. A. A study of the school adjustments of children who later in life became psychotic. *American Journal of Orthopsychiatry*, 1932, 2, 212–227.

LaMore, Mary T. An evaluation of a state hospital child guidance clinic. *Smith College Studies in Social Work*, 1941, 12, 137–164.

Lehrman, L. J., Sirluck, H., Black, B., and Glick, S. Success and failure of treatment of children in the child guidance clinics of the Jewish Board of Guardians, New York City. *Jewish Board of Guardians Research Monograph*, 1949, No. 1, 1-1–87.

Levi, Aurelia, and Ginott, H. G. The results of psychotherapy with children: another evaluation. Unpublished manuscript, 1961. Cited by H. G. Ginott, *Group psychotherapy with children.* New York: McGraw-Hill Book Company, 1961, 145–147.

Levitt, E. E. The results of psychotherapy with children: an evaluation. *Journal of Consulting Psychology*, 1957a, 21, 189–196.

Levitt, E. E. A comparison of "remainers" and "defectors" among child clinic patients. *Journal of Consulting Psychology*, 1957b, 21, 316.

Levitt, E. E. A comparative judgment study of "defection" from treatment at a child guidance clinic. *Journal of Clinical Psychology*, 1958a, 14, 429–432.

Levitt, E. E. Parent's reasons for defection from treatment at a child guidance clinic. *Mental Hygiene*, 1958b, 42, 521–524.

Levitt, E. E., Beiser, Helen R., and Robertson, R. E. A follow-up evaluation of cases treated at a community child guidance clinic. *American Journal of Orthopsychiatry*, 1959, 29, 337–349.

McCord, W., and McCord, Joan. *Psychopathy and delinquency.* New York: Grune and Stratton, 1956.

McCord, W., McCord, Joan, and Zola, I. K. *Origins of crime: a new evaluation of the Cambridge-Somerville Youth Study.* New York: Columbia University Press, 1959.

Mehlman, B. Group therapy with mentally retarded children. *Journal of Abnormal and Social Psychology*, 1953, 48, 53–60.

Michael, C. M., Morris, D. P., and Soroker, E. Follow-up studies of shy, withdrawn children: II. Relative incidence of schizophrenia. *American Journal of Orthopsychiatry*, 1957, 27, 331–337.

Morris, D. P., and Soroker, Eleanor. A follow-up study of a guidance clinic waiting list. *Mental Hygiene*, 1953, 37, 84–88.

Morris, D. P., Soroker, Eleanor, and Burruss, Genette. Follow-up studies of shy withdrawn children: I. Evaluation of later adjustment. *American Journal of Orthopsychiatry*, 1954, 24, 743–754.

Morris, H. H., Jr., Escoll, P. J., and Wexler, R. Aggressive behavior disorders of childhood: a follow-up study. *American Journal of Psychiatry*, 1956, 112, 991–997.

Norman, Vivian, Rosen, Beatrice, and Bohn, Anita. Psychiatric clinic out-patients in the United States, 1959. *Mental Hygiene*, 1962, 46, 321–343.

O'Neal, Patricia, and Robins, L. N. Childhood patterns predictive of adult schizophrenia: a 30 year follow-up study. *American Journal of Psychiatry*, 1958a, 115, 385–391.

O'Neal, Patricia, and Robins, L. N. The relation of childhood behavior problems to adult psychiatric status: a thirty year follow-up of 150 subjects. *American Journal of Psychiatry*, 1958b, 114, 961–969.

Phillips, E. L. Parent–child psychotherapy: a follow-up study comparing two techniques. *Journal of Psychology*, 1960, 49, 195–202.

Phillips, E. L., and Johnson, Margaret. Theoretical and clinical aspects of short-term, parent–child psychotherapy. *Psychiatry*, 1954, 17, 267–275.

Powers, E., and Witmer, Helen. *An experiment in the prevention of delinquency.* New York: Columbia University Press, 1951.

Rausch, H. L., Dittman, A. T., and Taylor, T. J. The interpersonal behavior of children in residential treatment. *Journal of Abnormal Social Psychology*, 1959, 58, 9–26.

Reid, J. H., and Hagan, Helen. *Residential treatment of emotionally disturbed children.* New York: Child Welfare League of America, 1952.

Robins, L. N., and O'Neal, Patricia. Mortality, mobility and crime: problem children 30 years later. *American Sociological Review*, 1958, 23, 162–171.

Rodriquez, A., Rodriquez, M., and Eisenberg, L. The outcome of school phobia: a follow-up study based on 41 cases. *American Journal of Psychiatry*, 1959, 116, 540–544.

Rosenthal, F. M., and Pinsky, G. D. Follow-up method in child guidance work. *American Journal of Orthopsychiatry*, 1936, 6, 609–615.

Rotenberg, Gertrude. Can problem adolescents be aided apart from their parents? *Smith College Studies in Social Work*, 1947, 17, 204–222.

Rubin, E. Z. Special education in a psychiatric hospital. *Exceptional Children*, 1962, 29, 184–190.

Seeman, J., Barry, E., and Ellenwood, C. Process and outcomes of play therapy. *American Psychologist*, 1956, 11, 428.

Seeman, J., and Benner, E. A therapeutic approach to reading difficulties. *Journal of Consulting Psychology*, 1954, 18, 541–543.

Shirley, Mary, Baum, Betty, and Polsky, Sylvia. Outgrowing childhood's problems: a follow-up study of child guidance patients. *Smith College Studies in Social Work*, 1940, 11, 31–60.

Weeks, H. A. *Youthful offenders at Highfields: an evaluation of the effects of the short-term treatment of delinquent boys.* Ann Arbor: University of Michigan Press, 1958.

Witmer, Helen. A comparison of treatment results in various types of child guidance clinics. *American Journal of Orthopsychiatry*, 1935a, 5, 351–360.

Witmer, Helen. The later social adjustment of problem children: a report of 13 follow-up investigations. *Smith College Studies in Social Work*, 1935b, 6, 1–98.

Witmer, Helen L., and Keller, Jane. Outgrowing childhood problems: a study in the value of child guidance treatment. *Smith College Studies in Social Work*, 1942, 74–90.

Witmer, Helen, and students. The outcome of treatment in a child guidance clinic: a comparison and an evaluation. *Smith College Studies in Social Work*, 1933, 3, 339–399.

Wittman, M. P., and Huffman, A. V. A comparative study of developmental, adjustment, and personality characteristics of psychotic, psychoneurotic, delinquent and normally adjusted teen-age youths. *Journal of Genetic Psychology*, 1945, 66, 167–182.

Zick, Frances. Outcome of intramural psychotherapy of children. *Smith College Studies in Social Work*, 1943, 14, 127–132.

From W. W. Lewis, "Continuity and Intervention in Emotional Disturbance: A Review," *Exceptional Children*, vol. 31, no. 9, May 1965, pp. 465–75. Reprinted by permission of The Council for Exceptional Children and the author.

Editors' Commentary

In a subsequent review, Clarizio[7] concludes that retrospective studies offer only modest evidence that the maladjusted child grows into a maladjusted adult. Both he and Morris's group[8] suggest that neurotic symptoms in childhood do not predict neurosis in adults. However, serious social maladjustment is predictive. In a study more closely related to the school situation, Zax and his associates[9] found that, compared to normal children, first graders with a high potential for being disturbed earned lower grades, scored lower on achievement tests, and were rated by teachers and peers as more poorly adjusted, when they reached the seventh grade. They do not believe that early mental health problems are transient.

Glavin[10] points out that 30 percent of "screened for problem" children who receive no planned intervention have persistent disturbance, but the majority of the emotional disturbances of young school children do not persist over four years. He also makes the point that these figures do not apply to profoundly disturbed children, only to those who remained in regular classes.

Kohlberg et al.[11] have written a thorough review of the relationship between childhood behavior and adult mental health. They point out that it is not the *absence of problems* that is predictive of adult status, but the *presence of various competencies* which makes the difference. In general, they find little support for the continuity theory that emotionally disturbed children will become mentally ill adults. Exceptions are found in biological predispositions to schizophrenia and in sociopathic conditions or character disorders that are the result of environmental factors—these two aspects are predictive of future difficulty.

From Kohlberg it is evident that significant physiological limitations and severe environmental conditions must be taken into consideration regarding risk in follow-up studies. The Thomas, Chess, and Birch excerpt that follows presents a reasoned viewpoint concerning the implications of biological aspects. The studies reported have continued since this article was written. The most recent report is a 1977 book by Thomas and Chess,[12] emphasizing the persistence of the child's underlying temperament and the need for a good "fit" with that temperament provided by the environment in home and school.

7.   **Harvey Clarizio,** "Stability of Deviant Behavior through Time," *Mental Hygiene* 52 (1968): 228–293.

8.   **D. Morris, E. Soroker, and G. Burruss,** "Follow-up Studies of Shy Withdrawn Children: Evaluation of Later Adjustment," *American Journal of Orthopsychiatry* 24 (1954): 734–754.

9.   **M. Zax** et al., "Follow-up Study of Children Identified Early as Emotionally Disturbed," *Journal of Consulting and Clinical Psychology* 32 (1968): 369–374.

10.   **J. P. Glavin,** "Persistence of Behavior Disorders in Public School Children," mimeographed (Philadelphia: Temple University, 1974).

11.   **L. Kohlberg, J. LaCrosse, and D. Ricks,** "The Predictability of Adult Mental Health from Childhood Behavior," in *Manual of Child Psychopathology,* ed. Benjamin B. Wolman (New York: McGraw-Hill, 1972), pp. 1217–1287.

12.   **Alexander Thomas and Stella Chess,** *Temperament and Development* (New York: Brunner/Mazel, 1977).

Temperament and Behavior Disorders in Children

Alexander Thomas
Stella Chess
Herbert G. Birch

Theoretical Implications of the Findings

The findings of our longitudinal study of children who developed behavior disorders clearly indicate that features of temperament, together with their organization and patterning, play significant roles in the genesis and evolution of behavior disorders in childhood. Both before and after they developed symptoms, groups of the children with behavioral disturbances differed in temperament from those who did not develop such disturbances. The clinical cases, as a group, were characterized by an excessive frequency of either high or low activity, irregularity, withdrawal responses to novel stimuli, nonadaptability, high intensity, persistence, and distractibility. No single temperamental trait acted alone in influencing the course of the child's development. Rather, combinations of traits forming patterns and clusters tended to result in an increased risk for developing behavioral disorders. Differences in types of behavior disorders and of symptoms, too, were found to be associated with differences in temperament.

A given pattern of temperament did not, as such, result in a behavioral disturbance. Deviant, as well as normal, development was the result of the interaction between the child with given characteristics of temperament and significant features of his intra-familial and extra-familial environment. Temperament, representing one aspect of a child's individuality, also interacted with abilities and motives, the other two facets, as well as with the environment, in determining the specific behavior patterns that evolved in the course of development.

Given our findings on the relevance of temperamental factors to the genesis and evolution of behavior disorders, we may explore their implications for general theory in psychiatry and child development. As is the case when any significant influencing variable is identified, there is an understandable temptation to make temperament the heart and body of a general theory. To do so would be to repeat a frequent approach in psychiatry which, over the years, has been beset by general theories of behavior based upon fragments rather than the totality of influencing mechanisms. A one-sided emphasis on temperament would merely repeat and perpetuate such a tendency and would be antithetical to our viewpoint, which insists that we recognize temperament as only one attribute of the organism. In our view, temperament must at all times be considered in its internal relations with abilities and motives and in its external relations with environmental opportunities and stresses. Consequently, the relevance of the concept of temperament to general psychiatric theory lies neither in its sole pertinence for behavior disorders, nor in its displacement of other conceptualizations, but in the fact that it must be incorporated into any general theory of normal and aberrant behavioral development if the theory is to be complete. Existing theories emphasize motives and drive states, tactics of adaptation, environmental patterns of influence, and primary organic determinants. The central requirement that a concept of temperament makes of such generalizations is that they come increasingly to focus on the individual and on his uniqueness. In other words, it requires that we recognize that the same motive, the same adaptive tactic, or the same structure of objective environment will have different functional meaning in accordance with the temperamental style of the given child. Moreover, in such an individualization of the study of functional mechanisms in behavior, temperament must be considered as an independent determining variable in itself, and not as an *ad hoc* modifier used to fill in the gaps left unexplained by other mechanisms.

A formulation of the role of the child's own characteristics that fails to give temperament serious consideration together with other mechanisms is illustrated in a recent discussion of autistic psychosis. The author, herself a longtime student of organismic individual differences in children, asserts an a priori hierarchy assigning prime importance to "mothering" and secondary importance to the child's characteristics: "Children who suffer from this illness have in common the lack or distortion of a mutual relationship with a mother person . . . in some instances this deficiency arises because there was no mother who responded to the baby as normal mothers do—an environmental deficiency. But the illness also occurs in children who were raised by normally responsive mothers who provide all that other children receive. But the child is so constituted that he cannot participate in the usual patterns of interaction, probably due to an inborn deficit yet to be specified. The child deficient in the capacity to respond is just as motherless as is the normally equipped child without a mother."

This formulation assumes that autism is a deficiency disease; and that the essential nutritive element is "mothering." It implies that there is one pattern of mothering that may be classified as adequate for all children and assumes, on hypothetical grounds, that such a universal "adequate" for the mothering process does exist. However, a recognition of temperamental differences and their significance for development makes it impossible to accept such universals, whether for the mothering process or any other environmental influence, and emphasizes the need to clarify and define "adequacy" in terms of the goodness of fit between the organism cared for and the pattern of care, if such care is to result in certain socially defined consequences.

A contrasting illustration, in which temperament is seriously treated as a determining variable rather than as an *ad hoc* consideration, can be cited from the recent literature. In a psychiatric study of children with poor school achievement, Ross defines a syndrome of behavioral disturbance which he calls "the unorganized child." He identifies the specific attributes of the child's individuality and parental functioning as independent but mutually interacting influences, and avoids any hierarchal designation of one as more fundamental than the other. Ross identifies the pertinent factors involved in the development of the unorganized child as the combination of the temperamental characteristics of high distractibility, short attention span, and low persistence in interaction with the parental attributes of overpermissiveness or disorganization of functioning. He further points out that specific manifestations of the syndrome will depend on whether these temperamental qualities are combined with high or low activity level and intense or mild responses. Specifically, Ross suggests that the unorganized child may show restlessness and a tendency to chatter disruptively if he also has a high activity level, daydreaming if he is less active, and tantrums when frustrated if he is also intense in his reactions.

Thus, a truly interactionist approach rejects the attempt to impose a priori hierarchal judgments of relative importance on child and environment in the developmental process. Moreover, it rejects the dichotomy of child versus environment and recognizes that the effective environment is the product of the selective responsiveness of the child to aspects of the objective situation to which he is exposed. An interactionist approach also cannot be satisfied with the application of global characterizations that children have "different constitutional dispositions" or that some mothers are "good" and others "bad" to explain all the vicissitudes of normal and disturbed development. What is required, first of all, is not merely an acceptance of the statement that children differ, but knowledge of *how* they differ and *how* these differences are continuously expressed as significant determinative factors in psychological growth. What is also required is not the categorization of parents as better or worse, more or less hostile, anxious, etc., but the delineation of those *specific* attributes of parental attitudes and practices and of other intra- and extra-familial environmental factors that are interacting with the *specific* temperamental and other organismic characteristics of the child to produce *specific* consequences for psychological development.

Motivational and Nonmotivational Factors

Although a long-term study must have a defined focus if it is to avoid the dangers of diffuseness and tangential pursuits, it is inevitable that such focused inquiry will have certain serendipitous outcomes. Such outcomes derive from the fact that what is being considered in detail is the developmental course of normal and aberrant behavioral styles, an issue which is more broadly encompassing than is temperament. Consequently, the sequential data on behavioral development necessary to assess the role of temperament in development are also entirely pertinent to a consideration of motivational features of functioning. As a result, the findings on symptom selection and evolution provide a substantial basis for considering the interrelations of motivational and nonmotivational factors, intrapsychic maneuvers, anxiety, and psychodynamic defenses in the development of normal and disturbed behavior. The implications of the findings for these issues can now be considered.

A major aspect of most theoretical formulations on the causes and nature of behavioral disturbances is the extent to which conceptualized intrapsychic purposes and aims are invoked as explanatory principles. Classical psychoanalysis and certain forms of contemporary learning theory present opposite and extreme positions with regard to the importance of such motives in the causation of disturbed behavior. For the orthodox psychoanalyst, motives are all-important. As stated by Freud in one of his final systematic formulations, "The symptoms of neuroses are exclusively, it might be said, either a substitutive satisfaction of some sexual impulse or measures to prevent such a satisfaction, and are as a rule compromises between the two." In other words, the primary force is considered as motivational, i.e., the aim to either satisfy or prevent the satisfaction of a basic drive. The motivational preoccupation of psychoanalytic theory has been ubiquitously evident in its search for the sources of psychopathological phenomena in underlying purposes, motives, and conceptualized goals and aims. A typical contemporary expression can be found in a discussion of child psychiatry in the *American Handbook of Psychiatry*. The general assertion is made that "there is evidence of repression and of the 'return of the repressed' in the symptoms of the neurotic child," and various specific symptoms are considered within this motivational framework. As an example, sleeplessness is stated to reflect "a vigilant attempt at protest against a frightening impression of the environment." At the other extreme, are the learning theorists, such as Eysenck, for whom "neurotic behavior consists of maladaptive conditioned responses of the autonomic system and of skeletal responses made to reduce the conditioned sympathetic reactions." With this formulation goes a denial of the existence of underlying motivational states. Thus, Eysenck states further that "there is no underlying complex or other 'dynamic' cause which is responsible for the maladaptive behavior; all we have to deal with in neurosis is conditioned maladaptive behavior."

Our finding that temperament–environment interactions play an important part in the development of behavioral disturbance in the young child suggests that it is frequently unnecessary and unparsimonious to postulate the existence of complex intrapsychic motivational states to account for maladaptation during the period of early development. The concern of such child analysts as Spitz, who have lamented the difficulty of studying intra-psychic states in young children, therefore appears unnecessary, inasmuch as the objective behavioral data obtainable for this age group appear quite sufficient for the study of the course of psychological development. . . .

Concepts of learning theory, based on conditioning, offer a non-motivational explanation for the manner in which specific maladaptive patterns may arise. It does not appear possible, however, to encompass the dynamics of symptom evolution in some of the older children entirely within the framework of a simple conditioned reflex model. Thus, as the growing child's subjective life expands and his psychological organization is increasingly influenced by ideation, abstraction, and symbolic representation, conceptualized motives and aims may, in some cases, begin to play an important part in symptom formation and evolution at older age periods.

To summarize, our findings would suggest that it is merely confusing to attribute elaborate psychological motivational mechanisms to the young child if a simpler explanation accounts for all the facts. In the older child, it may be necessary to invoke such motivational states when efforts to explain the behaviors in terms of simple mechanisms appear inadequate. . . .

Prevention of Behavioral Disturbance

The prevention of behavioral disturbances in childhood covers a vast array of issues, including those genetic, biochemical, temperamental, neurological, perceptual, cognitive, and environmental factors that may influence the course of behavioral development. The child's temperament is only one of the many issues to be considered by professional workers concerned with the prevention of pathology in psychological development, though often an important one. As our findings have demonstrated, the degree to which parents, teachers, pediatricians, and others handle a youngster in a manner appropriate to his temperamental characteristics can significantly influence the course of his psychological development. The oft-repeated motto, "Treat your child as an individual," achieves substance to the extent that the individuality of a child is truly recognized and respected. The other frequently offered prescription of "tender loving care" often has great value in promoting a positive parent–child interaction, but does not obviate the importance of the parent's actual child-care practices being consonant with his child's temperamental qualities.

Finally, the recognition that a child's behavioral disturbance is not necessarily the direct result of maternal pathology should do much to prevent the deep feelings of guilt and inadequacy with which innumerable mothers have been unjustly burdened as a result of being held entirely responsible for their children's problems. Mothers who are told authoritatively that child raising is a "task not easily achieved by the average mother in our culture" are not likely to approach this responsibility with the relaxation and confidence that would be beneficial to both their own and their child's mental health. It is our conviction, however, that the difficulties of child raising can be significantly lightened by advocating an approach of which the average mother *is* capable—the recognition of her child's specific qualities of individuality, and the adoption of those child-care practices that are most appropriate to them.

Editors' Commentary

Kupfer's group[13] has concluded that there are links between childhood and adult personality traits. The traits related to schizophrenia might be minimal organic dysfunctions. The implication is that problems with a biological substratum are resistant to change. However, descriptions of symptoms are not highly reliable, and thus prognoses vary even in supposedly biological conditions such as child autism. Wing[14] did a follow-up of sixty-three such cases into adolescence and young adulthood, and found 64 percent doing well, while another 25 percent had made useful progress though they were still "markedly abnormal." Most of the others were less difficult to handle than they had been as children. A few remained the same or regressed.

We have been considering the matter of heredity. There is also a "social heredity" so to speak. Certain conditions of a social nature set in early and tend to become self-prophecies. Kohlberg, we noted earlier, made the point that severe distortion of a child's environmental conditions has long-term negative predictive implications for that child's later maladjustment. The next study, also a consequence of long-term research, is of high importance for teachers, especially teachers of disturbed children. A fundamental problem of our culture is our failure to reverse antisocial behavior. Robins concentrates on sociopathic (or, in the extreme case, psychopathic) children, who have never internalized an acceptable set of values. They have no empathy for the feelings of others and little regard for the future. They learn little by experience.

Robins's work enables us to compare normal, neurotic, and sociopathic children as adults. Particularly telling is her discussion of the natural history of the sociopathic personality—in which the efforts at rehabilitation and the unfortunately negative role of education are clearly evident.

    13.   **D. J. Kupfer, T. P. Detre, and J. Koral,** "Relationship of Certain Childhood 'Traits' to Adult Psychiatric Disorders," *American Journal of Orthopsychiatry* 45 (1975): 74–79.

    14.   **L. Wing,** *Autistic Children* (New York: Brunner/Mazel, 1972).

Deviant Children Grown Up: A Sociological and Psychiatric Study of Sociopathic Personality

Lee N. Robins

Childhood Behavior Predicting Later Diagnosis

Feasibility of Long-Term Follow-Up Studies

This study describes the adult social and psychiatric status of 524 persons who, because they were seen in a child guidance clinic, were expected to yield a high rate of adults diagnosable as sociopathic personality. Their adult status has been compared with that of 100 normal control subjects. To complete this study, it has been necessary to locate patients 30 years after their clinical referral and control subjects 30 years after their graduation from elementary school and to obtain valid interviews from them about matters ordinarily treated as privileged and personal. From the interviews, supplemented by materials out of the records of many agencies, an evaluation of the kinds and seriousness of the subjects' adult antisocial behavior has been made, and the subjects have received a psychiatric diagnosis.

The success of the study in locating 90 percent of the subjects, in obtaining interviews for 82 percent of them and adult records for 98 percent means that subjects can be found and interviewed after 30 years, and that abundant record information concerning their adult lives can be located to verify those interviews. Pursuing information ordinarily considered personal and privileged through the structured interview was also surprisingly successful. Eighty-six percent of the sociopaths personally interviewed admitted enough antisocial behavior for psychiatrists to give them that diagnosis on the basis of the interview alone, before seeing record information. Only seven percent of them denied all adult antisocial behavior. While subjects were by no means totally reliable, they tended to minimize their antisocial behavior and push it back in time, rather than to deny it. On the basis of interviews and record information obtained, it was possible for two psychiatrists to reach an agreement as to whether 88 percent of the subjects were psychiatrically ill or well and to make a reasonably specific diagnosis for 71 percent. That it is possible to find subjects,

interview them, and make a diagnosis indicates that following populations thought to be disease-prone is a practical method for investigating the development of psychiatric syndromes, although the length and expense of the research indicate it is neither a cheap nor easy method.

The maladjustment of the patients showed itself in their high rate of arrests, low occupational achievement, their mental hospitalizations and numerous subjective symptoms, high divorce rates, alienation from friends, relatives, church, and all kinds of organizations, extensive use of welfare services, frequent moves, excessive use of alcohol, and the transmission of behavior problems to their children.

As a first step in specifying factors which identify those likely to have serious difficulties as adults, it was noted that children referred for antisocial behavior differed much more from the control subjects in their adult adjustment than did children referred for temper tantrums, learning problems, sleep and eating disturbance, speech difficulties, and all problems other than antisocial behavior. The more severe the antisocial behavior, whether measured by numbers of symptoms, by number of episodes, or by arrestability of the behavior, the more disturbed was the adult adjustment. Children referred to the clinic without numerous symptoms had no worse an outcome than had the control subjects. Clearly then, it was not the stigmatization as a "problem child" which created later problems, but rather the nature and severity of the childhood behavior which had occasioned referral.

The Natural History of the Disease Sociopathic Personality

A comparison of the childhood and adult histories of children diagnosed sociopathic personality with the histories of other patients and control subjects permits describing the sociopath's distinctive family history, symptoms, and course.

The disease occurred almost exclusively in boys referred to the clinic for antisocial behavior, particularly theft. Most of the sociopaths, in addition to a history of juvenile theft, had a history of incorrigibility, running away from home, truancy, associating with bad companions, sexual activities, and staying out late. Most of them were discipline problems in school and, having been held back at least one grade by the time they appeared in the clinic, most of them never even graduated from elementary school. More often than other patients, they were described as aggressive, reckless, impulsive, slovenly, enuretic, lacking guilt, and lying without cause.

Ordinarily referred to the clinic about age 14, the history of behavior problems dated back an average of seven years, beginning early in the school history. Before passing Juvenile Court age, almost four out of five appeared in court and more than half were sent to a correctional institution. Most of them had directed antisocial behavior toward their parents and teachers, and, more often than other antisocial children, they were also involved in offenses against businesses and strangers.

Girls later sociopathic were similar except that they were often referred to the clinic because of sexual activities, and their first difficulties began somewhat later.

Most of the sociopaths had a father who was either sociopathic or alcoholic. As a result, even more of them than of other clinic children came from homes that were impoverished and broken by divorce or separation.

As an adult, almost every sociopath had a poor work history, had been financially dependent on social agencies or relatives, and had marital problems. Three-quarters of them had multiple arrests leading to prison terms. They drank excessively, were impulsive, sexually promiscuous, had been vagrant, were belligerent, delinquent in paying their debts, and socially isolated. Most were disciplinary problems in the Armed Forces if not rejected because of their criminal records. In addition to their antisocial behavior, about half of them described themselves as "nervous," and they had a profusion of various somatic symptoms. The symptoms which best distinguish them from all other diagnostic groups were their poor marital histories, their impulsiveness, vagrancy, and use of aliases. With rare exceptions, they came to psychiatric attention only as a result of conflicts with the law or disturbances created while in prison or Service.

Sociopaths had a higher rate of injuries and deaths by violence than had other subjects. Children resulting from their unions had a high rate of problem behavior and failure to graduate from high school.

At time of follow-up, about age 44, 12 percent of the sociopathic group had given up their antisocial behavior, and an additional 27 percent had reduced it markedly. The remaining 61 percent were still seriously antisocial. The most common age at which improvement occurred was between 30 and 40 years.

The Independent Predictors of Sociopathic Personality

The best single childhood predictor of sociopathic personality was the degree of juvenile antisocial behavior. Sociopathic personality could be about equally well predicted by three measures of antisocial behavior: 1) the variety of antisocial behavior (what we have called number of symptoms); 2) the number of episodes; and 3) the seriousness of the behavior, as measured by whether or not the behavior was of the kind for which children appear in Juvenile Court.

Among children with a wide variety of antisocial behavior, the best predictor of the diagnosis of sociopathic personality was whether or not the child was ever placed in a correctional institution. Fifty-five percent of all severely antisocial children who became sociopaths went to a juvenile correctional institution, compared with only 33 percent of those who did not become sociopaths. The next most powerful predictor was the frequency and seriousness of their antisocial behavior. Almost all (88 percent) of the antisocial children who became sociopaths committed four or more arrestable acts, as compared with 71 percent of antisocial children with other diagnoses as adults. Three approximately equally good predictors were the kind of discipline in the home, the number of siblings, and a history of theft.

In descending order, other predictors of sociopathic personality in highly antisocial children were being male, committing antisocial acts against businesses, and being truant in combination with poor school performance.

Most of these predictors were common not only in the highly antisocial children who became sociopaths but in other highly antisocial children as well. About three-quarters of children with other outcomes also stole and experienced little discipline and more than half committed four or more arrestable acts, were male, and truanted. The largest percent difference between the two groups was with respect to institutionalization—a difference of 22 percent.

Predictors of sociopathy in less severely antisocial children were much more powerful, because while they occurred less uniformly in the sociopaths, many of them were almost absent in children free of antisocial behavior or only moderately antisocial who did not become sociopaths. As was the case for severely antisocial children, going to a correctional institution was the best predictor of sociopathy in less severely antisocial children. Inmates of correctional institutions accounted for 37 percent of the sociopaths in this group, but for only 10 percent of those who had other diagnoses. Next most predictive was having a sociopathic or alcoholic father. More than two-thirds of the presociopaths had such a father, compared with only 21 percent of children who later had other diagnoses. Committing four or more arrestable acts also predicted sociopathy in the less seriously antisocial children, as it did in the severely antisocial. Other predictors, in descending order, were impulsivity, aggression toward child strangers, running away, lying (except to avoid punishment), appearing in Juvenile Court, staying out late, being only children or one of four, and lacking guilt. The largest percentage difference between the two groups was in the proportion with a sociopathic or alcoholic father—a difference of 47 percent.

Many of the variables commonly reported as characterizing the childhoods of patients diagnosed sociopathic personality were not predictors of that disease when the level of antisocial behavior in childhood was taken into account. Although we found, as others have reported, a high rate of parental deprivation and repudiation, school dropouts, slum living, poverty, foster home or orphanage experience, and antisocial behavior on the part of the mother in the childhood histories of the sociopaths, these variables did not predict the disease independently of the child's level of antisocial behavior. The predictors found to be independent of the child's level of antisocial behavior, except for family size, have also commonly been reported as typical of the childhood histories of antisocial adults. Whether these variables do in fact reliably predict adult antisocial behavior can be demonstrated only if they are found to be successful predictors in other follow-up studies of populations of problem children. . . .

Implications of the Findings for Issues in Psychiatry

Child guidance clinic patients studied had a strikingly higher rate than control subjects of sociopathy, and also a somewhat higher rate of schizophrenia, chronic brain syndrome, alcoholism, and hysteria. But they had *no* higher rates of manic-depressive disease or of neurosis other than hysteria. Nor did any particular symptoms or family patterns in the patients predict these latter syndromes. While too few manic-depressives appeared in either patient or control groups to draw conclusions about them, these findings raise a question as to whether adult neurotic symptoms are in fact consequences of problems in parent–child relations or of parental loss in childhood, as is so commonly supposed. In any case, the kinds of juvenile problems and family constellations that led to the referral of these children do not appear to predict neurosis. Indeed, many of the childhood symptoms commonly thought to be early signs of neurosis appeared as often in children [who were] well as adults as in those [who were later] sick. Shyness, seclusiveness, "nervousness," irritability, tantrums, insomnia, fears, speech defects, hypersensitiveness, and tics were all unrelated to psychiatric outcome. Nor was the *number* of non-antisocial symptoms a good predictor of later psychiatric health. Serious antisocial behavior, on the other hand, was a particularly ominous childhood pattern. These findings suggest that the antisocial child deserves the most serious efforts at treatment if he is not to be a psychiatrically ill adult.

A suggestive finding of the study is the continuity of levels of antisocial behavior between childhood and adulthood, a continuity that cuts across the diagnostic lines we have been able to draw. The level of childhood antisocial behavior not only predicted sociopathy, but also predicted which schizophrenics and alcoholics would be combative and acting out, which relatively quiet and retiring. This tends to confirm two studies of the consistency of personality traits from childhood to adulthood (Tuddenham, 1959; Kagan and Moss, 1962) which also found aggressiveness an especially stable trait, particularly in boys.

The importance of the father's behavior in predicting the child's is also underscored in this study. Antisocial behavior in the father was associated not only with *juvenile* antisocial behavior in the patients, but also with antisocial behavior in adults who had been minimally antisocial as children. Antisocial behavior in the father, in addition, was the only childhood variable which predicted that sociopathic persons would not decrease their antisocial behavior with aging. The findings of this study lead us to recall A. E. Housman's lines:

> *When shall I be dead and rid*
> *Of the wrong my father did?*

But the findings do not permit any simple explanation of the mechanisms which relate the father's behavior to his offspring's. The fact that separation from the antisocial father by his desertion or divorce or by having the child adopted did not decrease the child's risks may seem to suggest a genetic factor, as Rosanoff *et al.*'s (1941) and Lange's (1931) twin studies argue. There are, however, practical consequences of having an antisocial father that tend to increase the number of independent predictors of sociopathic personality that a child may have: Children of antisocial fathers usually live in lower-class neighborhoods where they are likely to find other children who encourage them to engage in truancy and theft; they receive little discipline because the father is uninterested and hedonistic and because, if he fails to hold a job, the mother must become a breadwinner; they are more likely to be sent to a correctional institution when they come to Juvenile Court because the judge wishes to remove them from an environment he considers noxious. These consequences of having an antisocial father tend to occur whether or not the father remains in the home. In addition, the mother who chose to marry such a man may rear her child in his image even when he is absent or may herself be a "covert" sociopath from whom the child learns attitudes consistent with sociopathy. If the etiological factor *is* genetic, it is still necessary to explain the high prevalence of the disease in men as compared with women, the failure of the few women with the disease to transmit it to their children in the absence of a similar problem in their husbands, and the occurrence of the disease in some children without sociopathic fathers.

Whether or not the important etiological factor is genetic, certain factors frequently cited as etiological in the production of this syndrome did not appear to be so. Parental rejection, as measured by the parent's taking action against the child, treating him in a cold manner, or being excessively strict with him, did not predict sociopathy. Nor was parental deprivation resulting from the death or illness of a parent a factor.

This study provided no evidence that antisocial behavior and neurotic symptoms serve a common purpose, such as a defense against anxiety, so that an increase in one implies a decrease in the other. Antisocial children had as many non-antisocial symptoms as did children with non-antisocial symptoms only; and adult sociopaths who abandoned their antisocial behavior did not develop an excess of somatic symptoms in its place. It was noted, however, that with age, antisocial symptoms tend on the whole to decrease, somatic symptoms to increase. . . .

Some Inferences to Methods for Prevention and Treatment

Since children who will develop serious adult antisocial behavior usually have significant antisocial behavior in their early school years, it is reasonable to plan for their early treatment, not only because behavior patterns may be more amenable to change at that age, but because delay will add a serious educational handicap to the antisocial behavior. Since truancy and poor school performance are nearly universally present in presociopaths, it should be possible to identify children requiring treatment through their school records, refining the group most in need of care by using some of the predictors described above.

This study provides no answers concerning what, if any, methods of prevention and treatment will be effective. Yet the fact that a gross lack of discipline in the home predicted long-term difficulties suggests trying a program in which the schools attempt to substitute for the missing parental discipline in acting to prevent truancy and school failures. The public school might attempt to take over responsibilities that are usually the parents', just as the private boarding school does for upper-class children, perhaps by providing escorts for truant children in the morning and supervised study after school hours to guarantee that tomorrow's assignment is done before the child goes home. By randomly assigning boys who meet the criteria for presociopathic personality to such programs or to control groups and later comparing results, it will be possible to learn whether school discipline in the early grades can interrupt the development of antisocial behavior.

For adults already highly antisocial, suggestions for promising kinds of therapy have been sought in the adult histories of sociopaths in this study who have improved. Findings were meager and could plausibly be interpreted as the results rather than the causes of reform. Nonetheless, since they were the only hints available, the findings might be worth exploring for their possible therapeutic usefulness. The fact that sociopaths maintaining contacts with wives and other relatives tended to improve suggests encouraging wives and relatives to tolerate the irritability and hostility of the antisocial adult in order to maintain some sort of control of his behavior. The fact that brief prison terms may have induced reform also suggests that short incarcerations, preferably followed by prolonged supervision by parole officers to reinforce the family's control, may be useful. The fact that sociopaths holding jobs in which they had little supervision kept them longer than they did standard factory and office jobs suggests guiding them into occupations in which they have little sustained contact with supervisory personnel, occupations such as construction workers, cab drivers, and bartenders. Finally, one unexpected finding was the attribution of reform by some men to their desire to keep up payments on goods in their possession lest they lose them. While the impulsive and imprudent behavior of the sociopath may make it impossible to induce him to work in anticipation of purchasing objects desired, subsidizing down payments for him on desired goods which cannot be *kept* unless he works may sometimes be effective. Working to keep what one has may require less ability to defer gratification than does working in order to get something one does not have.

Next Steps in Research

Tests of the findings of the present study by replication and endeavors to turn observed associations into tools for therapy and prevention are not the only unfinished business.

The use of a clinic population to study this syndrome had the great advantage of providing a disease-prone population, so that sufficient cases of the syndrome were found at follow-up with a minimum wastage. But it had the disadvantage that one does not know how representative the children followed who turned out to have the syndrome are of all adults developing the syndrome.

Two techniques for overcoming this handicap can be suggested. Wastage can be avoided not only by following a clinic sample, but also by following children whose demographic characteristics suggest that there will be a high adult rate of the syndrome. We are currently doing such a study of a population of Negro men identified from public elementary school records. Negro men were selected because their high level of adult crime, unemployment, and marital instability suggests that they will yield a large enough proportion with adult antisocial behavior to allow the study of the relation of childhood factors to deviance in a population unselected by clinic treatment or court referral. This is not a perfect solution because one must still make the untestable assumption that the childhood factors predicting a syndrome in the sub-populations in which it is common are the same factors predicting it in the sub-populations in which it is rare, but one certainly can come closer

to obtaining an unselected sample than by choosing a clinic population.

A second way of solving the problem is to attempt to locate a representative sample of adults with a given syndrome, seek record information about their childhood behavior and their childhood family situation, and compare these results with the same information obtained for control subjects picked from rosters on which the sick adults appeared in childhood but on which their appearance was not dependent on special characteristics of the subjects themselves or of their parents. Such a roster might be birth records or elementary school records, and the control subject might be the next child of the same sex on the roster. The relevant childhood records with respect to which control and patient groups might be compared are, for their own behavior problems, juvenile police records, school records, and clinic attendance and for their social and family history in childhood, neighborhoods lived in and number of moves (as indicated by number and location of addresses on school records), welfare and police records of their parents, psychiatric hospitalizations of parents, and other records of parental problems. The source of a representative sample of adults with a syndrome would vary with the syndrome to be studied. For sociopathic personality, one might choose a sample of persons who simultaneously have police records, welfare records, and multiple divorces. Clinical interviews with persons simultaneously appearing on these three rosters could be used both to make a definite diagnosis and to locate the childhood rosters from which the control subject is to be chosen (*e.g.*, by asking place and date of birth to locate birth registration, or the elementary schools attended, to locate school rosters). This second technique is particularly useful for syndromes which are rare not only in the total population but in any demographically definable group. The only problem in the technique is one of so defining the adult target population that it does produce a representative sample of people with a given syndrome and relatively few people *without* the syndrome (to avoid wasting interviews).

The present study has attempted to solve one part of the equation between childhood patterns and adult outcomes. We have specified childhood patterns which appear to predict sociopathic personality in adults. We have only tentatively answered the question as to whether sociopathic personality can occur in the absence of these childhood patterns, by pointing to the rarity of this syndrome in the control population and in clinic patients free of serious antisocial behavior in childhood. A study of the childhoods of a representative adult sample of persons with the diagnosis of sociopathic personality would complete the equation.

Editors' Commentary

Both of the preceding studies were selected to examine Kohlberg's biogenetic and sociogenetic high-risk groups, and his position has been corroborated. Two other studies are important partly because of their differences. One, *400 Losers*, illustrates the problems of reaching the hard-core inner city youth with a work program.[15] The problem behavior of the youngsters continued in the work situation. If they had no work-oriented close identification figures, they were usually doomed to failure. The disastrous outcomes indicate yet again the difficulty of changing the inner and outer ecology systems. In another study of nine child murderers, it was found that their life experience had produced an emotionally empty state (psychopath) and a lack of cognitive coping capacity, since they could not use symbols to mitigate their impulses. They could not read. Many had been brutalized as well.[16]

The question of continuity of disturbance has also been studied by Shepherd, Oppenheim, and Mitchell.[17] Other long-term studies of mental health from childhood to adulthood can be found in Simmons[18] and the Isle of Wight Studies.[19]

We turn now to a few examples of studies related to program designs for helping disturbed children. The first deals with the least restrictive placement, mainstreaming with resource support.

15. **W. M. Ahlstrom and R. J. Havighurst,** *400 Losers* (San Francisco: Jossey-Bass, 1971).

16. **Charles H. King,** "The Ego and the Integration of Violence in Homicidal Youth," *American Journal of Orthopsychiatry* 45 (1975): 134–145.

17. **Michael Shepherd, Bram Oppenheim, and Sheila Mitchell,** *Childhood Behavior and Mental Health* (New York: Grune and Stratton, 1971).

18. **R. Simmons,** ed., *Research in Community and Mental Health*, vol. 1 (Greenwich, Conn.: JAI Press, 1978).

19. **S. Chess and A. Thomas,** eds., *Annual Progress in Child Psychiatry and Child Development* (New York: Brunner/Mazel, 1977), chap. 22.

The Effectiveness of Resource Programming

Paul T. Sindelar

Stanley L. Deno

Concern over the efficacy of special class placement, though still an unresolved issue, has been eclipsed in special education by emphasis on the reintegration of exceptional children into regular classrooms. Along with the "mainstreaming" of exceptional children, expanded special education services have, in effect, supplemented regular education programs. While supplementary services have taken many forms, including training regular class teachers and consultants for those teachers, most service models proposed to replace special classes have included resource programs. This article will review the research currently available regarding the effectiveness of these programs.

Resource programs are defined here as any administrative organization in which children, in regular classrooms, receive some proportion of their instruction from special education personnel. Children may receive no more than half their instruction from special education for the program to be considered a resource program. Thus, the use of resource programs, resource programming, or resource rooms implies regular class placement.

Descriptions of resource models abound in the recent literature (Chaffin, 1974; Deno, 1973; Fox, Egner, Paolucci, Perelman, & McKenzie, 1973; Hammill & Wiederholdt, 1972; Lilly, 1971; Reger, 1973; Wiederholdt, 1974). And the number of evaluations of special education resource programs is growing. But regrettably, careful and conscientious program description is often separated from program evaluation. Programs are described in articles in which they are not evaluated. At the same time, evaluations are reported for resource programs which have not been carefully described or developed. The net result is that while resource programming in service delivery multiplies, the efficacy of programs and program variables has not been established.

Special education rests on the assumption that programs can be provided for exceptional children which are in some (measurable) sense more effective than general educational programs. Special educators have naturally attempted to determine the efficacy of those alternative educational programs which they have organized. Efficacy research, though important, is not easy to plan and implement, and some considerable literature exists regarding the conceptual and methodological problems which have been part of the history of efficacy studies in special education. These issues continue to play an important role in interpreting research results.

Issues in Efficacy Research

Nelson and Schmidt (1970) described three characteristics of special education and its practitioners which inhibit the scientific pursuit of efficacy. First, special education strongly adheres to the past, prompted less by empirical data than by common sense. Second, since special education is apparently satisfied with an a priori problem solving approach, issues which seem "self-evident" are seldom put to scientific test. For this reason, practitioners may value program description more highly than program evaluation. The third characteristic is the failure of the field to critically examine and make operational its fundamental concepts. Thus, programs are evaluated when the independent variables are often unknown or at best summarily described.

Bruininks and Rynders (1971) reiterated these concerns in posing a series of questions to persons implementing and evaluating special education programs. They argued that program goals, targeted populations, program constituents, services, assumptions, roles (of both special and regular personnel), and criteria are issues which demand a priori resolution. The similarity between these issues and the characteristics enumerated by Nelson and Schmidt is obvious. Less obvious, however, is the question of whether these critiques have helped to improve special education research.

Beyond its failure to address the conceptual issues described above, efficacy research is also fraught with serious methodological problems. Cegelka and Tyler (1970) enumerated five weaknesses of most efficacy research. First, sampling is seldom a randomized process, and comparison groups are seldom comparable. Failure to use random samples, however, is a problem indigenous to much educational research, and quasi-experimental designs have been developed for use in natural settings (Campbell & Stanley, 1963). Although quasi-experiments are preferable to before and after descriptions of change, they fail to control for many of the threats to internal validity which can be controlled through random assignment. Ideally, a natural population of children needing resource room services should be defined, and random assignment to treatment should follow. Four of the studies or series of studies reviewed here have employed this procedure (Budoff & Gottlieb, 1976; Glavin, Quay, Annesley, & Werry, 1971; Jenkins & Mayhall, 1974; Smith & Kennedy, 1967). More often, naturally existing samples or matched pairs of subjects or schools have been employed. At present, no study of resource program effectiveness has yet matched the control obtained by Goldstein, Moss, and Jordan (1965) in their comparison of special and regular class placement. Goldstein et al. not only randomly assigned targeted subjects to special and regular class placement, but did so before the children entered first grade.

Cegelka and Tyler listed inadequate matching of subjects across conditions as second among the methodological shortcomings of efficacy research. Guskin and Spicker (1968) raised serious issues concerning the general use of matched pairs with exceptional populations. As a substitute for random assignment, matching frequently increases the number of threats to internal validity, since other uncontrolled status variables may interact with treatments. Nevertheless, Campbell and Stanley argued that nonequivalent comparison groups almost always increase the internal validity of a research design.

A third methodological criticism is that different placement histories of exceptional children potentially interact with current program placement, making the results of efficacy studies impossible to interpret. Thus, confounded effects of multiple treatments seriously limit the generalizability of experimental findings (Campbell, 1969). The study by Goldstein et al. illustrates one approach to controlling for the effects of school history. Conclusions based on long-term studies seem less subject to the threats to internal validity introduced by confounded histories.

The fourth common methodological weakness is the use of inadequate measurement instruments, particularly for personal and social adjustment. In fairness to most researchers, the criticism derives in part from the state of personality measurement. Personal–social constructs are often ambiguously defined, and the instruments used to measure these constructs are less reliable than instruments measuring achievement (Brown, 1970). Few of the measures developed have adequate standardization for use with exceptional populations. A second aspect of this issue is the investigator's choice of instruments. Although these tests do not meet the rigorous standards of achievement and ability tests, the responsibility to use the most valid and reliable instrument lies with the investigator. Further, the obligation to carefully describe the instrumentation used is seldom met.

Finally, Cegelka and Tyler pointed out that efficacy studies fail to control for teaching procedures and curricula. Treatment names often imply differences in instruction which either do not exist or are inconsistently applied. This, of course, is a failure to create and control differences in the independent variables implied by the treatment names. Cegelka and Tyler derived these criticisms from a careful review of the efficacy research on special class placement. However, the methodological weaknesses which limited the validity of these studies have not been resolved in the current efficacy research. This assertion will become clear in the literature review to follow.

The Present Review

Neither conceptual nor methodological criteria can serve to select current efficacy research for review. The reason is not that the critics have raised inappropriate issues, but that if these criteria were rigorously applied, an insignificant proportion of the available literature would remain for review. Thus, the single criterion for this review was the use of comparison groups to evaluate the efficacy of resource room programs.

Research on the efficacy of resource rooms conveniently divides into those studies comparing academic performance and those comparing personal and social adjustment. A further organizational strategy seems necessary owing to the diversity of populations sampled. The studies reviewed here include samples commonly labeled mildly retarded, learning disabled, neurologically handicapped, and emotionally disturbed. Other studies sample less technically defined populations, such as teacher referrals and slow learners. For the sake of economy, the research reports are summarized in tabular form.[1] Table 1 describes the results of efficacy studies which made comparisons on the basis of academic achievement. Tables 2 and 3 present the results of those studies in which personal–social development was the dependent variable. This body of research divides methodologically into two general categories: correlational and experimental studies. In the latter, placement is an independent variable of interest. Several studies appear in both tables, since both academic and personal–social development was measured. The results of research on academic achievement are discussed separately from the research on personal–social development.

Summary of Academic Achievement Studies

Four studies (Budoff & Gottlieb, 1976; Carroll, 1967; Smith & Kennedy, 1967; Walker, 1974) investigated samples from mildly retarded populations. As might be expected, this small body of research affords little insight into the question of efficacy of resource programming for such a population. It seems safe to conclude, however, that the superiority of resource programming for mildly retarded populations has not been established. This tentative generalization holds for comparisons with special class placement as well as regular class placement.

The findings from efficacy studies of nonretarded populations served in resource programs are more conclusive. Several studies (Glavin et al., 1971; Jenkins & Mayhall, 1974; Quay, Glavin, Annesley, & Werry, 1972; Sabatino, 1971) were well-designed and methodologically sound, providing a firm basis for interpretation. In contrast to studies with mildly and moderately retarded sam-

Table 1. Studies of Academic Achievement

Author(s)/date	Population/N/ assignment	Comparisons	Duration	Measures	Results
Carroll (1967)	Mildly retarded $N = 39$ In naturally existing groups	Resource program with special class	1 school year	Wide Range Achievement Test (WRAT)	1. Children, in both treatments realized significant gains 2. Special class group made greater gains on reading subtest than resource group
Smith & Kennedy (1967)	Mildly retarded $N = 96$ Randomly assigned	Resource program (45 min/day) with control activity (45 min/day) with regular class placement	Unclear (authors cite "short period of time" as major limitation— pretests 9/61; posttests 4/63)	California Achievement Test (CAT) Wechsler Intelligence Scale for Children (WISC)	1. No significant differences among groups on either measure
Walker (1974)	Mildly retarded $N = 58$ Matched on CA, IQ, and reading level	Resource program with special class placement	2-year program, 1st and 2nd evaluations	Word reading, vocabulary, and arithmetic subtests of Stanford Achievement Test (SAT)	1. Resource program group scored significantly higher in word reading and vocabulary than special class group 2. No difference in arithmetic
Budoff & Gottlieb (1976)	EMR $N = 31$ Randomly assigned	Resource program (45 min/day minimum) with special class placement	3 Evaluations (1) pretest (2) 2 months after assignment (3) 9 months after assignment	Metropolitan Achievement Test	1. At time 2 and time 3, no significant differences attributable to placement
Glavin, Quay, Annesley, & Werry (1971)	Behaviorally disruptive, or overtly withdrawn Experimental, $N = 27$ Control, $N = 34$ Random assignment of teacher identifications	Resource program with regular class placement	2-year program, 1st year evaluation	CAT	1. Resource program group scored significantly higher on reading comprehension and arithmetic fundamentals than regular class group
Quay, Glavin, Annesley, & Werry (1972)	(as above)	Evaluation following 2nd year of the program described	2-year program, 2nd year evaluation	CAT	1. Resource program group scored significantly higher than regular class group on:

Table 1 (continued). Studies of Academic Achievement

Author(s)/date	Population/N/ assignment	Comparisons	Duration	Measures	Results
					reading vocabulary, total reading; arithmetic fundamentals, total arithmetic
Glavin (1973)	(as above)	First year evaluation following termination of program	2-year program, 1st year postcheck	CAT	1. Resource program group scored significantly higher than regular class group on arithmetic fundamentals only
Glavin (1974)	(as above)	Second year evaluation following termination of program	2-year program, 2nd year postcheck	CAT	1. No significant differences between groups
Sabatino (1971)	Learning disabled $N = 114$ Matched on CA, sex, IQ, and perceptual impairment	Special class with resource prog. A (1 hr/daily); resource prog. B (½ hr/twice weekly); regular class placement	1 school year	14 selected subtests of WRAT, WISC, and Illinois Test of Psycho-linguistic Abilities (ITPA)	1. All 3 "special" groups gained significantly more than regular class group 2. Resource prog. A group superior to both resource prog. B and special class groups, which did not differ
Affleck, Lehning, & Brow (1973)	Learning disabled $N = 29$ Within-subject comparisons	Interpolated historical rates of improvement with rate of improvement in resource program	1 school year	Spache Diagnostic Reading Scales	1. Ss made significant pre-to posttest gains 2. Ss rates of progress significantly improved during resource program placement
Jenkins & Mayhall (1974)	A. EMR and LD $N = 6$ and $N = 24$ Random assignment B. LD, $N = 28$ ½ randomly assigned,	Special class vs. special class and resource prog. for EMRs; resource prog. vs. regular class	A. 3½ months	WRAT	1. Resource prog. group improved at significantly faster rate than either special or regular class group

Table 1 (continued). Studies of Academic Achievement

Author(s)/date	Population/N/ assignment	Comparisons	Duration	Measures	Results
	lowest 7 of remaining ½	for LDs; resource prog. (for reading only) vs. regular class placement	B. 1 school year	WRAT	1. Resource prog group significantly outgained regular group on reading subtest 2. No difference on arithmetic subtest

Table 2. Correlational Studies of Personal/Social Adjustment

Author(s)/date	Population/N/ assignment	Comparisons	Duration	Measures	Results
Lapp (1957)	Slow learners $N = 16$ Naturally existing groups Regular class children $N = 32$ Random selection	Resource program with regular class normals	Unclear. At least 1 school year. Subjects evaluated two consecutive springs	Sociometric questionnaire, Vineland Social Maturity Scale (VSMS)	1. Both acceptance and rejection scores lower for resource program group
A. Flynn (1974)	Mildly retarded in resource program $N = 61$; mildly retarded awaiting placement, $N = 61$; normal controls, $N = 61$	Resource program with regular class referrals with regular class normals	No information regarding length of treatment before subjects evaluated	Social Adjustment Scale	1. Normal controls scored significantly higher than either resource program group or referral group
B. Flynn & Flynn (1970)	Assignment as above	As above	As above	Teacher ratings; student satisfaction interviews	1. Teachers approve of resource program 2. Resource program group satisfied with school placement
Bruininks, Rynders, & Gross (1974)	Mildly retarded $N = 65$ Nonretarded classmates $N = 1,234$	Resource program with nonretarded classmates (with urban vs. suburban and same vs. opposite sex analyses)	In resource program for minimum of 18 months before evaluation	Peer Acceptance Scale (PAS)	1. No significant differences in social acceptance between resource program group and non-

Table 2 (continued). Correlational Studies of Personal/Social Adjustment

Author(s)/date	Population/N/ assignment	Comparisons	Duration	Measures	Results
					retarded classmates, for either urban or suburban groups 2. Urban, same sex ratings were significantly higher for resource program group; suburban, same sex ratings were significantly lower for resource program group
Guerin & Szatlocky (1974)	Mildly retarded $N = 27$ Natural groups Regular class normals $N = 54$ Random selection	Special class, partial integration; special class, full time; resource program, and regular class normals	No information regarding length of treatment before evaluated	Coping Analysis	1. Retarded girls more (positively) manipulative in peer interactions than nonretarded peers 2. Resource program and special class (full-time) groups showed significantly more self-directed behavior than special class (P.I.) group
Sheare (1974)	Nonretarded 9th graders $N = 400$ Random assignment	Two or more classes with EMRs (integrated normals) and none (segregated normals)	3½ months	PAS	1. Integrated normals more accepting of EMRs than segregated normals 2. Females more accepting than males

Table 3. Experimental Studies of Personal/Social Adjustment

Author(s)/date	Population/N/ assignment	Comparisons	Duration	Measures	Results
Carroll (1967)	Previously described (see Table 1)	Previously described	Same	Illinois Index of Self-Derogation (IISD)	1. Significant decreases in self-derogation for resource program group; significant increases for special class group 2. Special class group made significantly more self-derogating remarks than resource placement group
Walker (1974)	Previously described (see Table 1)	Previously described	Same	Bristol Social Adjustment Scale and IISD	1. No significant differences between resource program and special class groups in self concept 2. Resource program group showed significantly better social adjustment than special class group
Smith & Kennedy (1967)	Previously described (see Table 1)	Previously described	Same	VSMS Sociometric questionnaire	1. No significant differences between groups
Budoff & Gottlieb (1976)	Previously described (see Table 1)	Previously described	Same	1. 7 measures of Motivation 2. 2 measures of Cognitive Style 3. Teacher's Behavior Rating form (Not all administered at each testing session.)	1. At time 2, no significant differences attributable to placement 2. At time 3, resource program students scored significantly greater than special class students on measures of motivation and

Table 3 (continued). Experimental Studies of Personal/Social Adjustment

Author(s)/date	Population/N/ assignment	Comparisons	Duration	Measures	Results
					on measure of cognitive style
A. Glavin et al. (1971)	Previously described (see Table 1)	Previously described	Same	Behavior Problem Checklist	A. 1. Improved behavior for both groups in regular class 2. Behavior of resource program groups significantly better in resource room
B. Quay et al. (1972)			Same		B. 1. No significant differences between groups in regular class in attending behavior 2. Resource program group attended more in resource room than regular class
C. Glavin (1973)			Same		C. No significant differences between groups
D. Glavin (1974)			Same		D. No significant differences between groups

ples, these studies compared regular class placement with resource support to regular class placement with no resource support. All obtained results favoring resource programming. Although this emphasis may have occurred as an artifact of administrative organization (since special classes for the population studied are uncommon), it is nonetheless an important finding in support of special education resource programs.

In interpreting these results we should note that the samples examined represent diversely defined populations. Regardless of this limitation, reliable evidence exists that resource programs can be effective in improving the achievement of chil-

dren identified by teachers as exhibiting learning or behavior problems. However, the number of studies is not large, and what is needed to substantiate these initial findings is replications which (like Glavin et al., Jenkins & Mayhall, and Quay et al.) involve teacher referral on some prespecified criterion as a basis for defining the target populations.

In sum, it has not been clearly established that resource programs in general will be effective in improving the academic performance of all populations. The research results have been somewhat mixed. Where efficacy has been established, replication is lacking. Where well-defined populations (mildly retarded) have been repeatedly investigated, the results have proven inconclusive and the methodology comparatively weak. One clear trend has begun to emerge, however: The most carefully designed studies have, to date, obtained the most affirmative results.

Summary of Efficacy Studies Investigating Personal and Social Adjustment

Neither static assessment nor experimentation has established the efficacy of resource programming in improving the personal and social adjustment of children so placed. In fact, despite the substantial number of studies investigating this issue, no reliable generalizations can be derived. As mentioned earlier, the failure of this body of research to produce generalizable conclusions may derive in part from the multitude of measures and constructs and from the poor technical qualities of these measures. One encouraging trend is the use of direct observation of behavior in the classroom to assess social development (Glavin et al., Guerin & Szatlocky). Such data, although more difficult to obtain, resolve the issue of technical limitations and comparability of measures, while concurrently removing the issue from a theoretical to an empirical basis. Similar attempts would be welcomed in future research.

Recommendations

Although the research reviewed here does not clearly establish the efficacy of resource programs, evidence has begun to accumulate that such programs can improve academic achievement. Studies obtaining the clearest results (Glavin et al., 1971; Jenkins & Mayhall, 1974; Quay et al., 1972; Sabatino, 1971) are also those which most directly deal with the conceptual and methodological issues raised earlier. In addition, directions for future research can be inferred. One issue which must be addressed in future work is precisely what variables must be operative for resource programs to be effective. Of the studies reviewed, only that by Smith and Kennedy controlled for the possibility that any supplementary attention would accelerate achievement—the "Hawthorne effect." If the Hawthorne effect is a plausible hypothesis explaining resource program effects, then a "placebo" control group should perform as well as a resource program group, and the performance of both should exceed that of an untreated control group. In the Smith and Kennedy study where such comparisons were made, the groups did not differ significantly.

Clearly, the resource program was not effective, and just as clearly, no Hawthorne effect occurred.

An alternative to the traditional approach in which administrative arrangements are compared is the systematic investigation of independent variables illustrated in the work of Jenkins and Mayhall (1974). The resource program these authors investigated was constructed from a series of prior studies in which the independent variables most likely to improve performance in resource programs had been determined (Jenkins, Mayhall, Peschka, & Jenkins, 1974; Jenkins, Mayhall, Peschka, & Townsend, 1974; Mayhall, Jenkins, Chestnut, Schroeder, & Jordan, 1974; Mayhall & Jenkins, 1977; Moody, Bausell, & Jenkins, 1973). On the basis of these findings, the authors implemented a resource program treatment which incorporated one-to-one tutorial instruction, cross-age tutoring, direct service, daily measurement, and daily instruction. Evaluation followed the development of this program. The authors organized program development and evaluation in a sensible way without arbitrarily separating the two processes. Further, their approach allows identification of the essential independent variables which facilitate replication or extension of their research. It is encouraging that the results of the efficacy evaluation support resource placement.

Jenkins and Mayhall are not alone in having investigated independent variables (as opposed to administrative organizations). For example, Sabatino compared the effects of 1 hour of daily service to ½ hour, twice a week. Kennedy and Smith employed an experimental condition in which the effect of time out of the classroom was controlled. Budoff and Gottlieb contrasted the efficacy of resource programming for high and low potential EMR students. Bruininks and Rynders looked at the sex of the observer and location of school as potentially significant independent variables. This approach is wholly encouraging. Future research which examines variables within programs, rather than grossly organized and defined administrative arrangements, would be welcome.

A second recommendation involves the conceptual orientation of efficacy research. Specifically, evaluations should be used to improve existing programs as well as to certify them as successful or not. In short, formative evaluation should be combined with summative evaluation in efficacy studies. In such an approach, initial program evaluation is followed by program revision; subsequent evaluations by subsequent revisions; and so on until successful programs are constructed. The processes of program development and evaluation in such a design are clearly joined. Such a perspective in evaluation is not new. Light and Smith (1970) discussed this perspective in terms of the Head Start evaluation. These authors suggested that the results of an initial program evaluation can be used to design a second program which is more likely to achieve program goals. Such evaluation and development cycles continue until an effective program is established and maintained.

The Light and Smith approach to evaluation requires time and unstinting commitment to program refinement. What this approach provides, in turn, is a restatement of the goals of efficacy research. The question "Does this program work?" becomes "How does this program work?" An answer to the second question has greater relevance for both the practitioner and the researcher than does an answer to the first. It provides the information necessary for program replication and improvement, while an answer to the first question usually does not. Similarly, answering the second question would necessarily confront conceptual issues, though the first can be (and has been) answered without addressing these issues. Efficacy research would move a significant step forward through adopting this perspective—reuniting development and evaluation.

Note

1. A narrative review of the studies can be obtained upon request from Stanley L. Deno (108a Pattee Hall, University of Minnesota, Minneapolis, MN 55455).

References

Affleck, J. Q., Lehning, T. W., & Brow, K. D. Expanding the resource concept: The resource school. *Exceptional Children*, 1973, *39*, 446–453.

Brown, F. G. *Principles of educational and psychological testing.* Hinsdale, Ill.: Dryden Press, 1970.

Bruininks, R. H., & Rynders, J. E. Alternatives to special class placement for educable mentally retarded children. *Focus on Exceptional Children*, 1971, *3*(4), 1–12.

Bruininks, R. H., Rynders, J. E., & Gross, J. C. Social acceptance of mildly retarded pupils in resource rooms and regular classes. *American Journal of Mental Deficiency*, 1974, *78*, 377–383.

Budoff, M., & Gottlieb, J. Special-class EMR children mainstreamed: A study of an aptitude (learning potential) $\times$ treatment interaction. *American Journal of Mental Deficiency*, 1976, *81*, 1–11.

Campbell, D. T. Reforms as experiments. *American Psychologist*, 1969, *24*, 409–429.

Campbell, D. T., & Stanley, J. C. Experimental and quasi-experimental designs for research. In N. L. Gage (Ed.), *Handbook of research on teaching.* Chicago: Rand McNally, 1963.

Carroll, A. W. The effects of segregated and partially integrated school programs on self-concept and academic achievement of educable mentally retardates. *Exceptional Children*, 1967, *34*, 93–99.

Cegelka, W. J., & Tyler, J. L. The efficacy of special class placement for the mentally retarded in proper perspective. *Training School Bulletin*, 1970, *67*, 33–68.

Chaffin, J. D. Will the real mainstreaming program please stand up! *Focus on Exceptional Children*, 1974, *6*(5), 1–18.

Deno, E. *Instructional alternatives for exceptional children.* Reston, Va.: Council for Exceptional Children, 1973.

Flynn, T. M. Regular class adjustment of EMR students attending a part-time special education program. *Journal of Special Education*, 1974, *8*, 167–173.

Flynn, T. M., & Flynn, L. A. The effect of a part-time special education program on the adjustment of EMR students. *Exceptional Children*, 1970, *36*, 680–681.

Fox, W. F., Egner, A. N., Paolucci, P. B., Perelman, P. F., & McKenzie, H. S. An introduction to a regular classroom approach to special education. In E. Deno (Ed.), *Instructional alternatives for exceptional children.* Reston, Va.: Council for Exceptional Children, 1973.

Glavin, J. P. Follow-up behavioral research in resource rooms. *Exceptional Children*, 1973, *40*, 211–213.

Glavin, J. P. Behaviorally oriented resource rooms: A follow-up. *Journal of Special Education*, 1974, *8*, 337–347.

Glavin, J. P., Quay, H. C., Annesley, F. R., & Werry, J. S. An experimental resource room for behavior problem children. *Exceptional Children*, 1971, *38*, 131–137.

Goldstein, H., Moss, J. W., & Jordan, L. *The efficacy of special class training on the development of mentally retarded children.* U.S. Office of Education, Cooperative Research Project Report No. 619. Urbana: University of Illinois, 1965.

Guerin, G. R., & Szatlocky, K. Integration programs for the mildly retarded. *Exceptional Children,* 1974, *41,* 173–179.

Guskin, S. L., & Spicker, H. H. Educational research in mental retardation. In N. R. Ellis (Ed.), *International review of research in mental retardation* (Vol. 3). New York: Academic Press, 1968.

Hammill, D., & Wiederholdt, J. L. *The resource room: Rationale and implementation.* Philadelphia: JSE Press, 1972.

Jenkins, J. R., & Mayhall, W. F. *Development and evaluation of a resource program: The resource specialist model.* Unpublished manuscript, University of Illinois, 1974.

Jenkins, J. R., Mayhall, W. F., Peschka, C. M., & Jenkins, L. M. Comparing small group and tutorial instruction in resource rooms. *Exceptional Children,* 1974, *40,* 245–250.

Jenkins, J. R., Mayhall, W. F., Peschka, C., & Townsend, V. Using direct and daily measurement to increase learning. *Journal of Learning Disabilities,* 1974, *7,* 605–608.

Lapp, E. R. A study of the social adjustment of slow learning children who were assigned part-time to regular classes. *American Journal of Mental Deficiency,* 1957, *62,* 254–262.

Light, R. J., & Smith, P. V. Choosing a future: Strategies for designing and evaluating new programs. *Harvard Educational Review,* 1970, *40,* 1–28.

Lilly, M. S. A training based model for special education. *Exceptional Children,* 1971, *37,* 745–749.

Mayhall, W. F., & Jenkins, J. R. Scheduling daily or less than daily instruction: Implications for resource programs. *Journal of Learning Disabilities,* 1977, *10,* 159–163.

Mayhall, W. F., Jenkins, J. R., Chestnut, N., Shroeder, K., & Jordan, B. *Supervision and site of instruction as factors in tutorial programs.* Unpublished manuscript, University of Illinois, 1974.

Moody, W., Bausell, R., & Jenkins, J. The effects of class size on the learning of mathematics: A parametric study. *Journal of Research in Mathematics Education,* 1973, *4,* 170–176.

Nelson, C. C., & Schmidt, L. J. The question of the efficacy of special classes. *Exceptional Children,* 1970, *37,* 381–384.

Quay, H. C., Glavin, J. P., Annesley, F. R., & Werry, J. S. The modification of problem behavior and academic achievement in a resource room. *Journal of School Psychology,* 1972, *10,* 187–198.

Reger, R. What is a resource room program? *Journal of Learning Disabilities,* 1973, *6,* 607–614.

Sabatino, D. An evaluation of resource rooms for children with learning disabilities. *Journal of Learning Disabilities,* 1971, *4,* 84–93.

Sheare, J. B. Social acceptance of EMR adolescents in integrated programs. *American Journal of Mental Deficiency,* 1974, *78,* 678–682.

Smith, H. W., & Kennedy, W. A. Effects of three educational programs on mentally retarded children. *Perceptual and Motor Skills,* 1967, *24,* 174.

Walker, V. S. Efficacy of the resource room for educating retarded children. *Exceptional Children,* 1974, *40,* 288–289.

Wiederholdt, J. L. Planning resource rooms for the mildly handicapped. *Focus on Exceptional Children,* 1974, *5*(8), 1–10.

Reprinted from the *Journal of Special Education* 12 (1978): 17–27.

Editors' Commentary

Resource rooms are one level of handling disturbed children. Therapy may be considered the next level. There are many studies of traditional individual and group therapies. Usually they yield positive results overall, but individual results vary considerably, since there is little matching of the child to the method. Thus, in mismatched cases, therapists do not even discover what the possibilities for change are. Innovative procedures worth noting are classroom group therapy, as described in Chapter 3, and brief therapy which holds promise (though the most disturbed and acting out children require further treatment than brief therapy). To quote Leventhal and Weinberger, "On the basis of previous intake-diagnostic procedures, readmission rates, therapist ratings, problem checklists, and follow-up questionnaires, brief therapy is seen as a highly efficient and effective treatment approach."[20]

The next level of program design is the special class for disturbed children. Unfortunately, even in this "segregated" setting, teachers do not have all of the conditions for improvement under control—for example, they do not control the pupil's attitude, the family attitude, or even the quality and specificity of the interventions used to attack the problems designated in the IEP. Some pupils improve and some do not, and, of course, what one pupil needs to achieve maximum functioning eventually may not be what is required by the next pupil.

The next article reports on a broad survey of special classes for the emotionally disturbed, conducted with the help of the Council for Exceptional Children. The purpose of the study was to examine the effects of special classes. Definitive findings were elusive, because the research method had serious limitations, but the sample is fairly large and covers a wide spectrum of classes.

20.   **T. Leventhal and G. Weinberger,** "Evaluation of a Large Scale Brief Therapy Program for Children," *American Journal of Orthopsychiatry* 45 (1975): 119.

Public School Classes for the Emotionally Handicapped: A Research Analysis

William C. Morse   *Richard L. Cutler*
Albert H. Fink

An ultimate goal of this research was to determine the effects of special public school classrooms for emotionally handicapped children upon the children themselves.

Pre- and posttest data on school achievement were not broadly available, and plans to use these as a major criterion had to be abandoned. Retrospective data from both pupils and teachers were utilized instead, as were evaluative views of administrators and site visitors. In this chapter, both statistical findings and impressionistic views are presented.

Administrators' Evaluations of Programs

One simple criterion for evaluation of the programs was to pose the question to administrators, "Would you expand your program as it now exists if funds were available?" All but four program administrators indicated that they would. Several were enthusiastic or ambitious, and would add from ten to twenty more classes. Most were more modest, either in their aspiration or their evalua-

tion, and indicated that they would like two, three, or four more classes. A frequent suggestion for expansion set one class per medium size or large size building as a goal. Others defined their needs and wishes in terms of an extrapolation of the present percentage of children served. Estimates of the proportion of children needing special service ran as high as 20 percent of the total population, although the most typical estimate was 10–15 percent. Service by other special personnel was often included in these totals.

Administrators generally reported heavy demands for additional placements, which is understandable in the light of fairly well-established minimum percentages of known disturbed children. However, on the other hand, in several locations it was difficult to obtain the full complement of pupils for the classes. The reasons for this were nearly as many as the programs reporting the difficulty. Many of the most obvious school problems did not fit the available class in terms of age, pathology, or necessary psychiatric and parental acceptability. Often it was the vexing problem of transportation which prevented enrollment. More than half the programs studied reported waiting lists, and consequent pressures to move more children into existing classes or to develop new ones.

Needed Changes as Seen by Administrators

While some of the administrators' comments about needed change reflected unique local problems (e.g., "we need to have less clinical contamination" or "we can't seem to lick the transportation problem"), most administrators revealed a desire to serve more children, to enrich and broaden the programs, and to secure more adequate housing. Special equipment, e.g., teaching machines, typewriters, etc., was considered to be a need by many. Mentioned also was the desire to have the administration know the program better, and to be able to offer more or better inservice education. Additional help for the teacher, in the form of more consultation, aides, an itinerant teacher or substitute teacher, was an often expressed wish. While administrative frustration appeared in acute form only rarely, there was an occasional case, and it typically involved a lack of money or authority.

Ratings of Program Success

Table 1 presents ratings of overall program success.

The site visitors tended to see more extremes at both ends of the success continuum. Nearly three-fourths of the programs were judged by them to be either "encouraging" or "outstanding" in their success. Totals for comparable categories as rated by the school personnel totaled only 50 percent. On the other hand, the site visitors' judgments of clear failure outnumbered those of school personnel nearly three to one.

Table 1. Rating of Program Success

Category	Percent Site Visitors	Percent School Personnel
Clear failure	15	5
Limited success	11	21
Encouraging success	30	29
Outstanding success	40	21
No data	4	25

A good many reasons underlay the judgments of poor success found among school personnel.

The level of judged success was most often closely related to the appreciation of the teacher's efforts. Many administrators said that it all depended upon how good or poor the teacher was. If those persons doing the judging agreed with the teacher's methods, they found the program in one way or another successful. If they were not satisfied with what the teacher was doing, they tended to rate success lower. Other specific factors which seemed to be related to judgments of success and/or satisfaction were: (a) not enough structure; (b) too much expense; (c) lack of sufficient opportunity for outside treatment; (d) too few children going back to regular classes; and (e) class size and/or transportation problems.

It is obvious that the true concern about success or failure often goes much deeper and arises out of the total complex of problems previously discussed. This complex involves the establishment of goals, the screening and selection of pupils, the treatment, and finally the reintegration process. Since the goal often is to return the pupil to the regular class remediated and conforming, it is worth asking whether pupils with prognosis for quick recovery are selected. While it is true that few psychotics get into the programs, other criteria, such as family workability, age, etc., also need to be considered in the light of goals set. It is generally most difficult to set up that treatment program within the class which is most consistent with the nature of the pathology. A general approach is almost necessarily imposed on the classroom process, although it is apparent that more specific plans are not made as often as possible. Finally, there is a wide range in the efforts to return the child, as well as in the degree of acceptance he finds when he goes back.

Frequently, case successes stand out in the minds of school personnel. Generalization from the single case is tempting, either to support or to limit the program. Programs that operate for two years or more and return only 10 percent of their children to regular classes may still be regarded as successful because the children seem accepted and more comfortable, and are making some progress. The attitude of grateful parents also seems to play a large part in the feelings of school personnel. . . .

Teacher Prognosis Regarding Individual Pupils

Table 2 presents the views of the special teachers on whether their individual pupils will continue to need the special class.

Table 2. Perception of Pupil's
Continuing Need for Special Class

Will Need Special Class for Most of His School Life	Percent Indicating (N = 464)
Uncertain	35
Yes	6
No	42
No data	17

While the teachers' prognoses were not totally optimistic, there were indications of their belief in the recoverability of about half the children. This was in contrast to the relatively small number who were seen as becoming able to return to their regular classes.

Table 3 presents a summary of eventual expected placement. These figures are quite consistent with those seen in the previous tables, with slightly more than 40 percent of the children judged to be eventually capable of returning to a regular public school program. The larger "no data" percentage suggests less willingness to make longer term predictions.

Table 3. Teacher Perception of Pupil's
Eventual Placement

Type of Placement	Percent Indicating (N = 481)
Regular public school class	40
Special school placement	13
Vocational training	4
Drop out or expelled	2
Institution	5
Miscellaneous—job, private school	4
Uncertain	9
No data	23

Teachers predicted the degree of each pupil's personal adjustment and academic adjustment, as well as whether or not his general adjustment was expected to meet his parents' expectations. A summary of responses to the first two of these questions is presented in Table 4.

Table 4. Teacher Prognosis Concerning
Pupils' Personal and Academic
Adjustment

Degree of Adjustment	Personal Percent Indicating (N = 397)	Academic Percent Indicating (N = 406)
Complete	32	39
Limited	54	53
Very inadequate	14	8

Once again, there was evidence of the teachers' long term faith that a third or more of their children would return to essentially normal circumstances. The outlook for academic adjustment was only slightly better than for personal adjustment, even though it was clear that the teachers' main effort and orientation was toward the educational remediation of the children. The correlation between the two measures is $+.59$.

The teachers also indicated that a composite 56 percent of their pupils would be able to meet their parents' expectations for adjustment. The product-moment correlation between this estimate and the teachers' own prognosis for the child's personal adjustment is $+.40$. . . .

Pupil Prognosis for Return to Regular Class

Another aspect of program success concerned the pupil's perception of his own situation and prognosis. Tables 5 through 9 present summaries of findings which reflect on certain major aspects of his self-prognosis.

Table 5. Pupil Expectation Concerning
Return to Regular Class

When Pupil Expects to Return	Percent Indicating (N = 519)
Never	8
Not for a long time	10
After a few years	32
Soon, right now	45
No data	6

The pupils' collective outlook was somewhat more favorable than their teachers', and reflected a natural optimism and wish to have things back to normal. This finding was especially interesting in the light of data presented earlier, which indicated that most pupils were quite satisfied with their present classroom arrangement.

The distribution of responses over the categories [in Table 6] is strikingly similar to that in the previous table. Since the correlation between the two ratings is only +.38, this is not a simple projection. The ratings in Table 6, however, are related to teacher ratings at only +.15. It appears that teachers and pupils saw matters of individual prognosis quite independently.

Table 6. Pupil Perception of When His Teacher Expects Him to Return to Regular Class

When Teacher Expects Him to Return	Percent Indicating (N = 519)
Never	8
Quite a while	31
Soon	55
No data	6

Pupils anticipated the areas in which they would have difficulty when and if they did return to the regular classroom. Table 7 indicates the distribution of the pupils' responses.

Table 7. Pupil Anticipation of Difficulty in Regular Class

Area	Percent Indicating (N = 519)
No trouble	14
Academics—(specific subjects—34%)	54
Peers	10
Teacher	7
Miscellaneous	5
No response	10

Academics were the largest potential difficulty area, and expected trouble with specific subjects was a concern of about one-third of the pupils.

Troubles with teachers and peers affected less than one-fifth of the respondents. The concern with academic accomplishment in the regular class is particularly interesting in the light of the teachers' earlier reported discouragement in this area, as well as the teachers' emphasis upon interpersonal successes. In spite of the overall academic orientation of most programs and individuals, it appears that this is where the problems continue to exist.

Children also indicated in three specific areas what they felt their prospects were once back in their regular class. To the statement "I will be able to do the work," 87 percent of the 519 children indicated yes; only seven percent indicated no, and the balance gave no response. The respective responses to the statement "I will be able to keep the rules" were 86 percent, 8 percent, and 6 percent, and to the statement "I will be able to get along with the kids," they were 88 percent, 6 percent, and 6 percent. In terms of specific areas, the pupils' outlook was quite favorable. The high proportion of children who said that they expected academics to be their major problem must have felt, in the main, that they would be able to handle the problem. Once again, the pupils appeared to be able to make distinctions among the three areas, since the intercorrelations among the three ratings ranged from only +.20 to +.32—high enough to be significant with this large N, but not indicating much variance in common.

Pupil Aspirations for the Future

One of the major components in any pupil's motivational system is his notion concerning his prospects for the future. To a degree, this can also serve as an index of how realistic his appraisal of himself is. Students told what they proposed to pursue as a life activity once they were out of school. Table 8 presents a summary of these responses, catalogued according to Reiss' (1962) occupational index scheme.

Two-thirds of the children responding aspired to the first four categories, and the mean for all responses was 3.22, with $SD = 2.3$. The pupils aspired generally to occupations which were well within their intellectual capability to manage. In interpreting the data, however, one needs to recognize that many of the children are still young enough that fantasy, rather than reality factors, plays the major part in determining responses to such a question.

The children also felt fairly confident of reaching the goals they had set. In responding to a question specifically asking "How good are your chances of reaching the goal you have set?" 6

Table 8. Pupils' Occupational
Aspirations

Level	Example	Percent Indicating (N = 519)
1	Auto mechanic	25
2	Policeman	14
3	Salesman	15
4	Baseball player	11
5	Draftsman	7
6	Teacher	9
7	Scientist	6
8	Doctor	7
	No data	7

percent said "poor," 8 percent said "fair," 16 percent said "good," 50 percent said "very good," and 3 percent said "excellent." Eighteen percent of the sample of 519 children gave no response to the question. The mean of 3.4 falling between good and very good, indicates a reasonable degree of confidence.

Self-Perceptions of Change in the Pupils

One very important test of the success of such programs as those studied is the degree to which they induce change for the better in the children with whom they deal. It was not possible to assess these effects by extensive pre- and postprogram data.

It was necessary to rely upon retrospective data as a means of inferring changes which had taken place in the participating children, both from their own point of view, and from that of the teachers who had contact with them in the program.

Schedules A and B, which were completed by the individual children, or by trained recorders from data provided directly by the children when necessary, contained approximately 40 items which were used to assess pre- and postprogram conditions as seen by the children. These 40 items were grouped, a priori, into eight dimensions as indicated in Table 9. Each dimension contained approximately five items, and the median reliability of the dimension scores was +.60.

Schedule A required that the children respond in terms of conditions as they saw them in their previous school or class. Schedule B sought similar information on the present special class. Differences between previous and present scores on each of the eight dimensions were computed, and a t test for correlated arrays was then applied to each dimension. The items were scored so that a decline in mean dimension score indicated improved conditions from previous to present class. Table 9 presents a summary of this analysis.

In terms of the perceptions of the children themselves, the special classrooms offered significantly better conditions than did the regular classrooms from which they came. The children, as a group, saw improved relationships with teacher and peers, felt less anxiety and parental pressure,

Table 9. Children's Perceptions of Present and Previous Classes—Eight Classroom Conditions Dimensions

Dimension	Previous Mean	Present Mean	t	r	p
Peer relationships	2.23	1.95	8.12	.32	.001
School anxiety	2.41	1.80	18.50	.35	.001
Personal affect	2.52	1.82	17.51	.31	.001
Parental pressure	2.33	1.70	15.86	.37	.001
Teacher relationships	2.46	2.16	9.04	.22	.001
Behavior	2.49	1.81	18.82	.39	.001
Morale	2.36	2.12	8.77	.26	.001
Academic success	2.70	1.95	20.30	.27	.001

N = 406

and were happier, had higher morale, behaved better, and experienced greater academic success than in their previous settings. There was a considerable halo effect at work among the dimensions. At the same time, there remained little question that a general improvement in reactions to the school situation had occurred.

Changes in the Children as Perceived by Their Teachers

Another means of evaluating changes in the children as a result of their participation in the special class programs was obtained from teacher reports on perceived differences in pupil ability to control themselves, their affect, their academic achievement, and their personal relationships. Each teacher provided data on his children which indicated their condition on these dimensions as reported to him from their previous class, their condition when initially seen in the special class, and their condition at present. For each of the four dimensions, difference scores were computed between previous and initial, previous and present, and initial and present conditions. Table 10 summarizes the results of this analysis. In each case, t tests for correlated arrays were applied, and the items were scored in such a way that an increase in mean score from previous to initial, from previous to present, or from initial to present, indicated an improvement in the dimension.

Table 10 indicates a significant change in the perceptions of the teachers regarding the condition of their children, not only in the period during which they have had contact with them, but in the period between their previous class experience and their early contact in the special class. Several possibilities may be adduced to explain this peculiar finding. Perhaps the child's condition, as reported to the present teacher by the former teacher, was made to seem worse than it actually was. Perhaps the needs of the present teacher to see improvement were so great that they distorted his judgment or memory. Whatever the source, the changes seen by the teacher were in every case significant, and certainly indicate that things were better from the teacher's point of view.

Variables Related to Change in Individual Pupils

To go beyond the mere demonstration of these changes and to attempt to account for them in terms of other variables on individual pupils, a total of 78 variables, including the change scores on the eight pupil dimensions and the four teacher dimensions, was assembled. These were subjected to a correlation analysis. The variables included measures of pupil self-confidence and aspiration level, self-prognosis in specific areas, pupil age, family morbidity as judged by the teacher, etc., as well as the pre-, post-, and change scores on the specific pupil and teacher dimensions discussed in the previous section. . . .

This examination was not an encouraging one. A very large number of significant correlations appeared (in part because the size of the sample makes the requirement for significance very low),

Table 10. Teacher Perceptions of Changes in Children—Four Classroom Behavior Dimensions

Dimension	Means		t Tests		r	p
Control	Previous	3.87	Prev.-Init.	7.86	.74	.001
	Initial	4.33	Prev.-Pres.	17.87	.40	.001
	Present	5.47	Init.-Pres.	14.39	.52	.001
Affect	Previous	3.03	Prev.-Init.	6.14	.73	.01
	Initial	3.39	Prev.-Pres.	17.54	.30	.001
	Present	4.97	Init.-Pres.	15.35	.42	.001
Academic	Previous	7.17	Prev.-Init.	2.57	.30	.01
	Initial	7.58	Prev.-Pres.	8.06	.17	.001
	Present	8.55	Init.-Pres.	11.85	.50	.001
Relationships	Previous	2.96	Prev.-Init.	6.62	.73	.01
	Initial	3.35	Prev.-Pres.	20.40	.33	.001
	Present	5.00	Init.-Pres.	16.57	.39	.001

$N = 406$

but the pattern of relationships did little to clarify our knowledge of the factors which were operating to produce change. For the most part, pupil variables related to one another, teacher variables related to one another, but few significant relationships crossed the party lines. For example, considering the eight pupil self-description dimensions (peer relationships, school anxiety, personal affect, parental pressure, teacher relationships, behavior, morale, and academic success) on both the previous and present conditions, significant intercorrelations were found to exist among all pairs except three in the resulting 16 x 16 matrix. The range of significant correlations was from $+.10$ to $+.58$, with the median at $+.33$. These variables also related significantly to most of the change scores which were derived from them, as was to be expected. The several measures of pupil self-confidence and prognosis in specific areas also related significantly one to another, and to the eight dimensional measures and their derivatives, although less strongly.

A similar situation exists when the teacher variables are considered, although the teachers' ratings of such pupil characteristics as control, affect, relationships, etc., are less likely to be highly intercorrelated. It would appear that the teachers did discriminate among the variables, while the pupils were more likely to manifest a general halo effect in their perceptions. Once again, the teacher ratings of previous, initial condition in the special class, and present condition were strongly related within each teacher judgment variable, and also were related to the respective derived change scores. Beyond these expected patterns, meaningful intercorrelations were hard to find. A scattering of significant correlations appears throughout the matrix (far more than chance alone would provide), but most of these are so low or so remote in their interpretation as to be of only academic interest.

The level of these relationships is much too low to permit any but the most tenuous conclusions. However, a consistent pattern does seem to emerge, and while it is recognized that they may be the result of rating artifacts, response sets, etc., it is believed that they describe a meaningful syndrome which surrounds the improvements in the child's view of his school life. One would speculate that introduction into the special class, with reduced pressures and more tolerance from the teacher, produces a slight lessening of the child's overt pathology. The teacher in turn responds to this by seeing the child as better than he was described, and a narrow circle of hygienic relationships is developed. It is necessary to remember that every correlation plot has two ends, so that the opposite syndrome also exists for many children who do not see their lot as improved. However, the overall improvements discussed previously are of a significant magnitude, so that the proportion of children who are not benefitted is relatively low. Considering the fallibility of the measures, the difficulties with retrospective data, and the large and varied sample of pathologies, these findings represent an encouraging sign, even though they are obviously not conclusive.

Variables Related to Teacher-Perceived Change in Pupils

It was previously indicated that change scores were computed on four dimensions of pupil behavior as judged by their teachers. These four were: (a) control, (b) academic performance, (c) affect or feeling, and (d) general relationships. Three change scores were actually computed on each dimension, indicating changes from previous class condition to initial condition in the special class, from previous to present condition, and from initial condition to present condition in the special class. For the most part, changes which emerged were of the last two types, i.e., from previous to present condition, and from initial to present condition in the special class. From an examination of the changes, several interesting patterns emerge. The low magnitude of the correlations does not permit sweeping statements about those variables which relate to change as perceived by the teacher. However, there does seem to be a consistent pattern which involves not only teacher judgments, but also pupil perceptions of the improved conditions in their school lives in the special classroom. No causal significance can be attributed to these correlational findings, but it is quite clear that the pupil now feels that he is better off than he was. Whether this is a response to the relief from classroom pressure in the regular school, with consequent amelioration in his general relationships within the special class, or whether the teacher was an active, rather than an observing, agent in the change process is impossible to determine. For whatever reason, students seemed to feel better, and teachers were aware of this in their own view of things. What is cause and what is effect must await rigorous and controlled experimentation.

One other finding is worthy of mention. Running throughout the teacher change variable is the element of academic improvement, or at least less academic retardation. This appears consistently throughout all findings, as does the teacher's perception that the improved children were those with particular academic difficulty before they entered the special class. Once again, cause and effect are difficult to separate, but the importance of the academic process to both the student and the teacher cannot be overstressed. When the child improves academically, he sees his present condition as much more desirable than his former one. Teachers are generally very gratified at the fact that students seem not to be as badly off academically as they thought, and may respond favorably to such children. A most important element underlying the helping process in these classrooms centers around the teacher expectation of academic performance, previous pupil academic failure, and the introduction of academic success experiences into the classrooms.

References

1. **Reiss, Albert.** *Occupational and Social Status.* New York: Free Press, 1962.

Abridged from William C. Morse, Richard L. Cutler, and Albert H. Fink, "Public School Classes for the Emotionally Handicapped," a research project conducted for the Council for Exceptional Children, National Education Association, 1964. This project was supported in part by a grant from the National Institute of Mental Health to the Council for Exceptional Children. Reprinted by permission of the Council for Exceptional Children and the authors.

Editors' Commentary

Following this overall survey, a series of specific follow-up studies have been instituted. Even in an integrated series, it is impossible to get equivalent data from the various settings; these studies will probably raise more questions than they resolve. McKinnon completed a study on special classes.[21] He reports that relatively few of the disturbed children in schools get special help. Some 0.3 percent of all children are accepted, far short of the number of school pupils regular teachers identify as needing extensive help. In elementary programs, the mean referral age is 8 years, yet the mean acceptance age is 9½ years, a considerable lag. The pupils have all types of adjustment problems and, when referred, are learning at 62 percent of normal rate, although they have average IQs. During the typical 1½ years' stay in the classes, their learning ratio increases to over 70 percent. Behavior is considered improved, parents are encouraged, and the pupils are positive in their evaluation of the help. Follow-up data are obtained (on the average) over three years after the pupil leaves the class. Now 46 percent of the referred pupils are in regular classes and 21 percent are in special school programs at higher grades. Several have graduated or dropped out, but 11 percent are in in-patient hospitals. The older the pupil, generally the greater the academic retardation. Because of their low learning rate, these pupils tend to fall further behind those making normal progress. Although the children's behavior regressed somewhat after they left the special class, they are seen as getting along better in school and in social relationships, except for academics. The best candidate for a special class appears to be the younger child of relatively high socioeconomic status and relatively high IQ. Kotting and Brozovich[22] question how much change has been made in the school environment when the pupils reenter regular classes. They discuss the ideal candidate for the special class, the one for whom the prognosis would be high. And that child is the one unlikely to need the program at all. But, as Quay has asked, "Were the classes designed for the specific needs of disturbed children in the first place?"[23]

21. **Archie J. McKinnon,** "A Follow-up and Analysis of the Effects of Placement in Classes for Emotionally Disturbed Children in Elementary School" (Ph.D. diss., University of Michigan, 1969).

22. **B. P. Kotting and G. C. Brozovich,** *A Descriptive Follow-up Study of a Public School Program for the Emotionally Disturbed,* U.S. Dept. of HEW, Project No. 8-5068 (Pontiac, Michigan: Oakland County Schools, 1969).

23. **H. C. Quay,** "Facets of Educational Exceptionality: A Conceptual Framework for Assessment, Grouping, and Instruction," *Exceptional Children* 35 (1968): 25–32.

Asselstine,[24] after reviewing the twelve-year operation of a special class program, feels that two types of children are enrolled. One can be helped by individual tutoring in a regular school program. The other requires medical care, which is usually in short supply. Thus the special class is often a stopgap measure that does not provide the degree of help needed.

Recently, Hewett and others have evaluated their engineered classroom.[25] The program was able to increase attention to the task of meeting the primary goals. Gains in arithmetic were higher in the experimental group; reading gains were not. They feel that the checkmark system is superior to a teacher's verbal praise, at least at the initial stages, for these pupils. The temporary tangible rewards ceased to be necessary as the children made progress.

The following study brings us to the topic of institutional evaluation and deals with the well-known Re-Ed Model.

24. **D. Asselstine**, "Public School Special Classes for Disturbed Children," *Canadian Psychiatric Association Journal* 13 (1968): 375–381.

25. **Frank M. Hewett, Frank D. Taylor, and Alfred A. Artuso**, "The Santa Monica Project: Evaluation of an Engineered Classroom Design with Emotionally Disturbed Children," *Exceptional Children* 35 (1969): 523–529.

Re-education: A Mental Health Service in an Educational Setting

Anthony M. Gamboa, Jr.

John E. Garrett

Project Re-ED, a short-term residential treatment program for emotionally disturbed children, was first introduced in the early 1960s.[1] The major tenets of the Re-ED Model are: 1) Emotionally disturbed children will demonstrate and maintain improvement following a short-term (usually three to six months) period of residential treatment. 2) Educators can be trained to provide effective treatment services which traditionally have been provided by mental health specialists. 3) The most effective treatment model is one that attempts to improve all components of a child's ecology (home, school, and community) rather than only helping the child cope more effectively with those ecological variables that contribute to disturbance.

In 1968, the Re-ED Model was introduced to public education in a proposal submitted to the U.S. Office of Education, Title III of the Elementary and Secondary Education Act. Funds were awarded to a tri-county area in Kentucky for the establishment of a demonstration and research program for the education and treatment of emotionally disturbed children. The project was administered by the Jefferson County Public School System in cooperation with the Bullitt and Oldham Public School Systems and the Louisville Parochial Schools.

An integral part of the Re-ED Model is systematic assessment of student behavior. This is routinely accomplished through an assessment of the student's initial, interim, and terminal behavior. Attempts, however, to determine the stability of behavior six months after discharge are not routinely made. This study made such an attempt.

Method

Sample

The subjects of the study ($N = 116$) represent the total population served by the Kentucky Region III Re-Education Center during the period July 1, 1969 to June 30, 1972. The ages of the subjects ranged from six to twelve. The subjects had been identified as emotionally disturbed by school personnel and referred to the Re-Education Center for treatment.

Procedure

A *Cumulative Behavior Checklist* was used to assess student behavior at Intake, Discharge, and

Table 1. Analysis of Variance for Self, School, and Family Adjustment

Source of Variance	Self			School			Family		
	df	MS	F	df	MS	F	df	MS	F
Between	115	.22		115	.38		115	.42	
Within	232	.65		232	.68		232	.53	
Intake, Discharge, and Follow-Up	2	130.59	711.10[a]	2	66.14	582.02[a]	2	45.71	330.91[a]
Error	230	.13		230	.11		230		

[a]$p < .001$

six months after discharge, which is defined as Follow-Up. The checklist was divided into three areas of assessment: Self Adjustment, School Adjustment, and Family Adjustment. Items in each of these areas were rated on a three point scale (1 = nonadjustment, 2 = minimal adjustment, 3 = desirable adjustment). A total of 22 specific behaviors were listed under Self Adjustment, 13 under School Adjustment, and 12 under Family Adjustment. Ratings were made by Re-ED personnel after observation of students and through consultation with parents and teachers.

Results

An analysis of variance with repeated measures was computed to determine the effect of treatment over time. It can be seen in Table 1 that significant F-values were obtained for Self Adjustment, School Adjustment, and Family Adjustment.

A Newman-Keuls Range Test was computed to determine significant mean differences between Intake, Discharge, and Follow-Up for each of the three measures. Significant positive gains ($p < .05$) were found between Intake and Discharge and between Intake and Follow-Up for measures of Self Adjustment, School Adjustment, and Family Adjustment. Nonsignificant positive gains ($p > .05$) were indicated between Discharge and Follow-Up on Self Adjustment and Family Adjustment. In addition, a significant decrease in School Adjustment was indicated between Discharge and Follow-Up ($p < .05$).

A graphic representation of the mean scores obtained over time for each of the three measures can be seen in Figure 1. Although the trend toward continued improvement from Discharge to Follow-Up in the area of Self Adjustment and Family Ad-

justment was not significant, student behavior six months after discharge was significantly improved when compared to behavior upon entering the Re-ED treatment program. In addition, although the regression in behavior from Discharge to Follow-Up in the area of School Adjustment was significant, the mean gains made by the students from Intake to Follow-Up remained significant. Thus, student behavior was significantly improved six months after treatment in all areas of assessment.

Discussion

The results of this study appear to support the Re-ED Treatment Model. The subjects demonstrated significant improvement in the areas of Self, Family, and School Adjustment from intake to six months follow-up. In the areas of Self and Family Adjustment, parents perceived their children as maintaining improvement six months after discharge. Teachers, however, perceived significant regression in the area of School Adjustment from discharge to six months follow-up.

One explanation for the differing perceptions of the parents and teachers may be attributable to the expectancies of each. Most parents make a considerable emotional investment in sending their son or daughter to a residential treatment facility. Parents who arrive at such a decision apparently believe that such a program is beneficial and can be of help to their child. Upon release of the child from the treatment facility, parents expect and look for improvement in behavior regardless of the magnitude of the improvement. It is likely that parents notice the smallest improvement in their child's behavior and reinforce it by responding positively. Such reinforcement likely contributes to further improvement in the behavior of the child.

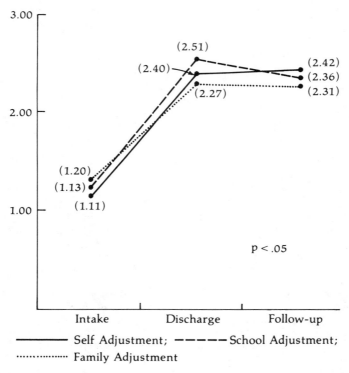

Figure 1. Means for Self, School, and Family Adjustment at Intake, Discharge, and Follow-Up

Teachers, however, may expect more dramatic improvement in behavior following treatment. In addition, teachers may have a predetermined set regarding the kind of behavior students should exhibit in the classroom. Anything less than a predetermined level of student functioning would be undesirable and perceived negatively. Thus, the gains made by the child would go unnoticed and, more likely than not, unrewarded. In effect, the expectations of teachers might have a deleterious effect on the child who had improved, but not dramatically so, while in treatment.

In order to insure continued student improvement in the public school, postdischarge consultation with the teachers of children who have been in a Re-ED program is needed. Such consultation should have as its focus the dissemination of behavioral information that delineates improvement made by the child as a result of treatment. An understanding by the teacher of improved child behavior would increase the likelihood of teacher reward for such improvement, and continued improvement could be encouraged. The teacher who is unaware of improved behavior in a child may actually punish improvement in that it is not compatible with a predetermined teacher expectancy. Thus, gains made by a child while in treatment would likely be diminished.

Consultation with the teacher by Re-ED personnel would alleviate the difficulties encountered by unrealistic teacher expectancy. Such consultation is essential and must become an integral part of all Re-ED programs.

Reference

1. **Hobbs, N.** 1964. Mental health's third revolution. *Amer. J. Orthopsychiat.* 34:822–833.

Reprinted from the *American Journal of Orthopsychiatry* 44 (1974): 450–453.

Editors' Commentary

Several recent studies have addressed the problem of institutional treatment evaluation. Davids and Salvatore[26] indicate how important follow-up studies are: predictions of "good prognosis" for subjects were not highly related to those subjects' subsequent adjustments, but "poor prognosis" was more likely to be an accurate prediction. The master analysis of residential treatment evaluation by Durkin and Durkin[27] covers both process and outcome issues in a review of many studies.

Summary

We can and must improve the ways we help disturbed children to mental health. As we observe the change from classic pathologies to drugs, alienation, and aggression (the new social pathologies), it is clear that education has more potential today as a basic mental health force. However, education alone cannot compensate for unhygienic societal conditions. Our new ecological understanding shows the critical part played by poverty, racism, and national policies based upon superficial values imparted to the young. Still, education has a substantial role to play in bringing mental health to disturbed children. Schools must become as concerned with emotional maturing as with intellectual stimulation, as concerned with the self-concept as with the achievement test scores. We cannot depend on secondary prevention or rehabilitation, but must devise processes to integrate feeling as well as thinking into education. Many of the proposals for special programs and ecological adjustments in schools, will lead in such a direction.[28]

Discouragement with the methods tried in the past has caused many to adopt any new method proposed. We have seen this happen before. We have heard that psychotherapy will help everyone and everything; drugs will empty the hospitals and calm the classrooms; operant conditioning will rehabilitate the autistic. We have sometimes used valid techniques in inappropriate places or overused certain techniques, and then we have criticized them for failing. But, after the frenzy over the choice of technique, what basic gains will we have made?

Far more diverse procedures will be available for those who work with disturbed children. All the techniques reviewed have use in selective fashion. A technique will be chosen after giving astute diagnostic attention to the child and his or her ecology. Interventions will be selective and parsimonious. The hard work of differential diagnosis is second only to the exhausting work of rehabilitation.

Mental health is not achieved until the many aspects of the child's life are in tune, as the ecological emphasis of education and therapy has pointed out. Unless children can master what are reasonable educational tasks for them individually, they cannot be well. Often, basic restoration has been achieved through educational success alone.

26. **A. Davids and P. Salvatore**, "Residential Treatment of Disturbed Children and Adequacy of Their Subsequent Adjustment: A Follow-up Study," *American Journal of Orthopsychiatry* 46 (1976): 62–73.

27. **R. P. Durkin and A. B. Durkin**, "Evaluating Residential Treatment Programs for Disturbed Children," in *Handbook of Evaluation Research*, vol. 2, ed. M. Guttentag and E. L. Struening (Beverly Hills, Calif.: Sage Publications, 1975), pp. 275–339.

28. See **William C. Morse, Craig D. Finger, and George E. Gilmore**, "Innovations in School Mental Health Programs," *Mental and Physical Health Review of Education Research*, 38 (December 1968): pp. 53–57.

Later this educational success evolves to finding a position in society. Children cannot be considered on the way to mental health unless they become as self-sufficient as possible in the adult world. Some will be able to reenter normal society. Others will need sheltered workshops and group living with built-in support. The task of education is to prepare them, whether in a public school class or a state psychiatric unit. To know about their world and their feelings, to be able to interact socially, to master skills—so much hinges on a flexible approach to education. Schooling—if it moves away from the prosaic and routine—will have more and more to do with rehabilitation. Teachers are most important.

Although education will assume a larger role, the multidisciplinary approach is just as necessary. Who should have the responsibility for assessing the risk of a potentially homicidal or suicidal adolescent? Are teachers able to take over all therapy, make complicated diagnoses, decide to use drugs? When reasonable ecological restructuring in the classroom is all the help a child needs, the educator may work alone or with minimal consultative planning. However, the need for joint efforts is clear to anyone who has worked, year after year, with very disturbed youngsters. The helping professions have finally recognized that their skills and potentials for assisting children are maximized when they work together as equals.

As we move ahead, the designs for offering educational assistance will be more and more varied. Interesting experiments are being conducted in all types of helping designs. The crisis teacher, the individualized learning center, the resource room, group counseling, and many other programs have been discussed. Since most disturbed children are still in regular classes, the new styles of direct assistance by special personnel and parallel work with regular classroom teachers will become more important. Drastic changes in educational content, mores, and administration will be required.

Finally, evaluation is always related to program purposes and goals. We are in the midst of a professional reevaluation of and revolution in our efforts to help the disturbed child.[29] New standards for practice are emerging.[30] Of course, it is easy to have a field day criticizing past practice (such as the "homes for the little wanderers") from our much "enlightened" vantage point, but we should recognize that the same will be done someday with our best efforts. Blanket indictments against classes or institutional treatment may be made without the slightest sophistication about the complexity of the issues. Yet we must read the critics as we search for new insights and higher goals, even if their so-called proof is often inadequate.

The fact of the matter is that we still have not clarified the process of acculturation for the normal child, the degrees of freedom for individuals, or the range of viable lifestyles in a democracy. Because of these questions, we are even more in doubt when it comes to the "disturbed" child. Intervention techniques are poorly understood. Because of the nature of child development itself, and the historical assumption of adult prerogatives, our problem is most difficult.[31] There are some who see every adult relationship with a youngster as *ipso facto* repressive; they advocate that adult interaction be replaced with the tyranny of immaturity, so little is their understanding of the reciprocal nature of human development.

29.   The fact that Head Start and many other programs have been faced with "accountability" pressure has resulted in many superficial efforts. Attention is finally being given to the philosophical as well as the psychological issues. See **Clifton L. Anderson,** "National Educational Research Design: A Collaborative Approach" (Ph.D. diss., University of Michigan, 1975).

30.   **Nicholas Hobbs,** *The Futures of Children* (San Francisco: Jossey-Bass, 1974); **William C. Rhodes,** *A Study of Child Variance,* vol. 4 (Ann Arbor: University of Michigan Press, 1972).

31.   **William C. Morse,** "Concepts Related to Diagnosis of Emotional Impairment" in *State of the Art: Diagnosis and Treatment,* ed. Kay F. Kramer and Richard Rosonke (Des Moines: Iowa Midwestern Educational Resource Center, 1975), pp. 113–171.

The legal system is actively attempting to define the rights and protections of the disturbed child as well as the disturbed adult. Unfortunately, the child-care professions have fallen so far behind that they now must heed the law on the child's rights even if the child loses needed protection in the process. As always, delinquents will be the most maligned because their behavior produces the greatest public fear reaction, and they have no organized parent lobby.

As we move into a new age of treatment, in which the nature of the healthy person has been considerably redefined and the modes of assistance have become expanded and less ritualistic, how can we professionals keep abreast? There are actually several steps we can take. First, we can continually deepen our understanding and judgment so that we apply a critical sense to the options. Second, we can participate in movements, both ad hoc and sustained, that are taking a stand for better care of the disturbed child. Sometimes this means applying pressure from the inside to make our organizations active. It may require money and time. Mandatory legislation is a promise, not a program: what about appropriations and high standards for actual programs? What about increasing the total spectrum of services for the disturbed, ranging from prevention to aftercare? To counter professional demoralization we must become involved.

Finally, there is self-evaluation. Of course, we are not child-beaters nor are we given to vicious abuse of those under our care. But each one of us must evaluate his or her own practice against the highest of standards. Have we avoided the human issue by relying on rules and regulations? Have we used our ability to maximize the sense of freedom possible for the children? Have we supported their rights in interactions with ourselves as well as with others? Have we tried something that we believed was right even if it involved some risk? Evaluation begins at home. In the last analysis, it is teachers and others relating directly with children who must usher in the new day. The creative forces must focus here to help those on the line provide a more authentic human experience for the disturbed child.

To the owner of this book:

We hope you have enjoyed *Conflict in the Classroom,* 4th edition. We'd like to get your personal reactions to the book so that it might better reflect your needs. Could you please take a moment to fill out this questionnaire? Thank you.

Your school: _____

Your instructor: _____

Department of: _____

_____

Course title: _____

_____

What did you like most about *Conflict in the Classroom*? _____

_____

_____

What did you like least about it? _____

_____

_____

Was the entire book assigned for you to read? _____

If not, what parts or chapters were *not* assigned? _____

Was there anything that you found particularly difficult to understand?

_____

_____

If you have any other comments, we'd be delighted to hear them. _____

_____

_____

OPTIONAL

Your name ————————————————————— Date —————————————

May Wadsworth quote you in the promotion of *Conflict in the Classroom*? ——— ———
                                                                          yes   no

Thank you for your help,

Nicholas J. Long

Ruth G. Newman

William C. Morse

———

FOLD HERE

———

FOLD HERE

| FIRST CLASS |
| PERMIT NO. 34 |
| BELMONT, CA |

BUSINESS REPLY MAIL
No Postage Necessary if Mailed in United States

Drs. Long, Morse, and Newman
Wadsworth Publishing Company
10 Davis Drive
Belmont, CA 94002